Douglas Haig and the First World War

From December 1915 until the armistice of November 1918, Sir Douglas Haig was commander-in-chief of the largest army his country had ever put into the field. He has been portrayed as both an incompetent "butcher and bungler" and a clear-sighted, imperturbable "architect of victory". However, in this magisterial new account, J. P. Harris dispels such stereotypes. A dedicated military professional, Haig nevertheless found it difficult to adjust to the unprecedented conditions of the Western Front. His capacity to "read" battles and broader strategic situations often proved poor and he bears much responsibility for British losses in 1915–1917 that were excessive in relation to the results achieved. By late 1917 his own faith in ultimate victory had become so badly shaken that he advocated a compromise peace. However, after surviving the German spring offensives of 1918, he played a vital role in the campaign that finally broke the German army.

J. P. Harris is a Senior Lecturer in War Studies at the Royal Military Academy, Sandhurst. His publications include *Men, Ideas and Tanks* (1995) and *Amiens to the Armistice* (1998).

Cambridge Military Histories

Edited by

HEW STRACHAN, Chichele Professor of the History of War,
University of Oxford and Fellow of All Souls College, Oxford

GEOFFREY WAWRO, Major General Olinto Mark Barsanti
Professor of Military History, and Director, Center for the Study
of Military History, University of North Texas

The aim of this new series is to publish outstanding works of research on
warfare throughout the ages and throughout the world. Books in the series will
take a broad approach to military history, examining war in all its military,
strategic, political and economic aspects. The series is intended to complement
Studies in the Social and Cultural History of Modern Warfare by focusing on the
'hard' military history of armies, tactics, strategy and warfare. Books in the
series will consist mainly of single author works – academically vigorous and
groundbreaking – which will be accessible to both academics and the interested
general reader.

A list of titles in the series can be found at:
www.cambridge.org/cambridgemilitaryhistories

Douglas Haig and the
First World War

J. P. Harris

CAMBRIDGE
UNIVERSITY PRESS

CAMBRIDGE UNIVERSITY PRESS
Cambridge, New York, Melbourne, Madrid, Cape Town, Singapore,
São Paulo, Delhi

Cambridge University Press
The Edinburgh Building, Cambridge CB2 8RU, UK

Published in the United States of America
by Cambridge University Press, New York

www.cambridge.org
Information on this title: www.cambridge.org/9780521898027

First published 2008

Printed in the United Kingdom at the University Press, Cambridge

A catalogue record for this publication is available from the British Library

ISBN 978-0-521-89802-7 hardback

Contents

Illustrations

Maps

Acknowledgements

A work of this nature cannot be completed in anything approaching a satisfactory form unless the author receives a great deal of help from a great many people. It is always a pleasure to be able to express thanks publicly to those who have given such assistance.

The project might not have seen the light of day had it not been for the support of Professor Hew Strachan of the University of Oxford. Professor Strachan was prepared to consider for the military history series of Cambridge University Press a book that, its author feared, had become unfeasibly large for publication by the purely commercial presses. Professor Strachan read the whole book in draft, provided much encouragement and gave the benefit of his scholarly expertise and advice. Michael Watson, History Editor at Cambridge, has also provided much friendly advice and useful criticism and played a vital role in seeing the book through to publication. The author also owes a debt to Helen Waterhouse, Jodie Barnes, Paula Devine and all others at Cambridge who have assisted with publication.

Professor Ian Beckett, Dr John Bourne, Dr Christopher Duffy, Dr Bryn Hammond, John Hussey, Dr Nick Lloyd, Chris McCarthy, Andrew Orgill, Dr Christopher Pugsley, Douglas Scott and Professor Peter Simkins all gave generously of their time to read portions of the book in draft. All made useful comments and several corrected some of the author's mistakes. For all opinions expressed and for the errors that remain the author is, of course, solely responsible.

Dr John Bourne of the Centre for First World War Studies at the University of Birmingham was a particularly abundant mine of information and a source of sound advice. Material from the Birmingham Centre's developing database on British generals proved particularly useful. Discussions (face-to-face, over the telephone and by e-mail) over many years with Dr Paddy Griffith have helped form the author's understanding of the Western Front. A fruitful collaboration with Dr Sanders Marble on an article for *War in History* also helped in this regard. David Filsell was enormously generous with his time in discussing some aspects of Haig's career and in lending the author rare literature from his personal library.

Librarians and archivists in all the institutions referred to in the bibliography have been most helpful. Patricia Methven and Kate O'Brien of the Liddell Hart Centre for Military Archives at King's College London deserve special mention. The author owes a particular debt to the library staff at the Royal Military Academy Sandhurst, without whose unfailing co-operation over a long period of time completing this project would have been practically impossible. He must thank in particular Andrew Orgill, John Pearce, Kenneth Franklin, Gareth Bellis, Ann Fergusson and Jane McCullen. Amongst other debts of gratitude to colleagues at Sandhurst the author must particularly acknowledge the encouragement and support of the Director of Studies, Sean McKnight, and of the Head and Deputy Head of the War Studies Department, Dr Duncan Anderson and Dr Simon Trew respectively. These colleagues not only gave important moral support, but also assisted in a practical way by releasing the author from teaching for a few critical weeks at the beginning of 2008. Dr Anderson was kind enough, during the same period, to relieve the author of some marking.

The author is most grateful to Her Majesty the Queen for permission to quote from documents in the Royal Archives, and to Earl Haig for his permission to quote from his father's papers. He is also grateful to the Trustees for permission to quote from a number of collections held at the Liddell Hart Centre for Military Archives at King's College London.

Introduction

Field Marshal Sir Douglas (later Earl) Haig is one of the central characters in the history of the First World War, a very major figure in British military history generally and a personality of some significance in British history as a whole. Haig's part in the fighting of the First World War took up only some four-and-a-quarter years of a life of more than sixty-six. His pre-1914 career, during which he took part in two of the wars of the late Victorian era, is certainly not without interest. Yet had he not played a major role in the First World War it is unlikely that a biography of him would attract many readers. So while the present book takes account of the experience Haig brought to that war and briefly examines his life in the post-war world, the focus is on the First World War itself.

Haig's part in that war became intensely controversial while it was still in progress and the controversy has never wholly abated. Haig's most extreme detractors have accused him of being a callous and incompetent butcher, responsible for sending hundreds of thousands of British and British Empire troops to unnecessary deaths.[1] A view of him as purblind and unimaginative (though not necessarily as brutal or callous) seems, indeed, to have become the predominant one in British popular culture.[2] Yet Haig attracted during his lifetime, and has continued to attract since, devoted admirers who have portrayed him as one of the great British commanders and as the key British architect of victory[3] in the First World War.

Debates about Haig's role in the First World War have now reached an interesting stage. A substantial proportion of the attacks on his performance between the 1920s and the 1960s employed two lines of approach, both now largely discredited and abandoned. The first of these was what might be termed the "British Way in Warfare" approach. Critics of Haig such as Winston Churchill, David Lloyd George and Basil Liddell Hart (who coined the term "British Way in Warfare") indicated that, largely owing to Haig's stance and that of Sir William Robertson, Chief of the Imperial General Staff 1915–1918, the British excessively concentrated their efforts on the Western Front and failed to take full advantage of opportunities in other theatres.[4] Sir James Edmonds and the other official historians of the British military effort in the war rejected this line of argument. John Terraine, author of a major study of Haig in the early 1960s, and one of the most widely read historians of the British experience of the First World War for the next couple of decades, endorsed the official historians' verdict and attacked the "British Way in Warfare" school in a more accessible and populist style than they could. Terraine repeatedly argued, as Haig had done during the war, that the Western Front was inevitably the decisive theatre. Adventures in other theatres were generally a waste of effort.[5] If the Germans had knocked France out they would have won the war as a whole. It was ultimately impossible for the British to have won the war without committing a mass army in the West and undertaking very major offensive operations with it. Though not everyone liked his manner of discourse, Terraine essentially won this argument. Practically all First World War scholars of real substance are "Westerners" now.[6]

A second line of attack, employed by Churchill in his *World Crisis* and taken up by several subsequent writers, was that Haig and his staff failed to make the most imaginative use of the military technologies that became available during the war. Something like the offensive mounted near Cambrai on 20 November 1917 could and should have been done, Churchill argued,[7] a good deal earlier in the war. Though, during the early 1990s, the eminent Canadian scholar Professor Tim Travers revived, with specific reference to 1918, the argument that Haig under-utilised the latest military technologies,[8] it seems fair to say that it has not carried the field. Most historians seem now to accept that, whatever his other faults, Haig was very open to technological innovation, that the British army on the Western Front was highly experimental and innovative and that the British pushed the available military technology to its limits in the war's final year.[9]

Yet the abandonment of these traditional lines of attack on Douglas Haig does not mean that his reputation as a general has been wholly and finally vindicated. The revolution in Western Front scholarship that has taken place since the 1980s (brought about through the work of Shelford Bidwell, Dominick Graham, Tim Travers, Robin Prior, Trevor Wilson, Paddy Griffith and a host of other able historians)[10] has highlighted other issues, practically all of which were raised in some form during the war itself. Haig's capacity to adjust from open warfare to quasi-siege warfare conditions, his selection and employment of his staff, his relations with and employment of subordinate commanders, his handling of his artillery, his choice of battlefields for offensive operations, his use of intelligence and his ability to "read" battles and strategic situations are amongst these.

In the pages that follow a serious effort is made to address all these issues and to incorporate them into a full re-evaluation of Douglas Haig as a man and a soldier.

What follows is neither a polemic in attack upon, nor one in defence of, Haig's reputation. Rather it is an attempt at a balanced, judicious consideration of one of the most important figures in British military history. Haig, it is argued, had genuine patriotism, a high level of professional dedication, much openness to technical and tactical innovation, a remarkable degree of political astuteness on some issues and very considerable skill as a political in-fighter. As a commander he had considerable force of character and the authority to secure, with rare exceptions, the compliance of his subordinates with his will. Coupled with this went a high level of physical and psychological resilience and, at least most of the time, a great deal of resolution. These qualities enabled him to play, it is argued, a vital part in shaping the campaign that brought final victory to the Allies.

Yet it is also contended that, even in the mobile warfare for which his military education had best prepared him, Haig was not a naturally gifted field commander, that he found it intellectually difficult to adjust to the unusual conditions that arose on the Western Front and that he cannot escape responsibility for casualties to his forces that were, for much of the period from the spring of 1915 through to late 1917, disproportionate to the results achieved. Haig, it is suggested, bore much responsibility for the near collapse of British civil-military relations by the end of 1917, the effects of which were so serious that they placed the Allied cause in jeopardy the following spring. His preparations for and handling of the German 1918 offensives were, it is further indicated, in some respects dangerously, almost fatally, inadequate and flawed.

Perhaps most controversially it is argued that Haig was not the perpetual optimist of legend. In 1914 he went to war full of anxiety about Britain's lack of preparedness and proved a nervous, somewhat battle-shy corps commander in the initial weeks of campaigning. Over-confidence and excessive strategic and operational ambition were, indeed, his besetting sins as commander-in-chief in 1916 and 1917. Yet the evident failure of his plans for 1917, combined with his diminishing faith in his allies and a growing fear of Bolshevism had, by the end of that year, made him doubt the realism of pursuing a complete victory. While he was keen to retain his command at almost any price, he became, in the early weeks of 1918, a keen advocate of compromise peace, apparently prepared to accept terms that would have left the Germans the real winners. His confidence in the Allies' capacity to defeat Germany decisively fluctuated greatly in the course of 1918, but remained somewhat fragile. From mid-October until a few days before the Armistice was signed, at a time when the German army was actually on its last legs, Haig was arguing that Germany must be offered very generous terms if the fighting were to end that year. In these last weeks he was, in effect, playing down the impact and significance of the victories his own army was achieving.

Ultimately it is intended to avoid the stereotypes of Douglas Haig both positive (as the clear-sighted, imperturbable great captain) and negative (as a stupid, callous, unimaginative butcher and bungler) and to reveal a human being of at least average complexity, possessing both considerable capacities and virtues and some fairly serious flaws.

1 Boyhood and early career

Background and childhood

Douglas Haig was born on 19 June 1861 at 24 Charlotte Square, in an affluent part of Edinburgh. His father, John Haig (1802–1878) was a wealthy whisky magnate whose principal residence was at Cameron Bridge in Fife. His mother, born Rachel Veitch, was nineteen years younger than her husband. Considered a great beauty in her youth, she came from a prominent Scottish family, which, at the time of her wedding in 1839, had fallen on hard times. Financial considerations and a sense of familial obligation may well have motivated her teenage nuptials with a rich businessman more than twice her age. Before Douglas, she had borne ten children, having delivered one about every two years since the marriage. Seven had survived. Douglas was her eleventh and last child: the eighth to survive infancy. His oldest brother, William, was twenty years his senior.[1]

Douglas Haig was directly but distantly descended from the Haigs of Bemersyde, a family of Norman origin and martial tradition, significant on the Anglo-Scottish borders since the twelfth century. In his later years he became proud of the Bemersyde connection and, through public subscription, acquired that property as his own home. Historians, however, have sometimes referred to the Field Marshal's illustrious border ancestry without making clear its remoteness.[2] Douglas Haig was certainly aware of his descent from the border family from an early age and there is evidence that he visited Bemersyde at least once during his childhood. During his early life, however, there was little if any social contact between his branch of the family and the Haigs who owned Bemersyde. For most of his army life, Douglas Haig's brother officers never heard him refer to his connection to the border family[3] and there is no evidence that it in any way inspired or advanced his career.

The social position of Douglas Haig's immediate family was based not on a medieval lairdship and a landed estate but on modern industry and commerce: not on martial tradition but on hard cash. Some of the Haigs had been distilling whisky since the late seventeenth century. A century later they had made it a big business. John Haig, Douglas's father, was the greatest figure in a vastly expanded nineteenth century Lowland industry and was its principal spokesman in its dealings with the government.[4] In Victorian Britain there were few obstacles to social advancement on the basis of wealth gained by commerce. In order to enter society's very highest ranks, the acquisition of the correct manners, attendance at the right educational institutions and appropriate marriages were of considerable importance. All this could quite easily be accomplished within a generation or two and Douglas Haig was a typical product of the process. The fact remains that the business that propelled him into the late Victorian social elite was alcoholic liquor. Through the marriage of an older sister, a stream of Irish whiskey[5] combined with his native Scotch to float his career.

Though his family owed its wealth to business, Douglas Haig showed no particular interest in a career in that field. Possibly this was a reaction against his father. John Haig had excellent qualities. A highly intelligent man who in his youth had won a prize for mathematics at St Andrew's university, he was reportedly of liberal views and considered to be a good employer. But, already fifty-nine at Douglas's birth, he seems to have exercised little positive paternal influence. Frequently ill with asthma (from which, in childhood, Douglas also suffered), gout and alcoholism, he was apparently away a good deal, sometimes abroad seeking cures at health resorts. This may have been for the best. He was reportedly given to outbursts of foul temper and foul language that frightened and upset other members of the family.[6]

Douglas's mother clearly had a far greater influence on the moulding of his character and general outlook on life. Since her marriage, Rachel Haig had immersed herself in family matters, almost entirely forgoing a social life. Devoutly religious, she insisted on hearing her children say their prayers night and morning and attempted to instil in them a strong sense of self-discipline and duty.[7] This was not easy in Douglas's case:

As a child he was headstrong, bad-tempered and intractable. He invariably wore the kilt, and as a minor punishment the drum which was his most treasured plaything bore as an inscription in bold lettering: "Douglas Haig – *sometimes* a good boy".[8]

Spending most of his early childhood at the family's Cameron Bridge home, Haig did not go to school until he was eight. He was thus much in the company of his mother and there can be no doubt that he ultimately absorbed some of her cardinal values. Haig's childhood was marred by severe asthma but he fought hard to overcome this by diet and exercise. Gradually, during boyhood and early manhood, he acquired a high degree of self-control. Such control, however, was imposed upon a nature that remained intensely passionate and somewhat highly strung. For most of the rest of his life Haig was given to occasional dramatic outbursts of emotion, most typically of anger, but sometimes of joy. It was only in his last years that his fierce temper was no longer in evidence.[9]

Clifton and Oxford

Between 1875 and 1879 Haig attended Clifton, a minor public school near Bristol. He went there instead of Rugby, as his mother had originally wished, because, still inattentive and a poor academic performer at pre-paratory school, it seemed unlikely that he would pass Rugby's entrance exams. At Clifton, although he never excelled scholastically or at games, he became, in both areas, a fair achiever. His delighted mother became eager that he should go to university and pursue a profession, but the exact nature of his future career apparently remained undecided. A year after leaving school he was able to gain admission to the University of Oxford without difficulty, though that was no vast achievement for a public school boy of his social background and financial means. More important, perhaps, by the time he left Clifton, Haig appeared well adjusted and comfortable in society, at least with other males of his own social class.[10]

As his school days drew to a close, Haig became an orphan, his father dying in 1878 and his mother in 1879. The former loss left him unmoved. The latter affected him more deeply. It did not, however, make him morbid. In his late teens he found himself possessed of a private income that was his by legal right rather than through paternal sufferance and he began to adopt a lifestyle to match. Postponing university entrance for a year, he accompanied his brother Hugo on a trip to the United States. He seems to have enjoyed the experience. Henceforth travel became a big part of his life. He was to return to the United States, to tour the Indian sub-Continent, parts of Australia and Western Europe and to campaign over great tracts of Africa. Some of this globetrotting was intrinsic to military duty and done at public expense. Much was self-motivated and self-funded.[11] If Haig's mind was insufficiently broad (as some have alleged) it was not for want of travel.

In 1880 he went up to Brasenose College, Oxford. There he lived the life of a young, fashionable, upper-class Victorian male. His academic studies, which included some Greek, Latin and religious studies, French litera-ture, Political Economy and Ancient History, appear to have been of little interest to him. Competent enough to get by without difficulty he worked hard enough to guarantee that he passed his exams. Yet he seems to have showed no desire to excel and possessed relatively little intellectual curiosity. He only read books that were necessary to pass his exams or of direct relevance to the profession he eventually chose. Other activities attracted more of his attention. He rowed, played a little golf, hunted and shot. In polo he distinguished himself, playing for the University in 1882. He was an active member of some of the most fashionable undergraduate clubs, enjoying wine and conversation. No dour Calvinist at this stage of life, he did not even disapprove of gambling in moderation. Even if few relationships he formed at Oxford went very deep, he was, to all appearances, full of good fellowship.[12]

Despite the formidable character and considerable influence of his mother, Haig, in his early twenties, was not noticeably religious. The beliefs that he did hold before the First World War do not appear to have been of a narrowly Presbyterian variety. He consulted fortune tellers and sometimes attended spiritualist meetings with his sister Henrietta. There is no evidence that he ever rejected the essential Christian doctrines in which he had been educated. But until he took supreme command on the Western Front his Christian observance seemed to contemporaries to be of a formal rather than of a particularly personal or passionate kind. He seems to have been still more indifferent to sexual passion and formed no known romantic attachments. As Charteris puts it:

He had no women friends: women neither interested him nor attracted him.

A close military colleague would surely not have been so blunt about this matter had it not become conspicuous to contemporaries, though it was perhaps more so in the first two decades of his army career than it was at Oxford. Haig, as a young man, and indeed into mid-life, was strikingly handsome. He was fastidious about his appearance to the point of being a dandy.[13] While he did not possess a glib tongue, there seems to have been every reason to believe that he could have been a success with women had he wished to. According to his future wife he had, until he married at the age of 44, a reputation as a "woman-hater". But it seems unlikely that he was ever a true misogynist. Perceiving the generality of women as frivolous and silly, he could respect the minority who struck him as serious-minded and he had a strong aversion to types of bawdiness that he considered insulting to the honour of the female sex as a whole.[14]

Given his seeming lack of sexual interest in women for so much of his life, it is not unreasonable to ask whether he may have been, at least latently, homosexual. From an enlightened, early twenty-first century perspective, that question should be straightforward rather than awkward or embarrassing. But it cannot be answered. There is a tantalising reference in Charteris's biography to a particularly close and enduring friendship that he struck up at Oxford with the (unnamed) son of a Hampshire landowner, a friendship that is said to have lasted well into later life. But there is no evidence to indicate homosexual practice or even inclination. For most of his life Haig gave little indication of interest in sex of any kind. There is a family story of an affair, only briefly preceding his marriage, with Daisy Warwick, the independently wealthy wife of the Duke of Warwick's eldest son. But no letters or other forms of written evidence have been produced. There is, however, no doubt that his relatively late marriage was fertile; it appears to have been remarkably devoted and affectionate on both sides, and it endured unto death.[15]

In an article written in the year of his death, more than twenty-seven years after the conversation was recorded, Haig is alleged to have expressed an interest in entering the army shortly after his arrival at Oxford. But such an interest is difficult to confirm from other sources. If it existed, it was probably not definite or strong. Other observers thought he had no particular sense of direction in his first two years at university. Yet he fitted well enough into the social milieu and no one seems to have thought him eccentric. His apparent lack of interest in women could be dismissed as a form of shyness. Entirely conventional in his tastes and habits, he was, in most respects, a typical representative of his social class, gender and age group at this moment in history. Conspicuously good at nothing except riding and polo and lacking any obvious ambition, it must have seemed quite possible that he might become just another upper-class drone.[16]

Yet how many people have a clear sense of direction between the ages of eighteen and twenty-one? As a young man under no compulsion to earn his living, perhaps the surprising thing is that Haig had found a definite purpose (and had seemingly become possessed of a driving ambition) before his twenty-third birthday. In 1883 Haig decided to apply to Sandhurst and to seek a commission in the army. It was the most important decision of his life so far. But it may not have been his idea.

Henrietta and Sandhurst

It is a paradox that, while, before his marriage, Haig appeared, to many observers, to be disdainful of women, feminine influence seems to have played a pivotal, determining role in his life. The influence of his mother has already been outlined. But the most enduring and, arguably, most important relationship of his life was with his sister, Henrietta. Up to the death of their mother, Douglas and Henrietta seem not to have been particularly close. Henrietta was ten years older and had married and moved to Ireland when he was only eight. Their mother's death apparently brought them much closer. She helped him get over the shock of it and appears gradually to have taken over the maternal role.

Henrietta's subsequent devotion to her brother has been ascribed to a thwarted maternal instinct, the Jamesons being childless. Her brother may also have offered Henrietta a vicarious outlet for ambition. Like most Victorian middle- and upper-class women, Henrietta had no career of her own. Her husband, whilst satisfyingly rich and well connected, was a sportsman and man of leisure. He clearly did not manage his family's business on a day-to-day basis and was not actively pursuing a profession.[17] Whatever the cause, the Douglas–Henrietta relationship became extraordinarily important to both parties. Though their voluminous correspondence diminished after Douglas's marriage, in other respects the sibling bond remained strong. For a couple of years, while the Haigs were in India, Henrietta acted as mother to their children. Decades later, Haig would die in Henrietta's London home, and she would outlive him by only a few months.

For the first few years after his mother's death Douglas Haig led, as we have seen, a rather carefree, sociable, apparently somewhat aimless existence. Henrietta, however, seems to have inherited their mother's intensity and familial ambition. Like her mother, she had married early, in 1869, at the age of 18. Also like her mother she had married money: Willie Jameson, another rich distiller. The Jamesons had better social connections than the Haigs had hitherto enjoyed. Willie Jameson had a considerable reputation as a yachtsman. This fashionable upper class sport was financed by his whiskey fortune. It was through the Prince of Wales' interest in sailing that the Jamesons became part of his social circle, being frequent guests at Cowes, Sandringham and Balmoral.[18]

Henrietta was, perhaps, both dissatisfied with the lack of direction in her brother's life and keen to make the most of her royal connection. Association with the royal family would inevitably have brought the Jamesons into contact with army officers, especially those from the "smarter" regiments. Henrietta was inevitably aware of her brother's pride in his appearance, his good physical shape, his appreciation of horses and his skill as a rider. She would have realised what a dash he would cut in uniform and how easily he could fit into the social ambience of an officers' mess. An intelligent, if not a highly educated, woman, Henrietta would also have appreciated the enduring influence of the royal family in the army. If one of her male relatives were to gain a commission, she might be in a good position to assist his career. Apparently she had already tried, without success, to persuade Douglas's older brother John to follow this path. During his last year at university, in March 1883, Haig and Henrietta went on holiday to the Continent together and it may well have been then that she persuaded him to apply to Sandhurst. However it happened, Haig seems to have gained, rather suddenly, a definite sense of purpose and direction. Apparently he came back a changed man. Gone were the carefree, relatively idle days of youth. He withdrew from college into more private lodgings in the town, curtailed his social life and temporarily abandoned his diary. He swotted hard to pass his final university exams, known as the Groups, which were necessary for admission to Sandhurst as a University Candidate.[19]

Haig apparently passed the university exams but was never awarded a degree. Oxford had a strict residence requirement. He fell short because in 1881 he had lost most of a term sick. All that remained to get the degree was to return to college for another term, but he decided not to do it. He did not need the degree itself for admission to Sandhurst. But he had to enter the Royal Military College before he was twenty-three or he would be disqualified on age grounds. He was already in his twenty-third year and was cutting it fine. In summer 1883, he proceeded to a military "crammer" based at Hampton Court to swot for Sandhurst's entrance exams. He was successful and entered the Royal Military College in February 1884.[20]

At Sandhurst Haig found himself at an immediate advantage compared to most of his fellow cadets. He was few years older than they were. He cut a striking figure. He was a well-travelled man of the world, with the self-confidence that tends to accompany financial security. Whilst not technically a graduate, he had been to Oxford, passed its exams and played polo for the university. In the small pool of the Royal Military College in 1884 these things were enough to make him a sizeable fish. Haig was determined not to lose his initial advantages. Assiduous in his attention to duty, he became a model cadet. He organised any time not taken up by drill or lectures to increase his competence in all areas of the curriculum. His diligence was rewarded. He did well at everything from Drill to Tactics and from Fortification to Military Law. His most outstanding results were in Military Administration and in "Marks Awarded by Professors": the rudimentary academic syllabus. His weakest suit seems to have been Gym.[21]

There was, however, a downside to Haig's exceptional dedication. According to Charteris, he formed no close friendships at Sandhurst. As a Senior Under Officer, he was apparently a strict disciplinarian, respected by, but not popular with, his fellow cadets. Extreme ambition had significantly changed his personality since his Oxford days. Easy fellowship was a thing of the past. With his narrow obsession with soldiering, lack of sociability and difficulty in forming close relationships outside his own family, he was apparently in some danger of becoming an insufferable careerist. Yet in December 1884, he passed out first in order of merit, gaining 2,557 marks out of a possible 3,350 and winning the Anson

1. Haig in his Hussar's uniform. National Library of Scotland.

Memorial Sword: the greatest honour available. He emerged from the Royal Military College a highly competent junior officer.[22]

Early military career

On 7 February 1885 Haig was commissioned into the Hussars. The normal life of a cavalry regiment at this period was, for the officers, rather leisured. Most of the routine training was left to the supervision of the warrant officers and NCOs. The Hussars had a first-class polo team of which Haig became a prominent member. Having been selected to play for England, Haig made his second trip to the United States, where his team triumphed that summer. Three months later, in November 1885, Haig embarked with his regiment for India. He was pleased to be going, expecting to find greater opportunity for active soldiering. Over the next few years, however, his regiment saw no action, being for the most part engaged in the humdrum routine of garrison life. Haig made the best of it. "Military Administration" had been one of his best subjects at Sandhurst and India offered plenty of opportunity in this field. In 1888 he was appointed Adjutant of his regiment. He was generally thought to perform the role most efficiently, though, at least in some quarters, he also developed a reputation as something of a martinet, known for a fearsome temper and a lack of tolerance for normal human frailty. He also became a determined self-advertiser and an assiduous charmer of superior officers, especially those from his own arm. His reputation as a mustard-keen, intensely ambitious, thorough and effective cavalry officer gradually spread through the army in India.[23]

India also took its toll on Haig as it did on many Britons. He caught tropical fevers including typhoid and, on at least one occasion, was dangerously ill. He was anxious about his health and became even more intensely fastidious about his food: a response by no means untypical of westerners obliged to live in tropical climes. Partly for health reasons, he took extended leaves in Europe in both 1889 and 1890, spending most of the time in London, but also touring France. It was apparently during this period that he first got into the habit of visiting spas and experimenting with a variety of health fads. Yet, despite the problems it caused for his health, he developed no general aversion to India or its people. He served there on two further occasions after the Boer War (when he might have been able to avoid it) and, as we shall see, he developed very enlightened views as to its political future. Taking full advantage of his first posting to the sub-Continent, he travelled widely there in 1891, exploring the North-West Frontier at one end and Ceylon at the other. Keeping up his practice of globetrotting, he journeyed to Australia the following year.[24]

While stationed in India, he also began to study the profession of arms more earnestly and systematically than was common with junior officers at this time. Far from parochial in outlook, he made serious efforts to learn French and German: the most important European military languages. There is some doubt as to how successful he was. By the mid-1890s he believed himself capable of making competent translations of German military documents. While in command on the Western Front (and after considerable extra tuition) he thought he could converse meaningfully in French. Against this, Charteris writes that he never achieved fluency in either language and many have testified that he was difficult to follow when speaking English. In all probability, in foreign languages, as in his native tongue, his level of literacy considerably exceeded his conversational skill.

By the early 1890s he had also started to commit his own military thoughts to paper. Some of them even got into print.[25] The Inspector of Cavalry in India appointed him as a Brigade Major at a cavalry camp in 1891. But this sort of thing was not enough in itself to get him the accelerated promotion he which seems to have become the focus of his life. Such advancement could be attained only by distinguishing himself on campaign or by passing the Staff College at Camberley. As there were no significant wars in these years, Haig decided to apply to the Staff College. He returned to England in September 1892 and joined a "crammer" to prepare for the June 1893 examination. He failed: dropping eighteen marks short in mathematics, a compulsory subject. Henrietta tried to pull strings for him, to get the authorities to use their discretion to overcome this minor academic shortfall. But the medical examination he had taken also revealed that he had a slight degree of colour-blindness and this also counted against him. Haig was bitterly disappointed and initially took the failure with ill grace, launching an unavailing protest that the Staff College examination had been unfair. Indeed, because of a change of examiner, the maths paper had suddenly become much tougher than those set in previous years and there had been an unusually high proportion of failures.[26]

Haig returned to the 7th Hussars in India in a downcast mood. He was based there until April 1894, when he was summoned to England to become *aide de camp* (ADC) to Lieutenant General Keith Fraser, the Inspector General of Cavalry, and to assist him with the autumn manoeuvres. Until the end of January 1895, Haig seems to have worked hard on cavalry training. For the rest of the winter he went on leave, spending much of it hunting in Warwickshire.[27] In April 1895, General Fraser retired and Haig's appointment as ADC formally came to an end. Haig, however, did not then rejoin his regiment in India. He had received notice that he would, after all, be admitted to the Staff College. This may have been partly a reward for his work with Fraser. Continued string-pulling by Henrietta may also have had an influence.

Haig had kept up an interest in foreign armies. He visited French cavalry manoeuvres on leave from India in 1893 and again in 1894. Not due to enter Camberley until January 1896, he decided, in the meantime, to visit Germany again and observe cavalry manoeuvres at Potsdam. The hospitality offered by German officers made the trip most agreeable. He showed his appreciation by arranging for Henrietta to send gifts and by trying to organise reciprocal hospitality for German officers wishing to visit the British army. On 31 May 1895 he met the Kaiser in Berlin and (strangely, in view of later events) they drank each other's health at the dinner table.[28] Between 1914 and 1918 Haig was, of course, an enemy of the German Reich, wishing to prevent its dominating Europe by force. But, perhaps remembering the kindness and consideration he had been shown in that country, he never endorsed the hysterical hatred of Germany vented in the worst sort of wartime propaganda.

His report to the War Office, *Notes on German Cavalry*, was not a very inspiring piece of work. It was good on the routine of administration and training, the aspect of soldiering with which Haig was most familiar, but had little to say on weaponry, tactics or German ideas on the operational and strategic employment of cavalry: perhaps reflecting the limits of his military thought at this stage. Haig, however, seems to have been greatly and rightly impressed with much of what he saw of the German army, in particular with the efficiency of its officer corps. He thought the German system of short-service conscription worked very well, and he admired the German philosophy of delegated command, today sometimes called *Auftragstaktik*, or, in the British army, "mission command".[29]

In June 1895 Haig returned to England, somewhat earlier than he had apparently intended, to take part in a "staff tour" (a sort of war game for the military training of commanders and staff officers) organised by Sir Evelyn Wood, one of the foremost British generals of the period. Colonel John French was commanding the cavalry on one side and Haig was on his staff. The tour started on 21 June. By 9 July Haig was back in Germany, a man of leisure. In this short space of time Haig had, however, boosted his career. Both Wood and French were to become important patrons. Wood wrote to Haig after the exercise stating that he had first heard of him through his military writing (possibly his report on the French cavalry) but that his conversation had proved still more pleasant and stimulating than the writing had led him to expect.[30] We should perhaps accept the evidence that Haig could converse agreeably on subjects that particularly interested him in the company of like-minded people. His problems of oral self-expression under more trying circumstances were to become notorious.

His official biographer, Alfred Duff Cooper, portrayed the Haig of 1884–1914 as a Spartan of self-discipline and self-sacrifice in the pursuit of military efficiency.

From the day when Douglas Haig went to Sandhurst in the year 1884, every hour of his life had been dedicated to preparation for a great ordeal. The military profession had been for him neither an easy alternative to idling, nor a pleasant excuse for leading an open-air life in congenial companionship. It had been on the contrary, a stern and high calling, which had demanded from its votary all the application and devotion of which he was capable.[31]

This picture is rather overdrawn, as an objective reading of Duff Cooper's own early chapters indicates. All things are relative, and by the standards of the Victorian army Haig was a true professional. From a modern perspective, however, he seems to have taken an extraordinary amount of time away from official duty. As noted, he justified his German trip of the spring and early summer of 1895 in terms of improving his knowledge of German cavalry methods. Another sojourn in Germany, later that summer, was spent at the well-known spa of Kissengen and explained on health grounds: the waters supposedly helping him recover from fevers he had contracted in India. Haig clearly used his considerable affluence to pursue his own particular interests and his own well being, remaining all the while perfectly easy in his conscience that his actions contributed to the greater good of the army and the Empire. Only a prude would, however, condemn a man for pursuing business and pleasure in judicious mixture, and Haig was judicious. For some of his contemporaries spas were merely holiday resorts at which the immoderate consumption of food and drink and the incautious pursuit of the opposite sex could outweigh the health benefits of taking the waters. Haig was too serious about looking after himself to fall into such traps. Yet, while not a Sybarite, he was certainly no Spartan. A doctor having discovered early in 1895 that he had a somewhat enlarged liver, Haig evidently regarded it as quite a hardship to be reduced to half a bottle of claret "for a whole day!!!"[32]

Haig attended British cavalry manoeuvres in the autumn of 1895 and then completed a revised *Cavalry Drill Book* that John French had begun but abandoned when he was appointed to the post of Assistant Adjutant General. This task, though a responsible one for someone not yet promoted beyond the rank of captain, seems not to have detained him much. The work he produced was progressive in terms of the methods of command and control recommended, but continued to stress that the charge with cold steel was the epitome of cavalry work. The booklet written to his own satisfaction, he again spent some of the early part of the winter hunting before entering the Staff College at Camberley in January 1896 at the age of 34.[33]

Staff College

Haig did the standard twenty-two month course at Camberley, studying topics including military history, strategy and tactics, fortification, staff duties and applied science. From all accounts he worked hard, just as he had at the adjacent Royal Military College Sandhurst a dozen years earlier. He kept himself so busy that he temporarily abandoned the diary he had begun at Oxford. As at Sandhurst, he seems to have been much too intense and self-absorbed to be popular with fellow students. Regarded as the class swot, he was seldom seen in the mess except for meals and kept himself to himself. He was also somewhat tactless. Within a few days of arrival at Camberley Haig annoyed his fellow students by requesting leave to meet the Prince of Wales at a shooting party that the Jamesons had arranged. Yet Haig here demonstrated a shrewd sense of priorities. In terms of his future career, meeting and gaining the patronage of the Prince of Wales was more important than popularity with classmates.

Yet there was inevitably a price to be paid for his tactlessness, for his habitually abrupt manner and his general lack of sociability. The appointment of the Master of Hounds for the Staff College Drag Hunt, regarded as a considerable honour, was conferred by a free vote of the students at the end of their first year. Haig was obviously the best horseman of his intake and should have been the natural choice. He was not elected. The appointment went to Allenby, a fellow cavalryman, who was later to command an Army under Haig on the Western Front and to make a reputation with an independent command in Palestine. Allenby was somewhat overweight and, according to some observers, distinctly ungainly on horseback. Haig might have seen his election as a hurtful rebuff. Yet, while he and Allenby had their differences later on, there is no evidence that Haig bore a lasting grudge over this relatively trivial matter.[34]

By the mid-1890s the Staff College was becoming a more prestigious and professional institution than it had previously been. G.F.R. Henderson, soon to publish the classic *Stonewall Jackson and the American Civil War* and generally considered a most stimulating teacher, was the principal instructor in military history. Haig responded very well to Henderson's teaching and Henderson apparently formed a high opinion of Haig, whom he is said to have tipped as a future Commander-in-Chief.[35] Even at this point, however, the British Army's Staff College lacked sophistication compared with the *Kriegsakademie*: the renowned training ground for the German General Staff. The German General Staff was the army's intellectual *corps d'elite* – providing its central think tank for making war plans and formulating military doctrine, as well as supplying staff officers for the headquarters of all major formations. In the 1890s the British had no General Staff of this sort. The British War Office and British generals in the field did need staff officers and Camberley tried to provide suitable training for such roles. It also tried to offer some intellectual preparation for command – at least up to the level of the small independent force that Stonewall had led in the Shenandoah Valley. Students at Camberley were, however, rarely encouraged to think of wars between the million-man armies made possible by the short-service conscription that the Continental Great Powers practised. Haig and his fellow students were not being prepared to join an elite corps that would shape the army as a whole.[36]

The most vivid account of Haig's Staff College career is that of James Edmonds, an academically gifted sapper who was to be the principal British official historian of the war on the Western Front. Edmonds indicated that he had managed to pass the unimaginative and undemanding Staff College course with very little work. (He had devoted much of his time to writing a single-volume military history of the American Civil War, for a long time considered a standard work on the subject.) In Edmond's estimation the majority of lectures consisted of "no more than the reading of some paragraphs of the regulation books (mostly out of date) and some pages of military history". He dismissed even G.F.R. Henderson's teaching on the American Civil War as pedantic and uninspiring: the enumeration of blades of grass in the Shenandoah Valley rather than the "broad principles of the leader's art". While there were outdoor exercises, of both a technical and a tactical nature, most of the tactical schemes were, in Edmonds's recollection, concerned with small units. Students seldom had to apply their minds even to the handling of anything as large as a brigade. Yet Haig's performance, even in such undemanding conditions, was, in Edmonds's estimation, weak. Tutors constantly asked Edmonds to assist him. In the end Edmonds had rebelled. On one staff ride he told Haig that he could no longer afford to impair his own chances by lavishing help on a less able colleague.[37]

Edmonds's account must be treated with caution. By the time he wrote the memoir quoted, he was, though still vigorous and extremely industrious, a disappointed and possibly somewhat embittered individual. His military career had not reached the heights that he might have expected. Even before the First World War, the less intellectual but better-connected and luckier Haig had overtaken him in the promotion stakes. While, during the war, Haig had risen to the very top of his profession, Edmonds's advancement was curtailed by a form of breakdown suffered under the stress of the retreat from Mons.[38] Yet Edmonds's version of Haig at Camberley cannot simply be dismissed. Edmonds was not the only contemporary observer who regarded Haig, at Staff College and after, as being somewhat narrow and rigid intellectually.[39]

It has been suggested that some ideas Haig absorbed at Staff College may have been inappropriate and ultimately damaging to his generalship. Yet most of what he was taught seems to have been entirely sensible. Staff College lecturers were aware of the growing firepower of modern weapons. They realised that it was necessary to win pronounced fire superiority before making an assault and that assaults should be carried out in an open order to avoid excessive casualties. There was instruction on the importance in modern warfare of fortification in general and of entrenchments and barbed wire in particular. Certainly Haig absorbed the doctrines that commanders must run risks in order to win, that it was impossible to achieve real victory by passive defence alone and that the moral forces in war were at least as important as the physical. But such notions were practically universal in the European armies of this period. Moreover, even from a post-1918 perspective, it is difficult to argue that they were, in the final analysis, wrong.

Neither is it reasonable to ridicule another notion that Haig picked up at this period: that campaigns might "normally" be expected to go through a number of distinct phases including the clash between advanced guards, the "wearing out" fight, the decisive attack and, finally, pursuit and exploitation.[40] A bright student would take it as read that, in a phenomenon as diverse as war in the nineteenth century had already proved to be, there would be variations from the norm. In all systems of practical education, much depends on the student's capacity to adapt principles and premises to changing circumstances. The reason that Haig found this difficult should be looked for in his limitations, rather than those of the Staff College curriculum.

The Sudan

Not long after leaving Staff College, Haig was to receive his baptism of fire in the 1898 Anglo-Egyptian conquest of the Sudan from the fanatical Moslem sect known as the Dervishes. Motivated partly by the desire to avenge the death, at Dervish hands, of General Charles Gordon in Khartoum in 1885, and partly by the perceived need to forestall French encroachments into the Upper Nile Valley, the intention was that the Egyptian Army should do most of the work. The latter had been reorganised by the British since they took effective control of Egypt in 1882. In 1898 Major-General Sir Herbert Kitchener was commanding general, or "Sirdar", of the Egyptian Army. That army had a number of British officers on contract and, for this campaign, was supported by a number of British regiments.[41] Haig's opportunity to participate derived partly from his professional qualifications and partly from patronage.

In January 1898 Kitchener had written to the Adjutant General, Sir Evelyn Wood, asking for three officers from the latest course at Camberley. Haig was one of Wood's choices. Wood's high opinion of Haig's writings on cavalry and of his role in the staff tour of June 1895 might well have been sufficient reason for this. Sir Evelyn, however, also wanted to exploit his patronage of Haig's career to obtain frank and detailed reports on

Kitchener, whom he did not altogether trust. Wood repeatedly invited Haig to:

Write to me as frankly as you will, you may be sure I will not quote you to anyone.[42]

Shortly before his departure for the Middle East, Haig was invited to Sandringham, where he again met the Prince of Wales. Like Wood, Prince Edward encouraged Haig to write.[43]

Haig arrived in Cairo on 3 February 1898. Over the next few days, he called at the Egyptian Army's headquarters, signed an agreement to serve with it for the next two years and then went shopping in the bazaar. On 8 February he left Cairo and journeyed up the Nile by steamer to join Kitchener at Wadi Halfa. The Sirdar received him in a "very cordial" manner and indicated that Haig would be given an Egyptian cavalry squadron. It was typical of Haig's earnestly self-improving style that within days of arriving in the Middle East he had begun to take Arabic lessons. It was equally typical of him that he made elaborate provision for his material comfort on campaign. The flavour of this wealthy Victorian's approach to war may be gained from a letter to Henrietta written on 17 February:

your little comforts came in most useful. I use the tea in the afternoon here and the cake in the luncheon basket was finished at Assuan on board the steamer ... At present I have two horses which I got at Cairo ... I have now bought two camels. I must have *two* to carry my plates, cooking pots and supplies! Then as to servants I have engaged a cook at £3 a month and the black fellow Suleiman as body servant. Then a syce [groom] for every two horses and a camel boy. So you see I have already got quite a retinue ... The sort of things I would like would be jam, tinned fruits, cocoa, vegetables, haddocks in tin, tongue, biscuits and a bottle or two of brandy or any sort of drink. Whisky I get here all right ... Spend whatever you like on these things, £50 or more ...[44]

On 20 February Haig received a telegram from Kitchener ordering him to proceed to Berber, above the Fifth Cataract of the Nile, to join the Egyptian cavalry brigade. He arrived there on 28 February. He reported to the commander of the Egyptian cavalry brigade, Lieutenant-Colonel R. G. Broadwood, of the Twelfth Lancers. Broadwood was four years senior to Haig in the army, had passed Staff College seven years ahead of him and had served in the Egyptian Army since 1892. Haig learned on 13 March that, apparently apprehensive of imminent action, Kitchener had changed his mind about letting him have a squadron. It was not now clear what Kitchener wanted Haig to do. What he actually did was to accompany cavalry patrols and to try to make himself as useful as possible to Broadwood. Broadwood apparently came to regard Haig as his principal staff officer. Haig was, however, annoyed at the Sirdar's sudden change of mind, which, as he commented in letters home, appeared entirely typical of the latter's autocratic and mercurial style of command.[45]

By mid-March Kitchener had concentrated a substantial force at Berber. In addition to the cavalry brigade of two regiments of four squadrons each, a horse artillery battery and a couple of maxim guns, this included a three-brigade Egyptian infantry division under Major-General Hunter, reinforced by a British infantry brigade. The whole force totalled about 14,000 troops. Its right flank rested on the Nile, where it was supported by three gunboats. The main Dervish army of about 40,000 under the Khalifa, their leader, was in the Khartoum area. Another army, of about 20,000 under his lieutenant, Mahmud, was thought to be a good deal closer, though its exact position was unknown. Kitchener decided to crush Mahmud's force before continuing his advance towards Khartoum, and to this end, in mid-March, pushed his forces twenty miles south of Berber to the confluence of the River Atbara with the Nile. A mud-brick fort was built at this point to serve as the army's base.[46]

On 19 March the Anglo-Egyptian forces, covered by their cavalry, began to probe up the right bank of the Atbara, which was largely dry at this time of year. This part of the Sudan was mostly bare desert. Reconnaissance was, however, more difficult near the riverbanks, around which there were palm trees and much scrub. On the early morning of 21 March Haig accompanied an Egyptian cavalry patrol. It moved out from a base near Abadar, where Anglo-Egyptian forces had a small block-house, towards Umbadia. Encountering a Dervish scout, the patrol pursued him for while but lost him. Having already advanced further than ordered, the patrol returned to base. Near Abadar, at about 1.45 p.m., a force estimated at about 100 mounted Dervishes attacked Egyptian cavalry outposts, some of whom were not fully alert. The Dervishes had apparently shadowed the patrol to which Haig was attached on its return trip. The Egyptian cavalry rallied quickly and counter-attacked, but lost eight killed and ten wounded, of whom two subsequently died, while, according to Haig's estimate, only accounting for some six or seven hostile troops.[47]

This minor outpost clash is usually regarded as Haig's baptism of fire. But he was watering his horse when it began and it is not clear how actively involved he became. In a long letter of 26 March, recounting the incident to Evelyn Wood, Haig gives no definite indication that he personally encountered physical danger, discharged a firearm, drew a sword or played any significant part in events.[48] His account is, indeed, so impersonal that it might seem that he did not want any responsibility for an action, however minor, of which the Dervishes had the better. In fairness it must be pointed out that he had only recently joined the brigade and that,

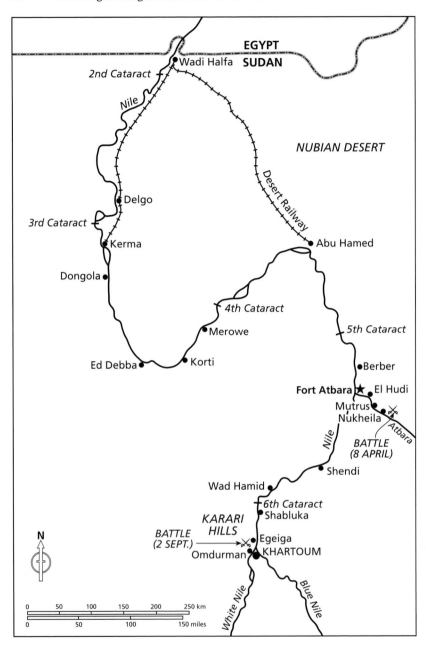

Map 1. The theatre of war in the northern Sudan 1898

as yet, he was probably insufficiently familiar with Egyptian troops and their Arabic language to exercise much leadership. At this stage he was, perhaps, inevitably something of a military tourist.

Haig took part in further patrols along the northern bank of the River Atbara on 27 and 30 October. The second of these located Mahmud's Dervish army in a fortified position at Nukheila. Kitchener moved his infantry up to Atbara on 4 April. On 5 April the Egyptian cavalry carried out a reconnaissance in force of the Dervish position at Nukheila, accompanied by General Hunter, who had been placed in overall command of Egyptian forces for this campaign. As the Egyptian cavalry approached their position the Dervishes, who had been rather passive over the last few days, suddenly sprang into action. They stabbed at both flanks of the Egyptian force: apparently aiming to cut it off and destroy it. Haig, as we have seen, had made no particular claim for his role in the skirmish of 21 March. In his diary, however, he placed himself centre-stage in his account of the more serious fighting of Tuesday, 5 April. Indeed, he practically credited himself with having saved the brigade. His description of the action was detailed, but whether his portrayal of his own role as central and decisive is fully justified is difficult to know. We can be reasonably certain, however, that he behaved competently. Broadwood commended him to Kitchener and in November that year he received a brevet majority, apparently in recognition of his services.[49]

Two features of Haig's accounts of early actions in the Sudan are worthy of comment. The first is the importance he ascribed to the Egyptian Cavalry Brigade's Maxim machine guns. In the fight of 5 April he claimed to have given personal direction to some of these, thereby helping check a Dervish thrust. With regard to the most modern military technology Haig was no Luddite. He recognised that such technology might on occasion save his skin and had a healthy interest in it. The second feature is his general fairness to the Egyptian cavalry and other native troops. After the action of 21 March he had observed that: "The pluck of the Egyptian cavalry is right enough in my opinion." With regard to the action of 5 April, Haig believed that the authorities had somewhat over-praised it, pleased that Broadwood's brigade had not simply fled from the Dervishes. But he recognised that its general conduct had been satisfactory. Haig had his share of imperialist arrogance, but he was far from being crudely racist.

After a brief artillery bombardment, Kitchener's forces assaulted the Dervish camp on 8 April – Good Friday. About 3,000 Dervishes were killed, their force was routed and their leader, Mahmud, captured. British and Egyptian casualties were 496, of whom 125 were British. There were eighty fatalities on the Anglo-Egyptian side of which twenty-four were

British. The Egyptian cavalry played only a small part. They were employed on the left wing and drove the Dervish horsemen back to the river. But they were not allowed to cross the river until late in the day. At some point in these proceedings Haig, according to a letter to Henrietta written from Berber on 12 April, rescued a wounded Egyptian soldier who was isolated on the battlefield and likely to have been killed.[50]

Haig was inclined to question Kitchener's decision to mount a frontal assault on the Dervish position when an attack on its right flank might have gained better results. He doubted the effectiveness of shrapnel shell against an entrenched enemy. He questioned the depth of the formation that Kitchener had used for the assault, thinking this might have contributed to the scale of Anglo-Egyptian casualties. (Very similar criticisms would be made of many of the British Expeditionary Force's attacks on the Western Front under Haig's own command in 1916 and 1917.) He suggested an alternative scheme of manoeuvre whereby only about half the army would be used in attacking the Dervishes' position while one infantry brigade and the cavalry, with some artillery support, would cut off the enemy retreat and annihilate his forces. But he did have the humility to admit that his scheme depended on a level of training, flexibility and initiative not universal in the forces available to the Sirdar. Kitchener might have been right, Haig finally concluded, to adopt simple tactics and to be content with a "moderate" rather than an annihilating victory.[51]

It was now the hot season. After the Battle of Atbara there was a lengthy pause in operations. Kitchener held a sort of "Roman triumph" in Berber on 13 April in which the chained Mahmud was humiliated and abused, an episode that apparently did not appeal to Haig. On a brighter note, Haig finally got a squadron of Egyptian cavalry, which he was able to spend the next few months training to his own satisfaction. Kitchener brought up reinforcements, including another British infantry brigade and the 21st Lancers and extra gunboats and transport vessels for his river flotilla. The Khalifa's 50,000-strong Dervish army still outnumbered Kitchener's forces by two to one, but this was more than offset by the British-Egyptian advantage in firepower. A significant proportion of the Dervish host consisted of spearmen and swordsmen, lacking firearms. Even Kitchener's Egyptian infantry had the single-shot Martini–Henri breech-loader and his two British brigades had the Lee–Metford bolt-action magazine rifle. Kitchener's troops, moreover, were well supported by machine-guns.[52]

In late August Kitchener moved his forces up river and shifted them from the right to the left bank of the Nile, landing them at Wad Hamid, about sixty miles north of the city of Omdurman, near which the Khalifa's army was concentrated. The Egyptian cavalry, covering Kitchener's southward advance, had reached the Karari Hills nine miles north of Omdurman by 31 August. On 1 September, as the Anglo-Egyptian army was making its final advance towards the city, the Broadwood's cavalry brigade protected its right flank – the furthest from the river. Haig took command of the lead squadron. On the evening of 1 September Kitchener's infantry halted at the village of Egeiga, south of the Karari Hills. There the troops fortified (with a thorn bush perimeter known as a *zariba*) a semi-circular position with its back to the river. In the event of an assault the fire of the gunboats would support the defence. Though a night attack was anticipated, none materialised.[53]

The following day the Dervish host advanced from Omdurman to give battle. The Dervish left wing under the Khalifa's son, a force numbering about 15,000, swung north around the right flank of Kitchener's infantry. There it confronted Broadwood's small mounted force of some 1,800 troops. Kitchener sent one of his staff officers, Captain Sir Henry Rawlinson, to tell Broadwood to withdraw inside his fortified perimeter. Broadwood, however, preferred to remain mobile and to attempt to draw the Dervish left northward through the Karari Hills – where it could not play an effective role in the imminent battle. This was a somewhat risky manoeuvre, the success of which depended on the Egyptian cavalry maintaining very good order. It was successfully accomplished and Haig played his part. As Rawlinson approached the Egyptian cavalry he found:

our contact squadrons under Douglas Haig gradually withdrawing as the Dervishes advanced ... When I reached him he was within about 600 yards of the enemy's long line, and I noticed that his confident bearing seemed to have inspired his fellaheen [Egyptian other ranks] who were watching the Dervish advance quite calmly.[54]

The Dervish main body's assault on the fortified position at Egeiga was totally smashed by Anglo-Egyptian firepower. Few Dervishes got within 300 yards of Kitchener's lines and the plain was left strewn with thousands of dead and wounded. A clearer demonstration of the defensive power of the machine gun and the bolt-action magazine rifle could not have been provided. In the aftermath of this slaughter, Kitchener's forces pushed on towards the city of Omdurman, gradually overcoming the Dervish reserves in the process. Some parts of the Dervish army, however, retained remarkable discipline and cohesion. During the early stages of the pursuit, Haig's squadron of Egyptian cavalry "came under a hot fire". He ordered it to dismount and fire "volleys by troops" while "waiting for the other squadrons to come up". Even when reinforcements arrived, it was found impossible to charge directly towards Omdurman as "there were too many resolute men remaining". Haig ultimately considered that the charge that three squadrons of Egyptian cavalry did eventually under-take "towards the mouth of the Shambat Khor" was ill advised. "It was a ridiculous idea for 3 squadrons to attack some 10 or more thousands of resolute and armed men all scattered across the plain. I lost only 5 men wounded, but 19 horses." During this phase of the battle, one regiment of British cavalry was handled with even less discretion.

The one British cavalry regiment present, the Lancers, was deployed on the left wing and tasked with leading the advance towards Omdurman along the river bank. Encountering some surviving Dervishes, this regi-ment attempted, without adequate prior reconnaissance, to sweep them away by a charge. The participation of Winston Churchill, who wrote of it in two of his books, has helped immortalise the incident. It resulted, however, in seventy unnecessary British casualties amongst the 400 cav-alrymen taking part for an estimated loss to the Dervishes of only fourteen or fifteen men. Total Anglo-Egyptian casualties for the battle as a whole were less than 500, as against 11,000 Dervish dead and 5,000 prisoners.[55]

In the right circumstances, Haig strongly believed in cavalry shock action and the use of cold steel. Writing to Evelyn Wood he was, however, utterly scathing about the action of the 21st Lancers at Omdurman. The regiment was embarrassed by its lack of previous combat experience and had been desperate to

charge something before the show was over. They got their charge but at what cost? I trust for the sake of the British Cavalry that more tactical knowledge exists in the higher ranks of the *average* regiment than we have seen displayed in this one.[56]

The Battle of Omdurman was the climax of the war in the Sudan. Though there was still some mopping up to be done, from Haig's point of view there was nothing further to be gained by hanging around in this part of the world. Terminating his contract with the Egyptian army, he left Cairo on 30 September and arrived in London on 5 October. Briefly he took command of a squadron of his own regiment, the Hussars, then stationed at Norwich. On 6 May 1899, however, he was appointed Brigade Major to the Cavalry Brigade based at Aldershot.[57]

The brigade commander was Colonel John French with whom he was already acquainted. Like Haig, French was widely regarded as a talented cavalryman. Like Haig, he was a serious student of his profession. In other respects they were totally different. At 5 feet 10 inches Haig was relatively tall for a man of his generation. French was very short. Haig was taciturn, French garrulous. Haig was celibate, or at least very discreet; French was a compulsive and flagrant womaniser. Haig was a painstaking master of administrative detail; French was volatile, impulsive and disorganised. Haig was financially careful and independently wealthy; French was feckless and (in 1899) insolvent.[58] French was so pressed by creditors at this particular time that he was in danger of personal bankruptcy and having to resign his commission. Haig made him a personal loan of £2,500, thus saving his career. There was nothing illegal in this and it violated no army regulation. The loan was openly acknowledged by both parties and interest charged.

Yet, not repaid for many years, the Haig loan put French in an invidious position. The latter's military career was to some degree at the mercy of his principal staff officer rather than the (more appropriate) reverse situation. How, in such circumstances, could French objectively assess Haig's performance? Haig's motives in this business have inevitably been questioned. Though their relationship was to decline catastrophically during the First World War, in this period he seems to have genuinely liked and respected French. The least sinister explanation for the loan (and the one that Haig himself gave) is that he wanted to save the career of a worthy officer.[59] On the other hand, we have no knowledge of his ever having given comparable assistance to an officer junior to himself, however talented. Whatever his motive in advancing the loan, he must have been conscious that he had gained massive leverage at a point potentially useful to the development of his career.

When he went to his next war, South Africa, in 1899–1902, Haig was most favourably situated. He had a good record of routine soldiering from his Sandhurst days onward and a reputation as a competent military administrator. He already had some active service behind him and, though his actual combat experience was very limited, he was believed to have performed well. He had his immediate superior literally in his debt. He was on friendly terms with the heir to the throne. Few were so well placed to seize the opportunities that a major war offers the military professional. Yet this conflict was to be a great destroyer of reputations, tarnishing many a bright prospect. How would Haig fare?

The opening phase of the South African War

On 9 October 1899 President Paul Kruger of the Transvaal gave an ultimatum to the British demanding that they withdraw some of their military forces from southern Africa. This brought to a head years of tension between the British authorities at the Cape and the republics of the Transvaal and the Orange Free State. Most of the citizens of these states spoke a version of the Dutch language and were known as Boers (farmers). Sir Alfred Milner, the British High Commissioner, had been trying to provoke a war in order to absorb the Boer republics and the British were in the process of reinforcing, rather than diminishing, their troops in the region. An army corps of three infantry divisions and a cavalry division under Sir Redvers Buller was on its way from England; other forces were coming from India. When Kruger's ultimatum expired, on 11 October, war between Britain and the Boer states ensued.[1]

On 14 September 1899, during the period of acute pre-war tension, John French, Haig's brigadier, received orders to embark within ten days for South Africa. The order for Haig to accompany him followed six days later. They left from Southampton, on board the steamship *Norman*, on Saturday 23 September. French occupied a cabin that had belonged to the ship's second officer. As no accommodation had been allocated for Haig, they shared it. They arrived at Capetown on 10 October, the day before war broke out. At Capetown they received a cable ordering them both to proceed to Natal. The railway up to Durban had been closed, so it was necessary to go by sea and there was some delay.[2] Haig was able to reflect on the military operations that might lie ahead. For the first phase of the war, at least, he was by no means intellectually unprepared.

As tension grew between Britain and the Transvaal, Haig had written, apparently to clear his own mind, a paper on previous military actions against the Boers, including the British defeat at Majuba Hill in 1881. He had gained some valuable insights. He realised that the Boers would be tough opponents, that they were accustomed to living rough and that they were good riflemen and fair horsemen. He realised that attacking Boer riflemen frontally would probably be costly in casualties, but that finding a flank to turn was also likely to prove tricky. In past campaigns the Boers had sometimes used their mobility to forestall attempts at envelopment and "kept prolonging their line". Cavalry would be needed to find and envelop a flank and then to intercept the consequent Boer retreat. Otherwise the Boers would escape and establish further defensive positions and a "series of rearguard actions" might result. Cavalry would consequently be crucial "to ensure the annihilation of their field force".[3]

Thinking further on this subject while waiting at Capetown, Haig came to the perfectly reasonable conclusion that, for this war, the British would need an unusually high proportion of cavalry in their army. By contrast he thought that they could get by with a relatively modest amount of infantry. Indeed, he reckoned that they would need little more than the 10,000 men that he expected the Boers to put in the field. (In fact he had massively underestimated Boer numbers. They had approximately 47,000 combatants from the outset. But he was, of course, a recent arrival in the country and not an intelligence officer.) Less excusably, he had made little allowance for the numbers that would be needed to guard enormously long lines of communication and to police occupied territory.

As in letters he had written from the Sudan, he greatly played down the importance of artillery, an arm the importance and effectiveness of which he tended to play down at this stage in his career. He argued that a "Boer enemy is not a suitable objective for artillery" because he "fights as an individual", by which he seems to have meant in very loose, dispersed formations. It was indeed reasonable to believe that enemy dispersal would reduce the lethality of artillery. But Haig, at this stage, seems to have had little understanding of its importance in a suppressive role.

Such were the strengths and weaknesses of Haig's tactical appreciation. When it came to strategy, he considered, reasonably enough, that the Boer field army was the centre of gravity and that once it was destroyed the whole of South Africa would be at the mercy of the British. Though he expected that Boers would try to exploit their mobility, he thought they would be bound to stand and fight for the Transvaal capital at Pretoria. Once the British had gained the initiative, a thrust in that direction was, therefore, the obvious thing to do.[4] Haig apparently failed, at this stage, to anticipate the guerrilla resistance that would follow the defeat of the main Boer field forces and the fall of Pretoria. But given that, at this stage, he knew the enemy only at second hand, through his reading of recent history, he can hardly be blamed for that.

Haig sailed with French for Durban on board the *Norman*, arriving on 19 October. They went from there, by rail, to Ladysmith, where they

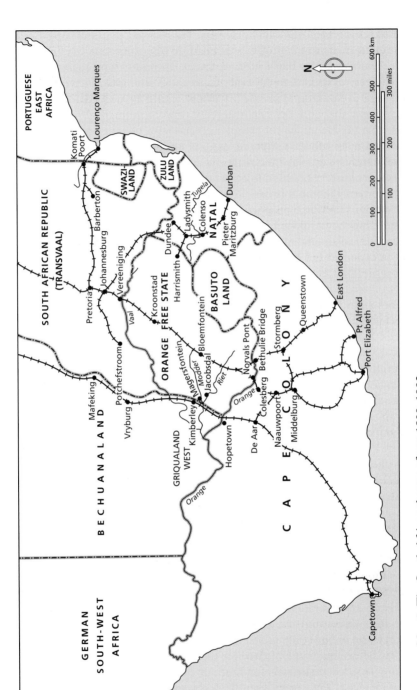

Map 2. The South African theatre of war 1899–1902

reported to Lieutenant-General Sir George White the following day. A substantial Boer invasion of Natal was now in progress. White had just heard that the Boers had captured the railway station of Elandslaagte, some twenty miles east-north-east of Ladysmith and seized a supply train there. The Boer occupation of Elandslaagte presented a particularly serious problem for a force of 4,000 British based at Dundee in the northern part of Natal. White did not yet know it, but that force had just fought, at Talana, a small action of which it had generally had the better, though its commander, Major-General Sir William Symons, had been killed. White did realise, however, that in order to avoid envelopment and destruction by the Boers, this force would probably have to fall back on Ladysmith. The Boers at Elandslaagte were a menace to its line of retreat.[5]

On 20 October White ordered French to recapture Elandslaagte. French's mounted troops for this operation, which came to him in dribs and drabs, consisted of a squadron of the 5th Dragoon Guards, a squadron of the 5th Lancers and five squadrons of the locally raised Imperial Light Horse (ILH). They started to ride out from Ladysmith at 4 a.m. on 21 October. Two batteries of obsolescent smooth bore seven-pounder guns moved with the cavalry while an armoured train with five companies of the Manchester regiment moved up the railway track from Ladysmith. Encountering Boer outposts about four miles west of the Elandslaagte at 7 a.m., French's force drove them back. The artillery brought the station under bombardment and caused the Boers to evacuate it. The Imperial Light Horse then galloped in and freed British prisoners from the train that the Boers had captured earlier.[6]

The Boer force at Elandslaagte, at about 1,000 men, was considerably larger than the British realised at this stage. Though it evacuated the station without much of a fight, it took up positions on a group of hills about two miles south-east of the station. Between them, French and White, with whom French was in touch by telegraph, decided to try to destroy this Boer force. To this end, substantial infantry reinforcements were brought in from Ladysmith under the command of one of White's staff officers, Ian Hamilton. The Boers were now heavily outnumbered. While Hamilton's infantry and dismounted troops of the ILH supported by reinforced artillery assaulted Boer positions frontally, but in a very dispersed formation, strong cavalry forces manoeuvred around the Boers left flank. These delivered a charge that the Boers were too distracted by Hamilton's infantry attack to be able to deal with. Some fleeing Boers were impaled on cavalry lances.[7]

The British forces at Elandslaagte suffered some 263 casualties all told. But the Boers had the worst of it. General Koch's commando sustained over 350 casualties, including 188 prisoners. Koch himself was killed.

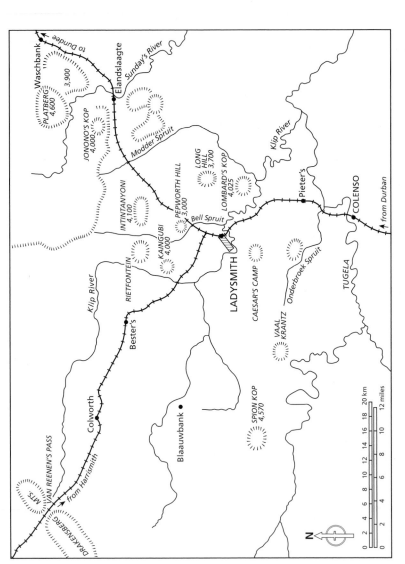

Map 3. Operations north of Ladysmith October–November 1899

It was a very small battle and only a very minor British victory. It helped the British force in northern Natal to escape into Ladysmith, but otherwise had no impact on the strategic situation. In the absence of other good news, however, this rather trifling affair was blown out of proportion by the newspapers and became the starting point for the very considerable military reputation that French would build in South Africa. Haig was French's principal staff officer but commanded nothing himself and it is difficult to say precisely how much credit he should be given. In the coming months, however, French's reputation would soar, French would sing Haig's praises and Haig's prestige would rise with his.[8]

When he had chance to reflect on it, Haig saw Elandslaagte as a confirmation of his previous tactical assumptions. Quite a few of these had, indeed, proved valid. But he continued to downplay the importance of artillery. It may have killed relatively few men on either side, but that was surely because neither side had used many guns and some of those that had been used on the British side were obsolescent. Its moral and suppressive effect, at various points in the battle, seems to have been of major importance. Haig did not deny this. But, as in the Sudan, he was remarkably contemptuous of artillery's lethality:

The effect of Artillery fire is chiefly moral! The teachings of peace manoeuvres and text books require to be considerably modified. Briefly, in our Army many have over-estimated the power of shrapnel fire.[9]

Meanwhile Boer forces continued to close in on Ladysmith. In an effort to disrupt the Boer concentration, White mounted a sizeable counter-offensive north of the city on Monday 30 October. French and Haig took a cavalry brigade onto Lombard's Kop on the British right where they became engaged in a prolonged dismounted fire-fight. Owing to disasters befalling forces to their left (most notably that to Colonel Carleton's force at Nicholson's Nek) they were compelled to fall back into Ladysmith by the end of the day. Thereafter White decided to keep his forces concentrated in Ladysmith and face a siege. Believing that their cavalry expertise would be wasted in such a situation, both French and Haig were keen to leave. White seemed equally keen to keep them.[10]

With the Cavalry Division

In the nick of time, French received orders from General Sir Redvers Buller, now in overall command in South Africa, that he and Haig should leave Ladysmith for Capetown forthwith. There they would take charge of the British Cavalry Division, which was expected to start arriving within the next couple of weeks. With White no longer able to oppose their departure, on 2 November French and Haig caught what turned out to be the last train out of Ladysmith for many weeks. It came under so much fire that, for a while, they were compelled to lie down on the carriage floor. Haig later discovered a Boer shell embedded in his luggage. At Colenso they caught another train to Durban and there embarked on the *Tintagel Castle* on 3 November, arriving at the Cape five days later.[11]

French and Haig were soon at work organising a camp for the Cavalry Division at Maitland, near Capetown. This kind of administrative exercise was far more Haig's forte than French's, but neither was given time to complete the task. On 18 November, before the Cavalry Division was fully assembled, Buller sent French to De Aar in the northern part of Cape Colony. The Boers had already captured the town of Colesburg and were raiding south from that vicinity. The situation was potentially serious. The authorities at the Cape feared that if the Boers seemed to be gaining the upper hand in the northern part of the colony, many of the Dutch-speaking inhabitants would join them.[12]

With Haig still acting as his principal staff officer, French was tasked with containing the penetration of Boer commandos into Cape Colony and with retaking Colesberg if possible. Only modest forces were available to undertake this task: initially only two half battalions of infantry, elements of the 5th Lancers and new South Wales Lancers, some Cape Police and two nine-pounder muzzle-loading guns. Yet the British in this sector responded aggressively and won moral superiority over Shoeman's commando. French was unable to recapture Colesburg but, over the next couple of months, while British forces suffered defeats elsewhere in South Africa, he prevented significant further Boer penetration into this part of Cape Colony. French and Haig seem to have been fortunate in being up against one of the less able Boer military leaders. Yet, given the defeats elsewhere, French's stock, already high after Elandslaagte, continued to rise and Haig's rose with it.[13]

British military operations in the last weeks of 1899 were intended to relieve the towns of Kimberley and Ladysmith. Forces under Lord Methuen and Sir Redvers Buller, the commander-in-chief, were to carry out these missions. On 11 December, however, Methuen suffered a defeat at Magersfontein on the Modder River and, on 15 December, Buller met a still more costly reverse at Colenso while trying to move across the Tugela River towards Ladysmith.[14] These "Black Week" defeats caused a sensation in the British press. The government decided to replace Buller with Lord Roberts as overall commander in South Africa, with Kitchener as Roberts's chief of staff. At the same time the military authorities in London decided that to have a mere major, Haig's substantive rank at this time, as Assistant Adjutant General (AAG, in effect chief of staff) of the Cavalry Division was inappropriate. A full colonel, the Earl of Erroll, was despatched to fill that appointment. French protested to Roberts in strong terms, praising Haig's work and expressing a desire to have him as AAG. While Roberts acknowledged Haig's contribution, he confirmed Erroll's appointment. Haig was, however, included on the divisional staff, as Deputy Assistant Adjutant General (DAAG) and remained French's most trusted adviser.[15]

Roberts left Buller in command of the field army advancing towards Ladysmith while he himself took charge of relieving Kimberley. Roberts decided to use the Cavalry Division under French as the spearhead of the British advance on Kimberley. Operating in secrecy and acting with great speed Roberts turned the eastern flank of Cronje's entrenched position at Magersfontein, French's Cavalry Division seizing inadequately defended fords over the Riet River at De Kiel Drift on 12 February and over the Modder River at Klip Drift on 13 February 1900. This was achieved with few human casualties but the horses were driven so hard that some 500 had to be shot. At Klip Drift there was a hiatus of more than a day in bringing up the cavalry division's transport. Cronje, the Boer commander at Magersfontein, used the time to try to extend his left flank towards Kimberley. On the morning of 15 February, however, its supplies having caught up, French's division advanced on Kimberley carrying two days' rations.[16]

Boer riflemen and artillery fired on French's advancing cavalry just a few miles north of Klip Drift. But French considered (correctly as it turned out) that only a light and porous screen of outposts blocked his path. In fact only about 900 overstretched Boers faced 8,000 British cavalry, 6,000 mounted infantry supported by fifty-six guns. Roberts had strongly emphasised the importance of a speedy relief of Kimberley. French, therefore, ordered his artillery to put suppressive fire on the principal Boer positions and his cavalry to charge through a gap between them. As at Elaandslaagte the previous year, British cavalry rode down fleeing Boers, killing some and capturing others. At the cost of about twenty casualties to French's division, including only seven killed, Kimberley was relieved. That night French and Haig dined in the company of Kimberley's most famous citizen, the super-rich businessman Cecil Rhodes, on horsemeat washed down with champagne.[17] The relief of Kimberley was one of the turning points of the war. Cronje's little army was now serving no useful purpose at Magersfontein. The Boer commander's escape route to the north was, however, made impracticable by the presence of British cavalry at Kimberley. He decided instead to retreat in an easterly direction along the Modder River towards the Orange Free State capital at Bloemfontein.[18]

Pulling out on the night of 15/16 February, Cronje had reached Paardeburg by 17 February. Roberts was anxious to trap him and, as soon as he realised the direction of Cronje's retreat, ordered French to make a cavalry dash from Kimberley. Despite the poor condition of the horses, which, in the relief of Kimberley, had already been driven very hard over a waterless landscape in ferocious heat, French took one brigade and rushed to Koedoesrand Drift, intercepting Cronje's retreat. British infantry then came up to surround Cronje's position and force his surrender. Kitchener, who took charge of British forces surrounding Cronje at Paardeburg, initially mishandled the operation. Bungled infantry assaults cost excessive casualties. Cronje remained trapped, however, and on 27 February 1900 surrendered his entire force of around 4,000 men.[19]

During the Kimberley-Paardeburg campaign, arguably decisive of the war, Haig had initially occupied a less prominent position than he had hoped. Lord Erroll had, on paper at least, been the AAG of the Cavalry Division, though some of the most important orders were issued under Haig's signature. But, on 21 February, French appointed Haig, over the heads of more senior officers, to command the 3rd Cavalry Brigade. When Roberts countermanded that appointment, French complained that he had not been satisfied with Erroll's performance as chief of staff. Erroll was transferred to Roberts's headquarters and Haig took his place.[20] To what extent the Haig–French financial loan played its part in French's determined efforts to advance Haig's career at this time is impossible to say. But there can be little doubt that Haig was demonstrating great keenness and great competence at this stage in his career.

Since the Roberts–Kitchener takeover in South Africa, British fortunes had undoubtedly improved. Haig, however, was far from satisfied with the performance of his superiors. In letters home he made a stream of pointed criticisms of Roberts and Kitchener and their headquarters. These were so continuous and so strident in tone that the Prince of Wales became rather sick of them and told Henrietta Jameson so. Haig remained self-righteous and unrepentant.[21] His future letters were not noticeably less critical, but Henrietta probably had the sense to be more selective in what she passed on.

After Paardeburg Roberts was keen to take the two Boer capitals, starting with Bloemfontein, capital of the Orange Free State, which happened to be the nearer. Roberts knew that Boer forces covering Bloemfontein were hastily arrayed at Poplar Grove, south of the city. He wanted to destroy these forces as well as taking Bloemfontein. To this end he ordered French to take the Cavalry Division together with two brigades of Mounted Infantry (MI) in a wide sweep around the Boer left flank. When British infantry assaulted the Boer position, the cavalry and MI would cut off their retreat.[22] Most of the Cavalry Division's horses were, however, exhausted and half-starved. Haig thought that the main problem was that Roberts had raised too many mounted troops. At the start of the war he had insisted that this conflict would require an unusually large proportion of mounted forces. But the British were now facing the tremendous logistical problems involved in maintaining many thousands of horses in high tempo operations over a semi-desert terrain. The supply of fodder and remounts to replace dead, sick or exhausted animals might have been sufficient to keep the Cavalry Division operating to its true potential. But much of the MI, the "Colonial scallywag corps" as Haig called it, was in his view grossly inefficient and, quite literally, a waste of rations. Roberts took a different view. Immediately after Paardeburg he was publicly critical of French for using more fodder than he was entitled to. Needless to say, this charge, which appears to have been grossly unjust, was not conducive to an effective working relationship between the Cavalry Division and the rest of Roberts's army.[23]

French seems to have believed from the outset that Roberts's plan to envelop the Boer forces at Poplar Grove gave the cavalry an impossible task. It is at least possible that neither he nor Haig tried too hard to execute it. While Bloemfontein fell to the British on 13 March, most of the Boer troops escaped to fight another day. After the fall of Bloemfontein, the British, logically enough, pushed on to the other Boer capital at Pretoria. The Cavalry Division played an important part in the campaign, culminating in the fall of that city on 5 June. But the perpetually exhausted state of the horses meant that it never operated at full efficiency. French and Haig were not able to help pull off any more dramatic envelopments of Boer forces. It was very rarely possible for cavalry to use cold steel and there were no notable charges like that of Elandslaagte. There were probably a number of factors involved in the relative ineffectiveness of French's cavalry at this stage in the campaign. But the sickly state of those of the Cavalry Division's original horses still surviving and the poor quality of many of the remounts were conspicuous amongst them.[24]

Counter-guerrilla operations

The occupation of the two Boer capitals did not end the war. Boer military forces had survived and continued to resist, increasingly employing hit-and-run guerrilla tactics. In November 1900 the British broke up their cavalry division, now considered too large for operations against a dispersed enemy. Until the peace settlement of May 1902 Haig was involved in counter-guerrilla operations in various parts of the Orange

2. Haig in the South African War. National Library of Scotland.

River Colony and Cape Colony. For most of this time he functioned either as a column or an area commander. Kitchener, who took overall command in South Africa when Roberts stepped down in November 1900, seemed to Haig to be shifting forces around too much rather than letting them focus on pacifying particular areas.[25]

Like other British officers, Haig initially underestimated the toughness and determination of Boer guerrilla resistance. Though he sometimes enjoyed the thrill of the horseback pursuit of Boer commandos, he found the experience of guerrilla warfare in many respects intensely frustrating.

He was aware that a high proportion of all South Africans of Dutch descent sympathised with the commandos. Many assisted them. Haig's frustration turned to a degree of bitterness. That in turn exposed a strong streak of ruthlessness in his nature. He actively supported (and himself practised) the official policy of burning the farms of civilians found aiding the guerrillas. He favoured executing citizens of the Cape caught in arms against the British authorities and thought this policy should be applied more consistently than it actually was. He mentioned in his diary, apparently approvingly, troops under his command summarily executing Boer prisoners captured wearing khaki.

During and immediately after the South African War, Haig's political attitudes seem to have been at their most illiberal and militaristic. He expressed a good deal of contempt for professional politicians and parliamentary politics. He appeared to want to militarise South Africa and not to forgive the Boers.[26] Such sentiments, however, seem to have developed under the pressure of war and to have been temporary. By the time of the Curragh crisis in March 1914 his attitudes were much more politically correct and, during the First World War, he was to display no bitterness against Smuts and other South Africans who supported the British Empire's war effort, whatever their previous allegiance.

In May 1901 Haig was promoted, becoming commanding officer of the 17th Lancers with the substantive rank of Lieutenant Colonel. It seems that he owed this particular appointment more to Roberts (whom he had bitterly criticised) than to French (whom he had most closely and faithfully served). French had earlier tried to give Haig a brigade, but for command of the 17th Lancers he favoured another talented officer, Herbert Lawrence, who had a lengthy period of service with the regiment and thus a strong claim. Roberts, however, considered Haig the most "capable and distinguished of all the young cavalry soldiers" and, now Commander-in-Chief of the British army, he arranged Haig's appointment to command the regiment.[27]

During the guerrilla phase of the war Haig found himself dealing with one of the most formidable of the Boer commando leaders, Jan Smuts: a Cambridge-educated lawyer who had been a senior judge in the Transvaal before the war. In July 1901, Smuts, with 500 mounted riflemen, swept south from the Transvaal, through the Orange River Colony and then west through Cape Colony. Over the next ten months he covered nearly 1,800 miles, wrecking railways and shattering isolated British units. Smuts spent a considerable part of this time in the area of the Cape for which Haig was responsible. In September Haig suffered the indignity of having "C" Squadron of his regiment badly mauled, by part of Smuts's force, about fourteen miles from Tarkastad, though he was not with the squadron when this occurred. Over the next few months he pursued Smuts, but had not managed to kill or capture him in May 1902 when the Boer leadership finally decided to end the war.[28]

Haig may not have been an outstanding success as a co-ordinator of mobile columns, but nor did he suffer, in the guerrilla phase of the conflict, the really humiliating disasters that befell some other officers. It may well be that both the lack of any remarkable success and the lack of any really major disaster were due to Haig's caution and hesitancy as a commander. Yet, earlier in the war, as a staff officer, he had undoubtedly played a role in some highly successful operations and he emerged from Britain's greatest conflict since the Crimea enhanced in both rank and reputation. Haig's promotion may also have owed something to Henrietta's lobbying and to royal influence, but South Africa had ruined the reputations of many officers, including some who had enjoyed royal favour.[29] At this stage in Haig's career, no amount of playing at army politics would have covered up, or compensated for, serious defeat in the field.

With the 17th Lancers in Britain; Inspector of Cavalry in India; marriage

Haig remained in South Africa, responsible for military administration in the western part of Cape Colony, for about four months after the war ended. On 23 September 1902, however, the 17th Lancers under Haig's command embarked from Capetown for Southampton. The regiment then headed to Edinburgh, where it was based for the next year. Haig found regimental routine extremely boring and was not especially pleased to be back in the city of his birth, judging it a poor location for cavalry. Under Haig's captaincy, however, the 17th Lancers won the Inter-Regimental Polo Tournament in 1903. In the final, played on 11 July in the presence of Queen Alexandra,[30] Haig's team beat the Blues, who had been the favourites to win the competition. As his next appointment, French wanted Haig to command of the 1st Cavalry Brigade at Aldershot, a job he would have much liked. But Kitchener, the commander-in-chief in India, wanted him as Inspector General of Cavalry there. When the post became vacant, in October, Haig filled it.[31]

Queen Victoria had died in January 1901 and Edward VII was now king. The Jamesons, his sister and brother-in-law, had been close to Edward when he was Prince of Wales. They maintained this friendship after Edward ascended to the throne. For about five years, Douglas Haig had been part of this gilded circle. In October 1903, shortly before he left to take up his post in India, Edward VII invited him to the royal residence at Balmoral in Scotland and there appointed him Commander of the Victorian Order. Perhaps more importantly, Edward encouraged Haig to write regularly from India, keeping his sovereign briefed on military affairs there. The role of royal informant was one with which Haig was long familiar and which he was more than happy to perform.[32]

As Inspector General in India over the next three years Haig worked hard on cavalry training and organisation. Though by no means opposed to cavalry's use of the rifle, he did not want it to become mere mounted infantry and continued to emphasise training in the use of cold steel and in the charge. Almost inevitably, he also became involved in a dispute between Lord Curzon, the Viceroy, and Kitchener, the Commander-in-Chief, over the overall control of military forces in the sub-Continent. Curzon wanted to preserve the existing system, by which responsibility was divided between the Commander-in-Chief and the Military Member of the Viceroy's Council. Kitchener naturally favoured unity of command under the Commander-in-Chief. Haig seems discreetly and adroitly to have taken the side of Kitchener, his immediate superior and, ultimately, the victor in the struggle.[33]

In 1905 Haig took some home leave, arriving in England in mid-May. The following month the King summoned him to stay at Windsor Castle to take part in the social round which accompanied Royal Ascot, the famous horse race meeting. At Windsor he met one of Queen Alexandra's Maids of Honour: the Honourable Dorothy Vivian, sister of Lord Vivian, who had served with the 17th Lancers in South Africa and been severely wounded in the attack by part of Smuts's commando on "C" Squadron. Within two days of their first meeting, Douglas Haig and Dorothy (Doris) Vivian were engaged. On 11 July they were married in the private chapel of Buckingham Palace, this apparently being the first time the chapel was used for a non-royal wedding. Both the suddenness and the brevity of the engagement were widely remarked. When one acquaintance referred to it, Haig is reported to have replied that he had decided more important questions in less time.[34]

Seemingly demeaning to the institution of marriage and to the status of women, Haig's remark about his courtship is rather shocking to modern sensibility. But he was notoriously poor at expressing his thoughts in speech. He may only have meant that he considered his personal happiness less important than military duty and that he had trained himself to make life or death decisions in seconds on the battlefield. Whatever he really felt, Haig had gained a wife, an acquisition generally thought appropriate, indeed almost necessary, for an officer of his rank. His choice, quite possibly suggested by his royal patrons, further consolidated his place in their favour. The available evidence indicates that both partners in the union rated it a major success.[35]

Army reform and the General Staff

Dorothy Haig spent the first year of her married life with her husband in India. But there is some evidence that Haig had been reluctant to return to India after his marriage. Army reform was being hotly debated. The War Office was the decision centre and Haig tried to gain appointment as Director of Staff Duties: an important General Staff post.[36] In the short term he was not successful. In March 1906, however, while back in the sub-Continent, Haig received a letter from the influential peer, Viscount Esher, informing him that he was to be offered the key General Staff post of Director of Military Training at the War Office. Haig was naturally flattered, especially when it was made clear to him that the King himself was "desirous that I shd accept the billet". He wrote to Henrietta that:

Although called Training, the Department also deals with "War Organisation" and "Home Defence", so that it is the most important Directorate in the General Staff at the present time.[37]

Esher, to whom Haig largely owed his appointment to the General Staff at a crucial period of army reform, was an *eminence grise* of British military affairs in the Edwardian period. He had served on the Commission of Enquiry into the army's weaknesses and failings during the South African War – a commission chaired by Lord Elgin. He was subsequently appointed to chair a small committee of his own on military reform. He had produced a series of reports recommending the reorganisation of the army at the highest level, substituting an Army Council for the Commander-in-Chief and introducing a General Staff whose chief would be the principal Military Member of the Council. These recommendations had been accepted and had begun to be implemented before Haldane's arrival at the War Office, but Esher was convinced that the process of reform still had a long way to go.[38]

During the enquiry on South Africa, Esher had heard Haig's evidence, had found him most impressive and reported upon him favourably to the King, confirming the latter's already good opinion. On 18 March 1903 Esher had written to his sovereign in the following terms:

Lord Esher presents his humble duty and begs to inform Your Majesty that the most interesting evidence taken to-day was that of Colonel Haig – 17th Lancers – an officer known to Your Majesty as a most capable cavalry leader. He is evidently a good organiser, and a helpful Staff Officer … In him Your Majesty possesses a very fine type of officer, practical, firm, and thoughtful, thoroughly experienced not only in war, but in military history.[39]

Balfour's Conservative government had appointed the Commission on the South African War and it was to this government that Esher had submitted his proposals for sweeping army reform. But, independently wealthy, Esher was not a career politician in the normal sense and considered himself above party politics. He exerted much of his influence on military policy through his relationship with the King. When Campbell-Bannerman's Liberal government came to power in December 1905, Richard Burdon Haldane, a Scot, a successful practitioner at the English bar, and a scholar of German culture and philosophy, became Secretary of State for War. Esher became an adviser to Haldane and was able to exert an influence on policy from an early stage in the latter's ministry.[40] Esher originally wanted Haig to be Director of Staff Duties and nagged Haldane relentlessly on this matter during his first few months in office. However, this post was held by Major-General H. D. Hutchinson, who was a favourite with General Sir Neville Lyttleton, the Chief of the General Staff and thus very difficult to remove. Instead, under pressure from both Esher and the King to find Haig a key General Staff position, Haldane decided to let him have the Directorate of Military Training.[41]

Haig's connection with Esher had thus provided his career with a massive boost – a key General Staff post at a critical time in the army's history. It is not completely clear how this connection was first established. It is quite possible that Haig and Esher had met in the social circle of Edward VII, perhaps while the latter was still Prince of Wales, before Haig gave evidence to the inquiry into the South African War in March 1903. In order to help explain Esher's very committed support for Haig's career it has been suggested, not altogether unreasonably, that the homosexual peer was physically attracted to the handsome cavalry officer.[42] There is no doubt that Esher was given to intense homoerotic passions, but he was also an intelligent individual with a real concern for issues of national defence who prided himself on the trust that the King placed in him.[43] It is most unlikely that he would have compromised his credibility by sponsoring the candidacy for key positions of a dunderhead or incompetent, however physically attractive. That Esher was prepared to sponsor Haig for key posts under a reforming war minister of exceptional intellectual gifts indicates the impression of intelligence, efficiency and professional knowledge that Haig was capable of making on astute observers at this stage in his career. It also tends to confirm our earlier suggestion that Haig's difficulty in expressing his ideas by word of mouth was intermittent and was probably dependent, to a considerable degree, on the subject matter and the nature of his audience.

On the surface of things Richard Haldane, the new Secretary of State for War, hardly seemed likely to be a success in this post. Obese and rather scruffy, he was not a natural choice for dealing with members of a profession that has always considered physical appearance important. He had little prior knowledge of military matters. He was imbued and somewhat preoccupied with arcane ideas of foreign derivation and was a member of a government considered by many officers to be dangerously radical. Yet he showed himself prepared to listen to military advice and benefited from comparison with Arnold-Foster, his Conservative predecessor, who had strong preconceived ideas and appeared not to be.[44] While still in India, in February 1906, Haig had written to his sister Henrietta:

Everyone I hear from in the soldiering line at home speaks well of Haldane, so the advent of the Radicals is certainly of great advantage to the Army in substituting him for Arnold-Forster [sic].[45]

Haig returned to England in June 1906. He met Haldane for the first time at Government House in Aldershot, where they were both guests of Sir John French. Haig and Haldane immediately established an effective working partnership, which was important to some of Haldane's reforms. Much of the initial success of this relationship may be attributed to Esher, who had expended a good deal of his time and effort extolling the virtues of each to the other. Mutual respect seems to have been strong from the outset. Ultimately Haig gave Haldane a degree of praise perhaps greater than he gave to any other contemporary.[46]

By the time Haig arrived at the War Office the process of forming a General Staff was already under way; indeed, it had commenced before Haldane's arrival. The next major task that Haldane set himself was to reorganise the various part-time military forces (the Militia, the Yeomanry and the Volunteers) into a single coherent force. It seems to have been in this reorganisation of the reserves that Haig played his greatest part in the Haldane reforms. Haldane eventually decided that his new "Territorial Force", the direct ancestor of the modern Territorial Army, should consist of fourteen infantry divisions and fourteen cavalry brigades. The intention was that these would be organised on similar lines and be equipped in the same way as the divisions of the Regular Army.[47]

One of the obstacles to Haldane's rationalisation of the reserve system was the opposition of the Militia Colonels to the incorporation of the Militia into the Territorial Force. The Militia Colonels were mostly major landowners whose control of the militia at county level gave them a useful form of patronage that they were reluctant to surrender. They seem also to have realised that Haldane's proposed reforms left them with many burdensome administrative responsibilities while depriving them of the more glamorous function of command. Haldane and Haig held a number of meetings with the Colonels in an effort to iron out these difficulties.

Ultimately, however, agreement proved impossible and Haig encouraged Haldane to abolish the Militia. Elements of what had been the Militia were used to form the Special Reserve, an immediate reserve for the Regular Army. Yeomanry (part-time cavalry) and Volunteer (mainly part-time infantry) units became part of the Territorial Force, the principal duty of which became home defence.[48]

Haig was also involved in Haldane's most famous reform: the creation, out of regular units and reserves based in the United Kingdom, of an organised expeditionary force of six infantry divisions and a cavalry division ready for prompt despatch overseas in a crisis. In order to help pay for this organisation and to effect economies that would win over his more anti-military colleagues in the Cabinet, Haldane abolished a considerable number of military units that he considered surplus to requirements. Savings of two million pounds were made in the annual army estimates. But all the units that disappeared were of either infantry or artillery. Not a single cavalry regiment was abolished. Considering the relative importance of the three arms in the next big war this might be considered not to reflect particularly well on Haldane's judgement. It is quite possible that it owed something to Haig's influence on his Secretary of State.[49]

In November 1907 Haig became Director of Staff Duties. In that capacity he played a part in another aspect of the Haldane reforms: the creation of an Imperial (as opposed to merely a British) General Staff system. Part of the key to the degree of success achieved was not being too ambitious. The self-governing parts of the empire – Canada, Australia, New Zealand and South Africa – opposed the centralised control of their military forces by the British War Office. Earlier negotiations had broken down for this reason. These countries were, however, prepared to harmonise the organisation of their forces with that of the British army, to introduce their own General Staffs on the British system and to send promising officers for further military education at Camberley. Arrangements along these lines were confirmed at a Colonial Conference held in London in July 1909.[50]

At "Training" Haig had put much work into the revision of the army's manuals. The most important of these, the master manuals, were the two-volumes of *Field Service Regulations: Part I Operations* and *Part II Organisation and Administration*. While Director of Staff Duties, Haig had to fight to get these accepted and published. *Part Two*, largely written within the Staff Duties branch, met with particularly intense opposition, mainly from the Adjutant-General's and Quartermaster-General's branches. They perceived it as trespassing on their preserves. Haig overcame the opposition and progress towards publication seemed unstoppable by the time he left the War Office. For the rest of his career Haig was proud of these booklets, especially the first. He thought the principles set down were fundamental to military operations conducted as late as 1918.[51]

Looked at from a post-First World War perspective, the *Operations* volume of the *Regulations* does have a rather archaic feel about it. Cavalry was seen as the principal means of reconnaissance and one of the principal means of exploitation. Aeroplanes as such were not even mentioned, though the use of balloons was carefully considered. The *Regulations* placed very strong emphasis on offensive action. In retrospect, a ruthless determination to succeed seems to be over-emphasised as against material factors such as weight of fire. "Half-hearted measures can never succeed in war, and lack of determination is the most fruitful source of defeat." The approach to the offensive generally recommended was to use suppressive fire in combination with enveloping manoeuvres: reasonable enough in itself. In retrospect it might seem that the problem of what to do when there were no open flanks to envelop should have been given more consideration. But British doctrine was, in general, not behind that of the major Continental armies.[52] Moreover, no set of regulations can deal with all contingencies. Indeed, while in India in 1911, Haig argued that:

Certain critics of the British General Staff and of our regulations have recently argued that a doctrine is lacking ... the British General Staff hesitates to teach and to publish a clear line of action ... The critics seem to lose sight of the true nature of war, and of the varied conditions under which the British army may have to take the field. It is neither necessary nor desirable that we should go further than what is clearly laid down in our regulations. If we go further, we run the risk of tying ourselves by a doctrine that may not always be applicable and we gain nothing in return.[53]

So, at least in theory, Haig believed in intellectual flexibility and pragmatism, in officers not being too rigidly bound by textbook ideas.

The most conservative aspect of Haig's military thought was defence of the importance of cavalry. This was presented in a fairly strident form in the introduction to *Cavalry Studies*, a book based on staff rides and exercises conducted while he was on his last job in India, and published with the assistance of Colonel Lonsdale Hale, a well-known military author of the period, in 1907. Haig claimed that the importance of cavalry would "always go on increasing". Increasing artillery firepower (a factor Haig had at last recognised) would, he professed to believe, demoralise the infantry and thus make it easier for cavalry to charge them. Cavalry could cross the fire-swept zone between armies faster than infantry, and the small-bore rifle (.303 and similar) had relatively poor stopping power against horses. Some historians have put considerable effort into setting these arguments in their proper historical context and explaining the thought processes behind them. It is, however, difficult to avoid the conclusion that they were, in the final analysis, rather weak arguments, and that the motive in putting them forward was excessive devotion to the arm of the service from which the author came.[54]

The treatment of cavalry in the official *Cavalry Training 1907* also made the sweeping and extremely dubious claim that: "The value of cavalry is now greater than at any previous period." But generally both this manual and the *Operations* volume of the *Field Service Regulations* were relatively forward looking in relation to the mobile arm. They emphasised cavalry's reconnaissance function, its greatly increased firepower (as a result of the adoption of the Lee–Enfield rifle and machine guns) and the importance of dismounted fighting as well as the charge. British thinking was somewhat more realistic in relation to cavalry than that of the leading Continental military powers. As late as 1914 Continental cavalry was generally equipped with the carbine rather than the rifle and Continental doctrine generally placed greater emphasis on shock action than did Haig and his colleagues when the *Field Service Regulations* were compiled.[55]

During his period of service at the War Office he had good news on the domestic front. His first daughter, Alexandra, was born on 9 March 1907 and his second, Victoria, on 7 November 1908. The Haigs's royal connection remained strong. Both daughters gained royal godparents. In July 1909 Haig was made Knight Commander of the Victorian Order and he and Lady Haig (as Doris now became) stayed for a few days with the King and Queen at their Scottish estate at Balmoral.[56] Yet despite his blessings and successes in this period, the War Office and London life did not altogether suit Haig. He was used to interspersing office work with more physical exercise (riding in particular) than he was now able to manage and his hours at the War Office were sometimes exceptionally long. Whether or not pressure of work was a contributory factor, his health broke down temporarily in April 1908.

Illness kept Haig away from the War Office until mid-June. During this period, and perhaps at others, much of his work devolved on his Deputy Director, the industrious if somewhat colourless Launcelot Kiggell, to whom Haig was deeply grateful. Kiggell, in turn, seems rather to have hero-worshipped Haig and to have constantly looked to him for guidance, becoming one of his protégés. The exact nature of Haig's health problem is not entirely clear, but, according to one account, a bout of the malaria he had contracted in India was followed by a severe attack of influenza. Haig had taken much time off sick in the course of his career. Years before his constitution was exposed to the rigours of India, he had lost a term at Oxford. At least one historian has, not unreasonably, diagnosed hypochondria, and Haig's siblings, amongst whom he was nicknamed "Dockie" (short for doctor), would probably have agreed with this.[57] It must, however, be remembered that Haig, like his mother, died relatively young.

Chief of the General Staff in India

During that same April, General Sir O'Moore Creagh, the commander-in-chief in India, approached Haig to become his Chief of the General Staff. Initially, Haig was not keen. Acceptance would mean separation from his children (whom he apparently considered too young to be exposed to the sub-Continent's health hazards) and he was anxious to ensure that the Staff Duties branch of the General Staff continued to work smoothly. Once Haig had used his influence to ensure that Kiggell should succeed him as Director of Staff Duties, however, he decided to accept the Indian post. He had a strong feeling that war with Germany was coming, but argued in a letter to Kiggell that he could play a vital role in preparing Indian troops for participation in a collective British Empire war effort. Doris, who would have an important social role to play, was to accompany her husband. The children were left behind under the care of Haig's sister Henrietta.[58] Before embarking for India in October 1909, the Haigs went to Balmoral to pay what turned out to be their last visit to King Edward VII. At this stage the King was still well enough to go out on the moors, but within six months he was dead. His passing was doubtless a cause of sadness to Haig and his wife, but they seem already to have been well acquainted with the new sovereign, George V, and would have close contact with the court well into the next reign.[59]

The new posting, in which Haig had the temporary rank of Lieutenant-General, lasted a little over two years. Haig left India to take command at Aldershot shortly before Christmas 1911. His long stint in the War Office had forced Haig to endure quite enough of the sedentary life for the time being. As Chief of the General Staff in India 1909–1911, he delegated a good deal of his routine office work to the newly appointed Director of Military Operations, Brigadier-General Hamilton-Gordon, who had accompanied him from Britain. Haig himself travelled widely through India doing the more congenial work of keeping in touch with staffs throughout the country and organising frequent Staff Rides.[60]

Inevitably, as Chief of the General Staff, Haig had to deal with some controversial issues. During his previous staff service in India, when Kitchener was commander-in-chief, he had been involved in drawing up a plan whereby elements of the Indian Army could be despatched as an expeditionary force overseas – perhaps to Europe – in the event of a major war there. The plan had been given the codename *Nathi* (Hindi for "imp"). Policy changed under Lord Morley, the pacifically minded Liberal Secretary of State for India, Lord Hardinge, the Liberal viceroy from 1910 and General Sir O'Moore Creagh, Kitchener's successor as commander-in-chief. The Indian Army, paid for from India's taxes, was to be used for the defence of India only. Plans for its use in support of a wider imperial war effort outside the sub-Continent were to be dropped and destroyed. Haig and Hamilton-Gordon, while not openly opposing the change of policy, partially evaded it and secretly preserved the *Nathi* plan.[61]

Haig's role in preserving *Nathi* indicates that he saw India as an integral part of a wider British Empire. In Haig's scheme of things, troops maintained largely by taxes imposed on the Indian peasantry would help fight the King–Emperor's wars wherever in the world these occurred and whether or not India's interests were directly concerned. Yet his attitude to the sub-Continent was certainly not crudely exploitative. He had upper-class Indian friends, most notably Sir Pratap Singh, the Maharajah of Idar. He thought India benefited from being part of the British Empire and he evidently saw himself, with some justice, as an enlightened, progressive imperialist. In mid-1911, in a letter to Launcelot Kiggell, he spelt out at some length his general views on policy in India:

As regards the granting of commissions to Indians, the Government have not yet decided … but they are being pressed by various influential sections of the community and there are many thoughtful officers of the civil service who think that the Indians really suffer under a grievance … Personally I feel that there are only two ways of treating India; either we must look forward to the time when India will be in the position of one of the Dominions, and we must prepare for it gradually, looking forward say another 100 years; or the other way is to keep India entirely as a vassal state and keep it entirely under control. For this we shall want a very much larger army than we have now, and it seems hardly possible, having started to give the people a voice in the Government to retrace our steps. There is thus, in my opinion, no other course than to give the sons of the fighting class an opportunity of becoming officers; only those however who show they are morally and intellectually fit for such appointments …[62]

Haig would surely not have believed that the British Raj in India had only another thirty-six years to run, but the same would have been true of practically all Britons at that time. By suggesting, in 1911, that India should gradually be prepared for the same sort of self-governing status within the Empire as Canada, Australia and New Zealand, Haig demonstrated a remarkably enlightened political vision.

Aldershot and the Curragh crisis

On 12 May 1911 Haldane wrote to Haig offering him the command at Aldershot that Sir Horace Smith-Dorrien was shortly due to leave. This was arguably the most important command in the peacetime British army, including, as it did, the units that were to form I Corps of the British Expeditionary Force. Haig was more than willing to accept this post. George V was, however, due to visit India for the "great Durbar" (a state occasion in which the King-Emperor's Indian subjects would have the opportunity to demonstrate their allegiance) from 7–12 December that year. The Viceroy, Lord Curzon, wanted Haig (as both a competent administrator and a friend of the royal family) to remain until then. Haig, who privately considered the Durbar "a terrible waste of money", complied with the Viceroy's wish. On 23 December, however, Haig and his wife embarked at Bombay for the voyage home.[63] Once home, they were reunited with the daughters they had left in the care of their Aunt Henrietta two years previously. The girls were so young that, after such an absence, they initially found it difficult to remember their parents. The adult Haigs, like other members of the British upper class at this time, seem to have accepted such separations as a fact of life. They had a few months of relative ease to reacquaint themselves with their children before Sir Douglas took over from Sir Horace Smith-Dorrien at Aldershot on 1 March 1912.[64]

Because he brought with him two staff officers with whom he had become acquainted in India, Haig's take-over of the Aldershot command was jokingly referred to as the "Hindoo invasion". Captain John Charteris became his Assistant Military Secretary and Captain H.D.C. Baird of the 12th Cavalry his ADC. The relationship with Charteris was to be particularly important in Haig's career. Haig had first encountered him during one of his tours of inspection directing Indian sappers in the building of a bridge. He was impressed not only with the efficiency of the operation itself, but also with the lucidity with which Charteris explained it. Haig had subsequently found Charteris a place on his staff in India. Charteris was widely regarded as clever, if rather superficial, and, in contrast with his boss, had great facility with the spoken as well as the written word. Though thoroughly disliked by Lady Haig, who considered him "dirty", he was, for about a decade, to be one of her husband's closest military colleagues.[65]

Haig had for some time been interested in the possibilities of military aviation. He had corresponded with Kiggell on the subject while he was in India. While he was in command at Aldershot, interesting developments were taking place nearby. On 1 April 1911 the Royal Engineers' balloon school at Aldershot became the base of a new Army Air Battalion and the army began to acquire heavier than air flying machines. The Royal Aircraft Factory was established at Farnborough shortly afterwards and on 13 May 1912 the Army Air Battalion became the Royal Flying Corps. The first aeroplane built specifically for the British army was designed and constructed by the celebrated American aviator S. F. Cody. Haig's official residence, "Government House" in Aldershot, was only about a mile from the Royal Aircraft factory. On one occasion Haig sent an ADC to see Cody and request an interview, only to be rather rudely brushed off. Cody died within a year, in a crash on Farnborough Common, apparently without having met Haig. By that time, however, aircraft were already playing a significant role in Haig's life.[66]

The first training season for which Haig was in command at Aldershot culminated in manoeuvres held in East Anglia between 16–19 September 1912. These were the largest peacetime manoeuvres ever held by the British Army and were a major military event, indicative, perhaps, of the increasing seriousness with which the highest authorities took the prospect of British participation in a European war. King George V himself attended, as did very senior French and Russian military delegations commanded by General Ferdinand Foch and the Grand Duke Nicholas respectively.[67]

The CIGS, General Sir John French, directed the exercise. Haig commanded "Red Force", consisting of 1st and 2nd Divisions from his Aldershot command and a cavalry division. Red Force represented an invading army. It was supposed to have landed on the coast of Norfolk and to be trying to advance southward – on London. Haig's opponent was Lieutenant General Sir James Grierson. His "Blue Force" also had two infantry divisions, but had only two cavalry brigades as against Haig's three. Blue Force was concentrated south of Cambridge, its mission to protect the capital, blocking Haig's advance. Each side had a Royal Flying Corps detachment consisting of a single airship and seven aeroplanes to assist with reconnaissance.[68]

In the ensuing operations Grierson was judged, partly owing to his effective use of aerial reconnaissance, to have checked Red Force's advance, and though the final exercise report tried to be as even-handed as possible, Haig was generally considered to have had the worst of it. The interpretation, popular at one time, that Haig lost because he ignored the potential benefits of airpower, has recently been exposed as a complete calumny. "In reality, Haig suffered for over-reliance on aerial reconnaissance rather than ... disregard of it." He was apparently reluctant to make any offensive move without good information as to the whereabouts of the enemy and seems to have been a bit over cautious in the early stages.

On the last day of the exercise, however, Haig hoped to win by turning Blue Force's right flank. His reconnaissance (aerial and cavalry) had informed him that this was undefended. But Grierson (who was equally alive to the importance of the aerial dimension) had carefully concealed his 4th Division in the sector in which Haig had hoped to make his decisive envelopment. Haig's forces were surprised and repelled by the defenders. Given the near equality of the forces on the two sides, the defender might well be considered to have had the easier task. But Grierson's force and staff were hurriedly thrown together, while Haig had his Aldershot team. Blue Force was, moreover, dispersed at the start of the exercise and Haig, according to Sir John French, had missed opportunities to defeat Grierson "in detail", crushing at least one major fragment of his force.[69]

The mere fact that Haig had the worst of the military contest was not, perhaps, too serious in itself. More potentially damaging to his reputation and career was his performance at the final conference. This was a very public affair, held in the great hall of Trinity College at the University of Cambridge. The King himself presided and many of the dignitaries of the university and members of the senior hierarchy of the army were also present. Haig had prepared a clear written account of his side of the exercise, drawing his own conclusions from what had taken place. Unaccountably, instead of reading this, he attempted, to the acute discomfort of his staff, to *ad lib*. To get the full flavour of the result it is probably best to quote Charteris an eyewitness who was, after all, strongly sympathetic to Haig. He

became totally unintelligible and unbearably dull. The University dignitaries soon fell fast asleep. Haig's friends became more and more uncomfortable; only he himself seemed totally unconscious of his failure.

A listener, without other and deeper knowledge of the Aldershot Commander-in-Chief, could not but have left the conference with the impression that Haig had neither ability nor military learning.

Haig's inadequacy on this occasion was made all the more conspicuous by the consummate ease and style with which Grierson summarised his own operations.[70] Yet his career suffered no apparent damage from this fiasco. How far royal influence helped to save him is not clear. It appears that, given his generally good record up to this point, an indifferent performance in one exercise, even when followed by a positively abysmal showing in the de-brief afterwards, was not enough to derail him. The following year he again commanded a corps in large-scale manoeuvres held in the Midlands on 22–26 September 1913: these were designed to simulate the sort of combat in which a British expeditionary force might become involved on the Continent. It is not clear whether Haig shone in these manoeuvres either, but his weaknesses were certainly not exposed as cruelly as they had been the previous year.[71]

The next event of real significance for Haig was the Curragh incident of March 1914. He had no part in the making of this famous crisis. He became involved only when it was at its height and then only in a peripheral way. Yet it is necessary to explain something of the background for Haig's part in the business to make any sense.

Asquith's Liberal government was heavily dependent on the support of the Irish Nationalists in the House of Commons. Partly in order to keep their support and partly in fulfilment of a Liberal policy dating back to Gladstone's time, the government introduced a Home Rule Bill. It passed the Commons in January 1913 and, under the terms of the Parliament Act 1911, was due to become law in June 1914 despite opposition from the House of Lords. The Roman Catholic majority in Ireland was, in general, strongly supportive of the measure. As usual, however, the country split on religious lines and the large concentration of Protestants in the north-east was violently opposed. In their view Home Rule meant "Rome Rule" – subjection to a Catholic majority – an intolerable state of affairs. The northern Protestants, who had support from the Unionists (Conservatives) at Westminster, formed a paramilitary force, the Ulster Volunteer Force (UVF), numbering 100,000 men by March 1914, to resist the imposition of Home Rule.[72]

The Irish crisis split England on party lines and introduced a degree of bitterness into politics unknown for at least a generation. Most army officers were Unionists and disapproved of the government's Irish policy. A small but significant proportion consisted of Irish Protestants: some from Ulster and some from the south. These people were particularly horrified at the idea of being ordered to crush the UVF, which might have meant firing on their friends. But there was concern in the Cabinet that the UVF, already possessing considerable numbers of firearms, would increase its stock by seizures from military depots in Ulster. To what extent the government actually wanted to bring about a confrontation between the British army and the UVF has remained a matter for debate, but the balance of evidence is, perhaps, against it. On 14 March, however, the Army Council transmitted an order to General Sir Arthur Paget, commanding British military forces in Ireland, requiring him to secure a number of depots in the north. Carrying out this order seemed to require moving British troops from southern Ireland to the north and this inevitably carried some risk of confrontation between the army and the UVF.[73]

Paget apparently became convinced that the government intended to confront and suppress the UVF. This impression seems not to have been altogether eradicated by an informal conference at the War Office that

Paget attended on 19 March. Sir John French, the CIGS, and the Adjutant General, Sir Spencer Ewart, were all present. Discussion seems to have been informal with nothing committed to paper. But one of the issues considered was what would be done with officers who refused to take military action they perceived as hostile to Unionism in Ulster. It seems to have been agreed that officers domiciled in Ulster would be allowed simply and informally to "disappear", no questions asked, until the crisis was over. Other officers would have the choice of obeying orders or resigning their commissions.[74]

On 20 March Paget held a meeting with the commanders of the main military formations in the Dublin area: Major-General Sir Charles Fergusson, commanding the 5th Division, and Brigadier-General Hubert Gough, commanding the 3rd Cavalry Brigade at the Curragh. As with the War Office conference the previous day, no formal records were kept of what was said. Paget seems to have indicated that, in the event of troops being ordered north to confront the UVF, officers domiciled in Ulster would be allowed to "disappear". All others would have to declare immediately whether they would obey orders. If they would not, they would be dismissed the service.[75]

Paget thus played a major role in precipitating a crisis. But the actions of the forceful cavalryman Hubert Gough (who may have been consciously exploiting Paget's ineptitude to embarrass and weaken the government) were necessary to bring matters to a head. Gough was admittedly in a most sensitive position. He was an Ulsterman by origin, and fiercely Unionist. But, no longer domiciled in Ulster, he could not take advantage of the unofficial right to "disappear". He decided that if his brigade were to be ordered to the north he would not go and that he would tender his resignation. Instead of leaving this as a purely personal decision, at the first opportunity he held a meeting with all the officers of his brigade. Announcing his own decision, he encouraged his subordinates to make theirs forthwith. Some sixty of about seventy officers decided to follow his example. The outcome of this meeting soon became known on both sides of the Irish Sea. In legal terms it was not a mutiny. Yet Gough's brigade had, in effect, made a collective and very public act of protest against government policy.[76] It was at this point, with "The Curragh" developing into one of the greatest crises in British civil-military relations since the seventeenth century, that Haig became involved.

Haig's Brigadier-General General Staff (BGGS), in effect his chief of staff, was Brigadier-General John "Johnnie" Edmond Gough VC, Hubert Gough's younger brother. Johnnie Gough had come to Aldershot in October 1913. He and Haig had not previously known each other, but they had apparently formed a good working relationship. On Friday

20 March, Hubert Gough wired his brother about events at the Curragh, Johnnie Gough getting the news at about 2 p.m. Haig was playing golf (a game which, since coming to Aldershot, he had taken up with great enthusiasm) that day at Littlehampton. Johnnie Gough telegraphed Haig that evening to inform him that he was contemplating resignation.

Receiving Johnnie Gough's communication on the morning of Saturday 21 March, Haig wired him back, telling him to calm down and not to do anything hasty:

> Hope you will not act precipitately. I feel equally strongly on the subject as you. There is no question of the Army fighting against Protestants or against Catholics. Our duty is to keep the peace between them.

Haig's personal authority with the younger Gough was clearly not as great as he might have wished. Gough submitted his resignation the same day, though Haig refused to pass it further up the chain of command.[77] Haig's *sang froid* at this stage in this crisis is indicated by the fact that he continued his golfing weekend, returning to Aldershot to deal with the situation only on the evening of 22 March. Once back at Aldershot, however, Haig quickly came to the conclusion that the situation was serious. He made it clear to the War Office that there was a real risk of the epidemic of resignation spreading from Ireland to his own command and it seems likely that this would indeed have occurred had forces at Aldershot been ordered to cross the Irish Sea.[78]

Cultural links between the Protestants of Ulster and those of Scotland were strong and Haig undoubtedly sympathised with the Unionist cause. His principal objective during the crisis, however, was apparently to prevent the resignation of valuable officers and to restore cohesion and discipline in the army. Keeping his head when some around him were losing theirs, he never tendered or threatened his own resignation. On Monday 23 March, he went up to London with Johnnie Gough where they talked to Hubert Gough at the family home in Sloane Square. He next went to see Haldane (by this time Lord Chancellor) at the House of Lords and walked with him to Downing Street. He then paid a visit to the War Office and another to Haldane at the Lords before getting back to Aldershot before 5 p.m.

At a meeting of his divisional and brigade commanders on Wednesday 25 March, he begged these general officers to stop their juniors "dabbling in politics", but indicated that they were all united against "coercing our fellow citizens who have done no wrong". As the crisis split the army and alienated many officers from the government, it has been said that Haig kept a foot in both camps. In a sense, this is quite true, but it does not seem that his behaviour was in any way perfidious. Indeed, he was being both constitutionally correct and politically astute. He tried to use his contacts to play the role of peacemaker, keeping close to the Gough brothers and expressing sympathy for their position, while also talking to the Liberal government through Haldane. In an effort to calm the situation the latter made a conciliatory speech in the House of Lords, though without much noticeable effect.[79]

Haig went up to London again on both the Thursday and Friday afternoons. On Thursday 26 March at a meeting at the War Office he heard that both the CIGS (Sir John French) and Sir John Ewart (Adjutant-General) had resigned after a guarantee that they had given to Hubert Gough was repudiated by the Prime Minsiter. Haig then went to see Haldane and Herbert Asquith, the Prime Minister. But the situation remained confused at the end of the week when Haig heard that Asquith had announced French's resignation to the House of Commons.

The Curragh affair subsided by the end of March, mainly because it became clear that there was absolutely no chance of the government using the army to confront the UVF. If Asquith's government had ever had any such intention it had clearly abandoned it by then. By that time, however, the War Office had been greatly disrupted: the Secretary of State for War, the CIGS and the Adjutant-General all having resigned. In the short term, Asquith himself took over as Secretary of State for War. On the eve of a great European War the affair increased mistrust between the army and the Liberal government and caused friction between officers who had adopted different positions.[80]

Haig had no general prejudice against the Liberal ministers and in later years seems to have blamed the Curragh affair largely on Sir John French. He apparently thought the CIGS should have made it clear to the government that ordering troops to Ulster was likely to precipitate a crisis destructive of military discipline and should have resolutely opposed any such move.[81] Whether Haig himself would have demonstrated such moral courage had he been CIGS at the time we cannot know. Ireland continued to teeter on the brink of civil war until the conflagration on the Continent temporarily overshadowed the crisis there.

3   Anxiously to war

Haig at the outbreak of the First World War

In summer 1914, the British government, preoccupied with events in Ireland,[1] was slow to realise how potentially catastrophic was the situation unfolding on the Continent. Naturally everyone knew of the assassination of the Archduke Franz-Ferdinand, heir apparent to the Austrian throne, by a Bosnian Serb member of a Serb nationalist group in Sarajevo on 28 June. Yet, from the British point of view, there seemed no necessity for this to lead to war. Until the Austrians announced their ultimatum to Serbia on 24 July, Sir Edward Grey, the Foreign Secretary, apparently believed that the Germans might help him defuse the situation.[2] It was only after learning of the Austrian ultimatum that Grey and his colleagues realised that the Austrian government was determined on war with Serbia and that the Germans were likely to support the Austrians. This almost inevitably meant war between Austria and Germany on the one hand, and Russia (Serbia's protector) and France on the other. If the Germans crushed France and Russia the balance of power on the Continent would be destroyed and Britain's position in the world gravely threatened. Great Britain, however, had no treaty obliging the nation to go to war on behalf of either Russia or France. So pacific were the feelings of the great bulk of the British Cabinet that, had it not been for the German violation of Belgian neutrality it is quite likely that Britain would not have intervened, at least not in the war's opening round.[3]

Whatever the level of enthusiasm for war amongst Britain's general population in August 1914 (and this is a matter of some debate) many of the nation's leaders entered the conflict racked with anxiety, in moods of the deepest gloom. Of the nineteen Cabinet members serving at the start of the crisis, Sir Edward Grey was, together with Winston Churchill, the First Lord of the Admiralty, one of the two most belligerent. Grey was no warmonger, but was unwilling to abandon France, a country with which Britain had enjoyed an *entente cordiale* (friendly agreement) since 1904, in the face of German aggression. Other ministers were so keen to avoid war at any price that Grey almost resigned and Herbert Asquith, the Prime Minister, along with him. Finally Grey and Asquith secured the agreement of most of the Cabinet to a British ultimatum to Germany to withdraw its forces from Belgium.[4] When that expired, on 4 August, Great Britain found itself at war. The remark attributed to Grey, that the lamps were going out all over Europe, not to be re-lit in his lifetime, is well known.[5] Though not all of them expressed it so memorably, most of his colleagues appear to have shared this deep sense of impending doom.[6]

It is, perhaps, hardly surprising that a Liberal Cabinet was deeply imbued with a horror of war. But in early August 1914 profound foreboding also seems to have been the dominant emotion of the King,[7] of the financial experts of the City of London[8] and of some prominent army officers, including Lord Kitchener[9] and Sir Douglas Haig. Haig had long realised the possibility of a major war between Germany and the British Empire. He perceived that the struggle might be a long one and had actively tried to play his part in preparing the Empire's military forces for it.[10] In the immediate aftermath of the assassination at Sarajevo, observing French military exercises in the company of fellow generals Grierson and Allenby, he fervently hoped that war could be avoided. In the circumstances of early August 1914 he seems to have accepted the need for Britain's intervention. But the judgement of his official biographer in this matter appears entirely correct:

When ... war broke out he greeted it in no spirit of enthusiasm. It was the moment for which he had been preparing, but to which he had not looked forward with any emotions save those of awe and dread.[11]

His profound anxiety and his sense of national unreadiness can be reliably documented from the war's first day.[12] Though this is less certain, it is possible that the normally self-confident, assertive Haig had some doubts about his personal readiness to fulfil his expected role.

War was traditionally seen as the professional army officer's opportunity. Sixteen years earlier Haig had rushed to join Kitchener in the Sudan. The Haig of 1914, however, was no longer a young man and no longer on the make in quite the same way. He no longer needed to seek the bubble reputation even in the cannon's mouth. He had matured and mellowed. At Aldershot, for the last few years, he had been enjoying a comfortable, pleasant and, for the most part, rather leisurely existence.[13] No impoverished Bonaparte of 1792, welcoming war as a means to display his genius and make his fortune, Haig had every reason to be content with the world as it was. By the standards of most of his countrymen he was rich. He enjoyed a good marriage and a happy family life. He basked in royal favour and had the respect of other important and influential men.[14] He was already near the top of his profession's promotion ladder. There was every reason to believe that, like Sir John French, he could have reached the top without another war.

Haig had made his reputation primarily as a military administrator and staff officer. He had commanded a mobile column in the counter-guerrilla phase in South Africa and had attempted, with limited success, to co-ordinate groups of columns. But he had never commanded a major formation on active service. On an objective reading of the available evidence it had to be considered doubtful that field command at corps level was his forte. Grierson had, it was generally reckoned, defeated him on exercise in 1912.[15] A proud and reticent nature, combined with a sense of professional self-interest, would have prevented the public expression of any self-doubt. Yet Haig had seen enough of war to recognise its professional as well as its physical perils. He had read enough military history to know that great wars can be the graveyards of military reputations made in peacetime or in smaller conflicts against lesser foes. Haig, in August 1914, therefore, was not exactly thanking God for having matched him with this hour. His initial advice tended to err on the side of caution, and, when he got into the field he would be far from keen to close with the enemy. He went anxiously to war.

Though Haig had held key military appointments in the years before the war, he was not privy to the details of the highly secret talks between the British and French General Staffs, held intermittently since 1906.[16] Staff officers had provisionally agreed in 1911 that the British Expeditionary Force (BEF) would concentrate in the area Arras-St Quentin-Cambrai, about forty miles to the north-east of Amiens. By August 1914, however, French General Staff had revised its plans. It now wanted the British Expeditionary Force, which Sir John French was appointed to command, to concentrate around Maubeuge, another thirty miles further to the east and nearer to the Germans.[17] The French high command anticipated that if the BEF arrived on the Continent in the first few days of the war, it would co-operate in securing the French left while the bulk of the French army mounted an offensive on the Franco-German frontier. But not being certain of the BEF's presence, the French had given it no definite role in their plans.[18]

On the afternoon of Wednesday 29 July Haig received a precautionary War Office telegram warning him that mobilisation was being considered. Six days later he received the order to mobilise. The arrangements for this were too well rehearsed to need any personal intervention on his part. On 5 August 1914 he drove to London to have a medical examination, which cleared him as fit for duty. He then attended a hurriedly convened, *ad hoc* Council of War under the chairmanship of the Prime

Minister at 10 Downing Street. Grey, Churchill and Haldane were all in attendance, as were the military members of the Army Council, Sir John French, Haig's fellow corps commander, Grierson and two of the country's most venerable veterans of Victoria's wars, Lords Roberts and Kitchener. It was apparently only at this meeting that Haig learned that the BEF was required by the French to concentrate at Maubeuge on the fifteenth day of mobilisation. Given that the British had started to mobilise their army three days later than the French or Germans, this scheme now looked dangerous and alternatives were discussed.[19]

Sir John French considered that Amiens might be a more suitable concentration area than Maubeuge. But he also suggested landing the BEF at Antwerp and, using that city as a base, operating more or less independently of the French army. Haig appears not to have endorsed this idea. He later pointed out that allowing the British army to become separated from the French so early in the campaign would have offered the Germans the opportunity to defeat both armies "in detail": throwing crushing weight first against one, then the other. Fortunately Winston Churchill, the First Lord of the Admiralty, vetoed the Antwerp gambit on the grounds that the Royal Navy could not guarantee to project the BEF's disembarkation so far east as Antwerp.[20]

A course of action Haig himself suggested at Downing Street on this day, however, also carried potential for disaster. Haig was aware that, in the German army, the British were facing an enemy of great size and exceptional quality. He also appreciated that the British Expeditionary Force (that he had, after all, helped to create), while finely wrought, was a brittle instrument. Much of its personnel consisted of reservists (mostly former regulars) whose superiority over Continental conscripts could not necessarily be taken for granted and it lacked the reserves of trained manpower available to states with systems of peacetime conscription. On 4 August, the day Britain entered the war, Haig had written a letter to his friend Richard Haldane, then Lord Chancellor. He pleaded that Haldane should return to the War Office and serve as Secretary of State for as long as the war lasted, arguing that "No one knows the details of the problems of organisation as you do." He went on to discuss his views on the employment of the Expeditionary Force:

This war will last many months, possibly years, so I venture to hope that our only bolt (and that not a very big one) may not suddenly be shot on a project of which the success seems to be quite doubtful – I mean the checking of the German advance into France. Would it not be better to begin at once to enlarge our Expeditionary Force by amalgamating less regular forces with it? In three months time we would have a quite considerable Army, so that when we do take the field we can act decisively and dictate terms which will ensure a lasting peace.

I presume, of course, that France can hold out, even though her forces have to fall back from the frontier, for the necessary time for us to create an army of 300,000.[21]

Though Haig denied it, Sir John French's recollection was that Haig gave the same advice in official conversations in the first few days of the war.[22] The diary of Henry Wilson, the Director of Military Operations, indicates that he had an hour-and-a-half's conversation with Haig and French at 10 Downing Street, immediately before the formal War Council started. During this Haig argued that the BEF should not cross the Channel for two or three months in order to allow the "immense resources of the Empire" to be developed. Neither from Wilson's diary nor from the secretary's notes is it clear to what extent Haig pressed this line of argument at the formal War Council itself, though he certainly offered the initial withholding of all or most of the BEF from the Continent as one of a number of options. In fairness to Haig it must be pointed out that his ignorance of the Franco-British staff talks left him in doubt as to how crucial early British military support was likely to be for the French. Others present at the meeting insisted that it was vital and, by its end, Haig apparently expressed a willingness to defer to them.[23]

Haig had some important insights in August 1914. He understood that the war was likely to be a long one, perhaps lasting for years rather than months. He rightly saw the need for a large British army. He correctly perceived that if Britain committed virtually the whole of its small regular army to the Continent, it would not have an adequate cadre to train the much larger forces needed as the war progressed. Yet his perspective at this moment, as on a number of later occasions in the war, was somewhat narrow: his difficulty in seeing the situation from an ally's point of view painfully obvious. A British failure to send any military forces to the Continent in August 1914 would, at the very least, have got the Franco-British alliance off to an exceptionally poor start. In the event, even with a fairly substantial BEF on the Continent, French survival was still a near-run thing. With France defeated and overrun, it is unlikely that the Russian army could long have remained in the field, and without Continental allies Great Britain could not have prevented the establishment of a German hegemony in Europe.

The Downing Street War Council resumed the following afternoon, Thursday 6 August, though Haig seems to have been less vocal on this occasion. The council decided to proceed with the deployment of the BEF to fight alongside the French army, though many details remained undecided. Meanwhile I Corps's mobilisation proceeded apace. On 9 August Haig visited Southampton, where I Corps HQ was being mobilised. On 11 August the King and Queen visited him at Aldershot. The King indicated his pleasure that French had been appointed Commander-in-Chief. But Haig, according to his own account (possibly retrospective rather than contemporary), felt it "my duty" to tell the King that, based upon his experience with French in the South African War, he had "doubts" about the selection.[24]

Amazingly, the initial concentration area of the BEF remained a contentious issue until 12 August, the day it began to embark for the Continent. At 3 p.m. on that date, Lord Kitchener, newly appointed as Secretary of State for War, held a meeting at the Office to consider the issue. Sir John French, his Chief of the General Staff (CGS), Major-General Sir Archibald Murray, Major-General Henry Wilson, the Director of Military Operations (DMO) at the War Office and representatives of the French General Staff attended. Wilson was about to join the BEF as French's sub chief of staff. He was a fluent French speaker and an enthusiastic Francophile. In his four years as DMO he had been responsible for working out provisional mobilisation plans with the French General Staff. He now insisted on complying with that organisation's current wishes and concentrating the BEF in the Maubeuge area.[25]

Kitchener, on the other hand, in one of his characteristic flashes of insight, correctly divined that the Germans were making a big drive north of the Meuse. (Why bother invading Belgium at all, and thus increasing the risk of British intervention, if the thrust through Belgium was not to be on a very large scale?) He thought the Maubeuge gambit too dangerous and wanted to concentrate efforts around Amiens. Wilson argued that, in addition to causing enormous administrative confusion, this might render the BEF irrelevant in the decisive actions of the campaign. Eventually Kitchener settled on what Wilson characterised as "a small and perfectly useless alteration" in the French General Staff scheme, "just enough to cause trouble and add confusion". Instead of detraining at Maubeuge the BEF was now to do so in the Le Cateau–Wassigny area about twenty miles to the south. [26]

Off to war

Haig learnt of the concentration area that was finally decided upon from Sir John French in London on Thursday 13 August. That same Thursday, after saying farewell to Doris at Aldershot, he proceeded to Southampton where he was due to embark, the following night, for the Continent. Fittingly, Henrietta and Willy Jameson, the fairy godparents of Haig's military career, drove down from London on the Friday to bid their farewells. Bringing a case of champagne, they met Haig and members of his staff in the drawing room of the Dolphin Hotel, where they all drank toasts to "success and a safe return".[27]

It would not, however, be luxury all the way to war. Haig and the II Corps commander, Lieutenant-General Sir James Grierson, together with their ADCs and senior staff officers, crossed the Channel on the night of Friday 14 August, on the *Comrie Castle*, an uncomfortable cargo steamer. No meal was served and the accommodation was not what Haig had come to expect. He found the discomfort annoying and doubted the efficiency of the naval personnel involved. When he arrived at Le Havre on the Saturday morning he was not a happy warrior. The fact that no accommodation had been arranged for him on the French side of the Channel did not improve his mood. The overworked base camp commandant had apparently collapsed under the pressure – an early psychological casualty of a war that was to see a great many more. Haig eventually found rooms at the Hotel Tortoni, which were respectable but not exactly the Ritz. He briefly got stuck in the lift, further trying his temper. War looked a little less hellish after a bath and a meal.[28]

It continued to look a bit more positive the following day. Haig and Grierson went to see the French general commanding the town. More bottles of champagne were produced and the health of both armies toasted. That same afternoon Haig went for a walk with Brigadier-General "Johnnie" Gough, his principal staff officer. They observed ships conveying British troops into the harbour and watched as

great crowds on the piers cheered again and again. The troops on board the ships answered with raucous sounds. There was great enthusiasm today, and it being Sunday, large crowds were about. We were saluted everywhere with great respect and little children ran up and grasped our hands as we walked along.

Haig seemed at last to be getting into the spirit of the Franco-British alliance.[29] That night the two corps commanders and their staffs boarded successive trains from Le Havre to Amiens. At 9 a.m. on the morning of Monday 17 August Haig's train halted at the small station of Serquex, where Haig was called to the phone and told that Grierson, in the following train, had died two hours earlier. Grierson was a respected colleague rather than a close friend and his death seems to have had no great emotional effect on Haig at the time. Ordering that the incident be reported to General Robb, commanding lines of communication, when they arrived at Amiens, Haig insisted that they continue with their journey.

Haig later heard that Grierson had suffered an aneurism of the heart. Widely considered one of the ablest generals in the army, Grierson had, as we have noted, got the better of Haig in the manoeuvres of 1912. A fluent French and German speaker, his skill in the former language, combined with a sober judgement, an affable manner and great charm might have been extremely useful in the maintenance of inter-allied relations. His death was a depressing start to the campaign and might have been read as an ill omen had anyone had time to brood. Fortunately Haig and his staff did not. Alighting from the train at Amiens, they went immediately to establish their first headquarters of the campaign at Wassigny.[30]

Sir John French heard the news of Grierson's death when he returned that evening to his own headquarters at Le Cateau. Earlier in the day he had endured a most frustrating meeting with the Anglophobic General Lanrezac, commanding the French Fifth Army, immediately to the BEF's right. Lanrezac had treated French with an ill-disguised contempt. Inter-allied relations were already on the slide. Things were, from French's point of view, only to get worse. He requested that the War Office send Sir Herbert Plumer, GOC Northern Command, to replace Grierson. But Kitchener, who was in the process of stamping his authority on the War Office and the conduct of the war, did not respond. On 19 August he instead despatched Lieutenant-General Sir Horace Smith-Dorrien. Smith-Dorrien was undoubtedly a capable officer, but French was bound to feel annoyed that his own choice had been rejected. To make matters worse, the War Office appointee was one with whom both he and Haig had clashed in peacetime and whom (as Kitchener knew perfectly well) French disliked.[31]

Smith-Dorrien had replaced French in the Aldershot command when French became CIGS in 1911. Smith-Dorrien, who had a fiery temper and could be difficult to deal with, managed to antagonise both his predecessor and his successor. As soon as he took over he had relaxed some of the irksome restrictions of garrison life on which French had insisted. He had also denounced the standard of the cavalry's musketry training and insisted on improving it. French seems to have taken these actions and comments as personal insults. When he succeeded Smith-Dorrien, Haig had, in turn, clashed with him over the seemingly trivial matter of the price to be paid for additional furnishings that Sir Horace had installed in Government House.[32] It is difficult to say how far this ridiculously petty dispute and a general sense of rivalry affected the wartime Haig–Smith-Dorrien relationship. But that was certainly never close. The principal British official historian of the war, Sir James Edmonds (who, in private, could be vitriolic about his brother officers), claimed of Haig and Smith-Dorrien that "neither of them would have been particularly sorry to see the other take a knock".[33] Whatever the truth of that, it is quite clear that French's relations with Smith-Dorrien were poor from the outset. The senior officers of the British army in France, shortly to go into battle, did not constitute a cohesive team.

The mobilisation and deployment of the BEF was, however, proceeding smoothly. It had begun crossing the Channel on 12 August: most of it leaving from Southampton, as Haig himself had done. By 17 August the great bulk of the four infantry divisions and one cavalry division initially despatched had landed in France, using the ports of Le Havre, Rouen and Boulogne. The concentration area was some twenty-five miles long by ten miles wide. It ran from Maubeuge in the north-east to Le Cateau in the south-west. The Cavalry Division was on the left, II Corps in the centre and I Corps on the right. On the British left were three French Territorial divisions: the 84th Territorial Division being their immediate neighbour on that side. XVIII Corps of Lanrezac's French Fifth Army was on their right. The British deployment was carried out without fanfare and even with a degree of secrecy. On 20 August von Moltke, the chief of the German General Staff, informed his First Army commander, von Kluck, that to the best of his knowledge "disembarkation of British troops on a large scale has not yet taken place".[34]

Haig was happy enough with arrangements in his own corps. Though some elements were still arriving as late as 22 August, by 18 August the great bulk of it was in position: 1st Division was around Le Nouvrion, Boue, Esquheries and Lavaqueresse, and 2nd Division around Wassingny, Mennevret, Longchamps and Lesquielles. Each division had an establishment of approximately 18,000 men and 5,600 horses. Each consisted of three infantry brigades of four battalions, plus three field artillery brigades, each of 18 18–pdr guns, a field howitzer brigade of 18 4.5–inch howitzers and a heavy battery of four 60–pdr guns. Each division also had its own integral engineers, signallers and supply troops, plus a cavalry squadron for reconnaissance. Controlling all this was I Corps's headquarters, consisting of twenty officers and eighty other ranks, plus an attached signals company.[35]

Haig apparently considered his corps headquarters highly efficient. His principal staff officer was Brigadier-General John Gough VC, whom we have already encountered at Aldershot, especially during the Curragh affair. Gough's official title was Brigadier-General General Staff (BGGS) and theoretically he had an equal status, under Haig, with Brigadier-General P. E. F. Hobbs, the Deputy Adjutant and Quartermaster General (DA and QMG). Like Gough, Hobbs ran a large and important staff department. Whereas Gough was primarily concerned with operations and intelligence, Hobbs's department dealt with personnel and supply. Two further officers on Haig's staff – Brigadier-General Henry Horne, Brigadier-General Royal Artillery (BGRA), and Brigadier-General S. R. Rice, Commander Royal Engineers (CRE) – held equal rank to Gough's and were "technically equal advisers to Haig as corps commander".[36]

In practice, however, Gough was universally regarded as chief of staff and "reigned supreme in that capacity". He was far and away Haig's most important adviser and carried, under Haig, the primary executive responsibility. Most of the orders issued by I Corps HQ bore his signature. A VC winner, former instructor at the Staff College at Camberley and a published military historian, Gough was one of the army's rising stars. Haig had the highest regard for his energy and administrative ability, placed great trust in his military judgement and appears to have considered him a friend as well as a colleague. During the 1914 campaigns Haig often dined with Gough, relatively rarely with his other officers. He seems to have spent more time with Gough than any other officer, except possibly his *aides de camp* (ADCs) Captains Charteris and Baird.[37]

In a "diary" account, almost certainly written much later, Haig indicates that he was happy enough with his corps headquarters. He regarded Major-General Samuel Lomax, commanding the 1st Division, as "an experienced and practical leader, much beloved by the men, most loyal to me". But he was a little less enthusiastic about the 2nd Division commander, Major-General Charles Monro. Monro had been a good regimental officer and an excellent former commandant of the Musketry School at Hythe. But he had little experience of divisional command, having recently replaced Archibald Murray (who had been selected as Chief of the General Staff at GHQ). Haig blamed "some years of service with the Territorials" for Monro's being "rather fat". All his brigade and battalion commanders were, Haig apparently believed, more than adequate to the challenges likely to face them. Neither was there much wrong, in his assessment, with the quality of his artillery and divisional cavalry. But, as with the rest of the BEF, much of I Corps', infantry strength consisted of reservists recently returned to the colours. One of his anxieties at this stage was that he would find himself in a major battle before these troops had been fully integrated.[38]

The advance to Mons: 21–23 August 1914

Haig had appreciated by Wednesday 19 August that the Germans were attempting, by their advance through Belgium, "to turn the French left which rests on Namur fortress". He seems, in other words, to have perceived that the German plan might be a large-scale envelopment. There is, however, little sign that this was fully appreciated at GHQ for at least another three days.[39] At 1 p.m. on 20 August, Sir John French's general headquarters (GHQ) issued BEF Operation Order No. 5. The following morning the army was to advance northwards, crossing the River Sambre. Detailed tables of march for the next three days were provided. The order stated that: "Information regarding the enemy will be communicated separately".[40] In reality GHQ had not been able to form a clear intelligence picture.

General Joffre, the French commander-in-chief, had intended to mount an offensive on the Franco-German frontier so violent that whatever the Germans intended to do would be massively disrupted. In the first two weeks of war, however, it was Joffre's plan that had suffered the principal disruption. Indeed, by 21 August, when the British advance began, it had virtually disintegrated.[41] The French First and Second Armies, attacking into Lorraine, had suffered heavy losses when on 20 August they were violently counter-attacked by the German Sixth and Seventh Armies and both severely defeated. Apparently undaunted by this major setback, on 21 August Joffre launched the French Third and Fourth Armies into the Ardennes – an operation that was to prove equally ill fated. This left both the BEF and the northernmost French Army, General Lanrezac's Fifth, dangerously exposed. Three powerful German armies were advancing north of the Ardennes, intending to crush the Allied left. On 21 August, the BEF began advancing into Belgium – II Corps on the left, Haig's I Corps on the right – the Mons–Bavai road the boundary between them. On that fiercely hot Friday, the BEF was thrusting its head into the lion's mouth.[42]

In the first fortnight of the war the Belgians had defended themselves with some determination, almost unaided by the armies of the Allies. The main obstacle to the German advance had been the modern fortress complex around the city of Liège. The defence of Liège had put the German advance a couple of days behind schedule. But super-heavy Krupp and Skoda artillery had forced the surrender of the last of the Liège forts by 16 August. Two days later King Albert began withdrawing his field army into the city of Antwerp and the Germans were able to drive deep into Belgium encountering little opposition. By noon on 20 August the Belgian concentration on Antwerp was complete. Von Kluck, who commanded the German 1st Army, on the extreme right, decided to detach two corps to seal up the Belgian army in that city, protecting his flank and rear while the rest of his forces pressed on. On the same day elements of Von der Marwitz's II Cavalry Corps entered Brussels.[43]

On Friday 21 August the BEF's advance met no resistance. There were already some disquieting reports of the scale of the German invasion of Belgium. But a dysfunctional GHQ was slow to take alarm. Unsuited for high command, French himself spent too much time trying to inspire the troops by force of personality and not enough time analysing his strategic and operational environment. All commentators agree that his Chief of the General Staff, Lieutenant-General Sir Archibald Murray, was out of his depth and floundering. Colonel George Macdonogh was a perceptive, intelligent officer, but seems not to have had French's ear. From most accounts, that seems to have been largely monopolised by his sub-chief of the General Staff, Major-General Sir Henry Wilson. Wilson, at this stage, apparently had much faith in the military competence of the French high command, exuded excessive optimism and was somewhat dismissive of disquieting reports.[44]

Historians have often commented on the breakdown of command and control in the BEF during the retreat from Mons. The fair degree of chaos that set in during the two-day advance to Mons has been less frequently remarked. By the afternoon of Saturday 22 August the BEF had become dangerously dispersed. Though I Corps had the higher proportion of regular soldiers, II Corps had advanced much further. It held Mons and a line along the Mons-Condé Canal west of the town. Perhaps because of the heat, or because he feared losing touch with the French Fifth Army to his right, Haig had halted his corps' march very early that day, around Maubeuge, ten miles south of Mons. A huge gap had thus opened up between the two British corps.[45]

Fortunately, both Allenby's cavalry division and the Royal Flying Corps sent GHQ reports that suggested the presence of large bodies of German troops not far to the BEF's front. At 1.30 p.m. on 22 August, therefore, GHQ ordered Haig to renew his advance north, closing up to the right of II Corps just south-east of Mons. At the same time it ordered Allenby's cavalry division to pull back and take up position on the left of II Corps. Haig, who had spent much of the afternoon visiting the HQ of General Mas-Latrie's French XVIIII Corps at Beaumont, seems to have received these orders late, at approximately 3.30 p.m., and no one seems to have acted to implement them in his absence. Haig's personal response to GHQ's order appears to have been neither prompt nor vigorous. The 1st Division moved that evening and marched through much of the night. But 2nd Division did not leave its billets until 3 a.m. the following morning and did not take up its assigned positions in the Mons sector until after battle had commenced.[46]

Sir John French, however, apparently continued to contemplate continuing the advance on 23 August until Lieutenant Edward Spears, the liaison officer with Lanrezac, arrived at his Advanced HQ at Bavai that night. Spears had spent all day at the French Fifth Army's HQ. He was aware that the BEF was now nine miles ahead of Lanrezac's left flank and that a gap of several miles existed between these forces. The French Fifth Army had taken a hammering and Lanrezac now had no further intention of moving forward; indeed, he might be pushed back – leaving the BEF isolated. Spears conveyed all this news to Macdonogh and the two of them went to brief French and Murray, his Chief of the General Staff. After

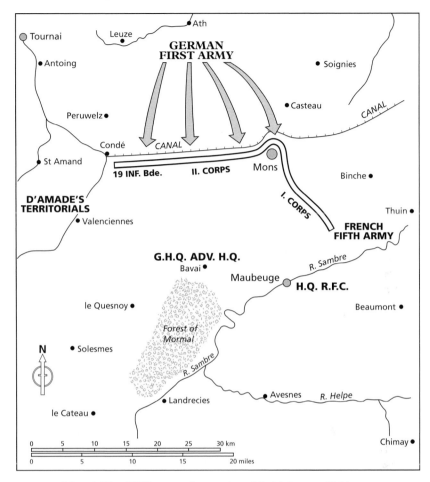

Map 4. The BEF's area of operations 20–24 August 1914

discussing the matter with Murray and Henry Wilson, French decided to halt the BEF's advance, at least for the time being, and communicated this to his corps.[47]

The Battle of Mons: 23 August 1914

At about 5.30 a.m. on the morning of Sunday 23 August Sir John French saw Allenby and the two corps commanders at Smith-Dorrien's head-quarters at Sars-La-Bruyère. According to Haig, French expressed awareness that he was confronted by at least three German corps "suitably placed for an attack on Mons and vicinity". But if French believed there was any serious risk of a major German attack that day his next move is difficult to explain. Departing on a trip to Valenciennes to inspect the 19th Brigade, which was assembling in that area, he removed himself from any chance effectively to command the BEF in the opening hours of its first battle. GHQ, initially left in the care of the ineffectual Murray, was to have no influence on the day's events. Fortunately, however, at least some elements of the BEF had already started to make serious efforts to fortify their positions.[48]

What was about to become the Mons battlefield lay in a rather dirty and depressing coal-mining and industrial region. It was littered with pit heads, slag heaps and miners' cottages. Fields of fire for infantry weapons were generally rather restricted and it proved practically impossible to find good positions for the artillery. The canal loop, north of the town of Mons, could easily have become a trap. On the other hand the BEF's front, principally held by Smith-Dorrien's II Corps, ran along the canal and was thus protected by an obstacle, though the numerous bridges (which there was no time to destroy) diminished the effectiveness of this considerably. Its right wing, mainly held by Haig's I Corps, was turned sharply back: "refused" to the enemy. The most serious danger was that of envelopment: the Germans sweeping round one or both of the BEF's flanks. Communication with French's Fifth Army on the BEF's right had, by this stage, been altogether lost and the three weak French Territorial divisions strung out to its left were very unlikely to block a determined German attack.[49]

Fortunately the fog of war seems to have hung even thicker over von Kluck's HQ than it did over Sir John's. Until the misty morning of Sunday 23 August Kluck seems to have been unaware that any really substantial force of British infantry was even in the vicinity. Kluck's troops simply blundered into the BEF and then tried to steamroller it out of the way, initially advancing in dense masses, very vulnerable to concentrated rifle fire. The German attack, commencing about 9 a.m., fell principally on Sir Horace Smith-Dorrien's II Corps, some five German divisions hitting his two. It is an indication of the clumsy nature of German operations that day that Haig's corps, which was not protected by a major water obstacle to its front, was subjected to only fairly minor attacks by a single German division.[50]

For Smith-Dorrien, however, Sunday 23 August was a nerve-racking day. As well as being by far the more vigorously attacked, his corps was intrinsically by far the more fragile of the BEF's two major formations. Haig's I Corps, though greatly fleshed out by reserves since the start of the war, was a substantial organisation even in peace. II Corps had, in normal times, a much more shadowy existence. In peacetime it was assembled out of units that only worked together for major exercises. In wartime it had a far higher proportion of reservists than had I Corps. Haig, moreover, had been commanding I Corps for years, whereas Smith-Dorrien had been in command of II Corps for only three days before the action at Mons.[51] Yet Sir Horace, a survivor of the disaster of Isandlwana in the Zulu war of 1879, held his nerve. The BEF's II Corps took all that the Germans threw at it, impressing them with its tenacity and inflicting heavy casualties. By mid-afternoon, however, Smith-Dorrien's situation was looking dangerous. The 3rd Division, in the canal salient north of Mons, was in some danger of being trapped and Smith-Dorrien had to take the decision to withdraw it. That inevitably meant pulling the 5th Division back from the canal also. As II Corps fell back under pressure, a gap tended to open up between its two divisions. In these circumstances Smith-Dorrien quite reasonably looked to Haig, most of whose troops had not yet been engaged, for assistance. At 5.35 p.m. that evening, a couple of hours after receiving Smith-Dorrien's request, Haig replied:

Dear Smith-Dorrien,

I felt sorry that I could not comply with your request to fill the gap between the left of your 3rd and the right of your 5th Divisions.

At the time I received your request our line east of Givry was being attacked from the direction of Binche. The best I could do was to relieve your detachment on Hill 93 by two battalions of Guards thus setting free two of Hamilton's battalions…

Shall I come over and see you about 8 p.m.? Unless you and I meet, co-ordination between our two Corps will be difficult '.[52]

Haig was not being untruthful when he indicated that Smith-Dorrien's request had coincided with an attack upon his own corps. But just how limited this was is indicated by the fact that I Corps suffered only forty casualties all day.[53] His response to Smith-Dorrien's request for help, the despatch of a mere two battalions from a corps that had scarcely been engaged to one that had been acutely pressed by superior numbers for several hours, appears niggardly, perhaps disgracefully so. It was, perhaps, the product, on a smaller scale, of that same narrowness of vision, the same lack of generosity of impulse in an emergency that had led him to suggest withholding the BEF from France at the outset of the war. At about 6.30 p.m., however, Smith-Dorrien and his chief of staff, Brigadier-General Forestier-Walker, arrived at Haig's headquarters at Le Bonnet, renewing II Corps' request for help in more forceful terms. At this point Haig was a bit more co-operative, sending three battalions under Brigadier-General Haking to II Corps' assistance. With their help, during the hours of darkness II Corps completed its withdrawal to a new line that Smith-Dorrien had started preparing earlier in the day, a couple of miles south of the canal. Feeling that the situation was fairly well in hand, at midnight Haig went to bed.[54]

Sir John French had returned to GHQ at Le Cateau early on the afternoon of 23 August. Mons, however, was thirty-five miles away and French remained ludicrously out of touch with the situation at the front. As late as 3 p.m. he seems to have had no idea that his army was engaged in a serious battle. He informed Lanrezac that he intended to co-operate with his offensive the following day and deprecated "pessimistic" reports from Smith-Dorrien. An intelligence briefing by Macdonogh at 6 p.m. seems not to have penetrated this complacency. It was only when he received a message from Joffre, at about 7 p.m., indicating that French intelligence believed the BEF to be confronting three German corps, that he seems to have abandoned thoughts of advancing on the morrow. But he still informed Smith-Dorrien at 8.05 p.m. on 23 August that he intended, on 24 August, to "stand the attack on the ground now occupied by the troops", a very unwise idea given the danger of envelopment, which should have been obvious by this stage.[55]

It seems only to have become obvious to French, however, when a liaison officer, Lieutenant Edward Spears, returned from Lanrezac's HQ around midnight. He reported not only that Lanrezac had abandoned all idea of attacking on 24 August, but that he had now ordered a retreat: a decision he had neglected to communicate to the allied force on his left. French was understandably furious. In these circumstances it was obvious, even to him, that there was no choice for the British other than to withdraw. GHQ had summoned the chiefs of staff of the two corps and the cavalry division to Le Cateau at about 11 p.m. At about 1 a.m. Murray told them that the BEF was to retreat about eight miles due south and take up a defensive position on a seven-mile front running west to east through Bavai, with that place near its centre. The corps staffs were to co-ordinate their retreat. Some accounts suggest that GHQ delegated too much to the commanders and staffs of the two corps and that this explains II Corps being left to fight practically alone on 24 August, for the second successive day. This is misleading. In a telegraphic order, sent at 1.40 a.m. on 24 August, GHQ quite specifically ordered I Corps to cover the retreat of Smith-Dorrien's formation.[56]

The retreat from Mons: 24 August–September 1914

Haig ignored this order. Inter-corps co-operation therefore failed from the outset and was to remain practically non-existent throughout the retreat. Poor personal relations between Haig and Smith-Dorrien may have been a factor. Relations between the two chiefs of staff, Gough and Forestier-Walker, were at least equally bad. On the night of 23 August Haig and Gough were, for obvious reasons, somewhat less exhausted than Smith-Dorrien and Forestier-Walker. Perhaps partly as a result, the staff work in I Corps was slicker. Realising that it would probably take him an hour or so to get back to I Corps HQ at Le Bonnet, Johnnie Gough telegraphed the order to withdraw to I Corps. Haig's staff officers had started to organise the retreat even before awakening him at 2 a.m. Forestier-Walker apparently did not telegraph ahead. It was another hour before he got back, by staff car, to II Corps HQ at Sars-la-Bruyère to deliver the critical message to Smith-Dorrien.[57]

At Le Bonnet Haig organised a rear-guard for I Corps. This consisted of 5th Cavalry Brigade, two battalions of infantry and two field artillery brigades, the whole under Brigadier-General Horne, who was ordered to make an offensive demonstration to cover the retreat of the rest of the corps. According to his own account Haig then saw divisional and brigade commanders and personally marked a map for General Monro and his staff, who seemed so sleepy they might otherwise fail to understand. The results of his and Gough's efforts were, within limits, impressive. I Corps showed the Germans a clean pair of heels. The movement began at 5 a.m. and the whole corps had reached its new position five hours later. Haig had looked after his own formation well enough. What he had not done was make any provision to assist II Corps. Indeed, his diary indicates that GHQ's order for him to do so was asking the impossible and that he therefore decided to ignore it. I Corps' rapid retreat that morning exposed Smith-Dorrien's right flank and German troops were allowed to march across what had been I Corps' front in order to attack II Corps.

Haig maintained his headquarters at Le Bonnet throughout the morning of 24 August. Sir John French came to see him, in an anxious mood, according to Haig, but impressed with the smoothness with which I Corps' withdrawal was proceeding. While they were conversing, sounds of heavy fighting were audible from the II Corps area to the north. Yet French and Haig sent no reinforcements to Smith-Dorrien and apparently made no effort to investigate his predicament. Smith-Dorrien's corps had, in fact, been under heavy attack since first light: its situation little short of desperate. At noon Smith-Dorrien came in person to see Haig to plead for I Corps' help in taking pressure off his troops and covering their withdrawal. By that time, however, virtually all of Haig's troops were in full retreat. II Corps was left to its own devices. It suffered another 2,500 casualties on 24 August. Yet somehow Smith-Dorrien's formation again maintained its cohesion and beat off its assailants. With no help from Haig, it ultimately managed to execute the planned withdrawal to the Bavai position. Some of II Corps' troops, however, arrived very late and in a state of complete exhaustion.[58]

On the afternoon of 24 August, I Corps occupied the new line, on the eastern side of Bavai, to which French's orders had directed it. Haig thought it a poor position and did not intend to remain there long. He established his headquarters at Vieux Mesnil, about five miles to the rear. Gough was summoned to GHQ again where he received orders to continue the retreat towards Le Cateau. GHQ allocated the old Roman road west of the Forest of Mormal (a thick wood nine miles from north to south and three to four miles west to east) to II Corps. I Corps was to keep to the east of the Roman road. Nothing much was known about the roads within the Forest. Haig therefore decided to move his whole corps to the east of it. On the night of 24 August the strain apparently began to take its toll on his health. He had a violent attack of diarrhoea lasting about two hours and fell asleep exhausted.[59]

The following morning BEF staff work went seriously awry. This time it was I Corps that was slow off the mark. II Corps began its retreat at 2 a.m. But, possibly having misunderstood his orders, Johnnie Gough, to whom, because of Haig's illness, the task fell, did not manage to get all of I Corps on the road until 8.30 a.m. Haig was feeling somewhat better that morning, but not well enough to ride, as he had the previous day. On 25 August he moved by staff car instead. Communications with French Fifth Army had now broken down almost entirely, and for the second successive day I Corps competed with some of Lanrezac's troops for use of the same roads. They got in each other's way and Haig's formation lost some of its baggage as a result.[60] I Corps recrossed the Sambre near Maubeuge.

Direct communication between the two corps then broke down as II Corps retreated west of the Forest of Mormal while I Corps went east of it. Instead of continuing the retreat to Le Cateau and taking up positions alongside II Corps as GHQ had instructed, during the afternoon Haig began setting up his corps HQ at Landrecies, immediately to the south of the Forest of Mormal, where 4th (Guards) Infantry Brigade HQ was also based. Perhaps because physical debilitation had affected his judgement, Haig had left himself and his headquarters in an exposed position: on the edge of a substantial wood not controlled by friendly forces, towards the rear of his own corps and uncomfortably close to the enemy's forward elements. He had left a gap a few miles wide between his own forces at Landrecies and the right of Smith-Dorrien's II Corps at Le Cateau.[61]

At about 5.30 p.m. some local civilians rushed into Haig's presence declaring that the Germans were upon them. Haig sent Charteris to investigate, moved to the town hall, as the most centrally located building, and tried to organise the town's defence. Gough went to check that the Guards were alert, but found them "sleepy and the measures taken rather half-hearted". Haig saw Brigadier-General Scott-Kerr and told him to ensure that his men remained vigilant. The first patrols sent out found no trace of the enemy in the vicinity.[62] Haig seems to have been on the point of dismissing the whole business as a false alarm when, at 7.30 p.m., a company of the Coldstreams picketing the road leading into the town was heavily attacked. At roughly the same time other German troops emerged from the Forest of Mormal and seized a bridge over the River Sambre from the 5th Hussars. Meanwhile, other German troops attacked elements of the 6th Infantry Brigade at Maroilles, about three miles to the east.

In the hours of darkness the town of Landrecies and its immediate environs became alive with rumours spread by both French civilians and (in all probability) desperately tired and nervous British troops. What happened next is not entirely clear, but it seems that small but daring German forces, some of them reportedly in French uniforms, began probes into Landrecies. Haig became alarmed. At 10 p.m. he sent an urgent appeal for reinforcements to GHQ. GHQ relayed it to II Corps. II Corps had, thus far, endured a vastly tougher campaign than had I Corps. Many of its troops were in such a state of exhaustion that they were in no condition to move. Smith-Dorrien responded that there was nothing he could do to help.[63] At one point in the crisis, Haig is reported as standing on a doorstep in Landrecies, revolver in hand, announcing: "We must sell our lives dearly", a report largely confirmed in Charteris's account.[64] This constituted (as we can see with the comfortable benefit of hindsight) a melodramatic overreaction, though certainly not a cowardly one.

The prospect of fighting to the death in Landrecies, however, seems soon to have lost its appeal. In the absence of the requested reinforcements, Haig decided to evacuate his headquarters to Le Grand Fayt, several miles to the south. He, Gough and Charteris left Landrecies by staff car apparently at around 11.30 p.m. It was pitch dark. The surrounding countryside was thought to be alive with marauding Germans. Though Haig and his entourage were in a hurry to be gone, they did not want to draw fire by using the car's lights. Inevitably it was a hair-raising ride. This part of the great retreat seems to have been a still more alarming experience for Major Ryan, Haig's medical officer, Captain Baird, one of his ADCs, and his soldier servant, Secrett, all of whom are reported to have followed on horseback, bringing Haig's horse with them.[65]

Haig later told the official historian, James Edmonds, that by the time he left Landrecies the initial German attack had been repelled and the town well organised for defence. But in that case why did I Corps' most senior officers adopt such a hurried and dangerous mode of departure? Charteris's explanation is that they believed the Guards in Landrecies (effectively I Corps' rearguard) were surrounded and that Haig thought it his duty to rejoin the main body of his corps. So the truth may be that while Haig considered Landrecies reasonably well organised for defence in the short term, he thought it likely that the Guards would be forced to surrender in a matter of hours. This would mean that he had decided to abandon the Guards rather than leading them in an attempt to break out to the south: perhaps a rational decision, but certainly not a heroic one.[66]

According to some reports, when Haig arrived at Le Grand Fayt at about 12.30 a.m., he announced that the Guards were heavily engaged and the BEF as a whole surrounded and facing annihilation, and ordered I Corps to dump baggage and even packs in order to expedite its south-ward retreat. Johnnie Gough reported to GHQ at 1.35 a.m. that I Corps was under attack by four German divisions and, as late as 3.50 a.m. on 26 August, Haig was still demanding reinforcements from II Corps. As it turned out, the Germans had managed to envelop neither the BEF as a whole nor even the Guards at Landrecies. All the German probes into Landrecies that night were repelled, though the Guards suffered some 270 casualties in the process.[67] Tuesday 25 August 1914 and the early part of the following morning were not Haig's finest hour. He had halted his corps in a dangerous position in the afternoon, not read the situation correctly that night and overreacted. The evidence is considerable that, at least for a few hours, his nerve, stretched by extreme tiredness and a recent bout of sickness, had at least partially given way. By mid-morning on 26 August, however, he seems to have recovered. He struck at least one observer as calm and composed. He even made efforts to mount an attack northward to relieve the Guards at Landrecies, though it soon became evident that this was unnecessary.[68]

By 26 August the BEF as a whole was in danger of losing all cohesion and sense of purpose. Sir John French's faith in Lanrezac had totally collapsed during the fighting at Mons. After being, under the influence of his sub-chief of the General Staff, Major-General Henry Wilson, grossly overconfident, he had now gone to the opposite extreme. He wanted to conduct the retreat as rapidly as possible. Sir John was, indeed, so demoralised that he was tempted to pull the BEF out of the fighting altogether. Archie Murray, his chief of staff, less than effective earlier in the campaign, had, by 26 August, suffered a temporary collapse from exhaustion. Henry Wilson had, by then, lost his earlier excessive confidence in the French army, but according to some reports, had become so despondent that he was unable to offer much positive leadership.[69]

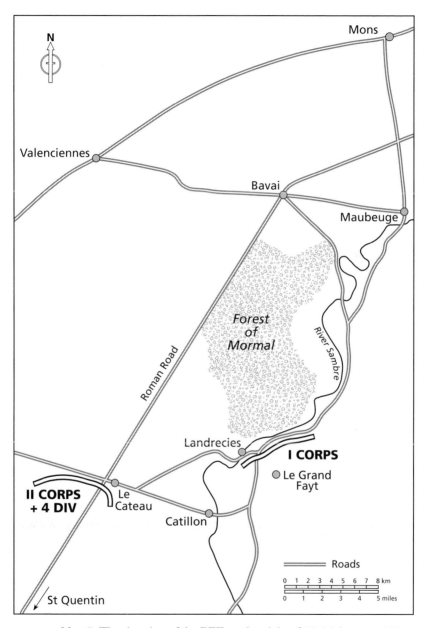

Map 5. The situation of the BEF on the night of 25–26 August 1914

With GHQ increasingly out of touch and ineffective, the corps had to look to their own salvation. While the Germans were harassing Haig around Landrecies on the night of Tuesday 25 August, Smith-Dorrien was coming to a momentous decision. His troops were, he believed, too exhausted to retreat further the following day without losing all cohesion. At 3.30 a.m. on the morning of 26 August he ordered them to stand their ground on the low ridge running west of Le Cateau and there to give battle. It was a momentous decision. It was taken against the wishes and advice of Sir John French and GHQ, but Smith-Dorrien seems to have reasoned that GHQ was too out of touch with II Corps' circumstances to be able to make an informed decision.[70]

While Smith-Dorrien's men were engaged in the desperate fight later known as the Battle of Le Cateau, I Corps continued its retreat. It did so, moreover, keeping east of the River Sambre on a path that was tending to take it further away from II Corps. For Haig personally 26 August passed in comparative calm. Most of his corps successfully completed a retreat of about ten miles to positions around Etreux. Though it is likely that sounds of battle were audible to I Corps troops for much of the day, it was not until 8.30 p.m. that Haig sent the following message to GHQ:

No news of Second Corps except sound of guns from direction of Le Cateau and Beaumont. Can First Corps be of any assistance?[71]

He received no reply. From his own words it is clear that Haig, in this instance, had chosen not to adhere to the old military maxim that commanders should "march to the sound of guns". By the time he contacted GHQ the battle was practically over. II Corps had defeated all the German attacks. It had suffered around 8,000 casualties and lost some thirty-eight pieces of artillery, but was able to continue the retreat the following day without serious interference. Lacking news of II Corps, which GHQ had apparently given up as lost, Haig and Johnnie Gough stopped for the night at a small inn on the main road just west of Iron. An old man and his daughter provided them with what Haig described as an excellent dinner of fried eggs and stewed rabbit. While they were enjoying their rabbit, Haig and Gough were apparently unaware that their corps had suffered a minor disaster earlier that evening. The 2nd Battalion of the Connaught Rangers, the rearguard for the 5th Brigade, had been badly mauled in the vicinity of Le Grand Fayt at about 6 p.m. The battalion had suffered such heavy casualties that it had virtually ceased to exist as a fighting unit.[72]

The wisdom of Smith-Dorrien's decision to fight at Le Cateau is still debated. At GHQ Sir John French, Archibald-Murray and Henry Wilson all thought him extremely foolhardy to give battle that day. Their initial reaction was apparently to give up II Corps as lost and concentrate on saving I Corps. Even when GHQ realised that the bulk of II Corps had survived the battle, there was no rush to congratulate its commander on his defensive victory. The general verdict of historians, however, has been more favourable to Smith-Dorrien. There is reason to believe that by turning to fight his pursuers at this moment Smith-Dorrien saved his corps from collapse. It is possible, though far less certain, that he saved the rest of the BEF from envelopment.[73]

It is indicative of the exhaustion that was beginning to overwhelm I Corps that Haig and Gough could not get it moving until 6 a.m. on 27 August. It was a grey and gloomy day, marked by heavy downpours of rain. The Germans were hot on I Corps' heels as it retreated on an axis through Guise to Mont d'Origny. In the early evening 2nd Battalion Royal Munster Fusiliers of 1st Infantry Brigade was surrounded near Etreux. After several hours' stiff fighting that seriously delayed the German pursuit of the rest of I Corps, the battalion was practically annihilated. It was I Corps' worst disaster of the war so far. Corps headquarters that night was at Mont d'Origny. On 28 August misty conditions were to give way to intense heat: further trying the endurance of Haig's troops. Considering the pressure, they were coping well. A French liaison officer noted that:

The men of the First Corps were tired and suffering from the extreme heat, but marched in perfect order. The regiments were ceaselessly singing Tipperary...[74]

That evening I Corps halted between La Frère and St Gobain Forest.[75] According to his diary, Haig was awoken at 5 a.m. on 29 August to receive a GHQ despatch demanding to know why he had agreed to co-operate with a French counter-offensive to be delivered that day. Haig denied that he had made any such agreement and said that GHQ should check its facts before making accusations. Then, according to Haig, French staff officers from Lanrezac's Fifth Army did arrive at his HQ requesting co-operation, but Haig said his forces were too exhausted to give it. Other accounts, however, indicate that Haig had agreed, on 28 August, to some limited co-operation with Lanrezac, only for this to be overruled by Sir John French, who had ordered that 29 August should be a day of rest for the BEF.

On Saturday 29 August some of Haig's troops had to repel minor German probes, but the bulk of them rested on their arms while Lanrezac's troops fought what was later called the Battle of Guise. It was the fourth occasion in a week that Haig's corps had largely stood by or fallen back while other people did the fighting. Despite the lack of British help, Lanrezac and the French Fifth Army performed well on 29 August. They played an important part in slowing the momentum of a German advance that was already in difficulties from logistic breakdown and the physical exhaustion of the troops.[76]

On the afternoon of 29 August Haig was summoned to see French at Compiègne. Nothing was achieved by this meeting beyond a decision to continue the retreat the next day. Haig got back to his own HQ at 8.30 p.m. He was on the move again at 3.30 a.m. the following morning. Corps headquarters that night was in a chateau two miles south-west of Soissons. The following day, 31 August, I Corps crossed the Aisne. Corps HQ was established at Villers-Cotterets. Someone at I Corps HQ, probably either Haig or Gough, took the decision to send away half the ammunition to release transport to carry men.[77] On 1 September the Germans made a determined effort to catch up with I Corps and 4th (Guards) Brigade had to fight a severe rear-guard action at Villers-Cotterets, suffering fairly serious casualties in the process. By this time the continuous retreating was getting on everybody's nerves, affecting even the normally harmonious relationship between Haig and Johnnie Gough. That night, after dining at their newly established corps HQ at Mareuil, Gough began to grumble at Haig's going on "retreating and retreating". There were other members of the staff present and Haig was not prepared to tolerate this kind of public grumbling and dissent. By his own account Haig "turned on [Gough] rather sharply and said that retreat was the only thing to save the Army and that it was his duty to support me instead of criticising".[78]

Yet Haig himself was fed up. When, on another occasion, Gough remarked that it appeared that Joffre did not intend to make a stand until he reached the ramparts of Paris, Haig reportedly replied, "Why Paris? It looks like Marseilles to me at this rate."[79]

Actually the crisis of the campaign was fast approaching. Joffre had no intention of retreating much further. But Sir John French had, by this time, almost totally lost faith in the French army. Since Mons, the tone of Sir John's letters to the War Office had fluctuated, but by the end of August had become despairing. On 30 August he indicated to the French high command that he intended to pull the BEF behind the Seine and out of the battle, at least for the time being. A complete allied collapse might easily have resulted. Joffre, whose principal strength was his composure under pressure, was thoroughly alarmed.[80] Fortunately so was Kitchener. The Secretary of State for War crossed the Channel to see French. They met in the British embassy in Paris on the afternoon of 1 September, Kitchener appearing in his Field Marshal's uniform. The situation was an awkward one. Kitchener, though a Field Marshal and thus still a serving officer, now held a ministerial post. The legitimacy of his giving orders in operational matters was open to question. In effect, however, an operational order was what he gave. The British army would remain in the "fighting line" and continue to co-operate with the French. French did not, of course, communicate to Haig the details of this meeting. But Haig, like everyone else in the BEF, was profoundly influenced by it.[81]

Kitchener's reassertion of allied unity was crucially important. Events were presenting the Allies, and the BEF in particular, with a magnificent opportunity. The troops of the German right wing were probably more exhausted than those they faced. German logistics had virtually collapsed and many units of von Kluck's First Army in particular seem to have been weak from hunger. On 29 August von Moltke altered the direction of advance of von Kluck's army. Instead of sweeping to the west of Paris, the German First Army was now to march east of the city. The main reason for the change was to avoid too big a gap opening up between the German First and Second Armies. Kluck's change of direction, however, left powerful French forces in the Paris area – the Paris garrison and the French Sixth Army – unmolested and available to strike the right flank of Kluck's army.[82] On 1 September, the day of the momentous Kitchener–French interview, Joffre incorporated the Sixth Army and one corps of the Third Army in the Paris garrison. General Gallieni, the Military Governor of Paris, an experienced and resolute officer, now had a very large military force at his disposal, poised on the flank of the German armies. That same day Joffre advised that, as the enemy was now so close to the capital, the French government should leave for Bordeaux. The government accepted this advice and left Paris on 2 September, giving Gallieni greater freedom to focus on operational matters.[83]

Yet, for the British, the retreat was to continue for the time being. Fortunately the German infantry seems to have been too tired by this stage to press I Corps as it had at Landrecies. There was, however, still much to depress the spirits. The Germans were close enough to I Corps' to be shelling it from time to time. There was continuing harassment by German cavalry. It was, moreover, fiercely hot and, though I Corps only retreated twelve miles on 2 September, such was the level of exhaustion of the troops that it was well into the evening before some units got to their billets. Much of the civilian population of north-eastern France was in the grip of a "Great Fear". Towns and villages seemingly became deserted as people fled the advancing Germans or at least hid themselves indoors to be out of harm's way. On the night of 2 September Haig slept in the town of Meaux, which he found "like a city of the dead – no-one moving in the streets except some aged men and women".[84]

By 3 September, Joffre had been planning a counter-offensive for some time. But Haig knew nothing of it. That day his spirits hit a low point.

Despite the Battle of Guise, his trust in the French army had practically collapsed. In a letter to his wife he suggested pulling the BEF out of the line and shipping it to Ostend. Objectively this made no sense. Without any apparent consciousness of how bizarre this was, he was reverting to the sort of notion that Sir John French had advocated in early August, merely substituting Ostend for Antwerp. Only extreme tiredness and psychological stress could have made Haig advocate a course which, coming from anyone else, he would probably have dismissed as the worst kind of armchair strategy.[85] That night he spent in "a shooting box evidently used by a syndicate of sportsmen from Paris" at La Fringale.

On 4 September the hot, monotonous, debilitating retreat continued. Haig spent what turned out to be the last night of the retreat in a chateau at Faremoutiers, three miles south-west of Coulommiers.[86] Going through the usual routine, Haig and his staff had the troops up well before dawn on 5 September. They were on the road by 3 a.m., moving south-west, towards Melun. Even when the sun came up, the day proved cooler than it had been of late, a mercy for the marching troops. Their spirits seemed to rise a little with this. They would rise further still at the news they were about to hear.

Haig had stopped to eat breakfast in an orchard next to the church in the village of Marles when Major Dawnay, a staff officer from GHQ, arrived with fresh orders from Sir John French. Aerial reconnaissance had now revealed that the German First Army had stopped pursuing the British. Von Kluck's formation was now going south-east rather than south, closing up towards von Bulow's German Second Army and at the same time threatening the flank of the Fifth French Army. Haig's corps was to be ready to assume the offensive the following morning 6 September. The retreat was over.[87]

So far I Corps' casualties had been fairly light: 2,261 of all types. The corps had marched some 160 miles, much of it over rather poor roads and in oppressive weather.[88] It had never starved or been without ammunition. Morale, though strained, had not collapsed. As the remainder of the year would show, I Corps had retained its cohesion as a fighting force. Haig could certainly claim some of the credit for this.

Haig's performance in the war's opening stage: Assessment

Despite being, at fifty-three, well into middle age, Haig had gone to war physically fit to lead. Grierson's military brain (from most accounts rather sharper than Haig's) had been of no further use to his country when, seriously overweight, he collapsed and died without hearing a shot fired in anger. Archibald Murray's constitution had also failed the test of war, though his problems may have been more psychological than physical. James Edmonds, the chief of staff of 4th Division, who had outshone Haig at Staff College and was later to gain fame as an official historian, had also undergone a form of breakdown during the retreat.[89] Though Haig had suffered a bout of diarrhoea on the retreat's first night, he had quickly recovered. With the marked exception of the Landrecies incident on the night of 25 August, he had appeared to bear up well under the psychological stress.

But there was a less positive side to Haig's performance. While he had some intelligent insights into the nature of this war, his suggestion that British troops be withheld from France in the opening round, had it been adopted, might have proved disastrous. Haig seems to have perceived quite early that the German move through Belgium was an attempt at large-scale envelopment. But the same narrowness of outlook evident in his initial strategic advice, as expressed to Haldane, could also be observed in his operational conduct. He had looked after I Corps well enough. On 22 August, however, by halting I Corps early in the day, he had left II Corps potentially isolated and exposed. On 23 August he had allowed II Corps to fight the BEF's first battle of the war almost unaided. On 24 August he had made no provision to cover II Corps' retreat despite a direct order to do so. On the night of 25 August and during the early hours of 26 August he had, by contrast, repeatedly, insistently and rather ridiculously demanded that Smith-Dorrien's exhausted troops rush to help him, at a time when I Corps was in no serious danger. As he withdrew I Corps to safety on 26 August, he apparently gave no thought, until very late in the day, to II Corps' genuinely desperate predicament.

Haig theoretically favoured bold manoeuvres and closing with the enemy, sometimes with cold steel. G. F. R. Henderson, Stonewall Jackson's biographer, had taught him military history and perhaps he did know all the blades of grass in the Shenandoah Valley. Up to this point in this war, however, he had not shown the slightest trace of Jacksonian aggression. He had gone to war full of doubts about the British army's level of preparedness and, in the opening stages of active campaigning, had proved a nervous, distinctly battle-shy commander.

4 From the Marne to the Salient

The Battle of the Marne and pursuit to the Aisne: 5–12 September 1914

In later years Haig used to say that he never knew there had been a Battle of the Marne.[1] Indeed, his behaviour at the time suggests a rather limited initial understanding of what was happening and some doubts as to how far he wished to participate. From 5–10 September, however, serious fighting did occur at some points over a 100-mile-wide belt of country stretching east from Paris, on either side of the River Marne. British involvement in Joffre's counter-offensive was crucial. But, tired from its retreat from Mons and under a shaken and confused commander-in-chief, the British army entered the campaign in a tentative, hesitant manner.[2]

During the retreat from Mons some significant changes had taken place that influenced the environment in which Haig was to operate in the forthcoming Marne and Aisne fighting. For one thing the BEF had been reinforced. Government fears of a German invasion of the United Kingdom having died down, the 4th Division came out to France on 24 August. Initially joining II Corps, it fought at Le Cateau on 26 August. On 31 August, however, the 4th Division, together with 19th Infantry Brigade, were placed under the command of Lieutenant-General Sir William Pulteney and formed the BEF's (initially very weak) III Corps. On Saturday 5 September, at the beginning of the Marne campaign, III Corps was on the left of the British line, at Brie-Comte-Robert.[3]

Also of great importance for the conduct of operations on the Marne was that the French Fifth Army, immediately to Haig's right, had a new commander. Joffre had been obliged to bully Lanrezac to get him to fight at Guise. Even the significant success of his army there appeared not to have lifted his despondent mood. On 3 September Joffre sacked him and replaced him with General Louis-Felix Franchet d'Espèrey.[4] Lanrezac's apparent defeatism and general disregard for the British had come close to destroying Franco-British relations. Franchet d'Espèrey, by contrast, was a determined, hard-driving commander with a distinctly ruthless streak matched by a capacity for courtesy and consideration towards allies that had eluded his predecessor. Franchet made changes in his subordinate commanders, removing those he thought tired or inefficient and replacing them with those meeting his standards of zeal. General de Maud'huy replaced General de Mas Latrie in command of the French XVIII Corps to Haig's immediate right. Haig, who was often to be bitterly critical of French generalship, was to establish cordial, respectful relationships with both Maud'huy and Franchet.[5]

At breakfast on the morning of 5 September, after his corps had been marching for several hours, Haig had (as we have noted) received orders that the retreat was at an end. His troops could get some rest before turning to strike the enemy the following day. Haig's diary reveals something of his state of mind at this time. He was glad that his troops could get a rest from marching. He had, however, told Sir John French at a meeting the previous day that while his men could stand their ground in a defensive battle, they were in no condition to attack. Haig was sceptical as to whether Joffre had any serious intention of mounting a counter-offensive, and whether, assuming that he had, the French army was in any state to respond.[6]

At 5.15 p.m. GHQ sent an operations order to the corps. The whole British army was to wheel to the right. By 9 a.m. on 6 September Haig was to have I Corps in position on a line at Rozay-en-Brie–Fontenay, about thirty miles east-south-east of Paris, from which it would attack more or less due east into the flank of the German First Army.[7] The following morning Haig moved I Corps into position as ordered. However, at about 9 a.m., an advanced guard of the 1st (Guards) Brigade reported a clash with German infantry about two miles east of Rozoy. Apparently uncertain as to the general position, Haig ordered I Corps to halt. At about 9.30 a.m. Sir John French arrived at Haig's HQ and discovered that no advance was in progress. Haig refused to move until he had clear evidence of solid support from II Corps on his left flank. He prevailed upon French to change II Corps' orders, redirecting its march so that it closed up tighter to Haig's left than had originally been intended. The counter-orders issued to II Corps inevitably slowed everything down.[8]

The bulk of Haig's corps apparently did not cross its start line until after 3 p.m., by which time it had become obvious that the Germans were in full retreat. Haig had delayed the BEF's participation in the Battle of the Marne for about six hours. Even then he scarcely cast caution to the winds. He ordered his forces to advance until 6.30 p.m., when divisions were to halt, covered by outposts, on the ground that they then occupied. I Corps' casualties that day were one officer and six other ranks killed, and five officers and thirty-nine other ranks wounded, scarcely indicating a vigorous contribution to the first day of the most crucial battle of the war. None of the BEF had made much impact on the Germans that day. But Smith-Dorrien's II Corps, a weaker and much more battered formation than Haig's, with far greater excuse to be weary and hesitant, had actually demonstrated much greater energy and offensive spirit. Despite having further to go to reach its start line and having been confused by the late change of orders that Haig had initiated, Smith-Dorrien's force had pushed several miles ahead of I Corps by nightfall. It had reaching the south bank of the Grand Morin without encountering significant opposition.[9]

Over the next few days the advance of the BEF as a whole was hesitant and slow. While some of this may be attributed to tiredness, there also appears to have been a distinct lack of drive on the part of commanders. Haig sometimes criticised others for hesitancy and timidity, but, at this stage in the war, he himself demonstrated at least his fair share of these tendencies. On the morning of 9 September Haig's forces had an unopposed crossing of the River Marne, but despite an almost completely unopposed advance, made only about seven miles that day. They made only ten miles the next day and, largely owing to Haig's hesitancy, lost the opportunity to capture some fifty-four heavy German guns that the French XVIII Corps had spotted on the road from Lizy sur Ourcq north-east towards Oulchy that morning. Yet I Corps took about 1,000 prisoners on 10 September. Despite foul weather, the moral of Haig's troops rose as they encountered masses of abandoned German equipment and numerous stragglers – obvious symptoms of the enemy's disarray.[10]

On 11 September, in response to a request from Joffre, GHQ altered the direction of the BEF's advance from virtually due north to north-east. Joffre's intention was to angle the BEF towards a gaping hole that had opened up between von Kluck's German First Army and von Bulow's German Second Army. The main danger to Kluck's army on 5 and 6 September had been the big flank attack mounted by Maunoury's French Sixth Army from the Paris area. Since then, Kluck had been pulling troops away from the BEF and the left wing of Franchet d'Espérey's French Fifth Army to deal with the threat from the French Sixth. Von Kluck's forces were thus tending to pull away from von Bulow's Second Army, opening a gap that was very dangerous from the German point of view and correspondingly inviting to Joffre.[11]

Haig pointed out that the wheeling motion required when the BEF changed direction on 11 September resulted in a marked slowing of its advance. The amount of road space allocated to the British by GQG (Joffre's headquarters) was, they believed, quite inadequate, compounding their problems and further killing their momentum. I Corps, on the inside of the BEF's turning circle, was practically standing still for much of the morning. At the same time, sheer physical tiredness after such prolonged exertions and the continuing foul weather, which had turned unseasonably cold as well as wet, inevitably diminished the ardour of the troops.[12]

On the evening of 11 September I Corps bivouacked just south of the River Vesle. On 12 September, for the second day running, the BEF met only light opposition from rearguards which the British cavalry were generally able to deal with. Again the advance was slow, I Corps making only about eleven miles. GHQ had set ambitious objectives: the seizure of crossings over the Aisne and the capture of the high ground on the far side. Part of Pulteney's III Corps, on the far left, did manage to get across the Aisne, but the other two corps stopped for the night a couple of miles short of the river.[13]

The Battle of the Aisne: 13 September – mid-October 1914

On 11 and 12 September, the Germans were given some respite. They were able to complete their retreat across the Aisne and to fortify positions north of the river. With a formidable water obstacle to their front, they occupied high ground which granted good observation for their artillery. The Aisne was about two hundred feet wide and, at twelve feet in some places, too deep to ford. The banks were steep, especially on the north side. From the north bank the ground rose for about three to four miles to a pronounced east-west ridge known, after an ancient road that ran along it, as the Chemin des Dames. The ground between the ridge and the river was broken by a number of pronounced spurs and re-entrants and was heavily wooded.[14]

Yet the Germans had not maximised their advantages, having, in some cases, botched their attempts to destroy the Aisne bridges. Despite the fire of German 15-cm and 21-cm howitzers, whose gunners had the bridges carefully registered, elements of 1st Division crossed at Bourg-et-Comin and elements of 2nd Division at Pont-Arcy on the morning of 13 September. None of Haig's troops, however, pushed far beyond on the Aisne that day and many did not cross at all. Some of those who did cross, on the half-wrecked bridges, were recalled before nightfall, apparently on the grounds that they might be destroyed by a German counter-attack if left where they were. Haig's sappers advised that the half-wrecked bridges were too precarious to rely on. They insisted on constructing pontoons to enable I Corps to cross the river in force. Once again, Haig's operations that day took on an appearance of hesitancy and confusion.[15] Accusations that he had lacked vigour and daring in the early stages of the Aisne battle appear to have circulated for years to come. Haig himself seems to have developed a sense of lost opportunity about this period of the war and it is likely that he was sensitive to such criticism.[16]

There is no doubt that had the Chemin des Dames fallen on 13 September it would have created an alarming situation for the German high command. The notion that the Allies might have exploited its seizure by executing a dramatic and devastating manoeuvre, swinging into the rear of von Kluck's 1st Army and crushing it, seems fanciful. The troops were too tired to accomplish anything so grandiose. Yet, with the Chemin des Dames in British hands, the Germans would have been forced to continue their retreat. Given the physical and psychological exhaustion of a high proportion of the German army by this stage, this would have meant the abandonment of much equipment and serious loss of personnel through straggling and desertion. It might have pushed German morale close to collapse.

We now know (as Haig did not) that the section of the Chemin des Dames ridge in front of Haig's I Corps was very weakly held. Some sections were apparently quite unoccupied until approximately 2 p.m. on 13 September, when the German VII Reserve Corps arrived. This formation had been besieging Maubeuge, but was released when that town fell on 7 September. The German high command had difficulty deciding how to use the newly released corps and it was not until 10 September that it left Maubeuge. Even then it was not sent directly to the Aisne sector. Moltke initially intended to use it in a scheme to envelop the northern flank of the French Sixth Army. By 12 September, however, the German high command had realised that it faced an emergency on the Aisne, and VII Reserve Corps was despatched there post-haste. When it arrived on the Chemin des Dames it had executed a march of forty miles in twenty four hours, an astonishing turn of speed by British standards and an indication that by no means the whole of the German army was exhausted.[17]

With the benefit of hindsight it appears true that a bit more haste on Haig's part on 13 September could have placed at least some British troops on the ridge before the German VII Reserve Corps arrived. Given the exhausted condition in which this German formation arrived at the Chemin des Dames, it is doubtful whether it could immediately have fought a battle to recapture it. But this whole argument rests on hindsight. The intelligence available to Haig on the morning of 13 September was sketchy and he may reasonably have surmised that the ground north of the river was already strongly held. The need to bridge a major river before going into a battle gave Haig a somewhat greater excuse for delay than on several previous days. Time had certainly been lost in British operations over the previous week. But the most inexcusable wastage of that precious commodity for which Haig was responsible, had occurred earlier, especially during 6–9 September.

After his period of crippling pessimism during the retreat from Mons, Sir John French's mood seems to have become very much more buoyant. GHQ's orders to the corps commanders on the evening of 13 September indicated that "The Army will continue the pursuit tomorrow and will act vigorously against the retreating enemy ... the heads of the Corps will reach the line Laon-Suzy-Fresne", an advance of about twelve miles.[18] GHQ's advocacy of boldness would have been entirely appropriate some hours earlier, but, as we have noted, the situation had changed.[19] The BEF completed its crossing of the Aisne on 14 September and pushed towards the ridge. Haig had little definite knowledge of the strength, positions or intentions of the enemy in front of him. He seems to have been by no means clear that he was sending I Corps into its first serious battle of the war. All he and his staff had done was to give the divisions their objectives and axes of advance.[20]

As on every day since 6 September, Haig's forces advanced to contact, trying to be prepared for anything they might encounter.

On the morning of Monday 14 September they were going uphill in rather broken terrain and in damp, misty weather, 2nd Division on the left and 1st Division on the right. From about 9 a.m., both divisions found themselves coming under heavy artillery, machine gun and rifle fire. The poor visibility made aerial reconnaissance practically impossible and impaired observation for the artillery. Combined with the complex topography it made the battle very difficult to control. In order to exert much influence Haig would, in any case, have needed a substantial corps reserve, and this he lacked. He was thus cast mainly in the role of a spectator, issuing occasional exhortations. It was to be a "soldier's battle".[21]

The German infantry was well supported by artillery (including heavy artillery) that had been given some time to register. The British artillery lacked observation. It could only be of much use by going forward practically to the infantry firing line to engage the enemy at short range. Lomax ordered 1st Division's gunners to do precisely that. Yet both of Haig's divisions gained ground and parts of Lomax's 1st Division actually crossed the Chemin des Dames. The Germans mounted violent counterattacks for much of the afternoon. These had subsided by early evening, however, and at 6.30 p.m. Haig ordered his whole corps to make a final bid to gain the ridge. By this stage heavy casualties had been sustained and progress was limited. During the night the troops that had gained the crest of the ridge, considered too much out on a limb, received orders from 1st Division to pull back some way down the forward slope.[22]

A report that Haig later submitted to GHQ, while full of pride in I Corps' achievement, seems fair:

The day's operations by my two divisions resulted in our gaining a foothold on about 4,000 yards of front on the main ridge north of the River Aisne, with strong flanking ridges covering a permanent crossing over the river ...

The Corps captured some 300 prisoners, 2 machine guns and 12 field guns. The guns, however, could not be moved and were recovered by the enemy after nightfall. Casualties had been fairly serious, approximately 160 officers and 3,500 other ranks, one brigade alone losing 3 of its 4 commanding officers. The chief difficulty lay in the wooded nature and steep slopes of the ground and the very accurate and effective fire of the enemy's heavy artillery...[23]

Unfortunately, on Haig's left flank, II Corps, never as robust a formation as I Corps, and weakened by its losses at Mons and Le Cateau, had not done so well. At no point had it gained the ridge. Haig alleged to Sir John French that, at a critical point in the battle, much of the 3rd Division, to I Corps' immediate left, had simply run away, though II Corps disputed this. The French XVIII Corps, on I Corps' right, had, as Haig admitted, made commendable efforts. But everywhere, on the morning of 15 September, the Germans held the crest of the ridge. For as long as they did so the Allies on the Aisne would fight at a disadvantage.[24]

The fighting on 14 September 1914 was a watershed. The Allied counter-offensive was finally checked. The German ability to stand on the Chemin des Dames helped preserve their army from disintegration. But paradoxically, it seems, in a much more positive sense, to have been a watershed in Haig's mental state. He had gone to war anxious and full of foreboding. He had, for many years, felt a profound respect for the German army and seems to have been doubtful whether the BEF could match it without, at least, more time to absorb and train its reservists. II Corps' battles at Mons and Le Cateau seem not to have quelled these doubts and, after its early debacles, Haig had been even more doubtful as to the competence of the French army.[25] He had gone into the counter-offensive on the Marne super-cautious to the point of being downright battle-shy, as he had been throughout the opening weeks of the war.

Naturally the outcome of the Battle of the Marne had already improved Haig's personal morale. Indeed, on 10 September, he had briefly dared hope that the war might be nearing its end. But, while the Battle of the Aisne badly dented that kind of optimism, it also boosted his confidence as a commander. Haig personally did nothing particularly remarkable on 14 September, but his troops did and he fully appreciated it. In a series of hurriedly improvised, essentially frontal, uphill attacks, the infantry of I Corps had proved, to Douglas Haig's enormous satisfaction and evident pride, that they were as good or better, unit for unit and man for man, than the Germans. Haig felt particular joy at this revelation precisely because, for him, it *was* a revelation. He was far too dour to have assumed it on the basis of mere patriotic sentiment. From 14 September Haig seems, at last, to have had some trust in the weapon he was wielding.

There was, however, a less fortunate aspect to Haig's response to the events of 14 September. His comments to Sir John French about that action have been interpreted, fairly convincingly, as part of what became a sustained effort to boost his own reputation and to play on the commander-in-chief's mistrust of Smith-Dorrien. Up to this point in the war, on any objective analysis, Smith-Dorrien had seemed the more assured and pugnacious of the two corps commanders. To Haig, therefore, he may have appeared as a potentially dangerous rival. During the Aisne battle Smith-Dorrien became aware that Haig was making allegations about II Corps to GHQ behind his back. Smith-Dorrien suggested that in future Haig raise any complaints about failures of inter-corps co-operation directly with him.[26] It is not clear whether this plea for a more brotherly and co-operative spirit had any effect.

I Corps and the rest of the BEF remained on the Aisne for the next month and the first period of trench warfare set in. On the evening of 15 September GHQ ordered that:

The Commander-in-Chief wishes the line now held by the Army to be strongly entrenched, and it is his intention to assume a general offensive at the first opportunity.[27]

The first part of this command was certainly fulfilled. The BEF dug in. But there was to be no further "general offensive" on the Aisne. In the trench warfare that followed the British were at a significant disadvantage because the Germans held most of the high ground and they were superior in heavy artillery. It was a lethal combination. At the beginning of the Battle of the Aisne the strength of the British army in France was approximately 164,000. Between 12 September and 3 October, the period of the Aisne fighting, casualties were 18,922. Overall, therefore, roughly one man in nine became a casualty. The proportion of losses amongst the infantry was much higher. Brigadier-General Edward Bulfin's 2nd Brigade, for example, had suffered 1,581 casualties, losing about a quarter of its fighting strength. Some of these losses were sustained in the small-scale assaults that both sides conducted to improve their positions throughout the second half of September. But a high proportion occurred in the sporadic shelling, sniping and patrol activity that would become the familiar routines of trench warfare on what would become known as the Western Front.[28]

Though the Battle of the Aisne rapidly degenerated into stalemate and trench warfare, there was, up to mid-September 1914, still an open flank

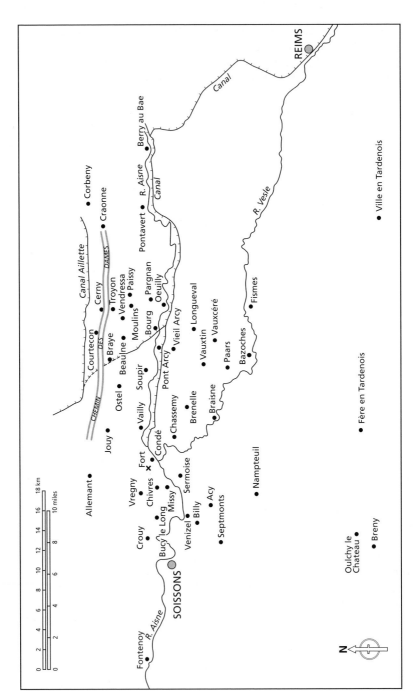

Map 6. The Aisne battlefield: September 1914

that either side might exploit. To the north of the French Sixth Army's sector on the River Oise there was a stretch of front extending over a hundred miles to the sea at Dunkirk, which was largely free of the troops of either side. The opportunities and dangers that this afforded were fairly obvious to both high commands. About the time that the fighting on the Aisne commenced, both sides had begun shifting troops to this northern sector.[29]

The shift to the north: 16–20 October 1914

On 13 September Moltke had ordered Prince Rupprecht of Bavaria to move his German Sixth Army from Lorraine to Picardy while second-line troops filled the gap thus created. Joffre mirrored this move by shifting de Castelnau's Second Army from Lorraine to the north flank of the Sixth Army, between the Oise and the Somme. Early in October the French created a new Tenth Army under de Maud'huy, formerly of XVIII Corps on Haig's right flank, to extend the front up to the Arras–Lens area. French cavalry divisions were used to extend the front still further north, to Flanders. At the same time Joffre transferred Ferdinand Foch, one of the most determined and aggressive French generals, from command of the Ninth Army in the Reims sector to that of the Groupement Provisoire du Nord (later the Northern Army Group), with its headquarters at Doullens.[30]

The British too were bringing troops to the northern part of the front. A hurriedly improvised Naval Division, comprising surplus naval personnel equipped (rather poorly) as ground troops, arrived at Dunkirk on 20 September. The idea was to relieve Antwerp, which had been under siege for over a month. The division reached Antwerp on 2 October, but was unable to prevent its fall a little over a week later. The British and the bulk of King Albert's Belgium Field Army, however, managed to extricate themselves and pull back to the River Yser.[31] By late September the British were also agitating for the BEF to be transferred to Flanders. This would put it in an area traditionally considered vital to British interests and in which proximity to the Channel ports would shorten its supply lines.[32] From Joffre's perspective, however, shifting the BEF created very considerable administrative and logistical difficulties. For the sake of harmony in the alliance, however, he consented to it and in the event it worked out well, making some of the highest quality troops available to the alliance exactly where they were most needed.[33]

Starting on 2 October, the BEF gradually withdrew from the Aisne, its positions being taken over by the rightward extension of the French Fifth and the leftward extension of the French Sixth Armies. Haig's I Corps was the last to leave. Pulled back south of the Aisne by 16 October, the bulk of it proceeded by train to Hazebrouck on 19 October. By that time II Corps had moved to Abbeville, arriving on 8 and 9 October. On 11 October, III Corps (which now included the recently arrived 6th Infantry Division) arrived in the Hazebrouck–St Omer area. GHQ had moved to Abbeville on 8 October and shifted to St Omer five days later.[34] Encouraged by Foch, Sir John French now intended that the British army should play a decisive role in enveloping the German right flank, thus bringing the war to a speedy and successful conclusion.[35] He sent II and III Corps into action within a few days of their arrival in Flanders. Smith-Dorrien's II Corps advanced towards La Bassée, with Pulteney's III Corps on its left. Rawlinson's IV Corps, consisting of the 7th Division and the 3rd Cavalry Division, had disembarked on the Continent on 6 October. It formed, for the time being, the far left of the British forces in the Ypres sector. Though the British were initially able to gain ground, by 19 October they were meeting very serious resistance from the German Sixth Army and their advance had largely ground to a halt. Smith-Dorrien was unable to take La Bassée and Rawlinson was stopped west of Menin.[36]

On 16 October, three days before his troops arrived in Flanders, Haig went by staff car from his HQ on the Aisne for a briefing from French at St Omer. French apparently indicated that the Germans in Flanders were in retreat and that "we would soon be in a position to round them up". Haig, despite his natural caution, did not at this stage dissent openly from French's prognosis. He was, in any case, pleased to hear that French did not intend to commit I Corps to battle as soon as it arrived in Flanders. It could expect a few days of badly needed rest.[37]

By 19 October, however, French had changed his mind. Haig was summoned again to GHQ at St Omer, where, at a meeting commencing at 6 p.m., French gave him his orders. Estimating German strength on the front between Ostend on the North Sea and Menin "at about one corps, not more", French ordered I Corps to advance without delay, its right wing passing through the city of Ypres. Once clear of Ypres, it was to march through Thourout, capture Bruges and drive the Germans back on Ghent. After French had finished with him that evening Haig returned to the corps HQ he had established at HQ Poperinghe, a small town west of Ypres, where he spent the night.[38]

At dawn on 20 October, in accordance with French's orders, the two divisions of I Corps marched north-east from the Hazebrouck area, where they had detrained. They assembled north-west of Ypres, behind the Ypres–Yser Canal. To I Corps' right and slightly to its front was Rawlinson's IV Corps. To its left, and also somewhat further forward, was a group of French Territorial Divisions under General Bidon. To their left, holding the Forest of Houlthurst, was a French cavalry corps under General de Mitry. The French cavalry were in touch with the Belgian Army, on the Allies' left flank. The Belgians held a canalised section of the Yser and extended the Allied line to the coast.[39]

That morning Haig established an advanced headquarters at the Hotel de La Chatelaine in Ypres. After lunch he rode to St Julien to visit the HQ of Rawlinson's IV Corps. Rawlinson's troops had been under attack since the previous day. Byng, of 3rd Cavalry Division, on Haig's immediate right, was apparently somewhat shaken and wanted to withdraw. On closer enquiry, however, Haig discovered that Byng had only sustained fifty casualties and considered that, in a war of this scale and intensity, such losses could not be considered particularly heavy. He nevertheless considered that Rawlinson could do with some assistance. He sent two battalions of the 4th (Guards) Brigade (2nd Division) to reinforce IV Corps at the boundary between Byng's 3rd Cavalry Division and Capper's 7th Division. Meanwhile, the rest of Monro's division entered the line north-east of Ypres and advanced as far as the crossroads a mile-and-a-half north-west of Zonnebeke. Haig returned to his main head-quarters at Poperinghe at about 7 p.m., where he spent the night.[40]

I Corps and the First Battle of Ypres: 21 October–12 November 1914

On 21 October Haig brought Lomax's 1st Division forward into the line, on the left of Monro's 2nd, and together they began to advance in a generally eastward direction.[41] But I Corps was moving into great danger. Since 18 October there had been intelligence reports (which Sir John French had played down or ignored) of substantial German reserves arriving at Brussels. These were, in fact, elements of the new German Fourth Army. Erich von Falkenhayn, then German War Minister, had begun to raise these reserve formations at the start of the war. They were mostly led by reservist or retired officers and were, to a large extent, manned by wartime volunteers who had only a few weeks' training. Unlike the British army, for the most part weary, battered and bloody, they were entirely fresh. Whether this would be enough to compensate for very basic training and accompanying tactical naiveté remained to be seen.[42]

Early in the Battle of the Aisne the Kaiser Wilhelm II had quietly dismissed von Moltke from his position as German chief of staff.[43] Falkenhayn succeeded him, combining the post with that of War Minister. Falkenhayn quickly decided to use the reserve corps he had created earlier – now combined as a new Fourth Army – to decisive effect in the north. On 10 October Falkenhayn had told its commander, Duke Albrecht of Wurttemburg, that:

The new Fourth Army will advance, regardless of losses, with its right flank on the sea coast, in order to cut off the fortresses of Dunkirk and Calais – these will be captured later – and then will swing southward, leaving St. Omer on its left.[44]

The arrival of the German Fourth Army in Flanders would force the Allies to modify their own grandiose strategic notions.[45]

As I Corps advanced on 21 October, French Territorial troops posted to its left were in rapid retreat. Some of them got in the way of the British advance. When Haig's troops reached the Langemarck–Zonnebeke road they came under heavy fire and the advance slowed. Then, at approximately 2 p.m., Haig heard that the French 7th Cavalry Division, now virtually the sole protection for 1st Division's left flank, had received orders, apparently from General de Mitry, the cavalry corps commander, to pull back. Commendably reluctant to endanger his allies, the divisional general insisted on getting written confirmation before complying and used the time to inform the British. Forewarned, Major-General Lomax of 1st Division posted some companies to protect his left.[46]

Unlike Mons, where the British army had halted and taken up a sort of defensive position before battle commenced, "First Ypres" thus began as a true encounter battle: at its outset both sides were trying to advance. Encounter battle, however, was not a game Haig wanted to play for any length of time. Hearing that Sir Henry Rawlinson's IV Corps, to his right, was under heavy attack and had lost ground, he ordered his divisions to halt and dig in. The Allies were now holding a pronounced salient around the city of Ypres.[47] For the rest of the Wednesday 21 October, the two divisions of I Corps found themselves under attack by five German divisions and suffered over 900 casualties. Superior British fieldcraft, shooting and infantry/artillery co-operation, however, wrought havoc with the German reservists. They found themselves advancing against an enemy they could not see. German co-ordination between infantry and artillery collapsed. The infantry made clumsy attacks in dense masses and were shot down in droves. Once they had lost most of their officers and senior NCO's, the remainder became confused and paralysed.[48]

Haig's corps did well that day, standing its ground. During the afternoon Sir John French paid a visit to Haig's headquarters, as did General de Mitry, the commander of the French cavalry corps on Haig's left. Though the British commander-in-chief talked of renewing the offensive at some unspecified time, he agreed that the "advance was to be discontinued for the present" and tried to impress on General de Mitry the necessity of protecting Haig's flank.[49]

Foch, however, insisted on fresh attacks, as did General Victor d'Urbal, who, on 20 October, took charge, under Foch's general direction, of all the French forces in Belgium. On the morning of 22 October, therefore, inter-Allied co-operation in Ypres temporarily broke down. While the British troops remained in their trenches, French troops of the 87th Territorial Division (mostly relatively elderly and unfit men) marched behind the British line at Bixschoote, shortly after 6 a.m., to mount an attack in the direction of the Forest of Houthulst. By 2 p.m. this attack had collapsed and some of the troops involved retreated back through the 1st Division. For most of the day the Germans furiously attacked the salient. With just two brigades, Lomax's 1st Division held a line stretching between Steenstraat on the Ypres Canal and Langemarck. During the afternoon the Germans mounted particularly massive and determined attacks in this sector. The division held its own except in the centre, at Kortekeer Cabaret, where the Germans broke in at dusk. In response Haig reinforced his corps reserve (the 2nd Brigade) with two battalions and ordered its commander, Brigadier-General Bulfin, now commanding five battalions, to counter-attack. In a well-executed assault mounted at 4 a.m. on 23 October, Bulfin restored the British line, took hundreds of German prisoners and released some British troops the Germans had captured the previous day.[50]

On 22 October Foch, whose headquarters was at Doullens, about sixty miles south of Ypres, ordered d'Urbal to use all the available French forces in Belgium to mount a counter-offensive in the direction of Roulers. Foch wanted d'Urbal to break the German line and swing round to the Lys, near Courtrai, apparently in an effort to envelop the right wing of the bulk of the German forces in the west. It was a grandiose conception, but suggests that Foch had little appreciation of the true balance of forces in Flanders.[51] Foch asked that Sir John French ensure that "the whole British Army should support this offensive, its left flank marching on Courtrai".[52] Foch's scheme required a major offensive effort from Haig's I Corps on 23 October. French wanted to comply with Foch's wishes and gave orders to Haig accordingly. But Haig concluded that those issuing such instructions were out of touch with the situation. He declined even to attempt to execute them, despatching staff officers to GHQ and to neighbouring French commands to explain his position. Haig's judgement was certainly correct. What is more remarkable is that by this stage in the campaign he felt he had a sufficient moral ascendancy over his commander-in-chief to be able to disregard orders with impunity when he judged them imprudent.[53]

Even in the absence of British support, d'Urbal made an effort to obey his orders on the morning of Friday 23 October. French troops, however, quickly met with fierce counter-attacks and made little progress. Later in the day, however, reinforcements arrived in the form of General Dubois' French IX Corps, which Joffre had sent up from Reims. The Germans had suffered very heavy losses over the last few days and the French IX Corps' arrival temporarily shifted the balance in the favour of the Allies. It also allowed some reorganisation of British forces. On the night of 23 October, the French 17th Division relieved Monro's 2nd Division, which, assembling just to the east of the town of Ypres, became I Corps' reserve. While d'Urbal took the offensive, on Saturday 24 October Haig was also able to take Lomax's 1st Division out of the line for a much-needed rest. But no part of Haig's corps was actually to get much respite.[54]

By Saturday 24 October, Major-General Sir Thompson "Tommy" Capper's over-extended 7th Division (of Rawlinson's IV Corps) had sustained very heavy casualties, mainly caused by the intense, remorseless pounding of the German artillery. That morning the division temporarily lost Polygon Wood. Monro's 2nd Division, after its brief rest, came back into the line, 5th Brigade helping to retake the wood. The remainder of 2nd Division took over the left of what had been the 7th Division's front and co-operated in the French IX Corps' offensive. But the 7th Division remained fragile. A German attack directed at the apex of the Ypres salient resulted in the loss of the higher ground around the village of Kruissecke on the morning of 26 October. As a result, a substantial part of the division temporarily disintegrated.

Hearing disturbing reports of this from IV Corps, Haig sent a staff officer forward to find out what was going on. Using his initiative, this officer ordered elements of 1st Brigade (1st Division) forward to plug the gaps in the line. At about 3 p.m. Haig rode out to see conditions for himself. He was disturbed to find apparently panic-stricken troops milling around in the rear. He sent in more of 1st Division to reinforce those elements of the 7th Division that had stayed in their trenches, before rallying the elements that had fled. Haig blamed the 7th Division's problems on troops having been left, "through the ignorance of their leaders", on forward slopes where they were unnecessarily exposed to German artillery. He placed particular blame on Brigadier-General Lawford of 22nd Brigade.[55]

After only the briefest respite, therefore, 2nd Division and the bulk of 1st Division had been compelled to go back into the line, though Haig was able to retain Bulfin's 2nd Brigade as a corps reserve. Visiting the front on 27 October, French informed Haig that he was now placing 7th Division under his command. Allenby's Cavalry Corps, to IV Corps's right, had taken control of 3rd Cavalry Division two days earlier. IV Corps temporarily ceased to exist as a fighting formation while Rawlinson and some of his corps staff went back to England to assist in the training of 8th Division, eventually intended to take 3rd Cavalry Division's place in IV Corps.[56]

As the German Fourth and Sixth Armies had failed to break through, Falkenhayn had created a powerful new striking force, under General von Fabeck, including the XIII, XV and II Bavarian Corps. Much of von Fabeck's group consisted of good quality troops. It was backed by a massive artillery concentration, including some 257 heavy guns and howitzers released from other sectors of the front. The arrival of von Fabeck's group gave the Germans in the Ypres sector a two-to-one superiority in numbers of troops and ten-to-one in guns. Fabeck's force was to enter the line between the Fourth and Sixth armies. Its mission was to break the Allied line between Zandvoorde and Messines and take Kemmel Hill, south and slightly east of Ypres. German occupation of this position might well have made Ypres untenable by the Allies. The stretch of front targeted was held by the 7th Division and Allenby's Cavalry Corps, formations that, like the rest of the BEF, were already severely depleted and close to exhaustion. The operation was planned for 30 October.[57]

Before the main offensive, Fabeck decided to mount a preliminary attack on 29 October to seize the high ground near Gheluvelt on the Ypres–Menin road. This operation was to be mounted mainly by Fourth Army troops that had been in the line for some time, rather than by Fabeck's newcomers, who were to remain fresh for the main effort the following day. The initial strike would be at the junction between Lomax's 1st Division and Capper's 7th Division. On 28 October, Haig, who had now moved his Advanced HQ from Ypres itself to the White Chateau near Halte, got some warning of this from a wireless intercept.[58]

The attack began promptly at 5.30 a.m on 29 October. The Germans came on in dense formations supported by very heavy artillery fire. A thick mist aided the Germans, at some points enabling the infantry to get within fifty yards of the British line without being seen. By 8 a.m. 1st Division was losing ground and the situation was looking very threatening. I Corps informed GHQ that there was now no chance of confining artillery shell expenditure to the thirty rounds per-gun per-day ration. During the morning the Germans took the crossroads east of Gheluvelt and much of the area south of the Menin Road. By 11.30 a.m., the situation was so serious that Haig was obliged to send in his main corps reserve: 2nd Brigade. Welcome support also arrived from Hubert Gough, who sent five squadrons of his 2nd Cavalry Division to support I Corps, in which, of course, his brother was chief of staff. The counter-attacks 2nd Brigade conducted were pressed home so vigorously that most of the ground was recovered, though the crossroads near Gheluvelt remained in German hands. Dusk, accompanied by a deluge of Flanders rain, brought the fighting to an end for the day.[59]

By the evening of 29 October, despite great resilience on the part of most of the troops, the BEF's position in the Ypres sector was becoming desperate. I Corps was severely depleted, indeed approaching exhaustion, and all its units were mixed up. That evening, however, Sir John French ordered I Corps to continue its offensive in conjunction with the French IX Corps. As if to demonstrate how out of touch he had become, French telegraphed Kitchener that evening indicating that, "if the success can be followed up it will lead to a decisive result".[60] This was fatuous. In reality all I Corps had really been doing on Thursday 29 October was fighting for its life.

Haig once again virtually ignored his commander-in-chief. He decided to remain strictly on the defensive, ordering that his divisions try to sort out their units and improve their fortifications as far as possible. The German assault began at 6.30 a.m. on Friday 30 October, after an hour of intense bombardment. I Corps stood up remarkably well against the initial onslaught. However, Allenby's Cavalry Corps on the right was forced to give ground, losing Zandvoorde. This forced 7th Division to withdraw its right wing somewhat in order to escape envelopment. Realising that the situation was becoming dangerous and having inadequate reserves of his own, that morning Haig appealed for help from General Dubois, commanding the French IX Corps to his left. Dubois promptly despatched a brigade that Haig used to shore up his right around Zandvoorde. When darkness fell, I Corps' line, astride the Menin road, had been driven back about two miles, but the defence was still coherent.[61]

Saturday 31 October was to be one of the most critical days fighting, not merely of 1914, but of the whole war. Falkenhayn apparently believed that he could break through at Ypres and, restoring mobility, roll up the front of the Allied armies from the north.[62] Whether German dreams of a decisive victory in 1914 were to be fulfilled would depend on how I Corps performed. At 6 a.m. three German divisions mounted an assault at a point on the Menin road about 300 yards east of Gheluvelt, near the junction of 7th Division and 1st Division. This was repelled, but was followed by a colossal pounding of the whole I Corps area by the German artillery, especially the locality around Gheluvelt. The bombardment was so intense and devastating that units east of Gheluvelt village, their primitive trenches buried or torn apart, were forced to pull back. Despite stern British resistance and heavy German casualties, a renewed assault then took Gheluvelt, in 1st Division's sector, soon after midday. By that stage Lomax, of 1st Division, had no reserves left and was obliged to ask Monro of 2nd Division for help.[63]

Monro was able to offer less than one battalion: three companies of 2nd Battalion of the Worcestershire Regiment. Brigadier-General FitzClarence, commanding 1st Guards Brigade, took charge of the battalion and brought it into position north-west of the village of Gheluvelt, portions of which were then on fire. From there, Major E. B. Hankey then commanding the battalion, led its 350 or so officers and men in a counter-attack which surprised the Bavarian troops of the 16th Reserve Infantry Regiment, who, thinking the battle already won, were in some cases looting or looking for water. The village was retaken, though at heavy cost to the Worcestershire battalion. But just as this dramatic counter-attack was in progress, disaster struck further to the rear.[64]

Up to 29 September Haig and his I Corps staff had used the Chateau of Hooge on the Menin road, some two to three miles east of Ypres, as a "Reporting Centre" (a sort of forward headquarters). On that date Haig, on one of his visits to the front, had apparently found Lomax and his 1st Division staff operating from a two-room cottage. Thinking these quarters too cramped, he had directed Lomax to use the Hooge Chateau, while he and his staff used the White Chateau, about a mile closer to Ypres. At some point between 12.50 and 1.15 p.m. (reports vary slightly) on Saturday 31 October, Lomax and Monro were conferring in the Hooge Chateau when, in quick succession, four big German shells struck it. Six staff officers were killed outright. Lomax was so severely wounded that he died some months later and Monro was stunned. Had these officers become casualties just an hour or two earlier, it might have proved decisive, for I Corps' cohesion could easily have collapsed. Hearing of the disaster, Johnnie Gough apparently directed Bulfin to go and take command of 1st Division, leaving 2nd Brigade under Lord Cavan's control. But this incident is not mentioned in Bulfin's diary, and Bulfin at this time was so preoccupied with the collapse of the 7th Division on his left (northern) flank that he was in no position to do anything about the situation at Hooge Chateau.[65]

Meanwhile, Sir John French was touring the front. As his staff car drove through Ypres he found the town jammed with the flotsam of battle, including artillery in flight from the front. So choked were the roads that he had to leave his car before he got to Haig's HQ. By the time he arrived at the White Chateau (at about 2 p.m. according to some sources, though the timing is disputed) he had already realised that the situation was critical. French found Haig and Johnnie Gough studying maps and obviously in an anxious state. Having heard of the German breakthrough at Gheluvelt an hour or so earlier, they had apparently only just received news of the Hooge Chateau disaster. Haig appeared calm, though his face had gone very white. He is reported to have said: "They have broken us

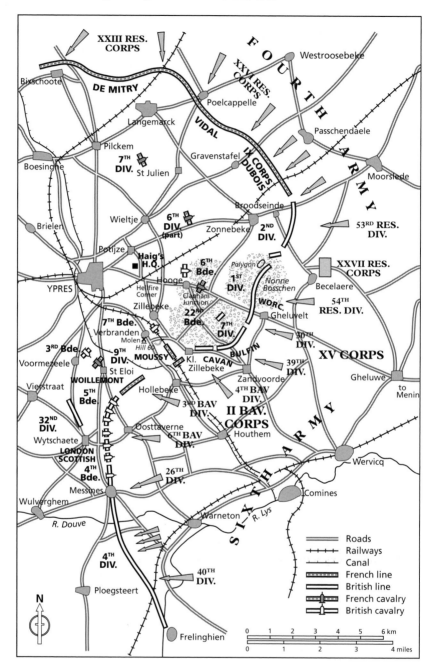

Map 7. The First Battle of Ypres: The situation on 31 October 1914

right in and are pouring through the gap."[66] If this account is accurate, he was, at that particular moment, somewhat exaggerating a bad situation. The Germans had not, despite diverse and contradictory reports, exploited their capture of Gheluvelt at all vigorously.

French left the chateau and walked off towards his staff car. At this point Brigadier-General S. R. Rice, Haig's chief engineer, whom Haig had sent to the front on horseback to establish the true situation, apparently came galloping back "as red a turkey cock and sweating like a pig". He reported the astonishing success of the 2nd Worcestershire's counter-attack. Haig's staff was heartened by the news. "It was just as if we had all been under sentence of death and most suddenly received a free pardon." But Haig himself was more cautious. He is reported to have "pulled at his moustache", always a sign that he was preoccupied and anxious, and to have said that he "hoped it was not another false report". Yet he sent an ADC to overtake French before he got to his staff car to give him Rice's news. Like Haig, French may have been initially sceptical. His staff car apparently left the scene at some velocity.[67]

Reports of Haig's activity on 31 October are conflicting, and timings are difficult to establish with exactitude. According to one account, even before Rice arrived with the good news, Haig had ordered his horse. Once French had left, Haig, in the company of Johnnie Gough and a small cavalcade of other staff officers, possibly at some point between 2.40 and 3 p.m., rode down the Menin road, apparently intending to make a personal assessment of the situation and to stamp his authority on events.[68] This ride seems to have played an important part in the development of Haig's own idea, and the image he wished to project to others, of his role in this war. In the midst of the greatest crisis for the British army in 1914, he had ridden forward majestically, in the face of confusion and danger, to put matters right. At least one historian has suggested that no such mid-afternoon ride took place, though he accepts that Haig may have ridden in the same direction earlier in the day when things were quieter. James Edmonds, the official historian, may also, at one point, have doubted Haig's version of events. The balance of evidence, however, is that the ride took place much as Haig portrayed it.[69]

Haig never explicitly claimed that this ride had had a decisive impact. Indeed, while it may have helped to boost confidence and morale amongst the relatively small numbers of officers and men who witnessed it, its material effect seems to have been, at most, marginal. The wisdom of Haig's leaving his headquarters in the midst of a crisis was, moreover, most questionable and might have led to a serious breakdown of command and control.[70] As he neared the front, Haig saw two of the brigadiers of 1st Division and Capper of 7th Division. Between 2 and 3 p.m., the front of that much-depleted division having been smashed in, Bulfin of 2nd Brigade (1st Division) organised a counter-attack into the left flank of the advancing Germans with his own troops and any others he could scrape together. Hearing of this, Haig apparently ordered troops of the 6th Cavalry Brigade, which he had commandeered that morning, from Allenby's corps, and now practically the only reserves he had left, to take part. Some of them actually did so, but no authority indicates that their involvement was of critical importance. Bulfin's counter-attack, however, was one of the outstanding feats of the war so far. For the second time that day, I Corps' collapse was narrowly averted. Later that same afternoon Haig received welcome reinforcements of French cavalry, giving him some prospect of continued resistance.[71]

The next morning Major-General H. J. S. Landon, who had taken over from Lomax as the commander of 1st Division, told Haig that his troops were so depleted and exhausted that they probably could not resist another serious attack. The German offensive that day, however, concentrated mainly on Allenby's Cavalry Corps to the south. Allenby's men lost the Messines–Wytshaete ridge, but somehow managed to re-establish a coherent defence behind that feature. Haig and his staff were shelled out of the White Chateau and had to withdraw their battle HQ to Ypres: a town itself increasingly devastated by German artillery.[72]

Heavy fighting continued into November, but it did not again reach the intensity of 31 October until 11 November, when the Germans made yet another determined effort to capture Ypres. For this they sent in another "Army Group" consisting of two corps under General von Linsingen. The Linsingen Group was the spearhead for the German attack mounted all round the salient that day, but focusing, as on 31 October, on Haig's corps astride the Menin road. The attack was prepared by the heaviest preliminary bombardment yet experienced by British troops. It commenced at 6 a.m. At 9 a.m. ten German corps attacked. The Germans penetrated Haig's front north of the Menin road to a depth of 500 yards, but could get no further. This was partly due to the fortification of battalion and brigade command posts and the preparation of a series of specially built strong points behind the lines: procedures recommended by Haig's chief engineer, Brigadier-General Rice.[73]

Though it took some time for them to realise this, by dusk on 11 November 1914 the Allies had won the First Battle of Ypres. The intensity of the fighting in this area greatly diminished as autumn gave way to winter.[74] The Allies' retention of Ypres seemed no less of a miracle than their victory on the Marne. In one sense, however, holding that town was a dubious victory. With the Germans in possession of most of the high ground around it, "The Salient", as it became known in the British army, became a "shell trap" for troops defending it. The canal line running behind Ypres might well have been a better position to hold, though that was not a decision for a mere corps commander like Haig.

By Wednesday 12 November, not knowing that the worst was over, Haig was becoming desperate that his corps should be taken out of line. Orders originating with Foch, but passed through GHQ, told him that I Corps should hold in place at all costs until relieved. What was left of it did so. Its relief was completed on 21 November. The BEF as a whole had been through a terrible test over the last few weeks and, at critical times, I Corps had borne the brunt of it. More than a fortnight earlier, on 4 November, 1st Division, 18,000 men at full strength, had already been reduced to ninety-two officers and 3,491 men. By the battle's end, 1st Guards Brigade, over 4,000 men at full strength, was down to four officers and 300 other ranks. Admittedly not all these losses were caused by wounds. The weather had turned cold and wet and between 20 October and 20 November over 15,000 men in I Corps had been taken out of the line sick: an average of about 717 per day. Yet, the fact remains that, one way or another, I Corps had been reduced to a skeleton by the end of First Ypres.[75] Remembering its shattered condition in mid-November 1914, Haig thought that the Germans had made a fatal error in slackening their efforts. It was a mistake he was determined not to repeat when the initiative lay in the hands of the Allies.[76]

Assessment

As on the Aisne, so at Ypres, Haig had done nothing particularly brilliant. But this was a battle that gave corps commanders little scope for brilliance. Rather it had demanded resilience and resolution. In these qualities, in these critical weeks, Haig was not found wanting. In particular he had performed sterling work organising the counter-attack to restore 1st Division on 22 October and in saving the 7th Division from complete collapse on 26 October. He had exercised prudence, conserving his resources, ordering his troops to fortify their positions and trying to maintain and manage some sort of corps reserve. Whilst his equanimity was doubtless strained at times, most of the evidence indicates that both his physical constitution and his psyche had stood the colossal strain reasonably well. In the final analysis, however, Ypres had been essentially another "soldiers' battle", won by the sheer stubbornness and determination of the great bulk of the Allied forces, French as well as British.

During First Ypres, Haig had enjoyed a number of advantages in relation to the other British corps commanders. At the start of the battle, his had been the strongest of the British corps. Practically throughout the campaign he had a shorter line to hold in relation to the size of force commanded than did any of the other British corps commanders. Though Haig's regard for Sir John French seems to have been in decline, French apparently trusted Haig more than any of his peers. Haig was thus able to get his own way relatively easily. He ignored orders from GHQ without adverse consequences and gained reinforcements more readily than his fellow corps commanders. Moreover, at a number of crucial points in the campaign, Haig had benefited from generous relief and reinforcement from the French army, which had troops on Haig's flank throughout its course.

With these advantages, Haig appeared the most resolute and dependable of the British corps commanders at the year's end. He emerged as the principal British hero of First Ypres still in the field. It was no fault of Haig's that others, who had been nearer the firing line most of the time and had personally led crucial counter-attacks, were no longer with the army. FitzClarence was dead and Bulfin temporarily disabled. Lomax, another rock of I Corps' defence, was badly wounded and would soon die. Haig, while giving these officers due praise, naturally reflected the glory they had helped to win. By his letters home, and by getting his wife to circulate his diaries to the right people, he successfully presented an image of himself as the outstanding British military commander of 1914,[77] far outshining Sir John French, whose attempt to withdraw the BEF from combat in September had already, to a large extent, discredited him.

With regard to the three weeks of intense, mainly defensive fighting, between 21 October and 11 November, the image was not merely a mirage. His performance during the war of movement, from 21 August to 13 September, a phase that had made a greater range of demands on his generalship, had, however, been much less impressive.

5   Army commander

Relief and leave

From 12 November 1914 the fighting around Ypres gradually and temporarily died down. Between 17 and 21 November what was left of Haig's corps came out of the line, the French IX and XVI Corps filling the gap. While his troops rested in the area around Hazebrouck, Haig took five days' home leave, starting on 22 November.[1] Doris, who had spent the last three months working in a small officers' hospital in Aldershot, presided over by Napoleon III's widow, the Empress Eugénie, met her husband at Victoria station. Though they had frequently exchanged letters, it seemed to Haig a hundred years since they had parted the previous August.

They spent most of the time at his sister Henrietta's home in Princes Gate. Their daughters, who had been living with Henrietta in Wales, came to join them. A family trip to the zoo on the last afternoon was one of the most relaxing activities. But the war could never be far from Haig's thoughts. During an interview at Buckingham Palace, on 24 November, the King assured him of royal gratitude for his service to date and royal confidence in his future performance. Haig saw the Prime Minister the following morning. There were two interviews with Kitchener, munitions and manpower being amongst the topics discussed, and there were less business-oriented meetings with Queen Alexandra (Edward VII's widow) and the Empress Eugénie. He returned to France on 27 November.[2]

Winter in the trenches, Christmas at Corps HQ

Fierce fighting had continued on the Eastern Front and the Russians requested a renewal of Allies' efforts in the west. On 14 and 15 December, as the British component of Joffre's winter offensive, Smith-Dorrien's II Corps participated in an unsuccessful attack on the Messines ridge south of Ypres.[3]

On 20 December, the Germans retaliated for the British attempt on the Messines ridge by striking at the already battered and somewhat demoralised Indian Corps around Givenchy. On 21 December elements of I Corps were obliged to go to the Indian Corps' assistance. Haig soon decided that it was necessary to relieve the Indians entirely and I Corps as a whole had to back into the line. For Haig's troops, the first winter in the trenches, coming on top of everything else they had suffered, was a thoroughly wretched experience. Especially after the New Year, it rained exceptionally hard. The water table in this region was always close to the surface. Inevitably the trenches became flooded. Men were often standing in a foot or two of bitterly cold, muddy water. In these circumstances it was inevitable that trench foot and other forms of sickness would take their toll. Haig was well aware of the suffering of his troops,[4] but could do only a limited amount to relieve it. In any case it was not in his nature to dwell excessively on such things.

Haig and his staff spent a much more comfortable Christmas at Hinges, two miles north of Béthune. Doris sent a present for everyone in the headquarters, including the servants. Before the war Haig had become friendly with the financier Leopold Rothschild, who sent fifty pairs of fur-lined gloves. Haig, his ADC's and his soldier-servant, Secrett, used part of Christmas Eve wrapping and labelling these presents. Distributing them the following day was a pleasant relief from the strain of command. Christmas dinner that evening was a splendid occasion, featuring turtle soup and a bottle of 1820 brandy – another Rothschild gift. Haig now knew that he was to become an Army commander. Though I Corps would remain under his aegis, he had to say a sort of farewell to some of his corps staff. In the afterglow of his Christmas dinner, Haig felt very privileged to have commanded I Corps and recorded that he had begun to feel a "higher power" was guiding his fortunes.[5]

The reorganisation of the BEF

On 26 December 1914 a new organisation came into effect for the BEF. Two armies were created. First Army comprised I Corps and IV Corps in the line, with the Indian Corps and part of the Indian Cavalry Corps acting as Army Reserve. Second Army took control of II Corps and III Corps. As the senior corps commander, already promoted to full general, Haig naturally became the First Army commander. Smith-Dorrien, despite his continuing personality clash with French, took command of Second Army. Allenby's Cavalry Corps went into GHQ reserve, later joined by the Indian Cavalry Corps. Lomax having being critically injured in the Hooge Chateau incident, Monro took over I Corps from Haig. Establishing his First Army headquarters at Lillers on 27 December, Haig took with him Johnnie Gough as chief of staff, and Charteris as head of his General Staff intelligence section. He also kept two ADCs, Captains Straker and Fletcher, who had been with him at I Corps. Finding their quarters at Lillers cramped and unpleasant, the First Army team moved to Aire on the River Lys on 1 February.[6]

The creation of new armies was followed in the New Year by changes at GHQ. Murray was generally considered a failure as chief of staff. In line with Haig's recommendations, it was not Henry Wilson, the sub-chief, who replaced him, but Major-General Sir William "Wully" Robertson. As Quartermaster-General, Robertson had done an excellent job of organising the army's movements and supply. From humble origins, Robertson had risen from the ranks on the basis of pure ability, and his professionalism was universally respected. Though Wilson had shown little insight or judgement in operational matters, fluency in the French language and good relations with French officers made his retention important to the alliance. He stayed on at GHQ as chief liaison officer.[7]

A mood of optimism

From the beginning of winter, despite the sufferings of the men in the trenches, a strangely sanguine mood seems to have taken hold at GHQ and also, to a lesser extent, at Haig's headquarters. Just a few weeks earlier the British army on the Continent had been within a hair's breadth of collapse and French and Haig had been at their wits' end. Yet, by the beginning of December (perhaps owing to the release of tension when the big German attacks in Flanders stopped), a somewhat unreal degree of optimism had set in.

Admittedly, the grand strategic situation, objectively considered, seemed bad for the Germans. They had failed in their attempt to knock France out. Despite their great victory at Tannenberg, in East Prussia, in August, they now appeared to be in some difficulty on the Eastern Front too. On hearing somewhat exaggerated reports of Russian successes in autumn 1914, however, French came to the quite unwarranted conclusion that a German collapse was imminent. He was prepared to venture this opinion when addressing British troops, including Haig's.[8] Though more cautious than French, Haig was not unaffected by this mood. Writing to Doris on 13 December, he indicated that the war was now going well. He thought that on the Western Front: "We have only a shell opposed to the French and ourselves, so if we succeed in cracking it, may be able to push the enemy back a very long way – say to the Rhine."[9] This view was not dispelled by the subsequent failure of II Corps' attempt on the Messines Ridge, a failure that Haig attributed mainly to a lack of grip and drive at II Corps and at GHQ.[10] Haig's notion that German defences in the west were now very fragile, and that their front could easily be broken once sufficient artillery ammunition became available, persisted well into the New Year.[11]

One of the sources of Haig's optimism during the first winter of the war may well have been John Charteris. Charteris had gone to the Western Front as one of Haig's ADCs, but despite the absence of a Staff College education or any formal staff training, Haig had soon made him I Corps' intelligence chief apparently on the basis of his linguistic skills. In one of many letters home to his wife, Charteris recorded a whole series of optimistic reports that had come to his attention and to which he apparently gave some credence. Sweden was now keen to join the Allies and would bring Denmark with her. Romania would enter the war on Britain's side in the spring of 1915. The Germans were so terrified of the Italians joining the Allies that they were trying to buy them off with the Austrian Tyrol. Hungary was about to split with Austria. Germany itself was on the point of seeking peace.[12] While there is no evidence that Haig fastened on to any of these rumours, they were part of the more collective mood in which he now operated.

Haig and French in harmony

During this relatively relaxed and hopeful period, Haig's relationship with Sir John French appears to have been fairly good. During the Ypres fighting Haig had come to doubt French's judgement and, as we have noted, on occasion had deliberately disregarded his orders. French, however, had generally been tolerant and supportive of Haig and was very complimentary about him in despatches home.[13] Haig liked praise, especially when accompanied, as in this case, by professional advancement and royal favour. In mid-December Haig had felt able to be frank with his commander-in-chief about changes he thought were needed at GHQ and was naturally pleased when he saw some of his suggestions (most notably the replacement of Murray with Robertson) adopted in the New Year.[14] Though some of his diary entries were rather patronising about French, Haig seemed reconciled to working with him for the foreseeable future. There was, moreover, a fair degree of agreement between the two generals on some major issues now facing the army.

How the British should conduct the war from this point onwards was a matter of debate at the highest levels during the winter. Some on the home front tended to think that the Western Front was so utterly deadlocked that the British Empire should transfer its principal effort elsewhere, the Dardanelles being one of a number of suggestions. French held a conference of Army and cavalry corps commanders on 4 January 1915. He read a letter from Kitchener that mentioned the possibility of the New Armies of wartime volunteers being employed on some front other than the Western. Haig's view was that:

we ought not to divide our Military Force, but *concentrate on the decisive spot* which is on this frontier against the German main Army. With more guns and ammunition and more troops, the Allies were bound in the end to defeat the Germans and break through.

Sir John naturally agreed with this. Haig, and all the other senior officers present, also concurred with French in his scepticism about the likely military value of Kitchener's New Armies, at least in the short term. Kitchener was thinking of deploying these troops out in entire divisions, corps and even Armies. All the generals present thought that New Army forces should be sent out in battalion or brigade strength only, and incorporated in the existing divisions.[15] Ultimately "Kitchener" forces would, in fact, arrive on the front as complete divisions, but would generally be grouped with other types of division in corps and Armies.

Allied strategic plans and Robertson's thoughts on operational method

During the winter, Sir John French, under the influence of his friend Winston Churchill, the First Lord of the Admiralty, became interested in the idea of an independent British offensive down the Belgian coast towards Zeebrugge, where the Germans had submarine pens. It was an idea on which Haig apparently looked more favourably than did most of French's other generals. To execute it, however, Sir John thought he would need large reinforcements, a great deal of shell and the co-operation of his French allies in transferring the BEF from its existing position (sandwiched between the French Eighth and Tenth Armies) to the coast. None of these preconditions could be met. Wilson, Joffre and Foch all opposed the idea and even Churchill lost enthusiasm during the New Year, as his interest shifted to the Dardanelles.[16]

Thus, Sir John's wish to develop an independent British Western Front strategy got nowhere. He had little choice other than to make what contribution he could to strategy formulated in Joffre's headquarters. Joffre's initial conception was a two-pronged offensive against the "Noyon salient": the great bulge in the German front between Arras in the north and Reims in the south. The northern prong of this manoeuvre was to be executed by the French Tenth Army commanded by General Maud'huy. Joffre doubted the British army's effectiveness in the offensive. Therefore the form of co-operation he most wanted was the northward extension of the British line, relieving the French IX Corps in the Ypres salient so that it could join the Tenth Army offensive.[17]

While the Germans on the Western Front were generally on the defensive in early 1915, they were prepared to mount opportunistic local offensives where they perceived the Allies to be weak. Between 25 and 29 January they mounted attacks in the Givenchy-Cuinchy sector. Still weakened by its losses at Ypres, Lomax's I Corps had some difficulty containing these, and Haig was initially worried that Givenchy might be lost. But the crisis passed, the Germans were repelled and Haig was soon on the lookout for offensive opportunities. Close to the centre of the First Army front, in the sector belonging to Sir Henry Rawlinson's IV Corps, the German position in and around the village of Neuve Chapelle formed a small salient protruding into British lines. On 6 February, Haig visited Rawlinson's headquarters and ordered him to draw up a plan for an operation to pinch out the salient. He indicated that he wanted to carry out the operation in mid-February.[18]

On 9 February GHQ wrote to the Army commanders demanding that each submit proposals for the first substantial British offensive operation of 1915. This ultimately led to the development of a somewhat more elaborate scheme for the Neuve Chapelle operation than was first imagined and put back its start date into March. A memorandum, dated 8 February, by William Robertson, the Chief of the General Staff at GHQ, on offensive methods under present conditions on the Western Front was enclosed. While its argument was essentially quite simple, it was in fact a pioneering piece of strategic and operational analysis. Robertson deprecated any attempt at complete rupture or breakthrough of the German defensive system on the Western Front, judging this to be impossible in the circumstances. A form of warfare nearer to "fortress" rather than traditional "field" warfare should now, Robertson believed, be the order of the day:

If the Germans are to be defeated they must be beaten by a system of slow attrition, by a slow and gradual advance on our part, each step being prepared by a predominant artillery fire and great expenditure of ammunition.

Though Haig had considerable respect for Robertson at this stage in the war, he seems to have made no direct response to Robertson's paper on operational method. His subsequent conduct would indicate either that he did not understand Robertson's argument, or he found that it so conflicted with his fundamental ideas about warfare that he could not accept it.

Planning the Battle of Neuve Chapelle

On 12 February Haig outlined for GHQ three possible offensive operations on the First Army Front. The one he recommended was an assault on Neuve Chapelle village, followed by an enlargement of "gap thus made in the enemy's front", and a drive "towards the line HERLIES-ILLIES" (in the Lille direction). This would involve capturing much of the Aubers Ridge. If mounted together with a co-operative movement by the French from the south, such an offensive could seriously endanger the German position at La Bassée. On 13 February Sir John French told Haig informally that he favoured the Neuve Chapelle proposal and, on 23 February, he informed Joffre that such an operation, scheduled for 7 March, would be the British contribution to the Allies' spring offensive.[19]

Haig was now proposing a much more grandiose operation at Neuve Chapelle than he had outlined to Rawlinson on 6 February. Possibly he was doing so because he wanted his First Army, rather than Smith-Dorrien's Second Army, to have the honour of mounting the first British offensive operation of 1915. But given that he was now contemplating a major Army-level offensive operation, it would have been logical for Haig, assisted by his First Army staff, to have taken direct, personal charge of its planning. He and his staff should logically have made an Army plan, leaving his corps and divisional commanders to fill in the details appropriate to their levels of command. Instead Haig, while outlining his intent, asked each of his corps commanders to draft a scheme for the attack as a whole. He then subjected these schemes to scrutiny and criticism, rather in the manner of a university tutor dealing with student essays. To use a somewhat different metaphor, Haig was adopting the position of a "back-seat driver", putting other people in charge of choosing a route, navigating and even manoeuvring the vehicle, while making comments and criticisms from the rear. Why did Haig approach the planning of his first major offensive operation as an Army commander in such a curious way?

No definitive answer to these questions can be given on the basis of the available evidence, but some suggestions can be made. During the 1914 fighting, Haig had initially been an anxious, extremely cautious, rather battle-shy commander. He had become more confident after the attack on Monday 14 September on the Aisne, but had inevitably found First Ypres very wearing on his nerves. After First Ypres he had talked and written more hopefully about operations against the German army. But, with his seemingly confident assertions of German fragility in the West, was Haig to some extent whistling in the dark? Indeed, even when claiming that the Germans were now vulnerable, he had normally added the proviso that the Allies would need plentiful artillery ammunition to exploit this. British supplies of this precious commodity were, in early 1915, still extremely limited. Was Haig, therefore, still far from sanguine about mounting a frontal assault on a well-trained, well-disciplined enemy in a fortified position? Did he, perhaps unconsciously, want to place an insulating layer, represented by a subordinate level of command, between himself and the detailed planning of such a battle?

It soon became apparent that Haig was relying mainly on Rawlinson and his IV Corps staff to plan First Army's first offensive. Haig's relationship with Rawlinson, whom he may have seen as a professional rival, is, therefore, relevant here. From an infantry (King's Royal Rifle Corps) background, and a protégé of Lord Roberts, Rawlinson's nickname in the army was "The Fox" (an epithet suggesting cleverness, certainly, but also a degree of deviousness). Rawlinson was friendly with Henry Wilson: another clever and scheming officer whom Haig mistrusted. Yet, while Rawlinson was known for intrigue, his ability was not all of the backstairs variety. His record in field command (chasing Boer commandos during the last phase of the South African War) considerably outshone Haig's, and he had been an able and popular commandant of the Staff College at Camberley. It is thus possible that Haig's delegation, in early 1915, of so much crucial work to Rawlinson was, at least in part, a manoeuvre in the internal politics of the army. Haig was, perhaps, asserting his control over his subordinate and putting him "on the spot", while trying to use that subordinate's supposed cleverness for his own ends.[20]

But what was the nature of the task that Haig had (for whatever reason) delegated to Rawlinson? In comparison with German defences on the Western Front later in the war those at Neuve Chapelle in February–March 1915 were primitive and weak. But in relation to the British army's offensive capacity at that time they appeared by no means contemptible. The German frontline had a parapet about four feet high and five feet deep with two rows of barbed wire to its front. Communications trenches ran back from the frontline – some of them towards the village of Neuve Chapelle and some to an old shallow trench, originally dug by British troops in 1914 and known to British planners in 1915 as the Smith-Dorrien trench.[21]

The intelligence available to the British on the position to be attacked was reasonably good. Much of it came from the RFC, whose airmen eventually photographed the German position to a depth of between 700 and 1,000 yards. From these photographs British intelligence was able to compile detailed maps. It seems, however, that either these photographs failed to reveal a line of concrete machine gun nests about 1,000 yards behind the frontline, or the intelligence officers reading the photographs failed to spot them.[22] First Army headquarters did know, however, that the Germans had only about twenty artillery pieces in the sector it was proposing to attack. With careful planning and preparation, therefore, it would be possible to ensure massive fire superiority, at least in the opening stages. The same was true of infantry numbers. The Germans had only about 2,000 troops in the sector to be attacked. It would be feasible for the British to attack on the first day with about 12,000. British opportunities, were, however, likely to be fleeting. It was estimated that the Germans would be able to bring in about 16,000 extra troops by the second day of the battle.[23]

An attack on Neuve Chapelle was being driven by the need for the British to do *something* on the Western Front early in 1915. Though it was as vulnerable as any point facing the British army on this front, it seems that no one involved, below Haig's level, really much fancied an operation against it with the limited resources available. Perhaps because he found the task so unappealing, Rawlinson did exactly what Haig had done. He referred it down to the next level of command, asking both his divisional commanders to produce schemes of attack.[24]

Davies of the 8th Division treated the problem as essentially one of siege warfare and suggested approaching the enemy position by sapping (digging trenches) towards it.[25] This was a classic approach to an attack on a fortified position. There were, however, a number of problems with it. One was that it would take time and Haig and the higher authorities were in a hurry. Another was that, unlike the normal situation when attacking a fortress, the British First Army did not have Neuve Chapelle isolated or invested. If the attackers did not achieve surprise (and that would be practically impossible using this method) the Germans would ensure that they had reserves so close at hand that it was most unlikely that significant success could be achieved.

Rawlinson, therefore, in commenting upon Davies' initial paper, ruled out a sapping operation. He insisted upon a "bombard and storm" approach. Yet he still came up with no detailed scheme of his own. Haig held a corps commanders' conference on the subject on 15 February. He insisted that the production of a workable plan was a matter of some urgency and demanded such from both Rawlinson and Sir James Willcocks, who commanded the Indian Corps on the right flank of IV Corps.[26] Up to this point Rawlinson had produced only papers for discussion, not a definite plan. Despite Haig's urging on 15 February, he remained reluctant to commit himself for some days to come. Given that this was now to be a major Army-level offensive, Rawlinson perhaps did not see why he should be saddled with the responsibility for submitting a plan for the whole operation. He also seems to have considered that capturing Neuve Chapelle was task enough and to have been profoundly sceptical about the chances of taking the Aubers Ridge.[27]

While plans for the Neuve Chapelle operation were being formulated, Haig had some distressing news. His chief of staff, Johnnie Gough, who was about to leave First Army HQ for the command of a New Army division, was visiting his old battalion, 2nd Battalion Rifle Brigade, in the line on 20 February when he was hit by a bullet, apparently fired from considerable range. It looked initially as if he might recover, but he died two days later. Haig had the greatest respect for Gough, who had shared his burden in the difficult times of 1914, and had come to regard him as a personal friend. He took the afternoon off to attend his funeral on 23 February. But even the loss of so well respected an officer as Johnnie Gough could not be allowed to interfere for long with the business of the war. Brigadier-General Richard Butler, the 3rd Brigade commander, who had served with Haig at Aldershot before the war, was appointed to take Gough's place at First Army.[28]

Rawlinson finally sent a definite plan for the Neuve Chapelle attack to Haig on 21 February. Again, this originated with Davies, the 8th Division commander, not with Rawlinson himself. In Davies's scheme it was to be a two-stage, two-day operation. On the first day, two brigades from IV Corps would put in an assault to the left of Neuve Chapelle and two brigades from the Indian Corps would mount a simultaneous assault to the right of the village. On the second day, the two brigades nearest the village, one from each corps, having executed turns through 90 degrees, would mount converging attacks (a pincer movement) to capture it.[29]

Haig quickly dismissed the Davies plan. It was too complicated and the converging attacks involved would entail the risk of self-inflicted casualties. Moreover, by not attempting to take Neuve Chapelle on the first day, this plan would allow momentum to be lost and give the Germans time to recover from their surprise, making the final capture of the village more difficult.[30] These strictures were entirely reasonable. Yet Haig still did not produce a plan of his own. Instead he demanded another, more feasible scheme from Rawlinson – this time in very short order. He expressed annoyance with Rawlinson on the grounds that he kept delegating planning to his two divisional commanders. (One of them, Capper of 7th Division, appears to have been rather slow to come up with anything.) Haig complained that: "If each problem is to be given to two Commanders where are we to stop."[31]

Haig's criticism of Rawlinson on this point was, in a sense, reasonable, but also very hypocritical. As this operation was to involve two corps it had to be considered an Army-level operation. It was, therefore, the responsibility of Haig's First Army HQ to conceive and develop plans. It was

Haig himself who had started the process of passing the planning buck downwards.

By 23 February Rawlinson and Davies, working together, had finally arrived at a scheme that proved reasonably acceptable to Haig. It involved a simple direct attack towards Neuve Chapelle by IV Corps and the Indian Corps, designed to take the village in a single day. Arrangements for exploitation beyond it were, however, hazy and the co-ordination of the attack with French offensive efforts was not discussed.[32] In fact, through no fault of Rawlinson's, there was to be no such co-ordination. Joffre made an attack by the French Tenth Army in the Arras-Vimy sector conditional upon the British relief of the French IX Corps at Ypres. When the Cabinet decided to keep back the 29th Division, which Sir John French thought he had been promised, for use in south-east Europe, he decided he could not undertake this relief.[33]

By Sunday 28 February, Haig knew, as a result of informal conversations with its commander, General Maud'huy (with whom he got on quite well), that the French Tenth Army would not support his offensive with an attack in the Arras sector. By the same date he had received a GHQ memorandum informing him that shell supply was severely limited and that he must be careful not excessively to deplete the BEF's reserves. As he noted in a memorandum to GHQ that day, the "nett result of this information is that our proposed offensive action must be considered an entirely independent operation". He further realised that "as we can only employ a limited number of troops and have only a limited amount of ammunition at our disposal it is clear that the scope of our operations is limited". Even if the Neuve Chapelle offensive was "successful at first", a point would be "reached ... in two or three days at most, when we shall have to re-establish our line". He also realised the "necessity for keeping sufficient fresh troops and ammunition in hand to meet the German counter-attack which can be counted upon".[34]

The common sense conclusion flowing from this was that the scope of the operation needed to be severely curtailed and that the seizure of the German salient at Neuve Chapelle was now all that could reasonably be aimed at. But, while asking GHQ to arrange supporting attacks by Second Army on the left, Haig somehow resisted the logic of his own argument. On Tuesday 2 March he told Robertson that he wanted GHQ to move a cavalry division closer to the front for the exploitation of a possible break-through. On the same day he told Rawlinson that "our objective was not merely the capture of Neuve Chapelle ... I aimed at getting the line Illies-Herlies and the line of the La Bassée road to Lille, and then to break the Enemy's front ... in the hope of starting a *general advance*." The contradiction between this and his stress, just two days previously, on the need to re-establish a defensive line within "two or three days at most" is astonishing. It raises questions about his capacity to apply sustained, consistent logic to the problems of Army command. At a First Army conference on Friday 5 March, Haig continued to insist on grandiose objectives.

> The advance to be made is not a minor operation ... It must be understood that we are embarking on a serious offensive movement with the object of breaking the German line ... The object is not to capture a trench here or a trench there, but ... to surprise the Germans, carry them right off their legs ... push forward to the ... Aubers ridge ... and exploit the situation by pushing forward mounted troops forthwith.[35]

Rawlinson, however, remained intensely sceptical about pushing on to the Aubers Ridge and even more so about the proposed use of cavalry. He asked, rather belatedly, for his divisional commanders' views on how to conduct such exploitation, but he seems to have considered that exploitation towards the Aubers Ridge should only be attempted "in the event of not very serious opposition".[36]

Preparations for battle

Despite some confusion as to the aim and scope of the operation, the preparation for the attack (or at least for its initial stages) had proceeded rapidly and efficiently. Indeed, this first British offensive under conditions of true positional warfare was organised with a degree of sophistication that seems positively precocious. One of the most remarkable features of the operation was the secret concentration of at least 340 artillery pieces and possibly far more (there are some discrepancies in our sources) facing the 2,000-yard attack sector. These included a substantial number of heavy guns brought in, some of them from England, specifically for this attack. The extra guns, over and above those the forces normally in this sector would normally hold, were all brought in at night and were concealed within ready made carefully camouflaged positions before daylight. Because the ground was still waterlogged and soft, and heavy objects would tend to subside, the guns had to be placed on firing platforms to achieve any accuracy. These too had to be carefully prepared.[37]

The newly positioned batteries had to be registered: to fire ranging shots to ensure that their shells would fall reasonably near the target when they started shooting in earnest. This registration shooting had to be observed (either from the ground or from the air) and adjusted until the battery was on target. But the registration of a substantial number of batteries might have been a clear intelligence indicator to the Germans in this sector that they were about to be attacked. So registration had to be conducted carefully and gradually and disguised within the normal, everyday pattern of shelling.[38]

The guns were given four principal tasks:

(a) cutting the German barbed wire: performed largely by the 18-pdr guns, the British army's main type of field piece, firing shrapnel shell;

(b) pulverising the enemy's earthworks and known strong-points: performed largely by the 4.5-inch field howitzers and by 6-inch howitzers and some heavier pieces, firing high explosive;

(c) counter-battery fire (fire on the enemy's artillery): mostly done by longer range guns, especially the 60–pdr guns, and heavy howitzers; and

(d) isolating the attack sector by placing barrages (curtains or barriers of fire) on the flanks and to the rear.[39]

The first phase of the fire plan was to be a thirty-five-minute preliminary bombardment. Haig and Rawlinson seem to have agreed that, in principle, the shorter the preliminary bombardment before the infantry attack, the greater the chances of success – as the greater the degree of surprise that might be achieved. Yet they considered that a certain minimum of destructive work needed doing. The question was, how long would this take? The artillery advisers tried to estimate how many shells would be required to destroy a given frontage of enemy trench and barbed wire. Using those figures Rawlinson worked out that the necessary work on the enemy's front-line trenches could be done with a thirty-five-minute programme. Haig at first guessed that three hours would be necessary, but Rawlinson's calculations convinced him.[40]

Another matter requiring attention was communication during the attack. Even at this relatively early stage in the war it seems to have been widely appreciated that command and control was likely to break down early in the battle, simply because the commanders would get no information as to what was happening once the attack started. Communication from the attacking infantry back to the front line trenches they had recently left would inevitably depend mainly on runners and would be hazardous, uncertain and probably very slow. There was considerable emphasis on ensuring that the formation headquarters involved remained in touch with each other by telephone once the inevitable German counter-bombardment began. Telephone cables were laid in triplicate to increase the likelihood of communications surviving.[41]

The initial infantry assault was to be delivered by three brigades: 23rd and 25th Brigades (8th Division) of IV Corps, and by the Garwhal Brigade of the Meerut Division of Lieutenant-General Willcocks's Indian Corps. Two further brigades would join the attack after the initial break-in: the 21st Brigade of Major-General Capper's 7th Division on the left and the

24th Brigade of the 8th Division on the right. Three successive objectives were given for the first day's attack. A halt was to be made on each objective while the artillery lengthened its range and shelled the next one. In order to help them cross the deadly ground between the two trench systems more rapidly, the infantry were to move in small columns (or worms) rather than extended lines. On 2 March the twelve battalions designated to take part in the initial attack were withdrawn from the line into billets around Merville, where they rehearsed the initial assault.[42]

Haig established a "reporting centre" (a sort of Advanced HQ) from which to supervise the attack at Merville some eight miles north-west of

3. Indian troops under bombardment near Neuve Chapelle. Courtesy of the Council of the National Army Museum, London.

Neuve Chapelle. He fixed the date of the attack for 10 March, provided the weather remained fine. Clear skies were needed for observation for the artillery and there had been some anxiety throughout the planning phase that the attack would literally bog down if the ground was too wet. Though it did rain on 9 March, and even snowed a little, the sky cleared that evening. Haig ordered the attack brigades to move to their specially constructed assembly trenches, immediately behind the front line.[43]

The Battle of Neuve Chapelle: 10 March 1915

The preliminary bombardment lasted from 7.30 a.m. to 8.05 a.m. before lifting 300 yards further east where it formed a physical barrier (the literal meaning of the term "barrage") to German attempts to reinforce their frontline positions and the village of Neuve Chapelle. The infantry assault, commencing at 8.05 a.m., met with mixed fortunes. On the far left, part of the sector that 23rd Brigade was attacking, much of the barbed wire was found intact. The German defenders were alive and putting up a serious fight. Why the wirie cutting, a field artillery task, had not been adequately done in this sector is unclear. It is rather clearer what had gone wrong with the heavy bombardment tasks. These had been assigned to heavy batteries that arrived from England only very shortly before the battle. They had not had time to ensure that they were properly registered or that their firing platforms were sufficiently stable. The 23rd Brigade suffered heavy casualties and initially could make no progress on its left. It had to ask for this section of the German front to be bombarded again before renewing the assault.[44]

On the far right, one battalion of the Indian Garwhal Brigade got lost, drifted too far to the right and ended up attacking a section of German trenches that had not been bombarded, with predictable results. Over most of the front, however, the wire was found cut or flattened. In some places all the German defenders were found dead or incapacitated. In others, trenches had to be cleared with grenade and bayonet. One way or another, however, German frontline resistance had been eliminated over most of the front within an hour so of the start of the infantry attack.[45]

Once the battle started, Haig's control of events was limited and much of his information imprecise. By approximately 9 a.m., however, he knew that the initial attack was making good progress in most sectors. Sensing that a breakthrough might be feasible, he requested that GHQ put a cavalry brigade under his control. The 5th Cavalry Brigade (of 2nd Cavalry Division) was duly ordered to Estaires, about six miles north of Neuve Chapelle, and placed at his disposal. Apparently getting more excited as the day wore on, and despite less encouraging news from the

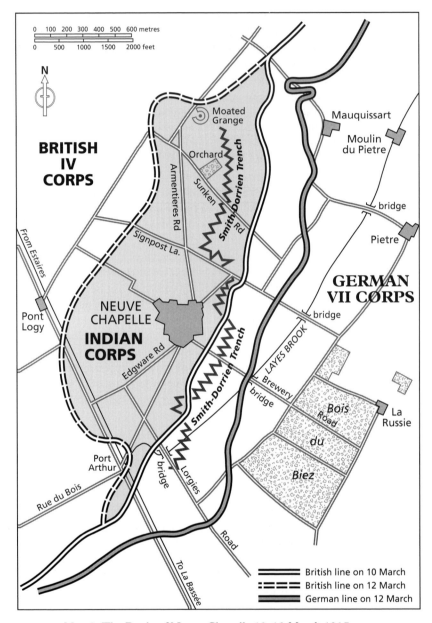

Map 8. The Battle of Neuve Chapelle 10–12 March 1915

left wing of his attack, Haig tried to order the rest of the 2nd Cavalry Division to join the 5th Cavalry Brigade at Estaires during the afternoon. He had no authority to do this. These forces were in GHQ reserve and did not belong to Haig. French countermanded the order. This minor *contretemps* with the commander-in-chief was, however, of no real importance. The opportunity for cavalry exploitation simply did not exist.[46]

Results that day had been mixed. Haig was disappointed that his forces had not pushed rapidly towards the Aubers Ridge after Neuve Chapelle was captured in mid-morning. The attack, however, had penetrated the German defences to a depth of 1,200 yards. The width of the rupture, initially only about 1,500 yards, had been expanded to about 4,000 yards. By nightfall, British and Indian troops held virtually the whole of the "Smith-Dorrien trench" – the German VII Corps' reserve line. German reserve companies, however, making use of recently completed concrete pillboxes, were still resisting a little further east. By nightfall, 748 German prisoners were in British hands. Casualties had been quite heavy on both sides, though, as Haig drew up his orders for the following day, these were not fully known. First Army's Operation Order No. 11, issued at 11.30 p.m. on 10 March, ordered a continuation of the advance at 7.00 a.m. The object remained the capture of the Aubers Ridge.[47]

The second day: 11 March 1915

Neuve Chapelle established a pattern for British attacks on the Western Front. Further experience would show that even if the initial attack were successful, the return on the effort invested in preparing the offensive would tend to diminish dramatically after the first day. Several factors contributed to this. On the first day the attacker might achieve a degree of surprise (though this would grow increasingly difficult for most of 1915–1917). By the second day this advantage had disappeared. On the first day the attacker's artillery could be quite effective, but would be much less so on subsequent days. (The forces of both sides were in different positions and these were often unknown to the gunners.) After the first day the numerical balance almost invariably shifted against the attacker. The defending side brought up reserves to seal off the break-in. These factors operated strongly around Neuve Chapelle on 11 and 12 March.

During the night of 10–11 March the surviving forces of the German VII Corps dug in hard east of Neuve Chapelle. That same night, four infantry regiments of the XIX Corps, the 6th Bavarian Reserve Division and three batteries of heavy howitzers arrived to assist the defence and help recapture the lost ground. It was, of course, entirely predictable that the Germans would reinforce this sector. Aerial reconnaissance, however, did not work at night, and the morning of Thursday 11 March was misty. Haig, therefore, did not know the scale of the reinforcement.[48]

As the British artillery had not registered the positions the German now occupied, the preliminary bombardment, beginning at 6.45 a.m., did them little damage. The British and Indian infantry assault quickly stalled in the face of intense rifle and machine gun fire and all attempts to renew it during the afternoon failed. British command and control to a large extent collapsed as German shelling cut telephone wires carried forward to the frontline trenches. For the British and Indians it was, in reality, a day of defeat. Their attacks were beaten back with heavy losses. Yet Haig wanted to continue attacking next day. Visiting the front early on the evening of 11 March, he ordered artillery to be brought forward to support renewed infantry assaults the next morning.[49]

The last day: 12 March 1915

The Germans forestalled a renewed British attack. At 4.30 a.m. on Friday 12 March they commenced an intense preliminary bombardment. This missed British and Indian frontline positions, but fell heavily on troops further back. At 5.00 a.m., in a thick mist, the German infantry assault began. It got close to the British trenches but was ultimately stopped by rifle and machine gun fire, resulting in heavy German casualties. During the afternoon Haig tried to get his forces to renew their offensive. This was unrealistic to the point of absurdity. The British had lost the element of surprise and no longer had the necessary superiority in firepower and numbers to succeed in a frontal assault. Many of their troops were completely exhausted. Commanders below Haig's level seem to have realised this. Most attacks that afternoon were not vigorously pressed. After telephone conversations with the two Corps commanders, Haig decided to call off the offensive and issued an order to that effect at 10.40 a.m.[50]

Results

In three days of fighting the First Army had incurred about 13,000 casualties, about one third of them fatal. Thirty German officers and 1,657 other ranks had been taken prisoner. German casualties overall seem to have been roughly equal to those of the British.[51] The Germans on the Western Front as a whole were now numerically inferior and could not afford to take losses at the same rate as the Allies. The British regular army and regular reserves were rapidly wasting assets and the Indian army was turning out to be a very brittle instrument.[52] Considering the numerous disadvantages under which the attacker operated in the conditions of the Western Front warfare, First

Army had actually done well to inflict losses of approximately 1:1. It is likely, however, that the Germans incurred the majority of their losses in the failed counter-attack of 12 March. British and Indian attacks after the first day had resulted in heavy casualties with virtually no gain and it was fairly obvious that these attacks had caused few losses to the Germans.[53]

The Davies case and French's despatch

Owing to the extreme shortage of artillery ammunition GHQ ordered a pause in major British offensive operations on the Western Front: a pause that lasted for the next two months.[54] Though some of the British newspapers expressed horror at the casualties, Neuve Chapelle was in some respects a promising start to British offensive operations under the new and peculiar conditions of a continuously entrenched enemy front. Haig received warm congratulations from both French and Joffre. However, Haig was disappointed not to have won a bigger victory. He was convinced that there had been a significant lost opportunity on the morning of 10 March: a failure to exploit vigorously in the direction of the Aubers Ridge immediately after the fall of Neuve Chapelle. A heated dispute arose over this matter – a dispute that focused especially on the handling of 8th Division's 24th Brigade, which operated in a support/reserve role at the start of the battle.[55]

A large part of the problem was that the 24th Brigade had not been kept together as a second-echelon force. Parts of it were used to assist the other brigades of 8th Division where they ran into difficulties. It was not until well into the afternoon that 24th Brigade, could be assembled for a push to the Aubers Ridge. Even then, Rawlinson who had always been sceptical about the idea of a breakthrough, was reluctant to order the advance without support from the Meerut Division of the Indian Corps, on the right of IV Corps. The Indians were in some disarray and were not in a position to offer such support. To compound these difficulties the transmission of orders broke down at critical moments.[56]

After the battle the inquest on the events of the first day turned ugly and disreputable, largely because of Rawlinson's personality and his difficult relationship with Haig. Like Haig, Rawlinson was keen to claim as much credit as possible for Neuve Chapelle and to deflect all criticism. Aware that Haig was unhappy about the failure to push on to the Aubers Ridge on 10 March, Rawlinson tried to place the blame on Major-General Francis "Joey" Davies, the 8th Division commander. Accusing Davies of a lack of drive, Rawlinson told him, on 12 March, that he was to be relieved of command and sent home. Rawlinson communicated this decision to Haig and wrote in the same vein to Kitchener and to Clive Wigram, the King's

ADC.[57] But if Rawlinson thought that Davies would tamely take on the role of scapegoat he had misjudged his man. Davies wrote a strong letter to Rawlinson, convincingly demonstrating that his actions had conformed to Rawlinson's orders throughout the battle. Realising that he could not ignore Davies's protest, Rawlinson, in effect, capitulated. He passed Davies's letter on to Haig with a covering note confessing the validity of Davies's case. Haig went see Davies to assure him that he was no longer blamed and that his job was safe.[58]

Rawlinson's dishonourable behaviour in trying to scapegoat a subordinate (and then withdrawing under pressure) became a serious embarrassment. The top people back in London had all now received a particular version of events: the little victory of Neuve Chapelle had not become a big victory because of Joey Davies and Joey Davies was being sacked. Making his own initial report to French, Haig endorsed Rawlinson's decision to send Davies home. When, however, Haig conferred with the commander-in-chief at GHQ on 17 March, French, now aware of Davies's protest and Rawlinson's confession, apparently wanted to sack Rawlinson.[59]

Rawlinson certainly merited dismissal on ethical grounds, but it is likely that French's stance also owed something to army politics and personal feelings. French apparently mistrusted and disliked Rawlinson. Though obviously a talented officer, serving as a divisional commander when war broke out, Rawlinson was conspicuously left out of the BEF in August 1914. Rawlinson was a protégé of Lord Roberts, whom French mistrusted, and was an infantryman known to be profoundly sceptical about the usefulness of cavalry. Haig shared some of French's feelings about Rawlinson, but argued against his dismissal. Though he considered Rawlinson "unsatisfactory in ... loyalty to subordinates" he had "many other valuable qualities as a commander on active service". Haig then told Rawlinson that any repetition of the sort of behaviour he had exhibited to Davies would mean his dismissal, but that his intervention with French had, at least for the time being, saved Rawlinson's career.[60]

Haig liked to portray himself as a man of plain and straightforward dealing. He may have seen himself in that light. Yet his driving ambition had, for many years, made him an earnest and sometimes ruthless player of the game of army politics, a game at which he was arguably far more adept than he was as a field commander. In the Davies case Haig securely held the moral high ground. Yet he also ensured that his ablest subordinate was in his debt and, to a considerable degree, at his mercy. After this affair it would be more difficult for Rawlinson to intrigue actively against Haig, whatever future disagreements they might have, or even to stand up to him in the event of genuine disagreement on operational matters. Haig's taking the trouble personally to reassure Davies that no blame now attached to him was also a sound move. It virtually guaranteed that one of Rawlinson's divisional commanders owed Haig a particular loyalty.

In the aftermath of Neuve Chapelle, Haig found himself in the strongest, most secure position that he had occupied in the army since the beginning of the war. This sense of security seems to have influenced the way he conducted his leave in England on 21–26 March. He felt no need to go politicking in London. He even politely declined a royal invitation. He spent the entire period in and around Folkestone, relaxing and playing golf with Doris.[61] When he returned to France, Haig found that a GHQ despatch on Neuve Chapelle had caused quite a stir at First Army HQ. It seemed to claim all credit for the victory for French and GHQ. Charteris, Haig's intelligence chief, seems to have been quite exercised on this subject. "It reads as if the whole operation had been planned by GHQ. As a matter of fact the whole thing was worked out from the very beginning here at First Army HQ and GHQ had nothing whatever to do with it." Haig, apparently quite confident in the security of his own position, refused to get too worked up over it, at least in public. Charteris was, in any case, stretching a point. Whatever was true on the intelligence side (for which Charteris was responsible), Haig had, as we have seen, delegated much of the real work of operational planning to Rawlinson.[62]

The Davies affair and the lesser matter of the GHQ despatch were about the attribution of blame and praise. Neither helped Haig and his staff to learn the real lessons of Neuve Chapelle. Indeed, there is little or no evidence of any depth of analysis of the recent battle at First Army. Butler had only just arrived and, perhaps, had yet had no time to understand his operational environment. Charteris's remarks on the matter were distinctly superficial, not progressing beyond the "hunt for the guilty" stage, and predictably concluding that guilt resided with IV Corps' HQ. If Haig himself could see beyond this issue he left no evidence of it.[63]

Lessons learned and lessons missed

In demanding to know why his forces had not gained the Aubers Ridge, Haig was asking the wrong question. (The right question was how the limited victory actually gained could have been achieved at lower cost.) With the resources available to him, and in the absence of French co-operation, the objectives that Haig had set for the operation had been excessively ambitious, as he had at least half-realised after his interview with Maud'huy on 28 February. Given the limits of the communications technology, the breakdown of command and control during the course of the advance had been practically inevitable. Even had troops of 25th Brigade advanced on the Aubers Ridge immediately after the fall of

Neuve Chapelle, without waiting for the support of other troops, it is doubtful that they would have reached it. The most detailed research indicates that there were still enough German troops between them and the ridge to have blocked their path.[64]

Had some elements of the 25th Brigade reached the ridge, it is questionable whether they could have remained there in the face of German reinforcements moving to the area, especially given that there would initially have been little immediate prospect of effective artillery support or resupply. Had other British or Indian infantry reached 25th Brigade later on 10 March, and had some artillery been able to get forward to support them, long-term success was still unlikely. Consolidating the British hold on the ridge in the face of the inevitable German counter-attacks would surely have taken days of intense fighting for which Haig knew the BEF did not have the shell.

In a GHQ memorandum forwarded to Haig on 9 February, Robertson, the Chief of the General Staff at GHQ, had, as we have noted, recognised the near impossibility of achieving a major breakthrough on the Western Front at this stage in the war. He had instead emphasised efficient attrition and advocated British infantry advancing by short steps, with massive artillery support. Henry Rawlinson had realised the inadvisability of aiming at a deep advance in the Neuve Chapelle operation, though he had allowed Haig to overrule him. Within a couple of days of the battle Rawlinson was attempting to formulate lessons from it along lines somewhat similar to those of Robertson. Unfortunately he did not present this analysis to either Haig or French – presumably because of the weak position in which he found himself with regard to these officers as a result of the Davies affair. Instead he sent his thoughts to Kitchener and to the King's ADC, Clive Wigram, with whom he continued to correspond, despite the degree of disgrace in which he now found himself.[65]

Rawlinson believed that the British and Indian forces at Neuve Chapelle had taken unnecessary casualties because they had tried to do too much. They had taken Neuve Chapelle itself with fairly light casualties. It was the determination to press on beyond that point and the completely unrealistic notion of passing the cavalry through (the result, in Rawlinson's opinion, of cavalry domination of the army) that had caused unnecessary loss. Rawlinson accepted that a major breakthrough on the Western Front was impossible for the foreseeable future. Yet he considered that breaking in (i.e. making some sort of penetration into the German defensive positions) should always be possible, provided enough heavy howitzers were available to pulverise the German trenches and provided that the German barbed wire could be clearly observed by the field artillery. Rawlinson argued in a letter to Wigram that:

What we want to do now is what I call "bite and hold". Bite off a piece of the enemy's line like Neuve Chapelle, and hold it against counter-attack. The bite can be made without much loss, and, if we choose the right place and make every preparation to put it quickly in a state of defence there ought to be no difficulty in holding it against the enemy's counter-attacks and inflicting on him at least twice the loss that we have suffered in making the bite ....[66]

This was very much an artillery-centred approach to Western Front operations. One of the objections to it was, as Rawlinson appreciated, that it entailed "the expenditure of a good deal of Art[illery] ammunition which we have not got". As he also admitted, when presenting a similar case to Kitchener a few days later, the "bite and hold" method would not "result in any decisive victory which could affect the final issue of the war". It could only very slowly force "the enemy's line back towards their own frontiers".[67]

Rawlinson, moreover, relied rather heavily on the Germans being prepared to dance to the British tune – to mount infantry counter-attacks in the face of British artillery superiority. If they came to realise that the British were not actually striving for breakthrough, but merely trying to suck them into battles of attrition, the Germans would, presumably, have become rather less obliging with the counter-attacks. Intelligent enough to see some of the weaknesses in his own preferred method, Rawlinson became intermittently pessimistic about all Western Front operations. He became something of an "Easterner", recommending a major effort to attack the under-belly of the Austro-Hungarian Empire in the Balkans.[68]

However, Rawlinson's was not the only proposal for future British Western Front operations based on an analysis of Neuve Chapelle. On 15 March, a memorandum submitted by Major-General Du Cane, the artillery adviser at GHQ, showed that he was thinking on much the same lines as Robertson and his analysis was in some ways better developed than Rawlinson's. Whereas Rawlinson had expressed his ideas in private letters to key figures in England, Du Cane's were formulated as a GHQ memorandum. The ideas this document contained were vitally relevant to all British military operations on the Western Front from Spring 1915 to at least the end of 1917, and it is worth examining (and indeed quoting) at some length.

Du Cane argued that "the tactical lessons" of Neuve Chapelle had a great bearing on the "strategic problem that confronts us". He thought that "the plan for the Battle of Neuve Chapelle was based on the conception of penetrating the enemy's front by a violent attack pressed continuously until the desired result was achieved". This was certainly true as far as Haig was concerned, though subordinate headquarters, where a good deal of the hard work of planning had been done, had never entirely embraced this grandiose scheme. But the critical point for Du Cane was that:

We failed to penetrate the enemy's front and it is necessary to form as definite an opinion as possible as to the contributory causes of this failure.

Du Cane attributed the failure essentially to a collapse of command and control after the initial assault, despite all precautions taken against this.

The leading infantry was therefore dependent on the initiative of subordinates and the system of artillery observation broke down to a considerable extent. The enemy thus gained sufficient time to bring up reinforcements and to oppose us with sufficient forces to make a further advance impossible without a pause to reorganise. Our losses and the expenditure of artillery ammunition were heavy.

If that is a reasonable account of what took place it is necessary to form a judgement as to whether we can expect any other result from a similar plan. If not, it will be necessary to modify our plan for the next attack and to base it on some other conception.

Du Cane saw two basic approaches to the achievement of a substantial Allied victory in future operations on the Western Front:

(1) The penetration of the front in the manner that we have attempted, and then rolling up one or both of the flanks produced by the penetration.

(2) The engaging of the enemy on a selected portion of his front, and by the concentration of superior resources in men, guns and ammunition, fighting him until his resources are so exhausted that he is obliged to withdraw to prevent the penetration of his front in conditions that would mean disaster, each step being consolidated before the next step is taken.

I will endeavour to explain more fully the second method. We select a terrain suitable for the combination of all arms and a line of advance that promises good strategic results if we are successful.

Facing the front which it is proposed to attack we assemble as secretly as possible a powerful force of artillery.

The first assault should be prepared and delivered as at NEUVE CHAPELLE, but it should not be pressed so far as to carry the infantry beyond the range of our artillery support.

The first step should be consolidated, counter-attacks repelled, and a fresh advance prepared for.

The next attack should take place as soon as possible, and should be made with fresh troops. The process should be repeated untill the enemy's resistance weakens palpably. The crisis has then arrived. We can now afford to denude our defensive front of troops and to make a bid for decisive victory by the concentration of every available man.[69]

As with Rawlinson's "bite and hold" concept, objections could be made to Du Cane's "step-by-step" approach. The most basic of these was that the British simply did not have the resources, especially in terms of artillery pieces and ammunition, which this method required. But this would apply to any significant attack that the British might attempt in the immediate future. Du Cane was trying to see beyond the pressing concerns of the moment and to contemplate in a rational manner the future of British offensive operations on the Western Front. In so doing, he had somewhat excelled Rawlinson.

Rawlinson's idea depended heavily on the Germans exhausting themselves in counter-attacks. Du Cane, while he expected counter-attacks, did not depend on them. His method did not rely on the Germans reacting in a particular way. At no stage in an offensive did he intend the British to relinquish the initiative. Du Cane's idea was, therefore, not so much "bite and hold" as "bite and bite". Each bite would be within the capacity of the teeth and jaws available. Each mouthful would be chewed thoroughly before proceeding with the next bite. No single bite would prove fatal to the German army. But a series would inflict wounds severe enough, if not to kill the beast, at least to make it retreat a substantial distance to lick its wounds in relative peace. Du Cane's notion that this process would ultimately culminate in a great climactic breakthrough may seem fanciful. In this he arguably demonstrated less realism than had Robertson in his paper of 8 February. But Du Cane's steps towards that point were eminently sensible and his presentation of a step-by-step *modus operandi* was more detailed than that of Robertson's February memorandum.

By mid-spring 1915, therefore, some senior British officers were developing a thoughtful, sophisticated approach to offensive operations on the Western Front: a "step-by-step" approach, which accepted that attempting a quick rupture of the German front was futile. Using "step-by-step" methods, the enemy would be kept under pressure by a series of short advances, each backed by concentrated artillery fire. In order to minimise casualties, British infantry would not be pushed further forward than its own artillery could effectively support it, at least until the enemy was evidently on the brink of collapse. Unfortunately Douglas Haig, whose own analysis of what had happened at Neuve Chapelle was superficial, did not endorse this approach. Indeed, he showed no sign of being prepared to engage with this type of thinking. Though sometimes depressed by the BEF's lack of the resources with which to achieve it, Haig would cling, at least until mid-1917, to the ideal of a swift, dramatic breakthrough. Haig was a member of the same army and thus part of the same military culture as Robertson, Rawlinson and Du Cane. The relative rigidity of his military thinking appears, therefore, to have been a quirk of personal psychology and an indication of personal intellectual limitations rather than a product of institutional background and professional training.

The background to the Battle of Aubers Ridge

The Allies were so starved of success in early 1915 that Haig's limited victory at Neuve Chapelle gained him a remarkable amount of praise. His staff had a strong sense that his "star" was "in the ascendant".[1] His self-confidence as a commander appears to have grown correspondingly. He wanted to make another attempt on the Aubers Ridge within a few days of his first attack's having stalled. The Battle of Neuve Chapelle, however, had left the British army's stock of shells dangerously depleted. Owing to the need to restore stocks and co-ordinate efforts with the French, the second half of March and the whole of April had elapsed before Haig had the chance to undertake another offensive.[2]

Up to mid-March 1915 the French high command had thought the British army competent enough in defence, but had considered its offensive power negligible. Neuve Chapelle appears to have obliged Joffre to revise his estimate of British combat power slightly upward, though he was much more fulsome in his assessment of this minor British victory when writing to Sir John French than he was privately. Haig seems to have been somewhat flattered that Foch (well known as a pre-war military theorist, as well as being commander of the French Northern Army Group) came to lunch at First Army HQ on 19 April and questioned him closely about Neuve Chapelle. It was a battle that Foch said Joffre had ordered French generals to study.[3]

There was good reason for the French, at this particular time, to flatter the British and seek close relations with them. Joffre now intended to mount the big, two-pronged spring offensive that he had postponed when the British had refused to take over any more of the front earlier in the year. The French commander-in-chief had outlined his plan for a late spring offensive at an Allied planning conference at his headquarters at Chantilly on 29 March. The object, as before, was to attack the German salient between Arras and Reims. The French Fourth Army would mount the right-hand thrust in the Champagne region, while the French Tenth

Army, now under General d'Urbal, would mount the left-hand thrust in Artois, with the initial object of taking Vimy Ridge. The two thrusts were to be mounted simultaneously, on 1 May or as soon as possible thereafter. Kitchener and Sir John French, both present at Chantilly, agreed that the British army would co-operate with a simultaneous attack by Haig's First Army on d'Urbal's left flank.[4]

On Thursday 22 April, while planning for the main Allied spring offensive proceeded, the Germans mounted an attack of their own on the northern side of the Ypres Salient, a sector that had been relatively quiet since the beginning of the year. Their infantry assault was preceded by the release from cylinders of chlorine gas: the noxious substance being borne on the wind into the trenches of the Allies. This first poison gas attack on the Western Front hit the French 45th Algerian Division and 87th Territorial Division and caused initial panic.[5] Though Haig did not have first-hand knowledge of events in the early stages of Second Ypres, on 24 April he expressed a growing contempt for the French army and its senior commanders that did not bode well for his future relations with them.[6]

Haig's First Army was not substantially involved in the Second Battle of Ypres, as the Flanders fighting in the spring of 1915 became known. This battle had, however, important consequences for the British army generally and for Haig in particular. It resulted in the notorious Salient becoming still more constricted and dangerous for Allied troops. Smith-Dorrien's Second Army, heavily engaged, suffered some reverses and lost ground to the Germans. Sir John French, whose feelings towards Smith-Dorrien seem never to have risen above the level of petty animosity dating from pre-war days, sacked him on 6 May, an event about which Haig displayed no sign of regret.[7] Sir Herbert Plumer, who had been commanding the V Corps in Second Army, replaced Smith-Dorrien: finally gaining the Army command that French had wanted for him in the immediate aftermath of Grierson's death in August 1914. Allenby of the Cavalry Corps took Plumer's command while Sir Julian Byng took Allenby's.[8] Smith-Dorrien's dismissal removed one of the few British generals whose prestige could rival Haig's, making it all the more likely that Haig would emerge as commander-in-chief if French's always difficult relations with his superiors in London became critical.

Planning the Battle of Aubers Ridge

In its mature form, Haig's plan for his May offensive, outlined at Army conferences on 27 April and 6 May, was to employ all three of his corps (from left to right: IV, Indian and I) in two converging attacks, the initial objective of which would be the Aubers Ridge. There would be an initial gap of some 6,000 yards between the two prongs of the British attack. The lesser, northern prong of the pincer movement (on First Army left) was to be mounted by the 8th Division of Rawlinson's IV Corps towards Rouges Bancs and Fromelles – somewhat to the north of Neuve Chapelle. His main attack, the southern prong of the pincer movement (on First Army's right), was to be mounted by the Meerut Division of Willcocks's Indian Corps and 1st Division of First Corps, attacking side-by-side, on a front of some 2,400 yards in the Neuve Chapelle-Festubert sector. Once the Aubers Ridge was secure, Haig intended to push towards Don on the Heute Deule canal – about six miles from the start line. GHQ reserves of two cavalry corps and three infantry divisions were supposedly available if things went well.[9]

A First Army order of 13 April expressed Haig's intent forcibly:

The operations for which preparation is now being are intended to be much more sustained, and it is hoped that they will lead to more far reaching results than could be expected from those at NEUVE CHAPELLE.

The object is to co-operate with a vigorous offensive which is to be made on a large scale by the French with a view to breaking the enemy's front for a considerable width and then to follow up with such action as will cause a general retirement of the enemy's line.

Our objective is, therefore, not a local success and the capture of a few trenches or even a portion of the hostile position on a more or less extended front, but to employ the entire force at our disposal and fight a decisive battle.[10]

As had happened with Neuve Chapelle, Haig had late doubts about the scope of the operation. On Friday 30 April he told Sir John French that (apparently owing to the fighting in the Ypres area) he had not been allocated sufficient infantry to "*sustain* our forward movement and reap decisive results". He said he was considering stopping the advance on the Aubers Ridge,[11] but he issued no orders to that effect. First Army's written orders for the attack, eventually mounted on 9 May, continued to urge a sustained, continuous offensive aiming at a complete rupture of the German defensive system and rapid exploitation towards Don.

Haig was right: his resources were inadequate for his task. But the most critical shortage was not infantry but artillery. It was not exploitation he should have been worried about but the initial break-in. The supply of guns and ammunition available to the BEF as a whole had been restricted as a result of the Dardanelles operation. (The landings on the Gallipoli peninsula occurred on 25 April, about two weeks before Haig was due to make his second attempt on the Aubers Ridge.) Faced with the task of mounting the British army's biggest offensive operation on the Western Front so far, Haig obviously wanted all the artillery he could get.

He had sought to borrow guns from Second Army, but the start of the Second Battle of Ypres on 22 April had virtually ruled that out.[12]

First Army's own integral artillery assets had increased only modestly since March. For Aubers Ridge it had 516 field and light artillery pieces and 121 heavies.[13] Unfortunately the Germans had substantially reinforced their forces and fortifications in front of the Aubers Ridge. The width of the parapets of their front line trenches had been doubled or even trebled and was now typically fifteen to twenty feet across. The parapets had also been substantially raised to a height of six or seven feet. German front-line trenches were now well provided with dugouts that could withstand all but direct hits from the heaviest shells. There was much more wire in front of the German positions and the number of machine gun emplacements had significantly increased.[14]

To complicate matters further, the depth of the German position to be assaulted had also somewhat increased. Whereas, in March, the British had been attacking a single major trench line, in May they would be tackling a much more mature defensive system consisting of three trench lines connected by well-constructed communications trenches. Over much of the front to be attacked, the German second line was itself wired. There were also many machine guns further back, in emplacements that could act as rallying points for troops whose trenches were overrun. Finally, at intervals along the front, the Germans had built redoubts or mini-fortresses that had all-round defences, their own wire and numerous machine guns. Some of these were set back behind the trench system itself.[15]

First Army gathered intelligence on the German defences in front of it by aerial reconnaissance, patrolling and trench raids. Though these could certainly not identify every detail of the German system, it was clear that it was becoming much tougher and deeper. Many of the new strong points and redoubts were definitely identified and given as targets to First Army's artillery. The problem was not so much a failure to identify targets. Rather it was the impossibility of First Army's limited number of guns dealing with all of them effectively in a brief "hurricane" bombardment of the type used at Neuve Chapelle.[16]

The Aubers Ridge attack of May 1915 was a very much bigger operation than Neuve Chapelle two months earlier. Though First Army's artillery resources had grown somewhat in absolute terms, they were significantly less in relation to the size of the task. It has been calculated that the British at Neuve Chapelle had one gun for every six yards, but at Aubers Ridge there was only one gun per eight yards. The problem was actually much more serious than this. During the preliminary bombardment for Aubers Ridge a substantial proportion of First Army's artillery was used to engage strong points and redoubts in the German rear – diminishing the intensity of the bombardment of the trench system itself.

The number of British guns bombarding the German trench system worked out at one gun per 30 yards for the March attack and one gun per 50 yards in the case of the May operation. It has been calculated that in the preliminary bombardment for the Battle of Neuve Chapelle, each yard of the German front had about 5lb of British artillery shell allocated to it – only about 2lb was used at Aubers Ridge. Because the German defensive system had been somewhat deepened, the impact of the British bombardment was inevitably reduced even further. Indeed, the intensity of the British preliminary bombardment of German frontline positions at the Battle of Aubers Ridge may have been only about one-fifth that of the equivalent bombardment for Neuve Chapelle.[17]

Its effectiveness was still further diminished by a reduction of accuracy. Some of the artillery pieces used were now, through constant usage, suffering from barrel wear – and thus tended to drop their shells short of their intended targets. The accurate registration of batteries also proved more difficult for the 9 May attack. The weather in the days immediately preceding the battle was particularly bad. Another, rather strange, factor – indicating the relative lack of routine artillery fire at this period in the war compared with later – was that many trees were still largely intact in this sector of the front. Whereas in March these had been bare, in May they were in full leaf. This significantly impaired the observation of objectives behind the German front. As if these problems with the intensity and accuracy of the bombardment were not enough, defective shells (the product of a munitions industry over-hastily expanded) was also a growing problem, perhaps more significant at Aubers Ridge than at Neuve Chapelle two months earlier.[18]

The final plan for the attack was incorporated in a First Army operations order dated 6 May. At that point it was intended that the attack be mounted on Saturday 8 May. The preliminary bombardment was to start at 5 a.m. and last until 5.40 when the infantry assaults would go in. The importance of the infantry hitting the German front line trenches soon after the preliminary bombardment lifting off seems to have been at least partially appreciated. Divisional orders directed the leading assault troops in some units to advance into no man's land under the cover of the bombardment to within eighty yards of the German trenches so that they would be in a good position to rush them when it lifted.[19]

Adverse weather conditions delayed the start of the Allied offensive. The attack of D'Urbal's French Tenth Army was originally programmed for Friday 7 May. Haig's attack was to proceed the following day. Torrential rain on Thursday 6 May and heavy fog on the morning of

Friday 7 May, however, set back the French preliminary bombardment, which, in contrast to that of the British, was of several days' duration. Joffre eventually decided to mount the French offensive on Sunday 9 May with the British attack going in simultaneously. It was an arrangement that Sir John French (who had favoured this all along) happily accepted and from which Haig did not demur.[20]

The Battle of Aubers Ridge: 9 May 1915

Sunday 9 May dawned clear and bright: in meteorological terms it was a glorious day.[21] In military terms, for Haig's forces, it was anything but. For most of the attacking British and Indian units, defeat was swift, bloody and complete. A first-hand account in a near-contemporary letter by a subaltern of 2nd Battalion the Welsh Regiment, of 2nd Brigade, 1st Division, vividly describes the battle, as many of Haig's attacking infantry experienced it:

We were told that after the bombardment there would not be many people left in the German first and second lines. We were all quite confident of the result and were very cheery ...

My platoon was not to leave the trench for two minutes after the first two platoons had gone. At 5.37 am the first two platoons jumped over the parapet ready to charge but they were met by a perfect hail of bullets and many men just fell back into the trench riddled with bullets ... My company commander then turned to me before my two minutes were up and said I had better try. So I took my platoon and the other platoon in the company also came and we jumped up over the parapet to charge but we met with the same fate ... I was the only officer left in my company ...[22]

By about 6 a.m., only about twenty minutes after it started, most of First Army's attack had come to a complete halt. In the southern sector – on the fronts of I Corps and the Indian Corps – it had failed utterly. Very few troops had reached the German parapet and the handful that had had been eliminated. There was scarcely a dent in the German front line. An attempt to renew the attack after a fresh bombardment from 6.15 to 7 a.m. brought no better result.[23] In the northern sector – the sector of Rawlinson's IV Corps – the situation was a little more complicated. In most places Davies's 8th Division (acting as a spearhead for IV Corps) had been stopped dead, but by 8 a.m. a small number of tiny lodgements had been made in the German front line – in some places the attacking infantry being helped by the explosion of mines. Desperate fighting continued within these lodgements and 8th Division made repeated efforts to reinforce the troops that had achieved them. In several parts of the front *ad hoc* efforts were made by divisional, brigade and battalion commanders to

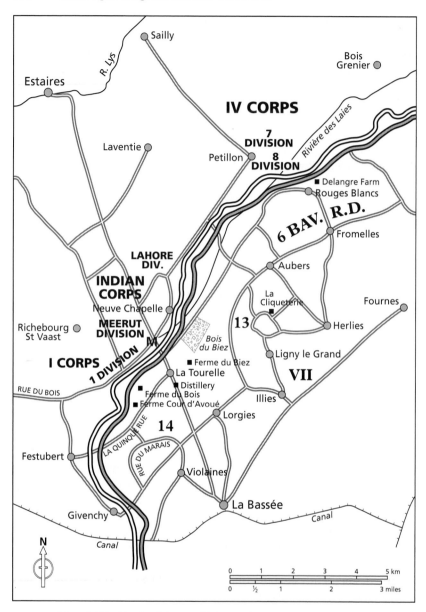

Map 9. The Battle of Aubers Ridge 9 May 1915: the position at zero hour

renew the attack, but these were uniformly unsuccessful. The situation was made worse by the response of the German artillery, which was now furiously shelling the First Army's front line and the communications trenches leading up to it.[24]

At his Advanced HQ at Merville, Haig heard some early disturbing reports but, for a couple of hours after Zero, had little conception of the severity of the defeat his forces had suffered. By 8 a.m., however, he knew not only that the initial efforts of I Corps and the Indian Corps had failed, but that attempts to renew the attacks with fresh forces had stalled. Half an hour later Rawlinson reported that IV Corps' assault had also been brought to a halt, but that it had penetrated the German front in a few places. Despite the generally gloomy picture that had now emerged, Haig ordered Rawlinson at 8.45 a.m. to "press the attack vigorously and without delay".[25]

A short time later Haig heard that the attack of the French Tenth Army to the south was making good initial progress and had breached the German defences on a wide front. The relative success of the French was certainly primarily owing to their superior resources in artillery and to their much longer and more thorough preliminary bombardment. Yet given the condescending, almost contemptuous, comments he had made about the French army in his diary just a couple of weeks earlier, it is possible that he felt somewhat shamed and frustrated by its relative success. He ordered the 1st Division and the Meerut Division, respectively of I Corps and the Indian Corps, to renew their attacks at noon, after another preliminary bombardment of forty-five minutes.[26]

In the late morning, leaving his chief of staff, Brigadier-General Butler, in charge at his Advanced HQ at Merville, Haig motored over to the nearby headquarters of the Indian Corps at Lestrem. There he met an inevitably downcast Lieutenant-General Willcocks. Willcocks was all too aware of the devastating losses his troops had so far suffered that morning and the massive dislocation that had ensued. He convinced Haig that the next attack needed to be significantly delayed. Haig amended his orders accordingly, giving 2.40 p.m. as Zero hour for this assault.[27]

Haig then proceeded to I Corps' HQ near Essars, where he saw Lieutenant-General Monro and found the situation little better. Having returned, apparently at some time before 11.20 a.m., to Lestrem, he was told that the Meerut Division would not be in a position to renew its attack at 2.40 p.m. Reluctantly he accepted a further delay until 4 p.m. Having heard nothing from Rawlinson for several hours, and apparently being desperate for progress somewhere, Haig repeated, at 11.45 a.m., his order of exactly three hours earlier – the 8th Division must press home its attack. In this atmosphere of apparent failure, chaos and frustration Haig took his lunch with Willcocks. He remained composed but tight-lipped – even less communicative than usual.[28]

The renewed attack of 4 p.m. was, as Haig should have anticipated, an unmitigated disaster. Informed of this (if not quite in those terms) by 5 p.m., Haig ordered that no immediate attempt should be made to repeat attacks that had failed, but that any inroads into German trench system should be secured. In reality the 4 p.m. attack had made hardly any penetration. Yet Haig refused to quit. He ordered the three attacking divisions (8th, 1st and Meerut) to be reorganised and reinforced and a fresh assault (preceded by a short intensive artillery bombardment) to be made at 8 p.m. Fortunately at 6 p.m. he received news that the communication trenches were so blocked as a result of German shelling (which had caused some sections to collapse and choked others with wrecked equipment and dead bodies) that the necessary reinforcement could not take place.[29] Another bout of pointless bloodshed was thus avoided – at least for the time being.

Annoyed, Haig ordered his corps commanders and their chiefs of staff to assemble at the Indian Corps headquarters at Lestrem at 7 p.m. To this gathering Haig expressed his acute displeasure at the lack of progress so far, and outlined the options as he saw them. The first was a night attack as soon as the attacking divisions could be reinforced, the second a renewed assault at daybreak. He asked for comments and found that the first option was widely opposed. It is not clear that there was much enthusiasm for the second option either, but that was the course Haig decided on. The conference ended at 7.30 p.m.[30]

Because Davies's 8th Division, in IV Corps, had suffered such massive casualties on the Sunday, Haig ordered that Major-General Hubert Gough's 7th Division relieve it during the night. The 7th Division would undertake the attack in the northern sector on the Monday morning. But upon careful investigation, Gough found not only that the 8th Division itself was a shambles, but that the communications trenches leading to the front were badly blocked. In addition the forming-up trenches had been so pulverised by the German artillery that troops occupying them would be terribly exposed. In these circumstances Gough decided that an overnight relief of the 8th Division by his own was simply impossible. He stood down his brigades and reported the situation to IV Corps' headquarters, which had to pass the unwelcome news to First Army. Rawlinson telephoned Haig before midnight with Gough's suggestion that his division be put into the line further south – near Festubert. Haig did not immediately take up this suggestion but accepted that it would be impossible for the 7th Division to attack the following morning.[31]

Yet Haig still persisted with plans for renewed attacks on Monday 10 May. At 11.30 on the Sunday night he ordered that I Corps should mount an afternoon assault at 4 p.m. on the Monday, to be supported later by the Indian Corps, if things went well. By midnight, however, First Army HQ was receiving reports that indicated that the renewal of the offensive at any time on the Monday would be very problematical. The casualty reports coming in were very depressing: losses were worse than Haig had hitherto realised and it became evident that much of First Army was still in serious disarray. Haig summoned his corps commanders to meet him at I Corps's headquarters at 9 a.m. There he announced his decision to cancel all attacks for that day. The Battle of Aubers Ridge was practically over.[32]

Results

During the night the Germans had finally eliminated the few minor incursions into their defensive system that the British had achieved (mainly in the 8th Division's sector) on 9 May. Haig's second battle as an Army commander was an absolutely unmitigated defeat – not a yard of ground had been gained. Casualties inflicted on the Germans were not known, but were obviously insignificant compared with First Army's own losses. These amounted to somewhere between 10,000 and 11,000 of which perhaps a quarter were fatal.[33] In relation to the numbers involved these losses were (very roughly) two-thirds as great as those of the much more notorious first day on the Somme: 1 July 1916. And whereas the casualties on the first day of the Somme were, in many cases, suffered by green troops, a high proportion of those lost on 9 May 1915 were veterans. Significant numbers belonged to the army's precious and fast-diminishing supply of pre-war regulars. Losses in some units and formations (notably the 1st Division) were so devastating that, though numbers were made up, it is arguable that morale and fighting spirit never fully recovered over the course of the war.[34]

Haig's failure was particularly galling when compared with (the admittedly modest) achievement of d'Urbal's French Tenth Army in the Arras–Vimy sector further south. After an intensive bombardment of four hours – compared with the forty-minute effort of First Army's gunners – the two French corps had penetrated the German defences on Vimy Ridge to a depth of well over a mile on a front of more than four miles. They had taken 2,000 German prisoners and captured twelve guns. Haig's failure had been so complete that the two German divisions in reserve behind the sector the British had attacked were moved south to face d'Urbal's forces. Inevitably the British army's stock with French general headquarters fell very low and Franco-British relations suffered. Joffre was clearly irritated by the lack of effective British co-operation with his spring offensive and both Haig and French were acutely embarrassed.[35]

Roots of defeat: "shell shortage" and the truth

Shell shortage became the BEF's excuse for defeat. Sir John French had, for some time, been considering going over Kitchener's head to complain about the inadequacy of the supply of munitions to his army. The final straw came when, in the immediate aftermath of Aubers Ridge, he faced a War Office demand that he should send 22,000 rounds of precious shell to Marseilles for shipment to the Dardanelles. French decided to leak details of his complaints to Kitchener on the subject of shell shortage to Colonel Repington – the military correspondent of *The Times*. He furnished the same information to David Lloyd George, the Chancellor of the Exchequer, who was eager to diminish Kitchener's control of the war effort. For several months there had been indications that Herbert Asquith, the Prime Minister, would need to broaden the basis of his government. The "shell scandal", coupled with the widespread belief that the government had mishandled the Dardanelles campaign, helped to bring matters to a head. Asquith formed a coalition government with the Unionists. Churchill was sacked as First Lord of the Admiralty and Kitchener's powers were reduced.[36]

Haig was exceptionally fortunate in the aftermath of Aubers Ridge. In the British camp at least, his generalship was subjected to very little serious scrutiny or criticism. It would have been difficult for French to scapegoat him, even had he wished to do so. He had not criticised Haig's plans before the attack, and having just removed one Army commander, it would have been politically almost impossible to remove another (especially one as well-connected as Haig) so quickly. Haig was also politically clever enough to avoid involvement in the shell scandal. Siding with an already discredited commander-in-chief against a figure as powerful as Kitchener (even if the latter's fortunes were now also somewhat on the wane) made little sense. Haig let it be known that he considered French's involvement in the press attack on the Secretary of State, "A most disgraceful state of affairs," thus strengthening his own position and helping further to weaken the commander-in-chief.[37]

Explaining Haig's defeat at Aubers Ridge mainly in terms of shell shortage was essentially false. Someone on the General Staff at GHQ, probably William Robertson, its chief, recognised this in a paper written a few weeks later. During the battle Haig had ordered a number of repeat bombardments of the German frontline and some of these were in fact carried out. This indicates that he had significantly more shell available than he had cared to use in his preliminary bombardment. He began the preliminary bombardment for his next major attack, the Battle of Festubert, on 13 May, within four days of the Battle of Aubers Ridge. This bombardment lasted for three days and consumed over 100,000 rounds of artillery ammunition. As First Army made slightly better progress on this occasion, the battle went on for ten days (albeit in a somewhat desultory fashion) and First Army's guns kept firing, if not always rapidly.[38] Whence came all of this shell so suddenly? Surely the only explanation was that most of it had been available all along.

The very perfunctory preliminary bombardment at Aubers Ridge must be explained in terms other than an absolute shortage of artillery ammunition. Haig was not obliged by shell shortage to keep the bombardment to a mere forty minutes. Rather, the "hurricane" bombardment, as used at Neuve Chapelle, was his *preferred* method. It had worked there – in the sense of helping First Army to achieve surprise and allowing the German frontline trenches to be overrun. For the operation of 9 May, trying to bring more rearward German positions under bombardment, Haig had hoped the same basic technique would work again.

It is clear that First Army's intelligence had provided Haig with a reasonable amount of information as to the increased depth and strength in the German defences in this sector since the Battle of Neuve Chapelle. To take reasonable account of this information in planning the preliminary bombardment, complex "operational analysis" of the type developed in the next world war was not necessary. Simple calculations would have sufficed. Rawlinson's staff had performed similar calculations for Neuve Chapelle and Haig had reviewed and approved them. For the attack of 9 May, however, Haig and the First Army staff had either not done the appropriate sums or ignored the results.[39]

Haig had, moreover, failed to adopt the approach to Western Front operations that Robertson had advocated since February and that Du Cane and Rawlinson had wished to embrace after Neuve Chapelle. One of the reasons the bombardment failed was that Haig was trying to get his troops to penetrate the full depth of the German defensive system in a single day. It was necessary to try to bring the whole of that system under bombardment at once, thus dissipating First Army's limited firepower. A "step-by-step" approach would have allowed a greater concentration of fire. The preliminary bombardment could have focused on the German trench system itself, had it been accepted that progress beyond it would require separate bombardments of deeper objectives (the strong points and redoubts further back) on subsequent days.

Haig must, therefore, personally bear much of the responsibility for Aubers Ridge. Yet that defeat also needs to be placed in proper perspective. Haig was not the first commander in military history to mount an inadequately planned, bloody and futile frontal assault on a strongly held position. It is, indeed, difficult to think of many famous generals who have not done so on some occasion. Haig's compounding of his initial mistake on 9 May 1915 by ordering repeated attacks of inevitably diminishing strength on largely undented enemy positions is also familiar in the historical pathology of generalship.[40] Haig had done generally very well at First Ypres. Neuve Chapelle had been a partial success. Though he had clearly not learned as much from Neuve Chapelle as had some other senior officers, his bloody defeat at Aubers Ridge on Sunday 9 May 1915 did not, in itself, prove him an incompetent commander. The real question was how well he would learn from that experience.

Learning from Aubers Ridge

Haig did in fact show a willingness to learn the most obvious lesson of Aubers Ridge. The German fortifications, he realised, were now too strong for the sort of artillery bombardment used at Neuve Chapelle to work. He concluded:

1. The defences in our front are so carefully and strongly made and mutual support with machine guns is so complete that, that in order to demolish them a long methodical bombardment will be necessary by heavy artillery (guns and howitzers) before Infantry are sent forward to attack.
2. To destroy the enemy's "material", 60–pdr *guns* will be tried as well as the 15–in, 9.2 and 6–in siege howitzers. Accurate observations *of each shot* will be arranged so as to make sure of flattening out the enemy's "strong points" of support before the Infantry is launched.
3. To destroy the physical power of the Enemy, and shatter the nerves of the men who work his machine guns, the bombardment will be carried on during the night ...[41]

Without making major changes to the climate, topography and vegetation of north-west Europe (and surely not even Haig had that much influence with "a higher power") it is difficult to see how he could realistically insist on the observation of every shell fired. It is by no means clear how he intended to ensure accurate observation of artillery fire at night: it seems likely that he simply failed to notice the tension (perhaps even contradiction) between his points 2 and 3. Yet, in response to a clear-cut defeat, there was, at least, some willingness to adapt.

Planning the Battle of Festubert

Haig came under pressure from GHQ (which was under pressure from the French) to resume offensive operations as soon as possible after stopping the Battle of Aubers Ridge.[42] For his next attack he again decided on a sort of pincer movement, but this time a little further to the south. The two pincers would begin about 600 yards apart. On the left, a brigade of the Meerut Division (Indian Corps) and two brigades of the 2nd Division (I Corps) would attack on a front of 1,600 yards. Further to the right Gough's 7th Division (transferred to I Corps after Aubers Ridge) would attack on a front of about 900 yards. The attacks of the two wings were not to be simultaneous. The troops forming the left pincer (who had been in the vicinity for some time and had plenty of time to make themselves familiar with the ground) would attack on the night of 15–16 May. The 7th Division, which was moved to its sector shortly before the operation, and did not know the ground well enough to do a night operation, was to go in at dawn preceded by a short, intensive bombardment.[43]

Three features of this operation suggest willingness on Haig's part to learn from experience and to try new methods:

(a) He decided on a lengthy preliminary bombardment: at least for the main attacking force. This began on 13 May and involved the expenditure of 100,000 rounds.

(b) Apparently in the hope that this might increase surprise and reduce casualties, Haig sanctioned the British army's first night attack of the war.

(c) The objective set for the first day was much more limited than that for either Neuve Chapelle or Aubers Ridge. The initial attack was intended merely to capture the German support line, which would involve an advance of about 1,000 yards.[44]

Festubert: Preliminary bombardment and battle, 13–25 May 1915

Continuous rain and poor visibility on 13 May made it difficult for batteries to register their targets and seriously interfered with the efficacy of the bombardment. The weather was, however, rather more clement on 14 and 15 May, and fire was, therefore, more effective. Haig judged that the bombardment had probably done enough to enable the infantry attack to go ahead with reasonable hope of success and, at 11.30 p.m. on 15 May, the attack forces of the Meerut Division and the 2nd Division went "over the top" and attacked the German trenches.[45]

Only one of the three attacking brigades, 6th Brigade of 2nd Division, on the far right, was able to take the German front line trench. The other two brigades reached the German front only in a few places and suffered very heavy casualties. Haig must be given some credit for common sense in his response to the failure of most of his initial attack. At 5.40 a.m. on 16 May, after the Indian Corps had made two failed attempts on the German trenches in its sector, he ordered all attacks on the left to stop. The Sirhind Brigade (the supporting brigade of the Meerut division) was to move to reinforce the 6th Brigade's success.[46]

By that time the 7th Division had made its dawn attack. Its 20th and 22nd Brigades had assaulted the German trenches at 3.15 a.m., after half-an-hour's intense bombardment. Both brigades had some success. On the right, the 22nd Brigade took all its objectives – capturing both the German front line and the support line. The 20th Brigade, to the left, also took the front line, but was then checked. First Army had made a vastly better beginning to this attack than to its predecessor a week earlier. Yet Haig's forces were in a rather awkward position. The British pincers had not closed. All that Haig had accomplished was to make two small and rather ragged incisions in the German front line. By approximately 9 a.m. on Sunday 16 May, his Army's advance had ground to a halt.[47]

After visiting corps and divisional headquarters on the Sunday afternoon, at 11.45 p.m. Haig ordered that I Corps only should attack the following day, at a time of its commander's choosing. The 2nd Division and the 7th Division were to make every effort to close the gap between them as well as renewing their drive in an essentially eastward direction. On the night of 16–17 May, however, the Germans made a slight withdrawal and established a new front. While the 2nd and 7th Divisions were able to effect a junction, the Germans were able to block any significant advance to the east. It rained hard for much of the day and by evening marshy conditions impeded the advance and waterlogged trenches made conditions miserable. On the following day, however, realising that his two attacking divisions were now approaching exhaustion, Haig decided to relieve them. Over the next few days the 1st Canadian Division relieved the 7th Division and the 51st Highland Division relieved the 2nd Division.[48]

In the somewhat desultory fighting that continued up to 25 May, very little ground was gained. By that time Haig's Army had advanced on front of about three miles to a maximum depth of a mile and established a reasonably coherent new front. The ground gained was, however, of no particular use and further progress in this sector was, for the time being, impossible. First Army had expended virtually all of its artillery ammunition and the Germans had created a new defensive line strongly held by reinforcements.[49]

Results

The cost to First Army of the eleven days of intermittent fighting that constituted the Battle of Festubert was steep by any standards: somewhere between 16,000 and 17,000 casualties. As at Aubers Ridge, some British units had suffered losses so severe that they needed to be totally reconstituted. First Army had taken approximately 800 German prisoners. Other than that, German losses were not known, though it was appreciated that they were likely to be far lower than were those of the British. The British official history suggested a total of 5,000 German casualties. The Germans too appeared to be learning. They avoided the mass infantry counter-attacks over open ground that so swelled their casualties at Neuve Chapelle, but used their artillery to great effect in pulverising positions the British had recently captured. For Haig and First Army, therefore, Festubert was a Pyrrhic victory at the most favourable interpretation, perhaps more realistically regarded as a defeat. The only things that the battle had achieved were to show the French that the British were still willing to fight and to tie down a modest number of German troops.[50]

The French were still fighting in the Vimy Ridge/Arras sector, but they were no longer making much progress. Joffre, however, hoped that he could make a greater offensive effort in June and that the British would contribute to this. By 27 May Sir John French was suggesting to Haig that he mount an attack at Loos. Haig did not like the idea. The British could not get good positions for their guns in that sector whereas the Germans already occupied some features that would give them commanding views of British positions. He wanted instead to mount the attack between Givenchy and Festubert. GHQ ultimately approved this. There is diary evidence that Festubert to some degree restored Haig's confidence after the Aubers Ridge debacle, but he showed little enthusiasm for mounting another offensive in the immediate future. He largely delegated responsibility for planning and executing the new attack to Rawlinson and his IV Corps headquarters, which had hardly been involved in the Battle of Festubert.[51]

On 27 May Joffre inspected the 7th Division. Asquith, now leading a coalition government, visited First Army a few days later. Both men made flattering remarks about Haig and his troops. Haig, who still had an almost childish delight in the praise of very important people, recorded their comments in great detail in his diary. Yet what had he achieved so far in 1915? One very minor and partial victory (largely planned by a subordinate), one clear-cut and extremely bloody defeat and one even bloodier stalemate: that was the sum of his military achievement in the first five months of the year. There were surely precious few laurels to rest on here.[52]

Haig's diary, however, also offers material that puts him in a somewhat better light. On 11 June Ben Tillett, a veteran trade union leader, visited Haig's headquarters. Tillett had once led a massive strike by the dockers that had much frightened the British establishment. Haig, while a social conservative and not entirely free of snobbery, was a pragmatist, prepared to draw support from men of proven ability, no matter what their background. Tillett told him that the working men he knew who now served in the ranks gave very favourable reports of their officers. It was clear to Haig that Tillett was a determined ally in the struggle with German militarism and he considered it "a very good thing he has come and visited the troops at the Front". Haig demonstrated here, as he quite often had in the past, a fair degree of political open-mindedness that contrasts with the relative rigidity of his thinking on operational matters.[53]

Planning the Battle of Givenchy

By the time of Tillett's visit to Haig's HQ, Rawlinson's IV Corps was on the point of mounting its next attack. Rawlinson had established his headquarters at Hinges on 29 May. After a considerable reorganisation of First Army, in late May Rawlinson's forces now consisted of the Canadian Division, the 7th Division and the 51st Highland Division. The German position on the Rue d'Ouvert that Rawlinson was charged with attacking was very well fortified and covered by quite deep belts of wire. Rawlinson considered it "a pretty stiff nut for us to crack. It will cost us many thousands of lives before we are in possession of it unless we get an unlimited supply of ammunition to smash the place to pieces before we go in."[54]

Rawlinson's delicate position in the internal politics of the British army in France (massively out of favour with Sir John French and therefore entirely beholden to Haig) would, however, have made any open dissent disastrous for him in career terms. Nor did Rawlinson enjoy the sort of relationship with Haig that would have enabled him to express his doubts, frankly but privately. They were not personal friends. After the Davies affair, in the aftermath of Neuve Chapelle, Haig had let Rawlinson know that he held his command on sufferance. He seems to have maintained with Rawlinson (as he did with most other subordinates) a psychological distance that would have made the sharing of confidences (and the sharing of doubts) practically impossible. In such a tense, frosty atmosphere the exchange of views necessary for serious military analysis was bound to be difficult.

Whereas "shell shortage" is a false explanation for defeat at Aubers Ridge, it was undoubtedly a major constraint in the planning for Givenchy. Given that the defences in the Givenchy–Rue d'Ouvert sector were known to be so strong, Rawlinson decided on a deliberate bombardment, as at Festubert. Rawlinson apparently appreciated his resources were quite inadequate in relation to the task: his gunners would be most unlikely to cut all the German wire in the sector he had chosen for attack and could not destroy the enemy's field fortifications or suppress his artillery. He seems, however, to have saved his worst fears for his diary and to have disguised his deep-seated pessimism from both Haig and the officers and men who would have to conduct the assault.[55]

Haig irritated Rawlinson considerably by insisting, on 12 June, that he draft plans for exploitation beyond the Rue d'Ouvert. Rawlinson himself was extremely doubtful that his men could get that far. He complied with Haig's wishes, but his lack of enthusiasm must have been obvious. The following day Haig expressed to his diary his confidence that the wire-cutting programme was going well and that the attack would achieve success – demonstrating either a remarkable lack of understanding or a remarkable capacity for self-delusion. Rawlinson, at the same date, and presumably looking at the same intelligence reports, was vastly less hopeful.[56]

Any attempt to understand the working of Haig's mind in this matter is bound to be speculative. Possibly he accepted that some sort of attack to assist the French army was unavoidable for political reasons (or at least that it was not worth the likely damage to his own career involved in trying to prevent it). Such thinking may have led him to delegate its planning and execution to a subordinate whom he knew to be reasonably able, but of whom he was not particularly fond. Yet, perhaps still not able fully to accept that British soldiers must go to operationally futile deaths to meet the political exigencies of the Franco-British alliance, he perhaps preferred to delude himself as to the likely outcome.

Givenchy: Preliminary bombardment and the battle 13–15 June 1915

The preliminary bombardment, involving some 211 guns, began slowly at 6 a.m. on 13 June. After 48 hours, at 6 a.m. on 15 June, it was somewhat intensified. It continued in that fashion until the 7th and 51st Divisions began their assault at 6 p.m.[57] The selection of this unusual hour seems in part to have been an attempt on Rawlinson's part to achieve a significant degree of surprise, though in this it seems to have failed. It may also have been a symptom of his "bite and hold" philosophy. Had Rawlinson been confident of capturing the German trenches and exploiting beyond them, a dawn attack would have made more sense. Attacking in the early evening was, however, more sensible on the assumption that little exploitation was to be conducted that day. Effective exploitation would require daylight, whereas it would be easier to reinforce and resupply troops who had gained a lodgement in the German front line in darkness, and even on a summer's night this would descend within a few hours of the attack.

The results of the Givenchy attack were as dismal as Rawlinson could have imagined. Over much of the front the attackers met intact wire and were mowed down before reaching the German front line. In a few places, where wire had been effectively cut, some lodgements were gained in the German trenches, but these were widely separated and there was great difficulty in holding them.[58]

By 4 a.m. on 16 June, the Germans had successfully driven all British troops from their trenches. The attack was renewed on Haig's instructions at 4.45 p.m. the same day. The attacking infantry again entered the German lines in some places, but by 8 p.m. had been driven out. On 18 June the offensive was aborted.[59] It was a defeat as unmitigated as that of 9 May, albeit on a smaller scale: First Army's second within little more than a month. For the cost of 3,500 casualties, not a yard of ground was gained. The Germans had defeated the attack using only local reserves. No troops had been diverted from French sectors of the front.[60]

Attempts at analysis

Meeting with representatives of the Ministry of Munitions after the battle, Haig insisted that he needed vastly more shell, especially of the heavier types. He also wanted more trench mortars (some of a super-heavy nature), a greatly increased supply of hand grenades of standardised types and more balloons (as well as aircraft) to assist with artillery observation. In other quarters he made representations that he required younger, more vigorous, battalion and brigade commanders – these were to be supplied by the accelerated promotion of promising captains and majors.[61]

This sort of formula for offensive success – more munitions plus more human dynamism, provided by officers of the "thruster" type – was one to which Haig would frequently return over the next few years. But even had the authorities at home been able to fulfil his wish lists immediately and in their entirety (which, of course, they could not), this would not have solved all the problems. Haig needed to rethink his methods. IV Corps' report on Givenchy, completed on 21 June, provided plenty of evidence of this. Rawlinson pointed out that

the hostile trenches are from seven to ten feet deep and that shell proof dug-outs have been constructed some five or six feet below the ground level.

Into these the garrisons no doubt withdraw during the artillery bombardment and the success of the attack therefore depends on the ability of our Infantry to reach the hostile parapets before the enemy can leave his dugouts to man them …

I much doubt if any kind of artillery fire however accurate and well sustained will have the desired effect unless it is sufficient to bury the garrisons in the deep dug-outs they have now constructed, and this is a matter of chance.[62]

Rawlinson's analysis pointed towards a vital general conclusion about the role of artillery in offensive operations on the Western Front. Except with regard to barbed wire, suppression rather than destruction was its proper role in support of an assault. In order to give attacking infantry a chance of success the artillery certainly needed to cut the German wire. But it could not guarantee to destroy their trenches and dugouts or to kill a high proportion of their garrisons. All it could do was beat down German fire, keeping the enemy infantry in their dugouts and bunkers or at the bottom of their trenches until the attacking British infantry reached and overran them. The effectiveness of this kind of suppression depended very largely on timing: on the synchronisation between bombardment by artillery and assault by infantry. Infantry needed to arrive on their objectives very shortly after the artillery lifted off them.

Rawlinson seems to have been tantalisingly close to grasping all this. But he had not yet quite made the final mental leap. Given enough shell to fire a prolonged suppressive barrage, it was in fact possible for artillery to achieve the "desired effect" of getting British infantry into the German trenches at a reasonable cost without having to "bury the garrisons in the deep dug-outs they have now constructed". Rawlinson, however, was somewhat ahead of Haig analytically. Faced with the novel problems of attack under Western Front conditions, Haig was demonstrating distinct intellectual limitations. On 16 June he declared himself at a loss to understand why the Givenchy attack had so dismally failed.[63]

On leave

On 8 July Kitchener and the Prime Minister both paid visits to First Army HQ. There was much general discussion on the course of the war and the future needs of the army in France. The following day Haig left for some home leave. He had hoped to spend the whole leave with his wife at the seaside at Westgate, where his ADC, Captain Alan Fletcher, had lent him a house. As with his last home leave, he seems to have made no effort to effect a meeting with his daughters. On Haig's previous leave, after Neuve Chapelle, he had politely declined the King's request for an interview. On this occasion, however, he accepted the request.[64]

The meeting at the Palace on 14 July was most cordial. The King expressed appreciation of his services, presented him with the honour of the GCB and assured him that no one had deserved it more. Two bloody defeats and an even bloodier stalemate in the last few weeks seem to have been in no way held against him. Given that his record so far in 1915 seems actually to have increased the degree of royal esteem in which he was held, it is interesting to try to imagine what he would have had to do to lose it. It was clear that the King had become completely disillusioned with French and wanted him replaced. Haig apparently said that the time to do this was immediately after the retreat from Mons. In static warfare, French's position was of little importance. Both the King and Kitchener, whom he saw later that day, encouraged Haig to write to them frankly. Clearly neither of them wanted him to hold back any criticism of French.[65]

On 17 May Haig returned to France,[66] where planning for the British army's greatest offensive so far had already begun.

7   The Battle of Loos

Haig's thinking on offensive operations in mid-summer 1915

In mid-summer 1915 Haig still kept faith in the ultimate victory of the Allies and had no doubt that the Western Front would be the decisive theatre. He still did not favour an approach based on short advances and gradual attrition: rather he eventually wished to conduct a massive, decisive breakthrough operation. Once sufficient heavy guns and ammunition were available he wanted to mount an offensive on a front of twenty-five or thirty miles,[1] perhaps even 100 miles. A broad-front offensive of this sort would force the Germans to commit their reserves. Once they were fully stretched, the Allies would use a "strong central reserve" to break through at a point where the Germans had proven weak. This decisive breakthrough might take place within five or six days of the opening of the grand offensive. Haig called this "applying old principles to the present conditions" and thought it would "win the war".[2]

He realised, however, that it would be many months before the British army could conduct or even participate in any such operation. The heady mid-March mood of optimism and aggression in the immediate aftermath of Neuve Chapelle had largely dissipated. Aubers Ridge, Festubert and Givenchy had sobered him. He, like other senior officers, accepted that the BEF was inadequately equipped to take the offensive with any hope of substantial success in the immediate future.[3] An appreciation of the immediate battlefield realities of the Western Front could not, however, be the sole determinant of British military conduct there.

The grand strategic situation in summer 1915

The BEF was just one element in the titanic struggle between the European powers. In the summer of 1915 that struggle was not going well for the Allies. The worst disasters were on the Russian front. There the Tsar's armies had lost most of Poland and perhaps a million troops had been killed and captured. Italy had joined the Allies in May, but her armies suffered heavy losses on the Isonzo in July and August and made no significant progress against the Austrians. Bulgaria joined the Central Powers in July, greatly increasing the threat to Serbia, which was overrun during the remainder of the year. Ignoring the needs and concerns of Great Britain's allies was, for those directing the British war effort, not a practical possibility. If the coalition fell apart the result would be defeat for all its members. In the late summer and autumn of 1915 the situation on the Eastern Front, where the Russians were suffering heavy defeats at German hands, was of particular concern to the western Allies.[4]

BEF expansion and the Loos sector

Its own prodigious expansion was another factor making it difficult for the BEF to do nothing. Between May and August it grew from sixteen to twenty-eight divisions. By August it had approximately 900,000 men altogether: eleven Regular, six Territorial, seven Kitchener, two Canadian and two Indian divisions. If its leaders judged it impossible to use this army offensively in the West, there was a real risk that the politicians at home would remove substantial parts for use elsewhere. (To GHQ's intense irritation there was never any shortage of such schemes.) At the very least the BEF's growing size obliged it to take over more of the front. Haig's First Army extended its line several miles south of the La Bassée canal in late June (after the Battle of Givenchy), so that Rawlinson's IV Corps on the far right faced towards the towns of Loos and Lens. It was in this area that Joffre wanted the British to attack in support of a renewed French offensive.[5]

Haig's assessment of the possibilities that this new area of responsibility offered for offensive operations varied somewhat over the next couple of months. But generally he was far from optimistic. In the immediate vicinity of the front the ground was, for the most part, very open and flat. This made it superficially attractive. But on more careful reflection (and probably having listened to his artillery adviser) he realised that, without some high ground, it would be difficult to get good observation for the guns and similarly difficult to conceal them. The Germans, on the other hand, had excellent observation over most of the British front.[6] A further problem was that the German and British trenches in some parts of this sector were widely separated. Crossing a broad stretch of no-man's-land was (at least in daylight) likely to cost the infantry heavy casualties. Yet a further difficulty was that about a mile behind the German front line, on the British right, there was a sort of conurbation formed by the mining towns of Loos, Lens and Lieven. It was a tangle of pitheads, working class housing and railway embankments that would considerably complicate exploitation, if attacking British infantry got that far.[7]

Joffre's plans and the British army

In mid-June Joffre informed Sir John French of his plans for a major autumn offensive. Again Joffre intended to try to force the Germans to abandon the Noyon bulge, this time with simultaneous converging attacks in Artois and Champagne. Again British co-operation was required on the left flank of the French Tenth Army: the British First Army being called upon to attack in the Loos sector.[8] On 19 June Sir John French ordered Haig to prepare a plan for such an operation.[9] After giving the matter some thought, Haig concluded that he might be able to capture a 1,200-yard stretch of German trenches in front of the village of Loos. He did not think that it would be possible to advance much further than that, mainly because the British artillery observers possessed no high ground from which they could see beyond the German front line. Just clearing the Germans out of their front line trenches would, moreover, absorb much of the effort of attacking British infantry.[10]

On 3 July Haig held a conference with his corps commanders (with the exception of Rawlinson, who was in England on leave). He informed them of his intention to take the German trenches in front of Loos (the IV Corps sector) and the Hohenzollern Redoubt (in the sector of Hubert Gough's I Corps, on the left flank of IV Corps, slightly to the north). Following his normal practice, especially when in one of his less buoyant moods, he delegated much of the detailed planning to his corps commanders[11] and between Friday 9 and Saturday 17 July went on leave to England.[12]

His leave did not change Haig's mind about the advisability of an attack in the Loos sector. Indeed, talks with the King and Kitchener, which indicated that both the Palace and the government were now thoroughly disillusioned with Sir John French, perhaps encouraged him to back his own judgement against such an operation. He informed Sir John that:

The resources at my disposal ... do not permit an offensive being undertaken on a large scale, such as might lead at once to freedom of manoeuvre, and it is therefore necessary, whilst being prepared for any eventuality in case of success, to limit the offensive to a definite operation within the scope of the force.[13]

But Haig's only suggestion as an alternative to the Loos attack was another attempt on the Aubers Ridge. He raised this with Robertson when the latter visited the First Army's headquarters on Wednesday 21 July. "By using gas", he claimed, "it seems possible to make sure of gaining this position in spite of the greatly improved defences which the Enemy has erected on it."[14] This was a bizarre notion. Haig had utterly failed to get British infantry to the Aubers Ridge in previous attacks, when the German front was less well fortified. On 7 July Haig had an interview with Lieutenant-Colonel Charles Foulkes who was in charge of developing the British offensive gas capability. But what convinced him that gas would make a difference vast enough to enable him to take the Aubers Ridge is far from clear. Though Foulkes' enthusiasm for gas was strong and infectious, his estimate of its potential seems to have been more modest than was Haig.[15]

In the short term, French appears to have supported Haig's proposal for a renewed attack towards Aubers. In early August, however, pressure from Joffre made the British commander-in-chief shift his ground once more. Sir John French reluctantly accepted that he must take some action south of the La Bassée Canal. He wanted, however, to restrict this to a mere demonstration. He suggested to Haig that "a storm of artillery fire laid down for a period of days on the German positions would harass and destroy their forward elements, and lead them to believe that a heavy attack might follow at any moment". A real infantry assault would be unnecessary.

As Haig recorded in his diary on 7 August:

I attended Conference at St Omer with Sir John French and his CGS (Robertson). Sir John explained his negotiations with Generals Foch and Joffre. French indicated that he had reluctantly agreed that:

... the British Army [will] ... attack between the canal to La Bassée and our right, which is opposite Loos, with the object of taking Hill 70 and the ridge to the north of it near Hulluch. This will cover the left flank of the French Tenth Army in its attack on the Vimy plateau.

... I am therefore to work out proposals for giving effect to the decision but my attack is to be made chiefly with artillery, and I am not to launch a large force of infantry to the attack of objectives which are so strongly held as to be liable to result only in the sacrifice of many lives. That is to say, I am to assist the "French, by neutralising the enemy's artillery and by holding the hostile infantry on my front".[16]

Haig still had no personal enthusiasm for an offensive south of the La Bassée Canal. But he may have feared that if the sole British contribution to the offensive were an artillery bombardment and an infantry "demonstration" the Franco-British alliance would be placed under excessive strain. When he held a conference with his corps commanders on Friday 13 August, he asked them to prepare something more than the bombardment and demonstration that Sir John had suggested, but much less than the full-blooded attempt at a rapid breakthrough that Joffre obviously wanted. I Corps was to take the Hohenzollern Redoubt and such other positions in that vicinity as it seemed reasonable to attempt. IV Corps was to take the German trenches in front of Loos. But the seizure of Hulluch, on I Corps' front, and Loos itself, on that of IV Corps, were to be left for a subsequent attack.[17] Haig's orders of mid-August, indeed, appear to represent a sensible, compromise approach. First Army would mount a real attack, but one with very limited objectives. At this stage, therefore, Haig seems to have been trying to absorb and apply the more obvious lessons of his experience in the first half of 1915.

Apparently through the agency of Sir Henry Wilson, the officer responsible for liaison with the French army at GHQ, Joffre, however, soon discovered the half-hearted manner in which the British intended to participate in his next major offensive. He objected in the strongest terms. British involvement in Allied operations required, he wrote to French on 12 August, "a large and powerful attack, composed of the maximum force you have available, executed with the hope of success and carried through to the end".[18] The British, in other words, must attempt a breakthrough whether they considered it practicable or not and whatever casualties this entailed. Sir John French's initial reaction was still to prevaricate. He indicated that the extent of British assistance must depend on the supply of artillery ammunition, a reaction that placed further strain on Franco-British relations.[19] French might have resisted pressure from Joffre had his own government supported him. But it did not. Alarmed by the dramatic German victories on the Eastern Front, culminating in the capture of Warsaw, Kitchener accepted the need for a major Franco-British effort to take the pressure off the defeated Russians and keep them in the war. He instructed Sir John French to that effect. Sir John had little choice other than to pass on to Haig the pressure for a full-blooded attack, though he acknowledged that achieving any considerable advance would involve "big losses".[20]

The impact of Kitchener's visit to the front in August 1915

To ensure the BEF's compliance with his instructions and thus the continuation of Britain's alliances with France and Russia, Kitchener visited GHQ and First Army HQ on Wednesday 18 and Thursday 19 August respectively. At First Army HQ he spoke to Haig's corps commanders in the garden of the chateau before seeing Haig privately. As Haig recorded it:

Lord K came into my writing room upstairs saying he had been anxious to have a few minutes talk with me. The Russians he said had been severely handled, and it was doubtful how much longer their army could withstand the German blows.

Up to the present, he favoured a policy of active defence in France until such time as all our forces were ready to strike. The situation in Russia had caused him to modify these views. He now felt that the Allies must act vigorously in order to take some of the pressure off Russia ... He had heard, when with the French, that Sir John French did not mean to co-operate to the utmost of his power when the French attacked in September. He [Lord K] had noticed that the French were anxiously watching the British on their left. And he had decided that we must act with all our energy and do our utmost to help the French, even though, by so doing, we suffer very heavy losses indeed.[21]

Haig was still not eager to mount an offensive of any kind. He was especially reluctant to attack in the Loos sector. If he had to attack there, he would have preferred to aim at very limited objectives and to keep the casualties down. Yet he was too ambitious and too canny to try to resist simultaneous pressure from Joffre, GHQ and the British government, as represented by Kitchener. In the climate of August–September 1915 he felt he had no choice but to mount a major offensive in the Loos sector. Realising this, he fell smartly into line, telling Kitchener that First Army was ready, wanting only more ammunition.[22] As Haig surely realised, this was not really true. First Army was also short of guns, especially the heavier types.

On 23 August GHQ instructed Haig to have First Army ready to attack on 8 September, an extraordinarily short period in which to plan an undertaking of the magnitude now contemplated. Yet Haig and his staff responded rapidly. By 28 August they had drafted a plan, which was sent to corps commanders.[23] The French, however, postponed their offensive several times, and Z day for the First Army infantry assault was eventually put back to 25 September. While the delays were in some ways useful to Haig, they also caused him considerable anxiety. Every delay, once physical preparations for an offensive had begun, offered greater risk that the enemy would realise what was afoot and reinforce the threatened sector.[24]

First Army's initial plans for the Loos offensive

Loos represented a big increase in the scale of British offensives. The Loos attack was mounted on a front of 11,200 yards compared with 1,450 at Neuve Chapelle or 5,800 at Festubert. But a total of only 533 guns were available to the two corps (I and IV) which would carry out the attack, divided fairly evenly between them. Judging by the BEF's recent experience, that was nothing like enough in relation to the stretch of front First Army was intending to attack and the sort of penetration it was now expected to achieve. Just how inadequate was the artillery in relation to the tasks assigned has been analysed in considerable detail for Rawlinson's IV Corps. Only 251 guns were available to support the corps' three-division attack compared with the 342 guns used to support the three divisions that attacked at Neuve Chapelle in March.[25]

The above figures, however, greatly understate the problem. The German system of fortification was now deeper and more complex. It has been estimated that whereas at Neuve Chapelle there was one gun for every six yards of enemy trench to be bombarded, the figure at Loos (in the IV Corps sector, at any rate) was one gun for every 141 yards. While the preliminary bombardment for Loos was to be much longer than for Neuve Chapelle and would involve a significantly higher proportion of heavy guns, this was not enough to compensate for the overall shortage of artillery. In terms of the weight of shell falling on German front line positions the Loos bombardment in the IV Corps sector was to be only one-fifth that delivered at Neuve Chapelle.[26]

The Neuve Chapelle bombardment, moreover, was concentrated into the forty-five minutes immediately prior to the infantry assault. The preliminary bombardment at Loos was to be delivered in four daytime periods, each of a twelve-hour duration, over the four days leading up to the assault. The night-time breaks in the programme of shelling (inserted because shelling in the hours of darkness could not be observed) would inevitably allow the Germans some respite to repair damage to their defences: a factor particularly important with regard to the wire. Haig and his staff seem to have realised that the artillery available to First Army was inadequate to support an attack on the breadth of front intended without the support of some other agency.[27]

Haig hoped that gas, for the use of which the British army was currently developing a capability, would be the answer. The first effective German use of gas on the Western Front had been on 22 April 1915 at the opening of the Second Battle of Ypres. On 3 May 1915 Kitchener ordered that preparations should be made for the British army to retaliate in kind. He charged Colonel Louis Jackson, the Director of Fortification and Works at the War Office, with making arrangements with industry and raising the specialist units. Sir John French asked Sir William Robertson, Chief of the General Staff at GHQ, to select a suitable officer of the Royal Engineers to take charge of chemical warfare effort on the Western Front, and Major (soon to be Lieutenant-Colonel) Charles Foulkes was appointed to this position on 26 May 1915.[28]

Foulkes's had no prior chemical knowledge. His qualifications were his energy and organising ability. Chlorine and phosgene seemed to him the obvious gases to use. Given that phosgene could not be obtained in the necessary quantity, the initial effort would have to be with chlorine.

Foulkes also quickly concluded that the primary delivery means would be cylinders placed in forward trenches to generate a large wind-borne cloud. In both respects he was following (consciously or not) German practice at Second Ypres. Foulkes was quick to make his work known to all those in authority and had, as we have noted, an early interview with Haig.[29] On 22 August Foulkes gave a demonstration of the technique of generating a gas cloud for Haig and his corps and divisional commanders at the new chemical warfare centre at Helfaut, near St Omer, where GHQ was based. Purpose-built steel cylinders containing the chlorine, each weighing between 130 and 160lbs, were fixed into position under the firing step on the front parapet of the fire trench. A length of flexible copper piping connected the cylinder to an eight to ten foot long iron pipe of half-inch bore. The iron pipe was laid over the top of the parapet, pointing towards the enemy and weighted down with sandbags. When the valve was opened the chlorine was released into the piping in the form of a yellowish-white vapour, which turned a greenish-yellow colour after it had left the pipe and made contact with the air. The chlorine vapour was heavier than air and would thus tend to sink into deep German dugouts, which had proved, in previous attacks, to be impervious to artillery fire.[30]

Only a few cylinders were employed in the Helfaut demonstration. Many more, and all the paraphernalia and trained personnel to go with them, would be required to make an attack on the scale contemplated a success. Even if the material could be provided and the troops trained in time, the crude method demonstrated depended entirely on the weather. Haig nevertheless declared himself impressed. He had never been reluctant to embrace technical innovation. He began to hope (and even to believe) that gas would enable him to snatch a dramatic victory from a situation that had all the ingredients of a major disaster. Though some officers (including Sir Henry Rawlinson, commanding Haig's IV Corps) remained intensely sceptical,[31] a massive gas cloud attack was built in to the First Army plan as that had developed by 28 August.[32]

After Joffre had postponed the date of his offensive from 5 to 25 September, Haig held a conference for his corps and divisional commanders at First Army's Advanced HQ at Hinges on 6 September. Haig's Army at this stage held an eighteen-mile front between Armentières, on the left, where it had a boundary with Plumer's Second Army and the Grenay-Lens Road, on the right, where it had a boundary with the French Tenth Army. First Army included, from left to right: III Corps (Lieutenant-General William Pulteney); the Indian Corps (Lieutenant-General Sir Charles Anderson); I Corps (Lieutenant-General Hubert Gough); and IV Corps (Lieutenant-General Sir Henry

Rawlinson). Gough had replaced Monro at I Corps on 13 July 1915, when the latter went to command the newly created Third Army. Haig had just replaced Willcocks with Anderson as commander of the Indian Corps because Haig thought Willcocks had become ineffectual and had allowed a pessimistic mood to prevail at his corps headquarters.[33]

In his opening address to the First Army conference on 6 September, Haig admitted that the coming operation was, in his words, being mounted "to help our friends although our own resources are not yet fully organised". Yet, based on some rather curious reasoning, he concluded that it was vital to aim at a strategically important breakthrough.

Anything I say regarding the scope of the forthcoming operation is based on the study of the maps, and on the principles which were taught by the late Colonel Henderson at Camberley.

It is not enough to gain a tactical success. The direction of our advance must be such as will bring us upon the enemy's rear so that we will cut his communications and force him to retreat. Briefly then, the question is how to turn our tactical success into a strategical victory?

Haig argued that "by capturing DOUAI, VALENCIENNES AND MAUBEUGE, the enemy will lose at least half the main branches of supply which come past LIÈGE".

Haig's plan was that while subsidiary attacks north of the La Bassée Canal tied down some enemy forces in that area, I Corps and IV Corps would, with a six-division assault, break the enemy's front south of the canal, a breakthrough that was to be followed by rapid exploitation. He concluded that

provided we and the Allies immediately on our right take reasonable precautions as to secrecy, and advance with the necessary vigour and strength on the line DOUAI–VALENCIENNES, decisive results are likely to be obtained.

He went on to emphasise secrecy and rapidity

the quicker we advance the smaller will be our losses and the less risk we run of being checked because:
(a) The enemy will have less time in which to collect troops for holding a new position or to make a combined movement and, as we know,
(b) Counter attacks by troops collected hastily and launched without adequate artillery preparation are doomed to failure.

In order to exploit to the full the success he intended to achieve, he expected "initiative amongst all ranks" and attacks to be pressed with the "*utmost energy*" north as well south of the Canal. Any group of enemy troops that withdrew was to be "pursued remorselessly". Once the enemy generally was on the run there would be the most "vigorous pursuit".[34]

The question of reserves

Haig expected GHQ to make cavalry reserves available for the offensive and cavalry officers had already reconnoitred the ground. On 6 September, however, the details of what cavalry formations would be made available had not yet been worked out.[35]

An issue eventually to cause major friction between Haig and GHQ was the question of infantry reserves. This was an important issue because, according to the First Army plan as it had so far evolved, I Corps and IV Corps would be committing all their divisions to the initial attack, not keeping any in corps reserves. Haig, moreover, had taken no steps to create an Army reserve from within the forces he currently controlled. Two of his corps, III Corps and the Indian Corps, would not take part in the main thrust, south of the La Bassée Canal. But rather than take divisions from these corps and use them as Army reserves, Haig was, as we have noted, planning to use them to mount subsidiary attacks north of the canal.[36]

Since the beginning of September Haig had been demanding that GHQ make XI Corps, its only infantry reserve, available to First Army for the Loos attack. XI Corps, however, still had to be considered an embryonic formation. It only formally came into existence only on 29 August 1915 and initially consisted only of two Kitchener's Army divisions, the 21st Division and the 24th Division. Both were recently arrived in France, hurriedly trained and yet untested in battle. On 1 September Haig discussed with Sir William Robertson the need to find a suitable corps commander for the new formation. Haig favoured Richard Haking, a "thruster" whose aggression at Aubers Ridge, where he had commanded 1st Division, had cost that unfortunate formation crippling casualties. But it was only very late in the planning process for the Loos attack that Haig began to press the issue of the exact location of the reserves immediately prior to the attack.[37]

In discussions at GHQ on 18 September Haig tried to insist on two divisions of GHQ's Reserve Corps (XI Corps) being brought to Noeux-les-Mines and Verquin by the morning of 25 September. Sir John French appeared doubtful of the wisdom or necessity of deploying these formations so far forward. Sir John (who was in poor health and losing his grip) never fully explained his reasoning. But the 21st Division and the 24th Division, in addition to forming the bulk of GHQ's infantry reserve, were so limited in their training and so totally inexperienced that they could hardly have been less suitable for employment in a major offensive.[38] Haig's demand that GHQ should make these desperately unsuitable formations available for use at Loos is one of the oddest aspects of his conduct at this time. Even if Haig's premise that a major breakthrough was on the cards were accepted, there was an obvious alternative to reliance on these half-trained troops for exploitation. The two divisions judged most battle-worthy (say the 8th Division and the Meerut Division) could have been taken from III Corps and the Indian Corps respectively and made ready for use south of the La Bassée Canal. This would have involved scrapping the supporting attacks north of that waterway, or reducing them to mere demonstrations. But it was always doubtful whether those operations could achieve much in any case. Haig had removed Willcocks of the Indian Corps partly because he insisted that most of his formation was in a bad way and would have difficulty undertaking major offensive operations.[39]

GHQ's written instructions arriving at First Army HQ on 19 September indicated that, on 24 September, the two reserve divisions Haig wanted would still be a long way behind the front. On 19 September, therefore, Haig despatched Butler, his chief of staff, to GHQ with a letter for French. This insisted that lead elements of the two reserve divisions intended to be available to participate in the offensive should have arrived at Noeux-les-Mines and Verquin by the night of 24–25 September. Butler returned to First Army HQ at 3 p.m. on 19 September and told Haig that Sir John had agreed to this demand.[40]

The final plan

The First Army plan in its final version was issued that same day, 19 September. The attack would be mounted on 25 September.[41] Zero hour would depend critically on wind speed and direction and could not be determined at this stage. Inevitably First Army staff had put much thought into meteorological matters. Experiments indicated that wind speed and direction were normally favourable for a gas cloud attack in the early morning, between 4.30 and 5.30 a.m. Captain Gold, a respected meteorologist, normally attached to the Royal Flying Corps, had joined Haig's First Army staff to help him make the final decision on the attack's timing.[42] The gas discharge would last forty minutes so as to outlast the effectiveness of the German gas mask of the period. It would be accompanied by a particularly intense artillery bombardment of the German first-line system. This was to be followed by an attack by all six divisions of I Corps and IV Corps on a six-mile front between the La Bassée Canal on the left and Grenay on the right. The aim of the four divisions attacking in the centre would be to break through the German first and second line defensive system on a four-mile front between Haisnes in the north and Loos in the south and then push on towards the Heute Deule Canal. The division on the left flank of I Corps (2nd Division) and the division on the right flank of IV Corps (47th Division) were intended to make limited attacks that would turn outwards to offer hard shoulders for the main offensive push – protecting its flanks.

Opposing Haig's six-division assault force of about 75,000 men, there were (as his intelligence indicated with a high degree of accuracy) only about 15,000 enemy troops within five miles of the battlefield. There were only about 6,000 in the front and support lines. A further 6,000 were in local reserve and 3,000 resting in billets. If First Army managed to penetrate the whole German defensive system before reinforcements arrived, the 3rd Cavalry Division, an Army reserve in the Bois des Dames, would exploit towards Carvin. It was also possible that GHQ would release further cavalry to exploit the breakthrough. The negotiations that had taken place over the use of XI Corps for exploitation have already been discussed. It was, however, apparently realised at GHQ that the Germans would be able to reinforce the attacked sector heavily within twenty-four hours. This would inevitably curtail opportunities for exploitation.[43]

As already noted, Haig intended to mount minor operations north of the La Bassée Canal. Their main purpose was to distract German attention and prevent the southward movement of reserves. In the most favourable scenario, if the Germans front seemed to be collapsing, they would enable the British to broaden their offensive. The Indian Corps was to attack Moulin du Pietre, opposite Aubers, and the III Corps, on the left flank of the Indian Corps, was to attack near Le Bridoux, three-and-a-half miles south of Armentières. GHQ had arranged with the Royal Navy that the Dover Patrol was to make a demonstration suggesting a landing on the Belgian coast. The Belgian army was also to make some demonstrations in its hitherto very quiet sector towards the northern end of the front.[44]

Though Haig had clearly convinced himself that, with the use of gas, a substantial breakthrough was a real possibility, he did not believe such a result feasible without gas. At one stage he hoped that he could get permission to delay the whole British attack beyond 25 September if the wind was unfavourable that day. On 16 September he had written to Sir William Robertson at GHQ:

Without gas the front of our attacks must be reduced to what our guns can satisfactorily prepare with the results normally attendant on small fronts; namely concentration of hostile guns on point of attack, large losses and small progress. In my opinion, under no circumstances should our forthcoming attack be launched without the aid of gas.[45]

The French, however, who were not going to use a gas cloud themselves, refused to contemplate the British starting their offensive later than 25 September. GHQ, under pressure from Kitchener to keep the French happy, overruled Haig on this issue. First Army must attack on 25 September, GHQ insisted, regardless of weather conditions.[46]

It is, however, indicative of the influence that Haig wielded that even at this late stage he was able to extract a concession from GHQ. He suggested alternative scales of attack for 25 September – depending on the weather. If wind conditions were right for the use of gas, I Corps and IV Corps would mount a full-scale attack employing all their divisions and attempting a complete breakthrough. But if the weather were to be unfavourable, First Army would attack with only two divisions south of the La Bassée Canal, with demonstrations by III Corps and the Indian Corps north of it. A wider attack using gas and the remaining four divisions of I Corps and IV Corps would follow on 26 or 27 September if the wind then permitted. Sir John French apparently agreed to this.[47]

Sir John French's concession to Haig permitted him to issue an alternative set of orders to his corps commanders. Were the weather to be unsuitable for the use of gas on 25 September, Haig might hold back the bulk of his infantry force but order 9th Division (I Corps) alone to assault the Hohenzollern Redoubt at daybreak. If this were successful the same division might then be ordered to attempt to seize a position known as Fosse 8 later in the morning. At about 10 a.m. on 25 September, 15th Division would storm the German first-line system immediately to its front and might then take the Loos salient – the village of Loos and the defences surrounding it. Other divisions of I Corps and IV Corps might join the attack if favourable opportunities presented themselves.[48]

Haig's decision to attempt a gas cloud attack (supposing that conditions were favourable) imposed a stupendous amount of extra work on his troops in the week before the infantry attack. Some 5,500 cylinders were deployed, each weighing 120–160lbs. They were brought forward from the railheads to within a mile-and-a-half of the trenches by lorry. From that point three-man carrying parties using special slings and wooden poles took them into the front line. About 8,000 men were employed in this labour. Though supervised by Royal Engineers of the Special Companies, the infantry, as usual, did most of the hard labour. The cylinders had to be carried along narrow communications trenches and, in order to maintain the element of surprise, all the work had to be done at night. Many of those involved regarded it as the hardest labour they had to perform during the war.

Such a massive and complex administrative exercise might easily have degenerated into complete chaos. That it did not is at least some tribute to First Army's staff work – in other respects it was distinctly defective. Complete circuits with "Up" and "Down" routes were organised along the communications trenches – a one-way system – so that carrying parties did not have to push past each other in the dark. The Germans had no inkling that all this work was in progress. They fired no counter-preparation programme with their artillery. Not a single cylinder was hit by German fire. The Germans seem to have had no definite idea that they would be facing a major British attack in the Loos sector on 25 September and none at all that they were to be subjected to a gas attack.

Yet, even with all this effort of organisation and labour, and assuming a favourable wind (a very major assumption), mounting an effective gas attack remained very problematical. Foulkes and his chemists reckoned that a forty-minute gas flow would be needed to overwhelm the simple gas masks the German army was then using. As a cylinder emptied in two minutes, this would have required twenty cylinders for each twenty-five yard stretch of front. However, only enough cylinders had been des-patched from England to provide twelve cylinders per twenty-five yard stretch. It was therefore decided to have breaks in the gas flow, the intervals to be filled by the emission of smoke from phosphorus smoke candles. Just before the infantry attack, triple candles were to be burned to provide a smoke screen. The actual release of gas and smoke was to be carried out by men of Foulkes' Special Companies.[49]

The final decision on the use of gas

Haig was inevitably in an anxious mood as the day of the attack approached. Captain Gold, Haig's meteorologist, was initially optimistic. At 9.20 p.m. on 24 September he predicted a fair westerly wind for the following morning. On this basis Haig ordered that the general offensive (with the use of gas) should proceed the next day. On receiving additional weather reports in the small hours of 25 September, however, Gold became less hopeful – though he was slightly more positive at 3 a.m. than he had been an hour earlier. In this atmosphere of uncertainty Haig ordered preparations for a gas release at sunrise (5.50 a.m.) to go ahead, the infantry assault to follow at 6.30.[50]

By 5 a.m. there was a good deal of light and a rainy night was turning into a warm, misty morning. There was some drizzle, but in most parts of the British front (though apparently not in 2nd Division's sector) the heavy rain had ceased. When Haig ventured from his headquarters into the open air he could discern no breeze at all. To gain a clearer indication he asked his senior ADC, Major Alan Fletcher, to light a cigarette. The smoke drifted lazily towards the north-east. A few minutes later the wind seemed to pick up slightly. At about the same time Foulkes gave Haig an assurance that his operators would exercise their judgement. They would not turn on the gas if they could see that in their location, at that particular time, it would be counter-productive. At 5.15 a.m., Haig gave the order "carry on".[51]

The Battle of Loos: 25 September 1915

Haig then climbed a wooden observation tower he had ordered to be built adjacent to his headquarters. He was evidently still racked with doubt. At the top of the tower the air was so still that he considered aborting the attack. One of his staff telephoned I Corps HQ to ask if this were still possible, but was apparently told that it was too late. (This seems rather odd. The most elaborate and careful arrangements had been made to ensure the rapid passage of a message in just such an eventuality.) But Haig seems to have accepted that the die was now cast. At 5.50 a.m. the gas was turned on. The artillery began an intense pounding of the German front line system. At 6.30 a.m. the infantry began its assault.[52]

As some protection against the gas Haig's infantry wore "smoke helmets" – crude gas masks consisting of flannel bags with eye-sockets made of transparent talc. As the infantry were supposed to advance behind the gas cloud rather than within it, the flannel was not initially pulled down over the face. But once this adjustment was made, as it would sometimes have to be, vision was restricted and all forms of communication became difficult. When properly secured around the user's head the "helmet" did offer some protection against gas. It was, however, almost equally proof against air, so that even if not gassed, the user tended to suffocate.[53]

Though some Germans later claimed that they strongly suspected that a British attack was in the offing (and though some claimed that they suspected a gas attack) the British infantry attack on 25 September seems to have enjoyed a significant degree of surprise. The feebleness of First Army's artillery bombardment compared with that on the front of the French Tenth Army to the right may have convinced the German higher command that nothing very serious was intended in this sector. The bombardment was indeed so weak that it is difficult to account for any of the attackers having had any success at all without taking some account of both surprise and the gas. But the gas behaved differently in different parts of the front. Everywhere it caused some problems. As soon as the primitive and defective delivery apparatus was switched on it leaked into First Army's trenches. The worst affected were often its operators, the men of the Special Companies, but in some sectors the infantry also seriously suffered from it.[54]

The 2nd Division, attacking astride the La Bassée Canal on the left wing of Gough's I Corps (and thus on the far left of the main effort), was

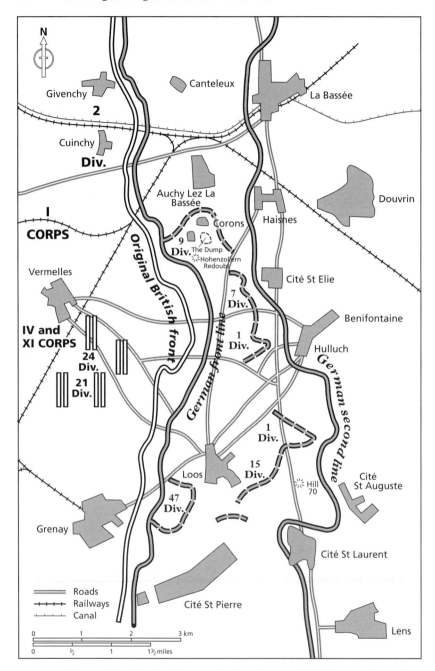

Map 10. The Battle of Loos: the situation at nightfall on 25 September 1915

particularly unfortunate with its gas. One of its battalions recorded that: "The air was practically motionless, with the result that the gas hung back considerably, and in our part of the line did more harm to our men than to the enemy." The officer commanding 6th Infantry Brigade of this division, realising the likely effects, actually refused to allow its gas to be turned on until given a direct order to do so by divisional headquarters. When the gas was released, the effects were as he had predicted. Over considerable parts of the 2nd Division's front of attack, moreover, the German wire was found intact. The division suffered a complete defeat. There was virtually no gain of ground and 2,234 of its members were reported killed, wounded or missing.[55]

Further south I Corps had rather more success. The 9th (Scottish) Division, a Territorial formation, would eventually become perhaps the most proficient, successful and admired division in the army. Loos was its first major action. Its fortunes on 25 September were very mixed, but overall its achievement was remarkable. The 28th Brigade, attacking on the left, next to the 2nd Division, was repelled from a German position known as the Madagascar trench with very heavy casualties. The 26th Brigade, on the right, however, overran the Hohenzollern Redoubt (thought to be the strongest first-line position attacked on this day) Fosse 8 and the Dump, and even got into "Pekin Trench" in front of the village of Haines in the German second-line trench system. At nightfall this brigade retained most of its gains, though it had been forced out of the German second line. The 7th Division, on the far right of Gough's I Corps, was that corps' most successful. It overran the German first-line positions practically right across its attack sector, but sustained heavy casualties in the process. It was not able to make serious penetration into the German second-line system – being stopped short of the fortified villages of Hulluch and Cité St Elie.[56]

The 1st Division, which was the northernmost division of Rawlinson's IV Corps, attacked virtually in the centre of the main British effort. The division had 1st Brigade on the left, 2nd Brigade on the right and 3rd Brigade in reserve. The 1st Brigade overran the German first line, though suffering heavy casualties in the process. It penetrated as far as the German second-line defensive system in front of the fortified village of Hulluch. But it made only very small indents into that system and these could not be maintained.[57]

A sudden adverse change in wind direction, almost as soon as the gas was turned on, caused significant casualties to 2nd Brigade and somewhat disrupted its advance. This was only the beginning of the brigade's problems. The German front line was immediately behind the crest of a ridge and had been undamaged by the bombardment. The thick belt of wire in front of it was completely uncut. The 2nd Brigade took heavy casualties and its attack stalled. Attempts to renew the attack led to further casualties, but the brigade remained stuck in No Man's Land. The situation was reported to Rawlinson, the IV Corps commander. He ordered double envelopment of the stubborn German troops in this sector: part of 2nd Brigade going through the gap made by the 15th Division further south, while 3rd Brigade went through the gap 1st Brigade had created to the north. The stalwart defenders of this part of the German front line system, low on ammunition, finally surrendered in mid-afternoon. But a breakdown of battlefield communications resulted in a huge 1,200-yard gap yawning between the two wings of 1st Division by nightfall.[58]

Slightly further south, in the 15th (Scottish) Division's sector, there was considerable initial success. The division had dug saps out into No Man's Land and connected them up to provide jumping-off trenches within 200 yards of the German front line. The preliminary bombardment here had been more successful. Much of the German wire was found cut. The advance was well covered by smoke and the gas in this sector may even have had a positive influence, though this is disputed. Though they suffered heavy casualties in the process, the Scots rapidly overran the German first-line system right across their front. They pushed on into the village of Loos before the Germans there had organised themselves and secured most of it. Many troops then swept on in the direction of Hill 70 – a critical piece of high ground in this sector.

By this stage, however, the Scots had lost many of their officers and NCOs. Their advance, while enthusiastic, became ragged, and many troops lost all sense of direction, turning off to the south rather than continuing to the east. Some troops swept right over Hill 70 and pursued the Germans beyond it. But attempts by various rather ragged groups to break in to the German second-line system resulted in heavy casualties and no lasting success. Hill 70 itself was never really secured. The Germans held a group of houses known as the Dynamitiere on its southern slope, just north of the village of Cité St Laurent. From there they were able to direct an intense rifle and machine gun fire onto much of the southern and eastern part of the hill. The eastern slopes were also swept by fire, including that of artillery, from the direction of Cité St Auguste. The division held only western parts of Hill 70 at nightfall.[59]

Meanwhile 47th Division, at the southern end of the British line, executed a limited attack designed to protect the right flank of IV Corps. The division was luckier with the gas than other formations and enjoyed an effective smoke screen provided by two batteries of Stokes mortars. It successfully anchored the southern end of the British line on a sort of slagheap embankment called the Double Crassier. In the confusion of battle, however, something of a gap developed between it and the 15th Division immediately to the south of the village of Loos.[60]

Haig, who had reluctantly ordered this great assault, the biggest in British military history up to this point, had lost all control of it as soon as it started. Despite his wooden tower, he was unable to gain much idea of the course of events. Mist and rain and low cloud reduced visibility for most of the day. The Royal Flying Corps had been largely blind. Haig's picture of events depended on reports sent back by his infantry. These initially gave an exaggerated idea of the successes achieved and little idea of the seriousness of the casualties. Haig apparently believed, in mid-to-late morning, that he was on the cusp of a great victory. It was a complete misreading of the battle.[61] But even the emergence of a great deal of evidence to the contrary over the next few hours would not shift him from it.

Soon after 7 a.m. Haig sent a message to Sir John French to have XI Corps ready to advance. At the same time he ordered the 3rd Cavalry Division to move to Vaudricourt. At 8.45 a.m. a staff officer from GHQ arrived at First Army's Advanced HQ at Hinges to congratulate Haig on the apparently good progress of the attack. Haig sent him back with a demand that French release XI Corps to him immediately. French quickly agreed to release the 21st and 24th Divisions to Haig, but retained the Guards Division under his own control. The two divisions now placed under Haig's command had arrived on the Western Front a fortnight previously. They "had received only four months of hurried training in England, had only a slight leaven of regular officers and non-commissioned officers, and were now coming into action for the first time". According to an authoritative source, Haig had promised both Haking, the XI Corps commander, and the two divisional commanders that the divisions would not be put in "unless and until the Germans [were] completely smashed and retiring in disorder". The two divisions "had been given to understand that all that was required of them would be a long march in pursuit of a demoralised enemy".[62]

At 2.35 p.m. Haig ordered Lieutenant-General Richard Haking, commanding XI Corps, to push the 21st and 24th Divisions into what he believed was a gap between Hulluch and Cité St Auguste and thence through to the Haute Deule Canal. In terms of what was actually happening on the ground these orders made no sense. The German second-line position between the places mentioned was essentially intact. The divisions were, moreover, still miles behind the front. In their inexperience, and in the absence of proper guides and proper traffic control, they kept getting lost or obstructed by other troops moving around in First Army's rear.

4. The Battle of Loos. British troops advance to the attack through a cloud of poison gas. With the permission of The Trustees of the Imperial War Museum, London.

The bulk of these divisions arrived at what were meant to be their positions of deployment before going into battle, east of the Vermelles–Grenay road, only in late afternoon and some not until after 6 p.m. They were further exhausted by a day's ill-directed marching, much of it in the rain. Their physical state and morale were not improved by the fact some units had not been properly fed. After 6.10 p.m. the main bodies of these divisions, responding to orders from their corps commander, Lieutenant-General Richard Haking, attempted to execute a night march as far the Hulluch–Lens road. Haking indicated that they were to attack the German second line that very night and exploit to the Haute Deule Canal and beyond. Later orders from Haig indicated that the assault should be postponed until dawn. For the inexperienced troops, however, the night march, in torrential rain, was in itself a ghastly experience. They had little real idea of where they were going, or of what lay in front of them.[63]

In the absence of infantry reserves Haig had, at 12.30 p.m., ordered the 3rd Cavalry Division into action near the centre of the main attack sector. Had this order been executed, it might have made the charge of the Light Brigade at Balaclava and the charge of the 21st Lancers at Omdurman look like rational operations of war in comparison. Major-General C.J. Briggs, however, declined to be a latter-day Lord Cardigan. He had earlier personally ridden forward to the divisional HQs of 7th, 1st and 15th Divisions. He thought that Haig's perception of the situation was far too sanguine. According to the official history, Briggs told Haig that "the situation did not admit of immediate compliance, but that he would move forward when the opportunity offered". Needless to say, almost no reasonable opportunity for mounted action presented itself that day.[64]

The results of Haig's operations of 25 September are not difficult to summarise. The minor operations by III Corps and the Indian Corps north of the La Bassée Canal had achieved practically nothing, at a cost of about 5,000 casualties. The main attack had (rather surprisingly in view of the paucity of the artillery support and the counter-productive effects of the gas over much of the front) successfully overrun the enemy first-line defensive system right across the front except in the 2nd Division sector in the north. No significant penetration into the German second-line system had been made at any point, and the losses, in relation to numbers engaged, were worse than those of the more notorious 1 July 1916 – the "first day on the Somme".[65]

A conservative estimate is that 470 officers and 15,000 other ranks were killed, wounded or missing – about one-sixth of those engaged. German casualties for this particular day are not known. While several German counter-attacks were shot to pieces, it still seems probable that German losses were less than half those of the British. British losses amongst senior officers were particularly serious. Nine Lieutenant Colonels (or acting Lieutenant Colonels) were killed and twelve wounded. The Germans still occupied a second-line system that was well constructed, properly wired and little damaged by British artillery. The positions Haig's forces held that night were, on the other hand, distinctly insecure. There had been little time to entrench properly. The British front was ragged and there were big holes in it. The largest was a 1,500-yard gap between the two wings of 1st Division. In the confusion of the battle, Major-General Holland, the divisional commander, and his superiors were unaware that this existed and it is not even mentioned in the report on operations given by IV Corps.[66]

The ragged nature of the British front mattered greatly because, as GHQ's intelligence had predicted, substantial German reinforcements (some twenty-two battalions – about two divisions) arrived on the battlefield within twenty-four hours of the start of the attack. There were as many German troops holding the second-line system at nightfall on 25 September as had been holding the first-line system the previous morning. The six British divisions that had attacked on 25 September were, of course, nearing exhaustion. The two new arrivals, 21st and 24th Divisions, were, owing to confused command arrangements and staff work, almost equally tired. Unlike the German arrivals, the British reserves were so inexperienced that they could hardly be expected to achieve much of significance.[67]

Yet the British First Army's performance on 25 September looked good in comparison with that of the French Tenth Army to its right. Most of the attack of General d'Urbal's Army had failed. His troops had generally managed to cross the German front line. Except on the far left, near the British, however, they had been subsequently beaten back. This failure occurred despite the very much stronger artillery of d'Urbal's Army compared with Haig's and the much more intensive preliminary bombardment that had been undertaken. In contrast with the British, the French in Artois had achieved no surprise at all. They found that their bombardment had proved relatively ineffective owing to the weather. Much of the German wire was uncut and German first-line positions on Vimy Ridge were held in considerable strength.[68]

The second day: 26 September 1915

During the afternoon of 25 September 1915, General Sixt von Armin of the German IV Corps had ordered counter-attacks and these started to happen that night. The most successful, mounted at approximately 1 a.m. on 26 September, struck troops of the British 7th Division in the position known as "The Quarries". The last British troops were forced out some time after 2 a.m., after being heavily shelled by their own artillery, which believed that the position had been abandoned.[69] The 21st and 24th Divisions of XI Corps, as we have seen, came onto the battlefield during the night, between the 1st Division and the 15th Division, in the IV Corps area. Haig's orders for 26 September, confirmed at 11.30 p.m. on 25 September, were that XI Corps should mount a four-brigade attack the following day between Hulluch and Loos. Meanwhile, 1st Division would renew its attempts to capture Hulluch, and the 15th Division, assisted by 62nd Brigade (of the 21st Division), would attempt to retake Hill 70.[70]

In retrospect these orders, especially those given to XI Corps, look absurdly overoptimistic. But having become overexcited on 25 September, having convinced himself that he was on the cusp of a major victory, Haig could not accept that whatever opportunity might once have existed had now passed. Others did appreciate this. At some time after 9 p.m. on 25 September, Major-General McCracken, of 15th Division, expressed grave doubts that his troops (now severely depleted and desperately tired) were in any state to retake Hill 70. Rawlinson, at IV Corps, overruled him, insisting that 15th Division renew its attack at 9 a.m. the following morning. Lieutenant-General Richard Haking of XI Corps, already having a reputation as a "thruster", did nothing to dampen Haig's overenthusiasm or to limit its destructive effects on his troops.[71]

First Army's attacks of 26 September all failed, some of them catastrophically. The 1st Division was easily repelled from Hulluch. The attack on the German second line by some elements of the 24th Division and the 21st Division between Hulluch and the Bois Hugo, commencing at approximately 11 a.m., was shot to pieces. Elements of the 21st Division had already been hit by a German counter-attack through the Bois Hugo, which developed at approximately 10 a.m., and thus took no part in the assault on the German second-line system. The 24th and 21st Divisions lost some 8,200 men in the course of the day, and large sections fell back in a state of disorder that, at least in some instances, amounted to rout. The 15th Division failed in its efforts to retake Hill 70. German counter-attacks put some elements of the division to flight. In the late morning Rawlinson had some reason to believe that this Division would disintegrate and that the village of Loos would be lost. He demanded reinforcements. Haig sent the 6th Cavalry Brigade of Brigg's 3rd Cavalry Division to Loos. By nightfall the remnants of 15th Division had rallied and the situation had stabilised.[72]

The 24th Division and the 21st Division were in such a state of shock and demoralisation by the night of 26 September that it was imperative to take them off the battlefield without delay. The Guards Division, the one remaining division of XI Corps, started to arrive on the battlefield during the afternoon, and enabled the two shattered divisions of Kitchener's Army to be pulled out. The balance of the 3rd Cavalry Division joined the 6th Cavalry Brigade in the Loos/Hill 70 sector that night, where it relieved the almost equally shattered 15th Division.[73]

The rest of the battle

After 26 September even Haig seems to have had little hope of break-through. Under pressure from GHQ and the French high command, however, First Army continued to mount limited attacks intended to help pin down German troops in Artois while Joffre continued with his bigger offensive in Champagne. But First Army made no significant gain of ground for the rest of the battle. Indeed, the Germans retook some of the ground they had lost on 25 September, regaining the Hohenzollern Redoubt in intense fighting between 1 and 3 October. Though British offensive efforts petered out after 13 October, when a final assault proved a bloody and practically unmitigated failure, the battle was not finally declared over until 4 November.[74]

Outcome and assessment

British casualties in the battle as a whole are estimated at about 50,000. There were over 6,000 confirmed fatalities with another 16,000 or so missing, a high proportion of which must be assumed killed. German casualties were almost certainly less than half those of the British. The Germans seem to have suffered fewer than 5,000 fatalities: probably less than a third of the British. Even in terms of pure attrition, therefore, Loos must be reckoned a British defeat.[75]

The Battle of Loos was launched because the British needed to prove to their allies (both Russian and French) that they were prepared to make serious offensive efforts on the Western Front. At least to begin with, Haig was pushed into mounting an offensive in the Loos sector against his better judgement. Recent scholarship tends to suggest that Sir John French never believed in the likelihood of a breakthrough at Loos.[76] GHQ's orders for the offensive, indeed, gave Haig some latitude. They did not force him to "go for broke" in pursuit of a breakthrough. Rather they allowed him, if he considered it more prudent, to adopt the "step-by-step" approach that Robertson, as Chief of the General Staff, had been advocating since February.[77]

Haig, however, was probably not much concerned with French's intentions for the offensive. He knew that Sir John was largely discredited in the eyes of his superiors and, as commander-in-chief, was living on borrowed time.[78] It seems to have been Kitchener's instructions (oral rather than written) rather than French's that Haig took seriously. Yet the fact remains that had Haig interpreted those instructions with greater sophistication and discretion he could have avoided the worst disasters of 26 September. Kitchener had, in effect, told Haig that, in order to save the wartime alliance, he had to undertake an offensive that *looked serious* to Britain's allies, even at the expense of a good deal of British blood.[79] By nightfall on 25 September Haig had done what was necessary in this respect, at least for the time being. His First Army had done better than the much stronger French Tenth Army to its right, the efforts of which it was meant to be supporting. Before Haig gave his final orders on the night of 25 September, he knew that General d'Urbal's attack had made little progress.[80] It would have been sensible to conclude that now was the time to consolidate the day's gains.

The real problem was that, during the planning phase, Haig had forced himself to believe that his offensive could be much more than a bloody gesture of solidarity with allies. He had convinced himself that it might result in a dramatic breakthrough and have a profound effect on the strategic situation on the Western Front. When bits of good news arrived at his Hinges headquarters on the morning of 25 September, Haig began to believe that his most optimistic forecasts were coming true. Despite the strong evidence to the contrary, which came pouring in for the rest of the day, Haig could not get it out of his head that he was on the cusp of a tremendous victory. He continued to give orders based on this erroneous reading of the battle. Thus the bloody gesture of alliance solidarity on which Kitchener had insisted became, under Haig's direction, much bloodier and more self-destructive than was really necessary.

8   Commander-in-chief

Aftermath of a debacle

By nightfall on 26 September 1915 Haig's attempt to use the 21st and 24th Divisions to achieve a complete breakthrough at Loos had proved a bloody and humiliating fiasco. His orders to First Army on the night of 25 September had been based on a complete misreading of the battle – a massive error of judgement.[1] Within a few days London was buzzing with rumours of the ensuing debacle and these were causing the gravest concern to the Prime Minister.[2] Haig, however, was neither sacked nor censured. Indeed, the controversy that followed the debacle worked to his benefit. In mid-December he was promoted to command the largest army his country had ever put in the field. How can this bizarre turn of events be explained?

Sir John French's vulnerability

Part of the explanation certainly lies in the extreme weakness of Sir John French's position as commander-in-chief. Overripe to fall long before Loos, his incompetence had, indeed, become fairly obvious within the first month of war. Since Kitchener had overridden his decision to pull the BEF out of the battle on 1 September 1914, relations between them, never easy, had often been difficult in the extreme.[3] Yet given that other members of the Cabinet found working with the taciturn, imperious Kitchener difficult,[4] French's awkward relationship with him need not, in itself, have proved fatal. Both ministers and the Palace were, however, also aware of serious doubts about French within his command.[5] After a conversation with Sir William Robertson, the widely respected Chief of the General Staff at GHQ, the King had concluded as early as 1 July 1915 that French must be replaced.[6]

Sir John French had done himself no favours by helping to initiate, through Charles a Court Repington of *The Times* and other press contacts, the notorious "shell scandal" of May 1915. French almost certainly

5. Field Marshal Sir John French. With the permission of The Trustees of the Imperial War Museum, London.

intended this as an attack on Kitchener.[7] But it was a blunt instrument, severely embarrassing to the government as a whole. For a commander-in-chief to attack the government he served was certainly improper by the normal rules of the game. Though the Prime Minister did not immediately and openly turn against French, he seems to have been added to the lengthening list of important people seriously disillusioned with the commander-in-chief.[8]

Like French, Haig had serious concerns about Kitchener's role in the war effort. Haig believed that Kitchener did not make proper use of the General Staff in the War Office and seems to have blamed him, to some degree, for allowing the development of pernicious side-shows, most notably the campaign at the Dardanelles.[9] Haig, however, was vastly more discreet than his immediate superior. He avoided all confrontation with Kitchener and, in contrast with French, had always adopted a deeply respectful attitude when dealing with the Secretary of State in person.[10] Kitchener may not altogether have trusted Haig, but he was prepared to use him against French, encouraging him privately to report any disquiet he had about French's handling of the army at the front.[11]

Haig, French and the informal inquest on Loos: Late September–mid-October 1915

Haig had reacted to the disastrous day of battle on 26 September 1915 with far greater political skill than Sir John French. Haig quickly realised that there was no possibility of denying that there had been a disaster. It was only a matter of who got the blame. Haig was determined it would not be him and French was the obvious candidate. Haig wrote to Kitchener on 29 September giving his version of events. The first point on which he insisted was that a tremendous, decisive victory had been narrowly missed on 25 September. "My attack was ... a complete success. The enemy had no troops in his second line, which some of my plucky fellows reached and entered without opposition ... We *were* in position to make this the turning point of the war." Haig's second point was that the loss of this golden opportunity was entirely owing to Sir John French, who had held the reserves too far back and not released them soon enough.[12] Haig to a large extent set the agenda for the subsequent debate on Loos, focusing attention on the alleged (and almost certainly mythical) lost opportunity of 25 September as a way of diverting attention from the real (and completely avoidable) debacle of 26 September.

Over the next few weeks Haig made these same points to Sir John French, Leo Rothschild, Lord Haldane, the King and his own corps commanders.[13] But consistency was practically the only virtue of Haig's case. It never became clear when and where had been the gaping hole in the German defences that Haig supposed the two reserve divisions could have gone through. In a report to GHQ on 3 October Haig suggested that it had been in the 15th Division's sector, but as GHQ's reply on 16 October pointed out, the evidence was against this. The non-existence of any substantial gap in the German defences has been confirmed by the most serious scholarship of the last couple of decades.[14] Yet it is not clear that Haig was consciously lying or deliberately presenting a distorted version of events to preserve his own reputation and damage that of someone else. Deceit and hypocrisy of that sort are, of course, the small change of career politics in many walks of life and Haig may have been guilty of them on occasion. But his predominant fault, and probably the one most relevant here, was rather different, and, for those under his command, much more serious. He had developed a remarkable facility for closing his mind to things he did not want to accept and for making himself believe what he wanted to believe.

It was French's incompetence (political as much as military) that allowed Haig to get away with this. Unlike Haig, he failed to report promptly to Kitchener that things had gone seriously awry in the early stages of the Loos battle. When Kitchener wrote to him on 6 October requesting French's version of the debacle of 26 September, French was evasive, indeed almost dismissive. In response to Kitchener's request for information on the notoriously mismanaged approach march of the 21st and 24th Divisions, French replied that he had seen these formations on the road and had noted their enthusiasm, discipline and soldierly bearing. He had taken the assurance of General Haking, the XI Corps commander, that they were well fed and properly rested.[15]

Over the next few weeks French made some silly, easily exposed mistakes in the presentation of his own case over Loos. Yet he (or his staff) also pinpointed some of the weaknesses in Haig's version of events, casting doubt, in particular, on whether there had been any real breakthrough on 25 September.[16] But by that time it was too late. French's ludicrously inadequate response to Kitchener's initial inquiry had practically doomed his chances of remaining in command. The (essentially correct) impression that French had lost his grip had become too firmly fixed in the minds of too many important people in London and the movement to get rid of him had become unstoppable.[17]

Haig's version of events did not, in fact, convince everyone. Richard Haldane, now no longer serving in the government, went to France on the Prime Minister's behalf to speak to both French and Haig about Loos. He and Haig conferred at First Army HQ at Hinges on 7 October. The former Lord Chancellor reported that French and GHQ were not to blame. Haldane appears to have wished to scapegoat neither French nor Haig. He presented failure at Loos as symptomatic of the national unreadiness for a war of this magnitude and suggested that blame needed to be shared much more widely. This was a philosophical way of looking at a military reverse. It had a good deal of validity. But it was not the sort of answer likely to find any favour in the crisis atmosphere of October 1915 and Asquith soon set it aside. Though he was characteristically slow to act, the Prime Minister seems to have decided by mid-October that French had to go.[18]

Sir William Robertson, Chief of the General Staff at GHQ, was in London in mid-October to give the GHQ view on strategic matters. Attending ministerial meetings there, he avoided (according to his own account) discussing French's fitness for command, despite much probing. In a subsequent telephone conversation with the King's secretary, Lord Stamfordham, and in an interview with the King himself, he was directly asked whether it was time for French to go. Even then he would not commit himself. Apparently he wanted to be sure of Haig's support and was not yet certain that the First Army commander was committed to Sir John French's overthrow.[19]

Robertson, Haig and the attack on French: Mid-October–early November 1915

Upon his return to France, Robertson paid a visit to First Army's HQ. There, on 17 October, he talked to Haig about the prospects for removing French. Haig indicated that it was not fair to the Empire to retain French in command in the main theatre of operations. He had discussed this issue with his corps commanders and they had agreed with him. Robertson was reassured. Noting that French now had hardly any support in the Cabinet, he declared that he was now clear on how to report to Stamfordham.[20] Haig's account of his conversation with Robertson on 17 October 1915 makes it clear that, by this stage, he was not merely briefing against French to French's superiors. He had also made himself the leader of a conspiracy within the BEF. He was openly discussing the competence of Sir John French with subordinates, commenting adversely upon it and encouraging their endorsement of his opinion. He was, in effect, drawing his corps commanders into a plot to overthrow the commander-in-chief. If someone less well connected had behaved like this, he might reasonably have been accused of gross disloyalty, even mutiny. Haig knew, however, that his was a conspiracy the King would support and that few significant ministers were likely to oppose. If mutiny had support at the highest level, and if it succeeded, then none dare call it mutiny.

The Haig–Robertson connection now became critical. Both officers came from the cavalry. They had known each other for years and seem to have had a degree of mutual respect, though they were not, and never really became, personal friends. Their backgrounds were totally different. William Robertson, whose army nickname was "Wully", was born in Welbourn, Lincolnshire, on 29 January 1860. His origins were humble. Both parents were born out of wedlock. His father was a tailor and postmaster. His mother had been in domestic service. William himself had been a servant for four years before joining the army as a cavalry trooper. He rose from the ranks and was the first ex-ranker to pass Staff College. A considerable linguist, qualified in half-a-dozen Indian tongues, he dropped his aitches and was not always strictly grammatical when he spoke English. He never acquired, and perhaps never wished to affect, all the attitudes that Haig associated with being a "gentleman", and Haig sometimes found his plain, plebeian manner of speaking rather irritating.[21] Yet in mid-October 1915 this unlikely pair formed an uneasy partnership that would last for more than two critical years.

Robertson's and Haig's initial and principal object was to remove French. There was, it is true, some commonality of purpose beyond that. Both officers wanted to assert the authority of the General Staff in the War Office and reduce that of Kitchener. They wanted the British war effort to be concentrated on the Western Front and to prevent the politicians diverting resources to sideshows.[22] In terms of the conduct of operations on the Western Front, however, they had very different ideas. Robertson was an early believer in "step-by-step" offensive methods: supporting a series of short infantry advances with concentrated artillery firepower, and in this way gradually grinding the enemy down. Haig, by contrast, continued to hanker after achieving a rapid breakthrough that would substantially change the strategic situation.[23]

It is likely that Robertson was well aware of this difference of opinion over operational methods before he joined with Haig to remove French. At GHQ in 1915 he was in a good position to evaluate Haig as a field commander and, though he might sometimes pretend to be an uncritical admirer,[24] it is unlikely that he was, in reality, particularly impressed. He was well placed to spot the flaws in Haig's case over Loos, having been involved, as CGS, in presenting GHQ's side of the argument.[25] Robertson's differences with Haig over operational methods would create serious tensions between them during the Somme offensive in 1916, and again during the Arras campaign in spring 1917, and would lead to a very serious breakdown of trust between the two generals in the latter part of that year. But here we are running a long way ahead of the sequence of events, to which it is necessary immediately to return.

In autumn 1915, getting rid of French was, in Robertson's mind, the overriding priority and, whatever reservations he might privately have about Haig, he was more than willing to co-operate with him to bring it about. Lord Esher, an astute observer, thought Robertson would ideally have wished to be commander-in-chief himself.[26] But Robertson apparently reckoned that his lack of experience as a field commander, coupled with Haig's seniority to him in the Army List, would militate against this. In the course of the autumn, therefore, Robertson and Haig seem to have reached an understanding that if they were successful in getting rid of French, Haig would become commander-in-chief, while Robertson would replace Archibald Murray as CIGS.[27]

Once Haig and Robertson began a co-ordinated attack, Sir John French's days as commander-in-chief were numbered. The King decided to intervene personally to resolve the command crisis and it seems clear that he had already practically decided that French had to go. He arrived in France on 21 October, moving into the Chateau de la Jumelle at Aire. Between visiting units, the King arranged to interview senior officers on their views of Sir John French. On Sunday 24 October he saw Haig's corps commanders. Rawlinson, Gough and Haking (in all probability briefed by Haig) united with Haig and Robertson in denouncing their commander-in-chief.[28]

An accident delayed George V's departure from France. On 28 October, while he was inspecting 1st Wing, Royal Flying Corps, at Hesdigneul, the troops' cheers startled the chestnut mare that Haig had lent him. The animal reared, slipped and fell, leaving the King trapped under it. In addition to sustaining very severe bruising, he fractured his pelvis in two places and was in great pain. It was to be weeks before he could walk, even with the aid of sticks. He seems never to have made a complete recovery.[29] Yet Haig's luck held – the King did not blame him for the misbehaviour of his horse. Rather he became still more displeased with Sir John French. Apparently fearful that the Germans might kill his sovereign in an air raid, French wanted to hurry his convalescence, urging a speedy departure for England. However good French's motives, the King, in his agony, did not want to be rushed: "Tell Sir John to go to hell!" was the royal response.[30]

The end of French's command: Early November–mid-December 1915

After he returned home in early November (by a rough Channel crossing that added severe seasickness to his other ills) the King agitated vigorously for French's removal and replacement by Haig.[31] Asquith seems already to have been clear by that stage that French would have to go.[32] By mid-November Haig felt confident enough to discuss the reorganisation of the supreme command with the still-influential Lord Esher, who operated as a sort of unofficial British liaison officer in Paris. Haig told Esher that Robertson should be CIGS and that Kitchener's powers needed to be curtailed.[33] A few days later Haig was in London discussing some of the same issues with Asquith and the Unionist (Conservative) leader, Andrew Bonar Law, who, in May, had entered a coalition government in which Asquith remained Prime Minister.[34] On 25 November Haig recorded in his diary a rumour he had heard from Robertson: French's dismissal was now imminent. The choice of successor lay between Robertson and himself. Robertson indicated that "he of course was quite out of the question and that there was no-one in it but me!".[35] The rumour that French was about to be removed was accurate. But who would replace him was, perhaps, not yet as certain as Robertson self-deprecatingly suggested.

Asquith wanted to handle French's replacement in a gentlemanly manner and to avoid any sort of fuss or scandal. At 5 p.m. on 23 November he had a meeting with Lord Esher, whom he had summoned from Paris. Asquith asked Esher to undertake the sensitive mission of getting French to resign with dignity and without the kind of fuss that might embarrass the government. After spending twenty-four hours considering whether he was willing to undertake what he regarded as a very disagreeable task,

Esher left for France on 25 November. But French proved awkward. Initially refusing to resign,[36] he then tried to set conditions, including the removal of Kitchener as Secretary of State.[37] The King, who, as we have noted, had been pushing hard for French's replacement for some weeks, became impatient. On 2 December Lord Stamfordham wrote to Asquith expressing the King's wish that the matter be settled without further delay.[38] Four days later Asquith wrote to Stamfordham, officially informing the Palace that Sir John had resigned. He was to be made a viscount and given command of Home Forces.[39]

French had actually resigned on 4 December,[40] but it was not until 10 December that Haig received a letter from Asquith, dated two days previously, offering him the command.[41] It seems that, at the point of French's resignation, there was still some debate as to who should succeed him and that Robertson was still being actively considered. Though his opinion no longer really counted, French had suggested Robertson as his successor, and on 4 December, Kitchener told Esher that he believed that the government intended to make Robertson commander-in-chief.[42] Asquith's letter to Stamfordham on 6 December 1915, however, stated:

He [French] suggests Robertson as his successor but I assume that we shall have to take Haig. K [Kitchener] and I both agree that Robertson should become CIGS here.[43]

This indicates little positive enthusiasm, on Asquith's part, for Haig as commander-in-chief. Robertson may, indeed, have lost the chance of the top job in France mainly because he was thought to be a far better choice than Haig for CIGS, rather than because the government was particularly keen to have Haig at GHQ. As one historian has put it:

Though suited for either position Wully was known best to the ministers for providing with decisiveness and clarity his views on military questions. Haig, on the other hand, was thought to be a poor choice as CIGS. The last thing the government needed was another incoherent military adviser.[44]

The King had, as we have seen, been involved in the command crisis throughout and royal pressure may have been one of the factors making Asquith think that he would "have to take Haig". On 14 December the King hinted to the Cabinet Secretary, Maurice Hankey, that it was he who had finally settled the matters both of French's removal and of his replacement.[45]

Haig's state of mind on becoming commander-in-chief

At noon on 19 December 1915 Haig succeeded French as Commander-in-Chief of the British Expeditionary Force.[46] Ambition had been the driving force of Haig's adult life. Inevitably he found his new status, as commander of the largest army his country had ever placed in the field, gratifying. Its attainment had, as we have noted, involved him in organising a conspiracy against a superior officer whom he had known for many years and whom he had once counted as a friend. It had meant denying (apparently to himself as much as anyone else) his personal responsibility for a major military debacle. Yet if there was the slightest twinge of conscience about any of this, his diaries and letters do not reveal it. If he was at all concerned that he might now duplicate, on a larger scale, disasters such as Aubers Ridge and the second day of Loos, there was no indication of that either. So little self-doubt did he display that one might think he had gained the command after a run of brilliant victories.[47]

His self-righteousness (when such an attitude was unwarranted) and his apparent self-assurance (when his competence was much open to question) are, for the modern student, amongst Haig's least appealing qualities. Yet his maintenance of an air of great composure and confidence for most of his period as commander-in-chief, was found by some contemporaries to be enormously reassuring, indeed inspiring. Some subordinates seem have become devoted to him largely as a result of this.[48] In boyhood Haig had, as we have noted, learned to exercise a high degree of control over a somewhat turbulent nature. Rather obsessive about his health, he was devoted to diet and exercise regimes and, most unusually for a man of his generation, gave up tobacco early in adult life. Since early manhood he had also been enormously fastidious about his appearance. All this rigorous self-control helped him put on a "mask of command",[49] making him seem composed even when he was deeply troubled.

Haig manifested no outward signs of being mentally or spiritually troubled when he assumed overall command on the Western Front – quite the contrary. But he now faced truly awesome responsibilities. It seems that the maintenance of his composure and self-belief now required more than just inner strength. He needed to draw heavily upon outside sources of comfort, reassurance and support. An uncritically admiring wife had reinforced his self-belief for many years. An equally adulatory older sister had been a crucial source of encouragement throughout his career. Royal favour also assisted him, as did the support of other prominent national figures. Yet, by the middle of this war, Haig seems to have required even more psychological sustenance than these sources could provide. He got it from religion.

This was no road to Damascus. Haig always tended to endorse the conventional values of his upbringing. Patriotism, support for the Empire and loyalty to the monarchy were amongst these. But so were officially approved versions of Christianity: his mother's Presbyterianism and the

6. General Sir Douglas Haig. With the permission of The Trustees of the
Imperial War Museum, London.

muscular Anglicanism of an English public school. Though he had also consulted fortune-tellers and spiritualist mediums, he had never renounced traditional Christian belief. Some observers assumed that his regular church parade attendance was merely a matter of military duty.[50] But it is not inconceivable that, even before the First World War, Haig's personal piety was somewhat more profound than was generally realised. The 1914 campaign was, perhaps, too hectic to allow much time for spiritual contemplation. But, at its end, Haig began to feel a "Higher Power" directing his destiny.[51]

There is some evidence of religious feeling growing on Haig in the course of 1915. At Christmas he heard a sermon by the Anglican Bishop of Khartoum, the Right Rev. L.H. Gwynne. Impressed, he had it printed and distributed to the troops.[52] But the most important experience in Haig's religious life at this period was his initial encounter with the earnest young clergyman George Duncan, whom he heard preach at the Scottish Church on 2 January 1916. Duncan's message was not theologically profound: "The nation is now learning to pray and nothing can withstand the prayers of a great united people." "Whatever your work is do it well and have God always with you."[53] The assurances that God was on the side of the British people, that he would listen to their prayers rather than anyone else's, and would aid each individual in his contribution to the war effort, were, however, exactly what Haig wanted to hear.

From this point onward Haig would regularly attend the Scottish church rather than any other: an expression both of his particular admiration for Duncan and of the increasingly personal nature of his religious experience.[54] Writing in 1918, Charteris, often an astute and not entirely an uncritical observer of Haig, believed that:

> He came to regard himself with almost Calvinistic faith as the predestined instrument of Providence for the achievement of victory for the British Armies. His abundant self-reliance was reinforced by this conception of himself as the child of destiny.[55]

Key appointments under Haig

With his appointment as commander-in-chief in France, Haig became one of the most important figures directing the British war effort. But Kitchener was still at the War Office and, though the Secretary of State for War's powers were greatly reduced after Robertson became CIGS, it was quickly brought home to Haig that his authority over the army he commanded had its limits.

As Haig left his old HQ at Hinges, Rawlinson temporarily took command of the First Army. However, Kitchener did not accept Haig's recommendation that Rawlinson should hold that position on a permanent basis.[56] Instead Rawlinson merely kept the job warm for General Sir Charles Monro. Having gone to the Dardanelles in October, Monro had taken command there from General Ian Hamilton and had soon decided to evacuate the Gallipoli peninsula. He executed this manoeuvre with considerable skill (practically the only part of the campaign that was so executed), and by 4 February was back in France, commanding Haig's old Army.[57] Yet Rawlinson, who had played a considerable role in the campaign to unseat French and to promote Haig, did not have long to wait for his reward. The very next day he was appointed to command the newly created Fourth Army.[58]

The General Staff component of GHQ at St Omer underwent something of a revolution at the end of 1915. Within a few days of Haig's takeover, some of the most experienced and capable officers at GHQ had left for London. Robertson, as Haig had recommended, succeeded Sir Archibald Murray as CIGS. Robertson took with him his sub-chief of the General Staff at GHQ, Robert Whigham, who became Deputy CIGS. Frederick Maurice, the operations chief at GHQ, who some considered Robertson's *alter ego*, became Director of Military Operations at the War Office. George Macdonogh, head of the intelligence branch at GHQ, became Director of Military Intelligence at the War Office. Removing all of these key people at the same time seems to have been a serious mistake. Well-informed contemporaries came to believe that none who replaced them had the same strength of character and independence of mind. But Haig seems to have raised no objection to their leaving. Those who replaced them (often dismissed by the wider army as compliant but mediocre) appear to have been the sorts of subordinate whom Haig was most comfortable to have in his immediate entourage.[59]

Haig wanted to replace Robertson with his First Army chief of staff, Major-General Richard Butler. Again Kitchener overruled him, considering Butler too junior. Instead the War Office sent Lieutenant-General Sir Launcelot Kiggell,[60] for whom Haig had, in any case, been trying to find a suitable position in France for some time. Kiggell had served under Haig when the latter was Director of Staff Duties in the War Office. Haig privately attributed to Kiggell a lot of the detailed work for which he had gained credit. Later Kiggell became commandant of the Staff College at Camberley. Undoubtedly he was, in a narrow sense, an efficient staff officer. Yet he was slow to develop independent ideas, lacking in self-confidence and much in awe of Haig.[61]

Butler became Deputy CGS, while John Charteris, who had been Haig's intelligence chief at First Army, replaced Macdonogh at GHQ. Brigadier-General J.H. "Tavish" Davidson, whom Haig also brought with him from

First Army, replaced Maurice at the Operations branch.[62] There was no prospect of Haig and Henry Wilson working effectively together in the same headquarters on a long-term basis. Wilson left his GHQ job as liaison officer with the French and went to command IV Corps in Artois, replacing Rawlinson in that position.[63]

The nature of Haig's new job

We have established that being commander-in-chief did not give Haig absolute control over the British army in France. Kitchener, as Secretary of State for War, could still decide some of the senior appointments made in the BEF. The Prime Minister and the Cabinet, of course, made grand strategy, with advice from the Admiralty, the War Office and occasionally from Haig himself. They had the final say on the distribution of troops between the United Kingdom, the Western Front and other theatres. Controlling the allocation of forces to Haig meant that they could, if they chose, exercise a good deal of control over the nature of the operations he undertook. So what exactly did it mean to be commander-in-chief of the BEF? What was the nature of Haig's authority and how did he exercise it?

Part of his function was to preside over a large and complex administrative apparatus. As one historian has put it:

The C-in-C was ... principal director of Britain's newest and greatest corporate enterprise, comparable in size to the administration of the largest city in the Kingdom (with the sole exception of London), the governance of which was the more delicate since it was based within a jealous and suspicious foreign state.[64]

In addition to planning operations, disseminating military doctrine and organising training, GHQ kept the vast army fed, clothed and supplied with weapons, ammunition, fresh manpower, horses, mules, fodder, motor vehicles, fuel, petrol, barbed wire, bandages and everything else it needed. It ran a postal service, organised hospitals and medical services and managed a transport network in rear areas that included canals as well as railways and road transport. The transportation system would ultimately be unable to cope with the demands of the Somme campaign in 1916 and would require a radical overhaul. But, for most of the war, most aspects of this administration were conducted remarkably well and this was reflected in the BEF's remarkably high standards of hygiene, nutrition and health.[65] Much of this administrative work went on from day to day without any personal intervention from Haig. He was, however, well aware of it through his regular programme of visits to all kinds of units. Haig owed his pre-war reputation very largely to his effectiveness as a staff officer and military administrator. These were roles of which he had greater experience before 1914 than he did of field command, and for which he perhaps possessed greater aptitude.[66]

Dealing with British and (less frequently) Dominion statesmen and other civilians of power and influence was practically a daily activity. Some of this work was done through correspondence but (at least with British VIPs) quite a lot was conducted in person. Some of it involved the formulation of strategy – Haig discussed major issues such as the introduction of conscription, the campaign in Salonika and the mounting of an offensive on the Somme with members of the Cabinet, sometimes at GHQ and sometimes in London. On occasion he was required to give his strategic opinions at formal meetings of ministers.[67]

But much of the time Haig spent personally dealing with politicians and other important civilians was really in the nature of public relations. Politicians, press barons and various other celebrities visited GHQ in droves. Haig was generally expected to spend some time with each of them.[68] Naturally he tried to limit this, both because he was busy with other matters and because he was not a good conversationalist. Social connections with the royal family and with other members of the British elite had helped Haig's career considerably. But before he became commander-in-chief, he had never had to concern himself with what the masses thought of him, and he seems to have had a degree of prejudice against journalists and the press. But his instinct for self-preservation and for the defence of his own interests to some degree overcame this prejudice. While he only rarely granted interviews to journalists, his staff did a good deal of press liaison work. Sir Philip Sassoon, Haig's private secretary, sometimes dealt with newspaper proprietors on Haig's behalf. John Charteris organised and ran a GHQ press liaison, public relations and propaganda machine, a function he combined (rather inappropriately) with that of intelligence chief. This work could not have proceeded without Haig's tacit approval.[69]

Haig's responsibilities obviously included deciding (in conjunction with the War Office, the British Cabinet and with allies) the strategic attitude to be adopted by the British army on the Western Front – whether defensive or offensive. He also had to decide how much of the Western Front the BEF was to hold and, if it were to mount major attacks, where these were to be made. It was Haig's decision as to which of his Armies should be committed to any operation and what troops (within the BEF in France and Flanders) should be allocated to each Army. To a large extent it was also his responsibility to decide the objectives of any major operation and to co-ordinate activities between the different Armies involved. In none of these areas, however, was Haig's authority absolute. The Prime

Minister, with the backing of the Cabinet, had the authority to intervene, overruling the commander-in-chief.[70] In the final analysis he had (as Asquith had already proved) the authority to dismiss the commander-in-chief, if he believed the national interest demanded it.

During the detailed planning for a campaign and once a campaign was in progress, the extent to which the commander-in-chief should tell his Army commanders how to achieve their missions seems to have been far from clear to Haig. His military education had taught him that a devolved style of command was preferable. "The Commander-in-Chief should only set out the strategic objectives – the details and execution ... should be left to subordinates."[71] But such a style obviously works best when subordinates are experienced and highly competent. One of the characteristics of the British army at this period was that it was expanding so rapidly that some senior officers were being promoted at a hyper-accelerated rate. Officers became corps commanders before having really proved themselves as divisional commanders, and in some cases became Army commanders before demonstrating their competence at corps level.[72] In these circumstances a devolved command style might be thought inappropriate. Arguably, more direction from the top was required.

A further difficulty, however, was that Haig's own career offered one of the most conspicuous examples of over-accelerated advancement. He had become an Army commander with a mixed record as a corps commander and commander-in-chief with (at least after Neuve Chapelle) a distinctly dismal record as an Army commander. Under Haig's command First Army had suffered 281,006 casualties for extremely limited gains and had suffered "a series of clear tactical defeats". In his previous appointments he had shown only limited signs of being able to deal with the intellectual challenges posed by the new type of war encountered on the Western Front. On the Somme, his first major campaign as commander-in-chief, Haig seems initially to have been uncertain about when to delegate and when to intervene.[73] He would actually intervene a great deal but, in doing so, would sometimes prove blinder than the one-eyed men he ruled.

GHQ: Montreuil and Beaurepaire

The physical setting from which Haig normally exercised his command changed on 31 March 1916 with the move of GHQ from St Omer to Montreuil. It is not known who first suggested Montreuil as the location of Haig's headquarters. Whoever it was, Haig clearly endorsed the suggestion. Montreuil was a very small town, devoid of industry. In 1906 only 2,883 people had lived there. It had the advantage of being on a main road from London to Paris, but it was not on a main railway line, which would have made it noisier and more difficult to secure. In terms of road transport and telephone links it was conveniently located for an army that had its main seaports at Dunkirk, Calais, Boulogne, Dieppe and Le Havre and the front of which stretched from Belgium to the Somme. Another factor was that pre-war Montreuil had been the base of the great École Militaire, the buildings of which afforded very suitable accommodation for GHQ.[74]

Haig and his personal staff did not live at Montreuil itself, but had a small chateau, the Château of Beaurepaire, about two miles outside the town. He only rarely visited the buildings of the École Militaire and remained something of a stranger to most of the 300 officers who, at the height of the war, served at Montreuil. Haig clearly wished to keep his command function as separate as possible from the routine administrative and logistical staff work of GHQ. He probably reckoned, quite reasonably, that if he became too much engrossed in the minutiae, it would swamp him. The most senior staff officers from Montreuil went to brief him at the chateau, in some cases on a daily basis, in others merely as circumstances required. Haig's deliberate remoteness from the bulk of GHQ seems to have given him a certain mystique, even, perhaps, a strange sort of glamour. One who worked there remembered that:

When the chief did appear at Montreuil all felt that they had the right to desert work for five minutes to go to a window to catch a glimpse of him as he passed from one side of the École Militaire to the other, or stopped in the great courtyard to chat for a moment with one of his officers.

Haig's personal staff consisted of an Assistant Military Secretary who helped advise him on personnel matters, a private secretary (Captain Sir Philip Sassoon), a Medical Officer (Colonel Eugene "Micky" Ryan: by training a surgeon but serving, in effect, as Haig's personal physician), an officer in charge of escorts and five ADCs. They lived with him in the chateau. Because of the importance of the alliance a French liaison officer was also resident there, as, later in the war, was an American equivalent. Philip Sassoon, one of Haig's most constant companions during the war, seems worthy of particular comment at this point. Born in 1888, a nephew of Leo Rothschild, a baronet and an MP, he was an urbane, sophisticated, smooth political operator whom Haig tended to employ in sensitive matters such as dealings with French politicians and British newspaper proprietors.[75] After the war he would negotiate with the Prime Minister on the equally sensitive matters of Haig's peerage and his financial reward.

GHQ included (from summer 1916) a small Military Secretary's branch, formerly part of Haig's personal staff, which was primarily responsible for military appointments, promotions and honours. The General Staff branch, under Kiggell, had as its principal branches the Operations section under Davidson and the Intelligence section under Charteris. As well as forming an intelligence picture and directing the operations of the Armies, the General Staff had responsibility for maintaining training standards, instituting new forms of training and developing and disseminating doctrine. The Adjutant-General's branch, which from 22 February 1916 was directed by Lieutenant-General G.H. Fowke, was in charge of personnel matters, especially discipline. By far the largest part of GHQ was, however, the Quartermaster-General's branch, in 1916 under Lieutenant-General R.C. Maxwell, which dealt with transport and supply. Also based at GHQ, but not coming under any of its major branches, were the Major-General Royal Artillery, the Engineer-in-Chief, the Director of Gas Services and the Inspector of the Machine Gun Corps. These officers were meant to uphold and develop the efficiency of their particular branch of the army and to advise Haig on their areas of expertise.

The GHQ structure did not remain static under Haig. The near collapse of the British army's logistics during the Somme campaign led, in October 1916, to the creation of a department of Transportation separate from the Quartermaster-General's department. This department was initially placed under Sir Eric Geddes, a transportation expert from the civilian world who had been recommended by the Secretary of State for War, David Lloyd George. Haig had absolutely no prejudice against civilian technical experts. He gave Geddes a good deal of encouragement and a very free hand.

There were also organisational developments at GHQ connected with the vital functions of doctrine and training. From the second half of 1916 onwards, the General Staff produced an impressive series of booklets to incorporate the tactical lessons of the Somme and subsequent fighting. Today eminent military historians regard some of these booklets as classics of their genre, though it is sometimes difficult to establish their exact authorship and even the particular branch of the General Staff from which they emerged. Ensuring that these manuals were read and their precepts were put into practice was extremely difficult in an army in which many units and formations had a highly developed sense of individualism and nonconformity. At least for the infantry, it is, therefore, often difficult to establish, for most of the war, a direct connection between what the latest doctrinal pamphlet said and how British troops actually behaved in battle. Haig's headquarters did, however, put considerable effort into tactical indoctrination and training.

A GHQ Training Directorate was established, initially under Brigadier-General Arthur Solly-Flood, in January 1917. This branch helped to develop and supervise an elaborate system of training schools, which was established throughout the BEF. Much crucial work had thus been done in this area before the creation of the office of Inspector-General of Training, held by Lieutenant-General Sir Ivor Maxse (a great self-publicist and therefore the BEF's most famous training guru) on 3 July 1918. Despite some recent and quite detailed research, however, historians know less about this indoctrination and training process than they would ideally like. The records of the Training branches of GHQ survive only in fragmentary form in private papers. And while there can be no doubt that he was interested in these areas, the role of Haig in the development of doctrine and training within his army is hard to establish.[76]

Haig's health and personal routine

Haig, however, could have made little use of the elaborate apparatus of GHQ had his physical or mental health collapsed. In order to stay healthy and to maintain some sort of control of the vast organisation that he commanded, he adopted a disciplined, regulated personal routine. This was nothing new. He had been ordering his daily existence in this way at least since Sandhurst, merely adapting the routine to suit his circumstances. In 1916 and 1917, according to some reports, he used to run round the grounds of the château before breakfast. In 1918, when he was feeling his age at bit more, this became a walk. After his morning exercise he recorded meteorological conditions, reading a barometer as well as using direct observation. After breakfast he went to his office and, if he had not had time to do it the previous night, wrote his diary entry for the previous day and a short letter to his wife. He would often then despatch diary pages to her by King's Messenger.[77] He would next deal with any correspondence between London and GHQ, position papers and memoranda addressed to him and see senior members of his staff. The most prominent of these, such as John Charteris, the intelligence chief, normally reported every morning at a fixed time.[78]

Following such meetings, having made decisions on the issues before him, Haig would have the relevant branch of the staff draft orders, which would normally be sent out under the signature of the chief of that branch. Operational orders sent to the Armies would normally bear the signature of the CGS, in 1916 that of Kiggell. Haig himself would often himself write (or at least play a major part in drafting) letters going to the CIGS or members of the Cabinet. If very important civilian guests were at GHQ, Haig would have to set aside part of the morning to seeing them, though with less important ones he preferred a senior member of the staff to take care of them until lunchtime. At lunch he would, of course, see his guests and invariably tried to be courteous. But he was often preoccupied and depended on ADCs or others to keep them entertained. After coffee he generally tried to slip away as quickly as possible.

Haig refused to become desk bound, perhaps remembering the temporary collapse of his health that had occurred while he was working at the War Office in the Haldane years. He spent almost every afternoon out of doors. If not burdened by visitors to GHQ he would sometimes slip away before lunch and have a snack on the road. He would be taken by staff car to visit units and formations of all kinds. He would often talk not merely with the commanders and their staffs but with junior officers and senior NCOs. He had a good memory and probably also had his ADCs take notes on what he saw and heard. Details were recorded in the diary and this helped him to accumulate what one historian has described as a "data bank" on the army he commanded. He would usually arrange for his staff car to be met, on its return journey, by an ADC with horses. He would then ride, sometimes at the gallop, for several miles back to GHQ.[79] Considered as a fitness regime for a middle-aged man doing a stressful job, this could hardly be bettered.

After looking at any fresh information that had arrived in his office he would then get ready for dinner where he would normally have guests. Though Haig himself seems never to have drunk heavily, his table was always well supplied with high quality wine and brandy, and this doubtless helped some guests to become very loquacious. Given that Haig was such a limited conversationalist, his ADC's were briefed, if conversation flagged (or perhaps if Haig personally seemed tongue-tied), to introduce topics known to interest him. After dinner he would sometimes invite particularly important guests to withdraw from the dinner table for a private conversation.

At about 9.30 p.m. he would return to his office to view reports that had come in that evening. He sometimes put questions to Kiggell at about this time, but would expect Kiggell to do most of the talking – Haig himself "thinking much and saying d–d little". He would then sometimes write up his diary for the day and write a letter to his wife – though if the hour had grown too late these tasks would, as already noted, be deferred until the morning. At no time in his life had he read particularly widely or deeply, but he would sometimes sample something from the Bible or the Pilgrim's Progress, and he seems to have been able to sleep even during the most stressful periods of the war. It is indicative of the concern he had always shown for his own health that he would allow his doctor, Colonel Ryan, often prompted by his soldier-servant, Sergeant Secrett, to order him to stop work and go to bed early if he looked excessively stressed or tired.[80]

Haig's "isolation"

One of the criticisms made of Haig and GHQ during the war, and repeated ever since, is that they were isolated from the rest of the army and from the realities of the war.[81] It should already be clear that it is not reasonable to accuse Haig of an entirely static form of "château generalship". He was out and about a good deal and saw a great many people. It does seem to be true that he rarely got closer to the front than divisional headquarters. But this was a big army. He could visit all the divisions at some time or other, but not all the brigades, still less the battalions. It seems to be true that he did not appear in front line trenches. But he would probably have seen this as pointless showmanship. Given his very limited ability to converse with the troops (to whom he always remained a remote figure),[82] it is difficult to see how any possible gain could have justified the risks.

Even when based at St Omer or Montreuil, Haig's programme of visits ensured that he was not physically isolated from the army he commanded. When a major campaign was in progress, he would normally establish an Advanced HQ much closer to the scene of the action.[83] A more serious and important issue, however, is the extent to which GHQ and Haig, in particular, became intellectually and psychologically isolated. There is a much stronger case to be made for this. Such isolation was not a function of the physical setting of GHQ and not a matter of physical laziness or cowardice on Haig's part or that of his staff. Nor was it really the fault of the staff system or the system of British military education that Haig had been through. It was part of Haig's fundamental character – the way his mind worked.

Ideas and innovation

It would be untrue, or rather it would be an oversimplification, to state that Haig's mind was unreceptive to new ideas. He understood, whether as a result of Staff College teaching or from general observation of the world around him, that he lived in an age of scientific and technical innovations and that such innovation could seriously influence the conduct of war. He could be very quick on the uptake with technical innovations and was, in some cases, inclined to overrate their short-term potential. His early appreciation of the importance of military aviation has already been mentioned. So has his quick adoption of chemical warfare. As we shall see, he would seize on the idea of the tank as soon as it was put to him and must be given much credit for the British army's assuming the lead in the whole field of armoured, "mechanical warfare".[84] Less creditably he was, for a time in 1916, bamboozled into supporting a charlatan of a sergeant who claimed to be developing a "death ray".[85] Making a leap of imagination, and indeed of faith, in response to a technical innovation (or even a suggested technical innovation) seems not to have been a problem for Haig. Similarly he had no difficulty taking counsel from people whose particular expertise was clearly outside his own area of professional competence: physicians, meteorologists, railway experts[86] and (to a degree) ministers of religion.[87] What he seems to have found much more difficult was productive discourse with equals and subordinates within what he regarded as his own area of professional expertise: essentially strategy and grand tactics, the latter being what modern armies call "operational art".

Haig and his staff

Haig's almost complete inability to engage in productive discourse, especially in this sort of area, was noticed even by people working closely and loyally with him. Charteris noted that he was "immensely tenacious of his own views". He read very few books which were not of a narrowly professional nature and "had not a critical mind". Charteris noted that Haig never actually argued, lacking "the dialectic cut". Instead he would simply announce that: "I don't agree with you. I think ... ".[88] His tenacity of his own opinions was perhaps, at this period, reinforced by his growing sense of divine mission and divine favour.

Haig demanded that GHQ should speak with one voice: a lesson that he had learned at Staff College and that had been reinforced by recent experience. He was bound to recall that he had become commander-in-chief in part by leading a sort of conspiracy by senior officers against Sir John French. A key figure in the conspiracy had been Robertson, French's CGS. Though he would not have admitted it, Haig probably lived with some anxiety that something similar might happen to him, especially during periods when the war was going badly. An important first step towards preventing such a catastrophe was to insist on loyalty in GHQ itself,[89] preventing anyone behaving towards him as Robertson had behaved towards French. For Haig, unanimity in GHQ was particularly important in its dealings with the Armies. There appears to have been perpetual anxiety within the GHQ staff that Army commanders would become practically independent lords of their own substantial fiefdoms, virtually ungovernable from above. Some at GHQ referred to the Army commanders as the "barons", sometimes as the "wicked barons".[90] Fear of excessive baronial independence was probably not without foundation. Army commanders were powerful people. Removing them was a very major step that could not be taken lightly or easily.

Haig's demand for loyalty at GHQ and his insistence that GHQ speak with one voice were, therefore, not in themselves irrational. These things were vital to his survival in office and his ability to command the BEF. But this should not have precluded free and frank discussions between Haig and the most senior members of his staff while policies were being determined and plans made. However, there is considerable evidence that Kiggell, Butler, Charteris and Davidson, and others working at GHQ, at least until the second half of 1917 rarely expressed truly independent judgements or made original suggestions. It was widely believed at the time that they (and especially Charteris) tended to reinforce Haig's preconceptions, telling him what he wanted to hear. It may be that some of these individuals were excessively timid, sycophantic or careerist. But they all seem to have sensed that independence of thought and expression was not what "the Chief" wanted. Lord Esher, who was by no means a hostile witness as far as Haig was concerned, noted that Haig's "general staff seems to be an excellent machine formed to carry out his ideas and intentions. They initiate nothing. All initiative remains with him."[91] For that Haig's fundamental attitudes, and, indeed, his whole persona, were largely to blame.

Relations with army commanders

A pronounced sense of estrangement was sometimes to develop between GHQ and the Armies.[92] This appears not to have been the result of lack of contact. Shortly after he took over as commander-in-chief, Haig initiated a system of Army commanders' conferences (initially weekly but later rather less frequent) at each Army's HQ in turn.[93] But these meetings seem to have been primarily occasions at which GHQ presented its policies to the Armies, and told them what it expected of them, rather than forums for the free and frank exchange of views. Haig seems to have let it be known he did not want Army commanders to introduce, at these meetings, concepts or proposals that were (in the current vernacular) "off message", discordant with the tunes that higher authority, in this case GHQ, wished to play.[94]

There is some circumstantial evidence to suggest that Haig was somewhat suspicious of Army commanders who did not owe their appointments to him. General Monro of First Army, for example, though he had served under Haig as a divisional commander in I Corps, was never used by Haig as an Army commander in a major campaign and was eventually shunted off to be commander-in-chief in India. Haig's relationship with Allenby, of Third Army, was also notoriously uneasy. Though Allenby went to some lengths to curry favour with Haig, giving him a horse, for example, he was not ultimately successful. After an admittedly poor performance at Arras in 1917 he would find himself relieved of command.[95]

General Sir Herbert Plumer, too, had been appointed to Second Army by Sir John French before Haig became commander-in-chief. He does not seem to have participated in Haig's and Robertson's efforts to overthrow French. Plumer was older than Haig and had been on the Directing Staff at the Staff College when Haig was a student there. According to some accounts, he had been less than impressed with Haig's performance and had made no secret of this. It has also been suggested that, had the Army as a whole been given a free choice as to Sir John French's successor, in December 1915, the choice would have fallen on Plumer rather than Haig.[96] If this is true, Haig's anxiety about Plumer's popularity may have been another cause of initial friction between them, though there is no hard evidence of this. After the loss of a position known as "The Bluff", two miles south of Ypres, on 14–15 February 1916, Haig accused Plumer (perhaps with some justification) of having inadequately fortified the Second Army front and indicated that he was contemplating the latter's removal. Plumer evidently wanted to keep his job. He made a sort of obeisance to Haig, offering to go home tamely if Haig lacked confidence in him. This seems to have convinced Haig that Plumer was no threat and he let him stay.[97]

Some contemporaries regarded Plumer as one of the ablest of the British generals of this war, though Haig seems to have thought his achievements in 1917 were largely due to the chief of staff, Major-General C.H. "Tim" Harington, whom Haig had sent him.[98] During that year the operational methods practised by Plumer's Second Army would be rather different from those that Haig normally advocated. Plumer was naturally cautious. He and his Second Army staff became, arguably, the ablest exponents of the "step-by-step" approach to offensive operations. But, after his initial carpeting by Haig in 1916, Plumer seems to have gone out of his way to avoid any confrontation with the commander-in-chief. His declared attitude to Haig and GHQ was one of "utter loyalty".[99] Henceforth, however mistaken he thought the course the commander-in-chief was pursuing, and however serious the losses likely to result, Plumer would ultimately defer to him.[100] Haig's approach to his Army commanders, like his attitude to GHQ itself, discouraged the expression of doubt or dissent. It has often been alleged that Haig's Army commanders were afraid of him and, while the degree of truth in this naturally varied between individuals and over time,[101] as a generalisation it seems valid. In some cases, such as that of Plumer, a degree of intimidation may, indeed, have been intended.

Early relations with the French

The course of Haig's relations with his Army commanders did not, as we have mentioned, always run smoothly. But the most important and sensitive issue confronting him was often that of relations with his French allies. During Sir John French's command, Franco-British relations had generally been rather poor and Haig was left in no doubt that the British government intended him to repair this situation as far as it was in his power to do so. The formal instructions Kitchener sent to Haig on 28 December stated that:

His Majesty's Government consider that the mission of the British Expeditionary Force in France, to the chief command of which you have recently been appointed, is to support and co-operate with the French and Belgian Governments in driving the German armies from French and Belgian territory and eventually to restore the neutrality of Belgium, on behalf of which, as guaranteed by Treaty, Belgium appealed to the French and ourselves at the outbreak of hostilities.

Haig's mission statement went on to indicate (even more strongly than had the one given to Sir John French) the importance of good relations between the Allies. Whereas Sir John French had been told to "coincide most sympathetically with the plans and wishes of our Ally", Kitchener told Haig that "the closest co-operation between the French and British as a united army must be the governing policy". Whereas French had been assured that he would "in no case come under the orders of any Allied general", Haig was told that "you will in no case come under the authority of any Allied General further than the necessary co-operation with our Allies above referred to". If this peculiar phrasing meant anything, it meant that Haig might, in some desperate contingency, be placed under Joffre or whoever else happened to be commanding the French army at the time.[102]

The idea of being placed under the authority of a French general was certainly not appealing to Haig and, when the possibility became real, early in 1917, he would resist it.[103] Yet months before he became commander-in-chief he had apparently realised that, irritating as he sometimes found them, being able to establish a working relationship with French officers might be vital to the future conduct of operations and thus to his career. In the summer of 1915, while still at First Army, he had begun reviving and developing his knowledge of the French language, taking lessons for about two hours a day with his liaison officer, Captain Gemeau, an officer who, while he was commander-in-chief, lived in his chateau and continued with the language instruction. John Charteris recorded that:

[Haig] made rapid progress, and ... was able to converse fluently, and also, by a curious twist of mentality, to express himself far more coherently and articulately in French than in English.[104]

Not all who heard Haig speak in French believed that he expressed himself clearly.[105] But in his early encounters with Joffre he certainly went out of his way to give a good impression and there is some evidence that he succeeded. Their first meeting as commanders-in-chief was a courtesy visit Haig paid to French general headquarters at Chantilly on 23 December. Haig recorded that:

General Joffre was quite hopeful ... said his armies would have unlimited ammunition in the spring, and he expected to drive the enemy back by April ... The old man was evidently very pleased with my visit ... He shook me by the hand ... and held it so long that I thought I was never to be allowed to go. Altogether it was a very satisfactory interview.[106]

It seems that relations between Haig and Joffre genuinely got off to a good start, though that might well have been because both generals were initially reluctant to press potentially contentious issues.[107]

On 29 December there was a much larger meeting at Chantilly. It involved the French President, Raymond Poincaré, the Prime Minister, Aristide Briand and the War Minister, General Gallieni, as well Joffre, Foch and other generals. Haig was clearly in a good mood following his promotion and Briand, for one, knew how to play on that. He flattered Haig that "if the present good feeling had existed between us from the commencement the situation would now be very different". This was precisely the right way to handle Haig, who found Briand "a most charming man and most alert". Poincaré further oiled the wheels by promoting Haig within the Legion of Honour.[108]

At New Year Colonel Pierre des Vallières replaced General Huguet as head of the French military mission at GHQ – a move made at French rather than British instigation. Huguet's post-war memoir indicates that he became deeply disillusioned with the British. He was fairly well liked by them, however, and his French superiors believed that he was too Anglophile to represent French interests properly. Des Vallières was a cavalry officer. He impressed Haig as knowledgeable and gentlemanly and managed to maintain good personal relations with Haig until he left GHQ in 1917. This, however, seems to have been a result of dissembling on des Vallières' part and a degree of blindness on Haig's. Des Vallières had Irish Catholic connections, and partly as a result of these had developed intense Anglophobia. He also saw himself as a fighting soldier and considered liaison work contemptible. That such a man was chosen as Haig's principal liaison officer seems to have been an extraordinary error of

judgement and, as we shall see, the quality of Franco-British liaison during 1916 left much to be desired.[109]

On the Western Front the mid-winter of 1915–16 was a relatively quiet
time. The Germans, however, were soon to unleash a devastating storm.
Under the intense pressure of these events, Franco-British relations
in 1916 would run far less smoothly than Haig had initially hoped. To
his credit, however, during his first weeks as commander-in-chief he was
making a serious effort to establish good relations with his principal ally.

9   The Battle of the Somme (1)

The controversial Somme

In terms of sheer scale the Battle of the Somme is one of the greatest campaigns of British military history and it is one of the most widely known. Much about it, however, remains obscure or at least intensely controversial. Historians do not agree about the purposes of those directing it,[1] the relative losses suffered by the opposing sides[2] or even who won.[3] The campaign would prove long and complex. Doing it justice will take two chapters. This first considers the planning processes, the preliminary bombardment and the dramatic and terrible first day of infantry assaults: Saturday 1 July 1916.

Franco-British strategic planning to 21 February 1916

Before Haig took over as commander-in-chief, a conference of all the Allied powers held at Chantilly on 6 December 1915 had agreed that the Russian, French and Italian fronts were the ones on which offensive action in 1916 must be concentrated. A decisive result should be sought by co-ordinated offensive action on these fronts. A general offensive of this nature was to be started "as soon as possible" and it was considered "highly desirable" that this "maximum effort" should "take place at the beginning of next March".[4] Obviously this was all extremely vague. No one was committed to anything in particular. In late December 1915, Joffre was still unclear about the form Allied offensive on the Western Front in 1916 would take. He recognised that the French army was not strong enough to conduct the Western Front operations of the coming year by itself and he could not dictate to Haig how the British army would be employed. Keeping his options open, he ordered each French Army Group commander to examine the possibilities open on his stretch of front.[5]

It seems clear, however, that Joffre personally favoured the main offensive's being mounted astride the Somme. In a memorandum addressed to Haig, dated Christmas Day 1915, Joffre indicated that the French Northern Army Group, under Foch, was studying the possibility of an offensive south of that river. He asked the British, without prejudicing the final choice of the location for the main Allied effort on the Western Front, to examine the possibility of an offensive between the Somme and Arras. The advantages that Joffre saw in an Allied offensive astride the Somme were twofold. First, the Somme valley was a place where the British and French armies were physically in touch and probably the place in which their efforts could most easily be combined. Secondly, during 1915, it had been a quiet sector and Joffre hoped that some degree of surprise might be achieved.[6] As a preliminary to offensive operations on the Somme, Joffre wanted the British to expand the stretch of front they currently held, relieving the French Tenth Army in the Arras sector, between the British First and Third Armies. Haig's immediate response was that discussion of reliefs should be postponed until the general form to be taken by Allied offensive operations in 1916 had been decided.[7] But in the name of maintaining good relations with his Allies he quickly relented, agreeing on New Year's Eve that the British First Army would extend its front southwards to relieve the left wing of the French Tenth Army during the first week of January. The relief of the rest of that Army would be considered for a later date.[8]

At New Year there was still no definite decision on the shape that the Allied campaign on the Western Front was to assume in 1916. GHQ was preparing plans both for major operations on the Somme and a big Flanders offensive. The Flanders operation was intended to comprise both an amphibious assault on the Belgian coast at Ostend (conducted in conjunction with the Royal Navy's Dover Patrol) and a breakout from the Ypres salient conducted by Plumer's Second Army. Whether the Flanders or the Somme operation was to be considered the main British effort for 1916 was undecided. Haig's preferred option seems to have been an attack on the Somme in mid-April followed by a major offensive in Flanders, in which the British Second Army would be supported by French and Belgian forces, perhaps in the early summer.[9]

Joffre was at least as concerned with when as where the main Allied offensive on the Western Front should be made. He thought it important that the main French effort and the main Russian effort should be simultaneous. Believing that the Russians were unlikely to be ready to attack before July, he wanted to delay the big French offensive until then. But Joffre also believed that for the big Allied offensive of the summer to have a chance of achieving significant success it must be preceded by *batailles d'usures*, or wearing-out battles. These would consume some of the German reserves and pull others away from the site of the forthcoming main Allied effort.[10] Yet the French army, in Joffre's assessment, did not have the manpower for both the wearing-out battles and the main effort. In order to economise French manpower Joffre wanted the British:

(a) To take over more front from the French.
(b) To do most, if not all, of the fighting of the wearing-out battles on the Western Front in 1916.
(c) To play a subordinate part in the big combined offensive effort of the summer.

The British were, however, still far less well off in terms of artillery and shell, and the divisions that Haig had under command in the early part of the year were, for the most part, seriously undertrained.

Joffre and Haig were both in awkward positions in early 1916. They were keen to be polite to each other and wished to avoid an ugly quarrel at almost any price. Yet Joffre was finding it very difficult to get Haig's agreement to the scheme of offensive operations that he ideally wanted. At a meeting on 20 January, Haig and Joffre agreed that the main British attack of 1916 would be mounted in the summer and that it would be designed to seize the Belgian coast. The British were to make a preliminary attack effort on the Somme, around 20 April, which would attempt to seize the first German defensive line, but not make a complete breakthrough. The main French attack would commence in June, but its location was left undecided.[11]

Only three days after this meeting, however, on 23 January, Joffre wrote to Haig to ask the British to make a second preparatory offensive in May to add to the one Haig had already agreed to in April. Joffre now wanted to plan for a contingency that their meeting three days earlier had apparently not considered: if the Germans mounted a really major offensive against the Russians in the spring, the Russians would need the western Allies to respond quickly to relieve the pressure. In that case Joffre wanted his army to attack with all available strength south of the Somme, while the British would attack with twenty-five divisions north of the river.[12]

With Joffre now proposing that the British engage in two distinct wearing-out battles in the spring as well a major summer offensive, alarm bells started ringing in Haig's head. He could foresee his Armies wearing themselves out in seemingly futile *batailles d'usure* before the French took any serious offensive action. Thanks to Robertson, now firmly ensconced as CIGS, he realised that this could spell serious political trouble in London. Robertson informed Haig that some members of the War Committee were not keen on any major offensive action on the Western Front in 1916 and were "quite definitely opposed to an attack on our part which is independent of a general allied offensive".[13] Haig therefore wrote to Joffre on 1 February to make it clear "what I am able to undertake and what my government is likely to approve my undertaking". He now insisted that the British would not undertake wearing-out battles until within two weeks of the date agreed for the main offensive on the Western Front – a considerable change in the British position.[14]

Haig was now determined to scale down the wearing-out operations that Joffre had proposed. Joffre (probably because he had little choice) decided to accept this, provided the main Allied offensive should be where it seems he had always wanted it: in Picardy, astride the River Somme. Preliminary *batailles d'usure* were being conducted by the British at Ypres and by the French somewhere further south and east. Haig now offered little opposition to this general scheme of operations. He had gained an important concession in that Joffre accepted that the British would not undertake subsidiary operations long in advance of the main effort and without French co-operation.[15] He had also found in a meeting with King Albert on 7 February that the serious Belgian co-operation that he had counted on for his proposed coastal operation would not be forthcoming. King Albert feared the subordination of the Belgian army to the British, probably anxious about the scale of casualties that such an operation would involve for his minuscule force. He expressed a preference that Belgian soil should be liberated by indirect means rather than by an offensive through Belgium itself, an offensive that might inflict further devastation on his homeland. Haig declared himself "quite astonished" that Albert "should have taken such a purely selfish view of the case".[16] But from that point onward, the idea that the main British effort of 1916 would be mounted in Flanders to large degree receded, though it did not altogether disappear before the start of the Battle of the Somme in July.

After 7 February, therefore, Allied planning for 1916 became, rather suddenly, more harmonious. When, on 14 February, Haig and Joffre met at Chantilly, it appeared that the major issues were settled. A British preparatory or wearing-out battle would be mounted during the two weeks preceding the main effort. This would probably be in Flanders. The western Allies intended to mount their main effort on the Somme on 1 July, with twenty-five British divisions north of the river and forty French divisions south of it. But the Somme operation might be brought forward to April if the Germans mounted a major spring offensive on the Eastern Front. Only one bone of contention between the western Allies remained – the relief of the remainder of the French Tenth Army. The French wanted this to happen quickly, but Haig would not guarantee it before "next winter".[17]

By 11 February the French high command had intelligence that a major German attack on the Western Front, probably at Verdun, was imminent. Joffre, therefore, was anxious that the British complete the relief of the

French Tenth Army. The French army was short of reserves and the relief of the Tenth Army would free up troops that might be needed urgently. Though his intelligence chief, John Charteris, apparently accepted that a German strike against Verdun was a possibility, Haig resisted this conclusion. If the Germans attacked, Haig believed, it would be more likely that they would strike the British in Flanders. He would not agree to the relief of the remainder of the French Tenth Army until after the major offensive of the summer.[18]

The impact of Verdun

On Monday 21 February, exactly a week after the Allies had harmonised their offensive plans for 1916 at Chantilly, the Germans launched a massive offensive at Verdun. The next day Joffre wrote to Haig renewing his appeal for the relief of the French Tenth Army in the Arras sector. If, for any reason, the British could not fulfil that request, Joffre pleaded that they should mount an offensive of their own to take the pressure of Verdun.[19] Haig reviewed various contingencies that might arise out of the Verdun offensive with Kitchener in London on 25 February. He did not consider his own Armies ready to take offensive action, but without in any way apologising for (or even acknowledging) his earlier misjudgement about German offensive intentions, he agreed to Joffre's request for the immediate relief of the Tenth Army.[20] As the battle at Verdun proceeded, the French talked much less of the British mounting *batailles d'usure* before the main Allied offensive. There was quite enough *usure* going on at Verdun, though it was happening to the French at least as much as it was to the Germans.

The German offensive at Verdun nevertheless brought significant elements of strain and discord back into inter-ally relations. It seemed to Haig that, even in its early stages, Verdun was making Joffre and his staff desperately anxious. But instead of prompting sympathy and stimulating a desire to help, French alarm and anguish bred British mistrust. Haig's confidence in Joffre and the French army declined sharply. He began to share Robertson's doubts that the French were really serious about a big offensive in the summer. Even if they were, would they have the capacity to do it? He started to believe that the British would soon have to take over from the French as the dominant partners in the wartime alliance on the Western Front.[21]

As the Verdun campaign continued, Haig's faith that a joint Franco-British offensive could be mounted in the summer began to decline. He began to reconsider the possibility of an attack on the Somme by British forces alone in late March or April, as a *bataille d'usure*, to be followed by a more ambitious British offensive in Flanders, perhaps in May. Haig made no attempt to keep this idea secret from Joffre, instead offering it as an alternative scheme to be implemented if French losses at Verdun made it impossible for them to play a major role on the Somme.[22] Joffre discouraged this proposal, still wishing to concentrate all efforts on preparing for a joint offensive on the Somme in July. But this did not stop Haig from ordering contingency plans to be made for a northern attack.[23]

Schemes for an amphibious landing at Ostend were explored in some detail. Lieutenant-General Sir Aylmer Hunter-Weston, who had commanded the 29th Division at Gallipoli, was sent to examine this possibility with Admiral Bacon. Though Hunter-Weston seems to have had serious doubts about an amphibious assault on Ostend, planning for a northern offensive continued into June 1916. Ultimately it was decided that a landing at Ostend could only be mounted as a climax to a successful British land breakout from the Ypres salient, through Roulers and Thourout. The object of such an operation would be the clearance of the Germans from the Belgian coast. Haig probably appreciated that, without active and close French co-operation, his forces did not have the strength to do anything so grandiose in 1916. But he still considered some sort of attack in the north to be a possibility as a follow-up to a limited offensive on the Somme if substantial French participation in that sector did not materialise.[24]

The longer the Verdun battle went on, the more the British realised that any summer offensive on the Somme would have to be made largely by them. Haig was conscious (at least some of the time) that most of his army was no more than a "collection of divisions untrained for the Field".[25] He favoured delaying the offensive into late July or even mid-August, enabling his forces to improve their standard of training and equipment. He was unwilling to attack earlier "except in an emergency to save the French from disaster and Paris perhaps from capture".[26] Robertson and the British government endorsed Haig's desire for delay. This approach even had some support from Georges Clemenceau, chairman of the Military Committee of the French Senate. Clemenceau feared that if a summer offensive went off at half cock and conspicuously failed it would greatly strengthen the defeatist element in French politics – people favouring a quick peace at almost any price.[27]

Paradoxically, Haig may have finally decided to fall in behind Joffre's wish for a joint Franco-British attack on the Somme at the beginning of July precisely because elements in the French government seemed all too ready to acquiesce in his own earlier wish to delay it. After despatching his private secretary, Captain Sir Philip Sassoon, to Paris to speak to French ministers in May, Haig sensed that "the French may give up the idea of an offensive while doing all in their power to induce *us* to attack".[28]

By late spring Joffre's headquarters were already indicating that the number of French divisions available for an offensive would now be reduced to somewhere between twenty-two and twenty-six, and it seemed that the longer the offensive was delayed, the smaller the French contribution was likely to be. By 1 May Haig and his staff seem to have doubted that the French would actually use more than ten.[29] The reduction of the intended French contribution provided an argument for delay so that the British contribution could be maximised. But when Haig mentioned to Joffre the possibility of delaying the Somme offensive until the middle of August, during a conference at Beauquesne on 26 May, Joffre replied that such a delay might mean the extinction of the French army. Haig agreed that the combined offensive should begin in late June and so instructed his Army commanders the following day.[30] A further inter-Allied conference took place on 31 May involving Poincaré, the French President, Briand, the Premier and General Rocques, the Minister of War, as well as Joffre and Haig. Taking place at Drury, near Amiens, on board a train that brought the ministers from Paris, it approved the existing arrangements for the Somme offensive.[31]

Haig, the British government and planning for the Somme

What, by mid-summer 1916, did Haig think was the purpose of an Allied offensive on the Somme? What did he really expect it to achieve and how did his views relate to those of the authorities in London?

It must be acknowledged from the outset that an attack in Picardy was not a personal project of Haig's. From a British strategic viewpoint he could see no particular advantage to this choice of battlefield. He and his intelligence chief, John Charteris, saw considerably greater opportunities beckoning in the northern part of the front.[32] Right up to the first infantry assaults on 1 July, Haig seems to have believed it at least possible that the French would be unable or unwilling to sustain an offensive alongside the British on the Somme. In that case he retained the option (at least in his own mind) of switching the main British effort to Flanders, though, in order to preserve inter-Allied harmony in the short term, this was no longer a possibility he discussed with Joffre.[33]

It is also important to realise too that, though the British government wanted Haig to co-operate sufficiently with the French to hold the alliance together, he was under no pressure from that quarter to gain the sort of decisive victory that might knock Germany out of the war. Indeed, during the planning phase, the key personnel in the War Office, through whom the government's wishes were normally expressed, seem to have considered any such victory so improbable that it would be dangerous to aim at it. Both Kitchener and Robertson apparently wanted Haig to conduct a 1916 offensive in a cautious, "step-by-step" manner, building up pressure on the Germans but minimising British casualties as far as possible. However, both Kitchener and Robertson seem to have been concerned (presumably because of what they knew of his temperament and past record) that Haig might get carried away and try to achieve some sort of dramatic breakthrough.

On 9 February, before Verdun, and at a time when the French army was still expected to make the main attack of the summer, Charteris found that Kitchener, who was visiting the Western Front at the time, was:

very emphatic against any talk of breaking through the German lines. He said someone from GHQ had been talking about a break-through, and that it must stop ... "There will be no break-through. You must lean against this line, press it, hit it as hard as you can, bend it. Some day you will find it is not there, going back, but you *will not* break through ..."

Immediately K. had gone I motored straight to DH and reported the whole conversation to him. DH was, as always, quite unperturbed. I fancy he himself has been using the term break-through to some of the visitors and it has reached K's ears![34]

Since February 1915 Robertson had been a consistent advocate of the step-by-step approach to offensive operations, in which a series of short infantry advances would be supported by massive artillery firepower.[35] Early in 1916 he seems briefly to have hoped that the cumulative effect of all the Allied offensives planned for that year (even if, on the Western Front, cautiously conducted) might prove decisive and bring Germany to its knees.[36] But, after the start of the Verdun battle, taking into consideration French fragility, the immature state of the British army and the British government's sensitivity to casualties, he changed his tune. In late May 1916 he was advising Haig to adopt a particularly cautious approach to the forthcoming Somme offensive.

The more I think of the future the more I feel we need to be relatively much stronger than at present in artillery. The French, too, give me the impression that they do not see the end of the war before next year and intend to go easy this year. Therefore I do not, at my end, propose to cause the Government to think of a great offensive promising far-reaching effect, but to show them the necessity of our cutting in soon so as to assist and encourage our allies and to well strafe the German. This I understand you to agree is the correct point of view to take. I think it is.[37]

But Haig was not entirely in agreement with Robertson. In reality he seems to have been in two minds. On 1 May Charteris recorded that Haig looked on the forthcoming Somme campaign as a "wearing out" battle, with "just the off-chance that it will wear the Germans right out", whereas Joffre thought "a breakthrough just possible".[38] But this was Haig at his most cautious and conservative. After Kitchener's comments to Kiggell in February, he seems to have been politically canny enough to avoid open use of the term "breakthrough". Yet there is considerable evidence that he found it difficult to rid himself of the hope that the Germans could be altogether ejected from their trench systems on the Somme, pursued with cavalry and perhaps forced to sue for peace before the end of 1916.

Haig's reply to Robertson's letter of 28 May was full of unresolved tensions. He indicated that he wanted to be ready to support the French by "a resolute attack when required by the military situation, and at the same time prepare to exploit to the utmost any success gained". The phrase "exploit to the utmost" suggests that Haig had not given up on the idea of breakthrough.

In his next two paragraphs, however, he struck a cautious note, indicating that it was important to leave his troops in a good position for the start of the 1917 campaign. That would mean not going "down in to the mud beyond the Pozières Ridge unless we have the force to take up a line on the heights beyond the valley at le Sars". This seemed eminently sensible. Haig, however, continued by stating his opposition to any reduction in his five divisions of cavalry on the grounds that:

It seems to me that troops and materiel are so imbedded in the ground in trench warfare that general retreat will be most difficult. We ought therefore to be prepared to exploit a success on the lines of 1806.[39]

This suggests that Haig imagined breaking right through German field fortifications and exploiting the breakthrough with a strategically decisive cavalry pursuit of the sort that Napoleon had executed against the Prussian Army after the battles of Jena and Auerstadt. This impression is amply reinforced by the plans he later made with General Sir Hubert Gough for the employment of the latter's "Reserve Army" (plans discussed below). Unfortunately, it seems that neither Kitchener nor Robertson considered himself to be in a position really to "grip" Haig and insist that he conform to their vision of a limited offensive.

By June 1916 the Cabinet's War Committee was very concerned that the Verdun offensive would lead to the collapse of France. The committee was thus prepared to authorise an offensive on the Somme without interrogating Haig too carefully when he appeared before them, on Wednesday 7 June, about the operational methods he intended to use. It is, indeed, doubtful whether its members had enough military knowledge to ask the right questions. Certainly Haig told Asquith, Grey and Hankey on Friday

9 June that to relieve Verdun and save France a prolonged campaign might be necessary. What he did not say was that he harboured ambitions for the campaign that went far beyond relieving Verdun and easing the immediate pressure on the French army. The committee's interrogation of Haig about strategic aims was no more rigorous than its investigation of his proposed operational methods.[40] Ultimately one of the most remarkable things about Haig in the latter half of 1916 was the degree to which he would operate without effective control from London. In truth Britain's leading statesmen were at least as much out of their depth in the grand strategic direction of a war as he was in its operational conduct.

Haig's army in mid-1916

So far we have reviewed the planning of the Somme offensive at the strategic level. Translating Haig's and Joffre's strategic conceptions into some sort of battlefield reality was a vast task, particularly given that it would be the first time that the British army had played the leading role in the principal offensive effort of the Allies on the Western Front.

By July 1916 the rapidly expanding BEF was approaching one-and-a-half million men. There were five Armies. From north to south these included: General Sir Herbert Plumer's Second Army (Flanders), General Sir Charles Monro's First Army (the Loos sector), General Sir Edmund Allenby's Third Army (the Arras sector) and General Sir Henry Rawlinson's Fourth Army (in Picardy, to the north of the River Somme). A so-called Reserve Army, under General Sir Hubert Gough, which came into existence on 22 May 1916, remained (appropriately) in reserve, its first headquarters being close to the 14th Century battlefield of Crécy. The five armies included twelve corps, comprising thirty-eight infantry divisions. Some of the latter, including the 9th (Scottish) Division and the 18th Division, were already beginning to emerge as elite formations, but the majority were seriously undertrained. There were five cavalry divisions, though these had rarely found much scope for mounted action since late 1914. Fourth Army, which would initiate British efforts on the Somme, had five corps, comprising sixteen divisions.[41]

In the British system as it had evolved by mid-1916 an Army was basically just a headquarters organisation consisting of a commander and about 100 staff. GHQ allocated corps to an Army for particular missions and could remove them again. No corps was regarded as a permanent fixture of any particular army. Nor, except in the case of Dominion (Canadian, Australian and New Zealand) troops, were infantry divisions regarded as permanent fixtures of particular corps. They too were rotated through the higher formations. These arrangements gave great administrative flexibility, but impeded the development of a sense of collective identity, cohesion and teamwork in the higher formations. These problems were compounded by the fact that the vast bulk of the army was composed of hurriedly trained wartime volunteers and characterised by, amongst many other weaknesses, an acute shortage of properly trained staff officers.[42]

Rawlinson's selection to command on the Somme

Haig selected Sir Henry Rawlinson and his Fourth Army staff to direct the British part in the principal offensive operation of 1916. Why he did so is not completely clear, but it is at least possible that he had made this choice even before he had decided where the offensive was to be mounted. Rawlinson spent some weeks in the early part of the year (at a time when Haig was contemplating making his main offensive effort of 1916 in Flanders) on reconnaissance around Ypres.[43] It might be supposed that Haig picked Rawlinson because he recognised his ability. Haig did indeed regard Rawlinson as intelligent, if somewhat scheming and duplicitous.[44] But his practice, both during the planning phase and the campaign itself, of overruling the Fourth Army commander in quite fundamental ways indicates that he was far from placing complete confidence in Rawlinson's judgement.

The likelihood is that Rawlinson was picked, at least in part, because, of the Army commanders serving in early 1916, he was the one who owed his elevation to that position most directly to Haig and thus the one Haig thought it would be easiest to control. Gough, who was elevated to Army command a few months after Rawlinson, and was also a Haig protégé, was the other Army commander who would eventually play a substantial part in the Somme offensive. This is unlikely to have been mere coincidence. Haig, like many other managers in both the military and the civilian worlds, seems to have felt most comfortable with subordinates who were, in a direct and personal sense, his people, owing their present positions and future prospects to his favour.

In February 1916 Haig ordered Rawlinson to move his Fourth Army headquarters to the Somme. At this time Allenby's Third Army held the stretch of front on which it was intended to mount the British part of the Somme offensive. Haig briefly considered an arrangement whereby Allenby would remain the sector commander with Rawlinson's Fourth Army, operating within Allenby's sector, in some senses under his authority, commanding the forces actually conducting the offensive. This strange arrangement was, however, never put into practice. With the start of the German offensive at Verdun, on 21 February, Joffre, as we have noted, desperately pleaded for the relief of the French Tenth Army.

This was accomplished by Third Army's extension of its front leftward. Rawlinson's headquarters then took charge of the stretch of front between the River Somme and the right of Third Army. During the Somme campaign of 1916 Rawlinson would be quite independent of Allenby.[45]

Rawlinson established his headquarters at Querrieu, six miles northeast of Amiens, on 24 February 1916.[46] His initial impression of the military geography of Picardy was favourable. He approved Joffre's choice of its gently rolling, well-drained, chalk-based countryside as the place to conduct the next big Allied attack. On 27 February he wrote to Clive Wigram, an aide at Buckingham Palace:

It is capital country in which to undertake an offensive when we get a sufficiency of artillery, for the observation is excellent and with plenty of guns and ammunition we ought to be able to avoid the heavy losses which the infantry have always suffered on previous occasions.[47]

The German defensive system on the Somme

Rawlinson recognised that the German field fortifications on this stretch of front had considerable strength. The Germans had been unmolested here in 1915 and had used their time wisely. Their defences were stronger than those at Loos. As at Loos there were two main German trench systems. A third system (unknown to the British when they began planning their attack) would be well on the way to completion by the time the battle began.

The German first-line system or "First Position" ("position" being the best translation of the German *Stellung*) was on the forward slope of a chalk ridge. Two belts of barbed wire, each of which was thirty yards wide and positioned fifteen yards apart, covered the First Position. Behind the wire were three trenches, each about 150 to 200 yards apart. The first trench was a sort of outpost line manned by sentries. The second was the main defensive position in which the front line garrison lived. The third was a support line from which local reserves could be fed into the battle. The German First Position on the Somme (rather like the second-line system at Loos) incorporated a number of fortified villages. These included Serre, Beaumont Hamel, Thiepval, Ovillers, la Boiselle, Fricourt and Mametz, place names that would acquire a terrible resonance before the year was out. Because it was on a forward slope the whole of the first line position was theoretically vulnerable to British artillery. But within this system there were many deep dugouts, some up to thirty feet underground, with room for up to twenty-five men, in which much of the trench garrison could be accommodated during periods of intensive shelling. Only a lucky direct hit by a very heavy shell would trouble the occupants of these shelters.

Behind the German First Position there was a series of intermediate redoubts: mini-fortresses with all-round defence, which, in some cases, linked the First Position with the Second Position behind the ridge. One of these was the Schwaben Redoubt, near Thiepval, soon to become notorious to British troops. Others included fortified villages at Beaucourt, Contalmaison, Mametz and Montaubon. The German Second Position was 2,000–4,000 yards back from the first, on the reverse slope. It had its own dense belts of wire, and repeated the three lines of trenches found in the First Position. Crucially the barbed wire covering the German Second Position, because it was on a reverse slope, could not be seen by British artillery observers on the ground. Though this wire could be bombarded it would be almost impossible to check the extent to which it had been cut or beaten down. Though Rawlinson was unaware of it at this stage, the Germans had also begun work on a Third Position about 3,000 yards further back.[48]

The troops defending the German fortifications on the Somme belonged to the Second Army under General von Below. Their strength would increase somewhat as the Allies' preparations for an offensive on the Somme became obvious. By 2 June, von Below was demanding reinforcements. But the opening of Russian General Brusilov's offensive against the Austro-Hungarian Army on the Eastern Front two days later caused a major strategic crisis for the Central Powers. General von Falkenhayn, the Chief of the German General Staff (the Verdun offensive was his brainchild), found himself obliged to send divisions from the Western Front to the Eastern. He decided that he could only spare four divisions plus some heavy artillery to reinforce von Below on the Somme. By 1 July 1916 von Below would have six divisions manning his defences with a further four-and-a-half divisions in reserve.[49]

Fourth Army's initial outline plan

Rawlinson and his chief of staff, Major-General Archibald Montgomery, were of like mind. They believed that an attempt to get right through the German defensive system in one rush was very unlikely to succeed and that it would result in extremely heavy casualties. They wanted to adopt a "step-by-step" or "bite and hold" approach – the sort of approach that Rawlinson had favoured since Neuve Chapelle and which had also been strongly advocated by Sir William Robertson and John Du Cane. Rawlinson fell seriously ill with influenza in the early part of March, and was obliged to take extended leave. Thus the initial attempt to produce an Army plan for the Somme attack was Montgomery's. Upon his return to duty towards the end of the month, Rawlinson found that the plan Montgomery had drawn up, on step-by-step principles, was "very good". Rawlinson knew, however, that that there might be difficulties getting it accepted at GHQ. Kitchener warned him that Haig had much more grandiose ideas about what might be achieved in the initial attack. But having discussed the matter with his corps commanders, and having discovered that they all liked the step-by-step approach that Montgomery had adumbrated, he sent it to Haig with only minor amendments.[50]

Fourth Army's initial plan, which, its authors anticipated, might be put into operation on 31 May (or perhaps even as early as 1 May), was for an assault by ten divisions on a front of 20,000 yards, between Serre in the north and the Montauban–Mametz spur in the south. It was essentially to be an attack on the German First Position and a few of the intermediate positions. In the critical northern part of the front the advance was to be between 1,000 and 2,000 yards only. The German Second Position was to be left alone. If the initial attack went well and the German First Position fell into Fourth Army's hands, the British would be in possession of a ridge that would give them clear observation over the Second Position on the northern part of the front. This would not, however, be true on the southern half of the front, where the ridge petered out. In the northern sector, the Germans could be expected to counter-attack to retake the ridge, but the Fourth Army planners intended to be ready for this and to beat them off, inflicting heavy casualties in the process.

The Montgomery–Rawlinson plan for the next step in the offensive was to make full use of the topography, focusing the British attack on the northern part of the German Second Position, which would, if the first phase had gone well, be dominated by the British artillery. After a pause of some three days, during which artillery would be moved forward, it was intended to capture the Second Position between Serre and Pozières and to take the fortified village of Contalmaison.[51] The rest of the German Second Position, south of Pozières, would thus have been turned and it might be possible to roll it up from the north. The Germans would then be fighting without the benefit of strong fortifications. Facing superior British numbers and firepower, they would then take casualties they could ill-afford or be compelled to make a humiliating retreat.

Yet the Fourth Army planners, while by not discounting the possibility of penetrating the whole system of German field fortifications within a few days, certainly did not count on doing this. From Rawlinson's point of view it did not seem that "the gain of 2 or 3 more kilometres of ground" was "of much consequence". Rawlinson thought that the object was "to kill as many Germans as possible with the least loss" to the British. He

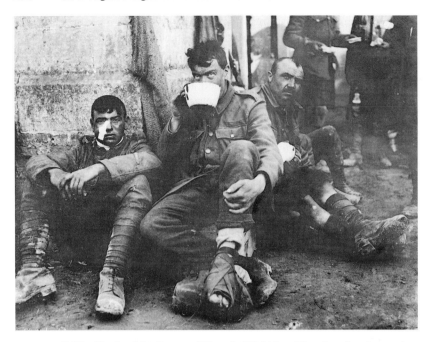

7. The Battle of the Somme: Wounded British soldiers in a dressing station in a churchyard at Morlancourt, near Albert. With the permission of The Trustees of the Imperial War Museum, London.

thought "the best way to do this" was "to seize points of tactical importance which will provide us with good observation and which we may feel quite certain the Germans will counter-attack".[52]

It must be emphasised that this was an Army-level outline plan. Much of the tactical detail concerning how to overcome local difficulties in their particular sectors would have to be filled in by corps and divisional commanders. Moreover, even as an outline, the Fourth Army scheme had some weaknesses. The most serious of these were:

(a) a failure fully to understand what it was reasonable to expect of the artillery; and
(b) an insufficient emphasis on the importance of timing when co-ordinating the infantry and artillery attack on the German First Position.

These weaknesses require further examination.

It seems that Montgomery and Rawlinson would ideally have preferred to assault the German First Position after an intense "hurricane" style of bombardment of the type used at Neuve Chapelle. Such a short, intense bombardment could have a stunning effect on the enemy and, by virtue of its brevity, might permit the achievement of a substantial degree of surprise. The principal reason that such an approach was not now practical was the dense belts of wire in front of the German positions. Unless thoroughly wrecked by the artillery, the wire would certainly kill the momentum of any infantry assault. It was not possible, with the numbers of guns that were available, to be sure that a short intensive bombardment would damage the wire adequately. Oddly, this point was not really driven home in the Fourth Army document sent to Haig. Rather Rawlinson emphasised that that a short, intensive bombardment would have to be conducted in daylight to be effective and that this would preclude an early morning attack. He proposed a fifty-sixty hour bombardment, though there would be some wire cutting fire prior to this.[53]

There was no question that the German wire had to be destroyed (or at least very badly damaged) if the infantry attack was to have any chance of success. This was principally work for the field artillery: 18–pdr guns and 4.5-inch howitzers held at divisional level. With the benefit of hindsight it seems, however, that the Fourth Army planners still placed too much emphasis on the actual physical destruction of trenches and the killing of their inhabitants, work that could only be done effectively by the heavier artillery, mainly howitzers of 6-inch bore or larger. As far as the German "front line system," or First Position, was concerned, Rawlinson believed that:

There should be enough howitzers and heavy trench mortars available to destroy a large proportion of the defences themselves.[54]

But this was to prove far too optimistic and, arguably, Rawlinson should have realised this. He knew from past experience that German field fortifications could be very strongly constructed and very hard to obliterate by shelling. He had specific intelligence that the Germans had deep dugouts in the positions in front of him on the Somme. He had already come across such dugouts in other parts of the front and had found them almost invulnerable to bombardment.[55] But in planning the Somme battle, perhaps because he had, in absolute terms, more artillery than ever before, he seems to have become overoptimistic about destroying the field fortifications of the German First Position.

Though they had gone some way towards it, at this stage in the war Rawlinson and Montgomery appear not have made a crucial mental leap. They had not yet accepted that the physical elimination of the enemy field fortifications and their garrisons (at least ones as well constructed as those facing Fourth Army north of the Albert–Bapaume road) by a preliminary bombardment was practically impossible. They had yet fully to understand that it was not necessary or productive to concentrate too much on *destruction* of field fortifications and their occupants in this manner. It was more effective to concentrate on *suppression*.

Suppression, in this context, would mean keeping most of the Germans underground, off the fire-steps of their trenches, or at least with their heads well below the parapets, until British infantry arrived. The critical thing for suppression to be effective was not so much the absolute weight of the bombardment, though it had to be at least accurate and intense enough to keep heads down. The key was timing and co-ordination with the action of the infantry. In the opening stages of the attack it was crucial that the infantry reached the German front line, without sustaining crippling casualties, within a very short time (ideally within seconds rather than minutes) of the artillery lifting off it. This was hinted at in the "Tactical Notes" that Fourth Army would issue in May, but it needed more emphasis than it got. Fourth Army as a whole was certainly not adequately indoctrinated with this concept at the opening of the Battle of the Somme.[56]

Haig's reaction to the Fourth Army plan

Despite these weaknesses, there was considerable sense in the Fourth Army outline plan. It adopted an essentially cautious, conservative, step-by-step approach to a formidably difficult task. But Haig did not like it.[57] One real problem was that Fourth Army had not taken sufficient account of the plans of the French army and, at this stage, the Allied attack on the Somme was still supposed to be predominantly French. But this seems to have been largely Haig's own fault, as he does not seem to have briefed Rawlinson adequately about the intentions of the French. These were, in fact, to achieve a crossing of the River Somme in the Péronne sector. Supporting this manoeuvre would require a deeper and more rapid advance by Fourth Army than the plan of 3 April indicated. Haig wanted Fourth Army to take the Thiepval–Ginchy Ridge (from which the Germans would otherwise overlook French operations north of the Somme) and then roll up the German Second Position south of Pozières. Thus, after the initial break-in, the main British advance would be to the south.[58]

French intentions became much less significant to British planning over the next three months as it became obvious that this would no longer be a predominantly French effort.[59] But Haig's objections to the Rawlinson scheme seem to have gone beyond its incompatibility with the initial French concept of operations. It had much to do with a fundamental difference in temperament between Rawlinson and himself. Haig thought the Fourth Army plan of 3 April made too little effort to achieve surprise and that it was too cautious. As he put it in his diary for 5 April, he was aiming at getting a "large combined force of French and British across the Somme and fighting the enemy in the open". He proposed that the lengthy preliminary bombardment should be dispensed with and reduced to a "short intensive bombardment immediately preceding the assault". He wanted to follow this with a much more ambitious initial advance. In the northern part of the front he wanted to capture the German Second Position between Serre and Pozières on the first day. In the south he wanted to secure the Montauban spur, Montauban village and the Briqueterie on the first day. Cavalry should be brought into action wherever possible "during the early stages of the attack". Haig denied that he was intending to take the whole German defensive system in one rush. But he was certainly inclined to push the first day's advance far deeper than Rawlinson would have preferred.[60]

One of Haig's greatest weaknesses at this stage in his career was his limited knowledge and understanding of artillery.[61] This is very evident in GHQ's comments on the Montgomery–Rawlinson scheme. With the number of guns they had available the Fourth Army planners simply could not guarantee to damage the German wire adequately on the stretch of front they were proposing to attack with a short bombardment. No one could deny the desirability of achieving surprise, but it simply could not be done in that manner. Even if the British artillery managed adequately to cut the wire covering the German First Position (which was very unlikely) it could not possibly have dealt effectively with that covering the Second Position. The Second Position wire was obviously more distant and much of it was on a reverse slope. These factors made it very much more difficult to hit. The points about the wire covering the Second Position had been well made in the Fourth Army plan of 3 April.[62] It seems that Haig's mind simply refused to engage with them: a classic case of an inability to engage in a proper discourse with subordinates.

Moreover, the issue of the wire was just one aspect of a more general artillery problem that Haig's insistence on attacking two major German positions on the same day would inevitably produce. The greater the initial penetration to be attempted, the greater the area of enemy field fortifications that needed to be bombarded. Given that the guns and ammunition available were finite, the greater the area to be bombarded, the lower the intensity of the bombardment. This would hold true whether the bombardment were long or short.[63]

But bombardment and wire issues were not the only arguments against Haig's insistence on a relatively deep advance on the first day. The Battle of Loos had demonstrated how much the momentum of even an experienced attacking formation was likely to be consumed by the first position it assaulted. Most of the divisions placed under Rawlinson's command on the Somme, like some of those under Haig's command at Loos, were New Army formations. Rawlinson and Montgomery regarded them only semi-trained and they thought that heavy losses had also reduced the effectiveness of more-established divisions, so that their discipline and cohesion were not what they had been the previous year. The Fourth Army planners believed that to assault one major German position in a day, and then to consolidate the ground won, was quite enough to ask of formations at this level of training. Asking more of them would result in serious disorganisation and excessive casualties.[64] This was an entirely reasonable argument. Haig overruled it without producing valid counter-arguments.

Most, though not all, historians consider that Haig's insistence on trying to penetrate the German Second Position on a substantial part of the attack frontage on the first day was a major error. The consensus is that the original Fourth Army suggestion of a step-by-step approach was the right one.[65]

Unfortunately for their troops the fundamental difference of approach between Rawlinson and Montgomery, on the one hand, and Haig, on the other, was never really resolved. The final plan of attack was a half-baked, distinctly dangerous compromise. Rawlinson won his point that a lengthy preliminary bombardment was unavoidable, but he gave way to Haig on the matter of the depth of the advance to be attempted on the first day. That was doubled from an average of 1,250 yards to one of 2,500 yards.[66]

One of the strangest aspects of Haig's planning for the Somme is that his hopes for it were not in any way scaled down to take account of the successive French announcements of reductions in the contribution that they were capable of making. Haig altered his intention as to the direction in which Fourth Army would advance after overrunning a section of the German Second Position. He now wanted this to be essentially due north, rather than due south to assist the French. But his overall conception of the campaign tended to become more grandiose over time. Conversations he held with Sir Hubert Gough on 21 and 27 June indicate that he expected Fourth Army to take the Pozières Ridge within a few days of the opening of the offensive. Gough, with his Reserve Army staff, would then direct the advance on Bapaume. Leaving a corps to defend Bapaume, "Gough with all the available cavalry and such infantry divisions as Rawlinson can spare will move northwards to clear the salient south of Arras by attacking the troops holding the front in flank and rear." Three cavalry divisions would be available for this work: two from GHQ reserve and one from Fourth Army.[67]

By late June Haig was full of confidence as to the prospects for the rest of the summer. That burgeoning sense of excitement and expectation that we have previously noted in him prior to major offensive operations was again taking over. He ridiculed Rawlinson's residual caution, noting that:

He has ordered his troops to halt for an hour and consolidate on the Enemy's last line! Covered by an artillery barrage!

Haig utterly rejected any such halt, insisting on a "rapid advance". As soon as the last line of German trenches had been gained, Haig wanted Rawlinson to push advanced guards beyond it.

By 29 June Gough was established in a headquarters at Toutencourt, slightly north of Rawlinson's at Querrieu. The 19th and 49th infantry divisions (the reserve divisions of III and X Corps) as well as three cavalry divisions were at his disposal for the exploitation of a breakthrough. Gough was himself at Rawlinson's disposal, rather than in an independent command. In the event of breach of the German front in this sector, he was supposed initially to exploit with the two infantry divisions in the direction of Le Sars, about four miles up the Albert–Bapaume road from the British front line. He was then to strike towards Bapaume with the cavalry. Somehow he was also to secure the high ground south of Bapaume to cover the deployment of the Fourth Army, which was then to attack northward, enveloping or rolling up German forces in the Arras sector. In his memoirs, with the benefit of hindsight, Gough could not conceal his sense of the unreality of all this. But there is no indication that, in late June 1916, he cast any doubt on the feasibility of the missions Haig gave him.[68]

Fourth Army's infantry and artillery tactics

Unless the British artillery had cut the wire and very thoroughly suppressed the opposition immediately to its front, the ability of Fourth Army's infantry to accomplish the sort of brisk advance that Haig intended was extremely limited. "Bangalore torpedoes" for blasting through obstacles was a device already known to military science, but these were not issued to Fourth Army's infantry for the initial attack on the Somme. Manual wire cutters, on the other hand, though issued, were likely to prove a poor way of getting through dense wire covered by rifle and machine gun fire in daylight. If they could get into the German trench system the British infantry might make good use of their rifles, bayonets, Lewis guns and grenades. (In contrast with the situation at Loos grenades were now fairly plentiful and the standard type, the Mills bomb, was a good and reliable weapon.) But if the German infantry were holding the parapets of their front line trenches in strength, before British infantry arrived there, the British were most unlikely to break in.

We now know that the traditional image of the British infantry on "the first day on the Somme" all advancing at a steady walk in successive waves, each wave consisting of an extended line with five yards between each man, is by no means entirely accurate. It is true that the attack in waves at a steady walk was advocated in Fourth Army's "Tactical Notes", issued in May: the thinking was that the inexperience of most of Fourth Army's troops would make more complex tactics difficult to execute. In reality, however, the "Tactical Notes" were just that: notes for the guidance of subordinate commanders. They were not prescriptive. Rawlinson knew that the ground and the enemy's defences on it varied a good deal. He thus delegated much to his subordinate commanders. These adopted a considerable variety of attack formations and advocated different styles and tempos of movement for the initial assault. But the formations, tempos and tactics adopted by the infantry seem, in the great majority of cases, to have made only a very limited difference to the outcome.[69]

Far more critical was the effectiveness of the supporting artillery. Rawlinson had the greatest concentration of guns and howitzers yet employed by the British army. These included 1,010 field guns and howitzers, 182 heavy guns (mainly 4.7-inch guns and 60-pdrs used for counter-battery work) and 245 heavy howitzers (ranging from 6-inch to 15-inch in bore). In addition Fourth Army had the support of forty French heavy guns and howitzers and sixty French 75mm field guns used for firing gas shell. There were also 288 medium and twenty-eight heavy trench mortars.[70] Rawlinson made recommendations for the use of all this firepower both in a series of Fourth Army conferences and in the "Tactical Notes" issued in May. Artillery employment in the opening stages of the Somme battle was also the subject of the British army's first ever Army Artillery Operations Order. Drafted under the direction of Rawlinson's Major-General Royal Artillery (MGRA), Major-General Budworth, and issued on 5 June 1916, it seems to have had two principal aims. The first was to encourage a co-ordinated employment of artillery and the common use of the best artillery tactics across Fourth Army. The second was to ensure that the supply of shell was adequate to the needs of the guns, at least in the early stages of the battle. It was far more successful in the second respect than in the first.

When dealing with shell supply Budworth's "Order" was prescriptive and detailed. For 6-inch howitzers, for example, the plan prescribed that, at the start of the preliminary bombardment, 200 rounds be dumped at the guns themselves, 650 rounds at dumps near the guns and 200 at the corps dumps. Seven trains per day were organised to ensure that the necessary quantities were delivered to the front and, by the start of the preliminary bombardment on 24 June, they were generally where they were supposed to be.[71] The supply plan depended on the construction (already underway) of a considerable network of roads and railways. In order for any sort of command and control to be exerted, 50,000 miles of telephone cable was laid, about 7,000 miles of which was buried to a depth of six feet to enable it to survive German shelling. All this involved a vast amount of physical labour, most of which (while directed by engineers or gunners) was actually performed by the infantry, reducing the time and energy they had for training.[72]

The degree of tactical co-ordination actually achieved by the Fourth Army artillery order was not, however, particularly impressive. This was not really Budworth's fault. In reality he was not in command of Fourth Army's artillery. When it came to tactics, as opposed to supply arrangements, over which he was apparently able to exert more influence, his "Order" was not really an order at all. It was a mere advisory document: having roughly the same status as the "Tactical Notes" that Fourth Army had issued to subordinate formations in May.

Budworth ordered a five-day preliminary bombardment. He outlined the tasks that Fourth Army's artillery needed to perform (notably wire cutting, trench destruction and counter-battery), but these were surely fairly obvious in any case. What he was not able to do was to fix the proportion of its guns any corps was to allocate to particular tasks or the weight of shell to be expended on particular types of target.

Both during the preliminary bombardment and during the initial infantry attack (eventually delivered on 1 July) each corps used its own artillery, as its commander, advised by his GOCRA (General Officer Commanding Royal Artillery), saw fit. At this stage in the war corps had the right to take direct control of the artillery of their integral divisions, but to what extent this actually happened during the preliminary bombardment for the Somme is unclear. There is evidence that the handling of the field artillery on 1 July was widely delegated to divisional level and in some cases lower.[73]

Budworth indicated that on the first day of infantry attacks the infantry should follow a moving artillery barrage: an advancing wall of shells. Everyone accepted this, but different formations planned different forms of barrage. The most sophisticated type of barrage in use in the British army at this period was what became known as the "creeping barrage" or "creeper". This type of barrage would normally commence ahead of the start line for the advancing infantry, but a long way short of the enemy front line. The infantry's first move would be to "close up" to the barrage, moving to within a hundred yards or less of it. The infantry would then follow the barrage as it advanced, in a series of short steps or lifts, usually of either fifty or 100 yards. Using this technique almost the whole of the ground over which the infantry advanced in the early stages of an attack would be swept by artillery fire immediately before the infantry reached it. The key thing was that the barrage should advance slowly enough that the infantry could keep pace with it – once the infantry had "lost" a creeping barrage its usefulness would be negligible.

As with most other types of barrage, a "creeper" was not expected to kill many enemy troops. It was intended to neutralise them, preventing them from firing by trapping them in dugouts or driving them to the bottom of their trenches or shell holes. Ideally the attacking infantry would be upon them within seconds of the artillery lifting off. The technique had the virtue (also a limitation) that the fire was preprogrammed. It did not depend on the infantry being able to send messages to the gunners while the attack was in progress, something rarely possible in practice. Radios were too heavy to carry. Landline, if taken forward, would not tend to survive enemy artillery fire. Runners would get pinned down or become casualties. Carrier pigeons were unreliable. Artillery staffs at GHQ and Fourth Army, led by Birch and Budworth respectively, advocated the creeping barrage technique. Rawlinson seems to have understood it fairly well and it was outlined and recommended in Fourth Army's "Tactical Notes" in May. But it seems that the authorities did not sufficiently emphasise the differences between the true "creeper" (the shortness of the lifts and the slow pace of the advance) and earlier forms of moving barrage. Nor did they adequately indoctrinate all the field gunners involved in the superior virtue of the "creeper" and insist on its adoption.[74]

The preliminary bombardment: 24–30 June

The preliminary bombardment, originally planned to last for five days (with the infantry assault scheduled for 29 June), began on 24 June. A great deal of aviation including four aeroplane squadrons with a total of sixty-eight aeroplanes and a kite-balloon squadron were made available to Fourth Army by 1 July. Thirty aircraft were allocated to counter-battery work alone. In order that artillery forward observation officers and RFC pilots and observers could direct the bombardment and monitor its results, it was important that the weather remained clement. But only one of the five days was really fine. On the others rain, low cloud and mist seriously interfered with the programme and, on 28 June, Rawlinson requested and Haig endorsed a two-day postponement of the infantry assault. The additional two days of preliminary bombardment were not particularly fine either. But given French anxieties about Verdun it was not thought possible to delay beyond 1 July. As well as the weather, another factor was adversely influencing the British bombardment as a whole: the loss of quality control in the rapidly expanded British munitions industry. This resulted in a substantial proportion of the shells fired failing to explode – a problem that was not fully appreciated until after the great infantry assault of 1 July.[75]

Before Z-day (the day of the initial infantry assault) Fourth Army's gunners had three main tasks: cutting or beating down the German wire; physically smashing trenches and strong points, and counter-battery (i.e., weakening the German artillery), by destroying guns or killing and wounding the gunners. It has been estimated that 1 million of the 1.6 million shells fired by Fourth Army from 24 June to 1 July were aimed at the German wire.[76] Most of the reports reaching Rawlinson and Haig during the preliminary bombardment indicated that the wire covering the German First Position was being adequately cut or battered down across most of the front. But as Rawlinson was aware, this was not happening in all sectors. He expressed particular concern about intact wire and the front trench not being sufficiently "knocked about" in the sector of the 34th Division, III Corps, just south of the Albert–Bapaume road.[77]

In the southern part of the front it was clear that much damage had been done to the field fortifications of the German First Position. But even there, some British patrols trying to enter German lines at night during the closing stages of the bombardment met serious opposition. Further north, in the sectors of VIII and X Corps, the German trench garrisons were sometimes strong enough and alert enough to prevent British patrols even leaving their trenches. Yet Fourth Army's intelligence gave way to gross over-optimism in this matter. Generalising excessively from the reports of relatively small numbers of prisoners (mostly taken in the XV Corps sector), a report of 29 June indicated that "Most of the dug-outs in the German front line have been blown in or blocked up."[78] Charteris and Haig, though they had access to the same data, did not correct this.

The five Fourth Army corps put different degrees of emphasis on the counter-battery mission and handled it with significantly varying degrees of efficiency. In general it seemed that this had been the least successful part of the preliminary bombardment. On the eve of the infantry assault it was clear that most of the German artillery was still active. This activity was greatest in the sector of the unfortunate VIII Corps. Hunter-Weston's headquarters had apparently allocated quite a large force of artillery to the counter-battery role but far too little ammunition (only twenty rounds per gun per day) and had tasked only one of the corps aircraft to spot for these guns. The problem was compounded because the German guns in this sector were exceptionally numerous.

The German artillery was considerably weaker at the southern end of the Fourth Army front. There were fewer guns there to begin with, their observation was not as good and they had been subjected to the most effective corps counter-battery effort. XIII Corps dedicated a large force of artillery and aircraft to the counter-battery role and these were handled with great efficiency. (It is also fairly clear that XIII Corps benefited from the proximity of powerful and efficient French artillery, which was undertaking counter-battery work in this sector.) The German batteries north of Mametz and Montauban were pulverised, German sources admitting that the field artillery of their 12th Division and 28th Division was entirely put out of action by enemy fire.[79]

Getting ready to go

As Z-day approached, Haig (as would be his usual practice for the rest of the war) established advanced headquarters nearer the front. For the Somme campaign Advanced GHQ was established, on 27 June, at the Chateau de Valion at Beauquesne, five miles south-south-east of Doullens.[80] This gave the commander-in-chief greater proximity to Rawlinson, whom he would be able to see face-to-face whenever he wished. But his ability to influence the battle was still very limited. He had no readily available infantry reserve under his own control, and was largely reliant on telephone reports from Fourth Army for information.[81]

By the evening of 30 June the infantry of Fourth Army was keyed up and ready to go. Though there were inevitably some failures of nerve on the part of individuals even before the attack started, morale seems to have been high. The infantry were to be formed up in their starting positions by 7.00 a.m. on 1 July. It would then be broad daylight, making it less likely that inexperienced troops would lose direction, but making them easy targets for any enemy troops still active. Rawlinson would have preferred a dawn attack, but the French were insistent on some hours of daylight for their final bombardment and it was considered important that their attack north of the Somme should be simultaneous with that of the British.[82] Sir Aylmer Hunter-Weston of VIII Corps had secured, from Fourth Army and GHQ, permission to explode a very large mine under the Hawthorn Redoubt, in the German front line, near Beaumont Hamel, at 7.20 a.m. (Mines in other parts of the front were due to be detonated at 7.28.) Also at 7.20, the artillery bombardment of the German front line was to reach maximum intensity. This would continue until 7.30 (Zero hour) when the artillery would lift off the German front line to deeper targets. At the same time the officers were to blow their whistles and the infantry attack would begin.[83]

Five corps of Rawlinson's Fourth Army would attack on 1 July, using a total of eleven divisions: Hunter-Weston's VIII Corps, on Fourth Army's

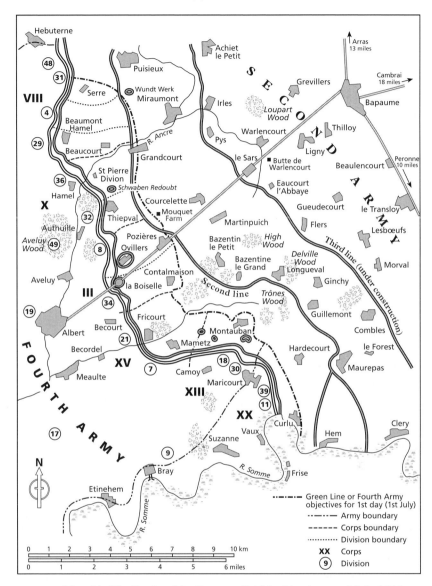

Map 11. The Battle of the Somme: British objectives on 1 July 1916

left wing, would attack with three divisions and the other four corps with two each. To the south, on Fourth Army's right flank, just north of the River Somme, there would be a simultaneous assault by XX Corps of General Fayolle's French Sixth Army, part of Foch's Northern Army

Group. South of the Somme two more corps of the same Army (I Colonial Corps and XXXV Corps) would attack two hours later. It was hoped that the Germans would, by this stage, have concluded that the attack would be entirely north of the river, enabling the belated effort south of it to achieve a substantial measure of surprise.[84]

Fourth Army's northern (left-hand) boundary was with Lieutenant-General Snow's VII Corps, belonging to General Allenby's Third Army. Late in the planning process Haig had decided that the two divisions of that corps, the 46th and the 56th should mount an attack on a bulge in the German front around the fortified village of Gommecourt. The Gommecourt attack was supposedly a diversion. The divisions involved were to make no effort to hide their preparations for an attack. Indeed they were intended to advertise them. That neither Allenby nor Snow was happy with the plan that GHQ had imposed upon them is hardly surprising.

The "first day on the Somme"

The VII Corps attack at Gommecourt at 7.30 a.m. on 1 July 1916 must be accounted practically unmitigated disaster. The 46th (North Midland) Division, attacking the northern side of the German bulge ran into much uncut wire and intense fire. Few men of this division penetrated the German front line and those that did were not able to hold their gains. The 56th (London) Division's attack made better initial progress. But the exposure of both of this division's flanks, coupled with the intensity of German artillery fire, which made it impossible to bring up reserves, ensured that it had lost practically all its gains by nightfall. It is, moreover, difficult to show that the Gommecourt operation afforded any significant assistance to Fourth Army.[85]

The explosion of the mine under the Hawthorn Redoubt at 7.20 a.m. seems to have been one of the worst blunders of what was, for the British, a truly horrific day. It alerted the Germans in the VIII Corps sector that they were about to be attacked ten minutes before the artillery lifted off their front line. By the time Lieutenant-General Hunter-Weston's infantry began their attack at 7.30 a.m., plenty of the Germans in this sector had left their dugouts and were manning the parapets. Most of VIII Corps' attacking battalions (belonging to 31st Division, 4th Division and 29th Division) met with intense rifle and machine gun fire in No Man's Land. Many of those who got that far also found the wire uncut. Only one battalion from 31st Division and a few from 4th Division made any penetration into the German defences at all. The attack of the 29th Division (a veteran division that had fought at Gallipoli) failed utterly.

In the sector of Lieutenant-General Morland's X Corps, initial results were better. Whether the preliminary bombardment had done greater damage to the German trench system is not clear, but there is no doubt that the wire had been more effectively breached. In the 36th (Ulster) Division's sector on the left, what was later called the "race to the parapet" was clearly won: the Northern Irish troops getting to the enemy front line before it was properly organised for defence. The divisional commander had moved his assault troops out into No Man's Land well before Zero hour. Many were able to form up in a conveniently placed sunken road, practically an extra trench. The distance they had to cross at Zero hour was therefore quite short and their movement was not significantly impeded by enemy wire. This division captured most of its objectives, including the mini-fortress of the Schwaben Redoubt. Results in the 32nd Division's sector were, however, more mixed, one attacking brigade doing well, the other failing. The 36th Division was subjected to intense fire from both flanks and fiercely counter-attacked. By the end of the following day X Corps retained almost none of the ground they had initially captured and casualties had been truly catastrophic.[86]

The attack of Lieutenant-General Pulteney's III Corps in the centre of the front, straddling the Albert–Bapaume road, was an unmitigated disaster. The 8th and 34th Divisions of this corps faced the strongly fortified villages of Ovillers and la Boisselle in which the defenders had generally survived the bombardment. The attacking divisions did not advance far into No Man's Land before Zero hour and clearly lost the race to the parapet. Casualties were massive and there was no substantial penetration of the German defensive system.

The four most northerly Allied corps attacking on 1 July 1916, the VII, VIII, X and III British corps, had thus all been defeated, sustaining very heavy casualties for minuscule permanent gains of ground. In the southern part of the front, however, things went significantly better for the Allies. Lieutenant-General Horne's XV Corps had not quite secured the fortified village of Fricourt before nightfall. However, the 21st Division made a successful advance north of the village, while the 7th Division pushed well into the German defences to its south. XV Corps' planned envelopment of Fricourt was thus well on the way to success and the Germans would soon abandon it. The southernmost British corps, Lieutenant-General Congreve's XIII Corps, was the most successful. Its 18th and 30th Divisions captured all their objectives and did so with casualties that were, by the standards of this bloodiest of days, relatively light. An unusually heavy effective preliminary bombardment, the most sophisticated use of a supporting barrage, and the movement of the attacking troops into specially constructed jumping-off trenches well out into No Man's Land before Zero hour all contributed to this corps' success. All three of the French corps also did very well, taking practically all their objectives. Precise figures for French casualties on the first day of the Somme are hard to find, but it is universally acknowledged that they were very low compared to those of virtually all the British corps.[87]

The overall results of the day are, therefore, not especially difficult to summarise. The Allied attack north of the Albert–Bapaume road and in the 34th Division sector, immediately south of it, had almost completely failed. The four British corps in that sector had all suffered defeats. But the five Allied corps operating further south (two British and three French) had been very much more successful. The British XIII Corps and all three French corps took practically all their objectives. The cost was appalling by any standards. The British (Third Army and Fourth Army) had suffered 57,470 casualties. Some 19,240 were killed outright or died of wounds. Over 500 were taken prisoner and over 2,000 were missing. A high proportion of this last figure must, presumably, be added to the number of fatalities. So the oft-quoted figure of 20,000 British dead from the "first day of the Somme" is probably quite near the mark and may even be an underestimate.[88]

Fourth Army headquarters lay at the hub of an impressive network of communications, giving Rawlinson access to information from all parts of the battlefield as fast as the technology of the day could convey it. Haig had placed himself close to Rawlinson and he motored to Querrieu to see him after lunch. Yet neither general had a clear idea of what was going on before night fell. A dense fog of war descended as soon the infantry left their trenches to begin the attack. Hundreds of messages came in to Rawlinson's headquarters, but many were wildly inaccurate and contradicted by others arriving later.[89] By nightfall Haig did realise that results had been very different on different parts of the battlefield, though his analysis of the causes of this was seriously flawed. He attributed failure on the VIII Corps front to "few" of its troops "having left their trenches". In reality VIII Corps had taken about 14,000 casualties that day. Another diary remark that "on a sixteen-mile front of attack varying fortunes must be expected" would have been exceptionally callous had Haig known the scale of the catastrophe his forces had suffered.[90]

No one, however, knew the casualties with any accuracy at this stage. Rawlinson's first guess for his own Army was between 16,000 and 20,000 – about a third of the real total. Like Haig, Rawlinson had a very imperfect understanding of the position that night. At 10 p.m. on 1 July he ordered operations "to secure, as early as possible, all important tactical points still in possession of the Germans in their front line system". The wording indicates a failure to realise that the Germans were still in control of the

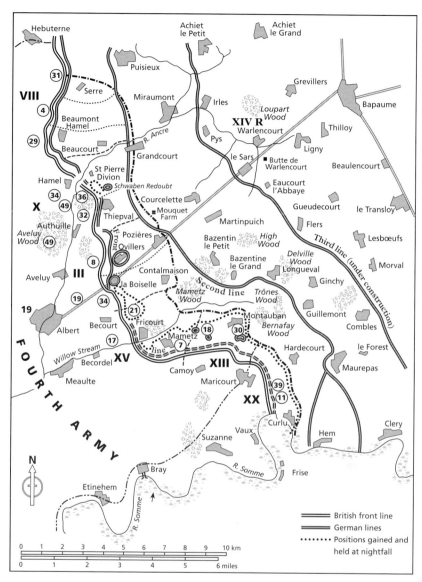

Map 12. The Battle of the Somme: situation at nightfall on 1 July 1916

great bulk of their First Position north of the Albert–Bapaume road. Few British troops would be active within that area by the end of the night.[91]

As noted, success was by far the greatest at the southern end of the front. The commitment of good quality, fresh infantry divisions in the XIII

Corps sector on the afternoon of 1 July, or even on the morning of 2 July, might have made a huge difference to the general course of the battle. Even a single fresh infantry division might have had a substantial effect. Though complete breakthrough and cavalry exploitation was almost certainly too much to hope for, the British would have stood a good chance of getting within striking distance of the German Second Position and might even have taken a section of those defences.[92] Had a substantial part of the German Second Position fallen to the British so early in the battle, the German high command would have been plunged into the deepest of crises. But despite all the fuss that had been made about infantry reserves at Loos, Haig and Rawlinson had, between them, failed to ensure their availability at what turned out to be the critical point at the opening of the next major British offensive. On 1 July, XIII Corps, like the other Fourth Army corps, had a division in reserve. This was the 9th Scottish Division, later widely considered to be the best in the army. But because British aims in this sector were so modest (just the capture of the German First Position) Rawlinson had no thought of this division being committed to offensive operations so early in the battle. Its units were dispersed in XIII Corps' rear areas.[93]

Though Gough had earlier shown a keen interest in the XV and XIII Corps sectors, Haig had, as noted, intended that Gough and his cavalry divisions be used further north, in a thrust towards Bapaume, and that subsequent exploitation should be northward from there. Apparently because he perceived his main axis of attack to be towards Bapaume and points north, Rawlinson had placed the only infantry divisions he had in Army Reserve (12th and 25th Divisions) under the administration of III and X Corps respectively.[94] From both Haig's and Rawlinson's points of view, therefore, the greatest success on 1 July came in an unexpected place (in some senses the wrong place). Their reserves were poorly disposed and both generals were, perhaps, mentally unprepared to exploit it.

Assessment

Of all the issues concerning 1 July 1916, it seems particularly important to try to understand why the French were so much more successful than the British and why XV and XIII Corps did so much better than the rest of the British forces. Even more crucially, we must ask why British casualties overall were so massive in relation to the ground gained and to what extent Haig was personally responsible for this. This last matter must get particular attention given that the holocaust of British troops on the "first day on the Somme" is widely regarded as one of the most serious indictments of Haig's generalship.

Factors often enumerated to explain the greater success of the French are their greater experience, their more powerful and efficient artillery and their superior infantry tactics. As far as the first day is concerned, the French artillery had been so successful that, at least in some parts of the front, it seems that the infantry had little need of tactical virtuosity. South of the Somme, where their attack went in later than that of the British, the French seem to have been aided by a degree of surprise.[95] Together these appear to offer a convincing explanation. But two further points need to be added. The first is that all the French corps attacked in the southern part of the front. In the southern sector even the comparatively under-gunned and inexperienced British were relatively successful. The most successful British corps was the most southern and all three French corps operated still further south. The second point, possibly even more critical, is that the south was the area where the attackers were expected by their own high commands (British and French) to achieve the least. The five most southerly Allied corps were only supposed to take the German First Position.

A factor surprisingly often left out of military analysis is the influence of the enemy. There is no reason to assume that German resistance was even all across the front. Indeed, it is certain that the Germans were at their weakest in the south. Their fortifications there were less developed and their artillery less numerous, especially south of the Somme.[96] The Germans seem to have prioritised defending the higher ground of the Thiepval–Ginchy Ridge, just as the Allies prioritised trying capture it. The absence of any pronounced ridge south of the Somme also left the Germans, who were, of course, inferior in the air, with relatively poor observation for what artillery they did have in that sector. That Allied success was greatest where it was least expected is very unlikely to be mere coincidence. The artillery resources of XV and XIII Corps were no greater than that of other Fourth Army corps in relation to the stretch of front they were attacking (though these corps, and especially XIII Corps, also benefited from French fire). Some of these troops benefited from the use of a closer approximation to a true creeping barrage and some won the "race to the parapet" by starting in No Man's Land. But their greater success (together with that of the French) probably also owed much to their artillery being able to concentrate its attention on the German First Position: not having to concern itself with bombarding field fortifications further back. XV Corps' artillery seems to have done an exceptional degree of damage to German field fortifications and the German wire had been effectively breached across most of the XV and XIII Corps sectors.[97]

This reinforces the arguments of historians who suggest that the greatest mistake in the planning for the first day of infantry attacks on the Somme was Haig's decision to double the extent of the penetration into the German defensive system that most of Fourth Army's corps were to attempt.[98] The likelihood is that this substantially increased the area that these corps attempted to bombard with their heavy guns and thus significantly dissipated the bombardment. Yet a caveat must be appended here. The command of British artillery was, as has been repeatedly stressed, much decentralised. With the possible exception of the Battle of Waterloo on 18 June 1815, the "first day on the Somme" is probably the most studied day in British military history. Yet no one has yet done the sort of microanalysis that might tell us the details of the fire programmes of all the corps and divisional artilleries during the preliminary bombardment and during 1 July itself. We really do not know the weight of shell devoted to different parts of the German defensive system.[99] It is surely unsafe to assume that corps and divisional artilleries devoted an equal amount of fire to all the German trenches that their infantry were theoretically supposed to overrun on the first day. It seems rather more likely that they concentrated a higher proportion on the nearer objectives, knowing that if their infantrymen were killed by fire from those, they would not have to worry about tackling those further away. So while we can reasonably assume that Haig's overruling of the original Fourth Army plan led to some significant dissipation of the bombardment, we cannot be certain of the degree of this dissipation.

There is no question that Haig bears the responsibility for trying to push the initial assault deep on one part of the attack sector – overruling the Fourth Army planners in this respect. But it also seems clear in retrospect that the attack was on too broad a front. For that Rawlinson and Montgomery must share the blame, though Haig's was the final responsibility. Narrow front attacks were generally perceived to be a bad idea because they could be exposed to intense flanking fire and because the enemy would usually be able to find reserves to throw in against them. A dislike of attacks on very narrow fronts (say three miles or less) was quite reasonable, though, in practice, Rawlinson would mount a lot of them over the next couple of weeks. Attacking on a sixteen-mile front (for the British alone) on 1 July, however, seems to have been going to the opposite extreme. Arguably the excessive frontage was even more responsible for causing the fatal dissipation of British fire than Haig's insistence on pushing the attack deep.

The prodigious British blood letting of 1 July was clearly a result of overreaching: of trying to do too much (in terms of both breadth and depth) too quickly, with too little artillery. The impulse behind this overreaching was very largely Haig's. Haig was under no real pressure to achieve dramatic results quickly. The French, though they insisted that a serious, sustained British effort should start by 1 July 1916, were in no position to dictate British operational methods. The French Sixth Army itself used a cautious approach: limited infantry advances prepared by intensely concentrated artillery fire.[100] The French could hardly have objected had the British done likewise. From his desk at the War Office, Robertson advocated careful, step-by-step methods. So (until he was killed when a ship intended to carry him to Russia hit a mine off the Orkneys in June)[101] did Kitchener.[102] Haig was in no position to complain, as so many commanders in other wars have complained, that an uncomprehending government was expecting him to make bricks without straw. The Asquith coalition's War Committee had no particular expectation of spectacular results from the Somme campaign. It put Haig under no real pressure to do more than the bare minimum necessary to hold the Franco-British alliance together.[103]

Had his forces gained a signal victory on 1 July, exceeding what Kitchener, Robertson, Rawlinson and Montgomery had thought practicable, we can be sure that Haig would have claimed a good deal of the credit. For the fact that his army grossly overreached itself, suffering vastly excessive casualties in relation to the results achieved, it is only reasonable that he should take much of the blame.

10   The Battle of the Somme (2)

After the "First Day"

About half the British troops who attacked on 1 July 1916 had become casualties by nightfall. Yet even the traumatised men who ended the day as prisoners of the Germans considered that there was little chance of the offensives being stopped. Too much time and effort had already been invested. Moreover, with the French army still on the rack at Verdun, cancelling the offensive at this stage might have jeopardised the entire Franco-British alliance. Up to late June Haig had been contemplating shifting his main effort to Flanders if things did not go well in Picardy. But there is no evidence that any such thought crossed his mind on the evening of 1 July. He had initially underestimated the first day's losses and, for the immediate future, he had ample manpower to keep the battle going.[1]

Haig's influence in shaping the future of the campaign after the disasters of the first day was of vital importance and, for once, of an entirely positive nature. On the night of 1 July, apparently not realising how completely the attack in the north and centre had failed, Rawlinson ordered the renewal of efforts to capture the German First Position and some intermediate positions beyond it, right across the Fourth Army front. Had this order been implemented, it would have resulted in the bulk of the effort being made in the north and centre, where the initial attack had most clearly failed. At this stage Rawlinson seemed to be giving little thought to the area where it had been most successful: south of the Albert–Bapaume road, in the XV and XIII Corps sectors.[2]

There can be no doubt that on Sunday 2 July Haig was more willing than Rawlinson to adjust British plans to take into account the result of the opening attacks. After trying to make sense of reports coming in that morning, Haig attended a church service conducted by the Reverend Duncan in a hut near Beauquesne at 9.30. He then went with Kiggell by staff car to see Rawlinson at Fourth Army HQ at Querrieu. In his discussion of future operations with the Fourth Army commander, Haig emphasised the southern sector. He instructed Rawlinson to devote much effort to the capture of the village of Fricourt on XV Corps' front and "questioned him as to his views of an advance from Montauban and his right, instead of from Thiepval and his left". According to Haig, Rawlinson needed some persuasion that this was the best course but soon agreed to it.[3] Over the coming weeks the British would focus their efforts on the southern sector.

In another respect, however, Haig seemed to show a strange reluctance to rethink his plans. On Sunday 2 July Gough's Reserve Army headquarters took control of the VIII and X Corps, leaving Rawlinson with III Corps, XV Corps and XIII Corps. This was rather odd. Gough's intended role had been to complete a breakthrough and exploit it. A cavalry officer, considered a "thruster", such a role might have suited his dashing temperament. All the prior arrangements for the intervention of the Reserve Army on the field of battle had, however, been predicated on the assumption that exploitation would be on an axis toward Bapaume and north from there, on Fourth Army's left. Though Fourth Army met stark and bloody failure on that wing on 1 July, and though by far the best opportunities were now on the right, Haig stuck to the plan that Gough should take over on the left.[4]

Thus Gough, the general originally tasked with exploitation, ended up commanding two corps that had been stopped dead in their tracks. On 2 July, Gough told Haig that he had taken a look at these formations and found them shattered and incapable of any major offensive action for a considerable time. This confirmed Haig's impression that it was better to concentrate efforts in the south. Haig now wanted to focus on breaking what, on 1 July, had been the German Second Position, between Bazentin le Grand and Longueval, and gave Rawlinson orders to that effect.[5]

In pursuing this eminently sensible course, Haig initially appeared to be endangering his relationship with the French high command. Joffre visited Haig's advanced headquarters on Monday 3 July with Foch and other senior French officers. Haig indicated that he was likely to make his main effort in the south and asked whether, if the British attacked towards Longueval, the French would co-operate by attacking Guillemont. At this Joffre, according to Haig's account, "exploded in a fit of rage". He tried to insist that the British renew the attack in the north and centre of the front, taking Thiepval and Pozières. Haig, according to his own account, remained "most polite" but insisted that he was "solely responsible to the British Government for the action of the British Army", and that plans had to be adapted to changing circumstances. At this stage Joffre apparently calmed down and by the end of the meeting Haig thought he had secured French agreement to co-operate with his plans.

Afterwards Haig condescendingly noted of Joffre that "the poor man cannot argue",[6] perhaps unaware that other people considered a singular lack of competence in discourse conspicuous amongst his own faults. Joffre's outburst at the meeting on 3 July was perhaps owing to the disappointment of an earnest hope that the British army would do the vast majority of the Somme fighting, with the French playing only a much lesser, supporting role. Joffre's thinking may have been that if the main fighting took place in the northern part of the front the British would inevitably do most of it. But with the initial British failure in the north and Haig's shift of the focus of the effort to the south, the French Sixth Army would be in the thick of it. The French were thus likely to have to bleed more heavily on the Somme than Joffre, frightened by his losses at Verdun, had hoped.

Early results at the strategic level: 1–12 July 1916

Joffre might have been a little less anxious had he known the effect that the Somme offensive was already having on the strategic situation. Seven German divisions were en route to the Somme by 2 July. A further seven were on their way by 9 July. Falkenhayn was forced to rethink his plans for 1916. Facing a deepening crisis on the Somme, by 12 July 1916 he had suspended major offensive operations at Verdun. Also abandoning a cherished scheme to use Prince Rupprecht's Sixth Army for a counterstroke against the British in the Arras sector, he took divisions from Rupprecht to shore up his defences on the Somme. By mid-July 1916 the Germans had completely lost the initiative on the Western Front.[7]

After 1 July, the French continued to have considerable success in their sector, but, uncertain where to make the main effort, they failed to maximise their opportunities. The best chance for a relatively deep and rapid advance was south of the Somme. But Joffre wanted this to be a predominantly British offensive and the British wanted French help north of the river. Close Franco-British co-operation, however, always proved extremely difficult to organise. Though the artillery of the French XX Corps gave some support to XIII Corps in its assault on the Bazentin Ridge on 14 July, Rawlinson was very disappointed not to get more direct and substantial help. Considered overall, however, French operations up to the middle of July were far more effective than those of the British resulting in the capture of 12,000 prisoners and seventy pieces of artillery.[8]

Fourth Army's struggle towards the Bazentin Ridge: 2–13 July

VIII and X Corps formally became part of Reserve Army on 4 July. They were, as Gough had pointed out, so smashed up that they were incapable of any serious offensive effort in the short term. Though some of their divisions were quickly relieved, over the next couple of weeks these corps gained little ground. Haig's plan for the continuation of the Somme battle as it developed over the next few days, therefore, was for Fourth Army to push forward with its remaining corps – III, XV and XIII – until it was in striking distance of the German Second Position on the Bazentin Ridge. Fourth Army would then mount a powerful, concerted assault. Rawlinson scheduled this for mid-July.

There were some favourable developments in the southern part of Fourth Army's front on 2 July. Fricourt fell to XV Corps and XIII Corps defeated a German attempt a retake Montauban. La Boisselle was taken on 3 July. Other opportunities, however, went begging. There appear to have been no German troops in Mametz Wood until 4 July and XV Corps might have secured it without a fight. Patrols spotted this, but action was not taken quickly enough. Rawlinson, however, reckoned he needed Mametz as well as Trônes Wood and Contalmaison before mounting the big, co-ordinated assault on the Bazentin Ridge he was planning for mid-July, a view with which GHQ concurred.[9]

Haig visited Rawlinson and his corps commanders on the afternoon of Tuesday 4 July to urge that these objectives be gained as rapidly as possible. Two days later he sent an order from Advanced GHQ urging the same thing.

Yet neither GHQ nor Fourth Army took control of the operations necessary to seize these intermediate objectives. Such operations were delegated to the corps. The corps commanders generally sub-delegated to divisions and sometimes on down to battalion level. This resulted in a series of rather unco-ordinated attacks, supported only by a fraction of Fourth Army's artillery strength. Such operations were mounted on fairly narrow fronts and thus created flanks vulnerable to the fire of German units that were not heavily engaged. Narrow front operations also invited counter-attacks – though these were usually unsuccessful. The struggle to place Fourth Army within striking distance of the Bazentin Ridge was thus an expensive one – resulting in around 25,000 casualties.[10]

Yet, however advisable a careful, step-by-step approach was in general terms, it is not clear that these hurriedly mounted, imperfectly co-ordinated attacks were the wrong way to proceed on this particular sector of the front at this particular stage in the campaign. Elaborately choreographed assaults involving several divisions normally took at least a week to prepare. It would have been of inestimable benefit to the Germans, whose forces in this southern sector were still somewhat disordered and off balance, had the British on the XV and XIII Corps fronts stopped attacking for that long. Arguably, the main fault of the Fourth Army forces in the southern part of the front, at least for the first couple of days of this period (2–4 July), was that they were insufficiently aggressive and opportunistic rather than insufficiently careful and co-ordinated.

Fourth Army's operations of 2–13 July kept the Germans off balance and shook them badly. By placing Fourth Army in a position to assault the Bazentin Ridge, they amounted to a significant victory, albeit a costly one.[11] Losses on 1 July had been vastly heavier on the British than on the German side. But over the next fortnight German forces on the Somme found themselves in a meat-grinder. Their high command's policy at this time was to fight for every foot of ground and always to counter-attack to retake lost territory. But they were facing superior, increasingly effective British artillery, which was enjoying the benefits of skilful observation by the Royal Flying Corps, which, together with the French air service, enjoyed marked air superiority. German counter-attacks, at this stage of the battle, were hurriedly mounted and generally much more disjointed than British attacks. Most were defeated. Within the first ten days of the opening of the Battle of the Somme the German Second Army had suffered 40,187 casualties.[12] Though some of the ground needed for Fourth Army's next grand slam was captured uncomfortably late, Rawlinson was able to go ahead with it on the planned date: 14 July.

Haig's relations with London in early July 1916

In the meantime, however, Haig was having difficulties in his relationship both with the authorities in London and with the press. The casualties of 1 July, when reported in the United Kingdom, especially in localities that had raised units that had been slaughtered, shook the public and inevitably caused concern to the government. After a meeting of the War Committee on 3 July, Maurice Hankey spoke to Lloyd George, who was about to replace Kitchener as Secretary of State for War. Hankey noted that, as he had "fully anticipated", the offensive had "utterly failed with very heavy losses". It had always seemed to him "utter folly". Lloyd George reminded Hankey of the paper he had written in December 1914 in which he had argued that it would be impossible "to break the front in the West and urged that victory was only to be obtained in the Eastern theatre of operations".[13]

Robertson had gone out to France on 1 July. His initial impressions were mixed, but subsequent reports of the slaughter seem to have shocked him.[14] He tried, however, to stick by his policy of presenting a united military front in dealing with ministers and, with them, put a brave face on events.[15] But given the scale of the losses, ministers were demanding to be kept informed of the progress of the campaign. Haig's communications with the War Office, however, were grudging and uninformative.

As Robertson explained to Haig in a letter of 5 July, this left him in an awkward position:

I have seen several Cabinet Ministers and the first question has always been how you are getting on and what you propose to do next. As regards the first I have said that you are getting on very well, but that it would be a slow business. As regards the second I have been able to say that I do not know what you propose to do next, that being the truth.[16]

It was a theme to which Robertson would repeatedly return over the next few weeks. In a postscript to a letter of 7 July the CIGS wrote:

I hope you will keep me informed of what you think as to your future prospects. This is really essential because of the many theatres and Allies which we here have to deal with. Our vast and complicated foreign policy necessitates the War Committee being kept fully informed of our prospects and doings in every theatre. I am not referring to detailed plans but to the General situation ... If you could send me a short letter which I could read to the War Committee I am sure it would be to the General interest, and to your interest in particular.[17]

Haig was generally assiduous in protecting his own interests. Now apparently convinced that these were at stake, he sent a report the following day. It explained that while he still saw taking the heavily fortified Thiepval–Morval position as vital, the "best prospects of success" now lay in "pressing our attack against it from the south". While doing this, he needed the French to protect his southern flank immediately north of the Somme. He assured the government that "ultimate complete success" was still possible, though only after a struggle lasting "several weeks". To achieve "complete success and exploit it to the full" he needed all the manpower the government could send him.[18] While this response was better than nothing, it did not keep the War Committee satisfied for long.

Government anxiety about public opinion inevitably meant concern about relations with the press. But, while somewhat uncommunicative with the War Office, Haig was being even more awkward with the Fourth Estate. It is perhaps understandable that he had refused Robertson's request to entertain newspaper proprietors immediately prior to the start of the Somme campaign on grounds of pressure of work.[19] But even after the campaign had opened, Haig found it difficult to set aside personal feelings in an effort to improve his relations with press and public. Conscious of the special political importance of *The Times*, on 4 July Lord Esher wrote to Haig asking him to play host for a visit by Colonel Charles Repington, that paper's military correspondent. Haig, however, had a very poor opinion of Repington (who had a rather poor opinion of Haig and had been a supporter of Sir John French). Haig's initial reaction was to snub Repington, indicating that he should apply through Charteris,

Haig's press liaison officer, like any other correspondent. Someone, possibly Charteris, did prevail upon Haig to grant an interview. But he conducted it with such coldness that there was little chance of this encounter improving GHQ's public relations.[20] At this stage Haig demonstrated no awareness that the size of casualties his forces were suffering might give the press and politicians legitimate cause for anxiety or dismay. Lady Haig, so useful to her husband in many ways, hated the thought of his pandering to press or public[21] and may well have encouraged this myopic attitude. Whether he realised it or not, it was vital to Haig's future that he improve his relations with the press. In the short term, the instincts of most editors and correspondents were to be patriotic and supportive. But had many of them turned violently against him, this might have proved fatal to his chances of remaining in command.

Haig had strong royal backing, but the support of everyone else of importance in London was limited and conditional. The Robertson–Haig relationship, for example, was formally correct, but even at this stage it was by no means close or trusting. In early July 1916 it was already under quite serious stress, not just because of Haig's reluctance to communicate. Robertson agreed with Haig on the need to concentrate effort on the Western Front. But he was already having serious doubts about Haig's operational competence, suspecting that an excessive adherence to "old theories" was "causing us very heavy losses".[22]

Throughout 1915 Robertson had been one of the principal advocates of a "step-by-step" approach to operations. He wanted attacks mounted with very limited objectives and supported by overwhelming firepower. He had, as we have noted, tried to get Haig to adopt a cautious approach to the Somme campaign, wanting limited attacks rather than "a great offensive promising far-reaching effect". He now evidently felt that Haig had ignored him and overextended his forces with tragic consequences. Robertson plainly doubted Haig's capacity to adjust to the realities of Western Front warfare, fearing that he would continue to set overambitious objectives and consequently continue to waste British lives. Yet Robertson was reluctant to confront Haig directly on these issues. Instead he wrote to Haig's subordinates, apparently hoping that his views would reach Haig indirectly. On 5 July he indicated to Kiggell that:

The more I think of it the more I am convinced that at any rate until we get through the enemy's defences the road to success lies through deliberation. All last year I preached this doctrine. I maintained then and still maintain that nothing is to be gained but very much is to be lost by trying to push on too rapidly. Before the war our theory was that anybody who could make ground should make it. This is a dangerous theory until we get through the enemy's trenches. People who can and do push on in front of the general line seldom … stay there. They are usually cut off or at any rate driven back. The fact is that the whole line must go forward together.

If the above view is sound it follows that the objectives must be exceedingly limited. In fact limited to such a distance as there is reasonable prospect of the whole line being able to reach. This theory tends to what is absolutely necessary, namely concentration of artillery fire. No nation in the world can turn out sufficient ammunition to deal with a long front … and at the same time to deal with great depth … What we have got to do is to plod on carefully, slowly and deliberately until we get through … and for this we want concentration and not dispersal of artillery fire … The thing is to advance along a wide front step by step to very limited and moderate objectives …

Robertson asked Kiggell to show this letter to no one.[23] It is difficult to know what he expected Kiggell to do with it. If Robertson, the Chief of the Imperial General Staff, who, at this stage, held military rank equal to Haig's, felt unable to confront Haig over military doctrine and operational method, how could Kiggell, an underling, assume this responsibility? If Robertson thought that Kiggell would be prepared to make veiled criticisms of his chief's operational methods combined with suggestions for their amendment, he had fundamentally misunderstood the Haig–Kiggell relationship. It seems, moreover, to indicate a certain lack of moral courage on Robertson's part that, in a letter sent to Haig on the very same day, he adopted a much more soothing tone. While counselling "deliberate and relentless pressure" rather than any attempt at breakthrough in future operations, Robertson expressed himself satisfied with the progress so far made.[24]

Kiggell did not reply to Robertson's letter for nine days. His eventual response, delayed until the immediate aftermath of the successful attack of 14 July, was superficially polite yet practically dismissive. If Kiggell had any capacity for military thought independent of Haig, he was not prepared to display it at this stage. He indicated that he, like Haig, favoured rapid advances where at all possible. At the moment it was not possible and limited attacks were, therefore, the order of the day. Rawlinson, in Kiggell's view, was doing wonderfully well and Haig was a magnificent, imperturbable commander-in-chief.[25] There was, Kiggell implied, really nothing to discuss. It seems that from Kiggell's perspective (which was also Haig's) Robertson was merely a sort of high-ranking office boy whose job was to mind the War Office on Haig's behalf while Haig and his army fought the war. Robertson's legitimate functions were to keep the politicians off Haig's back, to prevent their wasting resources on sideshows and to supply Haig's army, with the minimum of fuss, with all the men and munitions that Haig demanded. Robertson should, Kiggell implied, concentrate on those things, mind his own business and leave the conduct of operations to GHQ and the Armies in the field.

Some senior officers in the BEF, notably Rawlinson, to a large degree shared Robertson's concept of operations,[26] but Robertson found that he had little or no leverage with GHQ in such matters. Henry Wilson, an arch-plotter himself, considered that in July 1916 Robertson was manoeuvring personally to replace Haig as commander-in-chief.[27] It is, indeed, very probable that Robertson would have liked Haig's job and not entirely, or even principally, for selfish reasons. But he could not have removed Haig without expressing his doubts about him to the politicians, particularly the new Secretary of State for War, David Lloyd George, who formally took up office on 7 July. When he became CIGS, Robertson had started from the premise that it was necessary for the generals to present a united front in order to prevent the politicians wrecking the war effort.[28] No solid evidence has ever been produced to indicate that he was ready, in July 1916, to drop that principle in order to replace Haig. Adherence to it, however, prevented him from exercising any substantial influence over Haig's operations.

Planning the Bazentin Ridge attack: 2–13 July

The next step in the British army's Somme campaign was Fourth Army's assault on the Bazentin Ridge, which was scheduled for mid-July. This operation presented real problems. Even if all the preliminary operations that Rawlinson had delegated to his corps commanders were completed on time, the infantry of XIII Corps, on the right, would still be 1,500 yards short of the German front line. This was a distance too great to cross in the course of an assault. The solution that Rawlinson adopted was to send the troops out into No Man's Land in the hours of darkness and get them to advance stealthily as close as possible to the German positions they were about to attack.[29] The operation of 14 July is sometimes described as a "night attack", but the attack itself was always scheduled for dawn. Only the approach march was to be conducted in darkness.

There would be a vastly greater concentration of British artillery fire for the attack of 14 July (for which the preliminary bombardment began on 11 July) compared with that of a fortnight earlier. Rawlinson's Army had about two-thirds of the guns and howitzers it had employed on 1 July. But these supported an attack by only four divisions rather than the eleven of 1 July. In preparation for the attack of 14 July, Rawlinson gave his artillery an area to bombard only one-eighteenth the size of that shelled prior to 1 July and it has been estimated that the bombardment, when actually delivered, was five times as intense.[30] But the sheer intensity of fire was not the only thing that mattered. Timing, the critical matter of the "race to the parapet", was again crucial. The purpose of the night approach was to put British infantry close enough to the parapet of German front line trenches to get there before any surviving Germans in the vicinity had sufficiently recovered from the pounding administered by the British artillery to mount a coherent defence.

Haig deserves considerable credit for his refocusing of the British campaign on the southern part of the front in the immediate aftermath of 1 July. Rawlinson, as we have seen, was comparatively slow to readjust his thinking. But with regard to the detailed planning for the attack of 14 July, the roles were, in most respects, reversed. Rawlinson proposed an intelligent scheme and Haig was initially unable to see its merits. Rawlinson first informed Haig of his plan for a night assembly in No Man's Land during the latter's visit to Querrieu on 10 July. By the following day Haig had come out strongly against the proposal.[31] He told Rawlinson that:

Our troops are not highly trained and disciplined, nor are many of the staff experienced in such work, and to move two divisions in the dark over such a distance, form them up and deliver an attack in good order and in the right direction at dawn, as proposed, would hardly be considered possible even in a peace manoeuvre.[32]

Haig suggested an initial attack by XV Corps alone, without XIII Corps, from Mametz Wood. Having broken into the German positions, Haig proposed that XV Corps turn right and try to roll up the Germans in the direction of Longueval. XIII Corps would attack Longueval if the XV Corps operation were successful. Haig may have preferred to mount the initial attack with XV Corps only because Trônes Wood, on the right flank, was still in German hands at this time. Flanking fire from there might make things very difficult for the 9th Division of XIII Corps, which would form the right wing of the attack Rawlinson was proposing.[33] Haig's scheme, however, meant attacking on a narrow front and involved a complicated turning movement in the midst of battle: a manoeuvre perhaps even more difficult to execute than an approach march at night. Rawlinson, with the support of both corps commanders, argued for his original proposal. In the face of this phalanx of his subordinates (including the two corps commanders who had been most successful on 1 July) Haig eventually backed down. On 12 July he approved Rawlinson's plan provided that Rawlinson gave more attention to counter-battery fire and was careful not to commit cavalry prematurely.[34]

Haig's final caveat may seem surprising and requires some explanation. Haig had criticised previous Rawlinson plans for not considering the possibility of deep exploitation and particularly for not giving a role to the cavalry. Perhaps merely to avoid criticism on this score, Rawlinson did include the cavalry in his plan for the Bazentin Ridge attack. He ordered that if the initial attack were successful, the 2nd Indian Cavalry Division, to be placed under the control of XIII Corps, was to take High Wood and the German "Switch Line" on either side of it. Haig was sceptical of this scheme. He advised that "that large bodies of cavalry should not be pushed through at once as there would not be sufficient room for their action ... and they might be thrown back and cause confusion". He considered, however, that "a few squadrons" might be used with "good effect". He also offered Rawlinson an extra infantry division – the 35th to help exploit any advantage gained. Gough's Reserve Army was to assist with artillery, especially counter-battery fire.[35]

Though less sanguine than Rawlinson about the immediate prospects for cavalry action, Haig seems, as so often before, to have been in a mood of intense excitement as the big day approached. This found expression in a remarkable letter of exhortation despatched to Fourth Army and Reserve Army on 12 July, the day he finally approved Rawlinson's plan. Haig wanted it made known "at once to all the troops" that the Russians were gaining dramatic successes on the Eastern Front, that the Italians were doing well against the Austrians and that the French had achieved brilliant success on Fourth Army's right. As for the British themselves:

On the main front of attack our troops have broken, on a front of 12,000 yards, right through systems of defence which the enemy has done his utmost for nearly two years to render impregnable. We have inflicted heavy loss on him, capturing 8,000 prisoners and many guns...and other war material.

The enemy has already used up most of his reserves and has very few now available.

The defences which remain to be broken through are not nearly so deep, so strong, or so well prepared as those already captured, and the enemy's troops, exhausted and demoralised, are far less capable of defending than they were ten days ago.

The battle is, in fact, already more than half won. What remains to be done is easier than what has been done already ...

There is no room for doubt that steady, determined, united, and unrelenting effort *for a few more days* will definitely turn the scale in our favour and open up the road to further successes which will bring *final and complete victory within sight.* (Author's italics)[36]

It would be taking too harsh a view of Douglas Haig's character to view this as a cynical attempt to squeeze a bit more effort out of his troops. He almost certainly believed what he was saying. He was not, at this stage, anticipating a mere "wearing-out battle", dragging on for months, on the ground immediately in front of him. Rather he believed that the climax of the campaign would be reached within days and that his forces could break right through what remained of the German system of field fortifications in a few weeks at most. He was not quite rash enough to attach dates to this prognosis, but he strongly implied that there was a chance of a victorious conclusion to the war as a whole before the end of the year. That Haig was prepared to broadcast such sentiments, in such language, to everyone under his command, is a classic indication of his peculiar tendency, during much of 1916 and 1917, to extreme optimism. It suggests, too, the degree to which Haig's and Robertson's temperaments and their understanding of contemporary warfare were so utterly opposed. Finally, it demonstrates the extent to which Haig was operating independently of control from London. Haig had decided to attempt far more than anyone at home was asking of him or his army: the latter inevitably, at this stage, an immature instrument of war. Haig's forces were about to achieve a significant victory, but a limited one. He was fostering excessive hopes.

Trônes Wood and Bazentin Ridge: 14 July 1916

On the right, in XIII Corps' sector, the attack of 14 July might have appeared an operation with some of the makings of a disaster. The French apparently thought so and were reluctant to co-operate other than with artillery. As the troops assembled for the attack on the Bazentin Ridge, Trônes Wood was still in German hands. German positions there menaced the 9th Division's flank and threatened the success of the main attack. But renewed efforts by the 18th Division, more or less simultaneously with the main attack, largely neutralised German forces in the wood and cleared it in the course of the morning.

The main infantry attack began at 3.25 a.m., following five minutes of exceptionally intense artillery barrage on the German front line. By the time this intense barrage began, the British infantry had, in some places, crawled to within 100 yards of the German position. As soon as it started they got to their feet and moved still closer. When the barrage lifted to the next line of German trenches they were on the enemy in seconds rather than minutes.

From left to right, the divisions in the main attack were the 21st and the 7th (XV Corps) and the 3rd and the 9th (XIII Corps). XV Corps was dramatically successful in taking its initial objectives. But 9th Division encountered some uncut wire and there was heavy fighting for the village of Longueval. Rawlinson was hesitant about ordering XV Corps to push beyond its initial objectives until Longueval was in the hands of XIII Corps. This hesitancy probably wasted the opportunity to capture High Wood, which was practically unoccupied for much of the morning. By the time elements of the 7th Division attacked it that evening, the Germans were

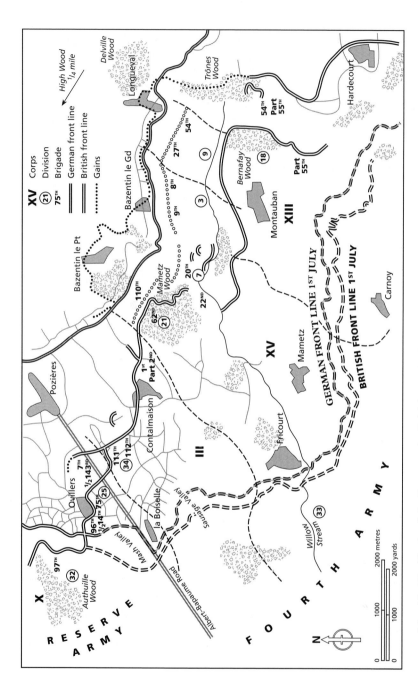

Map 13. The Battle of the Somme: the British attack of 14 July 1916

there in strength and the British were only able to take half of it. Elements of 2nd Indian Cavalry Division, who were ordered forward that morning, had difficulty traversing slippery ground and crossing trenches. But in the evening, while 7th Division was fighting for High Wood, two squadrons did get into action between there and Delville Wood, and killed or captured perhaps a hundred Germans for the loss of eight of their men.

The solid gains of the day included the whole of the German front line in the sector attacked, the villages of Bazentin le Petit and Bazentin le Grand, and most of Longueval. The cost had been very modest compared with the experience of most British formations on 1 July and the casualties inflicted on the Germans proportionally much heavier.[37] The Germans seemed to be in very serious trouble. In the southern part of their sector the British had, in the course of a fortnight, penetrated right through the German First Position and into what, on 1 July, had been the Second Position. The field fortifications now confronting the British in this sector really did not seem to be formidable compared to those already taken. Haig was naturally delighted by the outcome of the operation of Friday 14 July. He visited Rawlinson at lunchtime that day to congratulate him and GHQ was flooded with congratulations from both British and French sources.[38] Yet the success that day would prove something of a false dawn. The Germans were to show a remarkable ability to improvise defences, converting the woods that now confronted the British in this sector, particularly High Wood and Delville Wood, into formidable centres of resistance.

Haig's relations with "home" after 14 July

Up to mid-July Haig seemed on the brink of a public relations disaster. It was clear to the authorities in London that the Somme campaign had begun badly. The press as a whole seems to have been unhappy with GHQ's information policy and the military correspondent of *The Times*, though he wanted to help the army, really did not get on with Haig. By the end of the month, however, the situation had apparently been transformed in Haig's favour. Success on the Fourth Army front, culminating in the big attack of 14 July, certainly helped to ease the situation. But Haig also benefited from public relations work conducted by others on his behalf – efforts in which he was eventually persuaded at least to acquiesce.

Rather strangely, in view of their later relationship, David Lloyd George, who had replaced Kitchener as Secretary of State for War on 7 July 1916, seems to have played a substantial part in getting Haig a good press. For the sake of convenience we will leave the marked deterioration of the Lloyd George–Haig relationship that occurred over the course of the Somme campaign until the next chapter. Here we need only note that, in his early days as Secretary of State for War, Lloyd George naturally wanted maximum press support for the war effort. To this end it seems that he actually instigated the visit of Lord Northcliffe (owner of *The Times, The Daily Mail* and other newspapers) to GHQ over the weekend of 21–22 July, and there is no doubt at all that he encouraged the idea. For Haig and GHQ the Northcliffe visit was a great success. Superficially Northcliffe and Haig seemed to have little in common, but somehow they quickly established a rapport. Northcliffe was by far the most powerful of the press barons and once he had decided to back Haig most of GHQ's difficulties with the newspapers disappeared. Northcliffe told Charteris that he had never particularly liked or trusted Repington. If Repington did not behave himself from now on he would be sacked.[39]

Press approval inevitably strengthened Haig's position with the War Committee, the rest of the Cabinet and, indeed, with the CIGS. Yet Robertson apparently continued to have doubts about Haig's competence in operational matters and, by the end of the bloodiest month in British military history, the War Committee was again worried about casualties. On 29 July Robertson wrote to Haig:

The powers that be are beginning to get a little uneasy ... The casualties are mounting and they are wondering whether they are likely to get a proper return for them ... [T]hey will persist in asking whether the loss of 300,000 men will lead to really great results, because if not we ought to be content with something less than we are doing now ...[40]

Haig complained that this was "Not exactly the letter of a CIGS!" Robertson, Haig believed, should accept full responsibility for the casualties that the BEF was incurring under Haig's command.[41] In the disappointing aftermath of 14 July, Haig's communications with the War Office had again become sparse. Robertson raised this matter in another letter to Haig on 1 August. But Haig had already realised the need to defend himself and Rawlinson's letter seems to have crossed with one he sent to the War Office.

Haig explained to his government that the Somme offensive had relieved the pressure on Verdun, "proved to the Allies the fighting power of the British race" and inflicted heavy losses on the enemy. His intention now was to "maintain the offensive well into the autumn". It would not be "justifiable to calculate on the enemy's resistance being completely broken without another campaign next year".[42] This may indicate a genuine, if temporary, abatement of the extreme optimism that so often gripped Haig's mind. But it is also possible that he was deliberately feeding the CIGS and the War Committee a moderate, cautious line, which he knew they would find more acceptable, in order to avoid a direct order to curtail the campaign. This ploy, if such it was, seems to have worked. Despite criticism of GHQ by Sir John French, Winston Churchill and others, whom its members now considered "outsiders", on 8 August the War Committee sent Haig a statement of its continuing confidence and support.[43]

Royal backing for Haig had never wavered. In early August the King was agitating for his protégé to be promoted to Field Marshal. Granting this royal wish would make Haig senior to Robertson and might make him still more difficult for the War Office and the War Committee to control. Robertson was naturally reluctant to incur royal displeasure, but agreed with Asquith and Lloyd George that such a promotion was "rather early

8. General Joseph Joffre, General Sir Douglas Haig and General Ferdinand Foch walking in the gardens at Beauquesne, 12 August 1916. With the permission of The Trustees of the Imperial War Museum, London.

in the day as the battle of the Somme is not nearly finished yet".[44] There is, however, no indication that Asquith, Lloyd George or Robertson explicitly expressed to the Palace any doubts about Haig's conduct of the campaign. They did not rule out a Field Marshal's baton for Haig in the long run.

Command and operations: 15 July to 14 September

Immediately after the Bazentin Ridge attack of 14 July, Haig apparently considered his forces to be on the cusp of a dramatic breakthrough. To accomplish this he intended to mount another massive concerted attack within little more than a week. Preliminary orders for this operation were given on 15 July. Gough's Reserve Army was told to shift its boundary to the right, taking over the Pozières sector (on the Albert–Bapaume Road) from Fourth Army. Reserve Army was to commence operations to capture Pozières without delay, while Rawlinson's Fourth Army was to make ready for a concerted attack on High Wood, Ginchy, Guillemont and the German trench system known as the Switch Line on 22 July. The following day Fourth Army was to seize Falfemont Farm in co-operation with a French attack on Maurepas.[45] The attack of 14 July had taken a fortnight to plan and prepare. GHQ was now trying to put together a more complex operation in roughly half the time. This might have succeeded if German resistance had begun to disintegrate, but there was little sign of that. Reserve Army's repeated attacks on Pozières over the next few days were beaten off and the Germans fought for High Wood and Delville Wood on the Fourth Army front, with equal determination.

The big push of 22–23 July involved both Reserve Army and Fourth Army. It employed eight divisions belonging to five corps between Pozières on the left and Guillemont, at the junction with the French, on the right. Co-operation with the French was negotiated, but they asked for a postponement and Rawlinson decided to proceed without them. As with the operation of 14 July, a dawn attack was supposed to follow a night approach. But the hurried planning resulted in a failure of co-ordination: attacks going in at four different times. The number of guns used and the quantity of shell fired were inadequate in relation to the breadth of front attacked. Moreover, some of the German positions were on reverse slopes and poor weather had interfered with aerial observation. In these sectors the accuracy as well as the volume of fire was inadequate. The operation failed everywhere except on the extreme left, where the 1st Australian Division (Reserve Army), very recently arrived on the Western Front, took Pozières.[46]

For the next several weeks, progress was depressingly slow. In the Fourth Army sector between 15 July and 14 September the front advanced only about 1,000 yards across a five-mile stretch. Having tried to mount a large and very complex attack too quickly, between 14 and 22 July, the British on the Somme tended to revert to operations on a much smaller scale. Forces belonging to Fourth Army mounted attacks on forty-one of the sixty-two days, but, on an average day, only some six or seven infantry battalions were involved out of some ninety-six in Fourth Army as a whole. All the attacks mounted by Fourth Army between 15 July and 14 September gained less territory than the three square miles of the opening effort on 1 July and did so at a considerably higher cost in lives.[47] Gough's Reserve Army, which had a lesser role than Rawlinson's Fourth, performed even less impressively. Between 9 August and 3 September Gough mounted a series of attacks between Thiepval and Pozières in an effort to take the fortress village of Thiepval from the rear. These efforts focused on the German stronghold of Mouquet Farm (known to the BEF as "Moo Cow" or "Mucky Farm") and were conducted largely by three Australian divisions (4th, 1st and 2nd) of I and II ANZAC (Australian and New Zealand Army Corps). These divisions suffered some 23,000 casualties in six weeks: roughly equivalent to their loss in eight months at Gallipoli.[48]

The infrequency of large-scale efforts in the period 15 July–14 September and the dissolution of the British campaign on the Somme into a multiplicity of piecemeal operations indicates a breakdown of command and control. The Army and corps commanders and their staff may have been partly to blame for this, but, in the final analysis, responsibility rested with Haig and GHQ. GHQ had a variety of functions in this period, including liaison with the British government, liaison with the high commands of the other Allies and a good deal of complex military administration. However, now that there were two British Armies engaged in the same battle, one of GHQ's most important functions was to be, in effect, an Army Group headquarters. Haig, as well as being a national contingent commander, was now an Army Group commander. Arguably he was overtasked. With his head full of alliance politics and strategy and concerns about his relations with the government in London and, to a lesser extent, the governments of the Dominions, it was difficult for him to concentrate on performing the operational-level (or "grand tactical") functions appropriate to the commander of an Army Group. Nor, perhaps, was his staff appropriately selected and organised to perform as an Army Group HQ.

One possible course would have been to establish an Army Group headquarters as a distinct, intermediate level of command between GHQ and the Fourth and Reserve Armies. Indeed, both the Germans and the French already had Army Groups. From mid-July the Germans created an Army Group under General von Gallwitz to control their forces on the Somme, reorganised into First Army (von Below) north of the river and Second Army (Gallwitz himself) south of it. Gallwitz's doubling as an Army Group and Army commander was an awkward arrangement. This was finally sorted out in late August when Prince Rupprecht of Bavaria took over the Army Group command function, leaving Gallwitz to concentrate on commanding Second Army.[49] Organising all their forces on the Somme as an Army Group was a very rational thing for the Germans to do. Why did the British not adopt Army Group as a distinct command level in the First World War? Perhaps Haig positively wished to exercise direct control over his Army commanders. But another possible answer is that it seemed impractical, given the extreme shortage of properly trained staff officers and senior commanders (resulting from the small size of the pre-war army in relation to the mass force subsequently raised). Given that the British struggled to find competent officers to man the major headquarters they already had, there may have been a reluctance to create new ones. But it is hard to find evidence that the concept was even considered.

Between mid-July and mid-September 1916 Haig and GHQ demonstrated little "grip" on Reserve Army and Fourth Army, and British operations on the Somme were poorly directed. For the troops things were bloody and frustrating. From the other side, however, they looked even worse. British artillery was preponderant and the Germans were constantly deluged with shell. The British gunners received vital help from a Royal Flying Corps that impressed German ground troops as ubiquitous, determined and very skilful. Largely as a result, British fire was increasingly accurate as well as intense. The Germans were still counter-attacking far too frequently for their own good, trying to retake every piece of lost territory. In the Fourth Army sector they made seventy counter-attacks during the 15 July–14 September period in response to ninety British attacks. Given superior British firepower, these usually failed, often with disproportionate losses to the German side. Left in the trenches for longer periods, under much heavier fire and with the initiative obviously lying with the Allies, German troops were, moreover, under even greater psychological pressure than their British counterparts.[50]

There can, moreover, be little doubt that continuing and substantial British offensive efforts on the Somme were important to the preservation of the Franco-British alliance. Joffre's ideas of what could and should be accomplished in this campaign were at least as grandiose as those of Haig. Far from being satisfied that the British had helped take the pressure off Verdun, he was showing distinct signs of annoyance that they were not helping him fulfil these grander visions. On 11 August he denounced the multiplicity of piecemeal British attacks and tried to insist on a "grand slam" style effort by both Allies at once. Haig, however, did not believe that the time was ripe for this. For one thing he was awaiting the arrival of a new instrument of war of which he had great expectations: the tank.[51]

By early August Haig considered that the right wing of Fourth Army, where it connected with the French Sixth to the south of Trônes Wood, was the critical area. But a concentrated effort there meant co-operation with the French and, throughout the campaign, Rawlinson had found this very difficult to arrange. Possibly he was now also rather weary, for his leadership became singularly ineffective. He tended just to set objectives and delegate them to subordinates. Haig himself had a tendency to a "back-seat driving" style of command, based on exhortation, criticism and (rather more rarely) congratulation, rather than positive planning and clear direction. Nevertheless he became distinctly annoyed with Rawlinson, demanding that he delegate rather less and take a more active role in directing operations. The upshot was a Franco-British effort on 18 August, involving three of Fourth Army's corps. It was, however, hampered by several days of heavy rain preceding the attack, making observation for the artillery difficult. It proved to be a serious disappointment. The 24th Division took Guillemont Station, but the village of the same name remained in German hands.[52]

On 19 August Haig wrote to Rawlinson expressing his frustration with the slow progress in general and with the repeated failures to take Guillemont in particular. For weeks Haig had been contemplating another big push to secure the Germans' last prepared defensive line between Morval and Le Sars. But he thought it vital that Fourth Army should capture High Wood, Ginchy, Guillemont and Falfemont Farm without delay to secure the starting line for this operation. Haig criticised Rawlinson's methods in previous attacks, ordering him to engage the enemy "simultaneously along the whole front to be captured", and to employ "sufficient force … to beat down all opposition". Haig thought that Rawlinson was still not getting a grip on his subordinates:

In actual *execution* of plans, when control by higher Commanders is impossible, subordinates on the spot must act on their own initiative, and they must be trained to do so … [but] in *preparation* … close supervision by higher commanders is not only possible but is their duty … This close supervision is especially necessary in the case of a comparatively new army.[53]

There seems to have been much truth in Haig's strictures, but there was also an element of hypocrisy. If Rawlinson had not been exercising much control over the campaign for the last few weeks, neither had Haig. Yet Haig's criticisms did seem to energise Rawlinson. Some of Fourth Army's attacks over the next few weeks were better organised. The biggest effort, mounted jointly with Reserve Army on the left and the French on the right

9. Mr Lloyd George, General Sir Douglas Haig, General Joffre and Albert Thomas at Army Headquarters at Meaulte, 12 September 1916. With the permission of The Trustees of the Imperial War Museum, London.

(subsequently designated the Battle of Guillemont) began on 3 September. By 7 September, with the significant exceptions of Falfemont Farm and High Wood, Haig had his intended starting line for the next great grand slam attack.[54]

In the meantime Haig had met Joffre and all the most senior French war planners in a train at Saleux station on Sunday 27 August. Though the French were facing a mounting manpower crisis, they were still pressing for the achievement of dramatic results on the Somme, wanting a great climactic attack to begin on or about 6 September. Haig did not understand why the French were in such a hurry and considered their demands "tiresome". He told them at Saleux that he was planning the next big attack for 30 September. According to Haig's diary, Joffre replied that this would be too late, fatally so:

C'est trop tard. C'est la mort.

Haig indicates that Joffre was unable to give a reason for this view, though perhaps he simply failed to understand what the French commander-in-chief was saying. Poincaré explained to Haig that the weather in this part of the country normally broke around 25 September and remained unsettled for several weeks. Haig should not, therefore, delay the next big effort beyond 15 September. Oddly, while he meticulously recorded the weather on a daily basis (and though this was to be his third consecutive autumn in the north-western part of Continental Europe), Haig, up to this point, seems to have had no conception of the probable impact of the climate on the campaign. It is surely the ultimate comment on the abysmal state of Franco-British liaison (as well as being further comment on Haig's intellectual limitations) that the French, who were clearly aware of this vital factor, failed to get it to register in Haig's mind until late August.[55]

Planning the Flers-Courcelette Attack: 29 August–14 September

The attack of Friday 15 September (later designated the Battle of Flers-Courcelette) was to be by far the biggest since the start of the campaign on 1 July. Though it was to be primarily a Fourth Army operation, the British Reserve Army on the left and the French Sixth Army on the right were also to take part.

In mid-September Fourth Army faced three German trench systems (the first of which had been their Third Position on 1 July), plus a redoubt called the Quadrilateral just north of Combles. Very little of the British artillery could even reach the third German position and artillery observation (except from aeroplanes) did not even extend over the second system in most parts of the front. Rawlinson's planning was complicated by Haig's insistence that he exploit tanks to the maximum.

Haig had first heard about the development of "tanks" in December 1915 in a memorandum from Winston Churchill, recently arrived on the Western Front as a battalion commander. As First Lord of the Admiralty, a job he lost because of the failure of the Dardanelles campaign, he had played a crucial role in initiating their development. Haig was, in most respects, no great admirer of Churchill. But, as so often with new weapons technology, he was much taken with the tank idea and followed it up vigorously. He had wanted to get tanks for the beginning of the Somme campaign and was frustrated that they had not materialised by then. About fifty would be available for the big push of mid-September. GHQ made it clear that he was expected to make the fullest possible use of them. The Mark I tank (the type available in September 1916) weighed about

10. A "C" Company Mark I (C19 Clan Leslie) in Chimpanzee Valley preparing for action before the Battle of Flers-Courcelette. With the permission of The Trustees of the Imperial War Museum, London.

28 tons and over most types of terrain was slower than the infantry. It could crush barbed wire and eliminate machine gun posts either by driving over them or by fire. It was armed with machine guns. In one of its two variants it had a 6–pdr cannon mounted on each side. Though it was adequately armoured against rifle and machine gun fire, a direct hit from any kind of shell would knock it out. Given its mechanical complexity and its hurried development, it was inevitable that it should be much prone to breakdown. The crew's vision of the outside world from the interior of the vehicle was, moreover, always severely limited.[56]

While declaring himself reasonably impressed with what he initially saw of tanks, Rawlinson clearly wished to rely mainly on tried and tested methods. At this stage he was insistent that the three German defensive positions could not be overwhelmed in the one assault. His instinct was to tackle them step-by-step, concentrating his initial attack on the first German trench system, but also going for some defended localities beyond it, including the village of Flers, where the first and second line systems were close. It was there that he anticipated using the biggest concentration of tanks. He was contemplating attacking at night.[57] Rawlinson's approach made perfect sense except for one thing. Tanks could not be used at night: their vision was limited at the best of times. At night they were likely to more of a liability than an asset: there was a good chance that they would end up firing on British infantry.

Rawlinson knew Haig well by this stage in the war. He was almost certain that the commander-in-chief would attack his plan on the grounds that it was excessively cautious:

D.H won't like this but I am sure it is right. If we attempt too much we run the risk of doing nothing.[58]

Rawlinson was correct. Haig speedily dismissed his draft plan of 28 August. In a handwritten note 29 August, at the end of Rawlinson's outline plan, Haig remarked:

I think greater boldness should be shown at the outset. Tactical advantages we know may be obtained in the first few hours which ... will be more costly to obtain later.

So use tanks boldly, press success, demoralise enemy and try to capture his guns.[59]

This was Haig at his most ebullient. He had convinced himself that the enemy was desperately demoralised and that his forces were on the brink of a breakthrough to open country and "decisive results". He insisted on an operation aimed at "the destruction of the enemy's field forces".[60] However, as with the attack of 1 July, Haig did not use his own staff to take direct and positive control of the operational planning. Rather he engaged in another exercise in back-seat driving. He left Rawlinson as the principal operational planner, but, criticising the course he originally intended to follow, pushed him to adopt one in which he did not really believe and to go further and faster than he considered sensible. Haig insisted that all three German positions be attacked on the same day, wanted to break right through to the German gun line and wanted to exploit the breakthrough with massed cavalry. He was also unhappy about a night attack and insisted that the operation be mounted in daylight.

Haig's intervention on this occasion probably did not dissipate the intensity of the preliminary bombardment in the way that it seems to have done before 1 July. The German Third Position was outside British artillery range and no attempt was made to bombard it. The first two German positions would probably have been bombarded in any case. In the three days prior to the attack the British fired 828,000 shells at German defences. It has been estimated that the intensity of the preliminary bombardment was twice that employed on 1 July but less than half that used for 14 July. Fortunately the German defences now to be attacked were far less formidable than those encountered on 1 July. In addition all the attacking divisions on 15 September were to employ the "creeping barrage" technique. This method had been evolving constantly since the start of the campaign and had been gradually pervading the whole army. Now it was universally adopted and had reached a high degree of refinement. But there were problems in combining the creeping barrage with the employment of tanks. It was thought important to have tanks in the van of the attack, immediately in front of the infantry. But in that position it was likely that they would be hit by shells from the creeping barrage, which would also be moving forward just ahead of the infantry. So Rawlinson and his staff decided to leave "lanes" in the barrage (gaps in which no shells would fall) down which the tanks would move.

In a final, very late intervention, Haig extended the attack to the left to include an attack on Courcelette by the Reserve Army and on Martinpuich by Fourth Army's left wing.[61]

The Battles of Flers-Courcelette, Morval and Thiepval Ridge: 15–26 September

The preliminary bombardment began on 12 September, its accuracy somewhat diminished by extremely murky weather on the second day. Eleven of Haig's divisions attacked at 6.20 a.m. on 15 September from Courcelette in the north-west to just opposite the Quadrilateral in the south-east. On the left, 3rd and 2nd Canadian Divisions of the Canadian Corps Reserve Army attacked Courcelette. Fourth Army attacked with (from left to right) III, XV and XIV Corps, each employing three divisions. The French Sixth Army on the right mounted later attacks between Combles and the Somme.

Compared with that of 1 July, the operation of Friday 15 September was a major success. A 9,000-yard stretch of the German first line was overrun, as was a 4,000-yard stretch of the second line. High Wood was finally taken. About six square miles were captured – more than twice the ground taken on 1 July. The total cost in casualties seems to have been perhaps half that of 1 July. But British casualties were almost as heavy in relation to the numbers involved. All the divisions attacking on 15 September were nearing exhaustion by the end of the day and it would be several days before another major push could be made. The tanks had proved a mixed blessing. In some cases they arrived late or, because of breakdown, failed to show up at all. In other cases they broke down early in the battle or got lost and provided little useful service. In such cases the infantry had been deprived of the help of the creeping barrage and had gained nothing useful in return, suffering serious casualties as a result. Yet, in other cases, the tanks did very useful work.[62]

It seems likely, however, that the British would have gained equal results, and at significantly smaller cost, with Rawlinson's step-by-step approach, even if tanks had been able to play no useful part. The capture of the second German trench line system might have taken another day or two but the phased, carefully controlled nature of the operation would probably have left British infantry less depleted and exhausted and thus in a position to assault the third line rather sooner. As things were, when Rawlinson ordered another attack all along the line for 9.25 a.m. on 16 September, the response was rather ragged. It did not help matters that Poincaré's prediction about the weather apparently started to come true. Sunday 17 to Thursday 21 September were wet days.[63]

In total contrast with 1 July, the French, on 15 September, had performed very much less effectively than the British. They had gained little ground, and General Fayolle, commanding the French Sixth Army, considered that his forces would be in no position to mount another major attack until all the troops in the front line had been relieved. Haig therefore decided to postpone a concerted attack on what, on 15 September, had been the German third trench line until 21 September. British operations until then would be limited to gaining good jumping-off positions. Some significant ground was gained in limited operations over the next few days. On 18 September, for example, the 6th Division took the German "Quadrilateral" position from which they had been repelled three days earlier.[64]

The next big attack (later designated the Battle of Morval) was further delayed until 25 September because of the difficulties of the French and

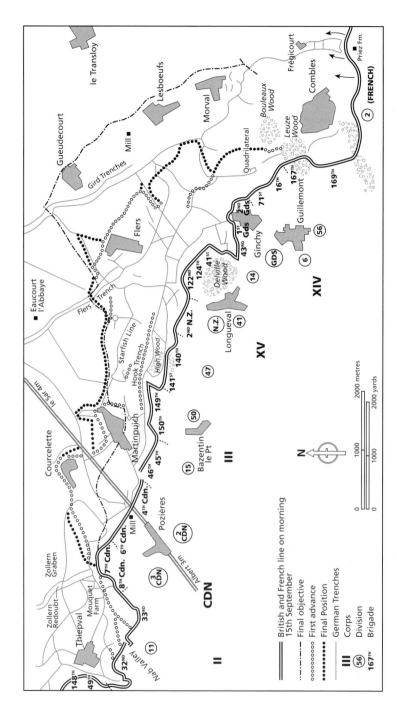

Map 14. The Battle of the Somme: the Flers-Courcelette attack of 15 September 1916

because the weather was interfering with aerial observation and thus with artillery fire. This attack was aimed at a single German trench system and at a group of fortified villages behind it – Gueudecourt, Lesboeufs and Morval. Rawlinson wanted a dawn attack but the French insisted on several hours of daylight immediately before the assault in which to conduct an intense, observed bombardment. Zero hour was fixed for 12.35 p.m. on Monday 25 September. The preliminary bombardment began on 24 September and was perhaps forty per cent more intense than that preceding the attack of 15 September. As on 15 September, a creeping barrage was employed, but this time no gaps were left for the tanks, which were held back for the clearance of the fortified villages. The operation proved a dramatic success. The entire stretch of trench attacked was rapidly taken, as were the villages of Lesboeufs and Morval. Only in the north, in the vicinity of the strongly defended village of Gueudecourt, was the attack temporarily halted. But the Germans in that area, some 370 of them, surrendered to a tank and infantry working with it the following day.[65]

Fourth Army had thus accomplished by 26 September what Haig had intended to do in one day on 15 September. It is highly likely that the same could have achieved at lower cost had the steady, step-by-step method advocated by Rawlinson (and consistently favoured by Robertson) been employed. Had there been less haste, there might have been greater speed. But even if Fourth Army had not operated with optimum efficiency, there can be no doubt that a very considerable victory had been won. It remained to be seen what could be made of it.

Late September was also a period of good news on the front of Gough's Reserve Army. Gough had, up to this point, made very little progress and was still trying to take German positions that had been Fourth Army objectives on 1 July. Gough's headquarters has been much criticised for a tendency to order hasty ill-prepared attacks and for exceptionally insensitive handling of subordinate formations – the latter often blamed on Major-General Neil Malcolm, Gough's chief of staff. In the Battle of Thiepval Ridge (as it was later designated), commencing on 26 September, Reserve Army seemed, however, to be showing a new effectiveness. The 18th Division, the 11th Division, the 1st Canadian Division and the 2nd Canadian Division attacked together in the largest Reserve Army operation yet mounted. All gained significant ground, Thiepval falling to the 18th Division and Mouquet Farm to the 11th Division. The 18th Division had aimed to take the Schwaben Redoubt on 26 September. It was not able to do so, but captured at least some of it in an assault that Sir Claud Jacob and his II Corps staff helped to plan, two days later.[66]

The October and November battles

In late September, despite Poincaré's warning about the weather, Haig once again believed he was on the cusp of a dramatic breakthrough.[67] Indeed, there were some legitimate grounds for optimism. At last there was real evidence, of a kind for which Haig had been eagerly searching for months, that German morale was low. German troops were now quite evidently fighting with less determination and they were surrendering much more readily. The German high command found it necessary to relieve all six of the divisions in line between Thiepval and Combles after 15 September. For the Germans, September was by far the worst month of the battle. By its end, they were, perhaps, closer to collapse than they would be again at any time before 1918.[68]

Haig was aware that his forces were not yet through to open country. While the Flers and Morval fighting was in progress, aerial reconnaissance had identified another German position, known as the Transloy Line. Two further lines, the first just in front of Bapaume, were in the course of construction still further back. But the Transloy Line did not appear to Haig (and actually was not) very formidable, compared with fortifications that his troops had already overrun. On 29 September, therefore, he gave orders for the renewal of offensive action on a massive scale by all British forces south of Gommecourt, involving elements of Third Army as well as Reserve Army and Fourth Army. Third Army would take high ground east of Gommecourt, while Reserve Army took the remainder of the Thiepval Spur, Serre and Beaumont Hamel. Fourth Army would push towards and take the Transloy Line, and then press on in the direction of Cambrai. These operations commenced on 1 October. Fourth Army initially achieved some success, gaining ground east of Le Sars.

From 2 to 5 October, however, it rained every day. Observation for the artillery was seriously impeded. The battlefield became a morass. Logistics, poorly managed by Maxwell and his department at GHQ, had been under strain for some time. They now came close to collapse. Despite Poincaré's weather warning, Charteris reacted, on 2 October, as if taken by surprise: "A horrible wet day. Is it the beginning of winter?" Several days later he decided to "study the weather records for this area" and discovered to his apparent amazement that "October is the wettest month of the whole year." This could hardly be considered timely intelligence. And while privately Charteris considered that it might be necessary to close the battle down, he seems not to have shared this conclusion with Haig.[69]

Foul weather on the Western Front always impeded the attacking side far more than the defending side. In this instance, indeed, it proved a powerful ally for the Germans, offering them some respite of which they made good use. They were again able to replace burnt-out divisions and they were able to increase their artillery strength. They also changed tactics in response to the proven effectiveness of the British creeping barrage. They started to keep a substantial proportion of their machine guns well back, so that British creeping barrages and the infantry following close behind them could not quickly put them out of action.[70] Yet Haig continued to make the most optimistic noises. He informed Poincaré on 2 October that he thought he might be in Cambrai by the end of the month. He reported to a sceptical Robertson, on 7 October, that the enemy was nearing breaking point. But the combination of adverse circumstances outlined above resulted in attacks mounted by Fourth Army on 7, 12 and 18 October gaining very little ground at a terrible cost. Much to Haig's chagrin, an Army that had captured considerably more powerful defences earlier in the year could make no impression on the Transloy Line.[71]

In mid-October, however, Haig and Rawlinson were in agreement that Fourth Army could not remain static in front of the Transloy Line. To do so would mean spending all winter at the bottom of a valley. Not only would the poor drainage be terribly bad for the men's health and comfort, but also the enemy's possession of the higher ground would favour his artillery. Consequently Fourth Army made three further efforts against the Transloy Line on 23, 28 and 29 October. All were costly failures. The shelling, coupled with further rainfall, turned the battlefield into an even worse quagmire. Moving supplies over most of it became all but impossible and the one serviceable road up to Fourth Army's front, from Longueval to Flers, was under constant heavy bombardment.

The condition of the troops was appalling. They were up to their knees in mud and water and living on cold food. They were so exhausted and so bogged down that they had to help each other even to get out of their trenches, and pressing home attacks was becoming a physical impossibility. So bad was the one road available that "fresh" troops exhausted themselves just getting to the front. By October fresh troops were, in any case, in exceedingly short supply. All fifty-one Divisions of the BEF had now fought on the Somme and its infantry strength had fallen dramatically. Fourth Army infantry battalions were down from their establishment of 800 men to an average of 350 and there was no immediate prospect of restoring their strength. Haig's staff informed him, in the most graphic terms, of the sufferings of his troops. But he remained determined to take the Transloy Line and, indeed, to press beyond it.[72] The streak of almost maniacal stubbornness in Haig's character certainly had much to do with this. But it was also the case that, despite the adverse weather, he was still under pressure from Joffre to achieve greater results by the end of the year. There were also indications that the Secretary of State for War, David Lloyd George, was losing confidence in Haig and intriguing against him. Haig may have been looking for some notable success to strengthen his position at home before closing the campaign.[73]

Haig's insistence on further efforts on the Fourth Army front produced something of a crisis of confidence in his command in early November. In support of a further attack by the French further south, Haig ordered that the XIV Corps, under Lord Cavan (which had replaced XIII Corps at the southern end of the British line), carry out a fresh assault on the Transloy Line. Cavan objected, telling Rawlinson that:

An attack from my present position with the troops at my disposal has practically no chance of success ...

I assert my readiness to sacrifice the British right rather than jeopardise the French ... but ... it does not appear that a failure would much assist the French and there is a danger of this attack shaking the confidence of the men and officers in their commanders.

No one who has not visited the front trenches can really know the state of exhaustion to which the men are reduced.

The last sentence undoubtedly constituted a swipe at Rawlinson and, probably, at Haig too. Rawlinson attributed the failure of a preliminary effort on 3 November to a lack of conviction on the part of the head-quarters of XIV Corps. At that point Cavan positively insisted that Rawlinson came to see conditions for himself. Having done so, Rawlinson finally concurred that the operation scheduled for 5 November was suicidal and futile. He informed Haig of this. Haig initially agreed to cancel it. But after an interview with Foch he reversed his decision and insisted that the XIV Corps attack go ahead after all. The result was a further 2,000 casualties for not a yard of ground gained. By 5 November Fourth Army had experienced almost a solid month of frustration and defeat. Fayolle's French Sixth Army, on Fourth Army's right, also had a somewhat disappointing day and French expectations for the rest of the year were massively scaled down.[74]

Fortunately, from the point of view of British prestige, there was to be greater success on the front of Gough's Fifth Army (as Reserve Army was now designated) in the valley of the Ancre. After the capture of Thiepval, Mouquet Farm and much of the Schwaben Redoubt in late September, progress in Gough's sector had been almost as disappointing as in Rawlinson's, though II Corps had an encouraging success in an attack on Stuff and Regina trenches, German positions south of the Ancre, on 21 October. Gough's forces were, of course, experiencing the same miserable weather. But at the beginning of November, Fifth Army did enjoy

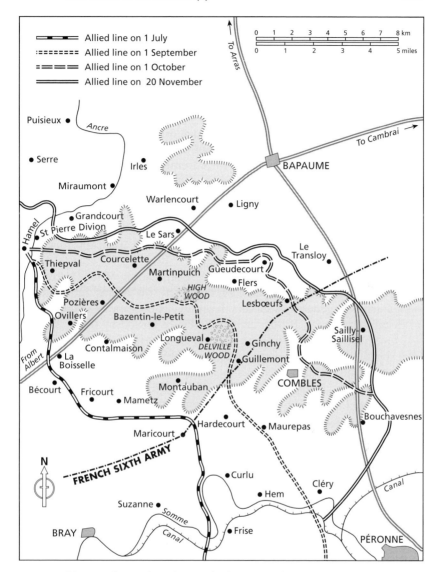

Map 15. Successive advances in the Battle of the Somme July–November 1916

some advantages over its neighbour to its right. Fourth Army had advanced a considerable distance since 1 July. Under the impact of the intense shelling that preceded and accompanied successive assaults on the Transloy Line, combined with the October rains, its supply system had all but collapsed.

The northern part of the Fifth Army front, astride the River Ancre, by contrast, had scarcely moved since 1 July. Its supply lines were, thus, much shorter. In the sector north of Thiepval, there had, moreover, been relatively little hard fighting since 1 July. While very muddy and slippery, the ground was still passable: not yet the utter morass found further south.

Gough intended to take advantage of these favourable circumstances in an operation that seems to have been very much his initiative, though one that Haig was happy to endorse. Gough originally intended to mount this operation at the end of October but foul weather delayed it several times. It was finally mounted on 13 November. In contrast with some of Fifth Army's earlier efforts this was a thoroughly planned attack, with clearly designated and very limited objectives. It was well supported by artillery, including 282 heavy guns and by a small number of tanks. It also involved the explosion of a large mine under the Hawthorn Redoubt, in practically the same spot where there had been a tragically mistimed detonation on 1 July.

Involving XIII (Fourth Army) and V Corps north of the Ancre and II Corps south of it, the Battle of the Ancre (as it was subsequently designated) was generally a success. It resulted in the capture of the villages of Beaumont Hamel, Beaucourt and St Pierre Divion by the evening of 14 November. Some 4,000 German prisoners were taken and the Germans were badly shaken. A renewed effort on 18–19 November pushed the advance slightly further, helping to secure British possession of at least part of the Redan Ridge for the winter.[75] This effectively ended the Somme campaign of 1916 and lent Haig some useful credibility for the conference of the Allies at Chantilly.

Assessment

The Somme campaign deserves its reputation as one of the most ghastly episodes in modern British history: four-and-a-half months of slaughter and suffering on an almost unimaginable scale. Yet the campaign wrested the initiative on the Western Front from the Germans. Together with the Brusilov offensive on the Eastern Front it helped save Verdun and the French army. It also wrecked a cherished German scheme for an offensive against the British in the Arras sector and contributed very largely to the general crisis experienced by the Central Powers in summer and autumn 1916.

In late August, General Falkenhayn, Chief of the German General Staff and architect of the German offensive at Verdun, lost his job. His strategy of bringing about a French collapse through the Verdun campaign was now perceived as a failure, and while the Somme battle was only one factor in bringing about this perception, it was a very important one. The new German team of Paul von Hindenburg (Chief of the General Staff) and Erich Ludendorff (First Quartermaster-General) had, however, experienced nothing like the mass industrialised warfare they encountered on the Somme and could find no easy answer to German quantitative inferiority in men, aircraft, guns and shell.[76]

On one measure, the result achieved by the British on the Somme, an advance to a maximum depth of about six miles in 141 days, seems extremely meagre in relation to the casualties sustained. Total British losses (killed, wounded, missing and taken prisoner) were around 420,000 and the French lost over 200,000. The best German sources put their casualties at around 500,000. Yet, at the start of the battle the defenders were in very strongly fortified positions and the bulk of the British army (the principal attacker) was inexperienced. Given these circumstances the discrepancy in casualties could easily have been still larger, though this certainly does not mean that the British army conducted the offensive with optimal efficiency.

In terms of morale the Germans seem to have been significantly more shaken by their Somme experience than were the British. Troops often find it psychologically easier to be on the attacking rather than the defending side: the defender feels like a passive recipient with little control over his own destiny. British troops on the Somme were, moreover, generally rotated through the battle faster than their German counterparts and were subjected to a level of bombardment that was far less intense. Recent research indicates that British soldiers who had served on the Somme and had become prisoners of the Germans by the end of the year indicated to their captors that they were proud of what they had been able to achieve. In contrast with the hopes Haig sometimes entertained, most ordinary British and British Empire soldiers do not seem to have anticipated a dramatic breakthrough ever occurring on the Western Front. Yet they remained confident in an ultimate victory, believing that this would result from German exhaustion. When probed on the time-scale for this, they considered that it might take another couple of years.[77]

At the end of 1916, indeed, confidence, in all ranks, seems to have been generally higher on the side of the Allies. The Germans felt themselves to be in grave danger. By contrast Haig and Joffre's successor, Nivelle (both rather more sanguine than the average "Tommy"), believed, as we shall see, that they could win the war in 1917. It seems logical to conclude that the Battle of the Somme (in humanitarian terms a catastrophe for all concerned) was, in military terms, a gruesome kind of limited victory for the Allies. But what was Haig's particular role in this?

An offensive on the Somme was not Haig's personal project. He did not select the place and regarded the start time as far from ideal from the

British point of view. Yet it was vital, if the Franco-British alliance and some hope of ultimate victory were to be preserved, that the British army play a major role in a major offensive on the Western Front in the summer of 1916, ready or not. Haig understood this clearly enough. After mid-July, however, when the crisis at Verdun eased, his perseverance with the Somme offensive cannot be explained by the need to preserve the French army from collapse. Nor does it seem likely that his overriding motivation was to please the French commander-in-chief. When it came to operational decision making for the British army, indeed, Haig prided himself on his ability to resist Joffre's demands. The meeting between the generals on Monday 3 July demonstrated this.

Haig's real motivation for persisting with the Somme offensive from mid-July seems to have been two linked beliefs: that the war could only be won if the German army could be defeated and that the Western Front was the only place to do this. At least up to early October, Haig had thought it was possible to inflict a truly decisive defeat on the German army on the Somme. Ideally this would compel Germany to end the war in 1916 on terms favourable to the Allies. Otherwise final victory might have to wait for the administration of a sort of *coup de grace* the following year. These ambitions for the Somme offensive may now seem excessive, but they appear to have differed little, if at all, from those of Joffre.

Haig is open to criticism less for his strategic intentions than for his operational methods. There was nothing in the least inevitable about the British army's catastrophic start to the campaign. Though, for many of the attacking troops, this was their baptism of fire, Haig had been planning and mounting attacks on the Western Front since early 1915. There was ample experience (most notably the Battle of Loos) from which to formulate a sensible approach. Kitchener, Robertson, Rawlinson, Montgomery and all of Rawlinson's corps commanders wanted to adopt a step-by-step method for the Somme campaign, concentrating on overrunning the German first-line system initially. Haig ignored them and overreached, fatally dissipating his firepower. About one-seventh of the total casualties for the entire 141-day campaign occurred on 1 July. By starting so badly Haig squandered the fighting power of his army, destroying much of its impetus and making it far less dangerous to the Germans than it otherwise could have been.

From 2 to 14 July, however, Haig continued to believe that a decisive breakthrough was a real possibility in the near future. German disarray on the southern part of the British front at this period arguably justified the high tempo of operations on which he insisted at that time. But he also promoted false expectations of decisive victory following hard on the heels of the big attack of 14 July. In its disappointing aftermath, and especially after the failure on 22–23 July, Haig appeared to lose control of the campaign for several weeks. At this period it seems that the British forces would have benefited enormously from the systematic application of the step-by-step methods that Robertson had long advocated. Such methods might even have led to a more rapid advance. Less haste might have resulted in more speed in the long run.

The fighting of 15–26 September undoubtedly constituted a victory for Haig's forces. But an equal result might have been achieved more cheaply had Haig allowed Rawlinson to do it his way. This success was, moreover, achieved too late in the year to reap the full dividends. That Haig was so slow to realise the likely impact of the climate on his aspirations for breakthrough is one of the oddest aspects of his performance in 1916. When the weather broke at the beginning of October, Haig then behaved as if he thought he could, by sheer willpower, overcome the frequent blindness of his artillery, the collapse of his logistics and the misery of his infantry. Predictably enough, this largely proved to be an illusion. The mid-November successes on the Fifth Army front saved Haig's face somewhat and left some British troops in slightly better positions in which to endure the winter, but that was all.

Nothing the British army could have done (and nothing that the British and French armies could have done together) in 1916 was likely to have brought Germany to its knees that year. But the more systematic application of a step-by-step approach might well have brought results equal to those actually achieved at considerably lower cost. It is even conceivable that the German army might have been forced to make a retreat of comparable depth to that which it conducted to the Hindenburg Line in early 1917 several months earlier, much more precipitously and with far greater attendant loss.

11   Lloyd George and Nivelle

Chantilly and Paris

On Wednesday 15 November 1916 Haig attended a military conference of the Allies convened by Joffre at Chantilly. Joffre proposed that the principal effort of 1917 should be a renewed Franco-British offensive on the Western Front. Haig supported him and the proposal was accepted by the other delegations. Despite a degree of dissent by the British Secretary of State for War, David Lloyd George, who favoured concentrating more forces in the Balkans, it was endorsed by a conference of statesmen at the Quai d'Orsay in Paris the following day. At another meeting later in the month, Joffre and Haig agreed to concentrate initial offensive efforts for 1917 on the sector between Arras in the north and the River Oise in the south.[1]

The Haig–Lloyd George relationship to December 1916

In 1916, though Lloyd George had the gravest reservations about the conduct of operations on the Somme, he and the other ministers on the War Committee had done practically nothing to restrain Haig. On becoming Prime Minister, on 7 December 1916, however, Lloyd George was determined to exert far greater control over the employment of Britain's largest field army. The following February there would be a confrontation so serious that, though each was to remain at his post for the rest of the war and though there would be limited truces between them, real harmony could never be restored. For as long as they both lived there would be a good deal of mutual antagonism between the two men, and once Haig was in his grave, Lloyd George would do his best to destroy his reputation.[2]

The personalities and attitudes of the two men were so antithetical that it had, perhaps, never been likely that they could work together harmoniously. Lloyd George, a Welshman of lower middle-class background, had a pre-war reputation as a radical. As Chancellor of the Exchequer, he had been responsible for the "People's Budget" of 1909, viewed by some as an exercise in class war. When the House of Lords had opposed this measure, Lloyd George had played a leading role in an attack on the Upper House that resulted in its being stripped of much of its power.[3] For someone of Haig's privileged background and generally conservative views, Lloyd George's radical past was probably enough in itself to engender mistrust. The minister's reputation for unsavoury connections and lack of scruple in financial dealings turned mistrust into distaste. Haig became convinced that, while Lloyd George was Minister of Munitions in 1915, his friends were "drawing large salaries and doing very little in the way of turning out ammunition".[4] On the occasion of Lloyd George's first visit to Haig's GHQ, in late January 1916, Charteris was impressed by the minister's intelligence, vivacity and charm. But he noted that "D. H. dislikes him. They have nothing in common." To make matters worse, Lloyd George immediately noticed Haig's mistrust.[5]

Even before his move to the War Office, Lloyd George had found himself angered by Haig's attitude. The War Committee had become concerned at the BEF's gigantic requirements for fodder and the strain that this placed on shipping and other forms of transport. In order to reduce the demand, the committee wished to cut the BEF's cavalry. Haig realised that the great bulk of the fodder went to animals used for transport purposes, not to the cavalry, and in any case he had dreams of the return of open warfare in which he thought cavalry would prove vital. Writing to Robertson on 20 May 1916, he indicated that the War Committee had "overlooked the fact that I am responsible for efficiency of the Armies in France". When Robertson passed it to the Committee, Lloyd George, then still Minister of Munitions, exploded at this "insolent letter". To whom was Haig responsible if not "to the Government, and through the Government to Parliament, and through Parliament to the people?" The War Committee could not be told by Haig to mind its own business. In Lloyd George's opinion the War Committee had "the perfect right to investigate any matter connected with the war that they pleased":[6] a view that was undoubtedly correct constitutionally.

Trouble between Lloyd George and Haig was therefore on the cards as soon as the former took over as Secretary of State for War on 7 July 1916. Yet it took months to develop into sustained mutual hostility. Robertson was initially able, to some degree, to act as a buffer between Haig and Lloyd George. While Lloyd George was still Minister of Munitions, Robertson had been grateful for his support in the introduction of conscription and had expressed this gratitude generously. Given their later intense antagonism, it is easy to overlook that Robertson made an initial effort to establish a good working relationship with Lloyd George as

Secretary of State and, for a while, seemed reasonably optimistic about his ability to do so.[7]

When he moved to the War Office, moreover, Lloyd George knew little or nothing about the conduct of military operations. He might dislike some of Haig's attitudes and think him a bit of a dullard, but he could not be sure that Haig would fail on the Somme. Had a major victory been won, Lloyd George would have wanted to share the credit, not to be regarded as having been an obstacle in Haig's path. Fate had linked Haig and Lloyd George and the unlikely pair had common interests, notably winning the war and, until that was attained, convincing the public that it was being conducted competently. These common interests, continuing in spite of growing tensions, account for Lloyd George's assistance in smoothing GHQ's relations with the press in July 1916, his despatch of the transport expert, Eric Geddes, to help solve the army's logistical problems in October 1916, and Haig's willingness to make the fullest use Geddes despite his distrust of Lloyd George.[8]

By September, however, Lloyd George was viewing the ever-increasing casualty lists and very limited advances of the Somme battle with mounting disquiet. Though he had insufficient military knowledge to develop a fully informed critique of Haig's operations, he was observant enough to realise that the French had often made at least equal progress at a lower cost in casualties. Quite intelligently, he inferred that this was something to do with their better use of artillery.[9] Robertson too had grave doubts about Haig as a field commander and his doubts too centred on Haig's use of his artillery. The Robertson–Haig relationship was already under strain.[10] Yet, as we have noted, Robertson refused openly to share his own criticisms of Haig's generalship with Lloyd George, apparently fearful that if a gulf opened between the CIGS and the GOC in France, the generals would lose all control of strategy.[11] The politicians might then divert resources from the Western Front and fritter them away in fruitless peripheral campaigns.

But Robertson's seemingly unconditional support for Haig was not necessarily going to keep the politicians focused on the West in the long run. Robertson warned Haig early in September that Lloyd George was again talking about diverting British effort to the Balkans.[12] When the Secretary of State paid a visit to the Western Front in the middle of the month, he made no overt criticism of Haig or GHQ and expressed no particular alarm about casualties. Haig got the initial impression that the visit was nothing but a "joy ride". "Breakfast with newspaper men and posings for the Cinema Shows pleased him more than anything else," Haig informed his wife. "I have no great opinion of L.G. as a man or leader."[13] The showmanship for the masses clearly irritated Haig. But he was even more upset when he discovered that the Secretary of State for War had engaged, behind his back, in somewhat more purposeful activity.

Lloyd George raised his concerns about British military methods and the doubtful competence of British generals with Foch. He clearly expected him to treat the conversation as confidential, but Foch promptly reported it to Haig, who was predictably furious. He expressed amazement that "a British minister could have been so ungentlemanly as to go to a foreigner and put such questions regarding his own subordinates".[14] When Haig informed Robertson, the CIGS offered to confront Lloyd George. Haig advised against this, saying that he preferred to let it drop. But Haig was probably not being entirely straight with Robertson. What he actually seems to have done was to complain to the press, probably using Charteris or Sassoon as the conduit. *The Morning Post* in particular brought Lloyd George under fierce attack.[15]

It is difficult not to have sympathy for Lloyd George in this matter. A civilian lacking any military training, he was trying to gain insight into operations of war for which he bore a high degree of responsibility to the British people. His suspicion that Haig often did not employ his artillery in the most efficient way and that the British army had suffered excessive casualties as a result was entirely reasonable: shared by some senior British generals at the time and by many reputable historians subsequently. But Robertson's doctrine that, when dealing with politicians, the army must maintain a united front[16] made it difficult for Lloyd George to get independent military advice from senior British officers. Was it not natural, therefore, that he should seek counsel from allies? Despite the press attack upon him, Lloyd George remained determined to investigate the French army's seemingly superior handling of artillery. One British officer who could be relied upon to express a judgement independent of Robertson and Haig was Lord French, with whom Lloyd George had long enjoyed cordial relations. Though the former commander-in-chief had no expertise in artillery matters, in October Lloyd George sent him on a mission to Joffre's headquarters to learn more about the French army's handling of this arm. Haig's relations with the man he had supplanted were now poisonous. When he found out about Lord French's mission, he was trebly furious: that it existed at all, that French had been chosen for it and that Robertson (who, he discovered, had known all about it) had not informed him.[17]

Haig may, indeed, have been angrier with Robertson over this incident than he was with Lloyd George. Given the little trust he now placed in Robertson, it may have occurred to him that a rapprochement with Lloyd George was in his best interests. When they met at a conference at Boulogne on 20 October, Haig decided to ask Lloyd George directly about the latter's conversation with Foch at which Haig had earlier taken such offence. An embarrassed Lloyd George defended himself on the grounds that the General Staff at the War Office told him only what they thought he needed to know, so he needed to seek information elsewhere. This was, of course, true enough. Haig expressed sympathy and promised to take the matter up with Robertson. (How Haig would have reacted had Robertson divulged to Lloyd George his serious doubts about Haig's generalship is all too easy to imagine.) After this meeting Haig reported to Doris that:

I get on very well with Lloyd George.[18]

But it soon became clear to him that Lloyd George did not altogether reciprocate this sentiment. For the British, October was, in many respects, the worst period of the Somme campaign. Lloyd George's confidence in Haig seems to have sunk to a new low and he came out against the renewal of the offensive in 1917. Under his influence the War Committee decided to examine "whether a decision might not be reached in another theatre".[19]

When Lloyd George failed to get the Allies to shift the focus of the next year's offensive effort away from the Western Front at the conference in Paris on Thursday 16 November 1916, Haig saw this as a victory. Wishing to consolidate it, he was in London the following week in an effort to ensure vigorous government backing for the resumption of offensive operations in the west in 1917. He found it difficult to get anyone to listen. The government was in crisis. Lord Lansdowne, a former Conservative Foreign Secretary, had circulated a memorandum advocating that, if his colleagues could not be sure of victory by next autumn, they should seek an immediate peace.[20] Asquith had proved an ineffective war leader and many of his colleagues had lost confidence in him. On 6 December, after complex political manoeuvring, he resigned. The following day Lloyd George became Prime Minister, leading a reorganised coalition in which the Unionist Party had a greater role.[21]

Haig was sorry for Asquith, whom he believed to be far abler and more intelligent than most of his colleagues, and whom he rather liked. He had to concede, however, that the outgoing premier's leadership, sometimes dampened with alcohol, had lacked vigour. Lloyd George, for all his faults, was certainly vigorous and, as Haig admitted, "really in earnest to win the war".[22] But Lloyd George's undoubted energy was, in Haig's perception (and also in reality), sometimes misdirected. As Secretary of State, Lloyd George had been something of an irritant for Haig. As Prime Minister there was every chance that he would be considerably more dangerous. There were, however, mitigating factors. Haig still had powerful press backing.[23] Even more importantly, he had the committed support of the King. The King's opinion still carried some weight with Unionists. Having split the Liberals in his break with Asquith, Lloyd George now depended on the Unionists, his old enemies, for political survival. As part of the deal with the Unionist leadership he not only agreed to keep Haig, but also accepted Lord Derby, a Tory peer amenable to royal influence, as his successor at the War Office.[24]

Yet serious disagreement between Haig and the new Prime Minister was not long in coming. At a meeting at 11 Downing Street on 15 December, Lloyd George indicated that, in order to rally British public opinion, he wanted a reasonably priced victory somewhere in the world early on in his premiership. It was not vital from his point of view that such a victory had any material effect on the struggle with Germany. He thought the Egypt/Palestine theatre was the best place. Taking Jerusalem would be dramatic and popular. He wanted Haig to release two divisions for despatch to that theatre and 200 heavy guns for the Italian front: the latter supposedly to be returned in the spring.[25] Haig resisted both requests. If he were to engage in serious offensive action in the West in 1917, he could hardly spare these guns, and he was surely right to be dubious about getting them back once he had released them.

On the issue of primacy for the Western Front, Robertson and Haig were, of course, in agreement, and for most of his time as CIGS Robertson would do his best to block all efforts to divert resources to what he regarded as sideshows. In an effort to out-manoeuvre Robertson and Haig and find strategic options away from the Western Front, Lloyd George organised a conference with the French and Italians at Rome in January 1917. But it was very difficult for the Allies to reach any definite agreement on any new strategic direction. The French seemed most interested in reinforcing Salonika, whereas Lloyd George saw the best opportunities in Italy. Robertson strongly implied that if more British troops were sent to Salonika he would resign.[26] In the meantime there were developments that, rather surprisingly, would focus Lloyd George's hopes on the Western Front for much of the first half of 1917.

Lloyd George and Nivelle: December 1916–February 1917

The very heavy casualties and limited gains of 1916 had placed even greater strain on French statesmen than on their British counterparts. Joffre and Foch had lost the confidence of their political masters. In December 1916 Briand's government sacked them, replacing them with General Robert Nivelle and General Louis-Felix Franchet d'Espèrey respectively. General Louis Lyautey, best known for his role in the conquest of Morocco, replaced General Pierre-Auguste Roques as Minister of War. As consolation for his loss of real authority Joffre was given a nominal post and made a Marshal of France. Haig's relationship with Joffre had (to put it mildly) not always been easy, but he was initially somewhat astonished at the elevation of Nivelle, of whom he knew very little.[27]

Nivelle, originally from the artillery, had been a colonel at the start of the war. His meteoric rise had been based primarily on his military performance in the field. He had succeeded Pétain in command of the French Second Army at Verdun and had undertaken a series of highly successful counter-offensives inflicting heavy losses on the Germans and retaking most of the ground they had captured since February, including the famous Fort Douaumont. Charming, articulate and Protestant, Nivelle was more acceptable to French Radical politicians than some brother officers who were devoutly Catholic. His mother being English, he was bilingual, which was a considerable asset given the growing importance of the British contribution on the Western Front. Above all Nivelle exuded confidence. He convinced some members of his own government (though by no means all his fellow generals) that he had found a formula for speedy victory.[28]

Nivelle quickly dropped Joffre's plan for a renewed Somme offensive, which he thought likely to be too long, drawn-out and bloody. As Haig recorded after their first meeting on 20 December 1916:

He is fully confident of breaking through the Enemy's front now that the Enemy's morale is weakened, but the blow must be struck by surprise and go through in 24 hours.

Having at last found someone whose belief in quick, decisive breakthrough equalled (or even exceeded) his own, Haig appears to have been, at least temporarily, bowled over. Nivelle seemed the perfect colleague – "a most straightforward and soldierly man" who was "better qualified that dear old Joffre to bring this war to a successful end".[29]

On the day after their first meeting, Nivelle sent Haig detailed proposals for Franco-British co-operation in next year's operations. The critical breakthrough operation was to be conducted by the French army on the Chemin des Dames in the Aisne sector, where Haig's First Army had fought in September 1914. But Nivelle asked the British to help in two ways. First he wanted them to extend their line southwards in order to release French troops for the breakthrough effort. Secondly he wanted them to mount a preliminary offensive between Arras and Bapaume to absorb German reserves. In this brief era of good feeling between the Allies, Haig was keen to help as much as possible, pressing Rawlinson to take responsibility for the front as far south as the Somme without delay.[30]

Much of the winter of 1916–1917 was extremely severe. There was great suffering in the trenches, especially in Fourth Army, which was stuck in the marshy trough into which it had advanced, at such enormous cost, in the autumn. Haig, however, personally lacked no material comfort, was pleased with the prospects for 1917 and had a cheerful Christmas and New Year. The burgeoning power of the British army was one source of satisfaction to him. By the beginning of 1917 it stood at fifty-six infantry and five cavalry divisions, backed by 1,157 pieces of heavy artillery: an unprecedented force by British standards, though still only about half the size of the French army. As Haig had noted after inspections, the Army's spirit appeared remarkably good.[31] Haig's confidence received one more boost in 1916. Just before New Year he received a letter from the King conferring upon him, in the most flattering terms, the rank of Field Marshal.[32]

As we have noted, Haig was initially inclined to look very favourably on Nivelle. But Haig's aspiration to conduct an offensive in Flanders at some point in 1917 became a source of tension between the two generals. Haig has been accused of being fixated on Flanders, having first made a reputation as a field commander by his heroic defence of the Ypres sector in the autumn of 1914. There may be some truth in this. Flanders had, as we have noted, been his preferred battlefield for the British army in 1916. In November 1916, before Nivelle's elevation, he had ordered General Sir Herbert Plumer, commanding the British Second Army in Flanders, to prepare plans for a major British offensive there in summer 1917. He considered that this might be mounted after the spring offensive between Arras and the Oise that he and Joffre had agreed on. Haig apparently thought that the Flanders operation might prove to be the climactic, decisive offensive.[33] On 20 November 1916 Haig had discussed the situation in the Channel with Vice-Admiral Sir Reginald Bacon, who commanded the Dover Patrol, and who was seriously worried about the increasing threat that German naval activity posed to the Channel ports. At the same time the War Committee was expressing the gravest concerns about the submarine menace and recommending that military action be taken to deal with the German bases on the Belgian coast. When Haig was in London the Admiralty had strongly encouraged him, at a meeting in Robertson's room at the War Office on 23 November, to mount a major offensive in Flanders the following year.[34]

On 2 January 1917 Nivelle sent Haig detailed proposals for his spring offensives. He intended a Franco-British offensive between Vimy and the Oise as a holding attack to draw in German reserves after which the main

French offensive would break through in the Aisne sector, on the Chemin des Dames. Nivelle thought the breakthrough could be accomplished in forty-eight hours. He intended to exploit any such breakthrough with a "mass of manoeuvre" of twenty-seven divisions. Haig replied on 6 January assuring Nivelle that he was prepared to do his part by mounting a preliminary offensive, designed to draw in German reserves. He expected that Nivelle would then launch "within a short period" of about eight to fourteen days a massive offensive with the French army. Haig reminded Nivelle of the latter's assurance that it ought to possible to tell after twenty-four to forty-eight hours whether his offensive was likely to lead to a decisive success.

If Nivelle's main offensive lived up to expectations, Haig was prepared to use the British army to help exploit its success. The object would then be to bring about the final collapse of Germany, or at least a major German retreat that would involve the abandonment of the Belgian coast. Haig, however, was not prepared to mount a preliminary wearing-out offensive of indefinite duration before Nivelle's main effort. That might use up the British army to no good purpose. Also, if Nivelle's big French attack failed, or turned into a prolonged and indecisive campaign, Haig reserved the right to curtail direct British support for it and shift his main effort to Flanders.[35]

It would surely be difficult for Haig's most acerbic critic to deny that, in January 1917, he was being reasonable with his allies. He was perfectly willing to help Nivelle to achieve his dream of a swift, decisive break-through. A massive rupture of the German defensive system on the Western Front would obviously be in the interests of all the Allies. If it forced the Germans to surrender this would solve all problems. If it forced them to retreat by a long way this might solve many of them, including the submarine threat from bases in Belgium. But if a breakthrough did not happen in the time frame that Nivelle himself had suggested, Haig wanted the freedom to use the British army to help serve Britain's own most vital needs. He wanted to mount an offensive that would help to keep her shipping lanes open, prevent her from being starved into submission and secure the link between England and his army across the Channel. In the final analysis, of course, a victory for the U-boats would have proved disastrous for the alliance as a whole.

The conditional, qualified support that Haig offered was not, however, good enough for Nivelle or the French government. On 8 January Haig went to London for a week's leave, to be followed by a London-based Franco-British planning conference. On the morning of Monday 15 January Haig went with "Tavish" Davidson, Director of Military Operations at GHQ, to 10 Downing Street, where they met Lloyd George,

Maurice Hankey, the secretary to the War Cabinet, and Robertson. Lloyd George asked Haig to outline Nivelle's scheme for offensive operations that year and to explain how he intended to co-operate with the British army. Haig's oral performance was probably as incoherent as usual in such circumstances and this may have irritated Lloyd George. Whatever provoked it, Lloyd George apparently launched into a diatribe on the incompetence of British generalship, relative to that of the French. The French, Lloyd George declared, were consistently able to achieve better results with fewer losses. Haig had wasted British life on the Somme and "the country would not stand any more of that sort of thing".[36]

The meeting broke up for lunch, but resumed in the afternoon. With Haig and Robertson humiliated by the Prime Minister, the scene was set for the entrance of Nivelle. He arrived, accompanied by the French ambassador and four staff officers, at 3.30 p.m. He outlined his plan with a fluency and conviction that contrasted markedly with Haig's presentation. Lloyd George was beguiled. Maurice Hankey, the War Cabinet secretary, noted: "Nivelle ... made a very favourable impression on the War Cabinet and me." Nivelle insisted upon the British army extending its front as far as the Amiens–Roye road, well to the south of the Somme, in order to release French troops for his great breakthrough. Haig argued that he could not do that and still have troops enough to mount the sort of preliminary offensive that Nivelle required of him.[37] At a further meeting the following day the War Cabinet overruled Haig, ordering him to comply completely with all of Nivelle's demands concerning the forth-coming military operations on the Western Front, with only one slight exception. Haig was given until the first week in March to comply with Nivelle's demands for the extension of the British front instead of having to complete this move by 15 February as Nivelle wished. But Lloyd George insisted that the date of the beginning of the British offensive should be fixed at 1 April precisely according to the timetable Nivelle had proposed.[38]

Robertson's memoirs suggest that he and Haig shared an equally neg-ative opinion of Nivelle and of the prospects for his spring offensive.[39] Contemporary records tell a somewhat different story. There is little doubt that Nivelle's celebrated charisma failed to impress Robertson. The CIGS seems to have been consistently sceptical of Nivelle's capacity to pull off a quick, decisive victory. But Haig's case was different. Of course, he disliked the way the War Cabinet was treating the British army as the mere handmaiden of the French. Inevitably he resented Lloyd George's attacks on his own professional competence. On the other hand he had himself initially been impressed and charmed by Nivelle. More significantly, he saw great benefits in the Prime Minister's rather sudden conversion to large-scale offensive action in the West. The dream of a massive, decisive Western Front breakthrough had obsessed Haig for the last couple of years. Even if, in the spring of 1917, the British army's role in executing it was to be a subordinate one, and even if he might have some doubts in matters of detail, in principle he approved of the endeavour. Haig proposed to abide by Lloyd George's instructions, noting that "we must do our utmost to help the French to make their effort a success. If they succeed, we also benefit. If they fail we will be helped in our turn, and we then have the right to expect their full support to enable us to launch our decisive attack, in the same way as we are now helping them."[40] On 7 February he spoke with Frederick Maurice, the Director of Military Operations at the War Office, then visiting the army in France. Haig said that in taking over more of the front from the French army the British army was sacrificing its own chances for conspicuous glory. But in the general interest, he was prepared to accept that:

> We willingly play a second role to the French, that is we are making a holding attack to draw in the Enemy's reserves so as to make the task of the French easier. We shall ... have heavy losses, with the possibility of no showy successes, *whereas the French are to make the decisive attack with every prospect of gaining the fruits of victory* [Author's italics]. I think it is for the general good that we play this role in support of the French, but let future critics realise that we have adopted it with our eyes open as to the probable consequences.[41]

At this stage, there was no indication whatever that Haig considered the Nivelle offensive fundamentally misconceived or doomed to failure. Within a couple of weeks of the Downing Street conference he was, very publicly, expressing enormous optimism about the campaigning season ahead. Combined with a certain tactlessness and (on this particular occasion) political ineptitude, this landed him in considerable trouble. John Charteris, the intelligence chief, normally managed GHQ's public relations and it is probably no coincidence that one of Haig's worst *faux pas* of the war occurred while Charteris was on leave. Encouraged by Lord Esher, by representatives of the Foreign Office and by some of his staff at GHQ, Haig granted audiences to a number of French journalists in late January and early February. On 1 February he noted that journalists he had just seen seemed "very pleased at my receiving them".[42]

Articles appearing in the French press reported the British commander-in-chief's complete confidence in decisive victory. Quoted as admitting the British army's continuing shortage of heavy guns, he nevertheless considered that the Allies could break the German front with their next big offensive. Making good use of their cavalry for exploitation, they might win the war that year. If they did not win outright in 1917, they should continue until they did. A "defeat palpable and unquestioned" must be inflicted on the German army. A "premature or halting victory" would enable German militarism to recover and take its revenge. Haig cast well-deserved scorn on recent German peace feelers, questioning the patriotism of British and French politicians who were prepared to consider a compromise peace.[43] When the resulting articles caused a row in England, Haig tried to claim that he had not really given an interview at all.[44] Some sympathetic authors have subsequently claimed that he was misquoted or his statements exaggerated. This cuts no ice. Haig had publicly made extremely overoptimistic prognoses on many previous occasions. He was also much given to questioning the patriotism and good sense of politicians. Charteris admitted that the newspaper articles were "not really very different from what the Chief actually said to the newspaper representatives or indeed to many other people not Press correspondents, at previous interviews".

The behaviour of the French journalists had been entirely correct. They had submitted their copy to GHQ before publication in the prescribed manner. Major Neville Lytton, responsible for GHQ's liaison with the foreign press, looked at it, and it was shown to a military censor who marked certain passages. Lytton then sent this material to Charteris, who was in England on leave. Charteris, by his own account, reviewed the articles in only a cursory manner and returned them to GHQ without objection. GHQ cleared them and they were published. In France this seems to have done no harm: rather the contrary. Haig, up to this point, was little known to the French public. His expression of great confidence in successful Franco-British co-operation in the immediate future and in the ultimate achievement of complete victory seems to have been precisely what many French people wanted to hear. As Charteris put it:

The net result as far as France is concerned, has been extraordinarily good; that is the curious point about it all. The French press has never been so pro-British as in the last few days.[45]

A letter requesting permission to make reference to these articles in the British press was not, according to his account, referred to Charteris. When *The Times* offered its readers an English translation of one of the articles on 15 February together with an editorial supporting Haig's views there was a hostile reaction by some MPs and some members of Lloyd George's government. Lloyd George himself was angry about the implied criticism of the Ministry of Munitions over the issue of heavy guns. Some politicians in all parties took marked exception to the apparent insult to their patriotism. Philip Snowden, Labour MP for Blackburn, favoured a compromise peace. Thinking that Haig had closed the door on that possibility, he stated in the House of Commons that his "blazing indiscretion ... had shaken the confidence of many people in his judgement". Fortunately for Haig, Andrew Bonar Law, Leader of the House and a crucial member of the War Cabinet (though someone whom Haig tended to despise), did his best to calm the situation and limit criticism of the commander-in-chief.

The War Cabinet, Lloyd George's inner policy-making group, demanded that GHQ explain how the gaffe had occurred. Haig despatched Major the Hon. Neville Lytton to London, where ministers gave him a ferocious grilling on Tuesday 19 February. Lloyd George and Lord Curzon wanted Haig's "head on a charger". Arthur Balfour, former Prime Minister, tried to put matters in perspective. He "rather laughed at the whole thing" and "eventually won the day". Haig was allowed to keep his job. Some influential people, including Max Aitken, the proprietor of the *Daily Express*, sent messages of support to GHQ.[46] Yet, in truth, Haig had acted thoughtlessly and spoken rashly. It was not for him to determine the terms on which the war should be concluded or the nature of the peace to follow it. Always jealous of his own prerogatives, he had recklessly trampled on those of others. Lord Derby, Secretary of State for War and generally Haig's most reliable ally in the Cabinet, was far from treating the matter lightly. Blaming (or professing to blame) Charteris, Derby pronounced:

He has let you down very badly ... He has destroyed in this country all confidence in his judgement, and everything which passes through his hands as having been approved by him will be a subject of suspicion.[47]

This attack by Derby seems, however, scarcely to have dented Haig's confidence in Charteris. While, in response to Derby's demand, he reduced Charteris's role in censorship, Charteris continued to be involved with GHQ's public relations while remaining intelligence chief.[48]

Logistics and the Calais Conference: January–February 1917

In the second half of February, therefore, relations between Lloyd George and the War Cabinet on the one hand and Haig on the other were extremely tense. Most of the War Cabinet seriously mistrusted Haig. In some ways this mistrust was excessive. Whatever the outrage to his personal feelings, in the aftermath of the January Downing Street conference Haig seems to have been doing his best to co-operate with Nivelle. He was, however, having real difficulties in preparing the British army for its promised spring offensive in the Arras sector. His operations on the Somme in the late autumn of 1916 had, it will be remembered, almost ground to a halt because of a supply crisis. Sir Eric Geddes, the civilian transport expert whom Lloyd George had recommended to Haig, had taken over as Director General of Transport at GHQ in October 1916 and was doing very good work, especially in the development of light railways. But the BEF's transport system was still beset by problems.

During the winter of 1916–17 many of the canals vital to the transport system of northern France froze so badly as to be unusable. To make matters worse, in late December 1916 the SS *Araby* sank in the mouth of the Bassie Loubet at Boulogne. This held up the operation of one of the BEF's most vital ports for nearly a month. The French *Directeur de l'Arriere* co-operated in finding the British extra berths in other ports, but the BEF's administrative system was, nevertheless, much dislocated. Though the *Araby* was cleared out of the way on 18 January, this still did not lead to a free flow of supplies to the front. There was an acute shortage of railway rolling stock in northern France, made more apparent by the fact that Geddes's reorganisation had helped significantly to increase the supply of goods to the ports. The rolling stock problem, in turn, was gradually overcome. But the French *Chemin de fer du Nord* railway company, on which the British were still heavily dependent, found that it did not have enough capacity in its system to move the rolling stock around as rapidly as the British required.[49]

Haig, of course, made his logistical difficulties known to Nivelle, suggesting that these might delay the start of the British spring offensive in the Arras sector. When they met over tea at GHQ on 16 February, Nivelle appeared understanding. Haig's difficulties with the French railways could be overcome, he indicated, and the attack would be delayed by no more than ten days.[50] Yet, while all was amiable on the surface, Nivelle and Lloyd George were apparently suspicious that Haig was using logistical problems as an excuse to drag his feet and that he did not intend to co-operate fully in Nivelle's spring offensives. When Haig suggested a Franco-British conference to help sort out his logistical difficulties, Lloyd George, Nivelle and the French government agreed. Indeed, they leapt at the chance. But they did so in order to hijack the proceedings for their own purposes. Robertson, who appears to have suspected that some such plot was afoot, disliked the whole idea of a conference. He thought that Haig was making trouble for himself by placing demands on the French railway system that were excessive in relation to the size of the British army. But, given that Haig had requested it, he was powerless to stop it happening. Robertson's suspicions of a plot were accurate. At the meeting of the War Cabinet before Lloyd George left for the Calais conference there was "much discussion about Haig's and Nivelle's merits and demerits ... conclusion that Haig is the best man we have but that is not saying much and that as between Haig and Nivelle Ll G should support the latter".[51]

Haig went from GHQ to Calais on Monday 26 February by staff car in the company of Eric Geddes. This suggests that logistics were still at the forefront of his mind. It is, however, difficult to believe that he thought that railway issues were all the conference was to be about, as some writers have indicated. The attendance of the British and French Prime Ministers, the CIGS and the French Minister of War was clearly not a surprise to him and people of their eminence would hardly convene just to discuss transport and supply. Yet, for Haig and Robertson, the actual course taken by the conference was not merely a surprise, but a violent shock.

Fittingly, given that transport was, at least ostensibly, a major item on the agenda, the conference was held in the *Hotel de la Gare Maritime*. After lunch Lloyd George and Briand made opening remarks and Geddes was allowed to present his account of the BEF's supply problems. But as soon as he had done so Lloyd George announced that the conference would divide. Geddes should discuss technical railway matters with French experts while the senior generals and politicians should discuss overall plans for the forthcoming offensive. Haig then found himself closeted with the two Prime Ministers, Lyautey, Nivelle and Robertson. Nivelle again outlined his plan. Lloyd George then demanded that Nivelle explain his disagreements with Haig. In fact the only real dispute was over the exact sector in which the British would attack. Haig was planning to assault the formidably defended high ground of Vimy Ridge, north of Arras. Nivelle wanted him to leave that position alone, but to extend his attack frontage well to the south of the River Scarpe.

According to his own account, Haig explained in French that making his attack south of the Scarpe would tend to push his forces towards a new and formidable German system of fortification that the British were calling the Hindenburg Line. That position would tend to block any further British advance. In any case he thought the capture of Vimy Ridge crucial to make the British front secure. His preparations for that operation were well advanced and he was not going to abandon it. Haig understood that Nivelle wanted the British to breach the German lines north of the Somme and to advance towards Cambrai, thus engaging a significant proportion of the German army on the Western Front. Haig had accepted this mission. How exactly he executed it should, he thought, be left to him.

At this point Lloyd George intervened in the discussion saying that strategy and tactics were beyond him, but that he wanted the command arrangements for the forthcoming offensive to be sorted out. He broke off the conference and "asked the French to put down in writing what they wanted". Lloyd George and Hankey then went for a walk through Calais. Soon after their return Hankey was summoned to Lloyd George's room, where Briand, Lyautey and Nivelle were also present. Lloyd George showed Hankey the document the French had produced. Hankey recorded that he tried to conceal his emotion, but that the French proposals took his breath away as they "practically demanded placing the British army under Nivelle … reducing Haig to a cipher".

Lloyd George's nervousness at this stage in the conference is indicated by the fact that he did not show up for dinner that evening, claiming that he was ill and dining alone in his room. Haig and Robertson, however, dined formally with their allies. After dinner the French presented, initially to Robertson, their scheme for unity of command in the forthcoming offensive. As Hankey had already noted, their proposal would have reduced British GHQ to little more than an administrative centre. Indeed, even some of its administrative functions were to be removed and exercised by a British Quartermaster-General's branch at Nivelle's headquarters. Operational command would be exercised entirely by Nivelle's headquarters, orders being transmitted to the British forces by Nivelle's British chief of staff. It was not difficult to guess who the French would want for that job: Henry Wilson, possibly the most Francophile officer in the British army, but mistrusted by Haig and Robertson. When he saw these proposals immediately after dinner, Robertson was incandescent with rage. He immediately sent for Haig, who appears to have been equally shocked.

Haig and Robertson went together to Lloyd George's room at about 10 o'clock that night. Hankey was also present. A furious and extremely ugly confrontation ensued. Lloyd George insisted that the French proposals must be accepted. To make matters worse, he told Haig that Nivelle insisted that Henry Wilson became the British chief of staff at Nivelle's headquarters. Hankey records that "Ll G was extraordinarily brutal to Haig. When Haig objected that the Tommies wouldn't stand being put under a Frenchman Ll G said, 'Well, Field Marshal, I know the private soldier very well. He speaks very freely to me and there are people he criticises far more than General Nivelle'." Eventually conceding that the French proposal might go too far, Lloyd George demanded that Robertson and Haig draft their own scheme to achieve unity of command and present it to him by 8 o'clock the following morning. The generals seem to have been in no rush to comply. But according to Haig they decided that they would both resign if forced to accept the French proposal.[52]

It was obvious to Robertson and Haig that the French scheme for unity of command was no surprise to Lloyd George. He was, indeed, largely responsible for it. At a meeting in Hankey's office on 15 February, he had suggested something like it to Commandant Berthier de Sauvigny, the

French assistant military attaché in London. That officer had passed the suggestion to Nivelle and the French government. The War Cabinet had authorised Lloyd George to seek, at the Calais conference, "such measures as might appear best calculated ... to ensure unity of command both in the preparatory stages of and during the operation". But it seems unlikely that most War Cabinet members knew the full scope of what Lloyd George and the French were intending. Lloyd George meanwhile kept the King, Lord Derby, the Secretary of State for War and, of course, Robertson and Haig completely in the dark.[53] Failing to inform the King was arguably unconstitutional. The sovereign had the right to be told and the right to express his disapproval, though the War Cabinet had the right to overrule him if it thought the national interest demanded it.

Early on the morning of 27 February Haig was summoned to Lyautey's room, where he saw both the French War Minister and Nivelle. The French generals commiserated with Haig about the "insult" implicit in what they described as "Briand's document". Lyautey claimed that the command scheme had been drawn up in Paris on Briand's instructions and that he had not seen it before boarding the train from Paris to Calais. Nivelle claimed that the proposal to place Haig under his command did not originate with him, but had been agreed between the two governments. He had only filled in the details. He had assumed that Lloyd George had explained to Robertson before the Calais conference that unity of command was on the agenda. There is little doubt that Lyautey and Nivelle were both lying, though Haig (who could be naïve at times, and was, perhaps, more inclined to attribute perfidy to politicians than to fellow military professionals) apparently believed them.[54] Yet tension that morning remained extreme. Still furious, Haig seemed in no mood for compromise. Before breakfast he wrote a letter, which he handed to Robertson at about 8.15, to be passed on to Lloyd George:

I have in the short time available considered the decision of the War Cabinet (of which Mr. Lloyd George informed us last night) viz. To place the British Army in France under the orders of the French Commander-in-Chief, and the proposals of the French to give effect to that decision.
   In my opinion there are only two alternatives, viz:
1. To leave matters are they are now, or
2. To place the British Army in France entirely under the French Commander-in-Chief.
The decision to adopt the second of these proposals must involve the disappearance of the British Commander-in-Chief and GHQ.[55]

A threat to resign could be inferred from the last sentence quoted, and Lloyd George apparently took the inference seriously. Only Hankey's intervention appears to have prevented the complete and simultaneous breakdown of Franco-British military relations and British politico-military relations. Realising the seriousness of the crisis, he had, in a manner entirely typical of his dutiful, obsessive oiling of the wheels of government, laboured all night to produce an acceptable compromise.

Hankey based his scheme on the precedents of Gallipoli and Salonika. There the commander of the larger army, respectively British and French, had been put in overall command but the commander of the smaller force had been left free to appeal to his own government if he thought the national interest was being disregarded. According to Hankey's proposal, moreover, Haig would be thus subordinate to Nivelle only during the forthcoming offensive. As soon as it was over, the previous command arrangements would be restored. Robertson summoned Haig after breakfast, at about 9.30, and showed him Hankey's paper, now approved by Lloyd George. While stepping back from his hard line position of an hour earlier, Haig was still not happy. He expressed willingness to follow general directives from Nivelle, but demanded "a free hand to choose the means and methods of utilising British troops" in his own sector of the Western Front, a principle that Lloyd George and the French conceded.[56]

The conference at Calais was a bitter and frustrating experience for all concerned. In complete contrast with his performance at Downing Street a few weeks earlier, Nivelle's handling of the proceedings had impressed no one. His demands had been couched in terms that were almost incredibly tactless and extreme. Lloyd George himself had acted with a degree of ineptitude rivalling Haig's gaffe with the press a few weeks earlier, miscalculating the likely strength of Haig's and Robertson's resistance and taking inadequate steps to deal with it. Lloyd George was now dependent for his political future on the support of the Unionists. Yet he had brought no Unionist minister with him. During the conference he realised that he might face the joint resignation of the CIGS and the commander-in-chief: a sensational event. It was reasonable to assume that it would be accompanied by vigorous protest from the Palace, which would exacerbate the crisis. A crisis on that scale would shake his ministry to its foundations. Lacking the immediate assurance of Unionist support in such eventualities, he made a substantial and rather humiliating retreat.

The aftermath of the Calais conference and the German withdrawal to the Hindenburg Line

While both Lloyd George and Haig were badly bruised at Calais, each tried to hide the extent of it from the principal woman in his life. While conceding that Nivelle had performed badly and that his own political career had been in jeopardy, Lloyd George tried to conceal from his mistress, Frances Stevenson, the degree to which he had backed down.[57] Haig, meanwhile, assured Doris that despite all the fuss his position was little changed. Command arrangements arrived at at the Calais conference would probably "work without difficulty" provided that there was no further political interference. But if "these Politicians" pushed him too far he would resign, secure in the knowledge that he would be welcomed back to the bosom of his family.[58] Haig had, perhaps, more reason to be satisfied with the situation than he realised at the time. If Nivelle were to succeed, Haig too would emerge victorious, albeit as junior partner. If Nivelle were to fail, the extraordinary lengths to which Lloyd George had gone to put the British army under his command would look ridiculous. Without any particular cleverness on his part, therefore, Haig found himself in a "no lose" situation.

An important source of comfort for Haig in late February and March 1916 (as throughout the war) was royal backing. Haig wrote to the King on 28 February indicating that he was reasonably satisfied with the command arrangements worked out at Calais. The King, however, should be alert to prevent any break-up of the British army with its divisions being placed under French corps: an alarmist suggestion that nothing in the proceedings at Calais justified. While he thought a change of commander at this stage unwise, Haig declared himself quite willing to resign if the War Cabinet wished it. The King immediately despatched a telegram of support. A follow-up letter, signed by Lord Stamfordham, indicated that the King had been much dismayed by Lloyd George's actions, that he believed the Army had every confidence in Haig and that royal confidence remained unbounded.[59]

At about the same time as he was receiving this royal support, Lord Curzon assured Haig of the War Cabinet's "thorough confidence". Writing to Doris, Haig used Curzon's remark as evidence that "most people, and all who really matter, are anxious to help and support me".[60] This, however, was simplistic and too rosy a view. Curzon was in the terminology of the time "trimming" – adjusting his metaphorical sails to suit the political wind. He apparently sensed that the issue of the command arrangements in France was now going against Lloyd George. In declaring the War Cabinet's "thorough confidence" in Haig, however, he was being far less than completely honest. Notes of a conversation he had with Lord Stamfordham a few days later demonstrate this. The Palace had clearly demanded from Curzon an explanation of the War Cabinet's decision to put Haig under Nivelle for the forthcoming offensive. Curzon justified it on the grounds that:

1. The French had practically twice the number of troops in the field that we had.
2. We are fighting on French soil to drive the enemy off French soil.
3. Independent opinion shows that without question French Generals and Staffs are immeasurably superior to British Generals and Staffs, not from the point of view of fighting but from that of generalship ...
4. The War Cabinet did not consider Haig a clever man. Nivelle made a much greater impression.[61]

How Haig would have reacted had he seen notes 3 and 4 of this conversation, which took place shortly after Curzon had assured him of the War Cabinet's complete confidence, is all too easy to imagine.

As might be expected, Haig's relations with Nivelle went downhill after Calais and Haig started to indicate doubts about the military wisdom of Nivelle's plans. Nivelle, at this time, gives the impression of a man who had been promoted too far too fast and was losing his grip. At Calais he had shown a certain degree of dishonesty and moral cowardice in his dealings with Haig: trying to conciliate the British commander-in-chief by minimising his own responsibility for the French scheme for unity of command. But he was clearly dissatisfied with the compromise solution reached at Calais and became increasingly fractious. Almost as soon as the conference was over he started to make demands on Haig couched in terms that the British commander-in-chief was bound to regard as peremptory and discourteous in the extreme.[62]

Meanwhile a German initiative invalidated one element in Nivelle's offensive plan. Hindenburg and Ludendorff, the command team that had taken Falkenhayn in August 1916, had decided to make a substantial, carefully planned withdrawal on the Western Front. The first signs of this were noticed on 25 February, just before the Calais conference. The Germans fell back on a front of 18,000 yards facing Fifth Army, giving up a group of villages including Warlencourt, Miraumont and Serre. A prisoner indicated that this was going to be part of a bigger German withdrawal to a carefully prepared fortified position that the Germans officially designated the *Siegfried Stellung*, but which the British called the Hindenburg Line.[63] Haig was not initially convinced. Thinking that a major retreat "seems to have greater disadvantages than advantages for the enemy", he believed that what had so far been observed might be a mere local withdrawal.[64] But he was reading the situation quite wrongly.

The Hindenburg Line extended from just north and east of Arras in a south-easterly direction to just west of Le Catelet, then essentially southwards to the Aisne east of Soissons. The withdrawal had two purposes: to put German troops in stronger positions and to release divisions to go into reserve or to be used on the Eastern Front. It was carried out in a series of well-planned stages between 25 February and 5 April 1917 and the Allies were quite unable to disrupt it. Codenamed *Alberich*, after a malevolent dwarf of Germanic legend, it involved the demolition of buildings, the felling of trees and the poisoning of wells across a swathe of evacuated territory up to thirty miles deep. When the manoeuvre was complete, the front was shortened by about twenty-five miles, freeing fourteen divisions.[65]

Though the German manoeuvre would not prevent Nivelle mounting his principal attack on the Chemin des Dames, the secondary French thrust that he had planned, in the Oise Valley, was pre-empted. The British attack on the Vimy Ridge north of Arras was unaffected, but British operations to the south of that city needed a rethink. Haig realised that the German withdrawal complicated matters, but gave different readings of the German move to different people. To Doris he argued that it was a "great sign of weakness"[66] on the part of the Germans. Writing for the War Cabinet on 2 March, on the other hand, he suggested that the German withdrawal might be designed to disorganise the Allies, while freeing troops for a gigantic attack elsewhere, perhaps in Flanders. German success in that region might sever the BEF's communications and prove decisive to the war. Unable to resist a piece of crude point scoring, he remarked that:

With such uncertainties and possibilities confronting us … the folly of definitely placing the British C. in C. under the orders of the French … becomes more marked than it seemed at the Calais Conference.[67]

When Nivelle saw Haig's memorandum in response to the German retreat to the Hindenburg Line he was intensely annoyed. Writing to Haig on 6 March, he insisted that the British should not reduce their contribution to the spring offensives "by a single man or gun". Haig thought:

It is difficult to receive these communications with patience. He has gone beyond the letter and also the spirit of the Calais agreement.[68]

On 7 March Nivelle wrote secretly to Lloyd George indicating that "the situation cannot improve as long as Sir Douglas Haig remains in command". He suggested replacing Haig with Gough.[69] Lloyd George appears already to have been "preoccupied with whether he should get rid of Haig". He asked Hankey for his views. Hankey by his own account sat up past midnight drafting a memorandum, which he dated 8 March. As Lloyd George had probably suspected, Hankey advised caution in dealing with the Field Marshal. This advice was so depressing to Lloyd George that he refused to read the memorandum, so Hankey "made him a long speech on the subject, weighing up the pros and cons and winding up strongly in favour of Haig. Lloyd George did not like it, having wanted

Hankey to "report the other way". He argued "hotly as he paced up and down the long Cabinet room". But Hankey "met him on every point". Hankey believed that if Lloyd George sacked Haig only Bonar Law would support him, and then more so out of loyalty than real conviction. In its most crucial paragraphs Hankey's memorandum concluded:

12. Personally I believe that, if Haig resigned, the Government would very likely be defeated, and that, even if they recalled him, they would be in jeopardy, unless Haig was at once appointed to some other active command. I do not under-rate the very strong case that would be made for the change, but even so I believe that the result would be to cause elements to coalesce which would never otherwise do so. The late Prime Minister would, I believe, on this issue, rally to him his old followers, and many waverers; they would be joined from sheer mischief by the disunited Irish, by the pacifists, and possibly by some Tories. Court and society influence, and all elements within reach of the General Staff would be thrown into the scale against the Government, and whether the Government were defeated or not they would be very seriously weakened. I have not the remotest idea how an appeal to the country would result, but at the present time an election on such a subject would not strengthen national unity.

13. On the political side, therefore, the arguments appear to me overwhelmingly in favour of Haig's retention. If, however, this is considered impossible, it is of first importance that he should not resign, but should be recalled, and should, if possible, be given a high military command e.g. at Salonica.[70]

In this crisis, Haig benefited enormously from Nivelle's arrogance and tactlessness. This tone of the French general's correspondence with Haig helped swing much of the volatile War Cabinet, once so convinced by the French general, very much against him. At the same time the Palace was using all its influence in support of Haig. At a meeting on 8 March, when Lloyd George was still thinking of sacking him, the War Cabinet decided that it was necessary to call another Franco-British conference to sort out continuing difficulties between him and Nivelle. Probably not realising how much weaker his position had become, Nivelle was continuing to make peremptory demands on Haig. On 9 March he tried to insist that the British increase their contribution to his spring offensive by mounting an attack in Flanders alongside the Belgians. But there was now no chance of his succeeding with such peremptory demands. That very day the War Cabinet instructed Lloyd George to emphasise its full confidence in Haig when the next Franco-British conference met.[71]

With a substantial and reliable majority in the House, a British Prime Minister, even in peacetime, can wield prodigious power. In wartime the potency of the office can become greater still. But any British premier's authority, whether in war or peace, is always, in the final analysis, entirely dependent on his ability to control the Commons. Lloyd George and

Asquith had split the Liberal Party between them. Most of it still acknowledged Asquith as leader. Given his radical past, Lloyd George and the Tories were not exactly natural bedfellows. Any major crisis or controversy touching on issues which they felt strongly could cause elements (possibly even the bulk) of that party to abandon him. The King and influential sections of the press were far more inclined to support the leaders of the Army than to trust Lloyd George. The Prime Minister had, of course, the option of calling a general election, but the political situation was most unusual and the result, as Hankey had pointed out, utterly incalculable. In spring 1917, therefore, Lloyd George was no Leviathan. He was more in the nature of political fixer, lacking any firm power base and surviving on his wits from day to day. The weakness of his position would be amply demonstrated over the next few days.

Arriving in London on Sunday 11 March, Haig had an evening conversation with Robertson, who seemed much depressed. Haig was then summoned to the Palace, where the King gave him the usual assurance of royal support and strongly urged him not to resign. The King feared that, in the event of Haig's resignation, Lloyd George would hold a general election. That would be massively disruptive and Lloyd George might win an overwhelming victory, which he might then use to threaten the monarchy as an institution. At 9.30 a.m. on the morning of Monday 12 March, Haig had a long talk with Derby at Derby's London home. The Secretary of State for War seemed even more depressed about the Calais conference than had the CIGS the previous evening. Later that same Monday morning Henry Wilson came to see Haig, at Haig's request, at Henrietta's London flat. Haig tried to persuade Wilson that it was the French, not he, who were now violating the Calais agreement. He also tried to enlist Wilson in getting this point across to Lord Milner, a key member of the War Cabinet whom Haig respected. Not for the first time, Haig was demonstrating a considerable amount of skill at this kind of service politicking and infighting.[72]

The same day, in an acrimonious interview, the King expressed his displeasure at Lloyd George's efforts, without consulting him, to put the British army under foreign command. Lloyd George was unapologetic, declaring his willingness to call an election on the issue if necessary. This was, as we noted, a contingency that really worried the King. But Lloyd George seems either to have been much less confident of the outcome than he pretended, or to have been unwilling to precipitate the kind of dislocation that holding a general election in the middle of a major war would inevitably cause. He was bluffing and soon backed down.[73] The Franco-British conference started on the afternoon of Monday 12 March and continued the following day. On Wednesday 14 March Haig signed the agreement arrived at. During the conference, Lloyd George told Nivelle that "Field-Marshal Sir Douglas Haig possessed the full confidence of the War Cabinet, and was regarded with admiration in England." While seeming to make some reasonable compromises, Haig and Robertson won most of their points. Haig conceded Nivelle's wish to have Henry Wilson at French general headquarters. But instead of being Nivelle's British chief of staff, answerable only to Nivelle and to London, Wilson was to be reduced to the status of a liaison officer, reporting to Haig. Haig and Nivelle were to harmonise their plans for the spring offensives, while Haig was authorised to proceed with operations in Flanders in the summer if Nivelle failed to achieve his breakthrough in the spring.[74]

Since the Calais conference Nivelle had been on a losing streak. This continued apace. Within days of his return, somewhat chastened, from London his political backing in Paris began to fall apart. Lyautey, the War Minister, while never totally convinced by Nivelle's plan, had gone along with it. But he was a professional soldier, not a politician. Attempting to address a night session of the Chamber on 15 March, he was howled down. Losing his cool completely, he retorted in abusive language and then quickly resigned. His resignation triggered the fall of Briand's government on 19 March. Its successor, with Alexandre Ribot as premier and Paul Painlevé as Minister of War, had little faith in Nivelle's offensive. The French army's security had been very lax. The Germans had captured compromising documents in trench raids and the operation's details had become talking points in the café's of Paris.[75] The chances of Nivelle's offensive achieving major success were fading. His star seemed to be setting before the spring offensives were due to begin and the possibility that its continued rise would result in a total eclipse of Haig's had, perhaps, already passed.

Haig's attitude to the Vimy-Arras offensive

The Arras operation of 1917 was no more a personal project of Douglas Haig's than the Somme offensive of the previous year had been. Its basic location, timing and objectives were decided by the French high command. A British attack towards Cambrai from the Arras sector was intended largely as a means of tying down German reserves and distracting attention from the main French breakthrough effort in Champagne, on the Chemin des Dames.[1] Though they had not altogether succeeded, Nivelle, the French government and the British Prime Minister had done everything they could to minimise Haig's freedom of action, reducing him to a cipher. Haig, however, was always much more inclined to positive co-operation with Nivelle than either Nivelle himself or Lloyd George appreciated at the time, and more than many historians have subsequently realised. Some commentators, hostile to Haig, have suggested that he adopted a more awkward and unco-operative attitude to his allies in early 1917 than was actually the case.[2] Others, more favourable to him, have credited him with more prescience of Nivelle's ultimate failure than he really demonstrated.[3]

When Briand's ministry fell in March, most of Nivelle's domestic political support, as we have noted, disappeared with it. Painlevé, the new French war minister, had little confidence in the Nivelle plan. Nor, by this stage, did a significant proportion of Nivelle's subordinates. At least one senior French general realised that Nivelle was far more to blame than Haig for the February–March crisis in Franco-British military relations. In late March General Franchet d'Espèrey, commanding the Northern Army Group, reportedly told Nivelle that British officers were easy to work with if you were honest and straightforward with them. Nivelle's problem, as with some remorse he now realised, was that he had tried to be devious.[4] In this climate, had Haig wished it, and had he taken a strong stand on the issue, it is conceivable that he could have had the whole programme of Allied spring offensives cancelled. This might not have been a good idea. Enormous effort had already been invested in preparing the opening stages of the Vimy-Arras operation. The whole offensive, however, could easily have been converted from a major, relatively open-ended operation of a "bite and hold" nature. Vimy Ridge itself might have been seized, the Germans driven back perhaps three or four miles in front of Arras and the ground gained consolidated and defended against possible German counter-attacks. The French might have confined themselves to similarly limited efforts in the Aisne-Champagne sector. Haig, however, advocated no such watering down of the plans that Nivelle and he had made. Indeed, he gave every indication of keenness to go full steam ahead. Despite all the apparent megalomania, dishonesty, petulance and paranoia that Nivelle had exhibited towards Haig, Nivelle had no more loyal supporter in spring 1917 than the British commander-in-chief. This, however, says little for Haig's military judgement.

Haig had evidence from various sources that things were far from well with the French army.[5] By contrast, his intelligence indicated that the morale of the German forces on the Western Front was fairly good. The withdrawal to the Hindenburg Line combined with the unleashing of unrestricted submarine warfare was a strategy that, according to reports of prisoner interrogations, made sense to German soldiers. They were hopeful that it might bring speedy victory. Haig's intelligence staff also knew that the withdrawal had more than doubled the strength of German reserves on the Western Front as a whole. There were now thirty-four divisions in reserve as opposed to thirteen for much of the previous year.[6] Haig was aware too, by late March, of the outbreak of revolution in Russia. He could not be expected to know precisely what effect this would have on the Russian war effort. But it was surely reasonable to anticipate serious disruption, especially in the short term. The entrance of the United States into the war in April came too late to be a factor in GHQ's calculations before the Arras offensive. Given America's total lack of preparedness for war, this event was not, in any case, likely to have much direct military effect for a long time.[7] Yet none of the dark clouds over the overall strategic picture appears to have shaken Haig's essential optimism.

Apparently buoyed by reports of privation and strained morale on the German home front during the harsh winter of 1916–17, Haig remained to a high degree confident of the prospects for 1917. Indeed, he and his intelligence chief, Brigadier-General John Charteris, seem to have been convinced that a German collapse was likely before the end of the year. They hoped that the launch of Nivelle's offensive on the Aisne might prove the trigger for this.[8] Even if the spring offensives did not produce immediate German disintegration, reserves would be drawn in and used up and the general strain on Germany increased. A British summer offensive in Flanders (for which Haig had ordered contingency plans to be made) might then deliver the knockout. Right through to mid-April, therefore, Haig continued to give support to Nivelle's project to a degree that now seems extremely misguided[9] and he displayed a degree of trust in Nivelle personally that appears distinctly naïve.

After a meeting with the French commander-in-chief on 23 March, Haig noted how "pleasant" and "straightforward" Nivelle had been. He was satisfied that he and Nivelle were in complete agreement. The Calais conference had, of course, been a terrible mistake. But Haig was now convinced that Nivelle was not responsible and wanted both alliance partners to put that sorry business behind them. Despite the German withdrawal, Haig believed that the Allies should proceed to execute their plans for the spring offensives with as little deviation as possible.[10] When he saw Painlevé, the French War Minister, the following day, he conveyed precisely the same message. He emphasised that he considered Nivelle "a capable general" with whom his relations had "always been excellent".[11] The second part of this statement was clearly a falsehood, but there was no malice in it and no intent to deceive: it represented a kind of wishful thinking. Nivelle's charm had initially worked as well on Haig as on most other people and Haig had always intended the friendliest relations and fullest co-operation consistent with Great Britain's vital interests.

GHQ, the Armies and the plans

The British had a fairly good knowledge of the German defences in the Vimy-Arras sector. They carefully monitored their evolution from the beginning of the year until the offensive was mounted at Easter. The German Sixth Army under Colonel-General von Falkenhausen, a component of Prince Rupprecht of Bavaria's Army Group, defended the fourteen-mile stretch of front that the British initially intended to attack. Sixth Army normally had two divisions defending a four-mile line on Vimy Ridge, a further five holding the ten miles in front of Third Army and several more in reserve. British intelligence identified a series of distinct and fairly formidable lines of defence behind the German front, the greatest being the so-called Drocourt-Quéant Line. In effect a northward extension of the Hindenburg Line, this was six or seven miles from the British front: far too distant to be subjected to an effective preliminary bombardment. It was thus going to be practically impossible to rupture the whole German defensive system in this sector in a single rush.[12]

Three British Armies were given roles in the Allies' spring offensive: General Sir Henry Horne's First Army, General Sir Edmund Allenby's

Third Army and General Sir Hubert Gough's Fifth Army. First Army's role was to seize and hold the Vimy Ridge, thus providing a strong defensive flank for Third Army's main effort further south. Third Army was to break the German front east of Arras and then exploit to the south-east, in the direction of the important German communication centre of Cambrai. If Fifth Army could close the gap between it and the retreating Germans in time for Z-day it would join the fray, attacking at the northern end of the Hindenburg Line.[13]

British planning to take the Vimy Ridge antedated Nivelle's scheme for an attack on the Chemin des Dames. Indeed, it had begun back in May 1916 when, shortly after taking over this sector from the French, First Army, then commanded by General Monro, lost a substantial amount of ground on the ridge to a small German offensive. As we have noted, Nivelle had wanted Haig to drop plans to capture the ridge in order to concentrate his efforts further south. But this Haig (respectfully and on the basis of reasoned argument) had refused to do.[14] General Sir Henry Horne had submitted the First Army plan for the Vimy Ridge operation on 2 January 1917, more than a month ahead of even the first version of Third Army's plan.[15] This was to be his first major offensive operation as an Army commander. A fellow Scot, born the same year as Haig, Horne was very much a Haig protégé. Since the start of the war he had risen remarkably rapidly. Originally a gunner, he had been Haig's artillery adviser at I Corps in 1914. He had commanded the 2nd Division in 1915 and the XV Corps for much of the Somme campaign. He took over First Army on 30 September 1916. Horne has remained perhaps the most enigmatic of Haig's Army commanders. Not charismatic and not, perhaps, particularly insightful, he was generally sensible, quite cautious and arguably rather lucky.[16]

Part of Horne's good fortune lay in having the Canadian Corps as part of his command for much of the war. Entirely integrated into the British command structure, yet also a sort of national army in miniature, the Canadian Corps would develop into the most formidable in the BEF. As at Easter 1917, it would frequently be First Army's spearhead.[17] Lieutenant-General Sir Julian Byng's Canadian Corps headquarters did much of the detailed planning for the Vimy Ridge attack and Canadian Corps would execute it. From a distinguished English aristocratic family, Byng had commanded the 3rd Cavalry Division and later the Cavalry Corps on the Western Front before taking command of the IX Corps at Gallipoli in August 1915. The Canadian Corps, to which he was appointed in May 1916, was his second command after his return from the Mediterranean. Though he and many key members of his staff were British, Byng won the complete respect of his troops. A cavalry officer originally, he adapted remarkably well to the planning of infantry and artillery operations under conditions of positional warfare. Like Robertson, Rawlinson and Du Cane, he became, in general, an advocate of a cautious, firepower-centred, step-by-step approach to offensive operations.[18]

As it matured over the next few months, the plan was for all four Canadian divisions to mount a simultaneous assault across a four-mile front, with the 4th Division on the right and the 1st Division on the left. The intention was to take virtually the whole ridge on the first day. Artillery preparation was to be exceptionally thorough, intense and prolonged. There was to be a three-week preliminary bombardment. Intense counter-battery fire and an exceptionally intense and deep-creeping barrage would support the assault itself. On Z + 1 (the second day of infantry operations) there was to be a subsidiary attack, known as the "Northern Operation", on positions to the left of the main crest of Vimy Ridge. A brigade of the 24th (British) Division and brigade of the 4th Canadian Division would capture the Bois en Hache and Hill 120 respectively.[19]

Sir Edmund Allenby submitted his plan for the Third Army attack east of Arras on 7 February. He intended a staged but remarkably rapid penetration into the German defensive system: an advance of up to four-and-a-half miles on the first day of the infantry attack. Amongst the prizes he wished to secure in the first few hours was the fortified village of Monchy le Preux, which offered commanding views of much of the ground immediately east of Arras. Keen to achieve a significant degree of surprise, Allenby wanted to confine the preliminary bombardment to the forty-eight hours immediately preceding the infantry assault, but to make it extremely concentrated. Haig liked Allenby's ambitious plans for a rapid advance, but was far less convinced of the wisdom of his proposals for the preliminary bombardment.[20] This was a technical controversy, albeit a vitally important one. But, perhaps owing to Allenby's personality and his difficult relationship with Haig, it was to develop considerable emotional intensity.

Like Horne, Allenby was born in the same year as Haig, but unlike Horne, he was far from being a Haig protégé. Allenby, like Haig, was from the cavalry. Contemporaries at Staff College, they had sometimes been seen as rivals. Allenby's record on the Western Front had thus far not been distinguished. Commanding the Cavalry Division in 1914, he had largely lost control of it during the retreat from Mons. In the fighting at Ypres in 1915 he had gained a reputation for a callous disregard for casualties, but this had not stopped Sir John French appointing him to command Third Army in October 1915. The Gommecourt attack on 1 July 1916, Allenby's first major operation as an Army commander, had been one of the sorriest episodes of an exceptionally bloody day. Not a popular commander, Allenby could appear to be something of a martinet and a bully. Even before 1914 his combination of physical bulk and violent temper had earned him the nickname "The Bull".

Perhaps because of his poor Western Front record, because they had once been rivals, because he saw Allenby as a French protégé or because of a combination of all these factors, Haig showed scant respect for Allenby's opinion as expressed at Army commanders' meetings. Allenby noticed this and was hurt by it.[21] Communication between the two generals was difficult. Both were painfully inarticulate and Allenby admitted to being shy. During the planning for Arras, John Charteris noted that:

Allenby shares one peculiarity with Douglas Haig, he cannot explain with any lucidity at all what his plans are. In a conference between them it is rather amusing. D. H. hardly ever finishes a sentence, and Allenby's sentences, though finished do not really convey exactly what he means.[22]

Haig sent his response to Allenby's scheme for the Arras offensive on 12 February, five days after receiving it. As noted, the main criticism fell on Allenby's artillery plan. Though an enthusiastic advocate of hurricane bombardments a year earlier, he now rejected the method. He argued that given the extent of the preparations necessary it would be impossible to disguise British intent to attack in the Arras sector. The only elements of surprise possible would concern the precise timing of the infantry assault and the exact extent of the front to be assaulted. The length of bombardment would, he implied, make little difference in these respects. Haig, moreover, doubted that the wire cutting necessary could be done in forty-eight hours. Haig's artillery adviser, Major-General J. F. N. Birch, argued that the intensity of the fire in Allenby's scheme would make it difficult to monitor its effects. In particular it would make it practically impossible to check how far the wire was being cut: an issue on which the success or failure of the first day of the offensive crucially depended.[23]

Allenby insisted that practical tests undertaken on his instructions with both a 6–inch howitzer and an 18–pdr gun had proved that the intensity of firing that he proposed was possible without damage to the weapons or the exhaustion of their handlers. But Haig and Birch were not prepared to back down. Each had interviews with Allenby on the subject, but "The Bull" seemed immovable. According to some accounts, Haig came close to sacking Allenby over this issue. In the end GHQ out-manoeuvred Allenby by changing his artillery adviser, sending Holland to command a corps. Holland's replacement, Major-General R. St Clair Lecky, toed the GHQ line. For Allenby to ignore both GHQ and his own artillery adviser would have amounted to professional suicide. Apparently realising this, he conceded the point.[24]

In its mature form, the plan was for the Third Army to attack on a front of nearly ten miles between a point near Farbus Wood in the north and Croiselle in the south. Three corps, Sir Charles Fergusson's XVII, Aylmer Haldane's VI and Sir Thomas Snow's VII, would make the attack, using ten divisions in the first wave. Another two divisions would be ready to go in as the day progressed. Z-Day (the day of the first infantry assault) was intended to be Easter Sunday – 8 April. It was to be preceded by four days of fairly intense preliminary bombardment and there was to be a good deal of wire-cutting fire in the seven days prior to that. Zero hour was to be 5.30 a.m. Four main German positions were to be assaulted on the first day. The Black Line was to be captured at Zero plus 30, after which there would be a halt of an hour-and-a-half while the bombardment continued. The Blue Line was to be taken by 8.14 a.m., after which there was to be a halt of nearly four hours before the attack on the Brown Line. That was to be captured at 1.30 p.m. There would then be a further halt of about two hours before the assault on the Green Line was mounted at 3.30 p.m. The final version of the plan still intended an infantry advance of up to four-and-a-half miles on the first day.

Infantry was intended to achieve this depth of penetration by the novel method of "leap-frogging" entire divisions. On the Somme battalions and brigades had frequently passed through others to attack more distant objectives. For the Arras battle, two of Third Army's corps, XVII and VI Corps, would attack, north and south of the River Scarpe respectively, each with three divisions in the first wave. Each of these corps would keep a division in reserve, to be passed through the Brown Line for the attack on the Green Line. The same method would have been used for the VII Corps on Third Army's right, except that, as part of their "Alberich" retreat, the Germans had already abandoned some of the ground it was originally intended to seize. By the time the attack began, therefore, VII Corps already occupied the Black Line. Indeed, its right was on the Blue Line. Its objectives were, therefore, relatively shallow and its configuration reflected this, with all four of its divisions in the front line.

As with most major operations planned under Haig's direction, the cavalry was given a significant role. The Cavalry Corps headquarters and two cavalry divisions (2nd and 3rd) were put at Allenby's disposal for the exploitation of success achieved on the Third Army's front. The 4th Cavalry Division was allocated to General Sir Hubert Gough for a possible operation at the northern end of the Hindenburg Line. The 1st Cavalry Division, though positioned in the rear of Third Army, was to be kept in GHQ reserve and was available to be committed in support of either Third or First Army, depending on how the battle developed. If the attack appeared to be going well, the Cavalry Corps was to attempt to pass through the Green Line almost as soon as the infantry reached it and then turn southwards, its first objectives lying on the left (north) bank of the Sensée River.[25]

Its sheer ambition (in terms of both the initial infantry advance and the cavalry exploitation, which was intended to begin later on the same day) was one of the most remarkable aspects of the British plan for the Arras attack. The Green Line was well beyond the range of the British field artillery from its starting positions. Guns and ammunition would have to be rushed forward to provide the infantry with a creeping barrage in the final stages of the intended advance. Yet even if the Green Line were captured along its entire length, the British would not by any means have penetrated the entire German defensive system. They would still be a couple of miles short of the formidable Drocourt-Quéant Line.[26]

Haig, his generals and their staffs had laid plans that gave them a good prospect of a substantial break-in on to the German defensive system on the first day. There was, however, practically no coherent planning for follow-up operations. Even if the attacking infantry captured all the objectives set for Z-day, on the basis of what was known of German troop strengths, defences and dispositions, as well as experience gained on the Somme, it was reasonable to anticipate that the battle would still be less than half won. Contemplating operations after Z-day in terms of mere exploitation, as both Allenby and Haig apparently did, was grossly unrealistic.

Preparing to strike

The most unusual feature of the Vimy-Arras battle was the exceptionally large-scale use made of tunnels, caves and underground shelters for protecting and concealing the infantry concentrated for the offensive. Tunnels under Vimy Ridge and large caves under south-eastern suburbs had existed since the Middle Ages, the result of the quarrying of chalk. The British (and especially a New Zealand Tunnelling Company that did much of the work under Arras) greatly developed these systems. Eventually a network of 10,901 yards of tunnels was created in the Arras sector alone (leaving aside the Vimy tunnels) and these were used to accommodate about 24,500 men prior to the attack.[27]

In one important respect the British were in a less favourable position while preparing for the Arras offensive than they had been before the Somme. The level of air superiority they had then enjoyed had seriously diminished. The Allies collectively still had far more aircraft than the

Germans. German fighters were now qualitatively significantly superior to those currently available to the British. Sir Hugh Trenchard, commanding the RFC on the Western Front, took it as his Corps' duty to carry out all the work that the ground forces required regardless of cost. In order to neutralise German observation balloons and facilitate close reconnaissance and observation, the RFC mounted an air offensive on 5 April. The RFC achieved most of what the ground forces required, but at a very high price. It had about 275 aircraft shot down and suffered 421 casualties of which 207 were total. "Bloody April" is still notorious in the history of British airpower.[28]

The preliminary bombardment for the First Army attack began as early as 20 March, that for Third Army at 6.30 a.m. on 4 April. They employed a combined total of 2,817 guns and howitzers – the greatest assembly of artillery yet made by the British army. British artillery pieces outnumbered those of the German forces opposite by nearly three to one. On the Third Army front most of the guns, howitzers and mortars involved kept up a steady rate of fire during daylight hours with some pauses for aerial photography, so that damage could be assessed. At night there was less firing because it could not be observed. Intense, irregular bursts of harassing fire were, however, put down during the hours of darkness to disrupt any attempts by the Germans to repair their defences or to bring up supplies. In the ten hours before Zero, there was an intense counter-battery effort using a mixture of lethal gas and tear gas. As Zero hour approached the use of lethal gas was reduced so that it would not be a hazard to the attacking British infantry.[29]

Engineers, aviation and artillery were thus all making vital important contributions even before the infantry attacks began. Another technical arm was also intended to play a part. Some forty tanks were made available to Third Army, twelve to Fifth Army and eight to the 2nd Canadian Division in 1st Army. Two types, Marks I and II, were available. Both had rather poor mechanical reliability and cross-country performance and their numbers remained very limited throughout the battle. Yet, particularly on the first day, they were to render some very useful assistance.[30]

On 5 April Haig had an appointment with Nivelle at Montdidier to discuss the final arrangements for the offensive. Though he put a brave face on it for Haig, Nivelle was, by this stage, deeply troubled. He knew that neither his subordinate commanders nor most of the French government now believed in his plan, though by a strange process of reasoning the government had decided to let it go ahead. To add to his troubles the weather had been exceptionally foul and this had interfered with artillery preparation. General Joseph Micheler commanding the French Reserve Army Group in the Aisne-Champagne sector wished to delay his attack for

11. Forward observation officers observing fire during the preliminary bombardment for the Arras offensive at Cuthbert Crater on 8 April 1917. With the permission of The Trustees of the Imperial War Museum, London.

forty-eight hours. Given that the British had also been having problems with the weather, Haig was not altogether averse to putting his own attack back by twenty-four hours to Monday 9 April.[31]

The offensive begins: 9–12 April 1917

Haig only formally established an Advanced GHQ for the Arras campaign (at Bavincourt, ten miles south-west of the city) on 22 April. At its beginning, on 9 April, he placed himself and some of his personal staff at Heuchin, near Third Army's HQ at St Pol.[32] The infantry attack that day commenced at 5.30 a.m. Though the calendar suggested spring, the severe winter of 1916–1917 continued. Snow lay on the ground and snow, sleet or rain fell for much of the day. But while the sun did not smile on the first day of the British spring offensive, fortune generally did. The contrast with 1 July 1916 was, indeed, astonishing. The infantry had enjoyed

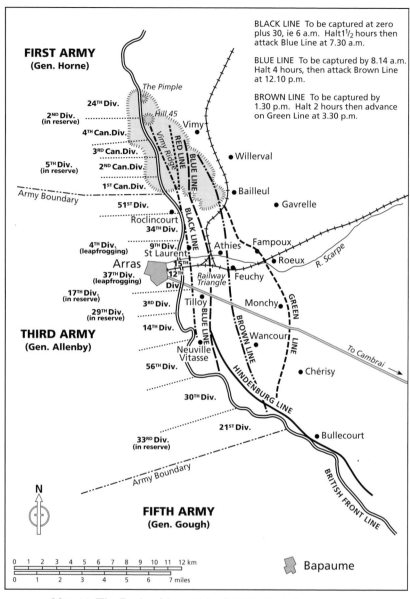

FIRST ARMY
(Gen. Horne)

BLACK LINE To be captured at zero
plus 30, ie 6 a.m. Halt 1½ hours then
attack Blue Line at 7.30 a.m.

BLUE LINE To be captured by 8.14 a.m.
Halt 4 hours, then attack Brown Line
at 12.10 p.m.

BROWN LINE To be captured by
1.30 p.m. Halt 2 hours then advance
on Green Line at 3.30 p.m.

The Pimple

24TH Div.

2ND Div.
(in reserve)

Hill 45

4TH Can.Div.

Vimy

3RD Can.Div.

Willerval

5TH Div.
(in reserve)

2ND Can.Div.

1ST Can.Div.

Bailleul

Army Boundary

51ST Div.

Gavrelle

Roclincourt

34TH Div.

4TH Div.
(leapfrogging)

9TH Div.

Athies

Fampoux

St Laurent

Arras

15TH

Roeux

R. Scarpe

37TH Div.
(leapfrogging)

12TH

Railway
Triangle

Feuchy

17TH Div.
(in reserve)

Div.

Monchy

29TH Div.
(in reserve)

3RD Div.

Tilloy

GREEN LINE

14TH Div.

BLUE LINE

Wancourt

BROWN LINE

THIRD ARMY
(Gen. Allenby)

Neuville
Vitasse

To Cambrai

56TH Div.

HINDENBURG LINE

Chérisy

30TH Div.

21ST Div.

Bullecourt

33RD Div.
(in reserve)

BRITISH FRONT LINE

Army Boundary

N

FIFTH ARMY
(Gen. Gough)

0 1 2 3 4 5 6 7 8 9 10 11 12 km
0   1   2   3   4   5   6   7 miles

Bapaume

Map 16. The Battle of Arras 9 April 1917: the infantry plan of attack

excellent artillery support, including the greatest barrages (both creeping and standing) fired by British artillery in the war so far. Though they were a relatively minor factor, Third Army also reported that:

The Tanks, some of which were attached to each Corps, did excellent work and assisted the infantry to a large extent, especially in the capture of the strong points of TELEGRAPH HILL, the HARP and the Railway Triangle.

By the end of the first day Byng's Canadian Corps had largely secured Vimy Ridge. Allenby's Third Army had gained its first two objectives, the Black and Blue lines, and much of the Brown Line. The furthest objective, the Green Line, had not been reached and the cavalry had not been able to go through. But by the evening of 9 April Third Army alone had recorded the capture of 5,600 prisoners and thirty-six guns.[33] Because German reserves were badly deployed at the start of the offensive, there were good opportunities for Third Army's infantry to press ahead rapidly in some parts of the front on the afternoon of Easter Monday. It is possible that, with more initiative and effort, Monchy-le-Preux might have been taken. But the foul weather sapped the troops' strength and, as Allenby complained to Haig, most of his infantry was not well trained for fluid operations. Long periods of trench warfare had left many British troops like "blind puppies", with little tactical sense and prone to excessive caution.[34]

There is some controversy as to whether there was a real chance for mounted action on the Easter Monday afternoon. The best opportunity was in the sector of Lieutenant-General Sir Charles Fergusson's XVII Corps, north of the Scarpe. But Allenby had placed no cavalry brigade under Fergusson's command, though, according to his own testimony, Fergusson had asked him to do so. Allenby had considered the possibility of cavalry exploitation only south of the Scarpe. After a conversation with Fergusson on the evening of Monday 9 April, Haig became concerned that an opportunity for cavalry exploitation was going begging. He telephoned Allenby about it,[35] but a cavalry brigade reached Fergusson's sector only on the afternoon of 10 April, too late to be of any use. With the benefit of hindsight this seems to have been of little real importance. Some of Fergusson's post-war comments indicate that he considered that this lost opportunity, if such it was, was probably not of great significance:

I doubt whether one Brigade let loose on the Douai plain without any definite objective would have done more than create some temporary discomfort and local confusion.[36]

Whatever his feelings about the lack of cavalry exploitation north of the Scarpe, Haig was generally well pleased with the events of 9 April. Indeed,

12. The Battle of Arras. British infantry awaiting orders to move forward from a reserve trench near Tilloy-les-Mofflaines, 10 April 1917. With the permission of The Trustees of the Imperial War Museum, London.

he was elated. At 3 p.m. he wrote a triumphant letter to the King[37] and when he met Allenby and Horne at St Pol at 10.30 a.m. the following morning, the mood was one of general self-congratulation. Haig, however, was now able to exercise very little practical influence on events. He merely exhorted Allenby to press on, suggesting that if resistance from the Germans in Monchy le Preux was proving to be a problem, Allenby should turn the position from the south.[38]

On the morning of Tuesday 10 April Third Army seems, in general, to have been tired, sluggish and lacking in a definite sense of purpose. In most parts of the front, it barely got going before noon. Most of the remainder of the Brown Line was then captured and consolidated. But long before infantry had secured the Green Line, Allenby prematurely committed his cavalry (2nd and 3rd Divisions), trying to get them through respectively north and south of Monchy. They met intense machine gun fire and lost a good many horses (though relatively few men) and achieved little.[39] That evening, Allenby, apparently dissatisfied with his Army's progress, issued an order for distribution to all ranks:

The Army Commander wishes all troops to understand that Third Army is now pursuing a defeated enemy and that risks must be freely taken. Isolated enemy detachments in farms and villages must not be allowed to delay the general progress. Such points must be masked and passed by.

Even in relation to the events of the first twenty-four hours of the offensive this missive made exaggerated claims. It was true that Third Army had inflicted a serious defeat on the front line divisions of the German Sixth Army. Despite the appalling weather, which inevitably sapped its spirits, Third Army's infantry could have done with a bit more vim and vigour on the Monday afternoon and the Tuesday morning to take advantage of this situation. But there had been no real prospect of its penetrating anything like the full depth of the German system of field fortifications. Allenby's order, moreover, came too late. German reserves were now arriving on the battlefield in substantial numbers. It was no longer a question of having to deal with "isolated detachments". A more methodical approach to offensive operations was now becoming appropriate.[40]

Despite mounting evidence that the offensive was losing momentum, Haig, who had just received hearty congratulations from Robertson and Derby, seems to have remained in a high state of excitement for several days. Charteris realised what the magnitude of the initial success meant to him:

I have never seen D.H. so stirred by success before ... It means a great deal to him personally ... After all this trouble at Calais ... there is no doubt in any of our minds that the Prime Minister would have got rid of him out of hand unless this show had been a success. It is a success, indeed it is more than a success, it is a victory.[41]

Despite some mishaps and frustrations, for the first three or four days there appeared to be good cause for celebration. In the period up to 11 April, Third Army captured 7,000 prisoners and 112 guns, to which must be added about 4,000 prisoners taken by the Canadians. The First and Third Armies suffered about 13,000 casualties during the same period, of which about one-third were killed. It is reasonable to believe that, as the British official history suggests, the British had inflicted about twice as many casualties as they had suffered in the opening days of the battle.[42] The bulk of the success had, however, been achieved on the first day. By Z + 1 most of the momentum was lost. It is true that, on Z + 2, Wednesday 11 April, the 15th Division of Third Army's VI Corps, with some help from the 3rd Cavalry Division, managed to take Monchy-le-Preux. But an attempt to widen the offensive with an attack by the 4th Australian Division of Gough's Fifth Army on the Hindenburg Line at

Bullecourt proved very bloody and was ultimately unsuccessful. The following day, Thursday 12 April, First Army took "The Pimple" and the Bois en Hache in its postponed "Northern Operation" and Third Army's VII Corps finally secured the villages of Heninel and Wancourt. But, even though Third Army was able to relieve six of the now exhausted divisions that had attacked on Easter Monday between 11 and 13 April, these were the last significant gains for some time.[43]

Break-in and breakdown: analysis

There can be no doubt that the British army had made enormous improvements in the art of the set-piece attack in the nine months between 1 July 1916 and 9 April 1917. The thoroughness with which the break-in phase was planned and the scale and sophistication of the preparations were, for a mass army thrown together in a few years and desperately short of properly trained staff officers, highly commendable. All the divisions attacking on 9 April 1917 had been on the Somme. While their infantry, some of which had replaced the casualties of the Somme, was at variable standards of training, divisional commanders, their staffs and the artillery undoubtedly benefited from their hard-earned experience.

Technical and tactical innovations such as tanks and machine gun barrages (machine guns being fired over the heads of advancing infantry), which had been first employed on the Somme, certainly gave some assistance to the infantry on 9 April. There had also been new initiatives in training, following the establishment of the GHQ Training Directorate under Major-General Arthur Solly-Flood on 30 January 1917. New training pamphlets such as the now celebrated "SS143 Instructions for the Training of Platoons for Offensive Action" (designed, in part, to make the platoon capable of fire and manoeuvre using its own resources, overcoming excessive reliance on artillery support) had certainly been issued, though, despite recent research, it is not clear how widely and deeply such new doctrines had yet been disseminated and absorbed. Cyril Falls, the much-respected official historian, is far from flattering about the British infantry's standards of initiative and flexibility after the initial break-in, and he considered that the general quality of the army's manpower had somewhat dropped after the massive losses of the Somme. Indeed, while Canadian and British infantry were well-drilled and rehearsed in the tactics of set-piece assaults, it seems safe to attribute the successful opening of the battle more to the massive and skilful application of heavy firepower (mortars and artillery, especially the latter) than to any other factor.

The growing British skill in the handling of this arm had caused the Germans considerable anxiety during the course of the Somme battle. They had been especially concerned about increasing British success in counter-battery work. Techniques such as using aerial observation to adjust fire, aerial photography and photographic interpretation, flash spotting and sound ranging had been continually developed and disseminated. During the fighting on the Somme the technique of the creeping barrage had been generally adopted and progressively refined. All the attacking forces used it on 9 April. A new type of contact fuse, the 106 (available only in limited numbers) gave improved effectiveness in some roles, especially wire cutting and counter-battery. One of the attacking divisions (the 9th Scottish) used smoke shell for the first time as part of the barrage fired by its field artillery. GHQ had launched a reorganisation of the field artillery after the Somme, reducing the number of guns in each division, but creating Army Field Artillery brigades: a move intended to prevent too many guns being kept out of action as divisions were moved around the front. Judging the precise influence of each improvement in equipment, technique and organisation is difficult, but on 9 April 1917 the overall effectiveness of the British artillery was evident to all. The German guns were greatly subdued and in some sectors all but silenced. In most cases the infantry found the German front line trenches pulverised and their wire cut. Where German defenders had survived in the front lines, the creeping barrage largely suppressed them.

The expansion and the increasing efficiency of the British munitions industry were arguably even more important to success than technical, tactical and organisational innovation. The sheer quantity of the munitions available made a vast difference. The attack of 1 July 1916 was on a front of 27,000 yards. The total number of guns employed in support of it was just under 1,750. The front attacked at Arras was slightly shorter: 25,000 yards, but 2,880 guns supported that effort. Even more telling are the comparative statistics of the weight of shell fired in the preliminary bombardments and the assaults of the first day: 52,000 tons for the Somme and 88,000 for Vimy-Arras. This had been delivered in six days for the latter offensive as opposed to eight days for the former. In June–July 1916 a high proportion of the shell used, particularly for the heavier guns, had proved defective. In April 1917 this was no longer the case. Much of the German Sixth Army, and especially the unfortunate men in the front line, had been subjected to an explosive battering of titanic force.[44]

Another important element in the initial victory was the largely fortuitous achievement of a considerable degree of surprise. Von Falkenhausen, the German Sixth Army commander, had become convinced that the British would not attack until about 15 April. It is unclear why he reached this conclusion. British security had obviously been tight enough not to reveal the true date, but there appears to have been no deception plan designed to suggest this later one. Von Falkenhausen had six *Eingreifdivisionen* (counter-attack divisions) available in addition to the five divisions that received the initial British attack. Understandably he wanted to keep these out of the way of the British bombardment. But he actually kept them between twelve and twenty-four hours marching time from the front and that was certainly excessive. These divisions were thus unable to influence the battle on the first day.[45]

That the attack quickly lost momentum is not at all difficult to explain. The tiredness of many of the attacking troops after heavy fighting on 9 April, made worse by foul weather and bitter cold, was an obvious factor. Some units seem also to have suffered from a lack of proper training for more fluid operations beyond the initial set-piece attack. The success of the first day was, as we have seen, very largely owing to the weight and accuracy of carefully planned artillery fire. This could not be repeated to the same degree on subsequent days. It became necessary to move guns forward over terrain that was sodden and churned up by shelling. This proved difficult and time-consuming, especially for the heavier guns, once moved, had to be re-registered in order to fire accurately, and this was bound to take more time. Moreover, in the more fluid situation, the gunners could not always be sure where their infantry was in relation to the enemy. In these circumstances artillery support was bound to be relatively ragged.[46] But the most important factor in slowing the British advance was, of course, the movement to the front of various categories of German reinforcements, most notably Falkenhausen's reserve divisions. Many of these were good quality troops who fought with real determination. In general their efforts to exercise their supposed mission of counter-attack were rather limited, but they were successful in shoring up the defence. By the evening of 12 April they had brought the British attack to a virtual halt.[47]

How far can Haig personally be given credit for the magnitude of the initial success and how far must he take responsibility for the rapid subsequent breakdown? The BEF was, of course, a very large and complex organism and much of its evolution since 1 July 1916 was not attributable to any personal inspiration on the part of the commander-in-chief. Other men's heads conceived and hands drafted most of the detail of the plans executed on 9 April. Haig, however, exerted a positive influence in at least two particulars. He insisted, against Nivelle's advice, on the seizure of Vimy Ridge and, in the face of stubborn resistance from Allenby, he ensured that Third Army employed its artillery in the most careful and systematic manner for the preliminary bombardment. Events vindicated him on both counts.

But Haig must also be held responsible for some of what went wrong on 9–12 April. It is not taking undue advantage of hindsight to suggest that the Green Line was an over-ambitious objective for Z-day. Analysis of any or all of the previous attacks by the British army on the Western Front operation over the previous two years should have pointed to that conclusion. Neither can Haig escape blame for the lack of realistic planning for anything beyond the set-piece assaults of Easter Monday. The principal mistake here was to imagine that sustained pursuit and exploitation could follow the initial assault. In reality the initial break-in could only be the beginning of a very hard fight. Sensible analysis of the Somme fighting and of the available intelligence on German fortifications and reserves on the Arras front should have made this apparent. Getting through the whole German defensive system and defeating all the available reserves would inevitably have required several major assaults, each backed by something like the firepower used on 9 April. Each of these assaults would have taken considerable time to prepare and the necessary logistical-operational pauses would have had to be written into the programme. A steady, systematic approach of this nature might, however, have tied down German troops at least as effectively as the disjointed efforts into which the battle degenerated after 9 April and might have done so at a significantly lower cost.

The offensive continues: 12–15 April 1917

Haig and Kiggell visited Third Army headquarters at St Pol on the morning of Thursday 12 April. They found Allenby out visiting his corps commanders, so Haig spoke to his chief of staff, Major-General L. J. Bols. Haig "pointed out that the Enemy had now been given time to put the Drocourt-Quéant line into a state of defence and to organise positions also in our immediate front. He has also brought up a large amount of guns. Our advance must therefore be more methodical than was permissible on Monday night and Tuesday after the victory ... Now we must try and substitute shells as far as possible for infantry ..."[48] The suggestion that, from this point onwards, shells ought to be substituted for the blood of his infantry was entirely sound. Unfortunately it was not implemented. Over the next few days Third Army's losses continued to mount alarmingly. This was by no means entirely Allenby's fault. Haig was sending mixed messages. Expressing concern for casualties and a preference for more deliberate methods at one moment, he was pressing Third Army rapidly to make significant gains of ground the next.

Later that day, Thursday 12 April, Haig heard from Nivelle that the French offensive was postponed by another twenty-four hours. Though this must have been frustrating, especially in view of First Army's successful "Northern Attack" that morning, he raised no objection. Continuing to play the part of loyal ally and dutiful subordinate, he replied that:

I have ... heard that the attack of the G.A.N. [French Northern Army Group] is again postponed one day. I understand that these postponements have been forced on you by the very unfavourable weather, which we also are experiencing.

My intention, which has not been modified in any way, is to push forward in the direction of CAMBRAI as rapidly and energetically as possible.

I regret that owing to the bad weather and the consequent state of the ground, my troops have not been able to follow up the successes already gained as rapidly as would have been possible under better conditions. The enemy has therefore had time to bring up reinforcements and is offering strenuous opposition, to overcome which, without great sacrifice of life, it is necessary to bring forward artillery: a slow and difficult task.

Every endeavour is being made to overcome these difficulties but it is still doubtful within what time I shall be able to organise an attack in force, adequately supported by guns, against the Quéant–Drocourt line, on the defences of which the enemy is working with great energy. It will be attacked as soon as possible and I will inform you as soon as I can form a reasonable estimate as to when the attack can be launched.[49]

Haig clearly meant every word of what he wrote to Nivelle. Despite his talk at St Pol, earlier the same day, of expending shell instead of infantrymen, it is clear that he was expecting Third Army to continue to fight forward "rapidly" and "energetically". But next day, Friday 13 April, Nivelle informed Haig that his Army Group commanders had requested yet another postponement. Nivelle was now acutely embarrassed. He informed Haig that he had made his acceptance of this further delay conditional upon his approval. Making a change in a French plan conditional upon the approval of a British general who, with great trouble, had been placed under his orders was a very odd thing to do and is surely indicative of the stress that Nivelle was now experiencing. Haig was also feeling the strain, but could hardly have been more loyal. He told Kiggell that "since the French had been given the main decisive attack to carry out we must do all in our power to make their operations a success".[50]

British hiatus and French defeat: 15–23 April 1917

By the time the French attacked on the Aisne, at 6 a.m. on Monday 16 April 1917, the British push east of Arras had been virtually stalled for three days. On Sunday 15 April Haig ordered an operational pause while preparations were made for another large-scale co-ordinated attack.[51] This decision was made none too soon. Indeed, it almost certainly resulted from a sort of generals' mutiny in the Third Army. On the evening of Saturday 14 April Allenby had issued orders that his VI and VII Corps were to reach, within forty-eight hours, the little River Sensee, between Vis en Artois and Fontaine le Croiselles. This would have constituted an advance of over a mile. In the face of the stiff opposition being encountered, with the still grim weather conditions and without any special artillery preparation, it was, to say the least, an extremely demanding goal. But if Allenby was driving his men ruthlessly, he was doing so on Haig's instructions. At a meeting at Third Army HQ at St Pol earlier that Saturday, Haig told Allenby that "I hoped the advance guards of Third Army would be over the Sensee in time for Gough to attack on Tuesday morning." According to Haig, Allenby responded that "there would be no difficulty about this ...".[52]

On Sunday 15 April three major-generals commanding front-line divisions, Wilkinson (50th Division), de Lisle (29th Division) and Robertson (17th Division), met to protest against Allenby's order. Two of the divisions concerned (the 50th Division and the 29th Division) belonged to Lieutenant-General Sir Aylmer Haldane's VI Corps, and Lord Loch, the chief of staff of VI Corps, was present at the critical meeting. Haldane's relations with Allenby were vitriolic. Though there is no indication that he was personally present, it is at least possible that he connived at, or even helped to instigate, what was, in effect, a kind of mutiny. The divisional commanders passed a "resolution" against further hasty, unco-ordinated, narrow-front attacks. Instead they recommended consolidating existing gains, especially Monchy le Preux, which had almost been lost to a German counter-attack the previous day. After that, they wanted a carefully prepared, broad-front attack to be mounted on both sides of the River Scarpe. It appears that the resolution was despatched directly to Haig, though by whom and by what means is not clear.[53]

This collective protest by a group of divisional commanders going over the heads of their Army commander to GHQ was an extraordinary procedure. It indicates a serious breakdown of leadership, command, control, and, therefore, discipline in Third Army. Yet, however improper it was by normal standards, the protest seems to have succeeded. Haig's order of 15 April complied with at least the most basic of the protestors' demands. Representing as it did a fairly dramatic change of Haig's plans within twenty-four hours, this is very unlikely to have been mere coincidence. There is no indication that any disciplinary action was ever taken against any of the dissident generals and it is difficult to say whether the action had a negative effect on their careers. Robertson and De Lisle both commanded corps before the end of the war, though, in Robertson's case, the command was only temporary.

In the immediate aftermath of their protest the generals concerned were informed that Allenby actually agreed with it. But if that were the case how did Haig get the impression, on Saturday 14 April, that the Third Army commander imagined "no difficulty" in getting his forces over the Sensee by the Tuesday morning?[54] Given that Haig and Allenby were both inarticulate of speech, a complete misunderstanding cannot be ruled out. But it seems more likely that, dealing with Haig face-to-face, Allenby's moral courage failed him. It is probable that it was their perception of Allenby's deficiency in that department that led his subordinates to circumvent him.

Haig held an Army commanders' conference at Third Army HQ at St Pol on 16 April. Gough, Horne and Allenby were all there. As the rebel divisional commanders had demanded, it was decided that there was to be a pause in offensive operations. At this stage, however, Haig was only prepared to concede a very brief intermission. There would be a preliminary attack by Third Army on 18 April to capture the village of Guemappe, followed by an attack by all three Armies two days later. Haig's conduct of the conference of 16 April suggests that he was trying to do three things at once: pacify the rebels in Third Army, maintain the momentum of the Arras offensive during the critical opening phase of French operations on the Aisne and reassert his own authority. These objectives were to some degree conflicting and his success was, in all respects, rather limited.[55]

The Guemappe operation, scheduled for 18 April, was soon cancelled in the face of renewed resistance from within Third Army. Then Horne protested that the weather was interfering with his preparations for the operation of 20 April and requested a postponement of that too, putting the main attack back to Monday 23 April. Even Gough, a Haig protégé and often regarded as a "thruster", now registered dissent. He declined to take part in infantry attacks on 23 April, indicating that Fifth Army would co-operate with its artillery only. "Sir Douglas Haig has almost always", commented the official historian, "deferred to the wishes of the commanders on the spot."[56] Such deference on Haig's part was, as we have seen, far from being a universal rule. The generals' revolt of 15 April and its immediate aftermath points up a theme that historians have not, perhaps, sufficiently explored: the fragility of Haig's authority in the face of collective or simultaneous dissent from formation commanders. Fortunately for Haig such dissent was rare. That it happened in this case probably reflected a combination of an extreme lack of respect for Allenby from a substantial section of senior officers, a sense that Haig was unlikely to support Allenby unconditionally and that Haig himself was out of touch with the situation on the front line.

It has often been implied that Haig and GHQ fully expected the failure of the French offensive in the Aisne-Champagne sector, but there is strong evidence to the contrary. On Sunday 15 April Charteris wrote to his wife noting that:

The battle is still going well for us but it is going to be a long affair. I think it will be the beginning of the end for Germany. Before this reaches you we should have good news from the French. Things may move very quickly then.[57]

In fact Nivelle's offensive, commencing on 16 April 1917, was not the unmitigated disaster of popular belief. It resulted in the capture of 28,500 prisoners and 187 artillery pieces in the period up to 10 May. It gained more ground than most previous French offensives. French casualties, however, were heavy: about 134,000 in the first nine days.[58] These were no worse than some of the offensives of 1914 and 1915, but the French army and people were now much wearier. The result was a massive crisis of confidence and discipline. Haig quickly got wind that all was not well. On Tuesday 17 April he recorded in his diary that "I could get no details from French as to results of today's fighting which is always a bad sign." On Wednesday 18 April a letter from Henry Wilson, who was attached to Nivelle's headquarters, tended to confirm Haig's suspicions and he became concerned about the effect on inter-Allied relations:

GQG [French general headquarters] is disappointed, and they will look about for some excuse. One of them will be that the whole German Army is facing them and that we have not succeeded in easing their load! This would be pure French, i.e. the woman's side of their nature, wounded vanity, jealousy and disappointment at their own failure and our success! I don't think, luckily, that the French losses are very heavy ...[59]

French losses were heavier than Haig realised at first, especially in relation to the already fragile state of French morale. But in this instance he worried unnecessarily about the French using the British as scapegoats. On the whole they preferred to blame each other.[60] On Wednesday 18 April Haig dined with Major-General Sir Frederick Maurice, Director of Military Operations at the War Office. Maurice brought news that Albert Thomas, the French Minister of Munitions, who had recently passed through London on his way to Russia, had spoken to Lloyd George. He had said that if the Nivelle's operations were not speedily successful the French government intended to "stop them and do nothing until 1918 when the Americans would be able to help".[61] Maurice enquired, on Lloyd George's behalf, how Haig intended to respond if the French soon ceased offensive operations. In a letter to Robertson the following day, Haig refused to countenance this possibility.

In my opinion the decision to cease offensive operations now until Russia and America are in a position to join in (probably not until next spring) would be most unwise ...

I consider that the prospects of success this year are distinctly good if we do not relax our efforts, and that it would be unwise, unsound and probably in the long run, more costly in men and money to cease offensive operations at an early date.[62]

Lloyd George would support Haig's line on this at a conference in Paris a few days later.[63] Haig soon received confirmation from the French military sources that their offensive was in serious trouble. But he found it impossible to accept that Allied plans for offensive operations in 1917 were totally disintegrating. He informed his French liaison officer, Gemeau, that "In my opinion the battle is taking a normal course"[64] and urged its continuance. Robertson could not take so sanguine a view of the matter. If the Allies' spring offensive were to be continued, the CIGS at least wanted Haig to think carefully about the methods used. In a letter of 20 April, while coating the essence of his remarks with a thick sugar of flattery, Robertson gave Haig what he himself described as "a sort of staff college lecture":

To my mind no war has ever differed so much from previous wars as does the present one, and it is futile, to put it mildly, hanging on to old theories when the facts show them to be wrong. At one time audacity and determination to push on regardless of loss were the predominating factors, but that was before the days of machine guns and other modern armament.

Robertson urged Haig to abandon all thought of "breaking the enemy's front". An obsession with doing that had, Robertson believed, been one of Nivelle's mistakes. The correct method, Robertson insisted, was to "aim at breaking down the enemy's army and that means inflicting heavier losses on him than one suffers oneself". Haig should adopt a cautious, firepower-centred, step-by-step approach characterised by "detailed and careful preparation", "thorough knowledge of the ground" and "well observed artillery fire". The necessity for this sort of approach was, of course, a theme on which Robertson had been harping since February 1915. The Nivelle offensive, Robertson indicated, was going to end in failure, a failure of which he had been a "true prophet". Haig should also realise that, because of the Revolution, Russia was going to be useless in military terms for the rest of the year.[65] Caution, both in operational method and in overall strategy, was, therefore, Robertson's keynote. In another letter, a week later, he struck the same note again. He did not demand that Haig cease offensive operations on the Western Front altogether; to do that would concede the initiative to the Germans and might be dangerous. But he strongly argued that the general strategic situation was now unfavourable to the Allies and that they should not expect decisive victory in 1917.[66]

When he wrote to Haig on 20 April, Robertson certainly realised that Haig's offensive had got stuck and may well have known of the generals' revolt five days earlier. This letter should probably be regarded as a major milestone on the downward path of Robertson's assessment of Haig's ability as a field commander and perhaps of his assessment of Haig's strategic judgement too. Probably it should also be seen as a highly significant episode in the decline of the Haig–Robertson relationship. Haig did not immediately react to Robertson's carefully worded criticism. But a couple of months later, after the CIGS had given further evidence of doubts about his judgement, Haig would suggest to the Prime Minister that Robertson be removed from the War Office.[67]

The renewed Arras offensive: 23–28 April 1917

As long as the French did not abandon their offensive in the Aisne-Champagne region, Haig was keen to maintain the pressure in the Arras sector. This was not the attitude he had taken during the winter. He had then indicated that if the French did not achieve a speedy breakthrough, he would want quickly to shift the main British effort to Flanders to deal with the submarine menace and expected the French to shift their effort northward to support him. Haig would still refer to the submarine menace whenever it suited him to do so.[68] But, while that menace continued seriously to worry the War Office and the War Cabinet, at least until May, it is not clear that it formed the real basis of any military decision that Haig took in 1917.[69]

From mid-April and through May 1917 Haig seems to have been motivated by three main factors. First, he was still so intensely excited by his initial success that it was difficult for him to come to terms with the reality that his troops had got stuck and that his offensive was now going nowhere. Second, he appears to have been fixated on extremely optimistic prognoses about the condition of Germany; his diary entries over the next few weeks indicate that he believed that if only the Allies kept the pressure on there was a very good chance of a German collapse before the end of the year.[70] Third, while he most wanted French support for his future operations in Flanders, he appears to have feared that if the French now stopped attacking in the Aisne-Champagne region they might stop attacking altogether for the rest of the year.[71]

Haig renewed his offensive at 4.45 a.m. on Monday 23 April, later and on a somewhat smaller scale than he had intended. Third Army mounted the main attack, with seven divisions, astride the Scarpe. First Army assisted by attacking towards Gavrelle with another two. Fifth Army provided artillery support. The 63rd (Royal Naval) Division took

Gavrelle. All of Third Army's attacking corps (from left to right XVII, VI and VII) gained some ground during the morning, but the advance was shallow and casualties heavy. In contrast with 9 April, the attack mounted on Monday 23 April achieved little or no surprise. There was far more German artillery present than a fortnight earlier, and whereas, on Easter Monday, the British artillery had the positions of most German batteries fixed and was able largely to silence them, this was not the case on 23 April. The attackers, therefore, sustained heavy German shelling from the outset. In the absence of surprise, the German counter-attack divisions were (in stark contrast with 9 April) correctly placed on 23 April. From around noon these went into action against VI and VII Corps, driving some of the British forces back to their start lines. Severe fighting continued during the night. The following morning VII Corps was able to regain some of the ground it had lost the previous afternoon. On 24 April the Germans counter-attacked First Army at Gavrelle and XVII Corps on Third Army's left, but regained no ground. Some veteran troops considered the fighting of 23–24 April 1917 the most severe they had yet experienced and Third Army's report noted that the enemy left "the battle field covered with his dead". Third Army had taken some 2,264 prisoners on 23 and 24 April and First Army another 479. Third Army reckoned it had sustained around 12,000 casualties of all types on these days.[72]

On Tuesday 24 April, while this exceptionally bitter fighting was still in progress, Haig informed Allenby that he wanted him to drive the Germans back to the Drocourt-Quéant Line by the end of the month. For this mission Haig could spare him no reinforcements, though four fresh divisions might be made available for the next big task: breaking the Drocourt-Quéant Line.[73] It does not seem to be going too far to say that Haig had, at this stage, lost touch with the reality of the battle. In the large-scale attack just mounted (an effort that had taken over a week to prepare) Third Army had gained, at best, only a few hundred yards of ground. To suggest that Allenby should simply press on, without reinforce-ments, to the Drocourt-Quéant Line appears absurd. This was especially true given that, having already faced a quasi-mutiny by some of Third Army's generals, Haig now had plenty of evidence of the exhausted and somewhat demoralised state of a substantial proportion of Allenby's forces.

That afternoon Haig went by staff car to Amiens to meet Nivelle. Before his 3 p.m. interview with the French commander, he spoke to Henry Wilson, who confirmed what Haig must already have suspected: that Nivelle no longer enjoyed the confidence of the French government. Haig, however, did not want Nivelle dismissed or his operations on the Aisne suspended. Indeed, he demanded Nivelle's assurance that "the

French Armies would continue to operate energetically".[74] Haig's behaviour seems odd. Why press Nivelle for a guarantee he was in no position to give? Nivelle must have suspected that his days in command were numbered, but gave the assurance anyway. Perhaps both generals were demonstrating a form of cognitive dissonance: a refusal to face the facts of the situation and to respond accordingly.

On 26 and 27 April Haig was in Paris seeking further assurances of a continued French offensive effort from Painlevé, the French war minister, and Ribot, the octogenarian premier. According to Haig, both gave the assurances sought, but each almost certainly knew it was valueless. Painlevé wanted to sack Nivelle, but Haig counselled against this, apparently believing that he was likely to get less co-operation and less offensive action from any likely successor.[75] Given that he was urging the French to go on attacking, however futile their efforts appeared, Haig seems to have felt honour-bound to order his forces to do the same. (If there was logic here it was of a distinctly tortuous kind.) So important did Haig consider the maintenance of pressure on the Arras front that, on Thursday 26 April, he had Kiggell conduct an Army commanders' conference in his absence, outlining offensive plans for the immediate future.

Kiggell told Horne and Allenby that British operations in Artois would continue unless the French offensives further south were curtailed. But uncertainty over French intentions was making long-term planning difficult, which was why, for the time being, the Army commanders would have to go on fighting with the same tired old divisions. Future offensive operations were to be conducted in two stages. On 28 April First Army was to capture Arleux and Oppy and Third Army was to take Greenland Hill and Roeux north of the Scarpe – objectives that defied all previous attacks. A much larger attack by First, Third and Fifth Armies was to follow on or about 3 May. This was supposed to bring Third and First Armies within striking distance of the Drocourt-Quéant Line, which would be assaulted in mid-May.[76]

Attempting another big push so quickly after the massive effort of 23–24 April was foolhardy. The British army's Western Front experience indicated that large-scale, well co-ordinated efforts could not be put together in that sort of time and many of the troops involved were already very weary. Saturday 28 April was, therefore, a dismal day for British arms. Again there was no surprise worthy of the name and the British counter-battery effort was unable to suppress the German guns and the BEF's losses were very heavy. Elements of 1st Canadian Division took Arleux and the British gained small amounts of ground in other sectors, but Oppy, Greenland Hill and Roeux all remained in German hands.[77] Much of Third Army was clearly in a state of extreme exhaustion. Morale, fairly high on Easter Monday, was now strained to breaking point.

The long, dismal last phase: 29 April–24 May

Between his last meeting with Painlevé on 27 April and the Army commanders' conference of 30 April Haig received unofficial confirmation of what had been rumoured for some time: Nivelle was to be sacked. This caused him to take, at least temporarily, a more realistic attitude to the chances of serious French offensive action for the remainder of the year. He told Horne, Allenby and Gough that:

As regards the French their losses had been heavy and they could not continue to co-operate by similar methods to those they had employed since their main offensive was launched on 16th April. There was the possibility of changes in the French higher command. This contingency would doubtless alter the military policy of the French, which would then probably be of a defensive nature with a tendency to avoid losses ... and await the active assistance of America in the field.

Haig seemed confident, however, of offensive action by the Italians and (contrary to War Office views) by the Russians.

He ordered that the major attack programmed for 3 May should go ahead as planned. While Haig's interest in breaking the Drocourt-Quéant Line seems to have diminished, he "stated his intention to move steadily forward to a good defensive position" and "to consolidate it pending the development of the situation on the fronts of the whole theatre of war in Europe".[78] The line he wanted to reach extended from Lens, through Acheville, Fresnoy, Greenland Hill, Bois du Vert and Riencourt. Once that line had been attained, Haig intended to switch British offensive efforts to Flanders.[79]

The attack of Thursday 3 May was to be a really big affair: First, Third and Fifth Armies operating on a fourteen-mile front. There was an inter-Army dispute over the start time for the operation: I ANZAC Corps in Fifth Army was to attack the section of the Hindeburg Line between Quéant and Bullecourt and wanted to do so by night, at 3.30 a.m. Allenby wanted Third Army to attack at dawn, at 4.05 a.m. On 2 May, with only a few hours to go before the operation began, Haig enforced an apparently arbitrary and ultimately somewhat disastrous compromise, insisting that all three armies should attack at 3.45 a.m. First and Third Army did not have time to make the necessary arrangements for a night attack and a good deal of chaos resulted. The last-minute choice of Zero hour also left attacking troops in large sections of the front silhouetted against the light of a nearly full moon, setting just behind them.[80]

Many who witnessed this day's fighting considered it, from the British point of view, the "blackest of the War" so far. The only success was gained on the far left by the 1st and 2nd Canadian Divisions, which managed to capture Fresnoy. In general, the German divisions in line managed to repel the attack without even having to call for the help of reserve divisions. The ground gained by British troops in the First Army and Third Army sectors in most cases was swiftly recaptured, in some instances by German counter-attacks mounted in no great strength. The Australian operation, in the Bullecourt sector on the right, also proved extremely bloody and largely a failure.[81] Even Fresnoy, the one significant gain of Thursday 3 May, was lost to a German attack five days later. The complete absence of surprise was clearly one factor in the defeat. Another was the failure of the counter-battery programme over much of the front and the consequently intense and accurate fire of a large amount of German artillery. The basic problem was that the operation had been thrown together far too quickly and was poorly co-ordinated. But there were also signs of demoralisation: a mixture of weariness and the loss of belief that those in command really knew what they were doing.

As far as First and Third Armies were concerned, the Battle of Arras dragged on dismally for another couple of weeks. There were one or two minor gains of ground, notably the capture of Roeux and the notorious nearby Chemical Works (which had already changed hands a number of times) on 11 May.[82] This, however, barely compensated for the demoralising loss of Fresnoy three days earlier. On Haig's orders Fifth Army continued its efforts at Bullecourt, mainly with I ANZAC Corps. These operations seemed to serve little rational purpose and helped make that place-name one of the most notorious in Australian military history.[83]

Assessment

It had all begun so well. At the opening of the offensive, as well as taking the commanding ground of the Vimy Ridge and making the deepest one-day advance since the stalemate set in, Haig's forces appear to have inflicted casualties very much heavier than those they had sustained. But even the statistics provided in the British official history indicate that the Battle of Arras, when considered as an exercise in attrition, was ultimately the least successful of the major British offensives mounted under Haig's command. Total casualties for the three British Armies involved were probably around 150,000: between a quarter and a third of them fatal. Over the same period the casualties of the German Sixth Army seem to have been only 79–85,000, though, to these, German casualties for the Bullecourt fighting (not done by Sixth Army and not accurately known) should be added.[84] The British casualty rate for Arras was approximately 4,076 per day, the highest by a large margin of any of Haig's major offensives.[85]

Haig's conduct of the battle after the first day raises, once again, serious questions about his judgement. The lack of realistic planning for events beyond the initial set piece assault has already been addressed. More vigorous exploitation of initial success on the evening of 9 April and on the following morning might, indeed, have gained useful ground at relatively low cost. But given its depth, and the availability of substantial German reserves, there should never have been any question of trying to get through the whole German defensive system by the exploitation of a single day's worth of set-piece assaults. The poorly co-ordinated efforts of 12–14 April resulted in excessive loss of British life for very limited gain of ground. Haig was just as responsible for this as Allenby. One minute he talked of substituting shells for the infantry's blood, the next he was demanding that infantry advance to places it could not possibly reach in the time allowed without bleeding profusely.

Arguably, one of Haig's problems (already discussed with regard to the Somme) was that he was attempting to operate at too many "levels of war" at the same time. The BEF was a very large Army Group. Haig was an Army Group commander and, therefore, an actor at what is today called the "operational level of war". Yet he was also very insistent on his role in helping to co-ordinate the overall military policy of the Allies on the Western Front and was keen to give advice on strategy for the war as a whole. He was, in other words, attempting to function at what would today be described as the "military strategic" (theatre command) level and to influence the very highest, "grand strategic" level too. All this proved too much for him. While worrying about French military policy for the rest of 1917 and dreaming of knocking Germany out of the war, he lost focus on the immediate operational and tactical realities confronting his Armies in the Arras sector.

The decision to halt small, unco-ordinated attacks and to consolidate ground won should have been made before the quasi-mutiny of 15 April. By that stage there was a serious crisis of confidence and morale in Third Army, which was followed by a partial breakdown in Haig's authority – a more general crisis of command and control. Combined with the strength and alertness of the Germans in this sector, it made any further progress extremely difficult. Though he did eventually order a series of large-scale attacks at Arras, Haig was too worried about maintaining initiative and momentum (largely non-existent after 12 April anyway) and did not give enough time for their planning and preparation. This way of proceeding normally had depressing and sometimes really dire results. Haig's arguments for continuing the offensive after 24 April now appear deeply unconvincing. The lack of enthusiasm with which his forces prosecuted the latter stages of the offensive suggests that they seemed so at the time. During the second half of 1917 there was a serious decline in the morale of the British army on the Western Front. This did not start in August in the rain and sucking mud of Flanders. A pronounced drop in the army's spirits was noticeable in May.[86]

Haig was, therefore, every bit as responsible for the miserable mess that had constituted most of the Arras offensive as was Allenby. Haig, however, got most of the credit for initial success while Allenby suffered the consequences of subsequent failure. The Third Army commander had, indeed, been out of his depth throughout. He had been excessively stubborn with Haig over the issue of the preliminary bombardment, about which he was almost certainly wrong. On the afternoon of 9 April, and throughout 10 April, he had seemed incapable of energising his troops. His "defeated enemy" order, when it came, was both too bombastic and too late. In mid-April, he failed to stand up to Haig when he really needed to do so, and tried to push subordinates too far too fast when the time for pushing had passed. When, in early May, he belatedly protested against the excessive demands being made on his exhausted troops, he irritated Haig, but failed to restore his ruined credibility within his command.[87]

In June Julian Byng replaced Edmund Allenby at Third Army. Distraught, Allenby broke down in Byng's presence.[88] Yet being sent to the Egypt-Palestine theatre proved a blessing in disguise. Given an independent command over British forces massively outnumbering[89] an enemy much worse equipped and rather less sophisticated than the one he had faced on the Western Front, he emerged as a conqueror and a hero.

13   Flanders Fields

A two-stage campaign

After the Battle of Arras Haig's next major project was a complex, extremely ambitious campaign in Flanders. This would eventually be mounted in two stages with a lengthy interlude between them. Commencing in early June, these Flanders operations would preoccupy Haig for most of the rest of the year. The second stage, from late July to mid-November, would eventually involve most of his army. Covering these operations adequately will take two chapters. This chapter deals with the overall strategic planning and with the short, successful opening round: the Battle of Messines.

Origins and early plans

Haig's Belgian operations of 1917 had a lengthy and rather complex genesis and to provide even the sketchiest outline of this it is necessary to backtrack somewhat. The devastated city of Ypres was the only major Belgian town that remained free of German military occupation at the end of 1914 and it was politically important for the Allies to retain it. But the First Battle of Ypres (October–November 1914) had left it in an awkward salient, further constricted as a result of the Second Battle (April–May 1915). The Germans held much of the higher ground around the Ypres Salient and enjoyed good observation over it, and it thus became notorious as a "shell-trap". Given that it was not politically acceptable to abandon Ypres, trying to capture some of this high ground made obvious sense. An area of particular importance in that respect was the Messines-Wytschaete Ridge to the south of the city.[1]

The Germans had initiated mining as a major element in the Flanders fighting early in 1915. The British took it up enthusiastically. They were soon doing it on a larger scale and to a greater depth than their adversaries. By September 1915 they were making detailed plans for the very large-scale undermining of the Messines–Wytschaete Ridge. The idea was to cause a series of massive explosions directly under German positions, immediately prior to an infantry assault. Major John Norton-Griffiths, who was one of the principal organisers of the British mining effort in Flanders, was a prime mover in the Messines mines scheme. He was strongly supported by Brigadier-General G. H. Fowke, the Engineer-in-Chief at GHQ.[2] Sir Herbert Plumer's Second Army headquarters supported the endeavour from the outset and in mid-January 1916, as part of a scheme for a broader Allied offensive in the Ypres sector, Haig also gave it his backing.

Flanders was bound to be of concern to any British commander-in-chief. The BEF's lines of communications ran across the Channel. That the French Channel ports might be lost to a German land offensive from Flanders had been something of a nightmare in 1914. Since then the Belgian coast, with its ports of Ostend, Blankenberghe and Zeebrugge, had become homes for German destroyers and U-boats. U-boats posed a threat not only to the BEF's maritime communications, but also to British shipping more generally. By November 1915 the Admiralty had become sufficiently concerned about a "growing danger to the transport of troops and supplies" to France to press for joint military and naval action against these ports. The General Staff at the War Office entered into joint planning with the Royal Navy's Dover Patrol, commanded by Vice-Admiral Sir Roger Bacon, and considered both a sea-borne attack and an advance along the coast to put British heavy artillery within range of Ostend. There were, however, significant problems with both courses.

The size of force that could be landed from the sea would probably not be difficult for the Germans to contain. It might, indeed, be crushed if a more powerful body of British or Allied troops did not connect with it fairly quickly. Yet an overland advance down the coast would also face substantial difficulties. In 1914, the Belgians had opened their floodgates and inundated a thirteen-mile stretch of the Yser valley. The two-mile zone of sand dunes between the flooded area and the sea was narrow frontage for a major offensive effort. Even if the Belgians closed their floodgates again the land would take weeks to dry out and the obvious attempt to do this would telegraph Allied intentions to the Germans. Yet a British General Staff study of the prospects for a coastal operation, completed on 12 November 1915, was by no means dismissive of the idea.[3]

Soon after his appointment as commander-in-chief, Haig began to take an interest in these proposals. On 26 December 1915 Admiral Bacon of the Dover Patrol came to see him at GHQ. Haig noted:

We discussed the co-operation of the fleet with my army on the Belgian coast. He said the front from Zeebrugge to Ostend was of vital importance to England, because the Germans commanded the eastern end of the Channel from there, and threatened England. We arranged to work out plans together.[4]

Haig, however, quickly concluded that any such operation would only work as part of a more general Flanders campaign. The biggest element in this would have to be a breakout from the Ypres Salient, bypassing the thirteen-mile stretch of flooded ground on the Yser.

Between December 1915 and April 1917 all the generals whom Haig charged with making detailed plans for large-scale offensive operations in Flanders predicted prodigious difficulties. Early in 1916 Haig tasked Sir Henry Rawlinson to study a breakout from the Ypres Salient to the north-east in the direction of the Forest of Houthulst. Meanwhile Sir Aylmer Hunter-Weston, recently returned from Gallipoli, was tasked to plan a landing on the Flanders coast in conjunction with Admiral Bacon of the Dover Patrol. Hunter-Weston considered that the only chance of survival of troops landed from the sea was a speedy link-up with much larger forces breaking out from the Ypres Salient. Only if an overland offensive were already making good progress, therefore, should there be a landing on the coast.[5] Rawlinson, meanwhile, could imagine no speedy and dramatic breakout from the Salient. It would be difficult to break out in the Forest of Houthulst sector without operations to secure relatively high ground on the right flank. Already an advocate of the step-by-step approach to Western Front offensives, Rawlinson argued that any "advance [would] have to be made by definite stages, with intervals of time allowed for the preparations necessary for undertaking each subsequent advance".[6]

Even during the 1916 Somme campaign, Haig never entirely forgot about Flanders. As that campaign came to an end, his interest in Belgium, further stimulated by the growing anxiety of the government about the U-boat menace, revived markedly. On 17 November 1916 Haig tasked Sir Herbert Plumer (whose Second Army had held the Salient for the past year) to plan a major offensive from the Ypres sector. Plumer and his talented and popular chief of staff, Major-General C. H. "Tim" Harington, considered that two Armies would be required, an assumption that had also underlain much of the 1916 planning. One Army would be needed to mount the breakout in the northern sector of the Salient while another secured the Messines Ridge and Hill 60 to the south. Initially Plumer appears to have assumed that he would command the northern army. With an approach not dissimilar to that of Rawlinson earlier in the year, Plumer and Harington considered a possible Ypres offensive in the judicious, cautious, step-by-step manner that was to become the Second Army trademark. They predicted that the Germans would put up a very hard fight. They made no forecast of taking the important railway centre of Roulers, thereby disrupting German logistics (always a pet idea at GHQ), still less of taking the Channel coast. They were unwilling even to discuss such matters until much of the most important high ground around the Salient was in British hands. Taking this ground was a massive undertaking in itself and an "essential prelude", as they put it, to anything more ambitious.[7]

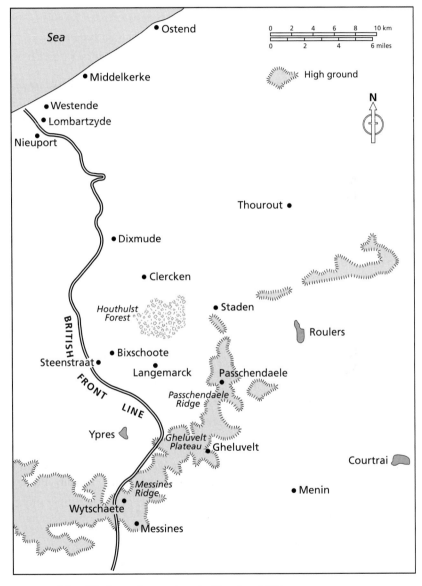

Map 17. Area of operations in Flanders 1917

When he received the Second Army proposals in mid-December Haig was unimpressed. On 6 January Kiggell wrote to Plumer indicating that Second Army's cautious, slow-moving approach was no longer appropriate. What Haig now required was:

Rapid action with a breakthrough of the enemy's defences on a wide front, and the infliction of a decisive defeat on the enemy.

An Ypres offensive in 1917 was most likely to be mounted, GHQ indicated, when the Germans had been much weakened by other attacks earlier in the year.[8]

GHQ's encouragement to think big and throw caution to the winds seems, however, to have had relatively little impact on Plumer and Harington. They continued to be guided by their own instincts and experience rather than by Haig's wishful thinking. What they presented to GHQ on 30 January 1917 was a plan for simultaneous assault by two Armies – one attacking the Pilckem Ridge and the other the high ground south of Ypres. The southern attack would be mounted over three days. The Spanbroekmolen Knoll would be seized in a preliminary operation, Hill 60 and the front crest of the Messines Ridge on the second day and the back crest on the third. The two Armies would then mount a converging attack on the Gheluvelt Plateau before the northern Army began its push north-east towards the coast. If the offensive from Ypres went well, two divisions would attack along the coast from the vicinity of Nieuport and another would be landed at Middelkerke. Middelkerke was much closer to Nieuport than Ostend. Landing there would make a link-up easier, but would pose a much less immediate threat to German U-boat bases.

Plumer, Harington and the Second Army staff had refused to underestimate the difficulties of a Flanders offensive and the scale of resources required. They reckoned that the operation as they had outlined would require more artillery than the British actually had in all of France and Flanders. They had still failed to come up with any scheme for a rapid advance to Roulers or a swift clearance of the Belgian coast. Again Haig was not happy. He had Plumer's plans re-examined by Rawlinson and his Fourth Army staff. Meanwhile, a committee under Colonel Norman Macmullen of the GHQ Operations branch was working independently on the same subject.[9]

Rawlinson and Montgomery suggested that mounting operations simultaneously against the Pilckem and Messines Ridges would be practically impossible because of the scale of resources, especially in artillery pieces, that this would require. Rawlinson suggested first attacking Hill 60 and the Messines Ridge and tackling the Gheluvelt Plateau and Pilckem Ridges in a subsequent operation to be mounted within seventy-two hours. Rawlinson was probably right that the attacks would need to be sequenced. But his time frame, particularly in view of all the movement of guns and ammunition and all the re-registering of batteries that would be required, was unrealistic. Even with all this high ground secured, however, Rawlinson did not believe that the northern Army would be able to exploit rapidly towards the Flanders coast. He imagined a series of hard fought battles, similar, as he put it, to the "Somme fighting", even before Roulers could be reached.[10] Roulers was, indeed, twelve miles from the existing British front line: a far greater distance than the British had advanced in the 1916 Somme campaign.

Predictably enough, Haig was unhappy with Rawlinson's proposals as well as Plumer's. But he seized enthusiastically upon a distinctly odd proposal from the Operations section of the General Staff at GHQ. In a memorandum of 14 February, based in part on a preliminary report submitted by Macmullen, the GHQ operations section proposed that the Gheluvelt Plateau be attacked simultaneously with the Pilckem and Messines Ridges. The slopes of the Plateau would be taken by conventional artillery and infantry attack. But the most novel part of the proposal was that the rest of the plateau should be seized in an attack by massed tanks, apparently with little infantry or artillery support.[11] This proposal seems to have been put forward with only hasty consultation with Brigadier-General Hugh Elles, who commanded tank forces on the Western Front. When examined more thoroughly by Elles's staff it was, largely owing to the boggy and heavily wooded nature of the plateau, quickly rejected as unfeasible. Yet, for the next couple of months, Haig seems to have regarded the Macmullen proposal as the official basis for a British campaign in Flanders in 1917.[12]

After the Arras and Aisne Offensives

As we have noted, the Arras offensive of Monday 9 April quickly ground to a halt. For the British, it ultimately proved bloodier in relation to its duration than the Somme campaign of the previous year and, after the first three days or so, did far less damage to the Germans. During the Arras campaign Haig faced, for the first time, active and collective dissent amongst his own generals and Robertson's doubts about Haig's competence as a field commander revived and intensified. Yet, strangely, Haig's position in relation to the British government, instead of further declining, became remarkably favourable. This was partly attributable to the dramatic success of 9 April: so striking (especially in relation to the events of 1 July 1916) that the War Cabinet appears not immediately to have noticed how bloody a failure most of the rest of the offensive was. The appalling losses and continual frustrations that constituted of most of the Arras campaign were apparently overshadowed by the more conspicuous failure of Nivelle. Lloyd George and War Cabinet colleagues who had supported him in his efforts to put the British army under Nivelle's control appear now to have been embarrassed to the point of mortification. Robertson, of course, was quick to demand that the Calais agreement should be terminated and the independence of the British army forthwith restored.[13] Lloyd George found this demand impossible to resist, and in the immediate future he also found it difficult to oppose Haig's proposals for the rest of the year.[14]

Nivelle's failure immediately raised the prospect of the French army relapsing into passivity for the rest of 1917 while waiting for the Americans to develop their military power. There was also a distinct possibility that the British War Cabinet would adopt the same policy. Haig, however, was very keen to prevent either the French or the British reacting in this way. He wrote to Robertson on 19 April that "results so far attained this year show that we have already reduced considerably, by previous efforts, the enemy's resisting power". He judged "that the prospects of success this year are distinctly good ... and that it would be unwise, unsound and probably in the long run, more costly in men and money to cease offensive operations at an early date".[15]

German powers of resistance had been sufficient to stop both the Arras offensive and Nivelle's Aisne offensive practically dead in their tracks within a matter of days. How Haig concluded from this that German powers of resistance were weakening is difficult to understand. It seems a classic case of twisting the evidence to fit preconceptions "situating the appreciation", as it is sometimes called in military circles.

Yet even if one did not share Haig's belief that the German army had been critically weakened, it was still possible to make an argument against lapsing into passivity on the Western Front. One (perhaps surprising) advocate of going ahead with an offensive in Flanders was Maurice Hankey, the War Cabinet secretary. Hankey had been by no means an uncritical admirer of Haig or Robertson. According to his own testimony, he had opposed the Somme campaign and there is no doubt that during its course he was intensely critical of Haig's generalship. In January 1917 he had been much impressed with Nivelle. But the German retreat to the Hindenburg Line had convinced Hankey that the Somme campaign had been far more successful than he had realised while it was in progress. The Calais conference and Nivelle's behaviour had made him disillusioned with the French commander. After Nivelle's failure, Hankey appreciated that the war was almost certain to drag on into 1918 and perhaps longer. His biggest fear was now that economic distress, perhaps even starvation, caused by the U-boat campaign would result in a collapse of civilian morale and he believed that while waiting for the Americans, the Allies must keep the Germans under continuous pressure on the Western Front:

> Guns, machine guns, trench mortars, tanks and munitions will this summer be so plentiful, and the results of the 1916 operations are so encouraging that the Allies would not have been justified in not making their main effort on the Western front this year ... At the same time it would be unwise to expect a *decisive* victory in 1917 ... [The enemy], by withdrawing from one strong prepared position to another ... and fighting a step by step rearguard action ... may avoid a decisive action. This renders it important to attack him at one point where he cannot fall back without surrendering some object of value ... and among such objects none is of such paramount importance ... as the Belgian coast ... At the present time ... the submarines and destroyers based [on Zeebrugge] are the bullets which strike their deadly blows at the heart of Britain's seapower. To capture Zeebrugge, or to get within artillery range and destroy its lock gates and deny it as an anchorage would be a serious blow at the German submarine campaign and an immense protection to our menaced maritime communications.[16]

Humiliated by his failure of judgement over Nivelle and getting this sort of advice even from Hankey, it is hardly surprising that, in spring 1917, Lloyd George found it somewhat difficult to oppose the views of his most senior generals. At the end of April and the beginning of May, it looked, in any case, as if those views might be quite cautious. When, on Monday 30 April, Haig addressed an Army Commanders' conference about his future plans, his tone was modest. The Arras offensive had long since ground to a halt and the Nivelle offensive had not met expectations. French policy for the rest of the year might, Haig warned, be purely defensive. He was not yet clear, he told his Army commanders, on his own policy for the rest of the year, though it might be possible, once a good defensive line had been reached at Arras, to "shift the centre of gravity up to the Second Army".[17]

On the afternoon after this conference, however, Haig told General Sir Hubert Gough of Fifth Army, rather more definitely, that he was planning operations in Flanders. Gough was to command the northern half of those operations, including landings on the Belgian coast. Haig instructed Gough to talk to Macmullen and to go and visit the tank workshops at Erin, where tanks were being prepared (at Haig's inspiration) to take part in a possible amphibious assault. While there may appear to have been some contradiction between Haig's statements to his Army commanders collectively and his instruction to Gough, it seems unlikely that he had engaged in deliberate deception at the Army Commanders' conference. Haig certainly wanted a major operation in Flanders, but he was not, at this stage, entirely sure that it was feasible, and in particular, did not know whether the authorities in London would authorise it.[18]

The following day, Tuesday 1 May 1917, Haig sent a memorandum on "Present Situation and Future Plans" by King's Messenger to the War Cabinet. This harped, in typical Haig fashion, on "guiding principles [that had] proved successful in war from time immemorial". The "first step was ... to wear down the Enemy's power of resistance until he is so weakened that he will he unable to withstand a decisive blow: then to deliver the decisive blow: and finally to reap the fruits of victory". How these platitudes were to be translated into practical plans may not have been immediately apparent to Haig's readers. But Haig now declared that he was convinced (echoing, consciously or not, the terms of Robertson's "staff college lecture" of 20 April) that Nivelle's problem on the Aisne had been that he tried to do the decisive attack before there had been enough attrition.

The Enemy has already been weakened appreciably but a long time is required to wear down such great numbers of troops composed of fine fighting material and he is still fighting with such energy and determination that the situation is not yet ripe for the decisive blow. Our action must therefore be to continue for the present to be of a wearing down character ...

Haig, however, went on to justify completing measures for a Flanders offensive aimed at "clearing the coast this summer". If the Belgian coast were to be cleared there would be "valuable results on land and sea". But even if that shoreline could not be captured, British forces would be:

attacking the enemy on a front where he cannot refuse to fight, and where, therefore, our purpose of wearing him down can be given effect to – while even a partial success will considerably improve our position in the YPRES salient and thus reduce the heavy wastage which must otherwise be expected to occur there next winter as in the past.[19]

By Haig's standards this was a fairly cautious statement of intent. The arguments he used were essentially the same as those that Hankey had deployed about a fortnight earlier. Flanders was the best place to prosecute a careful, attritional offensive campaign. This would maintain the pressure on the enemy and keep the initiative in Allied hands, whether or not it led to any more dramatic results.

At Lloyd George's invitation, Jan Smuts, the South African premier, attended a crucial War Cabinet meeting on 1 May, immediately prior to a conference of the Allies in Paris. Smuts had fought ruthlessly against the British in the war of 1899–1902 and, it may be remembered, had given Haig particular problems in the part of the Cape he then was charged with policing. But he had long since made his peace with the British and was playing an active part in the Empire's war effort. Lloyd George, who had been a "pro-Boer" during the South African War, seems to have regarded Smuts as a potential ally mainly because he seemed likely to take a broad "imperial" rather than a narrow Western view of the war. Smuts, however, who had visited Haig at GHQ and was in constant touch with Robertson, saw dangers in adopting an essentially defensive policy on the Western Front, as Lloyd George would have preferred. To do so would make it easy for the Germans to finish off Russia and, perhaps, Italy too. Smuts argued in Cabinet that "to relinquish the offensive in the third year of the war would ... be the beginning of the end ... pessimism and despair would be rife amongst the Allies" and the Germans would take encouragement from this. If it were not possible to break the German front in Flanders for the rest of the year it should be possible to break Germany's heart. This was a view apparently endorsed, or at least not definitely opposed, at this stage by most War Cabinet members.[20]

Haig too had been taking soundings ahead of the Franco-British conference scheduled for Friday 4 May. On Thursday 3 May he spoke to Pétain (who had become Army Chief of the General Staff, the French equivalent of CIGS, on 29 April and was to take over Nivelle's job on 15 May) about his plans for a Flanders offensive. Haig asked for assurances of continuing French offensive efforts to tie down and wear out the German army. He also wanted the French to take over some of the British front, relieving six British divisions. Pétain gave a general assurance of goodwill, but was vague about details. In reality Pétain's priority was to nurse the French army through the crisis of morale that had followed the Nivelle offensive. Pétain did not, at this stage, describe to Haig the collapse of discipline that had occurred in the French army. But he did point out that France was now desperately short of manpower – to the extent that he might have to dissolve a division a month for the foreseeable future. Haig would not have required a lot of subtlety to take the inference that French offensive action over the next few months was going to be very limited.

Haig had, indeed, recognised this as a possibility when addressing his Army commanders just a few days earlier. But when he had a particular project in mind he had a remarkable proclivity for hearing what he wanted to hear and ignoring the rest. He was already beginning to become obsessive about his Flanders project and the events of the next couple of days would send him into one his recurrent moods of seemingly uncontrollable, dangerously excessive optimism. At 9.30 p.m. the same evening Haig had, from his own viewpoint, a very satisfactory meeting with Robertson and Lloyd George. Lloyd George had firmly grasped the point that Haig preferred to ignore. It was unlikely that there would be much offensive action from the French for the rest of the year. Yet despite this, humiliated by the Nivelle fiasco and constrained by his own War Cabinet, he announced that he was in Paris to press for whatever plans Robertson and Haig decided upon. It was a remarkable change of tune since the Calais conference in February and Haig took great encouragement from it.[21]

The Paris conference of Friday 4 May was held in two sessions. The morning session, which met in Pétain's office, was for the generals. The afternoon session, for both generals and politicians, met in the Quai d'Orsay (the French Foreign Office). During the morning Robertson, Haig, Nivelle and Pétain agreed that the British would carry out the main offensive of the summer while the French would help "to the utmost of their power", which left things rather vague. The generals agreed that the politicians would be told the principles on which their action would be conducted, but not detailed plans. In the afternoon Robertson, who had chaired the morning meeting, gave a brief and somewhat vague report on the generals' deliberations. It indicated their determination to pursue a vigorous offensive, but insisted that the offensive be carried through using systematic, cautious, step-by-step methods – the same doctrine that Robertson had been preaching consistently since 1915.

It is no longer a question of aiming at breaking through the enemy's front and aiming at distant objectives. It is now a question of wearing down and exhausting the enemy's resistance ... We are all of opinion that our object can be obtained by relentlessly attacking with limited objectives while making the fullest use of our artillery. By this means we hope to gain our ends with the minimum loss possible.

Having unanimously agreed to the above principles, we consider that ... the time and the place of the various attacks ... must be left to the responsible generals ...[22]

Haig's diary entry for 4 May recorded that:

Mr Lloyd George made two excellent speeches in which he stated that he had no pretensions to be a strategist, that he left that to his military advisers, that I, as C-in-C of the British Forces in France, had full power to attack where and when I thought best.[23]

The Paris conference seems to have had a dramatic effect on Haig. Only a few days earlier, he had seemed to some degree doubtful about the British army's next move. He left Paris with the bit between his teeth, determined on a Flanders offensive. Unintentionally, Lloyd George had probably done as much or more than anyone else to put Haig into a mood of aggressive optimism. Apparently desperate to mend fences with Haig, he followed the commander-in-chief back from Paris to GHQ. There he was, Charteris noted, "full of praise of everything in the British Army in

France and especially of D.H." Turning on the charm as only he could, the Prime Minister was contrite about his previous underestimation of the British army in relation to the French. But he also treated his hosts to "an extraordinarily amusing imitation of Robertson at a Cabinet meeting" which "kept us all in fits of laughter", but which Charteris thought might have been an effort to "weaken the bond between the War Office and GHQ".

Taking from the Paris conference only what suited him, Haig interpreted its conclusions differently from other British participants. Robertson and Lloyd George both considered a big British offensive that summer conditional upon vigorous French support.[24] Haig, however, apparently chose to believe that he had given him a completely free hand and that the French army and the British government had committed themselves to support whatever he decided to do. The clearance of the Belgian coast became his stated aim and his mind was full of greater visions still. Haig informed his Army commanders of these intentions at a conference on Monday 7 May[25] and in a formal order of the same day. The main blow was "to be struck by British forces operating from the Ypres front with the eventual object of securing the Belgian coast and connecting with the Dutch frontier". The object of clearing the Belgian coast was restated twice in the same document. The Paris conference's caveat about aiming at distant objectives, if it had ever registered in Haig's mind, was already a dead letter there. Haig explained to his Army commanders that Flanders "operations will be carried out in two phases:–

(a) The attack on the MESSINES–WYTSCHAETE Ridge, to secure the right flank for further operations, will be delivered about 7th June.

(b) "Northern Operations" (some weeks later) with a view to securing the Belgian coast."

This newly stated intention to mount the Flanders offensive in two distinct stages with a gap of several weeks may have been owing to Haig's excitement after the Paris conference: to his impatience to mount the already well-planned Messines operation as soon as possible. It was open to the objection that the Messines attack might focus German attention on the Flanders sector and stimulate them to reinforce it, but when Haig communicated it to Robertson on 16 May,[26] Robertson made no immediate objection.

Few people of importance and insight, however, shared Haig's mood of "full steam ahead" confidence after the Paris conference. Esher, the government's unofficial advisor on Franco-British relations, realising France's exhaustion at this stage in the war, was profoundly sceptical about the chances of real French co-operation with British offensive efforts in summer 1917. A week after the Paris conference he warned Robertson not to count on any agreements the French had made there.[27] The military talks in Paris had, in any case, deprecated the pursuit of a breakthrough and the striving for distant objectives. Haig, however, now wanted firm and specific commitments from the French to help him with an offensive to clear the Flanders coast that summer.

On Friday 18 May 1917, he went to Amiens to see General Philippe Pétain, the hero of the defence of Verdun, who had succeeded Nivelle as commander of the French Armies of the North and North-West three days previously. Haig reviewed his plans for the Flanders offensive in some detail. He wanted Pétain's agreement to the French army relieving the British between the Omignon valley and Havrincourt while the British would relieve the French on the coast near Nieuport. Pétain agreed to the latter part of this, but not the former. Instead he offered an army of six French divisions to take a full part in the Flanders offensive. Pétain also outlined a series of four limited offensives that the French army was prepared to mount elsewhere on the front to help tie down some German troops while the British attacked in Flanders. The first of these was to be at Malmaison on or about 10 June, not long after Haig intended to attack at Messines.[28]

Pétain recognised that the initiative now lay in British hands. The decision on where to mount the main summer offensive (if any) and what form this was to take was inevitably a British one. He formally approved Haig's plan and agreed to give as much support as he could. But, in reality, he was not enthusiastic about it. Pétain told Henry Wilson, the British liaison officer at French headquarters, that, while he would do his best, he thought the liberation of the Belgian coast impossible "with the amount of assistance he could give".[29] Foch, appointed to replace Pétain as Army Chief of the French General Staff when Pétain replaced Nivelle, expressed the same opinion in even more forthright terms.[30] Wilson relayed Pétain's concerns to Haig.

By Saturday 19 May Haig had enough information to realise that he could expect, at best, very limited French offensive efforts for the rest of 1917. GHQ was well aware that "The French [were] having very serious trouble in their own army."[31] A week later, on Saturday 2 June, Major Neville Lytton, Haig's press liaison officer, warned him of a feeling of "despondency abroad" in France and indicated that French solders on leave had sided with strikers against the government. That evening, General Debeney, Pétain's chief of staff, visited Haig at GHQ and, without being too graphic, made it fairly plain that the French army was in a poor state of discipline. Except in the form of an artillery demonstration, the French would be unable to carry out the attack they had promised for

10 June.[32] Robertson had asked Haig to pass on to London any indication that the French would be unable to play a full part in operations that summer. Apparently determined that no one should curtail his plans, Haig failed to do so.[33]

Just how great were Haig's ambitions for the rest of the year, and how little affected by news of the crisis of discipline in the French army, is indicated by an order he sent to all his Army commanders on 5 June. He authorised this to be communicated down to corps commanders, though no lower than that, and not to the press.

After careful consideration of all available information I feel justified in stating that the power of endurance of the German people is being strained to such a degree that as to make it possible that the breaking point may be reached this year.

The mainstay of the German people ... is the hope of starving England by the submarine campaign.

With far less self-denial at home than the Germans have been enduring for some time this hope is doomed to disappointment. Suspicion that this is so is spreading in Germany and as this suspicion turns to certainty the feeling of hopelessness which is already evident in Germany will tend to grow beyond control.

If during the next few weeks, failure to stop the steady, determined, never-wearying advance of our Armies is added to the realisation of the failure of the submarine campaign, the possibility of the collapse of Germany before next winter will become appreciably greater.[34]

The quoted passage makes a number of important points abundantly clear. In Haig's mind the Flanders campaign was not driven by a desperate need to rescue Britain from the U-boats: the U-boat campaign was already doomed to fail. Nor was it a self-sacrificing effort to distract attention from a crippled French army. Haig was, to a remarkable degree, playing down the evidence he had of the French army's distress and was demanding from it a level of active offensive co-operation that more objective observers realised it was in no position to give. In Haig's mind the real purpose of the operations he intended in Flanders was to hasten the collapse of Germany: something he believed achievable by the end of the year.

The Battle of Messines

By this time Second Army was almost ready to mount its long-prepared attack on the German position on the Wytschaete–Messines Ridge.

At first glance that position certainly appeared very strong. The Germans had constructed two defensive lines on the ridge itself and a third position, the Oosttaverne Line, between 1,000 and 2,000 yards further back, on the reverse slope. All of these positions were very strongly wired and provided with concrete pillboxes to supplement the trench systems. While the British attack was being prepared, the Germans were revising their defensive system from a linear system to a more flexible one based on defence zones. They considered abandoning the ridge altogether and falling back to the Oosttaverne Line, though they eventually decided against this. When the British attacked on 7 June the ridge was held by some five German divisions, four of them belonging to Gruppe Wytschaete, commanded by General Laffert. A Bavarian division belonging to Gruppe Lille held the southern end of the attack sector, facing part of the II ANZAC Corps. Both groups belonged to the German Fourth Army, which was part of Prince Rupprecht's Army Group.[35]

Formidable as it was, the Messines Ridge position had weaknesses other than its vulnerability to mining. Just as the British in Ypres were in a salient, so were the Germans on the Messines ridge. They were thus subject to convergent artillery fire. Though the Messines ridge was commanding ground as far as the Ypres Salient was concerned, it was itself overlooked from positions behind the British front line, including Hill 63 and the famous Kemmel Hill. In addition the British had a marked local air superiority with over 300 aircraft active in II Brigade Royal Flying Corps, which was photographing the German positions and observing the fall of shell for the artillery. Six captive balloons of the 2nd Kite Balloon Wing RFC were in constant use. A further two were added just before the attack started. The weather in the weeks preceding the attack was exceptionally fine, stacking the odds very much in favour of the British.[36]

Plumer, Harington and their Second Army staff had from the outset made very precise calculations as to the artillery needed to tackle the German position.[37] But, as was his wont, Haig applied pressure during the planning process to extend objectives for the first day. On this occasion, however, Haig was able to send additional artillery to match and Second Army ended up with 1,510 field and 756 heavy pieces. Some 144,000 tons of ammunition was in Second Army's dumps when the bombardment began. Second Army outnumbered its opponents two to one in heavy artillery and five to one in field artillery, and had an artillery piece for every seven yards of the front it wished to attack. A further 428 heavy mortars further increased Plumer's firepower.

The preliminary bombardment began on 21 May, its intensity increasing dramatically on 31 May. Between 26 May and 6 June Second Army's artillery fired some three-and-a-quarter million rounds. The wire cutting was extremely effective and, though many of the pillboxes survived, most of the German defences were thoroughly pulverised. German artillery was heavily reinforced during the period of the preliminary bombardment and the new batteries were not always easy to locate. The German guns were never totally silenced, but in the last two days of preliminary bombardment, approximately a quarter of the field artillery and half the heavy artillery were put out of action by British fire.[38] The infantry that was to make the assault was from three corps: from left to right, X, IX and II Anzac. Each was to attack with three divisions up, keeping one in reserve. The divisions, almost evenly spaced across the 17,000 yards frontage, would, in most cases, have two brigades up and one in support. Army headquarters organised training meticulously: some attacks being repeatedly rehearsed over ground carefully chosen to resemble that over which the actual operation would take place. Large-scale models of the ground were also constructed for all ranks to view. Some seventy of the new Mark IV tanks were to help the infantry tackle likely German centres of resistance. Plumer's staff went to a great deal of trouble to ensure that they would be in the correct positions at the start of the battle without arousing the suspicions of the Germans. RFC aircraft over-flew the German positions on the night before the attack to drown the noise of approaching tanks.[39]

In general Plumer's and Harington's approach to planning and preparation for this operation could hardly have been more meticulous. In March, however, Haig made two fairly reasonable interventions. Plumer and Harington had initially wanted to compress their artillery programme into only four days. Haig knew from painful experience that intact enemy wire was one of the worst potential problems for attacking infantry. He considered that such a short bombardment might not suffice in this respect. As a result, Second Army significantly extended its wire-cutting programme. It could also be argued that Plumer's initial plan, which involved taking the Messines Ridge in two stages, was a little overcautious, not making full use of the shock to the German defenders likely to be engendered by the explosion of the mines. Haig wanted the whole ridge captured in one go and Plumer deferred to him on that issue.[40]

But a late change of plan between 10 and 19 May, probably at Haig's insistence, was much more dubious. In its order of 10 May, Second Army had seen the Oosttaverne Line as an objective for exploitation if all went well, but had not made it the target for a formal, pre-planned assault. This changed after 19 May, making operations for Z-day more ambitious and much more complicated.[41] In hindsight it seems that this late change was inadvisable and that, if it was urged upon them by Haig, which seems to have been the case, Plumer and Harington should have resisted more strongly. But the extent to which Haig was breathing down their necks can scarcely be exaggerated. On 20 May, after they had been planning for months, Haig sent them further notes for their guidance. For three full days, between 22 and 24 May, he visited the headquarters of all the corps and divisions about to take part in the attack, subjecting their commanders and staff to a rigorous grilling. Major-General Alan Montagu-Stuart-Wortley of 19th Division lost his job when he failed to cope with this interrogation to Haig's satisfaction.[42]

All this shows (as if the point needed to be reiterated) that Haig was no mere château general. He visited formations in the field and took a detailed interest in operations and tactics as well as high policy and strategy. But how necessary and useful this degree of intervention was in dealing with Plumer's well-run Army must be open to question. Admittedly Second Army had never previously mounted an offensive operation on this scale. But Haig intervened far less (e.g. with Gough's Fifth Army and the Bullecourt operations) when it was needed far more. Generally, however, Plumer and Harington took Haig's attempts at micromanagement in good part, putting the best face on what they could do little to prevent. Haig recorded in his diary on 22 May:

I find him [Plumer] a most pleasant fellow to work with and Harington and all his Staff work very kindly with GHQ. All are most ready to take advice.[43]

Gaining Haig's goodwill could pay dividends. As we have noted, Haig seems to have sent Plumer and Harington even more artillery than they had asked for. Giving in to Haig on some issues, moreover, probably made it easier to take a stand on others. As Z-day for the attack approached there were indications that the Germans might anticipate what was in store for them. Their own mining efforts brought them very close to those of the British and in late May Haig became anxious that they were about to make a withdrawal: a move they had indeed contemplated. On 29 May he suggested immediately exploding the twenty one massive mines then in place under the ridge, anxious that the effort involved in setting them might be wasted. Plumer and Harington did not believe that the Germans had any immediate intention of pulling back. They took a strong stand against immediate detonation and ultimately Haig did not insist.[44]

Zero hour was 3.10 a.m. on Thursday 7 June 1917. The British artillery had been almost silent for several hours. At that point nineteen gigantic mines were exploded. It was an awe-inspiring sight, with sheets of flame gushing from the ground and huge columns of earth lofting high into the air. People fifteen miles away thought an earthquake was in progress, though the oft-recounted tale that the explosions were heard in London may be mythical. The impact on the fighting spirit of German forces who were on the forward slope of the first crest of ridge is not difficult to imagine. Those not killed, disabled or buried alive were reported as running in all directions. The likelihood of serious resistance was further diminished as, immediately after the mine explosions, all the British artillery commenced firing at the most rapid possible rate. Two-thirds of

Second Army's 18-pdr guns, the mainstay of its field artillery, provided a creeping barrage in front of the attacking infantry. The other third, together with the 4.5-inch field howitzers, placed standing barrages on likely centres of resistance. Seven hundred machine guns also fired in support of the attack.

The initial advance of most of the Second Army's infantry was, indeed, relatively bloodless. There was little German rifle and machine gun fire from the crest of the ridge and the counter-battery programme was generally successful in subduing the German guns. Only one of Second Army's divisions took heavy casualties in the initial stages of the battle: Major-General John Monash's 3rd Australian Division – II Anzac Corps' right-hand assault division, on the southern wing of the whole attack. During its approach march through Ploegsteert Wood, the division was subjected to heavy gas shelling and took between 500 and 1,000 casualties. Apparently this was pure bad luck, the Germans not being aware that Zero hour for the British attack was imminent. The losses did not prevent the Australians mounting their attack at Zero and taking the first objective – the Red Line – within thirty-five minutes, as did all the attacking divisions.[45]

At the Red Line a "leapfrog" manoeuvre was performed. The two battalions of each attacking brigade that had performed the initial assault stayed on the Red Line while another two passed through to go for the second objective – the Blue Line, beyond the village of Messines. In some parts of the front German resistance became, at this stage of the attack, a good deal stiffer. New Zealand troops, for example, had quite hard fighting for the ruins of the village of Messines. Yet most of the Blue Line was taken on schedule at 5 a.m., after which there was a two-hour halt to consolidate ground won and beat off the anticipated German counter-attacks. These generally failed to materialise. While the infantry was at the halt, the artillery provided a protective barrage and hammered areas where German troops seemed most likely to form for counter-attacks.[46]

The next objective, known as the Black Line, was about 400 to 500 yards further on. It incorporated the second crest, at the far side of the almost flat plateau at the top of the ridge. This phase began at 7 a.m., the infantry assault being conducted, in most cases, by the third brigade of the attacking divisions – troops who had not yet undertaken any assault. During this phase the tanks (whose progress had been impeded by having to climb the slope onto the ridge and by the cratered nature of the ground) were finally able to render some assistance. Some of the hardest fighting was for the ruins of Wytschaete. But the 16th (Irish) Division had cleared these by 8.00 a.m. At 8.40 a.m. some troops, supported by tanks and low-flying aircraft, pushed forward to the Black

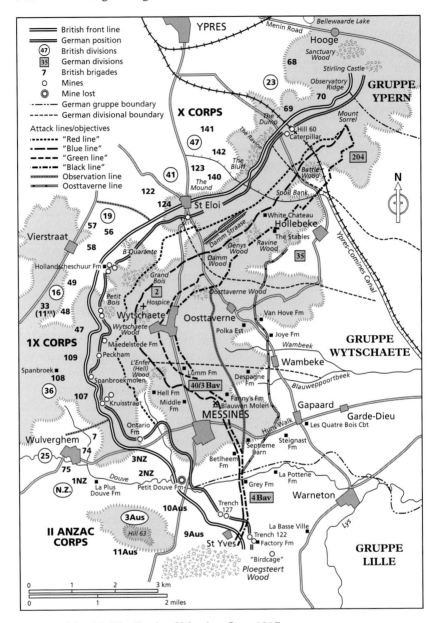

Map 18. The Battle of Messines June 1917

Dotted Line, from which they had some observation over the Oosttaverne Line and the valley below.[47]

By 9 a.m. the whole of the Messines–Wytschaete Ridge was in Second Army's hands and casualties had been remarkably low. At this point, however, fortune took a turn for the worse. Because preparations were being made for an assault on the Oosttaverne Line, involving the fourth division of each of the attacking corps, the ridge became overcrowded with troops and these started to suffer heavily as German artillery on the valley below came to life. The assault on the Oosttaverne Line was scheduled for 1.10 p.m. But there were delays in bringing forward all the artillery needed to support this fresh assault and Plumer decided to delay it for two hours. This extended the period during which the over-crowded infantry on the ridge were exposed to German artillery fire and permitted the Germans to reinforce the Oosttaverne Line. When finally the assault was delivered there was some breakdown of command and control, especially in the II ANZAC Corps. Australian troops ended up being heavily shelled by both sides.[48]

Confused fighting in the Oosttaverne Line and immediately beyond it continued until 14 June, and this pushed up Second Army's casualty toll for the battle to about 25,000 killed, wounded and missing: about half of this total from the ANZAC Corps.[49] It seems reasonable to suggest that the late change of plan that added the Oosttaverne Line to the list of objectives for 7 June was a mistake. With the British holding the higher ground of the ridge, within easy artillery range of, and with very good observation over, it, the Oosttaverne position might well have proved untenable for the Germans in the long run even without a British assault.[50] A carefully prepared assault on it a few days after the main ridge had been taken might have achieved the desired result at lower cost.

In addition to losing an important piece of ground swiftly and dramati-cally, the Germans themselves had sustained heavy casualties. Second Army had taken 7,354 prisoners. German sources record a total of 23,000 casualties including 10,000 missing, a figure that did not include the lightly wounded. Both sides recognised this as a notable British vic-tory.[51] When Haig saw Plumer at his headquarters at Cassel at 4 p.m. (at the highpoint of British success and before the somewhat bungled attack on the Oosttaverne Line) he "congratulated him on his success", while privately remaining somewhat patronising and grudging. He noted in his diary:

The old man [actually only four years older than Haig] deserves the highest praise for he has patiently defended the Ypres salient for two and half years and he well [knows] that pressure has been brought on me to remove him from Command of Second Army.[52]

It is not clear who had been arguing for Plumer's removal, but, as we have noted, Haig had initially been far from enthusiastic about Plumer as an Army commander. Plumer was probably right to believe that it needed a high degree of deference to Haig to keep him in command. It was impossible for Haig to avoid giving Plumer considerable commendation for Messines. But there is some evidence that, at least for a while, he resented the subsequent, meteoric rise in Plumer's reputation, preferring to attribute Second Army's success to Harington, for whose selection as Plumer's chief of staff he could claim credit.[53]

Above all Haig saw Messines as a personal victory and a vindication of his own decisions and ideas. As he put it in his diary: "operations today are probably the most successful I have undertaken". He clearly perceived Messines as a foretaste of further, potentially decisive victory. In reality, however, Thursday 7 June was a day of mixed news: of warning as well as promise. Not only did the Oosttaverne Line attack in the late afternoon involve heavy losses (yet another example of the danger of overreaching), but also Pétain specifically informed Haig, at a meeting at Cassel later that evening, that two French divisions had mutinied.[54] Two of Haig's most typical characteristics, already frequently remarked in these pages, were, however, again in evidence: an intense state of excitement following any significant success in the field and a pronounced capacity to filter out information that he did not want to accept. He became more certain than ever of the rightness of his chosen course for the rest of 1917: a truly massive offensive in Flanders.

A fortnight prior to the Messines attack, Haig had suggested to Second Army that it might be possible swiftly to follow up the attack on the Ridge with an assault by VIII and II Corps to the north: trying to gain a foothold on the Gheluvelt Plateau. If that went well, Gough might be supplied with reserves to enable him to begin an immediate attack on "the PLASSCHENDAELE [sic] – STADEN Ridge". Haig seems to have been having one of his visions of a sudden German collapse. Upon hearing news of the success of the 7 June attack, Haig immediately demanded that Plumer give consideration to assaulting German positions on the Plateau. Plumer was willing, but indicated that he would need three days to shift artillery north to support this fresh assault. This was perfectly reasonable. But Haig's response, on 8 June, was to transfer Plumer's two northern corps to Gough's Fifth Army. Gough had established his headquarters in the Salient only six days previously and was just getting orientated in this sector. When Haig asked him to organise an attack on the Gheluvelt Plateau, he replied, understandably, that he needed time to think about it. But given that the whole point was immediately to exploit any German disarray after Messines, it rather defeated the point. By 14 June Gough had decided that any favourable opportunity had passed. There was to be no immediate follow-up of the Messines success.[55]

Doubts in the War Cabinet and War Office

Despite the cheering news of a limited success at Messines, neither the War Cabinet nor Robertson and the General Staff in the War Office were at all certain, in June 1917, that a really large-scale offensive in Flanders was the appropriate next move. In the month that had passed since the Paris conference the grand strategic picture had darkened. Though Haig had apparently not passed on all the information that Pétain had given him about the crisis in the French army, Britain's political leaders knew by 6 June that there had been disturbances "practically amounting to mutiny" in some units.[56] Russia was expected to contribute practically nothing to the Allies' war effort for the rest of 1917. America offered hopes in the long run, but the British government expected no more than 150,000 American troops in Europe by the end of the year.[57]

All this bad news did not make the War Cabinet defeatist, but did make it very cautious. Generally both the General Staff in the War Office and the War Cabinet considered that Germany had greater residual strength than Haig was prepared to allow. Both were also worried about British manpower, which they considered a precious, finite resource. Both British manpower and British public opinion now needed, they believed, very careful handling. In response to a paper by Lord Milner, summarising the generally gloomy strategic situation, the War Cabinet established, on 8 June, a War Policy Committee comprising Lloyd George, Milner, Curzon and Smuts. The committee was to "investigate the facts of the Naval, Military, and Political situations and present a full report to the War Cabinet".[58] Lloyd George apparently hoped to use this review to cancel or at least to restrict Haig's proposed Flanders offensive.[59]

At the same time Haig became aware that the CIGS was now troubled by some of the same doubts burdening members of the War Cabinet. When Robertson met Ferdinand Foch, chief of the French General Staff, at Abbeville on Thursday 7 June, the French general appears to have conveyed to Robertson his grave doubts about an offensive in Flanders. Instead he tried to persuade Robertson that it might be worth sending help to the Italian front. The French believed that influential figures in Austria now wanted out of the war, but needed a serious offensive against them to give them excuse to make peace. Could not the British send 300 heavy guns to help the Italians take Trieste?[60] At GHQ on Saturday 9 June, Robertson passed on Foch's advice to Haig and asked him "to realise the difficult situation in which the country would be if [he] carried out large and costly attacks without full co-operation by the French. When Autumn came round, Britain would be without an Army! On the other hand it is possible that Austria would make peace if harassed enough. Would it not be a good plan to support Italy with guns?"[61] At this stage Haig seems to have expressed no anger at Robertson's apparent apostasy. The following day he considered that it might have been a temporary aberration that he and his Presbyterian chaplain, the Reverent Duncan, had succeeded in dispelling.

General Robertson (CIGS) left after having a talk with me and Kiggell after church. A night's reflection and Duncan's words of thanks for our recent victory seem to have had a good effect on him. He was less pessimistic and seemed to realise that the German Army was in reduced circumstances! I again urged the need for increased activity by the Allies *all round*. There must be no thought of staying our hand until America puts an Army in the field next year.[62]

Haig's belief that he had won Robertson over was at least partially correct. Robertson still did not share Haig's optimism. He did not believe there was any prospect of bringing Germany to its knees in 1917 and considered the capture of the Belgian ports unlikely. But, at least for the time being, he decided to maintain a united front with Haig and to continue to insist on the concentration of British military resources in the West. He was prepared to support an offensive in the Ypres sector provided that it was conducted in a careful, step-by-step manner. He wrote to Haig on 13 June urging him not to argue to the government "that you can finish the war this year or that the German is already beaten. Argue that your plan is the best plan – as it is – that no other plan would be *safe* let alone decisive, and then leave them to reject your advice and mine. They dare not do that." He now came down strongly against the idea of heavy guns for Italy, assuring Haig that "they will never go while I am CIGS".[63]

Robertson's letter apparently crossed with a memorandum dated 12 June that Haig sent to the War Cabinet and Haig used precisely the arguments for his Flanders offensive that Robertson had advised him to eschew: the German army "showed unmistakable signs of deterioration" and that final victory was "within reach this year".[64] At 11 a.m. on Thursday 14 June Haig chaired an Army commanders' conference at First Army headquarters at Lillers, sharing his most grandiose intentions for the Flanders campaign:

Underlying the general intention of wearing out the Enemy is the strategical idea of securing the Belgian coast and connecting with the Dutch frontier.

This was to be accomplished in stages:

1. Capture bridgehead formed of the Passchendaele–Staden–Clerken ridge.
2. Push on towards Roulers–Thourout so as to take coast defences in rear.
3. Land by surprise in conjunction with attack from Nieuport.[65]

The following Sunday Haig crossed the Channel. He was able to spend Sunday evening and much of Monday with Doris at the London flat before talks with Robertson and the government during the week. At 11 a.m. on Tuesday 19 June he addressed a meeting of the War Policy Committee. Using a three-dimensional "raised map" spread out on the Cabinet table as a visual aid, he made his presentation not only with great assurance, but also with a degree of clarity that usually eluded him. Ministers, however, were beset by doubts and asked Haig numerous questions all tending to show that "each was more pessimistic than the other". Lloyd George "seemed to believe that the decisive moment of the war would be 1918". But Haig

strongly indicated that Germany was nearer her end than [the politicians] seemed to think, that *now* was the favourable moment and that everything should be done to take advantage of it by concentrating on the western Front all available resources. I stated that Germany was within 6 months of the total exhaustion of her available manpower, *if the fighting continues at its present intensity*.[66]

There were further meetings of the War Policy Committee on 20, 21 and 25 June. It does not appear that any of the statesmen attending was convinced by Haig's talk of ending the war in 1917 and U-boats no longer figured prominently in the debate. It is true that Admiral Jellicoe, the First Sea Lord, contended, at the meeting on Wednesday 20 June, that if shipping losses continued at the current rate Britain could not continue the war into 1917. But, as Haig recorded in his diary, "No-one present shared Jellicoe's views and all seemed satisfied that the food reserves in Great Britain are adequate." In discussion with his Army commanders, Haig had, as we have already noted, already dismissed the U-boats as a serious threat to Britain's war effort and he showed no sign of changing his mind at this stage.[67] But if they were not desperately worried about U-boats, why did the War Policy Committee not unite against Haig's proposed Flanders offensive? One possible answer is that key members still considered the Western Front the vital one, accepted that it was dangerous to divert too many resources elsewhere, thought the Franco-British alliance needed a positive demonstration of British commitment to the war effort, and did not wish to lose the strategic initiative entirely by a passive policy of waiting for the Americans. Another is that while Haig had strategic aims (the collapse of Germany in 1917 and capturing the Belgian coast that year) that ministers generally considered unattainable, he reassured them by seeming to accept the need to use cautious, step-by-step, operational methods. Indeed, at the meeting on Wednesday 20 June, he declared that:

> He was fully in agreement with the Committee that we ought not to push in attacks that had not a reasonable chance of success and that we ought to proceed step by step. He himself had no intention of entering into a tremendous offensive involving heavy losses. His plan was aggressive without committing us too far.[68]

It seems that ministers drew the inference that if German resistance proved too strong and British casualties too heavy, the offensive could be stopped at any time.

The War Policy Committee remained divided on Monday 25 June at the last meeting Haig attended before his return to France. The Prime Minister still thought Haig's offensive had "no decent chance of success. Russian and French co-operation are too insufficient, our superiority in men and guns too slight, the extent of the advance required to secure tangible results too great in his opinion to justify the great losses." The likely casualties would, in Lloyd George's opinion, damage "our chances of success next year and cause great depression". Milner and Bonar Law tended to support Lloyd George, whereas Curzon and Smuts cautiously supported the offensive. The British ministers intended to consult with their French counterparts before making a final decision.[69]

Haig suggests removing Robertson: 24–26 June 1917

Ever since their respective appointments as commander-in-chief and CIGS, there had been tensions in the Haig–Robertson relationship. Robertson's instinct and policy, as we have repeatedly noted, was to maintain solidarity with Haig in dealing with the politicians. By mid-1917, however, he was finding this an acute and growing strain. Haig's view that Germany could be pushed over the brink of collapse in 1917 was not endorsed by the War Office's intelligence branch, under Macdonogh, and not believed by Robertson.[70] Robertson had been critical of Haig's operational methods both on the Somme and at Arras and had consistently tried to convince Haig of the need to adopt a cautious, step-by-step approach.[71] Though Haig had told the War Policy Committee that he would conduct the Flanders offensive in that manner, Robertson's fears that he would get carried away and exhaust the one reliable army left to the Allies were by no means entirely dispelled. Haig was certainly aware of Robertson's initial doubts and probably sensed that he had not managed to overcome them.[72] All this helps provide some explanation for the rather bizarre episode we are about to examine.

During his sojourn in London from 17–27 June, Haig had had several meetings with Sir Eric Geddes. Having done a great deal of vital work on the reorganisation of the BEF's logistics, Geddes had very recently moved to the Admiralty as Controller of the Navy. Perceiving the Admiralty's atmosphere to be one of inertia and defeatism, he believed that the First Sea Lord, Sir John Jellicoe, and the First Lord, Sir Edward Carson, were exhausted and had become ineffectual. Thinking that the Admiralty needed a firmer hand at the tiller, Haig and Geddes agreed, at lunch on Sunday 24 June, that it would be a good thing if Sir William Robertson were to become chairman of the Board of Admiralty: the position normally occupied by the First Lord. This would have meant Robertson's ceasing to be CIGS. Haig, however, wholeheartedly endorsed this suggestion, if he did not actually originate it.[73] Geddes knew that Lloyd George too was seriously concerned about the quality of leadership in the Admiralty. On Tuesday 26 June, he and Haig breakfasted with the Prime Minister at 10 Downing Street and there gave him their suggestion for moving Robertson. Lloyd George seems, naturally enough, to have leapt at the chance.[74] With Robertson out of the War Office he might expect to find it easier to get his own way on military policy in general and, in particular, to restrain Haig.

Why, then, should Haig lend his support to such a move? Patriotism and concern for naval efficiency cannot, of course, be dismissed as possible motives. But Haig seldom neglected the protection of his own interests. Probably the episode reflects his growing disillusionment with Robertson and a feeling that he had little to lose from a change of CIGS. Haig could not, of course, be certain whom Lloyd George would select to replace Robertson, but Henry Wilson was an obvious possibility. This would certainly have worried Haig at an earlier period in the war, but the pattern of personal and professional relationships had not remained static. When, after the fall of Nivelle, Wilson became *persona non grata* at French general headquarters, Haig offered him a corps. Wilson declined on the grounds that he was less qualified for it than many of those currently commanding divisions.[75] Indeed, field command was not Wilson's strength, as Haig well knew. But this makes Haig's offer all the more significant, indicating, as it does, Haig's wish to establish better relations with this most intensely political of generals.

Wilson had, moreover, recently expressed to the War Cabinet some cautious but positive support for Haig's proposed Flanders offensive.[76] Initially strongly opposed to that project, he had gradually changed his mind, thinking that something of the sort was necessary to distract German attention from the troubled French army.[77] Wilson, therefore, may now have seemed to Haig more positive about the Flanders offensive than was Robertson. Haig would soon be flattering him and trying to recruit him to rally War Cabinet support for the offensive: a role Wilson seems to have been willing enough to perform.[78] Though this is speculative, it is by no means inconceivable that, by 24 June 1917, Haig had already decided that he would be better off with Wilson than with Robertson as CIGS.

When Haig put the idea to him, however, Robertson refused to go to the Admiralty. Apparently still afraid of the political consequences of sacking the CIGS, Lloyd George left him where he was for the time being. Instead, Geddes replaced Carson as First Lord, while Carson was made a member of the War Cabinet by way of consolation.[79] To the end of his life Robertson never publicly admitted to any breach with Haig and never publicly complained of Haig's conduct towards him. It would, however, be a somewhat different matter in private.[80] It seems reasonable to regard the Admiralty episode as yet another milestone on the downward path of their working relationship.

Assessment

Considered as a whole, the Battle of Arras had been a worse conducted, less successful offensive than the Somme. During its course Haig's authority over his own army had partially broken down. Yet, paradoxically, the dramatic success of its first day, when coupled with Nivelle's evident failure, left Haig in a vastly improved position in relation to Lloyd George's government. His confidence having been boosted by this, the prospect of a decisive summer offensive in Flanders became a growing obsession in his mind: an obsession only reinforced by the limited success at Messines. The key members of the British government, embarrassed by their backing of Nivelle, had only doubts with which to confront Haig's certainties and failed to make any definite decision.

Despite the increasingly acute underlying tension with Robertson and the trying business of having to justify his strategy to a Cabinet committee, Haig apparently regarded his lengthy late-June stay in London as a success. He had managed to avoid a veto on his Flanders project and was reasonably confident that it would ultimately go ahead.[81] Arguing for the Ypres offensive and trying to move Robertson to the Admiralty seem, moreover, not to have been his only significant activities on this trip home. His son and heir was born the following March.

14　The Third Battle of Ypres

The German defences and Gough's plan: June 1917

On Saturday 2 June Gough had established his Fifth Army headquarters at the chateau of Lovie, three miles north-west of Poperinghe, in the rear of the Ypres Salient.[1] He and his staff had been busily studying the military geography of the Ypres sector and the German defensive system there. Flanders presented the defender, as well as the attacker, with peculiar problems. The water table was so high that it was generally impracticable to construct deep dug outs of the sort that had protected their troops on the Somme, and in some places the use of normal trenches was difficult for the same reason. Breastworks above ground had to be substituted. German fortifications in this part of the front were fast becoming perhaps the most formidable the British had yet encountered. In the early months of 1917 these defences had been essentially linear in character. There were four main positions. Much of the front line was on a forward slope and thus rather vulnerable. It afforded good fields of fire and might help slow an assault, but increasingly the Germans regarded it merely as a sort of outpost line and kept it rather thinly manned. The second position ran from Bixschoote southwards, on the reverse slope of the Pilckem Ridge, then across the Gheluvelt Plateau. The third ran south from Langemarck to Gravenstaefel about 2,000 yards to the rear of the second position and then joined it on the Gheluvelt Plateau. Behind this, another defensive line, Flandern I, ran in front of the Passchendaele Ridge and across the Gheluvelt Plateau to the rear of Polygon Wood. Both within and between the main defensive positions there were hundreds of reinforced concrete pillboxes, usually covered with turf to make them less conspicuous.

Haig's decision to attack the Messines Ridge weeks before completing preparations for the main Flanders offensive soon incurred penalties. Messines focused the German high command's attention on Flanders. Ludendorff sent his leading fortification expert, Colonel von Lossberg, to the headquarters of General Sixt von Armin's Fourth Army at Courtrai.

Lossberg, as Fourth Army's chief of staff, ordered that work should begin on further lines of defence known as Flandern II and III, the latter on the reverse slope of the Passchendaele Ridge. Other defences were soon under construction behind that. But these rearward positions were being built in a spirit of insurance. Lossberg hoped that the Germans could kill any attack within a defensive zone, some 6,000–9,000 yards deep, that he was developing between the front line and the Flandern I position. Indeed, he hoped to halt the Allies within about 4,000 yards of the German front line.

In Lossberg's thinking, the defence of this zone would rest more on a network of strong points (including large pillboxes or bunkers and smaller concrete-protected machine gun nests) than on lines of trenches or breast-works. Troops holding strong points, even if surrounded, were expected to stay and fight it out until reserve and counter-attack forces reached them. Given the virtual collapse of the Russian army and the weakness of the French at this period, the German defence of Flanders was not starved of manpower. By mid-July five divisions held the German lines directly in front of Gough's Fifth Army, with four in immediate reserve and another four further back. Supporting the German infantry were 1,150 pieces of artillery and the Germans held the higher ground, conferring good observation for these guns.[2]

Yet the British too enjoyed advantages: Gough and Haig were reasonably well informed about the German forces in Flanders and about the layout of their fortifications. This intelligence flowed, in part, from a pronounced air superiority that permitted detailed aerial observation and photography. The Allies had always enjoyed a numerical advantage in aircraft. But in the Arras campaign, the technical superiority of German fighters had forced the British to pay a very steep price for observation and photography on the German side of the lines. By the time of Third Ypres the arrival of new British aircraft, most notably the SE5 and the Sopwith Camel, was doing something to redress the German qualitative advantage, helping the British to get their vital aerial photographs and to do their artillery spotting at a cheaper rate. The British also had a hefty superiority in artillery. There were 752 heavy and 1,422 field guns in Fifth Army. Gough would have the use of a further 300 heavy and 240 field guns belonging to the French First Army, immediately to his north, and 112 heavy and 240 field guns belonging to Second Army to the south. And there was no shortage of shell for this ordnance.[3]

The quality of the BEF's tactical intelligence owed something to its increasingly confident and effective infantry. Frequent trench raids improved knowledge of the layout of front line defences and helped identify German units. The knowledge was to put to use. Rigorous training programmes were carried out in all four of Gough's corps. The British constructed models of the German defences and devised and rehearsed tactics for attacks on pillboxes and fortified farmhouses. In 1917 the British infantry platoon now had a useful mix of different weapons, including the Lewis light machine gun, rifle grenades and hand grenades, as well as LeeEnfield rifles. Infantry battalions also had light mortars that could be carried forward in the attack. The standard of training and indoctrination of British infantry also seem to have improved considerably since Arras. When combined with increasingly sophisticated infantry tactics and massive artillery fire support, they gave some hope of dealing with the tactical challenges posed by the German defensive system. British troops repeatedly practised tackling pillboxes, for example, and had the resources and skills to overcome with their own resources some of those not neutralised by bombardment.[4] Thus, while British commanders realised that the German defences in Flanders were formidable, they did not consider them impregnable.

Gough eventually decided to attack on a front of about eight miles, from the edge of the Houthulst Forest, on the left, to the Kleine Zillebecke road (on the Gheluvelt Plateau), on the right. On the first day of the attack he proposed to use two divisions of the First French Army (on Fifth Army's left) and nine divisions from Fifth Army's four corps. None of this was controversial. Nor was Gough's insistence on lengthy preliminary bombardment (16–25 July) before the infantry attack, planned for 25 July. The depth to which Gough proposed pushing his infantry on the first day, however, occasioned a sharp debate and the issue has remained controversial. Gough and his Fifth Army staff seem to have accepted that penetrating the entire German defensive system in Flanders in a matter of days, in a single continuous push, was out of the question. It would have to be tackled in a step-by-step manner and getting through all of it was expected to take weeks, if it could be done at all.

Gough, however, also believed that it would be easiest to gain ground at beginning of the offensive and that momentum would tend to slow after the first day. On the first day he hoped that he could reach a line running through Langemarck, Broodseinde and Polygon Wood on Z-day, an advance of between 4,000 and 5,000 yards. This would be done in four stages. The initial assault was expected to overrun the German front line system and reach the crest of the Pilckem Ridge and the edge of the Shrewsbury Forest on the Gheluvelt Plateau. After a 30-minute pause, the German second line would be assaulted. After this second advance there would be a four-hour pause. Then another bound would take infantry to a little stream called the Steenbeck on the far side of the Pilckem Ridge, while the troops on the right would reach and enter Polygon Wood on the

Gheluvelt Plateau. Finally the infantry was intended to take advantage of German confusion and, using its own initiative, to seize whatever further ground it could.[5]

Gough was proposing a first day's advance more than twice as deep as Plumer and Rawlinson had considered prudent earlier in the year, when German defences were far less formidable. Since becoming commander-in-chief, it had been Haig's habit to scrutinise his Army commanders' offensive plans intensely. He had, as we have noted, frequently intervened, sometimes constructively, sometimes with catastrophic results. Yet Gough, despite a very mixed record of command since the beginning of the war and particularly dismal recent results at Bullecourt, seemed to enjoy privileged treatment: there is very little evidence that Haig interfered in his initial planning. It is, however, likely that Haig had picked Gough because he had an aggressive, ambitious temperament and because he usually seemed eager to comply with Haig's wishes. It is also quite possible that Haig told Gough privately that, while he accepted the need for a step-by-step approach to overcome the complex German field fortifications in Flanders, he wanted the first step to be as impressive a stride as possible. Gough's testimony to the official historians, that Haig told him that he wanted the offensive to culminate, within a few weeks, in a dramatic breakthrough towards the Belgian coast[6] is, given Haig's past record, by no means incredible. What is quite certain is that Haig himself raised no objection to Gough's proposal for a 4,000-yard advance on the first day.

But Brigadier-General John "Tavish" Davidson, head of the Operations section, did ring alarm bells at GHQ. Davidson, who had held that appointment almost from the outset of Haig's command,[7] has so far figured little in these pages. He had made so few waves that it is very difficult to discern his influence on the BEF's previous operations. If he had raised any objection to Haig's over-ambitious plans on the Somme or at Arras, we have no record of it. Since Arras, however, he had clearly become a convert to the cautious, step-by-step approach to operations that Robertson had long preached and which Du Cane and Rawlinson had also advocated. Davidson may have been emboldened to intervene against Gough's plan by a belief that his immediate superior, Kiggell, and his ultimate boss, Haig, had undergone similar conversions. Haig had, as we have noted, promised the Cabinet's War Policy Committee that he would conduct his Flanders offensive in a step-by-step manner and Davidson may have been aware of this.

In a paper of 26 June, addressed to Kiggell, Davidson argued that the offensive should be conducted as a series of advances, each of which should aim to go to a depth of between 1,500 and 3,000 yards. Attempting to advance too far too fast would result in the supporting artillery fire being less concentrated, in communications breaking down and in the attacking infantry becoming disorganised. It would mean shifting masses of artillery big distances between assaults and thus in a slackening of British fire power at critical phases of the campaign. Above all it would mean excessive casualties to the attackers and the consequent diminution of their morale. Davidson's general principles were those that Robertson, Du Cane and Rawlinson had first advocated early in 1915 and were undoubtedly sound, though his suggestion that major attacks could be mounted at intervals of two or three days was too optimistic.[8]

According to Davidson's memoirs, Kiggell passed Davidson's memorandum to Haig upon his return from London on 27 June. Haig discussed it with Kiggell and Davidson that evening. Davidson records that "it seemed evident to me that Haig was ... in agreement with my memorandum. I made it clear that there was ample time to amend the plan of attack as might seem desirable and that some clarification of the situation with the army commanders seemed to be necessary." GHQ sent copies of Davidson's paper to both Army commanders.[9] Gough (or someone on his staff) drafted a response to Davidson's paper that was by no means ill-considered or unintelligent. Indeed, Gough's memorandum indicated general agreement with the step-by-step principles that Davidson advocated. Gough and his subordinate commanders were preparing "mentally and physically for a continuous series of organised attacks". Picking on a weak point in Davidson's paper, Gough expressed doubt that major attacks could be mounted every three days. He considered ten days a more realistic interval. But the real issue was how far to go on the first day. Gough argued that so much time and effort was being invested in preparing for this attack that not to reap the maximum benefit would be foolish. The attacking infantry should be encouraged to go as far as it could.[10]

Second Army had only a supporting role in the forthcoming attack and Plumer's forces were expected to make only a shallow initial advance.[11] According to Davidson and the official history, however, at a meeting in late June, involving Haig, Kiggell and Gough, Plumer backed Gough's proposal to send Fifth Army's infantry as deep as possible on the first day of the offensive.[12] During the planning for Messines Plumer had shown great caution in setting objectives for his own Army. His attitude on this occasion, therefore, surprised and dismayed Davidson.[13] Gough's version of events goes further in criticising Plumer. Gough states that he argued in favour of limiting the first day's advance, but was overruled by the combination of Plumer and Haig.[14] That would mean that Gough argued precisely the opposite case from what he had set down in a memorandum to GHQ just a few days earlier and seems scarcely credible. The account in Gough's memoirs, therefore, seems likely to be a deliberate falsehood designed to make him seem more prescient than he really was and to play down his responsibility for early reverses.

Haig's diary for 27–30 June makes no reference whatever to Davidson's memorandum. And while Davidson's account and the official history indicate that a critical meeting involving Gough, Plumer, Davidson and Haig took place on 28 June, Haig's diary only records meeting Gough that day. Haig makes no mention of what both Davidson and Gough clearly regarded as a vitally important debate about objectives for the first day's attack. The main point that Haig notes about his meeting with Gough on 28 June is that he tried to insist on Gough using more of his artillery against the Gheluvelt Plateau. Haig believed that German defences there were very strong and that Gough needed to give them more attention. If the Germans retained control of the Plateau after the first day, further progress might be difficult. Though Haig's concerns were valid, Gough arguably had inadequate artillery to give the Plateau all the attention it needed while also bombarding other objectives adequately. He seems to have responded little to Haig's prompting on this issue.[15]

A Fifth Army memorandum to its corps, on 30 June, helped to highlight unresolved tensions concerning the real object of the offensive and the methods by which it should be conducted. Though not diminishing the ambitious objective of a 4,000-yard advance on the first day, it emphasised "that our one object is the defeat of the German Army" and that "by comparison, the capture of this or that piece of ground … is … of minor importance". Haig's marginal comments, however, indicated that he did not want this line of argument pushed too far. Wearing out the enemy was important, but so was gaining commanding ground like the Passchendaele Ridge.[16]

Delay, spoiling attack and preliminary bombardment: July 1917

By the beginning of July detailed plans had been laid for the Flanders offensive. But before the infantry advanced, it was necessary to complete a vast amount of administration, to reassert and exploit the Allies' dominance of the skies and to conduct the greatest artillery bombardment in British history up to this time. There was also one other matter: the War Cabinet had still not formally authorised the offensive.

A series of delays increased both the chances of a political intervention to halt or scale-down the offensive and the risks of its chances being spoilt by the heavy rainfall, which Haig's staff knew to be common in Flanders in August. The first demand for postponement came from General Anthoine, commanding the French First Army on Gough's left. Owing to a shortage

of labour Anthoine reckoned he could not construct all the gun emplacements and ammunition dumps that would be needed to conduct the
bombardment and support the attack. Haig sent him 7,200 men to help
with this labour.[17] At a conference on Saturday 7 July, however, Gough
himself requested that Z-day be postponed five days until 30 July. Partly
owing to diversionary operations of dubious usefulness that Second Army
and First Army mounted in direction of Lille, there had been delays in
assembling the heavy artillery needed for the preliminary bombardment.
More ominously Fifth Army had lost some guns to German counter-battery
fire, which remained vigorous. Haig was disinclined to give Gough all the
time he asked for and said that the date of the operation could not be finally
fixed at this stage. At a conference held at Watou five days later, however,
Haig conceded a three-day delay making Z-day 28 July.[18]

On Tuesday 10 July, events on the coast further illustrated the annoy-
ing resilience of the Germans. On Thursday 5 July, General Sir Henry
Rawlinson had established his Fourth Army headquarters at Malo les Bains,
near Dunkirk, where he began preparing the coastal operations.[19] Fourth
Army had just one, rather weak, corps: V Corps, commanded by Lieutenant-
General Sir John Du Cane. On 22 June its two divisions (1st and 32nd)
relieved French troops in a small bridgehead over the River Yser, east of
Nieuport. This bridgehead constituted practically the only possible starting position for a thrust down the coast. Its fortifications were weak and
its defence depended largely on artillery. The relief was bungled, French
artillery being withdrawn before a high proportion of the earmarked
British guns had arrived. Correctly anticipating that a substitution of
British for French troops might mean trouble, the Germans struck the
bridgehead before it could be strengthened and expanded.[20] As Charteris
commented:

They attacked us with great determination and we have lost practically the whole
of a battalion, a real bad affair ... it does show that the Germans have plenty of kick
left in them. The German attack was admirably planned and carried out.[21]

Haig had argued for the Flanders offensive on the basis that the Germans
were visibly weakening. The strike near Nieuport undermined this argument and apparently alarmed the War Cabinet. Haig, however, assured
the authorities at home that German success had been entirely owing to
a local superiority in artillery and that the general military situation was
not seriously affected. Despite the now very cramped nature of the bridgehead, preparations for the coastal attack continued.[22] In retrospect,
it seems strange that this incident did not result in the War Cabinet's
more rigorously questioning Haig's estimate of the extent of German
military decline.

Given that the Germans generally held the higher ground and that most of their defences were on reverse slopes, winning air superiority was vital to the efficient use of British artillery. Haig was therefore concerned when he heard on 8 July, little more than a week before the preliminary bombardment was due to commence, that the War Cabinet had decided to take away two of his fighter squadrons for the defence of London. Though he realised that the British capital had recently suffered heavy air raids and that the public was alarmed, Haig protested against the diminution of his airpower at this critical time and managed to hang on to one of the squadrons. General Hugh Trenchard of the RFC reported on 11 July that the battle for air superiority was going well, a view he still held on the eve of the infantry attack.[23] The real problem with the conduct of the preliminary bombardment, which began on 16 July, was not enemy air activity but the weather.

For much of the period of the bombardment low cloud, mist and rain rendered visibility poor, and high winds made the important counter-battery technique of sound ranging less effective than normal. In total some 4.3 million shells had been fired by the time the infantry attack commenced. By 25 July Lieutenant-General Sir Noel Birch was reporting himself confident that the Allies had gained the upper hand over the German artillery and Haig echoed this judgement in his diary on 28 July. There had, indeed, been some destruction of German guns and gunners. But the Germans had been shifting batteries around a good deal and the British assessed some batteries as destroyed or neutralised that had merely been moved. In general German artillery in the run up to the attack, despite its losses, proved remarkably active.[24]

The overall effects of the preliminary bombardment were mixed. On the left and centre of the front the Allies were about to attack, the German defensive system within 2,000–3,000 yards of the front line was comprehensively pulverised. Wire was cut, trenches and breastworks smashed, and pillboxes and fortified farm buildings shattered. The Germans immediately facing Lieutenant-General Cavan's XIV Corps, on the far left of Fifth Army, found the bombardment so overwhelming that they pulled back from their front line positions behind the Yser Canal. British patrols noticed this and on 27 July Cavan's forces crossed in strength, securing their initial objectives four days early. On the Allied left and centre much of the forward-deployed German artillery had also been smashed. But the large number of German guns stationed behind the Passchendaele Ridge had largely survived. Further right, on the Gheluvelt Plateau, the British entirely depended on aircraft for observation. Given the problems with the weather, it was inevitable that results here were less impressive. German pillboxes quite close to the front remained intact.[25]

Largely because the army commanders were not satisfied with the progress of the bombardment, Z-day was delayed yet again. On 21 July General Anthoine wrote to GHQ asking for a postponement from 28 to 31 July. Haig was opposed to a delay. Rather than accept it, he proposed that the French First Army, whose role was only a supporting one, should mount a shallower attack. Gough, however, was unwilling to alter his plan. According to Charteris, the ensuing discussions were

definitely heated. The Army Commanders pressed for delay; D.H. wanted the attack to go on at once, and in the end he accepted the Army Commanders' view. He could indeed do nothing else, for they have to carry out the job. I came away with D.H. from the conference when it was all settled, and reminded him of Napoleon's reply to his marshals, 'Ask me for anything but time.' D.H was very moody ...[26]

Z-day was put back to Tuesday 31 July.[27]

Final, grudging, political authorisation

By July enthusiasm for this offensive in London seems to have been even lower than it had been in late June. The Prime Minister still had the gravest reservations and, reading between the lines, Robertson was little keener than Lloyd George. Just a few days after Haig returned from his meetings with the War Policy Committee in London, Robertson had gone to France to speak with the top French generals. He reported a conversation he held with Pétain on Friday 29 June. Robertson portrayed himself as initially taking a remarkably Haig-like stance. He had emphasised that:

the German is in a bad way, and ... we have a good chance of finishing him off if only we will all stick to it. But Pétain would listen to nothing of this nature ... He insisted upon talking about Diplomacy, the necessity of detaching some of the enemy Powers ... and he drew sad pictures about the tired state of the French Army and particularly the French Nation. In fact he talked like a man without a jot of confidence as to the future.

Robertson claimed that he drew no conclusions from this.[28] But the CIGS had already told Haig that he did not favour a major British offensive without substantial French support. Haig could draw his own inference. On 6 July Robertson again wrote to Haig warning that Lloyd George was still "keen on Italy", Smuts wanted to send a large force to Alexandretta and Milner favoured a Balkan theatre of operations. The situation had somewhat improved from Haig's point of view by 18 July, with most of the War Cabinet prepared to go along with a Flanders offensive. But Robertson warned Haig that the Prime Minster was still "sticking out against your plans". Robertson emphasised that the willingness of other ministers to lend their support might depend on Haig's using a "step by step system of advance", keeping the "extent of the advance" limited to distances at which the "assistance of the guns" could be effective. Though Robertson reported that these remarks had been made to him by "one of the Cabinet", they sound like a repeat of the "Staff College lecture" that he had given Haig during the Battle of Arras. Robertson further warned that the War Cabinet might stop the offensive at more or less any time if it felt that the losses were excessive in relation to the gains.[29] Perhaps suspecting that some of these remarks originated with Robertson himself rather than any of the politicians, Haig was plainly angry. On 21 July he replied:

> I note ... there is still a possibility of my being ordered to abandon the operation at some future stage ... [My] judgement ... is not trusted on this point, or even on the depth to which each advance should be pushed with due regard to the combination between Artillery and the other arms.[30]

Haig's letter crossed with one Robertson sent the same day. Despite the fact that "the Prime Minister [was] still very averse" and talked of switching the main effort to Italy or Palestine, the War Cabinet, at a "rough and tumble" meeting on Friday 20 July, had finally decided to let Haig proceed.[31]

Z-day: Tuesday 31 July 1917

As Z-day approached, Haig, as was his normal custom, moved himself closer to the action. He made ready to receive the initial battle reports in a camouflaged railway carriage at West Cappel. Later he would use a house in the town of Cassel where Second Army was also based, and later still would operate from a more formal Advanced GHQ at Blendecques, two miles south-south-east of St Omer.[32]

Zero hour was 3.50 a.m. It was supposed to be first light, but dense low cloud made it very dark. On the left, the French First Army was supposed to make a relatively shallow advance of approximately 2,500 yards to cover the flank of the British Fifth. The French artillery had done its work well and, at a cost of fewer than 1,000 casualties in each of the attacking divisions, the French conquered all the ground they had aimed to take and more. The results greatly boosted the morale of the troops, many of whom had been involved in the fiasco of the Nivelle offensive. On the far left of Fifth Army, Lieutenant-General Lord Cavan's XIV Corps, already across the Yser Canal since 27 July, also had a successful day. While the artillery duel before Z-day had by no means destroyed all the German guns in this sector, most of them were temporarily suppressed by vigorous counter-battery shelling with gas. Most of the German pillboxes between the front line and the little River Steenbeck had been destroyed or abandoned and the creeping barrage provided the advancing infantry of the Guards and 38th Divisions with effective support in the initial part of their advance. Pillboxes east of the Steenbeck were, however, mostly intact and fire from these gradually brought the advance to a halt just west of that stream. XIV Corps had generally advanced about 3,000 yards and had been stopped about 1,000 yards short of its objective. It had suffered a total of about 5,000 casualties, including 750 fatalities.

Lieutenant-General Sir Ivor Maxse's XVIII Corps, with the 51st and 39th Divisions, was intended to force the Steenbeck and capture the ruins of the village of St Julien. After a pause it was intended to push on to Gravenstafel, bringing it within 1,000 yards of the Passchendaele Ridge. Though the German front line was overrun relatively easily, a greater proportion of the pillboxes in this sector and some of the barbed wire beyond the front line remained intact. Carefully rehearsed infantry tactics and tank support, however, allowed the advance to be maintained. Maxse's infantry crossed the Steenbeck and, by 11 a.m., had advanced almost as far as Gravenstafel.

13. The Third Battle of Ypres. The 55th Australian Siege Battery in action with 9.2-inch howitzer near Voormezeele. With the permission of The Trustees of the Imperial War Museum, London.

Slightly further to the right, Lieutenant-General Watts' XIX Corps had made the greatest advance of the day, leading brigades of the 55th and 15th Divisions, reaching the St Julien Spur by early afternoon. On the left and centre, therefore, the Allies were doing extraordinarily well by midday on 31 July. Their advance (of up to 4,000 yards in places) had seriously shaken the Germans. But XVIII and XIX Corps had suffered serious casualties in making this advance and their front had become ragged. The leading troops were not actually beyond the range of supporting artillery, but, communications having broken down, divisional commanders and gunners did not know the positions of their leading troops with any clarity.

It was on the right, on the Gheluvelt Plateau, that British infantry encountered the stiffest resistance and made the shortest advance. Lieutenant-General Sir Claud Jacob's II Corps, attacking with the 24th, 30th and 8th Divisions, overran the German front line without much difficulty. But in the woods and bogs beyond it, the advance tended to slow. In some places uncut wire slowed it further and the infantry lost its creeping barrage, which, given the difficult terrain, was moving too rapidly. The German artillery was active in this sector and the 30th and 24th Divisions, in particular, were heavily shelled. The attack was halted, mainly by machine gun fire from intact bunkers and pillboxes. Nowhere did II Corps gain more than 2,000 yards. Supporting attacks by Second Army, on the right, gained very little ground. Because the advance on the Gheluvelt Plateau was so shallow, XIX Corps (especially the 15th Division) to the north was exposed to machine gun fire into its right flank and rear. Then, during the afternoon, Fifth Army's ragged centre was hit by a heavy counter-attack from three German reserve regiments. Its front rather ragged as a result of the rapid advance and heavy casualties, and unable to get the artillery support it needed, the British infantry here was driven back, losing vital ground including St Julien and the London Ridge.[33] The success of this German counter-attack inevitably reopened the question of whether Gough had tried to push troops too far too fast.

Yet, by the standards of the Somme battle of the previous year, the first day of the Third Battle of Ypres represented a major success. The total casualties sustained (about 27,000) were only about half those suffered on 1 July 1916 and the proportion of fatalities seems to have been substantially lower. And whereas German casualties on Saturday 1 July 1916 had been relatively light, on Tuesday 31 July 1917 the British had apparently inflicted as many as they suffered, perhaps more. Despite disappointments and reverses – the failure to clear the enemy from the Gheluvelt Plateau on the right and the loss of ground to the counter-attack in the centre – it had, overall, been a remarkably successful day's battle.[34] Had

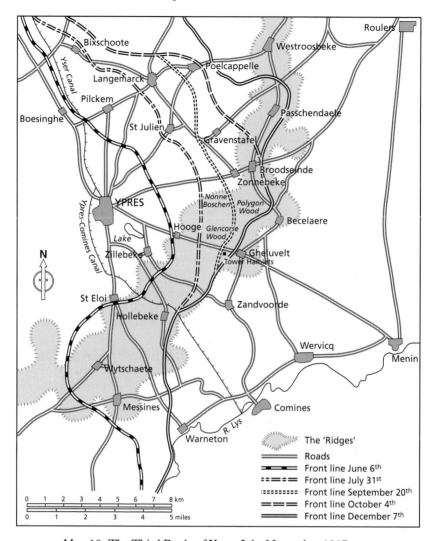

Map 19. The Third Battle of Ypres July–November 1917

the weather been fine and dry over the next month, the Germans would have faced an immense crisis. Even Haig's dream of clearing the Belgian coast before the end of the summer might not have seemed too fanciful. But, as Haig noted in his diary for 31 July 1917:

Heavy rain fell this afternoon and aeroplane [sic] observation was impossible. The going became very bad … This has hampered our further progress.[35]

August rain

Reports on the condition of German prisoners captured on 31 July convinced Haig that he had been right about the decline of the German army. On Wednesday 1 August he told a French officer about to go and brief Pétain that:

In my opinion now is the critical moment of the war and the French must attack as strongly as possible and as soon as possible so as to co-operate with the British in dealing the Enemy as strong a blow as possible.

Later that day he visited three of Fifth Army's corps, as well as that Army's HQ. The Germans launched major counter-attacks, but Gough's forces largely stood their ground. Haig took a particular pride in the 15th (Scottish) Division's defeat of the biggest German counter-attack, which was made in divisional strength. But the weather was obviously reducing the chance of further progress. In Haig's words it was:

A terrible day of rain. The ground is like a bog in this low-lying country.[36]

The rain would continue for much of the rest of the month. Rain in Flanders at this time of year was not unusual, but the extent of this deluge certainly was.[37] It fell on both sides equally, of course, and fighting in a morass was miserable for all. Yet, tactically and operationally, the weather strongly favoured the Germans. Rain and low cloud made observation for the artillery difficult and the Allies had far more artillery than their enemies. Mud tends to paralyse movement. In general it was the Allies who were trying to advance, whereas the Germans, most of the time, were merely trying to stay put. While Fifth Army remained largely paralysed by the weather and the condition of the ground, the Germans heavily reinforced their front in Flanders.

Gough was not known for his patience. Determined to make progress despite the break in the weather, on the evening of 31 July he ordered two further attacks. The first, scheduled for 2 August, was to be a limited advance by II Corps to complete the capture of what had been its second objective on 31 July. The second, scheduled for 4 August and to be mounted by II, XIX and the right of XVIII Corps, was intended to complete the capture of what had been the third objective on 31 July: recovering the ground lost to German counter-attacks on the first day. Also on 4 August the XIV Corps would attack towards and attempt to take Langemarck.[38] Neither attack proceeded on Gough's schedule. Apparently considering that his intervention of 26 June, questioning Fifth Army's plan for a 4,000-yard advance on the first day, had been vindicated by events, Davidson once more questioned Gough's judgement. He thought Fifth

Army should move fresh divisions into the line and wait for a few days of fine weather before resuming offensive operations on a large scale. Clear skies would permit aerial observation and photography of the battlefield, which would in turn enable more accurate gunnery. This time Haig came down on Davidson's side. GHQ ordered Gough to delay the attack he had ordered for Thursday 2 August. On that day Haig saw Gough personally and told him "to have patience and not to put in his infantry attack until after two or three days of fine weather, to enable our guns to get the upper hand and dry the ground".[39]

By Wednesday 8 August, Haig was showing a reasonably good understanding of German defensive methods. His diary indicates that, in response and at least for the time being, he now favoured the sort of cautious, step-by-step offensive approach for which officers like Robertson and Rawlinson had long argued, a method which, for some weeks, had been endorsed by Davidson and Kiggell at GHQ:

In view of the large reinforcements brought up by the Enemy and his manner of using them (viz. for counter-attack *after* our troops have reached the end of an offensive operation and are exhausted), instructions are sent to Gough by Kiggell directing him to reduce the length of his next advance to what the men can easily do in the bad state of ground (say about 2,000 yards) ... This ... may make our progress slow to begin with, but will pay us later on, I hope, when the Enemy's troops are worn out, and discouraged through failures in counter-attacking ...[40]

GHQ, therefore, made Gough wait until 10 August to mount his next big attack on the Gheluvelt Plateau. For this operation he did use fresh divisions, the 18th and the 25th, and he did set a very limited objective. But, though there were a couple of fine days immediately before the attack, the ground had still not dried out. Conditions were difficult for the attacking infantry, and poor observation made counter-battery work difficult. German artillery was not adequately suppressed. At the cost of some 2,200 casualties, only a very shallow advance was achieved.[41]

Haig had earlier insisted that Gough secure the Gheluvelt Plateau before attempting any further advance further north. But he did not stick to this, allowing Gough, on Thursday 16 August, after two days of heavy rain, to conduct another attack all along the Fifth Army front. Results were mixed. On the left, the French First Army and Cavan's XIV Corps did very well, capturing all their objectives, including the village of Langemarck. Further to the right, XVIII Corps took St Julien, but, in the centre and right of the Fifth Army front, the gains were very slight in relation to the casualties suffered. Allied forces on 16 August seem to have suffered about 15,000 casualties of all kinds, of which the overwhelming majority were in Fifth Army.[42] There were two further large-scale operations in this month. On Sunday 19 August a narrow-front operation by Maxse's XVIII Corps made brilliant use of tanks to capture, at amazingly low cost, a group of five bunkers that had hitherto blocked the corps' advance. But a bigger effort, involving XVIII, XIX and II Corps, three days later was an almost complete failure. Instead of stopping to regroup and rethink, Gough went on attacking until 27 August, despite renewed heavy rain from 23 August, which, on 26 August, became torrential.[43]

By this time there was serious disquiet about Gough and his Fifth Army staff, both in subordinate formations and at GHQ. Relations between Fifth Army and other headquarters, strained by doubts about Gough's operational competence, were exacerbated by the seemingly arrogant, tactless manner of his chief of staff, Major-General Neill Malcolm.[44] Inevitably Haig became aware of the disquiet about Gough. But, buoyed by Charteris's optimistic intelligence reports, he thought the campaign was going well overall. He reported to the War Cabinet on Friday 4 August that in the offensive so far the total of German casualties exceeded British "very considerably and not improbably by as much as 100% ... British Armies can be relied upon to drive the enemy from any position without undue loss."[45] In a letter of 9 August, however, Robertson made it clear that the War Cabinet's continuing support for the offensive could not be relied upon. At a conference of the Allies in London, over the last couple of days, Foch had indicated that he held out no real hope for offensive operations on the Western Front in 1917. During the same proceedings Lloyd George had yet again expressed his wish to concentrate efforts on the Italian front, a proposal for which he had both Italian and French support.[46]

Haig reacted with predictable outrage. A letter he sent to Robertson on Monday 13 August opened in moderate tones, but (probably reflecting the degree to which he was under stress) soon became something of a rant. He claimed that Flanders was obviously the decisive point and the only sensible thing for the government to do was to support him wholeheartedly, concentrating all resources there. Everyone under his command was, he claimed, convinced that they could bring about the decisive defeat of the German army in this campaign. This was an opinion based on "facts" such as that army's evident decline, which could be confirmed by any "occasional glance" at Charteris's intelligence reports. "Moreover", Haig asserted, "I have been in the field for 3 years and know what I am writing about." Foch's dissent from his view of the situation was "utterly stupid". Clearly that "old man" was "done".

Implicitly criticising Robertson, Haig indicated that some of his problems originated with the General Staff at the War Office. The War Office's "pessimistic estimates" in its intelligence reports did "much harm", causing "many in authority to take a pessimistic outlook". Indicating his somewhat deviant attitude to the intelligence function, Haig apparently wanted

Robertson to cheer up these reports in order to "help the nation on to victory". Haig stated that there was "every reason to be optimistic". If the war "ended tomorrow" Great Britain would find itself not merely "the greatest Power in Europe but in the World". (Haig's argument here is hard to follow. A compromise peace that left Germany in possession of the lands it had conquered since the beginning of the war would surely have made it the hegemonic power in Europe.) In the same letter Haig betrayed great fear of "the Socialists who are trying to rule us all at a time when the right-minded of the Nation are so engaged in the Country's battles". In what way and to what extent this fear was influencing his strategic outlook at this particular moment he did not explain. But the fear of socialist revolution if the war dragged on for another year or two may partly account for his extreme eagerness for continuing offensive action on a very large scale.[47]

To a conference of senior staff officers on Sunday 19 August Haig affirmed that "our Army's efforts this year have brought final victory near". He believed that "if we can keep up our effort, final victory may be won by December". The main obstacle to this, Haig believed, was a manpower shortage. He wanted the assembled officers to comb through other branches of the army looking for "every man who is in any way likely by training to become fit for service in the infantry".[48]

Haig's endemic optimism did not, however, prevent him gradually shifting control of the battle from Gough's Fifth to Plumer's Second Army HQ. Haig had emphasised the importance of the Gheluvelt Plateau. Very little progress had been made there and some adjustment was clearly necessary. Haig saw Gough and Plumer separately on 24 August and indicated his intention to shift the Army boundary. All formations on the Gheluvelt Plateau would, from early September, come under Plumer's control. Until the enemy was cleared from the Gheluvelt Plateau, Plumer would direct the general course of the campaign.[49] These arrangements were confirmed in a formal order of 28 August.[50] For the time being Gough continued to plan operations on the Plateau, to be implemented before Plumer took over. Having initially approved these operations, Haig changed his mind, deciding to leave further endeavours on the Plateau to Second Army. Gough, however, persisted, up to 10 September, with a series of narrow front attacks on fortified farmhouses on the St Julien spur. All were bloody failures, further damaging the Fifth Army commander's reputation.[51]

Haig went to London on Monday 3 September and remained there until the following Thursday. His main purpose was to oppose Foch's project of sending a hundred heavy guns from Anthoine's First Army in Flanders to Italy, though the visit also gave him the opportunity to see his pregnant wife. On 4 September he discussed the guns for Italy issue with Foch and with the War Cabinet. Surprisingly, no one seems to have pressed Haig to close down his Flanders offensive. Carson, Smuts and Lord Robert Cecil, representing the Foreign Office, all supported him on the issue of heavy guns for Italy, though Lloyd George was anxious that the guns should go. The issue was not finally resolved in London, but carried over to a conference of the Allies at Amiens on Friday 7 September. There Haig decided to give way, agreeing that the guns could be sent to Italy provided the French did their best to replace them before the next big attack in Flanders. Realising that he could not count on the French replacing these guns, he eventually decided to make more British guns available by not renewing operations in the First Army sector at Lens, which he had thought promising.

On 7 and 10 September, Kiggell spoke to Haig about the heavy cost of Gough's continuing narrow front attacks in the St Julien sector. Kiggell was clearly disillusioned with Gough and Malcolm, and his influence may well have been decisive in getting Haig to order that these operations should cease.[52]

The Plumer phase: 30 August–4 October 1917

In discussions with Davidson and Haig, Plumer had, as we have noted, supported Gough's pursuit of highly ambitious objectives for the offensive's first day. Yet as soon as he was put in the driving seat, he reverted to type. Thorough, very cautious planning and strictly limited objectives became the order of the day. Plumer had several important advantages compared with Gough in the earlier phase of the battle. First, in the short term, less was expected of him. No one now contemplated a rapid advance. Secondly, he had greater resources, especially in artillery, more of which had been concentrated in the Ypres sector as the offensive progressed. Thirdly, everyone had, at least for the time being, grasped the folly of trying to attack through deep mud; it was expected that Plumer should wait for the ground to dry out. Fourthly, at least for a few weeks, the weather co-operated with Plumer in a way that it had not with Gough. Even up to early October, however, Plumer did not have it all his own way. The Germans had reinforced their troops in Flanders. Plumer's forces would have to tackle a concentration of good quality German divisions in the most formidable fortifications military science could devise.[53]

In a plan submitted on 29 August, Plumer proposed that Second Army take the Gheluvelt Plateau in a series of short steps, while Fifth Army kept pace on the left flank. After three weeks delay (in mostly benign weather) to allow the ground to dry out, a total of nine divisions from four corps

(XVIII and V Corps from Fifth Army and I Anzac and X Corps in Second Army) attacked on 20 September. Six German divisions immediately faced the British attack. Another three, designated counter-attack divisions, were between 5,000 and 7,000 yards behind the front.

Considering that they were attacking frontally and into exceptionally strong fortifications, superficially this balance of forces appears unfavourable to the British. Massive fire support was the key to success. The British had a numerical superiority of about 3:1 in artillery and were able to achieve an unprecedented concentration of fire. It has been estimated that the preliminary bombardment on the Fifth Army front was of twice, and that on the Second Army front of three times, the intensity of that preceding the attack of 31 July. On Thursday 20 September the gunners provided a dense wall of fire, 1,000 yards thick, which swept over the ground the infantry intended to capture and remained for several hours as a static barrier against counter-attack. Even this level of fire support did not make the attack successful in all parts of the front and did not prevent about 21,000 casualties being sustained. But the attacking formations made an average gain of ground of about 1,250 yards and the casualties inflicted on the Germans were probably at least equally heavy. Three thousand Germans were taken prisoner. Just one of the British divisions buried 1,000 German bodies. Most of the numerous German efforts at counter-attack were shot to pieces, achieving nothing.[54]

Haig was rightly impressed with Plumer's victory (later designated the Battle of the Menin Road Ridge). But, as had already happened so often in the immediate aftermath of a degree of success, he became excessively excited, reviving his hopes of clearing the Belgian coast, even of a complete German collapse. He wanted the conquest of the Gheluvelt Plateau completed quickly and directed that an attack to take Zonnebeke and the Polygon Wood should be mounted on 26 September. A further effort, on or around 6 October, was to take the rest of the Plateau and the ruined village of Poelcappelle, slightly to the north.[55] Trying to mount another major attack so quickly inevitably caused problems. Between 20 and 25 September much of the British artillery had to be moved: giving the Germans some respite from its fire. A determined counter-attack against the British 33rd Division, just south of Polygon Wood, on 25 September, proved that the Germans still had some resilience. The German division involved suffered massive casualties. But there was not enough time for the British to regain the small amount of ground lost and this meant local disruption to arrangements for the big attack of the following day.[56]

The attack of Wednesday 26 September, later known as the Battle of Polygon Wood, involved, on the British side, seven divisions from four corps: two from the Fifth Army and two from the Second. After a single day's preliminary bombardment, the infantry attack commenced at 5.50 a.m. Nearly all objectives were taken, the 5th Australian Division capturing Polygon Wood itself. The Germans mounted nine counter-attacks, all of which proved very expensive. Two of these recaptured small amounts of ground, while seven were shot to pieces without making any gains at all. The attacking forces suffered some 15,000 casualties, but it is likely that as many were inflicted. It was a convincing victory that made the German high command very anxious.[57] Its effect on Haig was utterly predictable: his burgeoning excitement became impossible for his Army commanders to control.

Haig held a conference with Plumer and Gough at Cassel at 5 p.m. that very day. In order to keep the Germans off balance, Haig decided that the next attack should be brought forward slightly, to 4 October. Believing that "decisive results" were now possible, Haig now wanted to shift from "step-by-step" to breakthrough mode. He wanted the Passchendaele Ridge taken as soon as possible and for this to be followed by tank and cavalry exploitation towards Moorsede or Roulers. He talked to Rawlinson about mounting the long-contemplated coastal and amphibious operations soon afterwards. At a further meeting on Friday 28 September, he provisionally scheduled a big attack towards the Passchendaele Ridge for 10 October. He asked his Army commanders to submit their requirements for this operation and for subsequent rapid exploitation.[58] Plumer and Gough showed a remarkable degree of agreement in their responses. In the most tactful terms, each stated, in separate letters to GHQ, that he thought discussion of breakthrough and exploitation somewhat premature. Each indicated that German morale might collapse if the British continued to do well and if the Passchendaele Ridge were in British hands by mid-October. Cavalry exploitation might then be possible. But in the immediate future both wished to continue with the step-by-step approach that had worked for them for the last few weeks.[59] At a further meeting on Tuesday 2 October, however, Haig overruled them. As he noted in his diary:

I pointed out how favourable the situation was and how necessary it was to have all the necessary means for exploiting the success on the 10th, should the situation admit, e.g. if the Enemy counter-attacks and is defeated, then reserve brigades must follow after the Enemy and take the Passchendaele Ridge at once ... Both Gough and Plumer quite acquiesced in my views, and arranged wholeheartedly to give effect to them when the time came. At first they adhered to the idea of continuing attacks for limited objectives.[60]

How "wholehearted" was Gough's and Plumer's conversion must be a matter of opinion. Perhaps what this episode indicates was that neither man found it easy to stand up to Haig when he was in this sort of buoyant and aggressive mood.

Before the next attack, the Army boundary was shifted northward: II Anzac Corps, belonging to Plumer's Second Army, relieving Fifth Army's V Corps. A preliminary bombardment in the normal sense was not fired, though the gunners rehearsed their supporting barrage. Twelve divisions belonging to six corps (two of Fifth Army and four of Second) attacked at 6 a.m. The Germans had themselves been about to attack when the British hit them. This only increased their casualties, as the British barrage hit their crowded forward areas. German dead lay thicker on the ground than British infantry had ever seen before. Over 4,700 Germans were taken prisoner. Across most of the front the attackers secured all their objectives. Artillery and infantry played the main roles, but the ground was just dry enough to enable a dozen tanks to make an appreciable contribution to the success of Maxse's XVIII Corps in the centre. At the end of the Battle of Broodseinde (as this episode was later designated) Haig's confidence rose to new heights. But that very day the weather broke again.[61]

Haig's relations with the British government: late August–early October 1917

By the end of August it was clear that Haig's forces were advancing very slowly and at heavy cost. Given that it now seemed unlikely to fulfil any major strategic purpose, it seems puzzling that the War Cabinet did not intervene to end it. It was in this period that Robertson's performance as CIGS is most open to criticism. His intense personal dislike of the Prime Minister combined with an excessive adherence to the principle of military solidarity in dealing with the politicians left him increasingly anxious, but at the same time paralysed and impotent. By mid-September Robertson was warning Haig of the collapse of Russia and of the growth of disillusionment and anti-war sentiment in Britain. "There are gradually accumulating in the country a great many wounded and crippled men who are not of a very cheery disposition; there are others who are mere wasters and are without patriotism; and finally there are the various Labour Unions etc. On the whole there is a fairly formidable body of discontented or half-hearted people."[62] The inference that Robertson presumably intended Haig to draw was that a continuing very high casualty rate in Flanders might seriously damage morale at home.

Robertson came to GHQ in the company of the Prime Minister on Wednesday 26 September. Both Lloyd George and Robertson wanted to get Haig's views about recent, somewhat vague, German peace-feelers. At this point significant differences of outlook between CIGS and commander-in-chief resurfaced. Haig, at this stage, had no interest in a compromise peace. Heartened by Plumer's victory astride the Menin

Road and by the Polygon Wood battle (in progress that very day) he sang the old and, at this particular moment, not wholly inaccurate refrain that "the Germans were in a bad way". He thought that, with a bit more help from the French, he could finish them off. He insisted, too, that the British had a duty not to desert Russia. But Robertson apparently agreed with Lloyd George that Russia had effectively collapsed already and that neither Italy nor France was doing much real fighting. Robertson also agreed with Lloyd George that Britain could not "single handed defeat the German army". In these circumstances neither Lloyd George nor Robertson was prepared lightly to dismiss the idea of a compromise peace.[63] The CIGS, as he admitted in a letter to Haig immediately after his return from France, was now racked by doubt. The French and the Italians both now seemed feeble and the Americans were not likely to have much effect for a considerable time. In the short term, therefore, adopting a defensive posture on the Western Front while mounting some limited offensives against Germany's allies was a policy that no longer seemed to him as ridiculous as it once did. In order to maintain morale in Britain, might it not, indeed, be necessary to gain some offensive successes somewhere?[64]

By mid-autumn 1917 Robertson's position was becoming almost impossible. Trusting the judgement of neither Lloyd George nor Haig, he must have been aware that neither of them liked or trusted him. He tried hard, from force of habit as much as anything else, to limit the major offensive that Lloyd George was planning in Palestine and to minimise the despatch of British troops to other peripheral theatres. Inevitably this sent his relations with the Prime Minister from bad to worse. It seems likely that by the beginning of October, if not earlier, he would have preferred to close down the Flanders offensive. But, with Plumer in the driving seat, applying the operational methods that Robertson had been advocating since February 1915 and winning considerable victories in the process, this did not seem the time for a confrontation with Haig. Robertson wrote to Haig on 9 October indicating that Lloyd George was "out for my blood these days". He knew that Haig was "a little disappointed" with him for being unable to prevent the despatch of some forces to other theatres, but insisted, rather lamely, that "whatever happens you & I must stand solid together".[65]

The final phase of fighting: 5 October–10 November 1917

By this time the relatively dry, relatively successful phase of the Flanders campaign was over. Things had taken another turn for the worse. On Thursday 4 October, the day of the Battle of Broodseinde, the weather had again broken. Thirty millimetres of rain fell between 4 and 9 October.

Much of the battle area became a shallow lake with sucking mud beneath. Across much of it walking was only possible on wooden "duck boards" placed over the slightly firmer sections of the quagmire. Even for a fit man who had suffered no wounds, falling off the boards could mean death by drowning. Needless to say, the sophisticated tactics in which the BEF's infantry were now trained would not work under these conditions. Matters were hardly any better for the artillery. Moving shell to the guns through this morass became a Herculean labour. The guns themselves, to avoid their being lost in the mud, had to be mounted on wooden platforms. But, quite apart from the problem of target acquisition in conditions of poor visibility, accurate gunnery was hardly possible from a platform subsiding unevenly, and by incalculable degrees, into a marsh.[66]

But by the beginning of October Haig had convinced himself that the climax of the war was now at hand. He drew comparisons with the situation at First Ypres, on 31 October 1914, when the Germans had slackened their offensive efforts just as the Allies had reached breaking point, thereby losing an opportunity of decisive victory. There is ample evidence that he was aware of the ground conditions resulting from the renewal of the deluge on 4 October.[67] Yet he had become so excited by Plumer's three successive victories and so convinced that decisive results were now possible that halting the offensive at this point was not something he was prepared to consider. If an attack were to stand any chance of success in the conditions that obtained in Flanders after 4 October, however, it would need the most careful preparation. Keen to maintain tempo and keep the Germans off balance, Haig did not allow for this. At a meeting at Haig's Advanced GHQ at Cassel at 3 p.m. on Thursday 4 October, the afternoon of the Battle of Broodseinde, Plumer apparently counselled caution, indicating that he did not think that all German reserves had yet been consumed. Charteris, however, insisted that the Germans had "few more available reserves" and Haig insisted that the date of the next attack be brought forward by two days.[68] This would have meant attacking on Monday 8 October. The operation was to be mounted on a broad front, the French First Army attacking south and east of the Houthulst Forest, Fifth Army attacking with two corps and Second Army with three. Second Army's II Anzac Corps had the most important task: to advance 800–1,000 yards towards the high ground where the village of Passchendaele had once stood.

Even though Z-day was put back a day, to Tuesday 9 October, it proved impossible, over much of the front, to move the field artillery forward quickly enough to take part in the attack. Some of the batteries that were moved forward did not have adequate time to register. As with Broodseinde, there was no really systematic preliminary bombardment and what preparatory shooting the heavy guns were able to do was generally rather ineffective because the weather did not allow for good aerial observation. Over much of the front the infantry attacked on 9 October with relatively ineffective artillery support. This was an extremely serious matter because the Germans had managed to reinforce their own artillery and to move some fresh divisions to the Flanders front. The main gains in the Battle of Poelcappelle, as this effort was later designated, were on the flanks: the First French Army and XIV Corps gaining about 800 yards on the left and X Corps capturing a little ground on the Gheluvelt Plateau on the right. Practically no progress was made towards the Passchendaele Ridge in the centre of the front. It is likely that the main reason for the greater success on the flanks was that in these sectors there was less need for guns to be moved forward prior to the attack and that supporting artillery fire was, therefore, rather heavier and more accurate.[69]

Though hardly any advance was achieved towards the Passchendaele Ridge on 9 October, Plumer and Haig agreed that the attack should be renewed at 5.25 a.m. three days later. XVIII Corps (Fifth Army) and II Anzac Corps (Second Army) were set objectives of some 2,000–2,500 yards. Again there was no serious preliminary bombardment and the supporting barrage for some of the attacking divisions was feeble. Some elements of the 9th Division (XVIII Corps), one the finest divisions in the army, were torn to pieces by machine gun fire while its men were quite literally stuck in the mud. The First Battle of Passchendaele, as it was later designated, was practically an unmitigated defeat. There were about 13,000 BEF casualties for virtually no gain of ground.[70]

After First Passchendaele, Plumer recommended that operations on the Second Army front should cease.[71] Haig, however, had no intention of giving up. He still interpreted reports from Charteris to mean that German morale was near breaking point. He dismissed contrary analysis from the War Office intelligence branch under General Macdonogh on the bizarre grounds that Macdonogh was a Catholic and perhaps influenced by anti-British Catholic propaganda.[72] It is not clear that, even at this stage, Haig had abandoned hope of a spectacular German collapse. The "mass of high ground about Passchendaele" was, however, his next objective and he believed that, with that in British hands, the rest of the Passchendaele Ridge would soon follow. At a conference at Advanced GHQ at Cassel on Saturday 13 October Haig explained that he intended to reinforce Second Army with the Canadian Corps and Fifth Army with the 1st Division and the 63rd (Royal Naval) Division. He accepted that a more thorough preliminary bombardment was required for the next attack and that it should only be mounted when there was "a fair prospect of fine weather".[73]

Since its operation on the Vimy Ridge, on 9 April, the Canadian Corps had a new commander. As we have noted, Byng had replaced Allenby at Third Army in June. Lieutenant-General Sir Arthur Currie, a Canadian and, in peacetime, only a part-time soldier, had taken over command of the Canadian Corps. Currie was not keen to go to Flanders, being much more interested in participating in an operation that Byng was planning in the Cambrai sector. Yet it was to Flanders that the Canadians went, entering the line between XVIII Corps on the left and I Anzac Corps on the right. Currie was now commanding by far the most powerful BEF formation on the battlefield, facing towards Haig's next principal objective: Passchendaele. With both Plumer and Gough losing faith in the offensive, Currie was in the driving seat and seems to have realised it. He insisted on concentrating a mass of artillery, and on attacking in short steps each of a mere 500 yards.[74]

On Friday 26 October the Canadians had to advance through an appalling slough. On the left and right flanks, where British and Australian troops respectively mounted supporting attacks, conditions were even worse. The Canadians made their intended 500 yards, but the Australians on their right scarcely moved at all. The experiences of the 58th and 63rd Divisions of XVIII Corps, on the left, were so ghastly that Gough balked, telling Kiggell that Fifth Army should cease operations until the ground froze. Kiggell, apparently sympathetic, wanted to call a conference involving Gough and Plumer for the following day. Haig, probably fearing that the Army commanders would unite against the continuance of the campaign, vetoed Kiggell's suggestion. "In my opinion", he recorded, "today's operation at the decisive point (Passchendaele) had been so successful that I was entirely opposed to any idea of abandoning operations until frost set in."[75]

When the attack was renewed, on Tuesday 30 October, the Canadians gained their next 500 yards, though their infantrymen were sometimes reduced to pulling each other through the mud to do so. Again things were worse on their left, in the XVIII Corps area. The 58th Division reported that "the ground was impassable and so powerless were the troops to manoeuvre that they were shot down whilst stuck in the mud". This time Haig accepted Gough's recommendation that Fifth Army cease attacking, so the Canadians were left to carry on practically alone.[76] Currie's men took the remains of Passchendaele village, now merely a collection of reddish brick-stains in the mud, on Tuesday 6 November. Haig ordered another operation, on Saturday 10 November, to extend Canadian control of the ridge. Again a tiny amount of ground was gained at great cost. Then a renewed deluge made Haig decide to bring the campaign to an end.

The Canadian Corps had suffered about 12,000 casualties between 26 October and 10 November.[77] Its performance had been both heroic

14. Canadian stretcher bearers carry wounded through the mud during the Passchendaele fighting. With the permission of The Trustees of the Imperial War Museum, London.

and as efficient as was possible in the circumstances. But few historians have been able to convince themselves that, in this final phase of the Third Ypres campaign, anything of value was achieved. On 10 November Haig's forces still did not control the whole of the Passchendaele Ridge. Indeed the area of that ridge that they did hold, immediately around village of Passchendaele, formed such a minuscule and awkward Salient that GHQ was soon forced to acknowledge in writing that it was untenable in the face of any serious German attack.[78]

Outcomes

Third Ypres, or "Passchendaele", as the whole campaign has been generally remembered, remains an emotive subject in the United Kingdom and the Commonwealth. It has been difficult for historians of these nations to evaluate it objectively.[79] In terms of Haig's grander objectives for it, the campaign obviously failed. Germany did not collapse and the Belgian ports remained in German hands. It is true that the French army was able to make some recovery from the nadir of its morale in late spring 1917, a justification that Haig and his staff increasingly used after the fact. But how important the Flanders campaign was in enabling this recovery is difficult to say. The worst of the French army's troubles seem to have been over before Third Ypres began, and it seems doubtful that such an enormous and sustained offensive was necessary to fulfil the limited aim of distracting attention from the French. If that had been the primary aim, moreover, it would have made far more sense to make the main attack in a drier, better-drained part of the front, such as the Lens or Cambrai sectors. There, British firepower and hard-gained tactical skill might have been used to greater effect. Far from mounting the Flanders offensive with the primary aim of permitting French rest and recovery, Haig made constant entreaties that the French support him with greater offensive efforts of their own. Despite some retrospective claims by Haig and his staff, contemporary evidence that Pétain and Foch encouraged the British to conduct a campaign in Flanders is very hard to find. There is more definite evidence that both generals advised against it, deemed its success very improbable and went along with it with great reluctance.[80]

In absolute terms Third Ypres was far less bloody for Haig's forces than the Somme had been. As an exercise in the physical attrition of personnel, it seems to have been considerably more efficient than either the Somme or Arras. In Messines and Third Ypres together, the BEF is estimated to have suffered about 275,000 casualties, about 70,000 of them fatal. German casualties are less certain, but for Third Ypres alone they were certainly not much under 200,000 and perhaps a good deal more.

Estimates of the ratio of Allied to German casualties for Third Ypres by historians writing relatively recently vary between about 3:2 and about 1:1. The truth may be that Allied casualties exceeded German by about a quarter.[81] Given that it was attacking frontally into an area fortified densely and in great depth, often over appalling ground and against what was widely regarded as the best army in the world, such figures are not suggestive of tactical or operational incompetence on the part of the British army at this stage in the war.

For the troops taking part, however, some phases of Third Ypres had a quality more nightmarish than anything previously experienced. Whereas the British army came out of the Somme campaign with remarkably good morale, Third Ypres seems to have left much of it distinctly despondent. German veterans appear to have been in no better condition, but a much higher proportion of the British than of the German army had been through this particular mill. It seems clear, therefore, that, in terms of morale, Haig had done proportionally very much more damage to his own army than to the Germans.[82] The British army had been the only army of the Allies in a fair state of both morale and efficiency when Third Ypres began. Haig's conduct at Third Ypres, especially in the latter stages of the campaign, can be regarded as amounting to reckless endangerment of the Allied cause. As we shall see, the devastating effects of Third Ypres on British civil–military relations were to place that cause in even greater jeopardy.

15   The Battle of Cambrai

The erosion of Haig's position

By the end of Third Ypres Haig's stock was low, perhaps lower than he realised. Pessimism had an increasing grip on Britain's governing elite.[1] Growing numbers of important people doubted Haig's judgement and he had ever fewer firm supporters. The Unionist leader, Andrew Bonar Law, had told Lloyd George back in September that even Robertson had lost all hope of "anything coming of Haig's offensive".[2] Lord Milner, one of the politicians Haig most respected,[3] told Lord Curzon in mid-October that his "doubts ... about the ... policy of Hammer, Hammer, Hammer on the Western Front" were "becoming increasingly strong".[4] Curzon had grave doubts of his own. Even Smuts, who had supported the generals earlier, had shifted into the Lloyd George camp by the end of the Passchendaele fighting.[5]

The fissure between GHQ and the War Office, apparent for some time, was gaping wider. There had long been serious differences between Charteris and Macdonogh and their respective chiefs over intelligence analysis, the former being generally very much more optimistic than the latter. But these strains had become particularly serious during the Flanders campaign. Robertson was still trying to show a degree of solidarity with Haig, but the CIGS was not a man who found concealing his true feelings easy. Some members of the government realised that Wully's confidence in Haig's conduct of operations on the Western Front (always rather shaky) had now practically collapsed.[6] Lord Derby, the Secretary of State for War, continued to try to support Haig. But even he had concerns about Haig's judgement, particularly his excessive optimism and his choice of staff. For many months he had felt great anxiety (widely shared in the army) about the influence of Charteris.[7]

Though Haig gave little indication of being worried by it, by November 1917 there was strong evidence of a decline in the morale of his forces. Though there was little in the way of active indiscipline, censors who looked at soldiers' letters home now pointed to intense, almost universal, war weariness.[8] Gloom amongst the troops was beginning to affect attitudes in Britain. The growing number of soldiers who came home with serious long-term injuries was having a particularly damaging impact on domestic morale.[9] The civilian population, moreover, had its own reasons to be depressed, only some of which could be laid at Haig's door. To the news of the collapse of Russia and of the poor progress and heavy casualties of Third Ypres was added rising prices and taxes, food shortages resulting from the German submarine campaign and widespread industrial unrest, particularly on the "Red Clyde".[10]

During Third Ypres, Charteris realised that Haig had a public relations problem. In mid-September 1917 H. A. Gwynne, the right-wing editor of the *Morning Post*, suggested that GHQ use friendly newspapers to initiate a pro-Haig press campaign. Charteris apparently realised the dangers:

[I]f we use the Press to crack up DH we shall have LG outing him at once. If we let the correspondents have an interview with him we shall have a repetition of last February's episode. If we check Philip Gibbs [accredited war correspondent of the *Daily Chronicle*] writing his horror-mongering stuff we shall have his paper down our throat. If we say the Boche is beaten, or even that his morale is being lowered, we shall have the W[ar] O[ffice] itself saying we are over-optimistic and thus make it harder for Robertson to screw the necessary men and munitions out of LG. All the same I have taken steps to do what I can to give some effect to Gwynne's views, for they are right and it is worth taking the risk.[11]

It is, indeed, possible that Charteris had anticipated Gwynne's suggestion. A few days earlier Haig had received a visit from Horatio Bottomley, editor of the rabidly right wing, populist newspaper *John Bull*. Haig remarked in his diary that evening that he seemed "a true friend of the soldier … imbued with sound, patriotic ideas". It seems unlikely, therefore, that Haig would have objected to the Gwynne/Charteris scheme of using sympathetic (even if, in some cases, rather disreputable) elements in the press to defend his conduct of the war. He would have wanted no active part in this and, so that he could plead innocence if confronted, he would not have wished to be informed in any detail.[12]

Whether as a result of a conscious GHQ campaign or not, some of the press remained, up to the end of Third Ypres, reasonably supportive of Haig. Well into the autumn and, much to Lloyd George's annoyance, certain newspapers and magazines were sharply critical of government "interference" with the Field Marshal's plans. Yet the press was very divided: some of it was now taking a strongly pro-Lloyd George line on issues such as reinforcements for Italy.[13] Particularly ominous for Haig was that the *Daily Mirror*, owned by Lord Rothermere, Lord Northcliffe's brother, which had hitherto backed Haig, offered him only muted support over Third Ypres. Probably because the *Mirror* could find little in the

Flanders fighting that would be likely to encourage its readers, it tended to keep the campaign off its front page. So there was the somewhat bizarre phenomenon of one of the nation's most popular newspapers ignoring, or treating as second-class news, one of the greatest battles in British history while it was in progress.[14]

Worse was to come. By the end of Third Ypres, Lord Rothermere had become profoundly disillusioned with GHQ, its conduct of the war and his family's complicity with it. At a dinner party on 8 November he is reported to have pronounced that:

We haven't the pluck of these young lieutenants who go over the top. We're telling lies, we aren't telling the truth, that we're losing more officers than the Germans, and that it's impossible to get through on the Western Front. You've seen the correspondents shepherded by Charteris. They don't know the truth, they don't speak the truth, and we know that they don't.[15]

Just as his press support was being eroded, Haig was now clearly losing long-running debates on British military policy. One of these concerned the reinforcement of the Italian front. At the urging of General Cadorna, the Italian chief of staff, for much of 1917, Lloyd George had been keen to despatch British heavy guns and gunners to Italy. Haig had nothing but contempt for his Italian allies, with whom he fortunately had very few dealings. He and Robertson had resisted such a move. Robertson had at one stage indicated that he would treat the matter as a resignation issue.[16] On 24–25 October, however, an Austro-German breakthrough at Caporetto had transformed the situation, precipitating a crisis on the Italian front and raising the prospect of Italy's imminent collapse.[17] In response to Italian pleas the French despatched four divisions to Italy on 31 October and the War Cabinet ordered Haig to send two good divisions under an effective corps commander. Haig, complaining that this would jeopardise his Flanders operations, nevertheless obeyed orders, deciding to send the 23rd and 41st divisions under the Earl of Cavan, an exceptionally fine commander. The first of these troops started to entrain for their journey from Flanders to Italy on 1 November.[18]

This was far from the end of the matter. Six days later Haig was ordered to find further divisions for Italy and to release Plumer, with such of his Second Army staff as he wished to take, to assume command of the British forces in that theatre. Plumer did not want to go. Indeed, he was most upset by the whole business, thinking his transfer to a relatively minor theatre effectively a demotion. In his diary Haig asked rhetorically: "Was ever an Army commander and his staff sent off to another theatre in the middle of a battle?"[19] It was doubtless especially irritating that Lloyd George had picked Plumer, who had played such a major part in the

Flanders fighting, for Italy rather than another Army commander. But to suggest that this was "the middle of a battle" was really nonsense. Third Ypres, because of the condition of the ground and the exhaustion and general demoralisation of the troops, had almost run its course.

The establishment of a Supreme War Council was another, related issue on which, in early November 1917, the War Cabinet overruled Haig. The ostensible purpose of setting up such a body was to co-ordinate Allied strategy, but, in Lloyd George's mind, the actual motive was to wrest control of the British strategy from Robertson and Haig. Robertson's absence in Italy (where he was reviewing the strategic situation in the aftermath of Caporetto) in late October may have made it easier for Lloyd George to get his way on this issue in the War Cabinet.[20] On the morning of Sunday 4 November, Lloyd George, who was on his way to an inter-Allied conference at Rapallo in Italy, met Haig in Paris and asked his views on the Supreme War Council issue. Haig responded that

the proposal had been considered for 3 years and each time had been rejected as unworkable. I gave several reasons why I thought it could not work, and that it would add to our difficulties to have such a body. The PM then said the two Governments had decided to form it. So I said there is no need saying any more then!

Despite the evident fact that his opinion on this important matter was being brushed aside, it is not clear that Haig realised just how much political difficulty he was now in. Indeed, during the meeting with Lloyd George on 4 November, he seems, from his own account, to have been in a vivacious, rather cocky mood. He thought that "LG is feeling that his position as PM is shaky and means to try to vindicate his conduct of the war in the eye of the public and try to put the people against the soldiers!" Apparently not at all intimidated, Haig "gave LG a good talking to on several of the questions he raised, and felt he got the best of the arguments". At about 12 o'clock Lloyd George asked Haig to go for a walk. They went up the Champs Elysées to the Arc de Triomphe. Despite his past disputes with the Welshman and the deepening crisis in their present relations, Haig was not totally impervious to the Lloyd George charm. He was prepared to admit that the Prime Minister could be quite "a pleasant little man when one has him alone".[21]

In a discussion with Robertson, Plumer and members of the GHQ staff on 10 November Haig continued, as he had with Lloyd George six days earlier, to argue against further despatches of troops to the Italian front. He doubted that sending twenty British or French divisions could save Italy whereas forces of that size could make all the difference on the Western Front. He "pointed out the importance of the Belgian coast to

Great Britain" and wanted to ensure that "nothing should be done to stop our offensive next spring".[22] This statement indicates both Haig's poor appreciation of the grand strategic situation (in which the initiative was fast slipping into German hands) and an inadequate understanding of just how isolated and precarious his own and Robertson's positions were becoming and of how far power to direct the war effort was slipping from their grasp. By mid-November Haig had lost five divisions to Plumer's command in Italy. Three others were put on warning to go if needed. This obviously represented a massive actual diminution, and an even greater potential diminution, of the combat power available to Haig on the Western Front.[23]

At the same time an inter-Allied conference at Rapallo saw the formal launch of the Supreme War Council. On Wednesday 7 November, hearing this matter had been introduced without his agreement, Robertson had walked out in protest. After the conference, Lloyd George travelled back to London in stages. He stopped briefly at Aix-les-Bains, where, assisted by Hankey, and perhaps emboldened by Allenby's recent victory in Palestine, he wrote one of his most dramatic speeches of the war. He delivered it in the banqueting hall of the French War Ministry at Rue St Dominique in Paris on Monday 12 November, at a lunch given in his honour by Painlevé, the French Prime Minister. Lloyd George spoke in English, a language which most of his immediate listeners could not understand. His true target audience was the British people, to whom he appealed over the heads of Haig and Robertson. He went to some trouble to ensure that copies of the speech were very quickly conveyed to the British press. It was both a defence of the need for the Supreme War Council and an attack on the conduct of the war on the Western Front. Attributing the Central Powers' major successes against Serbia, Romania and Italy to lack of co-ordination amongst the Allies, he contrasted them with the limited gains made on the Western Front. He admitted that there had been great Allied victories in that theatre of war, but said that when he looked at the "appalling casualty lists" he wished it had not "been necessary to win so many".[24]

This was, of course, a scarcely concealed attack on Haig's professional competence. Yet the results indicate the limited strength of Lloyd George's position, even at this stage of his premiership. The speech created something of a sensation in the press, but its reception both there and amongst his political colleagues was mixed.[25] Most senior ministers supported him, but Carson publicly repudiated the Prime Minister's comments and Derby assured Haig of his "entire confidence". If Haig was concerned by the Prime Minister's attack he put a remarkably brave face on it. He considered that "LG has put the bulk of right thinking people against him," that the country would "never forgive him" and that his government might not last "another six weeks".[26]

Planning the Cambrai offensive

While the rows over Italy, the Supreme War Council and the Lloyd George speech were in progress, Haig had, despite the lateness of the season, been planning another major offensive on the Western Front. It is, indeed, possible that some of his confident and assertive attitude with regard to Lloyd George in the first half of November was owing to a gambler's faith that his last throw of 1917 would result in a big win.

Like most of the major British Western Front offensives before 1918, Cambrai had a somewhat complex genesis. Today it is generally remembered as the first "tank battle", and some historians, influenced by the writings of the military theorist and gifted author Lieutenant-Colonel J. F. C. Fuller, then a senior staff officer at the Tank Corps' Bermicourt headquarters, have, quite understandably, looked to that corps for its genesis.[27] Because of the heavy rain and the state of the ground after 31 July, Fuller and other senior Tank Corps officers seem to have decided, early in August, that tanks were going to be able to play little useful role in the Flanders fighting. They began to conceive schemes for their use in other parts of the front. In particular, Fuller developed the idea of large-scale "tank raids". As with normal trench raids, Fuller did not intend that these should lead to any permanent gain of ground. The aim was to inflict loss on the Germans, keeping them in state of anxiety and making it difficult for them to withdraw troops from the British sector of the Western Front for use elsewhere. The concept was, however, of dubious practicality and merit and, despite Fuller's assertions, it is not clear that it had much connection with the origin of the Third Army offensive that became the Battle of Cambrai.[28]

The basic concept of operations for that battle appears to have developed within General Sir Julian Byng's Third Army. In June 1917, two months after his striking success at Vimy, Byng had very reluctantly left the Canadian Corps to take over the Third Army from Allenby, who was going to the Middle East. Third Army's front was soon extended to the right to take over what had been the Fourth Army area. Rawlinson, as we have seen, moved up to Flanders to take command of the proposed coastal operations there. Byng's Third Army thus became a very large organisation comprising five corps and having a "ration strength" of some 629,408 men. Byng's role for the next few months was not, however, to be a glamorous one. Third Army's front became a quiet sector in which tired divisions which had been through the bloody mills of Arras and

Third Ypres were sent to recover. Byng, however, tried to prevent these divisions lapsing into passivity and inertia by a policy of carefully planned raids and he always had bigger operations under active consideration.[29]

When he took over in the Cambrai sector Byng inherited a plan developed under Fourth Army's aegis. In the middle of the Arras battle, on 25 April, Haig had ordered Fifth and Fourth Armies to devise a scheme for breaking the German Hindenburg Line defences south-west of the city of Cambrai. This might have complemented the efforts of First and Third Armies further north. At the time Haig gave this instruction, however, the Fourth Army was still trying to fight its way forward to the Hindenburg Line and it was not possible to give the idea immediate effect. Planning for an operation in this area was eventually delegated to Lieutenant-General Pulteney of III Corps, who submitted a plan to Byng's headquarters on 19 June. By that stage an attack in the Cambrai sector could only be a diversion from the larger efforts proposed in Flanders. The Hindenburg Line fortifications were formidable and caution had clearly been Pulteney's watchword. Probably drawing lessons from Third Army's poorly planned, ineffective follow-up of its break-in of 9 April, he proposed a steady, step-by-step advance that the official historian was to dismiss as "leisurely".[30] Byng was apparently unimpressed with the Pulteney scheme and did not pursue it.

According to the official history, during a visit to GHQ on 4 August, Brigadier-General Hugh Elles of the Tank Corps made proposals for offensive operations in the Cambrai sector. Davidson showed some interest. But ultimately GHQ proved too preoccupied with the Ypres operations to encourage the idea and it was dropped, at least for the time being.[31] The true father of the scheme for a major surprise attack in the Cambrai direction in the autumn of 1917 appears to have been Brigadier-General H. H. Tudor, who commanded the artillery of the 9th (Scottish) Division, holding a sector of the IV Corps front on Third Army's left. Tudor believed that taking advantage of innovations in artillery technique, it was possible to mount a surprise attack on the Hindenburg Line in the Cambrai sector. Tudor intended that a preliminary artillery bombardment should be forgone, though the infantry would be supported with an intense barrage and counter-battery work from zero hour. But even without a preliminary bombardment, the new artillery batteries moved into a particular sector for an offensive would make it very difficult to achieve surprise. Batteries could, of course, be moved in at night and carefully camouflaged before daybreak. But "registration" (the process of getting a battery properly oriented to its surroundings so that it could shoot accurately) normally involved the firing of observed ranging shots. The registration of a significant number of batteries would be difficult to conceal and would indicate to the enemy that an attack was imminent.

The most innovative aspect of Tudor's proposal was its reliance on the "silent" registration of batteries new to the sector by the use of maps, advanced survey techniques and a certain amount of physics and mathematics. Combined with other measures to achieve secrecy, silent registration and the forgoing of a preliminary artillery bombardment could, theoretically, allow a high degree of surprise to be achieved. What Tudor envisaged was essentially a surprise attack by the superior force of infantry supported, from zero hour, by intense artillery fire. But the use of a large number of tanks was always a vital element in the scheme. What made it so were the massive belts of barbed wire integral to the Hindenburg Line system. Without a lengthy preliminary bombardment the artillery could not cut these adequately, and without tanks the momentum of the infantry attack would be killed.[32] Tudor discussed his ideas with Brigadier-General De Pree, the chief of staff at IV Corps, and they evolved into a IV Corps plan which Lieutenant-General Sir Charles Woollcombe, the corps commander, presented to Third Army on 23 August. Tudor had apparently been more ambitious, but, as it emerged from IV Corps, the proposal was for a limited (single corps) attack employing three divisions, two cavalry brigades and eight field artillery brigades, plus the Third Army heavy artillery and an unspecified number of tanks. The idea was merely to seize a section of the main Hindenburg Line and its support system between the Canal Du Nord and the St Quentin Canal and to hold it against counter-attacks.[33]

Byng was interested in the idea and, between 29 August and 26 September, Brigadier-General Hugh Elles of the Tank Corps made three visits to Third Army's HQ to discuss it. Elles was keen because, in contrast with Flanders, the Cambrai sector had many advantages from the tank point of view. It was essentially a chalk down land, rolling and quite well drained. Having been a quiet sector, the ground was also relatively intact, not too pockmarked by big shell craters that might impede tanks. The thick grass over much of the prospective battlefield was likely to prove an aid to tank traction. Havrincourt Wood was ideally placed as a forming up position for tanks near the German front and there was still enough undergrowth to help hide them. Elles's enthusiasm appears to have encouraged Byng to expand the plan. Though the German fortifications of the approaches to Cambrai were formidable enough, German troops were relatively thin on the ground. There were only two divisions in the sector Byng was considering attacking and his intelligence officers reckoned it would take some forty-eight hours for other forces to reach the area. If, therefore, the two German divisions in line were to be overwhelmed quickly, considerable opportunities for exploitation might open up. Byng, himself a cavalryman, apparently imagined the Cavalry Corps sweeping north-east from the vicinity of Havrincourt and Marcoing, taking Cambrai and capturing bridges over the River Sensee to the north.

Third Army sent plans on these lines to GHQ on two occasions in September. On the first occasion Kiggell encouraged Byng to work up the plan in as much detail as possible, but indicated that GHQ was still preoccupied with operations in Flanders.[34] On the second occasion, on 16 September, Byng came to GHQ in person with a plan worked up in the detail requested. He wanted the five divisions he intended to use for the attack, each of which was short of about 3,000 infantry, to be brought up to full strength. Haig, despite the preparations in progress to renew the Flanders offensive, said that he would do what he could and sent Davidson to Third Army the following day to discuss details.[35] On Saturday 13 October Haig gave definite approval for the offensive. The following Monday Byng came to lunch at GHQ. Haig and Byng reviewed the plan in some detail, and arrangements were made for the infantry reinforcements to be delivered to Third Army and for a start to be made on training the divisions designated to take part in the attack to co-operate with tanks.[36]

On 26 October Byng briefed his corps commanders on the plan as it then existed. The objectives aimed at were remarkably ambitious:
(1) To break the enemy's front by a surprise attack with the aid of tanks.
(2) To pass cavalry though.
(3) To seize Cambrai, Bourlon Wood and the crossings of the Sensée River, cutting off German troops between the river and the Canal du Nord.
(4) To continue the advance northeast, rolling up the German front from the south.

After the initial break-in, the next step would be to seize crossings over the St Quentin Canal at Masnieres and Marcoing and then take a substantial German defensive position called the Masnières-Beaurevoir Line, behind the canal. Cavalry was to cross the canal once Masnieres and Marcoing had been secured. It would then carry out a wide range of tasks including the capture of Bourlon Wood, which stood on the high ground of the Bourlon Ridge, the city of Cambrai itself and the crossings over the River Sensée.[37]

Byng had made his reputation with the meticulously planned "bite and hold" operation on Vimy Ridge. He had subsequently continued to advocate methodical attacks with limited objectives.[38] This somewhat grandiose scheme for an offensive towards Cambrai might thus seem out of character. It might be suspected that, as with Rawlinson's initial plan for the 1916 Somme campaign, Haig had intervened to extend initial objectives he considered too modest. But in the Cambrai case it does not seem to have worked like that. Haig certainly did make suggestions for the modification of Byng's plan and, in the IV Corps sector, this did involve attempting a deeper advance on the first day than Byng originally intended. But Haig's interventions were, in general, designed to adjust the *direction* of the principal advance rather than expand the overall scope of the operation or increase the total amount of ground to be gained on the first day. Haig was, indeed, responding to a plan that was already fairly grandiose. Byng seems to have been excited by the opportunities presented by the combination of the low density of German forces in this sector and the novel methods of attack that now appeared practicable.

On Saturday 3 November, and a week later, when he came down to Third Army headquarters at St Pol, Haig made a number of suggestions for Byng's "consideration". His intention seems to have been to define the operation's purpose more clearly and somewhat to alter the main direction of advance following the initial break-in. The two most significant changes of emphasis in the final Third Army plan as a result were that:

(a) The mission of the Cavalry Corps was fixed as the "isolation" of Cambrai – by enveloping it from the south and east – and the seizure of bridges over the Sensée. The cavalry was not now supposed to seize the town of Cambrai as Byng had originally intended.

(b) It was now stated to be vital that IV Corps should take Bourlon Wood on the first day.

Haig considered Bourlon Wood "infinitely more important" than Cambrai.[39] Byng's biographer indicates that the Third Army commander protested that its capture on Z-day was not feasible, but that Haig "was adamant" on this matter. Byng's protest is not, however, documented in the work concerned and, whilst not intrinsically improbable, cannot be corroborated here. Haig regarded the advances of III Corps and the Cavalry Corps in the Cambrai direction as moves to secure Third Army's eastern flank and to confuse the enemy as to the main direction of the offensive.[40]

What then, from Haig's point of view, was the operation's true purpose? Cambrai was an important communications and transport centre for the Germans, but Haig seems to have regarded it as a secondary objective at best. What was so crucial, in Haig's opinion, about the Bourlon Ridge? What would be the advantage of seizing that if Cambrai itself were to remain, at least in the short term, in German hands? Haig's notes for Byng's "consideration" indicated that the overall object was the clearance of the quadrilateral represented by the Canal du Nord (to the west), the St Quentin Canal (to the east) and the River Sensée (to the north). The southern base of the quadrilateral was the German front line.

German forces within this quadrilateral were to be smashed. This and Haig's view of the role of III Corps and the Cavalry Corps as protection of Third Army's eastern flank indicates that he intended the main direction of advance to be almost due north, not north-east towards Cambrai, as Byng seems initially to have intended. Because of the configuration of the front at this point, Haig apparently considered that, after the capture of the Bourlon Ridge, IV Corps should actually be attacking to the west. V Corps, in Third Army reserve at the start of the battle and consisting of the Guards and the 40th and 59th Divisions, would go through the gap in the German front created by IV Corps and III Corps in their initial attack. Haig apparently hoped that the capture of the Bourlon Ridge would unhinge the German front and enable it to be rolled up, at least as far north as the River Sensée, perhaps as far as Arras.[41]

This concept of operations is open to serious criticism because it is doubtful whether Third Army had the strength to do much in the way of "rolling up". Though it was a formation of some nineteen divisions, all but five of these had been through the bloody mill of Third Ypres at least once and were not in the best condition.[42] Byng's capacity to disrupt any substantial section of the German front was particularly doubtful given that the Third Ypres campaign was closing down and that, with the collapse of Russia, German reinforcements might be expected to be arriving on the Western Front from the east. It is difficult to escape the conclusion that while Third Army was going into this operation using some innovative tactical and operational methods, the plan was overly ambitious. Given the general strategic situation in November 1917, a "bite and hold" type of operation was surely all that was realistic. Haig's much more ambitious concept of operations was, however, largely embodied in a modified version of Third Army's plan, codenamed GY, and issued at 7 a.m. on 13 November 1917.[43]

While developing this ambitious plan, Haig had sent Kiggell to London to plead for the retention of infantry divisions that had been earmarked for Italy. Kiggell was authorised to say that if he could use these divisions, Haig was confident of scoring a significant success on the Western Front. In putting this case, however, Kiggell could not have been helped by Haig's insistence on keeping the nature of the operation a complete secret. Lloyd George was predictably unimpressed and the Kiggell mission accomplished nothing. Haig's suggestion that three divisions could make all the difference in his coming offensive indicates that he thought the Germans still relatively weak on the Western Front overall and that they would be vulnerable if pressed hard. But on 13 November, after Kiggell had returned from London, Haig made a rather different argument for the Cambrai operation. Now closing down the offensive in

Flanders, Haig insisted that the Third Army attack must go ahead, for without it, the Germans, taking advantage of the strength of the Hindenburg Line, would be able to comb out troops from their defensive front and mount an offensive of their own, possibly against the French. That would stop all talk of reinforcements for Italy.[44]

This line of argument implies that Haig considered the Germans now strong enough in the West to be really dangerous to the Allies. That, of course, conflicts with the notion that a successful break-in near the Cambrai offensive might enable Byng's forces to roll up a significant part of the German front. Haig's attempts to justify this offensive thus appear confused and contradictory. Having become fixated upon a particular course of action, he was searching for justifications to pursue it. Even in changed circumstances, when his Flanders campaign had ground to a halt and a substantial part of the British army was being diverted to Italy, he was not prepared to abandon it. An extremely favourable account of his term as commander-in-chief published, at his instigation and with his blessing, soon after the war, comments:

Legends grew over Cambrai, one of these being that it was meant as a rebuke, a sharp lesson to a malcontent civilian power at home not to underrate the skill of the British Army in France.[45]

Perhaps Haig's tame historians protested too much. It seems highly probable that amongst the purposes of the Battle of Cambrai were the restoration of the BEF's morale and self-confidence, the boosting of Haig's and GHQ's prestige, and the administration of a "sharp lesson" to Lloyd George and his political allies. Yet Haig was keen to reassure others that he would behave sensibly if, in its opening stages, the offensive showed no great promise. He reportedly told Byng that, in such circumstances, he was prepared to stop it within forty-eight hours. In a letter of Thursday 15 November, he assured Robertson that "the nature of this operation is such that it can be stopped at once if it appears likely to entail greater losses than I can afford".[46] But he had, of course, given a rather similar assurance to the War Policy Committee with regard to Third Ypres.

Final battle preparations

Haig took a great interest in the preparations for this offensive and was keen to inspire the formations that would make the attack with as much aggression and initiative as possible. Between 12 and 15 November he visited divisions and tank battalions that would take part. On Friday 16 November he held a conference at the IV Corps HQ at Villers au Flos with Byng and Woollcombe, Pulteney and Kavanagh, commanding

IV Corps, III Corps and the Cavalry Corps respectively. Everyone apparently thought the preparations had gone well and had a high degree of confidence in success, or so they told the commander-in-chief.[47]

One aspect of battle preparation that had been conducted with unusual thoroughness was the combined training of tanks and infantry, and tank crews had been given special training in techniques for traversing the extraordinarily large trenches of the Hindenburg Line. Each tank carried a massive fascine (bundles of sticks) that could be dropped into a trench to enable it, and others following in its wake, to cross. The assembly of these fascines, fixing them to the tanks and fitting each tank with a release mechanism to allow the fascine to be dropped at the appropriate moment were major administrative exercises in themselves. The secret concentration of the tanks behind Havrincourt Wood and getting them into their start positions for the offensive was an even more complex undertaking.[48]

On the eve of battle, Monday 19 November, Haig moved to an Advanced GHQ at Bavincourt, about ten miles southwest of Arras.[49] Third Army was due attack on the morrow. The portion of front to be subjected to the main attack was about six-and-a-half miles long, and

15. Preparations for the Battle of Cambrai. A veiw of tank F4. With the permission of The Trustees of the Imperial War Museum, London.

stretched from a point two miles northwest of Havrincourt on the left to near Gonnelieu on the right. The principal effort was to be made by two corps: IV Corps on the left and III Corps on the right. Five divisions were to make the main initial assault: from left to right the 62nd and the 51st divisions in IV Corps and the 6th, 20th and 12th in III Corps. To the left of the 62nd Division, the 36th Division was to mount a supporting attack on the western bank of the Canal du Nord. It was to use only one brigade (the 109th), would have no tanks and would start later than the others, at 8.35 a.m. Its important, but subsidiary, mission was to prevent German flanking fire from the western bank interfering with the 62nd Division's operations on the east.[50] There were also to be some subsidiary attacks mounted as diversions by VI Corps on the left of the main thrust and by VII Corps to its right.[51]

The command arrangements for the cavalry divisions were somewhat complicated. The 1st Cavalry Division, commanded by Major-General Richard Mullens, came under the orders of IV Corps. Its mission was to take advantage of IV Corps' penetration of the Hindenburg Line, to move up on to the Bourlon Ridge and take the village of Bourlon from the north and east, before rejoining the Cavalry Corps. The 2nd and 5th Cavalry Divisions remained under the control of Cavalry Corps, commanded by Lieutenant-General Charles Kavanagh. The 5th Cavalry Division was supposed to lead the advance. It would cross the St Quentin Canal, isolate Cambrai, seize the crossings over the River Sensée and offer protection for Third Army's eastern flank. The Lucknow Brigade from the 4th Cavalry Division came under the control of III Corps. In combination with III Corps' integral cavalry regiment, it was to cross the canal south of Masnières and make a raid towards Walincourt. The 3rd Cavalry Division and two brigades of the 4th Cavalry Division would remain in reserve.[52]

A total of 1,003 artillery pieces were to support the attack. As planned, there had been no preliminary artillery bombardment and there was no registration shooting by the artillery. Yet the guns were critically important. They were to undertake two main roles: counter-battery fire against the German artillery and a barrage to support the tank-infantry advance. The latter was not the "creeping" barrage that had become standard by this point in the war. (A "creeper" advanced in very short steps of fifty or 100 yards, and was meant to go slowly enough for the infantry to "hug" it all the way to their objective.) Instead, a seemingly old-fashioned "lifting barrage" was employed, moving, in considerably bigger jumps, from one German defensive position to the next.[53]

The reasons for this are not spelled out in the Royal Artillery's history, but may be surmised. First, given the absence of normal registration shooting, the accuracy of the guns was bound to be somewhat reduced.[54]

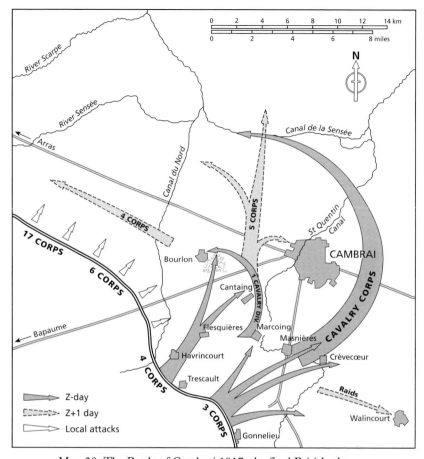

Map 20. The Battle of Cambrai 1917: the final British plan

It would thus have been more than usually dangerous for infantry to "hug" a creeping barrage in the normal manner. Secondly, in order to crush the wire, it was necessary that tanks moved forward in front of the infantry attack. Leaving "lanes" in the barrage, as had been done in the Battle of Flers-Courcelette, on 15 September 1916, had not proved to be a good system and there were so many tanks involved in leading the attack of 20 November that the barrage would have had too many holes in it to be effective. Thus the great belts of fire delivered by the artillery moved further ahead of the attacking infantry than was usual at this period of the war. A feature of 20 November, which was becoming a characteristic of British methods more generally, was the use of a great deal of smoke shell.[55] This would make tanks less vulnerable to direct artillery fire from any German gunners not suppressed by the counter-battery effort.

The Germans about to be attacked belonged to the 13th Corps, also known as "Caudry Group", commanded by General Freiherr von Watter. The corps was part of General von der Marwitz's Second Army, which formed the left wing of Prince Rupprecht's Army Group. Von Watter had the 9th Reserve Division, the 54th Division and the 20th Landwehr Division under command. Only the 54th Division and elements of the 20th Landwehr directly and immediately faced the five British infantry divisions, which would open the attack that morning. The 20th Landwehr Division was due for relief. An important fact of which the British were not immediately aware was that, on 19 November, the 107th Division, which was to carry out the relief, began to arrive in Cambrai from Russia.

How far were these forces expecting the British offensive? Prince Rupprecht had apparently warned OHL (German GHQ) on 18 November that, having failed in Flanders, the British might mount limited attacks elsewhere on the front. This was obviously only a vague warning, not very useful in an operational sense. Prisoners taken in a raid against the 36th (Ulster) Division the same day told their captors that the British were preparing an attack in the Havrincourt area. The Germans, however, seem to have perceived this as a local threat. The 54th Division's troops were placed on alert, but apparently not the other German divisions in the area.

Given how much the success of this particular attack depended on surprise, it was worrying that German artillery began to shell the Havrincourt sector quite fiercely at about 4 a.m. The waiting forces of IV Corps naturally feared that this might be a deliberate attempt to disrupt their attack. But it was not particularly accurate or effective and was over by 5.30. If the personnel of the German 54th Division thought they might be attacked that morning, they seem to have had no conception of the scale of what was coming. In the concealment of their preparations the British had been fortunate as well as careful. During the ten days prior to Tuesday 20 November there had been a good deal of fog and this was prevalent on the morning of the attack. Even more than the large RFC presence, this prevented effective German aerial reconnaissance. At Zero hour it was also still quite dark. A varying combination of darkness, fog and artillery smoke, therefore, provided cover for tanks and infantry in the early stages of the attack.

Z-day: 20 November 1917

The offensive started at 6.20 a.m. There were some 150 German guns in the area, but most of the batteries had been located by the British and were deluged by counter-battery fire. Practically across the whole front initial resistance was quite feeble.[56] In IV Corps, 36th (Ulster) Division played its role in protecting the left flank of the main attack by its actions west of the canal. The most successful division that day was the 62nd (West Riding) Division on the left of the main attacking force. By the end of the day, it had taken the village of Graincourt and got as far as the Bapaume–Cambrai road: an advance distance of about four miles from its start line.

However, the 51st Highland Division, on the right of IV Corps, was not so successful. Advancing north-east on an axis that would take it between Havrincourt and Ribecourt, it overran the outpost line and the main Hindenburg Line without much difficulty. But it hit problems in the Hindenburg Support System in the vicinity of the village of Flesquières. The village was strongly held by three battalions of infantry and two machine gun companies, backed by field artillery. The field artillery of the German 54th Division had been specially trained to engage tanks, having faced French models during the Nivelle offensive. The British artillery's smoke barrage had ceased at 8.35 a.m., leaving the tanks conspicuous targets and a high proportion of those supporting the British 51st Division were knocked out before they were able to crush paths through the wire. By about 10.45 a.m. the 51st Division's advance was checked and by noon it was completely stalled. Its infantry faced intact wire covered by machine guns. The division made attempts to renew the advance in the afternoon by outflanking Flesquières, but due to communications failures, confusion and perhaps a lack of enterprise and initiative in some quarters these failed. Flesquières remained in German hands when night fell.[57]

III Corps' advance suffered no such serious check until it reached the Canal de l'Escaut. The 6th Division secured Ribecourt and the Premy Chapel Ridge. Its lead tanks entered Marcoing at 11.30 and, with the help of tanks and infantry of the 20th Division to its right, it had control of the village by about 1 p.m. The main bridge at Marcoing was intact, but the Beaurevoir Line immediately behind it was staunchly defended. The 20th Division took Rue Vertes on the left side of the canal. But the main bridge across the canal to Masnières, apparently already damaged when the British arrived, was wrecked when a tank tried to cross it. There were some smaller footbridges. Infantry of the 20th Division crossed on these and began the fight for Masnières. But the Germans in that village resisted stubbornly. Meanwhile the 12th Division captured the Lateau Wood ridge to secure the right flank. The mission of the 29th Division (a reserve for III Corps) was to cross the canal at Marcoing and Masnières and take the Beaurevoir Line on the far side. The division advanced at

10.15 a.m. Elements of it did cross at Marcoing, but the stubborn defence of the Beaurevoir Line meant that little further progress was made on 20 November. Other elements of the 29th Division joined troops of the 20th Division in the fight for Masnières, but it was not cleared until the following day.[58]

The performance of the cavalry divisions, which, with very few exceptions, achieved nothing useful, was perhaps the most disappointing aspect of the day. The greatest opportunities were available to the Major-General Mullen's 1st Cavalry Division, which, in the early afternoon, might have had an almost clear run through Cantaing to Bourlon. In reality only tiny fragments of the division made any contribution to the day's fighting. This was partly owing to failures of communication. IV Corps had no system for sending radio messages to 1st Cavalry Division headquarters but had to relay them through the Cavalry Corps HQ. A message received at IV Corps from 51st Division falsely claimed that Flesquières had been captured and wasted the time and effort of part of the 1st Cavalry Division trying to get through there. But there were better opportunities elsewhere and there was a widespread feeling that it was owing to weak leadership and lack of initiative in the division that they were not seized.

The other cavalry divisions did little better. A small force of Canadian cavalry (the Fort Garry Horse of the 5th Cavalry Division) did get across the Canal de l'Escaut on an improvised bridge at a canal lock south of Masnières. At that point the Beaurevoir Line was relatively weakly held and the Canadian horsemen were able to inflict considerable losses on the German troops that they did encounter. But the Canadians suffered very heavy casualties in relation to their numbers and, lacking reinforcements, they were compelled to withdraw. By 5.30 p.m. on 20 November Byng had decided that the 5th and 2nd Cavalry Divisions should be pulled back from the Canal (where, because of the steep banks, it was difficult for them to water their horses) to the Fins-Villers Faucon area. For the time being he left 1st Cavalry Division with IV Corps.[59]

By evening on Tuesday 20 November 1917 Third Army had counted over 4,000 prisoners and had taken about 100 German guns. It had achieved a maximum advance of about four miles and its casualties were relatively light. This good news reached England very quickly. In some places church bells were rung in a celebration of victory. But the achievement of 20 November, though real enough, was limited. There had been practically no exploitation east of the Canal de l'Escaut. The Bourlon Ridge was still in German hands. The chances of achieving much more were diminishing by the hour, as the Germans recovered from their surprise and started to rush reinforcements to the area. There having been no cavalry exploitation, Cambrai was still in German hands, as were the railways leading to it. Much of the attack's initial momentum was spent. The troops who had mounted it were inevitably tired. As usually happened after a major attack, infantry–artillery co-ordination was now somewhat ragged and, according to the official history, only about 179 of the 378 fighting tanks available on the morning of 20 November were immediately capable of continuing the battle.[60]

Having visited Byng at Albert during the afternoon, in most respects Haig had a good picture of the situation on the Cambrai battlefield that evening. He was generally pleased, making little comment on the failure to break out east of the Canal or the lack of cavalry exploitation south and east of Cambrai. His main concern was for exploitation northward, onto the Bourlon Ridge.[61] The orders Byng issued that night amounted to a simple "press on". III Corps was to continue to try to take the Beaurevoir Line and IV Corps to take Flesquières that night and secure Bourlon as early as possible the following day. V Corps, tasked with exploitation northward, beyond Bourlon Ridge, would probably remain in reserve until noon. If the opportunity for cavalry exploitation towards Cambrai existed, it should be taken.[62]

The future development of the battle was likely to depend on the two sides' relative reinforcement and on the first day Haig sent a telegram to Robertson demanding that he be allowed to hold on to two divisions earmarked for Italy: the 47th and the 2nd. Strangely, however, he refused a pressing offer of French help. Pétain had apparently been excited at the possibility of taking part in this attack as soon as he heard that it was being planned. There had been a small Franco-British conference on 19 September, and with no real encouragement from Haig, Pétain had entrained French troops and sent them in the Cambrai direction. On the morning of 20 November they detrained at Péronne and waited upon events. But by 4.30 p.m. on 20 November Haig decided that there was no room for French troops in the attack sector and sent a message to Pétain to leave them where they were.[63]

Continuing the offensive

The tired troops of the British Third Army made only moderate progress on Wednesday 21 November. The Germans having withdrawn, Major-General Harper's 51st Highland Division was able to occupy Flesquières during the night of 20–21 November. The 62nd Division, with some help from the 51st, took Anneux. The 51st Division got into Fontaine and the 1st Cavalry Division took Noyelles. Byng sent the Guards Division and the 40th Division to reinforce the IV Corps in its drive on the Bourlon ridge and the government decided to allow Haig to retain, for the time being, the 47th and 2nd Divisions earmarked for Italy.[64]

There were, therefore, legitimate sources of encouragement for Haig on 21 November 1917. But there were also signs of trouble. Most of the high ground of the Bourlon Ridge that Haig so desperately wanted to take was still in German hands. Haig knew that night that the German 107th Division, recently arrived from Russia, was on the battlefield. It had counter-attacked between Rumilly and Masnieres earlier in the day. The British cavalry having failed to cut railway communications to Cambrai, there was nothing to stop further German reinforcements coming in. The battle was now two days old, and during the planning process, the forty-eight-hour time frame had been regarded as crucial. Yet, contrary to the spirit of the assurances he had given to Robertson before it began, Haig showed no sign of permitting this offensive to be terminated. There is no hard evidence that Byng asked permission to do so, but with Haig physically present in the battle area and touring Third Army's corps and divisional headquarters as he did on Thursday 22 November, Byng was bound to feel his freedom of action was curtailed.[65]

By the evening 22 November, the 62nd Division, which had almost reached the edge of Bourlon Wood, was nearing exhaustion. The 40th Division was to relieve it during the night, before attacking Bourlon Wood the following morning. Seeing no opportunity for cavalry action, Woollcombe, the IV Corps commander, had decided to withdraw the 1st Cavalry Division. By nightfall Haig knew that German resistance was now much stronger than it had been on 20 November and appreciated that time was not on his side. Yet he still did not stop the battle. Instead, when he saw Byng at 5 p.m. that evening, he

urged capturing Bourlon Wood *tomorrow*. If we did not get it tomorrow, it would be harder to take the next day and in view of the demands made on me for Italy I could not continue a wasting fight. I also told him about the cavalry division being withdrawn and he said that he would see to it that the division was sent forward for tomorrow's attack.[66]

IV Corps attacked at 10.30 a.m. on Friday 23 November. The 40th Division, in the centre, pushed through Bourlon Wood and into the Bourlon village immediately behind it. The 36th (Ulster) Division and the 51st (Highland) Division offered support on the left and right flanks respectively. About 120 tanks took part. In a remarkable feat of arms the 40th Division gained its objectives (at least for the time being) and the 36th Division took Tadpole Copse, near Moeuvres, west of the Canal du Nord. But the 51st Division and tanks met furious resistance in Fontaine. The failure to secure it was serious in that it left the right flank of the 40th Division in Bourlon Wood exposed and overlooked from higher ground.[67] During the night the 40th Division lost much of Bourlon village and, on Friday 24 November, German attacks into Bourlon Wood, especially from the Fontaine direction, became frequent and furious. Haig was still discussing the possibility of cavalry exploitation beyond Bourlon village, but in so doing was losing touch with the reality of the battle.

The extent to which Haig was taking over direction of Third Army's battle and the unhealthy degree to which he was fixated on the Bourlon Ridge are evident from his diary entry for that day:

I directed Kiggell to inform Byng that he must devote all his strength and, if necessary the reserve divisions at his disposal in establishing our position on the Bourlon ridge, and retaking it if lost.[68]

The dubious wisdom of Haig's demand that Byng's devote "all his strength", including reserves, to the Bourlon Ridge, soon became apparent. Even in the absence of hard intelligence, it was logical to suppose that, with no battles in progress anywhere else on the Western Front and with the Eastern Front practically defunct, the Germans would be rushing reserves to Cambrai. Haig accepted that Germans were now strong around Bourlon Wood. Given the frequency and violence of the counter-attacks, he could hardly do otherwise. But he insisted that they were weak everywhere else. On Tuesday 27 November he recorded in his diary:

Charteris reported no change in Enemy on Cambrai battle front since yesterday. His troops are very thin on this front except at Bourlon. In fact the situation is most favourable for us but unfortunately I have not got the necessary number of troops to exploit our success.

Haig had refused Pétain's offer of French troops on 20 November and he gave no sign of reversing that decision now. But given the shortage of British troops, he began to accept that, though the situation on the battlefield was still potentially "most favourable" from the British point of view, there was little to be gained from continuing the offensive. After unavailing attempts to secure the villages of Bourlon and Fontaine by the 62nd Division and the Guards Division, respectively, on the morning of Tuesday 27 November, Byng halted his attacks. Haig's diary for the following day, however, demonstrates an extraordinary inability to comprehend the strategic outlook. He thought that the Allies' offensives of 1917 had seriously weakened the Germans, that they were "very short of men" and that the Allies could and should resume the offensive on a large scale next year. Haig seems to have had very little comprehension of the radical change in Germany's favour of the balance of forces on the Western Front, which, as a result of the collapse of Russia, was already under way.[69]

16. A British Mark IV tank knocked out in Bourlon Wood during the Battle of Cambrai. With the permission of The Trustees of the Imperial War Museum, London.

The German counter-offensive

Haig's notion that the Germans were weak everywhere except around Bourlon was soon shown to be inaccurate. The German Second Army had, indeed, been preparing a counter-offensive for several days. On Friday 30 November fourteen divisions attacked all around the Salient that British efforts since 20 November had created. The counter-offensive was most effective south of the Bourlon Ridge, in the III Corps and VII Corps sectors, and made its greatest inroads from just south of la Vacquerie to a point just east of Epehy. As with the British attack of 20 November, surprise was not quite complete. Lieutenant-General Snow, commanding VII Corps, had noticed unusual activity on his corps' front and expected some sort of attack. He had been in touch with III Corps and with Third Army about it. Major-General Louis Vaughan, Byng's chief of staff, apparently accepted that there was some danger on the front of the 55th Division. But, as with the Germans ten days earlier, no one apparently appreciated the scale of what was coming. Snow did not actually demand reinforcements and Third Army did not send him any until after the attack had started. On the night of 29–30 November, VII Corps appears to have been the only one of Third Army's corps on any special state of alert.

The German counter-offensive began at 7 a.m. Infantry attacks, in some sectors led by specialist storm troops and supported by low-flying aircraft, succeeded brief but very intense artillery bombardments. Major-General Jeudwine's 55th Division in VII Corps was the first to be overrun. Though this division had not hitherto been heavily engaged, its defensive front was stretched dangerously thin. By about 8 a.m. the forward positions of the exhausted 12th and 20th Divisions, which had been in the line since the start of the battle, were also overrun. The villages of Banteux, Gonnelieu, Villers Guislan, la Vacquerie and Gouzeaucourt were lost. In some places British infantry fled in panic and gunners abandoned their guns without even disabling them.

Fortunately Byng still had some reserves at hand, though not all were anything like fresh. He had pulled the Guards Division out of the line after the intense fighting around Fontaine on Tuesday 27 November. Battered as it was, he now threw it, elements of the Cavalry Corps and some tank battalions against the German counter-offensive. The 1st Guards Brigade, which had been at Metz that morning, retook Gouzeaucourt in the early afternoon The 20th Division retook la Vacquerie. These actions helped to stabilise the situation on the southern part of the front. Further north, in the IV Corps sector, the Germans had from the outset met stout resistance and had suffered heavy casualties.[70]

The German intention had been to precipitate a major British collapse by suddenly pinching out the whole salient created since 20 November. Though they had not entirely succeeded, they had administered a very profound shock. Third Army lost well over 7,000 personnel on 30 November, over 6,000 of these as prisoners. The Germans had captured over 150 guns, more, apparently, than the British army had lost on any previous day in its history.[71] The questions this reverse raised about the competence of Haig and GHQ would reverberate for months.[72] Indeed, whatever claims were later made, there is no doubting that the German attack of Friday 30 November came as a big surprise to Haig. Charteris's briefings had in no way alerted him. Even when the counter-offensive was in progress, he was slow to comprehend the seriousness of what was happening.

I motored to Albert and saw General Byng a little before noon. I told him to use his reserves energetically and that I had ordered two divisions to Péronne and 2 others to Bapaume by train *in case* of the Enemy attacking in great strength.[73]

Haig's telling Byng how to use his reserves at this point was quite superfluous. It was no thanks to Haig that he had any. A few days earlier Haig had been encouraging him to commit everything he had to the Bourlon ridge. GHQ now moved in reinforcements from other parts of the front and (finally) asked for French assistance in the event of attacks directed at Fifth army's right. But as usual, there was, on Haig's part, no admission of error. Having earlier convinced himself that the Germans were weak everywhere except at Bourlon, he tried to hold on to that notion in the face of events. He initially refused to believe that the German attack had been "in great strength". All he was prepared to admit was that an attack "in great strength" might later develop. If, moreover, the German attack had not been particularly powerful, it followed that instances of local collapse were owing to incompetence or worse on the part of the routed troops. As we shall see this would indeed become the official version, saving the faces of senior commanders and their staffs.[74]

In his diary for Saturday 1 December Haig noted that:

About 11 o'clock, Charteris brought me copy of captured order showing that Enemy has organised his attack on big lines and is employing about 12 divisions.[75]

It was still an underestimate of the actual scale of the attack and it was now more in the nature of recent history than usable intelligence. It arrived just as Third Army's troops were bringing the German counter-offensive to a halt. There were further German attacks on 2 and 3 December, but these proved costly and made little progress.[76]

Closing it down

Though the German counter-offensive had been largely contained by Monday 3 December, Haig realised that his forces in the Bourlon–Marcoing sector were in an exceptionally exposed salient. He decided to pull them back to the Flesquières Ridge. It was perhaps his best decision of the campaign. It was carried out on the morning of 5 December with little interference from the enemy. Sporadic, sometimes very fierce, fighting continued in the Cambrai sector for several days and Haig was concerned about another big German attack as late as 19 December. This voluntary withdrawal, however, marks the effective end of the Battle of Cambrai.[77]

Assessment

By the end of the battle the British had made no net gain of ground. Yet despite the withdrawal from Bourlon, Third Army in the Flesquières sector was still in a dangerous salient. Third Army had taken 145 German guns but lost 158 of its own. It had captured over 11,000 German prisoners, but over 6,000 of its own personnel became prisoners at the opening of the German counter-offensive. Total British casualties

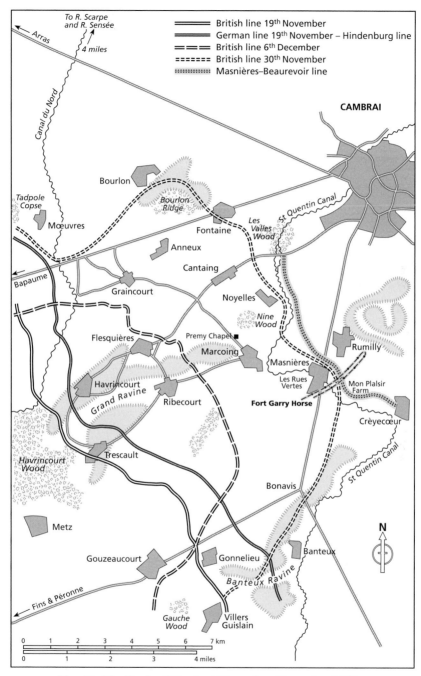

Map 21. The Battle of Cambrai November–December 1917

were about 40,000. Total German casualties are not known, but are likely to have been roughly the same. It is difficult to say who could least afford such losses at this point. That depends whether one is thinking long or short term. It is probable that the balance of advantage in morale lay with the Germans. Very likely an attempt to boost the prestige of Haig and his staff, this offensive had raised hopes, especially at home in Britain, only for these to be cruelly dashed.[78]

Even his greatest admirers have found it difficult to defend Haig's generalship at Cambrai.[79] Certainly he deserves credit for being prepared to use some of the most advanced technology available to mount a novel form of attack. But during the planning his analysis of the strategic situation had been very muddled. During the offensive itself, taking the Bourlon ridge had become an obsession with him, narrowing his vision fatally. Losing sight of the broader picture, he had encouraged Third Army to become dangerously unbalanced and vulnerable to counter-attack. As so often in the last few years, he had misread a battle. As for much of 1917, he had also misread the strategic situation. He thus grossly underestimated the danger of a counter-offensive. It will not do to put all the blame for this on Charteris. Haig knew perfectly well that Charteris was regarded by much of the army as dangerously overoptimistic and that this was an opinion strongly endorsed in the War Office. Yet up to the Battle of Cambrai Haig had consistently refused to replace his intelligence chief. In its aftermath, he would continue to defend and to try to retain him.

An aspect of Cambrai that has received relatively little comment is Haig's treatment of Pétain and the French. For much of the year Haig had been vociferously demanding more offensive action from his allies. When, however, Pétain made French divisions available for the Cambrai operation, Haig turned them down while continuing to complain to his own government of a shortage of troops. While active Franco-British co-operation could be difficult to arrange, in this case Pétain was most willing but Haig apparently reluctant even to try. This tends to reinforce the suspicion that one of the main goals of the Cambrai operation was to boost Haig's and the British army's prestige, and that Haig had no wish to share any glory available with another commander-in-chief and another army. It was only when the Germans unleashed their counter-offensive that Haig demonstrated any real interest in French help: just one example of his extremely questionable decision making during this campaign.

16   The last war winter

The impact of a debacle

Haig's stock was already low by the end of Third Ypres and the brief period of optimism in the early days of the Battle of Cambrai did him no good in the long run. Though reactions were perhaps more muted at the front, at home in Britain the German counter-offensive of Friday 30 November dashed hopes so cruelly that it might have been better if they had not been raised. Those in Parliament who applauded the British army's achievement of Tuesday 20 November, those who trumpeted it in the press and those who rang bells in the churches were all made to look foolish ten days later. For some the disappointment was so extreme as to amount to a sense of betrayal, and that, of course, turned to anger.[1]

At least one historian has suggested that the exaggerated public acclaim for Third Army's limited success on 20 November was far from spontaneous, that it was the result of a political and press campaign by GHQ and the War Office.[2] The detailed workings of any such campaign have never been brought to light, and given the tensions between the two institutions, a co-ordinated effort might have proved difficult. For the record, at least, Charteris poured scorn on the bell ringing.[3] Yet Lloyd George, who was generally astute in such matters, firmly believed that there was massive military manipulation of the media against him at this period.[4] Cheerleading in the opening stages of the Cambrai battle may well have been part of this. Media manipulation is, however, notoriously prone to backfire. Journalists and editors briefed by their military contacts to proclaim victory in the early stages of the Battle of Cambrai would have been reluctant, after 30 November 1917, to trust those contacts ever again. It was, indeed, an independent-minded journalist who pricked the bubble. Philip Gibbs, GHQ-accredited war correspondent of the *Daily Chronicle*, but never a GHQ toady, had happened to be in the Gouzeaucourt area when the German counter-offensive erupted. It was obvious to him that the counter-offensive came as a complete surprise to British troops there. He saw an officer in a field ambulance unit, literally caught with his trousers down, fleeing from his bath dressed in a towel. Gibbs' despatch of Saturday 1 December seems to have been picked up by the War Cabinet.[5]

Ministers were evidently upset to get first news of a serious reverse from the press. Major-General Sir Frederick Maurice, Director of Military Operations at the War Office, reported to them on Monday 3 December. But ministers seem, justly or not, to have regarded the report as tardy and inadequate. Two days later they interrogated Robertson at length. Commenting on the time lag in official reporting, one minister remarked: "If we had inflicted a corresponding reverse on the enemy, the news of our success would have been communicated within a few hours."[6] The War Cabinet was clearly concerned by the apparent failure of intelligence at GHQ. At the Cabinet on Wednesday 5 December, Lloyd George was, Robertson reported, in a foul mood. Haig had constantly insisted that the German army, after the battering it had taken at Third Ypres, was much weakened. He had recently argued for maintaining an offensive policy on the Western Front even though the Germans had moved thirty divisions from the Eastern to the Western Front. According to GHQ intelligence reports, the Germans had so far transferred only a small number of divisions to the West. How, then, had they proved capable of such an aggressive stroke as that of 30 November? Robertson was, as he explained to Haig, unable to answer this to the satisfaction of the statesmen.[7]

Replying to Robertson on Sunday 9 December, Haig wrote:

I gather that the P.M. is dissatisfied. If that means that I have lost his confidence, then in the interests of the cause let him replace me at once. But if he wishes me to remain then all carping criticism should cease, and I should be supported and trusted.[8]

This could be understood as Haig, realising just how vulnerable he had now become, at last adopting a properly submissive attitude to political authority. But it is perhaps more accurately read as a declaration of defiance, as a gamble that Lloyd George still could not be sure of the political support necessary to sack him. Robertson, surely being less than completely frank, replied that, as far as he could see, the War Cabinet had no lack of confidence in Haig personally. It was GHQ's intelligence analysis they mistrusted and it was high time that Charteris was dismissed.[9]

Haig's position was, however, deteriorating faster than either he or Robertson seems to have realised. The apostasy of elements of the press that had once supported him, most notably Lord Northcliffe's empire, was one aspect of this. Haig's personal tactlessness may well have been a factor here. On Friday 7 December the great press baron was at GHQ, where he spoke at length about the mission to the United States from which he had just returned. Haig's boredom was evident and Northcliffe took offence.[10] Perhaps more significantly, Lloyd George finally achieved substantial successes in a long campaign to increase his own influence with the press by getting Rothermere and Northcliffe successively to accept employment in his government. Rothermere took the new Air Ministry. Northcliffe, having very publicly rejected the Air Ministry, the appointment his brother accepted immediately afterwards, quickly accepted responsibility for propaganda aimed at enemy countries.[11]

Whatever the underlying cause, it became clear in December 1917 that *The Times*, long a source of support for Haig, had radically changed its tune. On Wednesday 12 December it sharply criticised GHQ over the reverse of 30 November, concluding that its readers could "no longer be satisfied with the fatuous estimates ... of German losses in men and morale which have 'inspired too many of the published messages from France'". It was clear that *The Times* shared a widespread perception that intelligence analysis was a particular weakness at GHQ. When this added to the a demand for the "prompt removal of every blunderer", it was clear that the knives were out for Charteris, though not for him alone. "Sir Douglas Haig's position cannot but depend", the article continued, "in large measure on his choice of subordinates. His weakness is his inveterate devotion to those who have served him longest – some of them perhaps for too long."[12] Charteris noted that "The attack on D.H. is in full swing. All our information is that L.G., Curzon and Churchill are out to down him, and will do so by attacking his staff."[13]

In a letter to Philip Sassoon, Haig's private secretary, the following day, Northcliffe indicated that in the United Kingdom at that moment:

There is the memory of a dead man or the knowledge of a missing or wounded man in every house. Outside the War Office it is doubtful whether the Higher Command has any supporters whatever.[14]

Charteris was the most immediately vulnerable member of Haig's entourage. When the damning *Times* article appeared he was already under attack from many quarters, including the War Office and the headquarters of major formations in France. Derby had written to Haig on 7 December, indicating that for a long time Charteris had appeared to him "and many others" to take "a quite unjustifiable view of the fighting value of the enemy". He pressed for Charteris's removal. Charteris was himself concerned that "the Government at home was striking [at Haig] through him". He indicated his willingness to go if it would help Haig's position.[15] Haig had a great personal liking for his glib, articulate, somewhat scruffy intelligence chief that suggests the attraction of opposites. He clearly believed Charteris both industrious (which he was) and efficient (which was much more questionable). At one stage Haig had suggested that

Lloyd George was seeking Charteris's downfall not so much because of dissatisfaction with his intelligence work as because he had influence with "correspondents and so with the press and consequently is in LG's way".[16] Haig told Charteris in conversation on Sunday 9 December that he considered the bulk of the criticism directed at him unfair. Haig's estimates of the condition of the enemy were not based solely on Charteris's reports, but also on what he learnt from "Army and subordinate commanders".[17]

Haig must be granted high marks for integrity in the affair of Charteris's removal. He wrote to Derby, on Monday 10 December, in precisely the same terms as he had spoken to Charteris the previous day. It was not reasonable to make his intelligence chief "the whipping boy for the charge of undue optimism brought against myself". Charteris had responsibility for collecting, collating and placing before Haig all information available on the enemy. But the responsibility for views put forward to the War Cabinet was Haig's alone. If the War Cabinet was not satisfied, Haig concluded, "[I]t is I and not Charteris who should answer for those views."[18] This was about as close as Haig ever came to admitting personal responsibility for errors, though even here there was no explicit admission that errors had been made. There was, however, no doubting that Charteris was now a distinct liability for GHQ as a whole. He had lost the confidence not merely of journalists, politicians and the War Office, but of a high proportion of the senior officers in Haig's army. Kiggell told Haig that Charteris, who, as Haig already realised, sometimes seemed arrogant and overbearing to equals and subordinates, was "much disliked in Corps and Armies". Haig was keen that no harm should come to "poor Charteris" and wanted him to be found "another good job", but by mid-December had decided, under irresistible pressure from the War Office, that Charteris should be removed from his intelligence post.[19]

Whether sacrificing Charteris would save Haig was, however, open to doubt. GHQ was under serious attack in the House of Commons. On Friday 12 December John Dillon, leader of the Irish National Party, taking up the article on Cambrai published by *The Times* that morning, wondered why the newspaper had knowledge "denied to members of this house". The Labour MP Jimmy Thomas, by no means unpatriotic and certainly not an opponent of the war, thought that "the blunders of the people at the top" were not dealt with in the same way as those of the people at the bottom. Bonar Law tried to answer on behalf of the government, but he himself had never had much confidence in Haig and appears not have been very effective. He blamed the sense of dismay that followed the reverse of 30 November "on the exaggerated hopes with which the initial success at Cambrai was greeted in this country". But an Irish heckler demanded to know who was responsible for these exaggerated hopes. Bonar Law tried to give an impression of War Cabinet calm and confidence that was actually far from the truth, yet he conceded a "full official enquiry".[20]

This concession, however, did not end parliamentary disquiet. On Wednesday 17 December, one MP asked on whose authority flags were displayed and church bells were rung to celebrate victory at Cambrai. Bonar Law denied that the War Cabinet was behind it. This, of course, suggested some branch of the military authorities. A couple of days later, Josiah Wedgwood, an independent MP who had served at Gallipoli and in France, had been wounded and had won the DSO, accused Haig by name of "super-optimism" and an "absurd" obsession with cavalry. Wedgwood's doubts about Haig's generalship considerably antedated 30 November 1917: "If there is going to be an inquiry into Cambrai", he suggested, "it is ten times more reasonable to have an inquiry into Passchendaele."[21]

The Cambrai inquests and the purge of Haig's staff

The whole management of the British war effort was now in crisis. Having played a key role in the establishment of the Supreme War Council, Lloyd George thought he could finally wrest control of strategy from Robertson and Haig. On 11 December, the day before the attack on GHQ appeared in *The Times*, Lloyd George had suggested to Derby that both should be removed. Lloyd George wanted to use the combination of Haig's failure at Cambrai and Allenby's recent success in Palestine to show to the public that the strategy for which he had been arguing was correct, and that Robertson's and Haig's obsessive focus on the Western Front was wrong. In order to avoid political crisis, however, each should be given a high-sounding but meaningless job, much as the French government had done with Joffre. Derby refused this suggestion, implying that he would resign if Lloyd George forced the issue. Derby was, however, prepared to remove several of Haig's most important subordinates whom the War Office now regarded as liabilities.[22]

In terms of the efficiency of the British war effort, it seems reasonable to suggest that a purge of Haig's entourage was long overdue. Derby and Robertson had probably not acted earlier for fear of precipitating a break-down in their relations with the commander-in-chief. But the situation was now so critical that action could no longer be delayed. Haig, in turn, seems (rather gradually) to have realised that accepting the dismissal of some of his closest associates was the bare minimum price of his continuance in command. Robertson came out to GHQ on Saturday 15 December. He pressed Haig to deliver a full report on Cambrai as soon as possible. At the same time he got to work removing those at GHQ that he and Derby considered inadequate. Charteris was at the top of the War Office "hit-list" and Haig was now ready to make that sacrifice. But at this stage in the post-Cambrai crisis Robertson went for a softer target, persuading Haig to remove his long-serving Quartermaster-General Sir Ronald Maxwell. Maxwell was now nearly sixty-five. Derby and Robertson had apparently long doubted that he was equal to his task. Control of transportation (once his main function) had already been taken away from him, after the BEF's logistics came close to collapse in 1916. Haig informed Maxwell of the decision to remove him on 16 December.[23] A week later Lieutenant-General Sir Travers Clark took his post.[24]

Snowdrifts and ice, which were making mail delivery difficult, resulted in Byng's telephoning his preliminary report on Cambrai to GHQ on 17 December. Third Army's enquiry into the events of 30 November was not yet complete, but Byng's preliminary findings were that there had been no surprise, that Third Army had expected the attack for days and that no general (or even senior) officer was to blame. In what became the most notorious passage of his report he continued:

I attribute the reason for the local success on the part of the enemy to one cause and one alone, namely – lack of training on the part of junior officers and NCO's and men.[25]

For a British general publicly to blame the quality of his troops for a battle-field reverse was extraordinary. With regard to the German counter-attack at Cambrai it seems to a large extent unreasonable and unjust. Doubtless there were mistakes and failures of nerve at junior levels. But the primary responsibility lay, as we have seen, much higher up the chain of command. At GHQ, a staff officer apparently somewhat watered down Byng's wording before passing his report to the War Office. Yet the essence of what Byng had written soon became common knowledge and caused some disgust. Efforts by an able and admiring biographer to explain it away are not, ultimately, very convincing. More than the reverse of 30 November itself, it casts a shadow over Byng's reputation to this day. Further inquests on Cambrai conducted in the War Office, by Jan Smuts on behalf of the War Cabinet and by GHQ, essentially confirmed this initial report.[26] The overused term "cover up" seems appropriate in this context. The alternative was, perhaps, bitter recrimination between the generals that might have destroyed confidence in the British army's leadership at a critical time.

Personnel changes over the weeks after Cambrai tell a version of the story rather different from that of the reports, though that version too was flawed and incomplete. Byng had refused to acknowledge that mistakes by any senior officer had contributed to the reverse of 30 November. Yet the three corps commanders involved were all removed over the next few months: Snow on 3 January, Pulteney on 16 February and Woollcombe on 11 March.[27] Pulteney of III Corps, admittedly, had rarely been a star performer before Cambrai and arguably he did not pay enough attention to Snow's warnings immediately prior to the German counter-offensive. But the justice of the other two sackings is more dubious. Woollcombe may be open to criticism for his failure to make effective use of 1st Cavalry Division on 20 November 1917. But it is more difficult to point to serious mistakes later in the battle. His IV Corps had, indeed, manfully resisted the German counter-offensive in the Bourlon sector. Snow of VII Corps was the corps commander who had read the combat indications most accurately and had tried to sound the alarm.

The least unjust of the post-Cambrai sackings was that of Charteris. He had greatly underestimated the speed and scale of German reinforcement of the Cambrai battlefield. He had believed on 12 November that "the Germans cannot get divisions from Russia before winter", though twenty-three had already arrived by that date. He had allegedly failed to pass to Haig intelligence he had received about the arrival of the German 107th Division at Cambrai before the battle, not accepting evidence provided by junior intelligence officers and not wishing to "weaken the C-in-C's resolution to proceed with the attack".[28] If, moreover, he had appreciated the danger to III and VII Corps immediately prior to 30 November, he had not made it apparent to Haig. Haig's remark to his wife that Charteris's removal and the subsequent reorganisation of the intelligence branch had "nothing to do with the Cambrai battle" was inaccurate.[29] Charteris had been making enemies for a long time, but it was Cambrai that terminated his intelligence career.

In addition to his excessive optimism and his tactlessness when dealing with everyone except Haig, Charteris's persistent fault seems to have been an overeagerness to please the boss combined with a reluctance to confront him with unpleasant facts. He always seems to have been at least as much preoccupied with public relations as with intelligence. These were, of course, quite separate fields in which no one officer should have been simultaneously involved. It is at least possible that Charteris had allowed his intelligence analysis to be adulterated by a wish to build confidence in the British war effort and put British military performance in the best possible light. Herbert Lawrence, who had commanded the 66th (East Lancashire) Division in 1917, replaced Charteris as intelligence chief at the end of the year. Haig, however, succeeded in providing Charteris with a soft landing. Charteris remained at GHQ as Deputy Inspector General of Transportation.[30]

The purge of Haig's senior staff officers, of which Maxwell and Charteris were the first victims, was not over. Kiggell was next. Kiggell had often seemed merely a massively industrious chief clerk, overawed by Haig, lacking the capacity for independent thought and out of touch with the reality of the fighting. The anecdote most frequently repeated about him is that when he saw the mud of the Third Ypres battlefield at close quarters he expressed horror and astonishment that he had shared responsibility for sending men to fight in it. There is, however, very little solid evidence to support this story and many scholars now believe it to be false.[31] Indeed, it is, perhaps, particularly unfair that a dubious anecdote about the mud of Third Ypres has stuck to Kiggell. By the time of that battle he was showing not only more operational insight, but also slightly greater assertiveness. Under the influence of his immediate subordinate, John "Tavish" Davidson of the operations branch, he had become a convert to a cautious, firepower-centred "step-by-step" approach to operations, an approach he had seemed to dismiss when Robertson tried to persuade him of its virtues in July 1916.[32] Mistrusting the generalship of Hubert Gough, whom he considered rash and wasteful of soldiers' lives, in August 1917 he had made a definite attempt to rein the Fifth Army commander in.[33]

Yet it is doubtful whether Kiggell could ever have given Haig the benefit of the fully confident, fully independent military judgement that he so desperately needed. Always a worrier, in December 1917 Kiggell was formally diagnosed as suffering from nervous exhaustion.[34] The War Office was well aware of Kiggell's condition and, while Haig was in London over the New Year, Derby told him that he was "unwise to retain a tired man". Apparently still keen to keep Kiggell, Haig said that, in the event of his becoming too sick to continue, his deputy, Butler, could take over. But Derby "at once said that neither he nor the Cabinet would approve of Butler" as Chief of the General Staff at GHQ. Butler, Derby indicated, was "not liked by any of the 'Authorities' at home".[35] Though an able administrator, he was clearly considered another Haig acolyte whose independence of mind and strength of character the authorities in the War Office believed to be insufficient for the task in hand.

War Office pressure triggered a series of changes. On 24 January, Lieutenant-General the Hon. Sir Herbert Lawrence replaced Kiggell as Chief of the General Staff at GHQ.[36] Lawrence had only recently replaced Charteris as intelligence chief and in that position Brigadier-General E.W. Cox, who had formerly served in War Office intelligence under Macdonogh, replaced Lawrence.[37] Haig secured the command of III Corps for Butler,[38] though that turned out to be a move of dubious wisdom. Major-General G. P. Dawnay took over Butler's work at GHQ.[39] The general verdict of contemporaries, echoed by historians, has been that these personnel changes resulted in significant improvements in efficiency and effectiveness.[40] To a large extent, however, this favourable verdict is probably a reflection of the afterglow of the "Hundred Days" victories in the latter part of 1918. To what extent the changes at GHQ contributed to those victories is not easy to say. During the Hundred Days Lawrence's influence on Haig was not, as we shall see, wholly positive, and there are serious question marks over the performance of the General Staff at GHQ in the run up to, and in the early stages of, the German spring offensives.

The contrast between Kiggell and Lawrence was, however, a marked one. A Haig protégé since they had served at the War Office together under Haldane, Kiggell had always been deferential. The professional paths of Haig and Lawrence had also crossed before the war, but in a less harmonious manner. Lawrence had resigned from the army on 12 May 1903 because Haig had been appointed over his head as colonel of the 17th Lancers, a regiment in which Haig had not previously served. Like Haig's, Lawrence's family background was one of wealth and privilege, but whereas Haig's father had been a mere distiller, Lawrence's had been Viceroy of India. This, combined with a strong sense of his own abilities, gave him an air that has been described as "regal", a marked contrast with Kiggell's highly-strung subservience. After leaving the army Lawrence had built a successful city career, which further increased his personal wealth, his self-assurance and his independence of spirit. He rejoined on the outbreak of war. Whereas Kiggell had made his career as a staff officer and lacked experience in the field, Lawrence had served at Gallipoli and had won a small battle at Romani in the Sinai in summer 1917. He commanded the 66th Division on the Western Front from February to December 1917 and brought some of his staff officers from that division to assist him at GHQ. Despite his former tendency to surround himself with "yes men" (or "fat counsellors" as Charteris himself once put it), and though he had often appeared to hate "being told any information, however irrefutable, which militated against his preconceived ideas or beliefs", Haig seemed to adjust with little difficulty to working with Lawrence and the other new and more independent-minded appointees.[41] This is a tribute to a type of professionalism on Haig's part, albeit one in which an acute instinct for career survival played a dominant role.

Haig's vulnerability; his willingness to consider a compromise peace

Haig's career did, of course, survive. But over Christmas 1917 (apparently a somewhat gloomy festive season at GHQ) and well into the New Year this seemed doubtful. Haig was acutely conscious of a violent press campaign against him and was practically certain that Lloyd George was behind it. In conversation with Lord Milner at GHQ on 26 December, Haig seemed to be pleading for a truce with the Prime Minister. He assured Milner that he considered it his duty to assist Lloyd George to the fullest extent of his power and "not to countenance any criticism of the PM's actions". In fact he had already "stopped criticism in the Army". He argued that "it would be better that I go at once, rather than that LG should proceed with his policy of undermining the confidence which troops now feel in their leaders, and eventually destroy the efficiency of the Army as a fighting force. Moral[e] in an army is a very delicate plant."[42] Lloyd George did not respond to Haig's plea for a truce at this stage. The Prime Minister still hoped to oust both Haig and Robertson and the campaign against them in the Northcliffe press continued with increasing ferocity. Haig's concern that this would damage the morale of his army was probably perfectly genuine. He appreciated that the BEF was already in a weakened and depressed condition. Arguing, earlier in the month, against any great extension of the British front in France, he had explained to the War Cabinet that:

The British Armies in France have been engaged practically continuously since last April in exhausting offensive operations involving considerable wastage and great fatigue. Every division has been engaged in battle several times and while on the defensive fronts, necessarily thinly held during the operations, they have had heavy work ...

The whole Army is therefore much exhausted and much reduced in strength ... [Of] the divisions at present in reserve behind the British front, only those belonging to the Australian and Canadian Corps are fit for duty in [the] front line.[43]

Though Haig did not spell it out here, both he and the War Cabinet knew that exhaustion and heavy casualties had resulted in a substantial fall in the BEF's morale. Though serious mutiny was not considered probable, desertion, drunkenness and other forms of indiscipline were on the increase.[44] Given his army's fragile state, and the prospect of the transfer of a large number German forces from the now largely defunct Eastern Front, Haig had apparently (and very grudgingly) recognised by early December that it might be necessary to go on the defensive at least for a few months. To a conference with the Army commanders at Doullens, on Friday 7 December, Charteris had forecast "an attack by Germany in great strength in the spring, not later than March".[45] Haig, however, was (for once) sceptical of Charteris's (for once) essentially accurate analysis. He accepted that the Allies had temporarily lost the initiative, but considered it improbable that the Germans would risk everything on a massive spring offensive. Charteris noted that:

D.H. does not agree about the German strategy for 1918. He says that the correct strategy for them is to play a waiting game and not commit themselves to a big attack. He does not think they will make a mistake that will lead to their complete collapse. While this would obviously be their correct strategy, their internal troubles will outweigh strategy. At least I think so.[46]

By 20 December Charteris thought he had converted Haig to a belief in "a big German attack in the spring",[47] but Haig remained very much in two minds about it. At least for the next few weeks he tended to believe that the Germans would not go for broke, but would confine themselves to limited offensives in the coming year.

Both GHQ and the War Office were seriously worried about the manpower situation for 1918. Derby pointed out in early December that, if Haig's army were not kept up to strength to face a possible German onslaught, "the war might well be lost". The Army Council pointed out quite accurately in early January that merely standing on the defensive was no guarantee of lower casualties. Lloyd George and his closest political allies, however, regarded all estimates and statistics emanating from the military as extremely dubious and it was perfectly true that the General Staff, both in the War Office and at GHQ, was prepared to massage figures to influence policy.[48] As in previous years Derby, Robertson and Haig wanted to concentrate military manpower on the Western Front and keep Haig's divisions up to strength as much as possible. They were convinced that the war could only be decided in that theatre. Modern scholarship indicates that Lloyd George and his War Cabinet colleagues also believed that the war would be decided in the West: the traditional description of some them as "Easterners" being to some degree misleading. But they did not want to take the offensive on the Western Front until the Americans had fully deployed their military power, which would probably take until 1919 and perhaps even longer.[49]

The biggest single problem in the way of a rational formulation of British strategy at this period was a complete breakdown of trust between the War Cabinet, on the one hand, and the military authorities in the War Office and GHQ, on the other. The War Cabinet's negative perception of Haig's generalship was, moreover, absolutely central to this problem of civil–military relations. What confidence Lloyd George ever had in Haig had been much eroded by the end of the 1916 campaign on the Somme. The events of 1917, especially what Lloyd George perceived as Haig's incompetent handling of the Ypres offensive and his mounting of an unnecessary and unavailing attack in the Cambrai sector, had completed the process. To give more than the bare minimum of manpower to Haig was, in Lloyd George's mind, to invite him to send it for slaughter.[50] Apart from the human tragedy of such casualties and the possible political consequences, the manpower needs of the British war economy had to be considered. The War Cabinet now perceived that national manpower was stretched to breaking point. The War Cabinet's strategy, therefore, as it gradually emerged that winter, was to accept that the war probably could not be won in 1918. In the coming year it was considered that the Allies would most likely remain on the defensive on the Western Front.[51]

The War Cabinet (like Haig himself) did not consider it certain that the Germans would mount a really major offensive in 1918. Lloyd George personally seems to have strongly doubted it. Assuming a continued stalemate in the West, the War Cabinet intended that the main British offensive effort of 1918 should be a knockout blow against the Turks: following up on Allenby's capture of Jerusalem on 21 December. The collapse of Turkey might precipitate a falling away of Germany's other allies and this could be expected to weaken Germany's overall strategic position without excessive loss to Britain. British manpower could be conserved while the Americans built up their army on the Western Front preparatory to a general offensive by the allies in 1919 or perhaps 1920.[52]

Lloyd George may have been too canny to put it in writing explicitly, but it seems likely that his policy was to deny Haig any surplus manpower that might incline him to resume major offensive efforts in 1918. Indeed, a memorandum by Hankey, dated 18 April 1917, suggests that rationing Haig's manpower had become War Cabinet policy as far back as that.[53] What seems strange in retrospect, and what no historian has, perhaps, adequately explained, is why the War Cabinet gave so little attention to the worst case scenario: that the Germans would in fact decide to go for broke with a really violent offensive in the West. For if they did so and succeeded, anything the Allies did elsewhere in the world would be of little account. With the benefit of hindsight it is easy to see that, while worrying about the manpower situation in 1920, the War Cabinet did not take sufficiently seriously the risk of losing the war in the spring of 1918.

Haig's diary for Christmas 1917 and the New Year of 1918 gives little direct insight into his emotional state, but this was surely strained. His confident expectations of final victory in 1917 had been disappointed. His army was, as we have noted, desperately tired and depleted and somewhat demoralised. He was disillusioned with Britain's allies. The French were weary. The Americans were unready and likely to remain so for a long time. He was under attack in the national press for miscalculation, failure and waste of British life. He knew that the Prime Minister wanted to sack him. Yet, on the other hand, he had a devoted wife, two growing daughters and, relatively late in life, another child on the way. These were not only sources of comfort, but also reminders of the potential pleasures of peace and domesticity and of a more normal existence.

To Haig's mind, steadiness of purpose was one of the greatest virtues. But he was neither impervious to normal human emotion nor immune to the pressures of the world around him. Even his sense of divine mission did not render him incapable of doubt. There is no indication that, even at this low point in his fortunes, he considered resignation – quite the contrary. Admitting personal inadequacy and surrendering status were foreign to his nature. But, like most other people in Europe at the beginning of 1918, he was very weary of war. He was now uncertain that the crushing victory over Germany he had confidently expected a few months ago was a realistic objective, worth the effort required. He feared bloody, war-spawned revolution of the Bolshevik sort, and was somewhat anxious about the growth of Socialist sentiment of a less violent type in his own army.[54] On Friday 28 December, shortly before he came home on New Year leave, he remarked in his diary that recent German peace proposals, which we now know were not seriously intended,[55] deserved careful consideration:

Germany's peace offer appeared in last night's wireless and a more detailed account this morning. General opinion is that it will be difficult to ignore this offer ...[56]

New Year in London

No longer necessarily averse to a compromise peace, Haig was beginning to question the purposes for which Britain was continuing the war. On Wednesday 2 January he went to Buckingham Palace for an interview with the King. Despite George V's presenting him with his field marshal's baton, this meeting between general and sovereign seems to have been the gloomiest of the war. They agreed that, in the event of a German spring offensive, heavy casualties and some loss of some ground were to be expected. Haig gave his views on war aims:

I told the King that it was very desirable to tell the Army in a few unambiguous sentences, what we were fighting for. The Army is now composed of representatives of all classes in the nation, and many are most intelligent and think things out. They don't care whether France has Alsace and Italy Trieste; they realise that Britain entered the war to free Belgium and save France. Germany is now ready, we have been told, to give all we want in these respects. So it is essential that some statement should be made which the soldier can understand and approve of. Few of us feel that "the democratising of Germany" is worth the loss of an Englishman! I also pointed out that the removal of the Hohenzollerns from Germany is likely to result in anarchy just as was the case in Russia. This might prove a great evil for the rest of Europe.[57]

Haig was wrong about the German willingness, at this point, to give up wartime conquests. But he was right to be frightened (as Lenin was right to be hopeful) that social chaos and civil war might spill out of this international conflict and engulf much of Europe.

Yet, while the general mood in London that New Year was anxious and subdued, it was not one of unrelieved gloom. Lloyd George, while still scheming to get rid of both Robertson and Haig, could, when it suited him, turn on his notorious charm and appear pleasant, relaxed and full of bonhomie. This seems to have put Haig off his guard and tempted him into indiscretion. Writing of a War Cabinet meeting that he attended on Monday 7 January, Haig noted that "All were most friendly to me." According to his diary, Haig said that the next four months would be the critical period on the Western Front. The Germans could be expected to transfer thirty-two divisions from the Eastern Front at the rate of about ten per month. This would make March the real danger period. It was not clear whether a German attack would focus on the British or the French. If on the French, they would be likely to demand either British reserves or an extension of the British front. For fear of weakening the British army, Haig was reluctant to provide either. What he would prefer to do would be to continue the British offensive in Flanders. By doing so the British would "retain the initiative and attract the German reserves against us". This would be vital, as it was "doubtful" whether the French could stand for long "a resolute and continued offensive on the part of the Enemy".

But if Haig did raise the prospect of a renewed British offensive in Flanders at this meeting, the others present do not appear to have understood him. There is no suggestion of it in the minutes, in which the discussion focuses on defence. Perhaps Haig's poor self-expression helped him in this particular instance; the prospect of his restarting the Ypres offensive would surely have horrified his listeners. But perhaps Haig made the suggestion of renewing the Flanders offensive only in his diary and not at the meeting itself. At the meeting Bonar Law asked Haig whether, if he were a German commander, he would think that a "smashing offensive" was worth the inevitable losses. Haig's diary account and the minutes agree about his answer to this question. He said that he would favour limited offensives rather than attempt a knockout blow.[58]

Hearing Haig play down the prospect of a really major German offensive at this meeting (which he also attended) thoroughly alarmed Robertson. Immediately afterwards he got Haig to put in a paper emphasising the danger of the worst-case scenario: that the Germans would mount an all-out attack in the spring. But to Lloyd George this was just another annoying indication of Haig's intellectual inadequacy and confusion. Nor did Haig redeem himself at a "cheery" luncheon party with Lloyd George and Derby two days later. Derby bet Lloyd George 100 cigars to 100 cigarettes that the war would be over within a year. Lloyd George apparently accepted the bet. Haig agreed with Derby on the basis that the domestic situation in Germany would make her continuance beyond the autumn impossible. But, while indicating that the next four months were likely to prove critical, Haig once again shot himself in the foot:

Germany having only one million men as reserves for this year's fighting, I doubted that they would risk them in an attempt to "break through". If they did it would be a gambler's throw. All seemed to depend on the struggle now going on in Germany between Military and Civil parties. If the Military won, they would certainly attack and try to deliver a knock out blow against the Western Front, probably against France.[59]

Not only did he again raise doubts as to whether the Germans would attempt a knockout blow on this occasion, but he again suggested that if they did, it would be against the French, not the British. He could hardly have done more to weaken his position when bidding for the manpower resources he so desperately needed.

Trenchard's removal and pressure to extend the British front: January 1918

Returning to GHQ in the New Year, Haig found himself beset by problems. First, he discovered that he was to lose one of his most loyal and trusted commanders. Lieutenant-General Hugh Trenchard, who had commanded the Royal Flying Corps on the Western Front since 1915, was to become Chief of the Air Staff in the new Air Ministry in London. Haig resented the move at this critical stage. He remonstrated with Derby to try to get it delayed for a few months, but to no avail.[60] While Haig was to establish a good working relationship with Lieutenant-General John Salmond, Trenchard's successor, he could have done without the disruption at this critical period.

This was by no means the worst news. In response to the manpower shortage and at the insistence of the War Cabinet, on 10 January the War Office reluctantly ordered Haig to reduce all British infantry divisions on the Western Front from twelve battalions to nine. This necessarily involved great disruption of the main fighting component of the army at almost the worst possible time. Less seriously, but also to Haig's displeasure, and despite his remonstrance, his cavalry strength was reduced from five divisions to three.[61] Just as the manpower situation was biting, moreover, Haig came under renewed pressure to extend the British front.

The original source of this pressure was, of course, the French army. The British government had agreed to an extension of the British front during Third Ypres, leaving the details to be worked out between Haig and Pétain.[62] Haig had then used the despatch of British troops to Italy after Caporetto and the Cambrai battle as excuses to delay. But in January the matter went through the Supreme War Council based at Versailles, where Sir Henry Wilson was the British military representative. The Council concluded that the British should extend their line to some point between the Ailette and the Soissons–Laon road. Haig thought the extension of his front dangerous. He believed that this issue raised the matter of the status of the Supreme War Council in an acute form. "The government now have two advisers! Will they accept the advice of the Versailles gentlemen (who have no responsibility) or will they take my advice?"[63] In fact Haig would have to accept for the next several weeks that his advice on critical issues was being overruled, but his responsibility in no way diminished. The only alternative was resignation and that was not an option he seems seriously to have considered.

Press campaigns and the Hankey–Smuts mission: January 1918

Meanwhile the campaign against Robertson and Haig in the Northcliffe press was building to a climax. Northcliffe clearly intended to help the Lloyd George cause against Robertson and Haig. But it seems that he did not consult Lloyd George about the details of the campaign, and a poorly timed and especially violent piece rebounded against the Prime Minister. On Monday 21 January, the journalist Lovat Fraser of the *Daily Mail* mounted an especially violent attack, in an article entitled "Things Hidden", on the "ridiculous 'theory of attrition'". He accused the generals of wasting British life on the Western Front with a "strategy of the Stone Age". Like Lloyd George, Lovat Fraser advocated making the major effort in 1918 in other theatres. The virulence of the criticism of British generalship on the Western Front went too far for most army officers and for the majority of the Unionist MPs upon whose political support Lloyd George depended. It was widely regarded as unpatriotic and a symptom of the press baron's megalomania.[64]

At lunch on Friday 18 January, Lloyd George had suddenly asked Smuts to go to the Western Front, "to find out who are the rising men". He wanted to see if a suitable replacement could be found for Haig.[65] On 19 January Robertson informed Haig that Smuts and Maurice Hankey, the Cabinet secretary, would be touring the front together to get to know the generals there and report to the Prime Minister.[66] Whether Robertson realised that this was a mission to replace Haig is not clear. If so he gave Haig no explicit warning. Smuts and Hankey spent the first evening of their five-day tour of the Western Front with Haig at GHQ. Their arrival coincided with the publication of the Lovat Fraser article: the culmination of the press campaign against Haig. Haig, therefore, seems to have suspected the true purpose of the mission, but Smuts and Hankey "went out of their way to assure" him that Lloyd George had no wish to replace him.[67]

Hankey found that "the atmosphere of complaisant optimism that formerly pervaded GHQ" was now "conspicuous by its absence". The bitter and bloody fighting of 1917, the collapse of Russia, the growth of German strength on the Western Front, the BEF's acute manpower shortage and French pressure to extend the stretch of Western Front held by the British all played their part in this. So did a degree of disillusionment with the Americans. The latter were understandably reluctant to supply drafts for British and French formations, except in an extreme emergency. But they seemed unlikely to be capable of taking the offensive themselves in 1918. Indeed, according to Hankey, the general opinion at GHQ was that they would be unable to do so before 1920. Most surprising to Hankey was the common talk, at GHQ, of a compromise peace, talk in which Haig shared. Haig told Hankey and Smuts that Britain had so far gained more from the war than any other power including Germany. He

doubted whether we would gain more by continuing the war for another twelve months. At the end of that period we would be more exhausted and our industrial and financial recovery would be more difficult, and America would get a great pull over us. There were ... dangers from the collapse of Italy or France or both.[68]

Though he had made a similar statement in correspondence with Robertson during Third Ypres, it is difficult to understand the reasoning behind Haig's claim that Britain had got more out of the war than any other power. Possibly he was thinking of Britain's conquest of Germany's African colonies (a process not yet complete) and of territory the British had captured from the Turks in the Middle East. In a war aims speech of 5 January, Lloyd George had cast doubt on whether any of this territory was to be annexed to the British Empire,[69] but even if it were all annexed, it may be doubted that such peripheral gains were equivalent to Germany's conquest of much of Eastern Europe. If the German Empire were to be left in control of these European conquests, was it not likely to become a superpower with hegemonic status on the Continent? In that case the relative power positions of Great Britain and Germany would surely have shifted radically in Germany's favour.

As far as the main purpose of their visit was concerned, it is clear that Smuts and Hankey found no groundswell of opinion in the army in favour of Haig's replacement by any other general. Indeed, Smuts reported that officers were greatly upset by the Lovat Fraser article, which had the unintended consequence of rallying them in support of Haig. Smuts and Hankey found it impossible to recommend anyone who they thought would do better than Haig with the possible exception of Lieutenant-General Claud Jacob of II Corps. Jacob, however, was practically unknown to the British public and to move him up two steps at once to become commander-in-chief would have been a very great gamble. Lloyd George apparently did not fancy it.[70]

Indeed, the parliamentary response to the Northcliffe press campaign, and the Lovat Fraser article in particular, made dismissing Haig at this precise moment practically impossible politically. Haig had been under serious attack in the House of Commons over Cambrai just a few weeks earlier. But the House was then, as it has remained, a volatile assembly, prone to dramatic mood swings. On Thursday 24 January the Unionist War Committee passed a resolution in support of Robertson and Haig. It demanded that the Prime Minster condemn the campaign then being conducted in the Northcliffe press. At least for a week or two (a week being a proverbially long time in politics) Haig's job was safe.[71] On Saturday 26 January, Asquith, at the front mainly to visit his badly wounded son, Arthur, dropped in at GHQ. Now an inveterate political enemy of Lloyd George, Asquith was doubtless pleased to be able to assure Haig that the Northcliffe campaign against him had rebounded on the Prime Minister in the Commons. Lloyd George had found that it "did not pay" to attack Haig, though Asquith predicted that "the attack on Robertson might be continued".[72]

At this moment Lloyd George was, indeed, facing not only the failure of the Northcliffe press campaign, but also a violent counter-attack by a former Northcliffe employee. In the early stages of the war, relations between Haig and Repington, who was then the military correspondent of *The Times*, had been strained. Before the war and during its early stages Repington had formed a fairly low opinion of Haig's abilities,[73] and had not been careful to conceal this. Haig had reciprocated by treating Repington with contempt. When, in the early stages of the 1916 Somme campaign, GHQ managed to form an alliance with Northcliffe, Charteris had hoped that this would have the advantage of keeping Repington under control and out of Haig's hair.[74] Between early December 1917 and mid-January 1918, however, a sort of reversal of alliances had taken place. Northcliffe had turned violently against GHQ and moved into the Lloyd George camp. Repington, whatever his doubts about Haig's abilities, was a convinced Westerner and thought that Lloyd George was leaving the British army on the Western Front dangerously exposed. He broke with Northcliffe and transferred his services to the *Morning Post*.

On Thursday 24 January, the very day of the Unionist protest in the Commons against the Northcliffe press campaign, Repington published an article attacking the Prime Minister over manpower:

The one question which concerns most deeply every man, woman and child in the United Kingdom is whether Sir Douglas Haig's armies will not be sufficiently reinforced to enable them to compete with the enemy on fair terms, and in my opinion they will not be.

It was obvious to Lloyd George that the War Office had furnished Repington with both British manpower statistics and estimates of German strength on the Western Front. Repington knew, for example, that the government intended to supply Haig with only 100,000 category "A" recruits in 1918. Lloyd George was furious with the War Office for the obvious leak. Repington, once reviled by Haig, was now one of his few active allies in the press and Haig praised him for "having stated the true case in his articles in the *Morning Post*". But Repington's campaign seems to have done little to awaken public opinion to a proper sense of the acute danger now developing in the West.[75]

The General Reserves issue and the fall of Robertson: late January and February 1918

Between 29 January and 2 February Haig attended a conference of the Supreme War Council at the Trianon Palace Hotel at Versailles. Haig and Pétain both rang loud alarm bells about the manpower weakness of their forces. Pétain spoke of losing twenty-five divisions by the autumn just from "normal wastage". But Haig was "pleased at the way Pétain backed me up and this without any prior talk or argument". Generally Haig was more in tune with his French allies than he had been for many months. He found himself strongly admiring Georges Clemenceau, the new French premier, whom he considered "the soundest and pluckiest of the lot ... a grand old man, full of go and determination". Clemenceau was clearly unhappy about the prospects on the Western Front and very dubious about Lloyd George's scheme, supported by the Military Members at Versailles, for an offensive against the Turks. The conference, however, concluded that the Allies would remain on the defensive for the time being on the Western Front. Clemenceau reluctantly conceded that "he could not prevent Great Britain doing what she thought best" in the matter of an offensive against the Turks, though he got Lloyd George's agreement to delay such an effort for the next two months. Robertson made a formal expression of dissent, stating that he thought this strategy for 1918 "quite unsound". But Haig did not speak up in his support, later excusing himself on the grounds that "LG never asked my opinion".

The final day of the conference was, from Haig's point of view, in some ways even worse. It was decided that Foch, as President of the Military Committee at Versailles, was to determine the size of the Allies' General Reserves and to issue orders to the national commanders-in-chief as to where and when these reserves should be used. Though this proposal seemed designed to make Foch a "Generalissimo", and though Haig did not like it, he did not oppose it directly. He did not think he could release any forces from his own command to form part of such a General Reserve. But at this point none were being demanded of him. Far more serious, in his view, was the demand, accepted by the conference, that the British substantially increase the length of the Western Front they held. Again Haig was not prepared to put his job on the line to resist this proposal, even though, given his army's depleted state, he thought it very dangerous. To his heavily pregnant and seriously worried wife, he put the best possible interpretation on events. As "far as I am concerned", he wrote, "the Versailles Conference went off quite well ... Anyhow don't let the Versailles Conference trouble your little head. The machinery is so big and clumsy it will take some time before it can work fast enough to trouble me. So I don't mean to be influenced by it against my better conscience."[76]

By the beginning of February it was clear that Lloyd George and Robertson were on a collision course. Robertson was so furious with Lloyd George and so sure that the Prime Minister was jeopardising the British war effort that, though he told Haig he had no intention of resigning,[77] he seemed be courting dismissal. Robertson was only prepared to accept the agreements that the Allies had made at Versailles at the beginning of February on condition that the government should merge the posts of CIGS and British Military Representative at Versailles. He intended to occupy both posts. With Robertson adopting this stance a crisis, as Derby warned Haig, could not be long delayed. Derby clearly intended to back Robertson in any confrontation that arose and assumed that Haig would do likewise,[78] but that assumption was soon to prove invalid.

Haig travelled to London on Saturday 9 February in order to respond to the crisis developing between Robertson and Lloyd George. According to Haig's diary, as soon as they met at Victoria station, Derby told Haig that the Cabinet had decided to sack Robertson and that Haig's view on that was not required. They went to Downing Street where Haig told Lloyd George that, though he thought the scheme for the handling of the General Reserve a bad one, he was prepared to work under it. Haig agreed to Lloyd George's proposal that Robertson and Wilson should change places. Robertson would go to Versailles, help control the General Reserve, hold the post of Deputy CIGS and be part of the Army Council. Wilson would come to London as CIGS, a post that would revert to the somewhat lower status that it had enjoyed in the pre-Robertson era.[79]

From Haig's point of view, the notion of having Robertson at Versailles seemed reasonable enough. Having spent Sunday 10 February with Doris, Haig saw the CIGS at the War Office on the Monday morning. Showing no particular concern for Robertson's *amour propre*, Haig went so far as to tell him that it was his duty to accept the transfer (and the reduction in status). Nor did Haig have much sympathy with Robertson's outrage at the notion of Henry Wilson's replacing him in London. At noon Haig went to see the King at Buckingham Place, and "urged HM to insist on Robertson going to Versailles", before returning to GHQ that evening.[80]

While the crisis continued in London, in France it was appearing increasingly probable (though still not beyond doubt) in Haig's mind that he would shortly face a large-scale German offensive. Particularly vulnerable was the Fifth Army, on the Somme, which he visited, using his headquarters train, from 13–15 February.[81] From a telegram received from Derby in the early hours of Friday 15 February, Haig learned that crisis point had been reached between Robertson and Lloyd George. Haig also gathered that Lloyd George was misrepresenting his position, indicating that he positively favoured the scheme for the management of the General Reserve to which Robertson so violently objected. In reality Haig had only said that he was prepared to work under this scheme, not that he approved it. While himself staying on the train, where he dined with Gough that night, Haig sent his secretary, Philip Sassoon, back to GHQ at Montreuil to book a trip to London for the following day.[82]

The train took him to Doullens on the morning of Saturday 16 February. There he had an interview with the French Minister of Munitions at 9.15 a.m., before holding an Army commanders' conference between 10.00 and 12.30. These conferences were regular events, but this one was exceptionally serious. Cox, Charteris's replacement as head of intelligence at GHQ, indicated that a major German offensive was shortly expected. After lunch Haig went by car to Boulogne, where he boarded a destroyer, which sailed at 3 p.m. A special train got him to London by 5.30 where Derby met him at the station. Derby's car took Haig to his recently acquired family home at Kingston Hill, into which he and Doris intended to welcome the child they were soon expecting. It was the second successive weekend on which Haig had been able to see Doris.[83]

On the morning of Sunday 17 February Haig received visits from Robertson and Derby. Derby picked him up at 11.30 a.m. and took him to Lloyd George's home at Walton Heath. There Haig and the Prime Minister conferred privately at some length.[84] Lloyd George made it clear that the government regarded Robertson's refusal to comply with its wishes as tantamount to resignation. Haig gave no support to Robertson and showed less interest than Lloyd George did in finding Robertson a suitably prestigious alternative post. Lloyd George told Haig that Derby had threatened resignation in support of Robertson. According to Lloyd George, however, Haig reacted to the prospect of Derby's resignation "with an expression of contempt".[85] Derby had bent over backwards, since the formation of the Lloyd George coalition, to help and support Haig. The Tory peer's judgement of men and issues was often very sound. But Haig had, as Lloyd George now realised, no real regard for him.[86] Indeed, Haig felt as little personal loyalty to Derby as he did to Robertson.

Haig returned to his home at Kingston Hill that afternoon. There, at Lloyd George's request, he had a meeting at about 4.30 p.m. with Sir Henry Wilson, who was about to take over as CIGS. A few days earlier Lloyd George had offered Plumer, whom he imagined might be a popular choice with the army, the chance to replace Robertson as CIGS. Plumer had turned it down, opening the way for Wilson. Haig now stated that he needed Plumer, who had been serving in Italy, back on the Western Front as an Army commander and Wilson agreed to that. They also agreed that Rawlinson should replace Wilson in his Versailles post. At about 6.30 the same evening Derby came to Haig's house, apparently seeking Haig's advice on whether he should resign over Robertson's dismissal. Despite his fundamental contempt for Derby, Haig helped Lloyd George keep Robertson isolated and helped to make life easier for Wilson by telling the Secretary of State that "in the interests of the Army" he must not resign.[87]

On the morning of Monday 18 February, Haig went to see Bonar Law at the latter's request. Lloyd George, excusing himself on grounds of illness, had asked Bonar Law to read a statement in the House indicating that Haig now approved of the way the Supreme War Council was set up. Bonar Law wanted to know if this were true. Haig said that he did not approve it, but would do his best to work under it. He warned Bonar Law that he was so stretched on the Western Front that he could not afford to earmark any of his divisions as part of the Supreme War Council's "General Reserve" and that he would rather resign than do so.[88] Later that day Bonar Law announced in the House of Commons that Robertson had been appointed to Eastern Command.[89] This was a humiliatingly minor post for someone of Robertson's eminence, but Robertson, who had no private means, had little choice but to accept it. Within a few weeks he was made Commander-in-Chief of Home Forces, a rather more suitable position.[90] Back at GHQ, on Tuesday 19 February, Haig congratulated himself on having defused a civil–military crisis.[91]

Assessment

The winter of 1917–1918 represented a low point for Haig's reputation and career. He was commanding a depleted and somewhat demoralised army, and for a while he was under dangerous levels of attack on his professional competence by influential newspapers in cahoots with the Prime Minister. As usual his diary gives little insight into the depths of his consciousness. But he was now far from sure that it was worth continuing the war long enough to secure (and sustaining the further losses that seemed likely to be involved in securing) a clear-cut victory over the German Empire. Confidentially he was advocating a compromise peace – a peace that would almost certainly mean leaving the Germans in control of a significant proportion of their wartime conquests in Eastern Europe. Only a few months previously he would have found such an attitude cowardly and defeatist. In February 1917 he had, indeed, been in serious trouble for publicly insisting that no half-baked settlement was acceptable. Germany, he had then pronounced, had to be completely crushed.

While he increasingly regarded clear-cut victory in this war as chimerical, and while he sometimes indicated that he was prepared to stand down if the Prime Minister wished it, in practice Haig demonstrated great determination to remain commander-in-chief. Indeed, he showed that he was prepared to make a great many compromises over military policy (some of them quite dangerous) and to jettison virtually anyone else in order to hang on. His callousness and seeming disloyalty towards Robertson and Derby appear, however, to contrast with the greater care and consideration he had shown for the welfare of Charteris, Kiggell and Butler.

The difference was that the last three were subordinates (indeed, almost acolytes) who had served him devotedly without challenging his authority or overtly questioning his judgement. Derby and Robertson, on the other hand, had quite vocally questioned his wisdom on some issues. On occasion they had even tried to caution, correct and lecture him. In Haig's mind, therefore, these people were certainly not loyal retainers and to some degree he may have perceived them as potential competitors for any credit that might be going if the Allies did win the war. Given that they were not giving him the uncritical support to which he thought he was entitled, he felt no obligation towards them. Robertson was now gone. Haig had made it clear to Lloyd George that he would not stick his neck out in Derby's defence. But how long this kind of flexibility would enable him to retain his own position would inevitably depend on events.

17   The German March offensives

Haig's doubts

From mid-December 1917 GHQ's intelligence staff predicted a large-scale German offensive effort in the following spring with increasing certainty and in increasing detail.[1] From then until it began, on the morning of Thursday 21 March 1918, Haig was trying to get his army ready for the onslaught. Until very shortly before it started, however, he had some doubts as to whether it would really occur. Considering (rightly) that an all-out offensive would be a desperate gamble for the Germans,[2] he thought they would do better to conserve their strength and try for a compromise peace. Showing considerable signs of war-weariness himself, Haig strongly favoured such a settlement throughout the winter and into mid-March.[3] Having a generally high opinion of the German capacity for rational thought in military matters, Haig needed a great weight of evidence to convince him that the enemy was about to do something really rash. But by early March, while he still had lingering doubts which, foolishly, he did not entirely keep to himself, for practical purposes he had accepted that the Germans were about to launch, against his Third and Fifth Armies, the first of what seemed likely to be a series of major offensives.[4]

Front extension, manpower and balance of forces

At New Year, in his dealings with the War Cabinet and the Prime Minister, Haig's trumpet had made a very uncertain sound.[5] This, coming on top of his apparent wastage of British blood at Third Ypres, and his serious misjudgements at Cambrai, had put him in a very poor position to bid for manpower in 1918 or to argue against the extension of his front: an extension for which the overcommitted French army had long pressed. (The French army held, indeed, a far longer stretch of the Western Front in relation to its numbers than did the British army, though quite a large stretch of the front the French army held was relatively inactive.) In mid-January 1918 the British sector of the Western Front was ninety-five miles long. By 4 February it had been extended to 123 miles – an increase of almost thirty per cent. At the same time, as the result of restricted drafts, the infantry strength of the British (as opposed to Dominion) divisions on the Western Front had dropped from twelve battalions to nine. (Though GHQ did not really favour this reorganisation and though it was imposed mainly as a result of the manpower shortage, there was certainly something to be said for diminishing the quantity of manpower in relation to firepower at divisional level.) A total of 134 infantry battalions in France effectively disappeared (disbanded or amalgamated) and another seven were converted to pioneers. And whereas, in autumn 1917, Haig had sixty-two British and Dominion infantry divisions on the Western Front, by mid-January he only had fifty-eight. His cavalry strength was also cut from five divisions to three: a fact by no means unimportant given that cavalry could function as infantry when the need arose. The manpower statistics are complex and controversial, but one assessment is that Haig had about 70,000 fewer fighting troops at the beginning of 1918 compared with the beginning of 1917 – a drop of about seven per cent.[6]

It seems that British rifle strength on the Western Front was thus substantially reduced, while the front was lengthened, at a time when both War Office and GHQ intelligence were predicting major German offensives. This provides a *prima facie* case of culpable negligence on the part of the War Cabinet. Even on a more complete review of the evidence it is impossible to exonerate Britain's political leadership. As already noted, there is some evidence that Lloyd George was pursuing a conscious and deliberate policy of restricting the manpower available to Haig, fearing that he would waste any surplus in futile offensives.[7] It is true that the government's maintenance of remarkably large forces in the Middle East while the outcome of the war was still undecided in the main, Western theatre of operations was to a certain degree the fault of Robertson and the General Staff in the War Office. The War Office had deliberately exaggerated the size of the forces that would be needed to mount a successful offensive in Palestine in a futile effort to discourage the War Cabinet from launching such an enterprise. The fact remains, however, that in spring 1918 the British Empire had a surplus of troops in peripheral theatres such as Palestine–Egypt and Mesopotamia,[8] and was dangerously weak where it really mattered, on the Western Front. The fact that two divisions were rushed from the Middle East to the Western Front[9] when the German offensive began tends to confirm this point.

A Manpower Committee, established under Lloyd George's chairmanship in late 1917, gave the army a lower manpower priority than the Royal Navy, the RAF, food production and even timber felling. The War Office thought the army needed, in 1918, some 615,000 "category A" (i.e., fully fit) men, but the Manpower Committee allocated only 100,000 men in this category. While some reaction against Haig's apparent profligacy with soldiers' lives at Third Ypres was to be expected, this was surely taking things too far. Events tended to show that Lloyd George's view that the Allies were adequately insured on the Western Front for 1918 was a massive, extremely dangerous error. Yet the War Cabinet did face real manpower constraints, some economic and some political. With the best will in the world, it would almost certainly have been impossible to obtain all the fit men that the War Office and GHQ were demanding.[10]

To take one example of the political constraints, it would have been rash to the point of insanity to apply conscription in Ireland. Some military advisers, including, at one point, Haig himself,[11] pressed for this to be done, and the War Cabinet was still considering the idea in April 1918. But the mere suggestion of conscription was enough to cause, from the British viewpoint, a marked deterioration in the Irish political and security situation.[12] At the same time the government was meeting opposition from the trades unions to its attempts to comb out labour from the factories, and public opinion seemed unhappy about extending the age of military service. Though Lloyd George and his colleagues did institute another comb-out of industrial manpower in January 1918, they were reluctant to push things to the point of industrial and social crisis. Indeed, Haig's interpretation of the manpower question in the early weeks of 1918 was not so much that the War Cabinet was deliberately starving him as that it was suffering a failure of nerve in dealing with Ireland and the trades unions.[13]

The question of manpower in relation to the British army on the Western Front in 1918 is, indeed, a complex one. While the War Cabinet had much to answer for, the military authorities, including Haig himself, are by no means beyond criticism. There is evidence to suggest that some military manpower was, at the critical time, in Britain rather than France as result of decisions by military personnel rather than by politicians. Some 120,000 men of the "general reserve" were kept in the United Kingdom, partly on the grounds that it would help the British economy if they spent their pay at home. Haig had apparently assured the War Office that he was fairly certain of being able to hold a German offensive for at least eighteen days, and General Staff in the War Office judged that it would have no difficulty in transporting these reserves to the Western Front within that period.[14] Another manpower issue under military control was that of leave. When the German spring offensive began, there were over 88,000 British soldiers from the Western Front on leave in the United Kingdom. In an army suffering from somewhat depressed morale, the complete cancellation of leave for any length of time would have been a dangerous step to take. Yet the British army has never faced a greater crisis than it did in March 1918, and it needed all the manpower it could get. The timing of the onslaught was predicted with a high degree of accuracy and the British knew by early March that the Germans had stopped leave in their own army. It is, therefore, rather remarkable that such a significant proportion of British troops were (quite lawfully) absent at the critical moment.[15] This was not Lloyd George's responsibility; it was Haig's.

Haig's inaction on the leave question may have been partly owing to an underestimation of German numerical superiority. On 13 January, during his brief period as intelligence chief at GHQ, Lawrence told Haig that even after they had finished transferring divisions to the West the Germans would "have too small a superiority over the British and French to ensure a decisive victory".[16] Within a few weeks, however, GHQ's estimates of the scale of German transfers to the West were revised dramatically upwards and it was considered that they might eventually have 220 divisions, vastly outnumbering the French and British forces combined.[17] But the speed of transfer seems to have been somewhat underestimated. GHQ estimated that there were 178 German divisions in mid-February against 165 Allied divisions. In mid-March, with no significant change in the Allied forces available for combat, it had identified only 185 German divisions, though, in reality, by 21 March, there appear to have been 191 or 192.[18]

The new defensive system

In order to be able to deal with the distinct possibility of major German offensives the following spring, on 14 December 1917 GHQ had ordered that the British army should adopt a defensive system closely modelled on the one that the Germans had used at Third Ypres. Defence in depth was to be the watchword. There were to be three zones of defence: the Forward Zone, the Battle Zone and the Rear Zone. Each was to be organised in depth. It was intended that the Forward Zone should be relatively lightly held (though sufficient to force the enemy to fight for it) and its defence based largely on machine guns. The Battle Zone was to be laid out on the best ground available for fighting behind the Forward Zone. (The Forward and Battle Zones, as the scheme worked out in practice, were normally one or two miles apart.) The Battle Zone was to be at least 2,000–3,000 yards in depth. Even the most serious enemy attacks were if at all possible to be stopped in this zone, using, where necessary, counter-attacks by corps and Army reserves. But there was also to be a Reserve Zone four to eight miles behind the Battle Zone.[19]

It is commendable that the British were trying to adopt the most up-to-date methods of defence and that they were prepared to learn from their enemies. But there were major problems in trying to do so at this particular time. The Germans had been strategically on the defensive on the Western Front for most of the war and had invested enormous effort both in the physical construction of defences and in the training of troops in defensive methods. The British army had done far less of this. Between December 1917 and March 1918, the fighting troops of the British army were weary, to some degree demoralised, understrength and overstretched and there was a serious shortage of labour troops. Matters were acutely complicated by the extension of the British front. The particularly overstretched Fifth Army found itself in an area that was very poorly fortified and had a very poor infrastructure with relatively little time and inadequate labour to do anything about it. Consequently, across the part of the front on which the Germans were actually to attack in March, the Rear Zone generally existed only on maps, and the fortifications of the Battle Zone remained, on the Fifth Army front, somewhat underdeveloped. Time infantry spent on construction, moreover, could not be spent training. The British army remained undertrained in the methods of dynamic defence appropriate to the new lay out, and GHQ was aware of this.[20]

Haig's dispositions

Fifty of Haig's fifty-eight infantry divisions (not counting two Portuguese divisions on which little reliance was placed) were formally assigned to Haig's four Armies: from north to south, Second, First, Third and Fifth. (There was no Fourth Army at this stage. Rawlinson, whose headquarters normally had that title, was British Military Representative at Versailles.) Haig had only eight divisions in his GHQ reserve. Two of these were located in the rear of each of the Armies, though they were supposed to be ready to move in any direction, as the situation demanded. The weakness of his reserves would be Haig's biggest problem in conducting an effective defence. But he could only increase his reserve by pulling divisions away from Army commanders who, in most cases, already thought themselves badly overstretched.

Though Haig had made a seemingly even distribution of the GHQ reserve divisions (two behind each Army), the British front, on the eve of the offensives, was by no means evenly held. Fifth Army, commanded by General Sir Hubert Gough, was exceptionally thin on the ground. It defended an enormous forty-two-mile stretch with only twelve infantry divisions and three cavalry divisions: a cavalry division having less than half the combat power of an infantry division in defensive fighting. To give an indication of just how fragile Gough's formation had been left in relation to the rest of Haig's army, it is worth noting that Byng's Third Army, immediately to Gough's left, had fourteen infantry divisions to hold a twenty-eight mile front. It is difficult to find any contemporary (i.e., pre-21 March 1918) explanation by Haig of why he left his right, where his forces joined with those of the French army, so extremely weak. The danger was obvious. Lloyd George later alleged Haig's pique as the explanation, that he refused to defend adequately a stretch of front that he had been obliged to take over against his better judgement. At least one recent historian of these events has given his explanation some degree of credit.[21] Whether "pique" is an adequate explanation is open to question. There can be little doubt, however, that both Gough and the General Staff at GHQ concluded in February that Fifth Army's front was indefensible with the forces available in the face of any major and sustained offensive. In such an event, a fairly big retreat was considered almost inevitable and was written into GHQ's plans.

Fifth Army's problems and GHQ's "solutions"

In mid-December 1917 Gough had moved his headquarters, on GHQ's instructions, from Flanders to Nesle, twelve miles south of the town of Péronne.[22] There his Fifth Army took control of VII Corps and the Cavalry Corps from Third Army. This had been a quiet sector and Gough considered its defences inadequate. But the real problems came when Fifth Army extended itself rightwards in two major shifts (of twelve and eighteen miles respectively) in mid and late January. In the sectors taken over from the French (a stretch of about thirty miles) Gough found that only front line defences existed. Battle Zone and Rear Zone fortifications had to be created virtually from scratch. In order to construct these necessary defences, as well as to do vital work on such behind-the-lines infrastructure as railways, roads, bridges and aerodromes, Gough realised that he was going to need a vast amount of labour. GHQ was aware of the problem and the number of Labour Corps troops allocated to Fifth Army rose from 17,400 men on 30 December to 48,000 on 9 March. But most of this total arrived after 27 January and there was insufficient time to carry out all the work necessary. The great majority of the labour was needed, Gough claimed, to create vital infrastructure such as roads, railways, depots, water supply dumps and hospitals, and very little was available to build fortifications.[23] It is certainly arguable, however, that some adjustment of priorities was appropriate and that he should have seen to that.

At the end of January, Gough had intelligence that General von Hutier's Eighteenth Army had taken over responsibility for much of the German front facing the Fifth Army. Gough knew that Hutier had conducted a successful German attack on the Russians at Riga in November 1917. When combined with other evidence, such as the increasing concentration of German reserve divisions and the construction of new German aero-dromes, this made him almost certain that a big attack on his front was to be expected. Gough was well aware that German methods in their recent offensives had involved relatively short artillery bombardments, designed to help achieve surprise. This would give no time for reinforcements to be brought to his front and he was clearly very doubtful of being able to defend his sector adequately with the forces he had. He thus asked for reinforce-ments of both combatant and labour troops.[24]

On 4 February, Davidson sent Gough a paper on "Principles of Defence on Fifth Army Front". This largely accepted Gough's assessment of the particular vulnerability of his sector, much of it devastated by both the 1916 Somme fighting and the systematic vandalism of the German retreat to the Hindenburg Line. Davidson seems to have appreciated that it was the lack of infrastructure (roads, railways and properly buried telephone lines) as much as the inadequacy of the field fortifications that was going to make the sector difficult to defend. Davidson also appears to have realised that it would be impossible to solve these problems before the Germans struck.

In the devastated state of the Fifth Army area communications are one of the primary difficulties for a determined defence of the Battle and Rear Zones.
    We have not the means to render these communications really efficient south of the line Roisel-Péronne.

Davidson's solution, which, a few days later was endorsed by Lawrence and Haig, was to accept that, if Fifth Army were hit hard in the southern part of its front, it might well have to make a substantial retreat.

Although it is considered that we should make our preparations to fight east of the Somme, we must, however, be prepared to be forced back to the line of the Somme. It is therefore of first importance that an emergency zone should be constructed at once along the line of the Somme and Tortille and connected at once by a switch to the existing defensive zones north of Péronne ...

But a retreat to the Somme would create its own difficulties. The loss of Péronne would make it difficult to keep forces in the central and northern portions of the Fifth Army area supplied. If those forces could not be supplied, and were forced to retreat, that might expose the flank of Third Army on their left. Davidson's suggestion for dealing with problem involved the building of yet more fortifications:

In view of the importance of Péronne it is considered that a bridgehead should be constructed at sufficient distance from that place to cover the crossings there and to protect the railway communications through Brie. This can best be done by the construction of a switch from the present rear zone about Marquaix via Bouvincourt to the emergency zone about Pargny.[25]

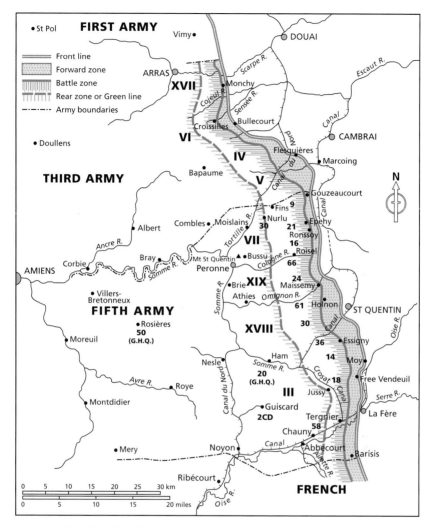

Map 22. The Fifth Army area March 1918

As we have seen, Davidson and Gough had clashed, in June 1917, over Gough's plan for the opening stages of the Third Ypres offensive. In that instance Davidson's critique of Gough's planning and Davidson's advocacy of more cautious, step-by-step methods had been generally sensible. But his suggestions in response to Gough's defensive problems in early 1918 were somewhat absurd. Gough was struggling to fortify his Battle Zone and Rear Zone properly. Davidson offered no real solution to that problem. GHQ still wanted Gough to fight for these zones and thus Gough had to do his best to fortify them. Davidson, however, also recommended the creation of two extra systems of fortification, not hitherto contemplated: a line about twenty-five miles long behind the Tortille and Somme rivers and another line of about the same length covering Péronne, making an extra fifty miles of fortification altogether. Gough points out in his memoirs that the Hindenburg Line was seventy miles long and that the Germans had taken six months to construct it using a vast army of civilian labour. Given his shortage of labour and given that the German offensive was expected in March, what hope did he have of constructing the fortifications GHQ demanded in the time available?

Davidson's ideas were, however, confirmed in a GHQ order to Fifth Army of 9 February. Lawrence signed the order, but Haig was, of course, the ultimate authority behind it. GHQ indicated that it did not now consider it vital to hold the Battle Zone in the Fifth Army area:

It may well be desirable to fall back to the rearward defences of Péronne and the Somme while linking up with the Third Army in the north, and preparing for counter-attack.

Fifth Army was ordered to create a system of fortification called "the emergency defensive zone" behind the Somme and, further north, behind the Tortille. The building of this zone was to be given a high priority, but an even higher one was assigned to the fortification of a bridgehead around Péronne. Once Fifth Army had fallen back to the Tortille, to Péronne and to the Somme, it was to conduct "strong counter-attacks from the direction of Péronne and from the south, possibly assisted by the French Third Army".[26]

GHQ's demands that previously unplanned but extensive and substantial defensive positions be constructed within a few weeks were impossible for Fifth Army to carry out with the resources available. GHQ was making demands on a subordinate formation as absurd as it ever had, casting some doubt on the common belief that its realism and efficiency had been transformed by the dismissal of Kiggell, Charteris and Butler and the arrival of a new team. In the event of a major offensive, Gough's overstretched Army was expected first to resist as manfully as possible in the early stages of an offensive. Secondly, if the attack persisted on a large scale, it was to carry out a lengthy fighting retreat: an exceptionally difficult type of manoeuvre in which British troops had been given little practice since 1914. Thirdly, it was to occupy and hold new defensive positions (which to a considerable extent existed on maps only, not on the ground). Fourthly, it was supposed still to have the energy and resources to conduct major counter-attacks. Gough quite reasonably argued in his memoirs that as a plan for dealing with a really major offensive against his grossly overstretched Army this was all rather preposterous.[27] The only possible justification for the Davidson–Lawrence scheme is that the staff officers concerned thought Fifth Army most likely to be subjected to a substantial but *subsidiary* German attack: not the colossal onslaught actually unleashed on Thursday 21 March.

When Haig was in the Fifth Army area from 13–15 February, however, he found Gough (or so he recorded in his diary) "fit, active and in the best of spirits". Everyone seemed hard at work on preparing to meet the German offensive. Haig emphasised to Fifth Army brigadiers and commanding officers that they needed "to be ready for a *heavy attack*". Referring to the Crozat Canal sector in the south Haig wishfully thought that "if only we had another month to work, this sector *ought* to be very strong". But tacitly he seems to have recognised that the existing state of the fortification was far from adequate. Gough dined with Haig on the latter's train on the night of 15 March, but Haig gives no indication that Gough was expressing extreme alarm or that he was screaming for reinforcements.[28]

There are two explanations for Gough's lack of any really dramatic personal protest to Haig about the extreme vulnerability of his Army prior to 21 March. The first is that he realised that he was now walking on eggshells in career terms. His performances as an Army commander at Bullecourt and in much of the August fighting at Third Ypres had established a reputation (justified or not) for reckless disregard for the lives of his troops. Senior members of his staff had become intensely unpopular with subordinate formations. Much to his chagrin, GHQ had recently removed some of them, including Neil Malcolm, his long-time chief of staff. But Lord Derby, still Secretary of State for War, believed that this did not go far enough. Gough, Derby believed, was a liability and did not "have the confidence of his troops". Both he and Lloyd George considered Gough's removal from command before the offensive started "a very urgent matter".[29] Gough could hardly have been unaware of the widespread feeling against him. By the early months of 1918, Haig was one of his few remaining supporters and by far the most important. Gough may well have considered that Haig's continuing support was likely to depend on his uncomplaining co-operation.

A second explanation (and Gough's own) is that, in a series of conversations in February and March, Haig outlined his strategic thinking and asked for Gough's understanding and co-operation. According to Gough's memoirs, Haig explained that his principal anxiety was for the Channel ports. These were closer to the German front than any significant objective further south and their loss would jeopardise the whole of the British army in France. It was only Gough's sector that was sufficiently far from those ports for Haig to feel that he could allow any real elasticity in the defence. He was thus prepared to leave the Fifth Army sector lightly defended in order to afford greater security in more sensitive areas further north. It may be that Gough to some degree accepted this logic, despite the risks it entailed for his own forces.[30]

Intelligence appreciation, morale and relations with Wilson

On Saturday 16 February Haig held an Army commanders' conference at Doullens. GHQ's intelligence officers were now convinced that a big German offensive was imminent. They thought that the Germans would probably attack in March or perhaps even earlier. An attack on the British front anywhere between Lens and the Oise was considered possible. (In a letter to Byng four days earlier, Lawrence had indicated a portion of the Third and Fifth Army front as GHQ's best guess.) Flanders seemed improbable in the immediate future, as the ground was still too wet. The first German strike was not expected to be the main one. Initial attacks would probably be designed to use up the Allies' reserves and wear their forces down, before they launched their main effort. At this stage GHQ's intelligence thought it most likely that the main German attack would come in Champagne – a view apparently shared by their French opposite numbers.[31]

In late February there was continuing evidence that morale in Haig's forces was somewhat fragile. Haig heard from Lieutenant-General Sir Aylmer Hunter-Weston of VIII Corps that some soldiers had berated MPs visiting the front about the horrors of the war, demanding to know why these continued and what they were fighting for. Haig tried to be philosophical about this, telling Hunter-Weston over lunch at GHQ that:

I thought the best remedy was to let the MPs see some of the best and most thoughtful of our soldiers. There is no doubt that we have, in this very large Army, men of all opinions – ultra Socialists, pacifists and conscientious objectors, as well as real hard fighting patriots.

What the proportion of "patriots" was in relation to the others even Haig did not claim to know, but as his forces prepared for their greatest test so far he must have appreciated that he could not count on all his soldiers fighting well. There is no evidence that Haig lost sleep over this, but it was surely a source of some anxiety to him.

A better piece of news, from Haig's point of view, was that the change of CIGS that had occurred in mid-February was not giving him too much trouble. While at Versailles, Sir Henry Wilson had appeared to Haig to be intending to reduce the General Staff in London "to a local office for *Home* Defence" and concentrating as much power as possible in the hands of the Supreme War Council. That, however, had "changed with his advent to power as CIGS". He did not now "appear so anxious to make the Versailles staff under Rawlinson very strong".[32] After his move to London, moreover, Wilson became much more preoccupied with the Western Front and less interested in adventures in distant theatres. Lloyd George joked that Wilson was really just another "Wully" but still preferred the lighter, less confrontational style of the new CIGS and did not wish the old one back.[33] At the same time Haig had little reason to regret his decision not to risk his career in defence of Robertson.

On Saturday 2 March Haig presided over another Army commanders' conference at Doullens. Brigadier-General Edgar Cox, Haig's intelligence chief, provided a review of what was known about German intentions.[34] The conclusion was that a very big offensive was imminent. There was now no doubt that this would initially strike the British Third and Fifth Armies, though it was also believed that the Germans were making plans for an attack in Flanders when the ground dried out. The best guess was that in attacking the British Third and Fifth Armies the Germans' purpose was that of "cutting off the Cambrai salient and drawing in our reserves". As in mid-February, both British and French intelligence believed that the main German effort would eventually be made against the French army in the Champagne region, possibly with subsidiary attacks at Verdun and in Alsace and Lorraine. In making this analysis they seem to have been taken in by a German deception plan.

Haig "emphasised the necessity of being prepared to meet a big hostile offensive of prolonged duration". Picking up a theme that he and his senior staff officers had been playing since December, he emphasised the need for depth in the defence:

There was a tendency in some divisions to place all the brigades in line instead of keeping one under the hand of the GOC Division ... All Commanders should retain some part of their force to meet the unforeseen!

But Haig weakened these accurate and rather dire intelligence forecasts (and his own generally sensible statements about the need for depth in the defence) with much less apposite remarks. Sometimes quoted out of context, these have been used to suggest an extreme degree of complacency on his part. Haig told

Army commanders that I was very pleased at all that I had seen on the fronts of the 3 Armies which I had recently visited. Plans were sound and thorough, and much work had already been done. I was only afraid that the Enemy would find our front so very strong that he will hesitate to commit his Army to the attack with the almost certainty of his losing very heavily.[35]

A number of comments in Haig's defence seem appropriate here. First, while he allowed for the possibility that the enemy might "hesitate", and while this was a foolish thing to say in the circumstances, Haig did not deny Cox's evidence of a massive German build up against his Third and Fifth Armies. Nor did he contradict his own earlier statement that "a big hostile offensive of prolonged duration" was to be expected and prepared for. The use of the phrase "front so very strong" was certainly silly, but may have been a misguided attempt to boost the morale of his subordinates. Haig had already accepted that Fifth Army was very vulnerable and would probably be forced to make a big retreat if attacked in any strength. His statement that the Germans were facing "the almost certainty of losing very heavily" proved accurate, and we now know that, in the planning stage, Prince Rupprecht, a German Army Group commander with a vital role to play, was pessimistic and hesitant about the whole endeavour.[36] The official record of the conference that GHQ sent to the Armies after the meeting, moreover, mentioned nothing about the possibility of the Germans "hesitating" and made no particular claim for the strength of the British defences. It simply indicated that a German offensive on the fronts of the British Third and Fifth Armies was imminent, that this might "develop into a protracted struggle" and that commanders should satisfy themselves that they were ready to deal with it.[37]

An issue that has remained controversial is the extent to which Haig and his staff understood innovative German offensive methods such as the "Bruchmüller" artillery tactics and infantry "storm troop" tactics. Some points can be made with certainty. By February, at the latest, GHQ understood that the Germans would be aiming at a dramatic breakthrough at some point in their spring offensive, not just limited advances. It was also appreciated that they would try to achieve surprise.[38] Haig's diary mentions German "*stoss-truppen*" at Cambrai in 1917 and they are referred to in a GHQ intelligence summary of 7 January 1918.[39] Haig was thus certainly aware of their existence and, almost certainly, of their tactics. Accounts of the methods the Germans had used in Russia and in Italy in 1917 were widely circulated to British headquarters before the spring offensive began, though some doubt was cast on how well these were likely to work on the Western Front.[40] There is, however, no doubt that, since early February, Gough had seen the relevance of such methods to his poorly defended sector with its underdeveloped infrastructure.[41]

In early March, with a massive German offensive expected at any time, Haig was concerned that he was short of an Army commander. When

Plumer had been sent to Italy towards the end of the Third Ypres campaign Rawlinson had taken over his Army. But on 17 February Haig had agreed that Rawlinson should immediately be transferred to Versailles, where he became the British military representative on the Supreme War Council, replacing Wilson. In return the government had agreed that Plumer should come back to the Western Front. Though an immediate attack in the Flanders sector was not considered likely, the ground in that sector still being too wet, Haig still wanted an experienced Army commander in charge. On 4 March he reminded Derby:

As you know signs are accumulating of an attack being likely at an early date, it is therefore most important that Plumer and his staff take over command hitherto held by Rawlinson and get settled down. A week lost now may never be regained.[42]

On Wednesday 6 March Haig conferred with Pétain at the latter's headquarters. Since the extension of the British front earlier in the year Haig had been concerned about the weakness of his right and had sought assurances of French assistance if the southern wing of Fifth Army came under heavy attack. Though no details were settled at this meeting, Haig's diary indicates that it was entirely amicable. The two national commanders shared a common intelligence appreciation: that the Germans were shortly to attack the British, but that they would also soon strike the French army in the Reims-Champagne sector. Both generals apparently believed that they could co-operate effectively to defeat German moves and considered that they were better off not contributing divisions to a General Reserve controlled from Versailles. It was a sanguine assessment soon to be put to the test.[43]

Between Thursday 7 and Saturday 9 March Haig proceeded to carry out inspections of the front in the Fifth Army and Third Army sectors. The fact that he started his inspection in the III Corps sector on the far right of the British line, gradually working up into the southern part of Third Army, is another indication that GHQ now had little doubt as to where the initial German blow would fall. Haig realised that Lieutenant-General Richard Butler's III Corps, which held the extreme right of the British line, was greatly overstretched. "I think it has a very wide front to defend with three divisions", he noted, "but for a considerable part of that front there are river and marsh obstacles which are said to be impassable at the present time." The late winter and spring was very dry and some of these obstacles were to prove quite negotiable two weeks later. A further potential problem for this overstretched formation, in the most critical of positions, was that its commander was new and untried in his role, having been at GHQ until 25 February. Haig was sufficiently concerned about Fifth Army and III Corps in particular to make one change in his dispositions:

As a result of my visit I ordered the 50th Division to move south to reinforce Fifth Army area from Fourth Army.[44]

London, a son and the return of Plumer: mid-March 1918

Haig crossed the Channel on Tuesday 12 March. There was to be a meeting of the Supreme War Council in London two days later, but it was also good for Haig to be at home for domestic reasons: Doris was due to give birth. The following day Haig saw Derby at the War Office, where he complained about the manpower situation: by June his forces would be 100,000 below their proper establishment. At 10a.m. on Thursday 14 March he was at Downing Street telling Lloyd George and Bonar Law that, by June, he might face very serious manpower problems "if the enemy attacked" – another unfortunate phrase. Perhaps trying to exploit Haig's use of the term "if" with regard to a German offensive, Lloyd George and Bonar Law, according to Haig's account, tried to get him "to say that the Germans would not attack". This Haig refused to do. They reminded him of the doubts he had expressed about an all-out German offensive back in January. But Haig now said that:

[T]he Germany Army and its leaders seemed drunk with their success in Russia ... so that it is impossible to foretell what they may not attempt. In any case we must be prepared to meet a very strong attack on a 50-mile front, and for this drafts are urgently required ...

Two sessions of the Supreme War Council were held that day with a long lunch break between them. It is difficult to say what, if anything, was achieved, but Haig was amused to hear Clemenceau silence Foch when the latter became pushy on the issue of the General Reserve. Haig had lunch with Doris and his sister Henrietta at the latter's London home. Afterwards he took his heavily pregnant wife for a 45-minute walk in the park, presumably to help bring on labour. There was, however, no immediate result.[45] Next day Haig took part in a lengthy discussion of Allied bombing policy. He favoured concentration on military targets and regarded the bombing of German towns as a waste of effort: an opinion he had firmly and, for this moment in history, quite rightly held since 1916.[46]

Between 11 and 12 o'clock on the night of Friday 15 March Doris gave birth at their Kingston Hill home, attended by Colonel Ryan of the Royal Army Medical Corps whom Haig had apparently brought to London to deal with this contingency. When Ryan announced that Doris had delivered a healthy boy and was doing well, Haig gave way to one of his rare outbursts of emotion. Even more inarticulate than usual, he expressed himself by kissing the medical officer "like a Frenchman". Much to Haig's delight, congratulations on the birth flooded in from friends and admirers: the latter including many perfect strangers. The following morning, before returning to GHQ, he called in at Buckingham Palace where the King gave his own congratulations and offered his opinion that morale in the country was now fairly sound.[47]

By the time Haig returned to France, Plumer was back in his old job, commanding Second Army in the Flanders sector. Apparently in a pugnacious mood, Plumer talked of renewing the Flanders offensive of the previous year. Haig realised that he was out of touch and told him that this would not be possible: there was a manpower crisis and the Germans seemed about to mount a massive attack of their own. After dinner on 19 March Lawrence came to see Haig and told him that the long-expected German offensive was now almost certain to be on 20 or 21 March.[48]

The onslaught: 21 March 1918

It was also Lawrence who informed Haig, while he was dressing at 8 a.m. on Thursday 21 March, that the offensive had begun. The Germans had opened a preliminary bombardment at about 4.45 a.m. This lasted some five hours and was followed by infantry assaults across a fifty-mile front from the River Sensee in the north to the Oise in the south.[49] The timing of the attack, the basic location (against Third and Fifth Army) and the frontage (fifty miles) were all much as predicted, though, if forced to commit itself, GHQ's intelligence staff might have placed the centre of the German attacking forces somewhat further north.[50]

The problem was that Haig had left his forces in the southern part of the attack sector so weak that they were completely overmatched. The German Seventeenth Army, Second Army and Eighteenth Army, carrying out the first stage of the German offensive, code-named *Michael*, had seventy-six divisions available, 6,608 guns and 3,534 heavy mortars. The British Third Army and Fifth Army had twenty-six divisions and 2,686 guns between them. For the Fifth Army the odds were still worse than these figures suggest. A recent monograph indicates that on 21 March 1918 British troops on the southern wing of Fifth Army, facing the German Eighteenth Army, were outnumbered eight to one. On the first day the Germans fired 3.2 million rounds at the British Third and Fifth Armies.[51] Applying Occam's razor, there is really no need to seek explanations for initial German success on the Fifth Army front in terms of weaknesses in British morale or tactical understanding (though that is far from saying that such weaknesses were absent).[52] It is doubtful whether any troops in the world could have stood their ground for long under that weight of fire and against that weight of numbers on an imperfectly fortified front, supported by an inadequate infrastructure. An officer based at a British brigade head-quarters wrote a description of what it was like to be subjected to the preliminary bombardment conducted by Colonel Bruchmüller, the great German artillery expert.

I was almost blown out of my bunk by a concussion like an earthquake. I thought a shell must have hit us but the concussion went on ... I then went to the telephone pit and told the signaller to get me on to each battery in turn. The bombardment could not have been going on for much more than a minute, yet every line was cut. And ... all had been buried six feet deep ... It was impossible to find out what was happening.

The Germans were assisted in making their initial break-in by exception-ally foggy conditions. Over much of the front, these lasted well into the afternoon and resulted, in some cases, in the distress flares sent up by British infantry in the Outpost Zone being missed and the British defen-sive barrage consequently not being fired at the appropriate time. Across a good deal of the fifty-mile attack sector the Outpost Zone fell very quickly. But the Germans generally had to fight hard for the Battle Zone and, in most places, had not penetrated it by the end of the first day. The German achievement on 21 March 1918 was not in fact as remarkable as is some-times suggested. They had made an average advance of less than three miles. It was an achievement of the same order as that of, for example, the British Third Army on 9 April 1917, but not much more than that. They had captured some 13,000 prisoners and perhaps 150 guns. This was certainly a big haul for one day, but in relation to the exceptionally vast scale of the offensive, not so astounding. None of the three German armies had reached its first day's objectives. On the northern wing of the German attack, General von Below, commanding the German Seventeenth Army, was seriously disappointed at the progress, as was OHL: the German high command.[53]

Haig, on the other hand, appears to have been in a surprisingly sanguine mood all day. He sent a message to the CIGS demanding that drafts must now be rushed to him and asked for French help on Fifth Army's right in the Oise Valley. In general, however, he pronounced himself satisfied with the day's fighting:

Having regard to the great strength of the attack...I consider that the result of the day is highly creditable to the British troops: I therefore sent a message of con-gratulation to the Third and Fifth Armies for communication to all ranks.[54]

Haig correctly appreciated that the Germans had gained far less ground than they had hoped and he clearly saw this as a kind of victory. He would have remembered that, in the British attacks of the previous year, the first day was generally the most successful. After that the momentum tended to be lost. But that was because German fortifications normally had very substantial depth, because the defenders were able to throw in substantial reserves and because, in some cases, the attackers did not have sufficient fresh troops ready to hand to maintain momentum. None of these factors applied in the British Fifth Army sector on 21 March 1918. Over the next few days Fifth Army's troops would continue to face massive attacks, but Haig had minimal reinforcements immediately available. Though some effort had been put into making arrangements with the French to reinforce the Fifth Army in the event of an emergency, these simply did not provide the scale of reinforcement required quickly enough to meet such an acute emergency. Indeed, the French Third Army, which was supposed to be the immediate source of assistance to the British Fifth, existed only as headquarters without troops. A further problem was that once Fifth Army began retreating, it would have few solid fortifications behind which it could rally. Fifth Army was thus facing not only the prospect of a lengthy retreat, but also the risk of disintegration and destruction. This was, to say the least, not the right moment for a message of congratulations. Given that communications over much of the Fifth Army area forward of corps headquarters had already broken down, German shelling having cut a high proportion of the cables,[55] it is unlikely that many troops received Haig's missive. But that was hardly a matter for regret.

There seems, indeed, to have been very limited communication of any kind between Fifth Army and GHQ during the course of 21 March. There is no record of a telephone conversation between Haig and Gough. Haig seems to have made no arrangement to go and see Gough and no member of the GHQ operations staff went to Fifth Army. Gough records that he spoke to Davidson on the telephone that morning, but Davidson told him that GHQ could send him only one additional division and that might take seventy-two hours to arrive. Gough spoke to Lawrence on the telephone that evening, but Lawrence "did not seem to grasp the seriousness of the situation" and doubted that the Germans would press the attack with the same intensity the following day. Gough recounts that he strongly disagreed.[56] If Gough's report of Lawrence's apparent complacency on the evening of 21 March is accurate, the most likely explanation is that Lawrence still believed that the attack on the British Third and Fifth Armies was not the main German effort and considered that the Germans would soon switch the focus of their attack to the French army in Champagne. That, as we have noted, had been GHQ's best guess on 2 March.

According to his own account, Gough had spent much of Thursday 21 March 1918 trying to gauge the situation, initially by telephone conversations with corps headquarters and later by visiting and talking to corps commanders. But Fifth Army seems to have issued no written orders to its corps during daylight hours on 21 March. At 9.45 p.m., however, Gough ordered a general readjustment of his front. Butler's III Corps was to pull back behind the Crozat Canal, and the other corps would also give some ground. Fifth Army HQ announced its move to Villers Bretonneux and ordered its corps headquarters to retreat too.[57]

Crisis for Fifth Army: 22 and 23 March 1918

Tired by their exertions the previous day, the Germans were slow to renew major assaults on the morning of Friday 22 March, not really getting going until about 11 a.m. By that stage, however, Gough was alarmed at the general situation. He realised that the enemy had made deep penetrations into his Battle Zone in three places (Ronssoy, Maissemy and Essigny) the previous day.[58] In view of his losses and, in the absence of substantial reinforcements, he thought that his Army might be annihilated if he fought to the bitter end to restore and hold that zone. At 10.45 a.m. on Friday 22 March 1918, therefore, he authorised a general retreat should the Germans renew the attack that morning in any force:

In the event of serious hostile attack Corps will fight rear-guard action back to the forward line of Rear Zone and if necessary to the rear line of Rear Zone. Most important that Corps should keep in close touch with each other and carry out retirement in complete co-operation with each other and Corps belonging to armies on flanks.[59]

Once Gough left decisions on when and how far to retreat to the discretion of corps commanders, there was a tendency for Fifth Army to lose cohesion.[60] During the afternoon of Friday 22 March General Sir Ivor Maxse ordered his XVIII Corps to fall back to the rear line of the Rear Zone, which, in his sector, was just east of the Somme. But he then quickly concluded that halting his corps with its back to a major river was not a good idea, and, during the night, his troops crossed to the west bank. Apparently at some stage on Friday 22 March, Maxse did inform Gough that he intended to pull back behind the Somme. The move is confirmed in a Fifth Army order issued at 9.57 p.m. But it inevitably resulted in a big gap the next morning between XVIII Corps and Lieutenant-General H. E. Watts' XIX Corps immediately to the north. Apparently there was also some failure of communication between Maxse and Watts and between Gough and Watts for Watts, claimed that Maxse's retreat behind the Somme took him by surprise. When Watts' XIX Corps and its northern neighbour, Lieutenant-General Sir William Congreve's VII Corps, fell back in compliance with Maxse's move in the course of Saturday 23 March, the position of Third Army's V Corps, which was trying to extricate itself from the Flesquières Salient and already in acute difficulty, was further jeopardised.[61]

Meanwhile, Gough had telephoned Haig at 8 p.m. on 22 March and indicated that the Germans had penetrated parts of Fifth Army's Rear Zone. Fifth Army would thus have to fall back to the Péronne bridgehead and the Somme "in accordance with [Haig's] orders". Haig authorised this. Haig's only significant interventions on the second day of the offensive were to telegraph Pétain to inform him of Gough's decision and to ask for more help. Pétain had already despatched three divisions to the Crozat Canal sector to shore up III Corps at the southern end of the British line, for which Haig expressed sincere appreciation.[62] Maxse's pulling of XVIII Corps behind the Somme on the night of 22–23 March forced Fifth Army's two northern corps to retreat rapidly on Saturday 23 March. It then became unreasonable to expect the northern wing of XIX Corps to stop in a position that there had been no time to fortify properly, east of the river. The Péronne bridgehead concept (never more than a GHQ pipe dream) had no discernible impact on events. By dawn on Sunday 24 March practically the whole of Fifth Army north of the Oise was behind the Crozat Canal, the Somme and the Tortille.[63]

Crisis in Third Army: 23–24 March 1918

The period 23–26 March represented the most acute period of crisis during the first of the German offensives of 1918 and one of the most acute crises of the entire war. Until the early hours of Saturday 23 March, Third Army, much stronger than Fifth Army in relation to the stretch of the front it held, had generally resisted the German onslaught fiercely. It had given some ground, but only a few miles at most. It appeared to be maintaining a coherent front. But a major emergency developed on its southern wing that day.[64]

As far back as December, GHQ had told Byng that the Flesquières Salient was to be regarded as untenable in the event of a major German offensive. It was not a suitable place to fight a decisive battle. Apparently considering that Byng was tending to ignore its instructions in this matter, on 10 March 1918 GHQ sent him a direct order to hold this salient as a "false front": to be lightly held and evacuated quickly in the event of a major attack.[65] But Byng seemed to have little belief in GHQ's defence-in-depth philosophy and, in the weeks prior to the offensive, it was a matter of serious concern to GHQ that he was concentrating his forces too far forward and neglecting his more rearward defences.[66]

At the beginning of the offensive Byng held the Flesquières Salient strongly, with three divisions of V Corps. His Battle Zone behind the Salient, however, seems to have been left very poorly developed. Though V Corps, on Byng's orders, evacuated the apex of the salient by 6 a.m. on 22 March, Third Army did not sanction the evacuation of the salient as whole until 1.30 a.m. on 23 March. Fanshawe appears to have been somewhat slow in passing the order on. By the time V Corps' withdrawal commenced, the 47th Division (on the extreme right of Third Army) was in real difficulty. The Germans had managed to get round its right flank. It was forced off its intended line of withdrawal and compelled to retreat north-west. By 6 p.m. on 23 March there was thus a three-mile gap between Third Army and Fifth Army. As the retreat continued that night it tended to widen. V Corps as a whole had been much battered in the Flesquières Salient, where it had particularly suffered from intense bombardment with gas shell. Nearing exhaustion already, under the further strain of the retreat it came close to collapse.[67]

On Saturday 23 March Haig visited both Byng and Gough for the first time since the offensive began. At his Albert headquarters (from which he felt compelled to retreat that evening) Byng put on a bold front for Haig, reporting himself "on the whole quite satisfied with the situation". Haig apparently left Albert with little idea of the magnitude of the crisis facing V Corps. He then moved to Villers Bretonneux, ten miles east of Amiens: the location to which Fifth Army's headquarters had retreated the previous day. He saw Gough in the early afternoon but was able to offer little practical help. He had lunch at a chateau at Dury, which had just been established as his Advanced GHQ. There, at 4 p.m., he met Pétain. The latter had already formed an Army Group, consisting of two Armies under General Fayolle, to operate in the Somme valley supporting the British right. Haig recognised that:

P. is most anxious to do all he can to support me. The basic principle of co-operation is to keep the [British and French] Armies in touch. If this is lost and the Enemy comes in between us, then probably the British will be rounded up and driven into the sea! This must be prevented even at the cost of abandoning the north flank![68]

Up to the afternoon of Saturday 23 March, therefore, Haig and Pétain were, at least ostensibly, working well together. Pétain was organising support for the British right without having to be asked, and Haig, showing appreciation of Pétain's loyal support, had apparently resolved to stick by the French even at some risk of jeopardising his cross-Channel communications. In reality, however, the speed of the British withdrawal had disconcerted Pétain, and within the next thirty-six hours trust and co-operation between Haig and himself were to break down to an extremely dangerous degree. After his meeting with Pétain, Haig left Advanced GHQ at Dury and returned to his house at Beaurepaire, near Montreuil. There, at 7 p.m., he held a conference with Plumer, Horne, Lawrence and Davidson. He arranged that Plumer should hold his Flanders front with eight divisions, releasing 3rd, 4th and 5th Australian Divisions to go south.[69] This was something he should arguably surely have done days, if not weeks, earlier. The ground was still too wet in Flanders for an offensive to have much chance of success. Plumer made no difficulty about releasing these formations. Haig commented:

It is most satisfactory to have a commander of Plumer's temperament at a time of crisis like the present.[70]

The crisis intensifies: Haig, Byng and Pétain on 24 March

Haig went to church on the morning of Sunday 24 March and took some comfort from the sermon. The morning news did not seem so bad. By afternoon, however, the situation looked darker than ever. Haig knew that the Germans were over the Tortille and advancing on Amiens: a rail centre of great importance to the supply of his troops in the Somme region. Haig dined with Byng at his Beauquesne HQ at 8.30 that night. As usual, Byng and his staff put on a brave face. Haig, however, was clearly troubled. He told Byng to make sure that he stayed in touch with Horne's First Army in the Arras sector, but apparently accepted that a fairly rapid retreat would continue on Third Army's southern wing and that the Germans were likely to reach Amiens, perhaps to capture it. He told Byng that his intention was to concentrate all the reserves he could by thinning out his line in the north, and, with these, to strike southward "when the Enemy has penetrated to Amiens". The prospective counterstroke he outlined here seems to have been intended to recover Amiens if that place fell to the Germans and to restore touch between Third and Fifth Armies if that were lost.

At 11 p.m. that night, Haig met Pétain at Haig's Advanced GHQ at Dury. They agreed that Gough's Fifth Army should now form part of the French northernmost Army Group under General Fayolle. According to his diary, Haig asked Pétain to concentrate a large force at Abbeville "to co-operate on my right". To Pétain this must have seemed extraordinary. Abbeville was on the Somme, certainly, but some thirty miles north-north-west of Amiens. Confusingly, an undated British typescript record of the meeting (probably drawn up later than Haig's manuscript diary and with a view to the defence of the commander-in-chief's reputation) indicates Amiens not Abbeville as the place where Haig wanted Pétain to concentrate French forces. But if at this late night meeting on Sunday 24 March Haig really said "Abbeville", the place mentioned in the original, manuscript version of his diary, it might well have indicated to Pétain that he had given up Amiens as lost. Pétain might well have drawn the further inference either that Haig had lost his nerve or that he had accepted that his forces in the Somme valley were now in a condition bordering on complete collapse. So far Pétain had been helpful in moving divisions to shore up the British right. Indeed, though he now told Haig that he was expecting an attack in Champagne at any moment, he said he would spare whatever troops he could for Fayolle's Army Group. He may or may not have told Haig that, while continuing to do his best to help the British, he had now decided to give covering Paris a higher priority than staying in touch with them. (The manuscript and typescript versions of Haig's diary differ on this point.) The decision to prioritise covering Paris, however, was certainly one that Pétain had communicated to his subordinate commanders earlier in the day.[71]

Pétain's prognosis for the development of the German offensive programme (that the main focus would shortly shift to the French army in Champagne) had been GHQ's from mid-February until at least 2 March. Gough's report of Lawrence's telephone conversation with him on the evening of 21 March suggests that it was still GHQ's best guess up until that point. It may have continued to be so until late on 22 March. An intelligence briefing given by Cox on the morning of 23 March, however, indicated that the current German offensive was an all-out effort. The actual German aim, Haig now believed, was to drive a wedge between the British and the French armies and, having isolated the British army, to destroy it.[72] But, even on 24 March, Haig had no definite information that the Germans would not attack in Champagne and he could hardly blame Pétain for still thinking that they would.

Haig later claimed (in a revised, typescript version of his diary) that he was deeply dissatisfied with Pétain's response at this interview. Pétain had seemed unbalanced and obsessed with the protection of Paris to the detriment of co-operation with the British. But this is far less evident in the brief account provided in the original, manuscript version of the diary. Pétain, on the other hand, probably had good reason to leave this late-night encounter believing that the British southern wing was irretrievably disintegrating, that Haig had despaired of holding Amiens and that, with his request for French flank protection as far back as Abbeville, he might be thinking of soon pulling his remaining forces back towards the Channel ports. Recent scholarship indicates that, over the next two days, Pétain continued to do his best to help the British and that he realised, on

Monday 25 March, that he was now unlikely to be attacked in Champagne in the immediate future. Nevertheless, by Tuesday 26 March, the cumulative strain seems to have been too much for him. He was apparently close to despair and had lost confidence in being able to restore cohesion to the Allies' defence on the Somme.[73]

The crisis peaks: 25 March

At about 11 a.m. or 11.30 a.m. on Monday 25 March, Sir Henry Wilson, the CIGS, arrived at GHQ to see Haig. According to Haig's subsequent version of events, Wilson came in response to a telegram Lawrence had sent on Haig's instructions shortly after 3 a.m., a telegram that also demanded the presence of Lord Milner. But the manuscript and typescript versions of Haig's diary differ appreciably at this point.[74] The typescript diary (Haig's preferred version of history) is unconvincing. Wilson's footwork would have had to be exceptionally fast to enable him to arrive at GHQ by 11.30 a.m. in response to a telegram received in London after 3 a.m., and it is difficult to imagine Haig summoning Milner at that hour. Milner was not even serving in the War Office at this stage and was certainly not at Haig's beck and call. Even Haig's preferred version does not reflect particularly well on him. He must have been in a very high state of anxiety to demand that Wilson, a man whose military abilities he had once regarded with contempt, should rush to France to bail him out of a crisis. But that version does at least give Haig a central role in the drama. In reality events had slipped out of Haig's control. Others, most notably Lloyd George, Foch and Wilson, had recognised this. They were intervening over his head. Perhaps more in retrospect than at the time, Haig seems to have found this humiliating and sought to rewrite the record.

By the time Haig claims to have summoned him, Milner was already in France, Lloyd George having asked him, after a War Cabinet meeting on Saturday 23 March, to go as his emissary. Milner left London on 24 March and had passed through GHQ, where Davidson gave him a briefing, before Haig had returned from his late-night meeting with Pétain. From GHQ Milner had gone on to Versailles, arriving there at 2.30 a.m. on Monday 25 March. Spending the night in a hotel, he spoke to Rawlinson early the following morning, and then went on to see Clemenceau in Paris. On the afternoon of 25 March, he attended a conference at Pétain's headquarters at Compiègne.[75] Wilson's presence at GHQ during the late morning of Monday 25 March seems to have been mainly the result of a telephone conversation with Foch at 5.30 p.m. on Sunday 24 March, though another with Haig later that evening confirmed the necessity for it. Wilson had thus decided to go to France some hours before

Haig's late-night meeting with Pétain and did not come in response to anything said at that meeting. Wilson left London by special train at 6.50 a.m. on 25 March and crossed the Channel by destroyer.[76]

What seems certain is that on the morning of Monday 25 March Haig told Wilson that the outcome of the war depended on the scale and promptitude of French support for the British army. He needed the help of twenty French divisions north of the Somme and thought that would require a decision by Clemeneau – overruling Pétain if necessary. Wilson's version is that he suggested that the situation required greater unity of command and proposed that Foch take responsibility for co-ordinating the French and British armies. Haig needed some persuasion but eventually agreed. Wilson's version makes sense in that Foch and Wilson were old friends. But it is also quite possible that the idea of making Foch responsible for Franco-British co-ordination originated with Milner.[77] In the course of Monday 25 March the Germans continued to advance. Wilson and Haig proposed a high-level Franco-British conference, involving the French Prime Minister, at Abbeville that afternoon, but were unsuccessful in arranging it. A conference was eventually scheduled for Doullens at midday on Tuesday 26 March. Haig, however, saw Colonel Weygand, Foch's chief-of-staff at Abbeville at about 4 p.m. Haig gave Weygand a note addressed to Clemenceau demanding (according to Haig's manuscript diary) that the French concentrate "as large a force as possible north of the Somme, about Amiens". But Haig apparently failed to express his meaning clearly. Weygand came away from this meeting thinking that Haig intended to mount his defence west of Amiens: that he had no confidence in holding the city.[78]

Doullens conferences: 26 March 1918

On Tuesday 26 March Haig attended three conferences at Doullens. The first, commencing about 11 a.m., was with Plumer, Horne and Byng. Haig insisted on the importance of holding Amiens, and Horne offered to pull one of his Canadian divisions out of the line to make it available to be sent south if required.[79] Of course, nothing said or done at this meeting could have any immediate result. Though, in general, German pressure was slackening, co-operation between Third Army and what was left of Fifth Army broke down to some degree that day. Part of VII Corps had been transferred to Third Army at 4 a.m. on Monday 25 March 1918. Its rapid withdrawal resulted in touch being lost with Fifth Army's left at Bray by the Tuesday evening.[80]

At 11.40 a.m. the second conference of the day began. It was a meeting of Haig, his Army commanders and some senior staff officers with Milner and Wilson. Haig said that sixty-nine of the 193 German divisions identified on the Western Front were involved in the current attack. But he could "hold on" if the French would bring "all available troops" to cover "the direct road to Amiens". Milner said that he had assurances from Clemenceau and Foch that the French would do whatever was necessary in this respect.[81]

The third and most celebrated Doullens conference of 26 March started at noon. It was an august gathering including Poincaré, Clemenceau and Milner on the political side and Foch, Pétain, Wilson and Haig on the military. Everyone agreed that Amiens must be held and Milner proposed that Foch should co-ordinate operations in that sector. According to his own account, Haig then said this proposal did not go far enough. Foch should be given authority to co-ordinate the activities of the British and French armies on the Western Front as a whole. Everyone agreed to this.[82] The precise extent of Foch's powers was not clearly defined at Doullens and, while the tendency of subsequent inter-Allied meetings was to increase his authority, it was never to become absolute.

Haig's immediate reaction to the outcome of the third Doullens conference was one of relief. After his return to GHQ he went out riding. It was one of his favourite forms of relaxation and one in which he did not seem to have engaged since the German offensive began. Wilson, who encountered him during the ride, thought he suddenly looked ten years younger.[83] Haig later tried to persuade posterity that he, in contrast with some others, had remained unruffled throughout the March crisis. In the altered, typescript version of his diary he suggested that, at Doullens, Pétain was "in a funk" and had "lost his nerve". Even in the original manuscript version, he remarked that both the King and Prime Minister, who each visited the front over the next few days, looked as though they had been suffering from "funk".[84] Historians can make themselves ridiculous trying to be psychologists. But it here seems reasonable to suggest that Haig was easing his mind ascribing to others an emotion of which he now felt ashamed in himself.

Foch was not slow to assert the authority granted by the Doullens conference, ill-defined and limited as it was. Shortly after the conference finished he arrived at Fifth Army's HQ at Dury. With a fine touch of melodrama he entered, delivered a furious and rather insulting tirade in the French language, demanded to know why Gough was not personally at the front, ordered that "There must be no more retreat; the line must be held at all costs" and walked out.[85] He next went to see General Fayolle, the "Reserve Army Group commander" with whom he apparently interacted in a somewhat more civil manner. They arranged for three French divisions to go to Amiens and for Debeney's French 1st

Army to enter the line between Humbert's 3rd Army (currently on the French left) and the battered British Fifth Army, reducing the latter's front. It was, however, easy enough to order "no more retreats". It was much more difficult to make that a reality on the ground. The right wing of Debeney's 1st French Army was bashed in almost as soon as it entered the line. Montdidier was abandoned on the evening of Wednesday 27 March and a gap temporarily opened between the French First and Third Armies.[86]

The Germans lose momentum: 26–28 March 1918

Yet, while he probably did not realise it initially, Foch had taken over at a favourable moment. The loss, on Tuesday 26 March, of Albert (a town that had been well to the British rear throughout the Somme campaign of 1916) more or less represented the German high tide north of the Somme, as did the loss of Montdidier further south.[87] By 28 March the first German offensive of 1918, codenamed *Michael*, had practically ground to a halt. This was a development to which Foch had made only a limited positive, practical contribution. His main influence (and this may well have been decisive) was moral and, in a sense, negative. He insisted that the British and French armies rally, stick together and defend Amiens. He did not panic and did not authorise any more major withdrawals. In particular he did not authorise a French withdrawal to cover Paris.

A crucial factor in halting the offensive was the sheer physical exhaustion of German troops. In the Somme valley they were now struggling across zones devastated in the 1916 battles. The roads and drainage system had been smashed and the ground was pitted with shell holes. It was difficult enough for the infantry to traverse, and exceptionally so for the artillery. German horses were in poor shape even before the offensive began, and this contributed to a partial breakdown of German logistics. Much of the time, as British intelligence realised, the German troops were not even being fed properly. The Royal Flying Corps, moreover, was subjecting them to massive and relentless low-flying attack.[88] Major-General Sir Frederick Maurice, the Director of Military Operations at the War Office, thought that 25 March was the turning point. He considered that the British army had suffered about 53,000 casualties (certainly a major underestimate), but noted that 88,000 men on leave had been returned to France and another 106,000 had been sent out. More important, perhaps, was the *ad hoc* reorganisation of Allied forces that (as we have noted) had taken place over several days, reinforcing the Fifth and Third Army sectors with French and British divisions and dramatically reducing the length of the Fifth Army front.[89]

Ludendorff's concept of operations had changed since the start of his offensive on 21 March. His original intention seems to have been for *Michael* to swing north-west: towards the Channel coast. In reality, however, he had no very definite strategy. His approach was essentially opportunistic. Pleased with the success of von Hutier's Eighteenth Army against the southern wing of the British Fifth Army, and disappointed with the Seventeenth Army's progress further north, he used a high proportion of his forces on the line of least resistance: seeking to drive a wedge between the British and French armies. This has sometimes been dismissed as an error, but it can be seen as an intelligent piece of opportunism that came remarkably close to complete success. Arguably Ludendorff's real problem was that he was too muddleheaded to adequately concentrate his forces at any particular point. While failing to do enough to exploit the gaping hole between the British Third and Fifth Armies, which opened up on a number of occasions between 22 and 26 March, he went ahead, on 28 March, with another long-contemplated scheme for an offensive by the German Seventeenth Army in the Arras sector, at the junction of the British First and Third Armies. It was codenamed *Mars*.[90]

GHQ's intelligence branch predicted *Mars* with impressive exactitude.[91] At 7.30 a.m. on Thursday 28 March, in the Arras sector, astride the River Scarpe, at the junction of the British First and Third Armies, the German Seventeenth Army mounted an assault with nine divisions. This followed a four-and-a-half-hour preliminary bombardment by 1,250 guns. At the same time the offensive was renewed in a less concentrated form along the whole of the front of the British Third Army. North of the Scarpe the Germans were able to overrun the Outpost Zone, but did not make much progress beyond it. Further south they gained very little ground. The Arras sector was generally well fortified and strongly held and the Germans did not enjoy the assistance of the heavy fog that had helped them on 21 March. "Storm troop tactics" were not in evidence during *Mars*. In most places British infantry reported the Germans coming on in dense formations and being shot down in droves – "repulsed with slaughter", as Haig put it.[92]

Assessment

German attacks as part of *Michael* continued north and south of the Somme up to 5 April. But these did not have the force of earlier efforts and they met adequate levels of resistance. Though this was not clear at the time, by 28 March the Allies had won the opening round. They had lost a lot of ground, but none of it vital. The British Fifth Army had been pulverised and reduced to a mere shadow of its former self, but it had not altogether disintegrated. There was no real rout: no Western Front

Caporetto. Allied (predominantly British) casualties were heavy, but those of the Germans were possibly heavier: 212,000–230,000 are the estimates of a recent monograph. In the long run the Germans could afford these far less.[93] Though morale in Haig's army was distinctly low by autumn 1917, it had not cracked under this offensive. Indeed, in the bulk of the BEF (though not in Fifth Army), it had apparently started to rise again by about 26 March.[94] In fighting on this scale there were inevitably instances of ineffectual resistance, panic and dereliction of duty. But, as the German casualty figures tend to show, a degree of doggedness was rather more predominant.[95]

Between 23 and 26 March Haig appears to have been under acute psychological strain. By proposing, on the night of 24 March, that French troops should be concentrated in support of his right flank as far back as Abbeville, he gave Pétain legitimate reason to believe that he had given up Amiens as lost and that he had little faith in the capacity for continued resistance of British forces on the Somme. Had they been left to themselves, it is quite likely that, over the next couple of days, co-operation between Haig and Pétain would have broken down completely. Contact between the French army and the great bulk of the British army might then have been lost. Had the Germans achieved that much, there is every chance that, by continuing to focus their attacks on the British army, they could have destroyed it as a fighting force, perhaps resulting in its evacuation from the Continent. Given the extreme immaturity of the American army and with the French army heavily outnumbered, the Germans might then have been in a good position to impose peace on their terms. Owing to the intervention of individuals, including Lloyd George, Milner, Wilson, Clemenceau and Foch, this potential catastrophe was avoided. By the evening of 26 March Haig was feeling much more relaxed and within forty-eight hours the most extreme phase of the crisis had passed. The famous "backs to the wall" order still lay a fortnight ahead. But, with the inestimable luxury of hindsight, it is possible to say that, for the British, by 28 March, the worst was already over.

18　The turn of the tide

Gough's dismissal

The worst of the first *Michael* offensive was over by 29 March and its last spasm died away after 5 April, leaving three rather less furious days before the next storm broke. Haig's intelligence staff realised that any respite would probably be brief. The Germans were known to have a large number of divisions still in reserve.[1] A crisis atmosphere persisted. But while trying to work out where the next blow would fall and to take steps to meet it, Haig was also clearing debris left by the opening round.

The career of Sir Hubert Gough was amongst the wreckage. Haig had, as we have noted, left an Army commander who had been a personal favourite but who had become unpopular with much of the rest of the army and discredited in the eyes of the government, with a grossly over-stretched Army in an untenable position. It certainly seems unjust to heap on Gough all the blame for what happened to Fifth Army on 21–26 March. But the events of those days added Pétain and Foch to the long list of important people whose confidence he had lost.[2] In these circumstances there was little chance of his remaining an Army commander. We have already seen how Haig dealt with some intensely loyal subordinates who eventually became liabilities, most notably Charteris and Kiggell. His tendency in such cases was to show as much reciprocal loyalty as possible short of sacrificing his own career. When he finally dropped such people, he tried to provide soft landings. That was very much his approach to the Gough case. When he met Wilson and Milner while out riding on the evening of 26 March, shortly after the Doullens conference, the subject of Gough came up. By his own account Haig said

whatever the opinion at home might be, I considered that he had dealt with a most difficult situation very well. He never lost his head, was always cheery and fought hard.[3]

But Foch's grossly insulting behaviour towards the British Fifth Army commander on the afternoon of 26 March suggests that he knew he would

461

not have to work with him for any length of time. Foch and Wilson (who were old friends) had both been at the Doullens conference earlier that afternoon. It is highly probable that they had discussed Gough's removal then.

On 29 March Haig noted that

Foch has brought great energy to bear on the present situation, and has, instead of permitting French troops to retire south-west from Amiens, insisted on some of them relieving our troops and covering Amiens at all costs. He and I are quite in agreement as to the general plan of operations.[4]

At this stage, therefore, Haig needed Foch and Wilson far more than he needed Gough. Wilson wanted Henry Rawlinson, another old friend, to take over what was left of Fifth Army and Haig evidently offered no serious opposition to this. On the day of the Doullens conference Rawlinson was told that the command was his. Haig's Military Secretary told Gough that he was to be replaced at about 5 p.m. the following day. After Foch's elevation, Rawlinson assumed command of Fifth Army at 4.30 p.m. on Thursday 28 March.[5] In Haig's eyes, however, Gough was in no sense in disgrace. He was a dinner guest at GHQ on the evening of Friday 29 March, where Haig told him that he and his staff were to come out of the line and undertake a reconnaissance of the Somme valley from Amiens to the sea. A defensive line behind Amiens might still be necessary and Gough and his staff (now to be called "Reserve Army") were to decide where this should be.[6] The term "Reserve Army" had a certain historical resonance: Gough's Army had been called that when it was formed in 1916. In spring 1918, however, with no reserve to command, Reserve Army was little more than a means of letting Gough down lightly.

By Tuesday 2 April Rawlinson's reconstituted Fourth Army staff had completed the takeover of the headquarters at Dury and the remnants of Gough's former command were now termed Fourth Army. A Reserve Army headquarters opened at Crécy on the following day. In May it would become the kernel of a new Fifth Army under General Sir William Birdwood.[7] But Gough was, even nominally, in command of the 1918 Reserve Army for only a few days. Lloyd George had no intention of allowing him the soft landing that Haig had prepared. Talking to the Prime Minister on 3 April, after a Franco-British conference at Beauvais, Haig got the impression that:

LG expects to be attacked in the House of Commons for not tackling the man-power problem before, also for sending divisions to the East at a critical time. He is looking for a scapegoat for the retreat of the Fifth Army. I pointed out that "fewer men, extended front and increased hostile forces" were the main causes. He was much down upon Gough. I championed his case ... [If] LG wishes him suspended he must send me an order to that effect.[8]

Derby sent Haig a telegram to that effect the very next day: Gough was to be relieved of any and all commands and sent home. He was, as Haig had rightly put it, a "scapegoat". Arguably he had deserved the sack for mistakes earlier in the war. Perhaps he should have co-ordinated the retreat of his four corps rather more effectively in March 1918. But in the circumstances no commander could have prevented Fifth Army taking massive casualties and making a big retreat. Gough's performance in 1918 did not in itself merit the humiliating treatment he eventually received: placed on half pay and left conspicuously unemployed for the rest of the war.[9] When he had lunch with Gough on Friday 5 April Haig "told him of the orders received from the Secretary of State for War for him to go home". Haig indicated that he had supported Gough "to the utmost of my power" and that it was the Cabinet that had taken the decision.[10] But there is no real evidence that Haig had stuck his neck out in Gough's defence. His protests had been much too limited and private to put the government under any pressure. After the war Haig reportedly admitted to a friend of Gough's that he had realised that "the public...demanded a scapegoat". Gough and he were the only ones possible and Haig was "conceited enough" to think that the Army could not spare him.[11]

Lunch with Gough that Friday may, however, have pricked Haig's conscience enough to precipitate a half-baked gesture of sympathy with him. The following day, in a private letter to Derby, he offered his own resignation.[12] This was not, however, an active threat to resign unless Gough were treated better, but a passive offer to go if the government wished. It was an offer he had made before and was largely meaningless. As he knew perfectly well, the government was free to dispense with his services at any time, with or without his agreement. His ready acceptance of it might minimise administrative disruption, royal censure and political fall-out, but it was certainly not a requirement. On this occasion Haig's resignation offer was taken more seriously than he had probably expected. Derby read the letter to the War Cabinet meeting on 8 April. Lloyd George, Curzon, Bonar Law and Hankey discussed it at a less formal gathering afterwards. On this occasion, according to Hankey, what saved Haig was not the support he had once enjoyed in Parliament. That had nearly all evaporated after the March retreat. The main problem, as at the time of the Smuts–Hankey mission in January, was that there was "no very obvious successor". Hankey thought "Plumer in whom the troops are said to have confidence" was "as stupid as Haig himself".[13] Wilson also gave Haig some (rather negative and unenthusiastic) support. Given that no outstanding personality had emerged as a replacement, Wilson suggested that the government wait for Haig's report on the March fighting before making a decision.[14]

Reform At GHQ

While Gough was being replaced and Haig's career was still in the balance, less dramatic but perhaps equally important developments were taking place at GHQ. During the course of March and April the General Staff was reorganised into two sections: Operations and Staff Duties. The new Operations section, under "Tavish" Davidson, now a major-general, included both what was formerly Davidson's operations branch, known as "Oa", and now under Brigadier-General John Dill, and Intelligence under Brigadier-General Edgar Cox. A large part of the point of this was apparently to integrate intelligence better with operations, while somewhat cutting down the size of what had become, in Charteris's time, a vast and unwieldy intelligence empire. The new Staff Duties section, under Major-General Guy Dawnay, took charge of subsections dealing with the BEF's organisation, Training, Machine Guns and Anti-Aircraft, though the machine gun sub-section was short-lived. In June the officers in charge of censorship and publicity were moved out of the Intelligence sub-section and placed under Staff Duties. In June there was a further reorganisation on the logistics side. The most obvious of these was that the separate Transportation department that had been established under Eric Geddes was put back under the Quartermaster-General now that the more competent Lieutenant-General Sir Travers Clarke had replaced Maxwell in that post. At the same time Clarke established better contact and better relations between the QMG's department and the wider army.

Haig's personal role in these reforms has never been elucidated. They followed in the wake of personnel changes that had been imposed upon him against his wishes. While there is no evidence that he resisted them, it seems equally unlikely that he personally inspired them. As with the personnel changes that preceded them, some historians see these reforms as vital to Haig's army's ability to survive the spring offensives and ultimately to mount a successful counter-offensive. Certainly the vast improvement in the British army's logistical performance on the Western Front, in progress since late 1916, can be attributed in large measure to greater expertise and better organisation at GHQ. On the operations side, however, it is much more difficult to establish clear links between changes in personnel and structure at Montreuil and the effectiveness of the army in the field. Successes in the second half of 1918 probably owed something to improvements at GHQ,[15] but possibly a good deal more to the greater delegation of decision making to Army and corps commanders and more still to changes in external circumstances.

Haig, Foch and the Beauvais agreement

In late March and early April, Haig was still intensely and quite rightly worried about further German offensives and (after only a few days of honeymoon with Foch) about the attitude of his French allies. At the beginning of April he still did not believe that the French army was doing enough to support him in the Amiens sector and wanted the French line extended north to cover the valley of the little River Luce, south of the Somme. Haig again found that he had a rapport with the French premier, Georges Clemenceau, whose energy and determination he had long recognised. When they met at Dury on Monday 1 April, Clemenceau was eager to help. He summoned Foch by telephone. Foch came and signed the necessary order on the spot. Clemenceau told Haig that he was quite sure that the British would be able to co-operate effectively with Foch, but was less certain of Pétain. The French premier valued pugnacity and, according to Haig, considered Pétain somewhat "nervous". Haig had no difficulty in concurring with Clemenceau's proposal that Foch's position should be strengthened so that the Generalissimo could override Pétain if the need arose.[16]

Lloyd George, Clemenceau, Foch, Pétain, Haig and Pershing (the last-named not having been present at the Doullens conference) all met at Beauvais on 3 April. The description of Foch's powers was amended somewhat to give him overall charge of the "strategical direction of military operations". Grand tactics and the right of appeal to national governments were left to the national commanders-in-chief. Pétain would have realised that he would rarely get much joy appealing to Clemenceau over Foch's head. But for Haig and Pershing the right of appeal was an important one. Haig also used the Beauvais meeting "to ask the Governments to state their desire that a French offensive should be started *as soon as possible* in order to attract the Enemy's reserves and to prevent him from continuing his pressure against the British". Foch and Pétain both indicated their willingness to help in this way.[17]

Yet nothing of the kind materialised over the next few days. By Friday 5 April Haig was increasingly doubtful that the French would mount any serious offensive, believing that their army was too war-weary. He thought it still possible that the Germans might take Amiens and push on towards Abbeville near the Channel coast, a move that would practically sever the link between the British and French armies. He therefore discussed with General Asser, who commanded his lines of communication, the construction of some new south-facing defensive positions "with the object of covering Rouen and Havre".[18]

Haig was also pretty certain that the British army would be subjected to another massive attack, well to the north of the Somme, over the next few days. The latest intelligence he had received suggested this might be an attempt at the double envelopment of Vimy Ridge. It was also considered possible that there might be a small attack on the Lys, in the First Army sector, where the Portuguese held a short stretch of front. In these circumstances, doubtful as he was of French combat effectiveness, Haig thought he needed whatever help he could get. He sent Davidson to see Foch at his Beauvais headquarters on 6 April. Davidson suggested three possible courses of action:

(1) The French could launch an offensive – as they had agreed at the Beauvais conference.
(2) They could take over the British front as far north as the Somme.
(3) They could mass reserves behind Vimy Ridge – the sector where the British considered the next German effort most likely.

But Foch made no definite response. Haig therefore wrote to him later the same day making the same demands.[19] Foch agreed to meet Haig at Aumales on Sunday 7 April. At that meeting Foch did not demur from Haig's belief in the imminence of another major German offensive against the British. But he seems to have been unconvinced that the Germans would strike further north. Barring the door to Amiens was still his first concern. He was perfectly happy to order an attack to drive the German away from that city provided Rawlinson's Fourth Army would co-operate with General Debeney's French First. At this stage, as Foch must have known, Fourth Army largely consisted of the shattered or exhausted remains of Gough's command. It was in no condition for serious offensive action. Haig may have been right that this was just a ploy on Foch's part to avoid mounting a major French counter-offensive at this stage. Foch was prepared to place four French infantry divisions and three cavalry divisions south-west of Amiens, but not to grant Haig's request that the French take over the whole front south of the Somme. Nor was he prepared to move substantial French forces further north. Haig was dissatisfied and asked Wilson to come out to France to argue the British case.[20] One explanation for Foch's reluctance to mount a major offensive or to despatch French divisions north of the Somme is that the French themselves were under attack further south. On the morning of 6 April, General von Boehn's German 7th Army (immediately to the left of von Hutier's 18th) opened an offensive codenamed *Archangel* in the direction of the Oise-Aisne Canal. Over the next few days this relatively small offensive made good progress, the Germans taking more prisoners than they suffered casualties. It helped secure the German left flank in that vicinity and served as something of a diversion for the more serious effort being prepared further north.[21]

On Monday 8 April Haig heard that a German airman in French captivity had told his interrogators that the German reserves were concentrated in the Tournai–Douai–Cambrai sector. This confirmed his belief in an impending German offensive well to the north of the Somme, but did not really pinpoint the threat. In response Haig asked his chief French liaison officer at this time, General de Laguiche, to intercede with Foch to relieve six British divisions in the Ypres sector. This would allow Haig to create a reserve of British divisions. Foch's chief of staff, General Weygand, came to see Lawrence at GHQ, but expressed his regret that Foch could not comply with Haig's request. When Wilson showed up at GHQ on the morning of Tuesday 9 April to assist Haig in his dealings with his allies a local disaster was already unfolding.[22]

Georgette

Whereas GHQ's intelligence staff had predicted *Michael* and *Mars* with a fair degree of accuracy, the same was not true of *Georgette*, mounted in the Lys sector of southern Flanders held by the British First Army on the morning of 9 April. An attack of some sort in this sector was not a surprise, but the scale of it was. It is, however, difficult to blame Cox and his team. The Germans had no clear programme for these offensives and were constantly changing their minds about what they wanted to do next. They made the critical decisions about their attack on the Lys only a week or so before the operation began.

The Lys sector, between just north of Armentières and the La Bassée Canal, was tempting to the Germans because they knew that it was weakly held. At the beginning of April there were some six-and-a-half divisions to a front of about eighteen miles. Two of these divisions were Portuguese and were judged to be of very low quality. The Germans believed that others had been badly battered in the *Michael* fighting and that their fighting power had thus been significantly reduced. This vicinity was also tempting to the Germans because of its proximity to the Channel ports. A substantial advance here would jeopardise the British army's supply lines and might precipitate a British collapse. The main problem was that the ground was still sufficiently waterlogged to make a rapid advance difficult. The final plan for *Georgette* was for General von Quast's German Sixth Army to focus its attack on the Portuguese, break through, cross the Lys and head for the important communication centre of Hazebrouk. Ludendorff had originally hoped that the German Fourth Army under General von Arnim would be able to mount a simultaneous attack on von Quast's right. But with fairly intense fighting continuing in the Somme sector, there was insufficient artillery available. Prince Rupprecht's Army Group, therefore, scheduled the Sixth Army attack for 9 April and the Fourth Army attack, slightly to the north, for 10 April.[23]

The condition of the Portuguese corps had long been a matter of concern to the British. Its officers seemed generally rather ignorant and inefficient. Relations between officers and men were poor and morale low. The two divisions were not getting adequate drafts from Portugal to keep them up to strength. Noticing that the Portuguese were fast deteriorating, General Horne of First Army arranged for them to hold their two-division front with just three brigades in the line and one in reserve, in order to allow the other two brigades to rest and recuperate in the rear. The four brigades still at the front were temporarily incorporated in the British XI Corps. Horne had apparently promised that he would reduce the Portuguese front, but this decision had not been implemented when the Germans struck.[24]

The preliminary bombardment for *Georgette* began at 4.15 a.m. on 9 April. The Germans had a marked superiority in guns, used gas shell effectively and found the British artillery response rather feeble. The infantry attacked at 8.45 a.m. About two-thirds of the Portuguese troops ran away. The remainder offered little resistance. The divisions on the immediate flanks of the Portuguese flanks remained relatively firm and the British moved up reserves behind the Portuguese to try to prevent a complete breach. But by 4 p.m. von Quast's forces had advanced up to six miles and established a bridgehead over the Lys east of Sailly. They had taken 6,000 prisoners and 100 guns.[25]

Foch came to GHQ to see Haig at 1 p.m. on Tuesday 9 April. Though his intelligence branch was still underestimating the scale of the German attack in Flanders, Haig was clearly in an agitated frame of mind. He demanded that the French take over more of the British line. Foch resisted this. The most he was prepared to do was to proceed with his plan to place four French divisions west of Amiens, in the British Fourth Army sector. Haig thought this would complicate Fourth Army's administration without taking any real pressure off his forces and he was far from keen on it. He insisted that the German objective was to destroy the British army. It was vital, he argued, to reduce the length of the British front in order to:

1. Form a British Reserve to keep the battle going, and preserve the Channel ports, the Bruay coal fields and Amiens.
2. Give the Enemy a smaller target to strike at and reduce the wastage of British units.[26]

Early the following day, von Armin's Fourth Army opened its attack on the IX Corps of Plumer's Second Army, north of Armentières. The Germans met serious resistance in this sector and gained relatively little ground, though enough to leave the town of Armentières in a dangerous salient. British forces in that sector, mainly belonging to the Lieutenant-General

Sir John Du Cane's XV Corps, were in danger of being trapped. At 10.45 that morning, therefore, First Army ordered Armentières' evacuation. The Germans captured a few thousand more prisoners that day and a few more guns, but deep mud impeded movement and the attackers, as well the defenders, were nearing exhaustion.[27]

Haig's mental state was now as stressed as it had been at any time since he became commander-in-chief in December 1915. He continued to plead for French help. At 11.30 a.m. on Wednesday 10 April, he wrote to Foch demanding that the French "take over *some portion* of the British line". For the second time in two days he demanded French assistance "in order to ... continue the battle". Haig clearly believed his army to be (perhaps like his own nerves) close to breaking point and that the war might soon end in defeat for the Allies. Foch and Weygand, his chief of staff, visited Haig at GHQ at 10 p.m. that night. According to Haig's diary, Foch said that he had decided to move up "a large force of French troops ready to take part in the battle". What this apparently amounted to was a French agreement to extend their front north of the Somme coupled with a decision to send a single division, the 133rd, to Dunkirk by rail.[28]

On Thursday 11 April, Haig remained desperately anxious and with good reason. The Germans committed a further seven divisions to *Georgette*, so that the balance of forces stood at thirty-one German divisions against thirteen of the Allies. Haig thought Plumer badly needed reinforcements, but in his own army only the 1st Australian Division and the 4th Canadian Division had not already been heavily engaged. After the evacuation of Armentières there appeared to be a serious threat that Hazebrouk might be lost. If that crucial communication centre fell into German hands it was possible that a gap would open up between the Second and First Armies. Haig's fears for the Channel ports were greater than ever. After paying a visit to Plumer's Second Army headquarters in the morning, he wrote yet again to Foch. This time he demanded that at least four French divisions should be sent to the sector between St Omer and Dunkirk. At this stage Foch was not prepared to offer any more than an extra cavalry corps.[29]

Haig was not generally given to rhetoric or to making emotional appeals to the troops. It is an indicative of his state of mind that on this day he issued one of the most melodramatic (and thus memorable) orders of the day in British military history:

Every position must be held to the last man: there must be no retirement. With our backs to the wall and believing in the justice of our cause, each one of us must fight on to the end ... Many amongst us are now tired. To those I would say that Victory will belong to the side that holds out longest. The French Army is moving rapidly and in great force to our support.[30]

One historian has reasonably suggested that Haig's intention with this order was to work a sort of emotional blackmail on Foch: to get him to provide the massive French military support that the order indicated was already on its way. But it is not possible to show that it had much impact either on Foch or on British troops. British resistance in Flanders continued to be stubborn rather than fanatical. Positions that were considered tenable only at exorbitant cost continued to be abandoned. In places the German Sixth Army advanced four miles on 12 April. After that, however, both it and the German Fourth Army gradually ground to a halt. A number of factors were at work. The state of the ground made bringing up ammunition and supplies difficult. The attacking troops were becoming exhausted. The German commanders and their staff were in some doubt whether to give *Georgette* overriding priority, or whether to try their luck elsewhere on the Western Front. But probably the most important factor was a dogged defence.[31]

For the next couple of days Haig's nerves remained stretched. In a lengthy conversation with Clemenceau at Doullens on Friday 12 April he was still saying that the British would need more help if they were to "*keep the war going*". Clearly he still thought that without substantial French help his own army might collapse and the war come to a speedy and ignominious conclusion. Next day, after visiting Second Army, Lawrence told him that Plumer had abandoned the Passchendaele Salient though he intended to hold the Pilckem Ridge.[32]

During this second period of intense crisis when the British felt in desperate need of French help, they appointed a very senior officer, Lieutenant-General Sir John Du Cane, as principal liaison officer between Foch and Haig. It is not completely clear whose idea this was, but Wilson discussed it with Foch on Tuesday 9 April, the first day of *Georgette*. Du Cane took up the appointment on Friday 12 April, having been told by Haig to represent British interests strongly. Two days later, Haig missed church in order to attend a conference with Foch at Abbeville and told him that the "Enemy was likely to continue his effort towards Calais because by taking that place he might be able to dictate peace to England!" By that stage, however, the actual situation in Flanders was better. The Germans had lost momentum and were gaining little ground, though, in order to shorten the line and accumulate reserves, the British Second Army pulled back voluntarily north of Ypres surrendering ground won at great cost in 1917.[33]

French observers commented in somewhat disparaging terms on British command and control in the face of *Georgette*. They admitted that Plumer was a cool customer who refused to panic, but considered that many other senior British officers were excessively given to pessimism and had little idea how to control a mobile battle. There may have been truth in these strictures. Nevertheless, with only limited help from the French, the British had fought the Germans to a complete standstill in the Flanders-Lys sector by 19 April. A vital factor here, which strongly impressed itself on French observers[34] and on Haig, was the remarkable resilience of British other ranks. As Haig mentioned in his diary on Monday 15 April:

Field Censor reports that, judging from the letters written by the men, the moral of the troops is extremely good. "It can be safely said that it has never been higher". "As soon as the German offensive started, the tone of the letters improved and grousing ceased ... replaced to a great extent by a confident tone."[35]

The resilience of British morale was particularly significant given the fragility of that on the other side. German soldiers had, for the most part, been very hopeful on 21 March. By the second half of April, however, many seem to have sensed that they could not win the decisive victory promised and there were some serious outbreaks of indiscipline.[36]

By Thursday 18 April Haig had relaxed sufficiently to give some praise to the French for having mounted a counter-attack near Hangard on the Somme front. Foch, by this stage, seemed more willing to help and next day Haig received a letter from him saying that he wanted to keep fifteen French divisions in the British rear as reserves and for Haig to send him tired British divisions in exchange. This gift-horse had obvious attractions. But the immediate crisis in Flanders having now passed, Haig viewed it with some suspicion, concerned that it might lead to a merging of the French and British armies under Foch's overall control.[37] That same Friday Lord Milner, who had been doing important liaison work for the British War Cabinet in Paris, called at GHQ on his way back to London, where he would take over from Derby as Secretary of State for War. (Derby was coming out to Paris as British ambassador.) Lloyd George may have considered Derby's removal part of a continuing process of isolating Haig and perhaps still hoped to replace him. Haig, however, was happy to work with Milner, whom he rather admired.[38] It cannot be said that Milner was equally impressed with Haig, as he took a dim view of his record in 1917.[39] Given the absence of an obvious successor, however, Milner was now in no rush to replace him and their conversation on the afternoon of Friday 19 April seems to have been entirely amicable. Haig recorded Milner as saying that he hoped that he and the army would treat each other with mutual respect. On the issue of the intermingling of British and French formations Haig and Milner agreed that they would accept it as "for a time necessary" but they both considered any permanent "Amalgam" unacceptable.[40]

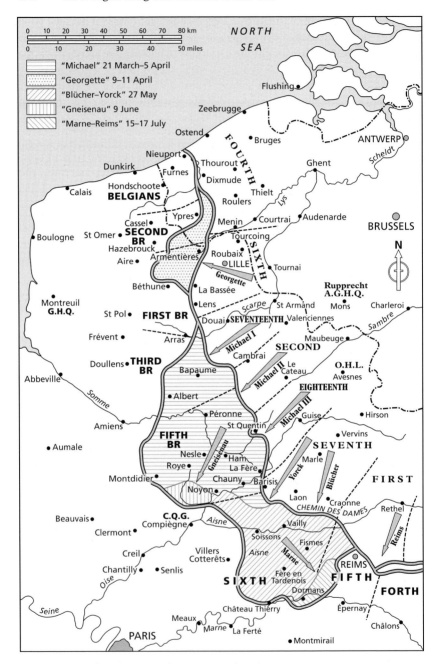

Map 23. German offensives March–July 1918

German offensives against the British were renewed in the last week of April. On Wednesday 24 April Rupprecht's Army Group mounted another thrust in the Amiens direction. Assisted by tanks, the German infantry pierced the British line just north of Hangard and captured the village of Villers-Bretonneux. The vicinity of that village became the scene of what seems to have been the first tank-to-tank combat in history, a fight that went in favour of the British. That night a counter-attack by troops of two Australian and one British brigade recaptured much of the lost ground. The village of Villers-Bretonneux was recovered the following morning. On 25 April the Germans decided to cease offensive operations in this vicinity.[41]

Unfortunately for Haig's nerves, this was accompanied by a renewal of *Georgette* that was (at least initially) alarmingly successful. At 3.30 a.m. on 25 April General Sixt von Armin's German Fourth Army opened an intense bombardment of Allied positions on and around the 156 metre Kemmel Hill, which offered commanding views of the Ypres Salient and the Flanders plain in general. To the consternation of Plumer, who had told Haig that he considered it impregnable, infantry of the German Alpine Corps took the hill from the French 28th Division. Early on the afternoon of 26 April Haig visited Second Army's Advanced HQ at Cassel, where he discussed the situation at some length with Plumer and Harington. Plumer now wanted to pull back his main defensive line to the Ypres Canal, leaving outposts on Pilkem Ridge. In view of German gains south of Ypres, Haig considered that it might be time to abandon the Ypres Salient.[42]

Given the enormous number of lives that the British had lost in defending and expanding it, the abandonment of Ypres would have been a momentous step. That Haig, whose reputation as a tough and determined commander had very largely been made in defence of this area in 1914, was now virtually resigned to relinquishing it is truly remarkable: indicating a high degree of pragmatism, the fragile state of his personal morale or perhaps a combination of the two. But this crisis passed almost as soon as it arrived. Two men were primarily responsible: Foch and Ludendorff. While Haig was ready to abandon his "backs to the wall" policy, Foch vehemently insisted upon it. He sent a series of messages to Haig and to Plumer demanding that there must be no further retirement. What emerged was a compromise. British and Belgian forces withdrew a couple of miles, but stopped just east of the city of Ypres itself. Ludendorff, meanwhile, had unwittingly assisted the Allies. Thinking they were now too strong in Flanders for decisive results to be obtained, he ordered the German Fourth Army to be cautious in following up its victory at Kemmel Hill.

The German offensive in Flanders had petered out by the end of April. Ludendorff decided to make his next effort in the Champagne region, hoping that this would force the French to withdraw many of their troops from the British sector. In that event he thought he might be able to renew his offensives against the British army with real hope of crushing it.[43]

Inter-Allied relations, the May lull and the Maurice case

Much of Haig's time in late April and early May was occupied by a series of high-level inter-Allied conferences. At a meeting attended by Clemenceau, Foch, Milner, Wilson and Haig on Sunday 27 April, Wilson pressed Foch on whether covering the Channel ports or keeping the British and French armies united was his priority. Foch indicated the latter: a priority spelt out more definitely a few days later. At the same time an agreement that the British government had made with the Americans was putting the Franco-British alliance under some stress. The British were supplying most of the shipping to bring American troops across the Atlantic. Whereas the American tendency was bring across complete divisions to be formed into a proper American army, the British insisted that this would not help the immediate crisis. The war might be lost before a complete American army could be formed. The immediate and desperate need was for infantry drafts to fill gaps in the British army, under such violent attack since 21 March. The British had thus prevailed upon the Americans to give priority to sending infantry and machine gunners. During May 120,000 such troops were to be provided to the British. Haig was obviously pleased. The French, on the other hand, were angry that these arrangements had been made without consulting them. For different reasons, Pershing was also annoyed.

As Haig noted after a conference of the Supreme War Council at Abbeville on Wednesday 1 May, the American commander hankered after *"a great self-contained American Army"*. Haig ridiculed this on the grounds that the Americans lacked competent commanders at divisional level and above. Neither, in his judgement, did they have officers competent to form the staff for divisions, corps and Armies. He considered it ridiculous to imagine that an independent American army could be in operation "in less that two years" and thought Pershing "very obstinate and stupid" for insisting on such a thing. Haig was always outraged at any attempt to diminish the independence of the British army or his own authority over it. His inability to sympathise with comparable feelings in another national commander indicates a certain narrowness of view, a certain lack of generosity of spirit, which we have sometimes encountered before in his dealings with allies.[44]

Since 21 March the Germans had focused their attacks on the British. The latter had suffered approximately a quarter of a million casualties and twelve of Haig's sixty-two infantry divisions were reduced to skeletons. In Haig's estimation, the Germans had brought his army to the brink of collapse on a number of occasions. He and his intelligence staff had become understandably preoccupied with the threat to British sectors of the front and found it very difficult to believe that the Germans had, even temporarily, shifted their attentions to the French. In a letter to his wife on 2 May, Haig described the Germans as having become "uncannily quiet" and confessed that he did not know what to make of it. In mid-May Cox's officers began picking up rumours of a German attack on the French in the Reims area, but they were initially inclined to dismiss this as part of a German deception plan: possibly designed to cover a renewed offensive in the Arras sector. Only in the last couple of days before the Germans actually struck on the Chemin des Dames on 27 May did GHQ's intelligence branch become certain that a German offensive against the French was imminent. Naturally they passed their intelligence to their allies.[45]

During May (an interval of relative calm for the bulk of the British army in France) there was the diversion of the "Maurice case", a sensation in the British press and Parliament. In an effort to pre-empt parliamentary attacks on his government over the March retreat, Lloyd George had denied that there had been any real shortage of manpower in the British army in France, claiming that in early 1918 the army was actually stronger than it had been a year previously. On a subsequent occasion Bonar Law had told the Commons that the extension of the British line had been undertaken as a result of an agreement between the British and French high commands without government interference. The implication was that Haig had failed to warn the government that his army in France was over-extended in relation to the threat it faced. Even Lloyd George's admirers amongst modern historians have accepted that his government told less than the whole truth in its statements to Parliament on these issues.[46]

On Tuesday 7 May Major-General Sir Frederick Maurice, until recently the Director of Military Operations at the War Office, published a letter in the *Morning Post* attacking what he denounced as dishonesty on Lloyd George's part. The War Cabinet, he indicated, was responsible for the depleted state of the army in early 1918. It had ignored warnings about the dangers of this depletion and was, by implication, responsible for the spring reverses. One of Maurice's objectives may have been to support Haig. But although Maurice was at GHQ shortly before the newspaper article appeared, there is no evidence that Haig was consulted about it. Maurice's action, indeed, constituted a breach of military discipline and of official secrecy[47] and Haig was keen to distance himself from such dangerous illegality. Writing to his wife on the same day that Maurice's letter was published, he expressed the opinion that:

This is a grave mistake. No one can be both a soldier and a politician at the same time. We soldiers have to do our duty and keep silent, trusting to Ministers to protect us.[48]

This, however, sounds like the official line, which Haig wanted Doris to pass on to the King and other interested parties. His real feelings in the matter seem to have been rather different. On Thursday 9 May, Lloyd George not merely survived the "Maurice debate" in the Commons, but gave a brilliant oratorical performance that routed his enemies (most notably Asquith) and confirmed his authority.[49] When he heard about this, Haig was unable to maintain his pose of dignified aloofness from the political arena. Writing to Doris again the following Saturday he remarked:

Poor Maurice! How terrible to see the House of Commons so easily taken in by a clap trap speech by Lloyd George. The House is really losing its reputation as an assembly of common sense Britishers. However, I don't suppose that Maurice has done with LG yet.

This was wishful thinking. The Maurice case was practically over and Lloyd George had won. Doris had heard rumours that Lloyd George would follow this up by bringing Haig back to England as Commander-in-Chief Home Forces. Haig responded by adopting the constitutionally correct position that he was ready to serve wherever the government placed him.[50] But the problem of finding a replacement for him persisted. Haig, though his position was still not safe, remained where he was for the time being.

During mid-May Foch was already contemplating counter-offensives against the salients that the German offensives had created on the Lys and to the south-east of Amiens. On Friday 17 May, Haig and Lawrence visited Fourth Army's headquarters at Flixecourt and told Rawlinson to start preparing an attack from the Villers-Bretonneux sector.[51] Together with an attack by Debeney's First French Army south of Roye, this was intended to form a pincer movement against German forces threatening Amiens. However, almost three months were to pass before an Allied counter-offensive in this sector materialised. Foch's and Haig's proposals of mid-May cannot, therefore, be seen as leading directly to the attack mounted on 8 August.

The French bear the brunt: late May to mid-July

On Monday 27 May the Germans struck in Champagne in an offensive codenamed *Blücher*. The attack was preceded by a Bruchmüller artillery bombardment even more intense than that of 21 March 1918. Once again the Germans hit a weakly-held sector. Once again the poor dispositions by the Allies assisted them. The Chemin des Dames ridge, on which the French front rested, was such a prominent feature, acquired at such cost in 1917, that General Duchêne, commanding the French Sixth Army, was determined to hold it in strength. In this he was going against the advice of his Army Group commander, General Franchet d'Espèrey, and that of General Pétain. Both wanted Duchêne to use the ridge as an outpost line while keeping most of his forces in a Battle Zone between it and the Aisne. But Duchêne dug his heels in and deployed a substantial force, including the British IX Corps, commanded by Lieutenant-General Hamilton Gordon, on the ridge.

The five divisions of IX Corps, all of which had been battered in previous German offensives, were supposed to be having a rest in a quiet sector. Instead they were hit by probably the most intense artillery bombardment of the war so far, followed by an assault by massively superior numbers of German infantry. Inevitably they suffered very heavy casualties and they and French forces alongside them were swept off the ridge. Having had a large part of his Army deployed forward and thus shattered in the initial Germans attack, Duchêne now faced an acute crisis. The Germans swept forward irresistibly towards, and then over, the Aisne.[52]

Foch could see no strategic purpose in the Chemin des Dames attack and his initial reaction was that it must be a diversion to draw reserves away from Flanders, a conclusion that seems to have been at least partially correct. At GHQ too Haig's intelligence officers seem to have expected an early resumption of German attacks in Flanders. But Haig demurred. He guessed as early as 28 May that now that the enemy had achieved a breakthrough in Champagne he would "devote all his energy to exploiting his success" against the French.[53] In this instance Haig guessed correctly. Though Ludendorff had not yet definitely abandoned hope of resuming offensive operations in Flanders, he did indeed get carried away with his attacks on the French army and the German offensive in Flanders was never to resume.

The late May and early June fighting produced a serious crisis, not only in the French army but also in the Franco-British alliance. Just as the French had taken a poor view of British resistance to the *Michael* and *Georgette* offensives, the British generally proved very pessimistic about French chances of surviving *Blücher*. Wilson, who had been the most Francophile of British officers and the one with the greatest respect for the French army, believed a French collapse quite possible and considered that the British might have to abandon Ypres and Dunkirk. He ordered detailed planning to begin for the British army's evacuation from the Continent. Meanwhile, the British actually packed up much of their archive in their Paris embassy, in preparation to evacuate.[54]

Despite his correct prognosis for the development of German offensive operations, Haig was obstructive and slow about sending help to the French army. On 31 May Foch met him in Paris prior to a Supreme War Council meeting scheduled for the following day. Foch asked Haig to send south some American divisions that were training with the British. Foch wanted to use these formations to relieve French divisions holding a quiet sector along the Swiss frontier. French divisions so relieved could then be used to check the German offensives. Haig gave Foch various arguments against this seemingly logical course. He said he would consider the matter and let Foch know his answer the following day. Haig did, however, agree to consider forming a corps of three divisions as a general reserve that could be used anywhere on the Western Front, but this did not satisfy Foch, who remained "more anxious" than Haig had ever seen him. Lord Derby, who was also present, noticed that Haig himself looked "anxious and tired".[55]

By the beginning of June the entire German offensive was already beginning to lose momentum. But this was not yet clear to the Allies when they held the sixth conference of the Supreme War Council at Versailles, on 1–3 June. Under the stress of events, the conference was acrimonious and serious Franco-British mistrust came to the surface. On 1 June there was a preliminary meeting of the British delegates, including Lloyd George, Milner, Wilson and General John Du Cane (appointed in April to be Haig's principal liaison officer with Foch). Haig indicated his pessimism about the French army. He thought that since the failure of the Nivelle offensive and the consequent mutinies, the French had neglected discipline and training, and that French troops, therefore, were disinclined to fight. Reserves thrown into the Aisne battle had melted away. Haig was not sure it made sense to place potentially good troops like the Americans under French command.

At a Franco-British session at 2.30 that afternoon, the French expressed some anger that the British army was continuing to shrink. Foch practically accused the British government of withholding desperately needed manpower: an accusation that incensed Lloyd George, appearing, as it did, to resurrect issues that he thought his victory in the Maurice case had buried. Though Haig had some degree of agreement with Foch on this issue, he sensibly avoided siding with a foreigner against his own government. Foch did not, at this stage, pursue the matter of the American divisions that he wanted Haig to release, indicating that he and Haig could easily settle that issue between them.[56] On 3 June, however, Foch told Haig that with Pershing's agreement he intended to send some of the American divisions currently training in the British sector south to relieve French divisions. He and Pershing were acting quite properly to avoid a French collapse and to save the alliance. Yet Haig was displeased:

> My views are that it is a waste of valuable troops to send half-trained men to relieve French Divisions. In 3 weeks' time these Americans will be fit for battle. I doubt that the French divisions they relieve will ever fight!

Though Haig had no choice but to release the formations concerned, he did so with a poor grace, insisting that their British training cadres should stay behind. In Foch's opinion and to the Marshal's intense annoyance, Haig was also administratively obstructive about the movement of these forces.[57] To be fair to Haig, it must be pointed out that his intelligence staff kept warning him that Rupprecht's Army Group, facing the British sector, still had large reserves. These might be used to renew German offensive efforts in Flanders at any time. Haig still had a particular responsibility to the British government for the preservation of the British army. While its survival still appeared in doubt, his reluctance to see the British sector stripped of reserves is understandable. When, on 4 June, Foch ordered Haig to create a reserve of three divisions to be placed astride the Somme for possible use in the French sector, Haig complied. But he sent a protest to his own government against releasing any further divisions from the British sector while Rupprecht's Army Group still looked dangerous. Haig was still in an anti-French mood, repeating in his diary his claim that the real problem was that much of the French army would not "face the enemy".[58]

Three days later a major Franco-British conference held at the French War Ministry in Paris overrode Haig. Foch insisted that, in this emergency, he needed the full powers of a Generalissimo. He must have the right "to order troops of any nationality wherever he thought fit at the shortest notice". Lord Milner, the Foreign Secretary, who represented the British government at this conference, agreed with Clemenceau that Foch must have these powers. Haig objected that this decision diminished his capacity to ensure the survival of the British army and he wanted the government to acknowledge this officially. Yet he had no choice but to go along with the decision.[59]

As had happened in April, it was the easing of German pressure that led to a gradual reduction of the internecine strife amongst the generals of the Allies. In the first half of June, despite successive attacks on the French army, the Germans were clearly failing to obtain decisive results against it. Haig's armies had not been subjected to a major attack for about six weeks. In these circumstances Haig's nerves relaxed to a point at which he was able to use civil language about French martial qualities and even to make favourable diary references to Foch.[60]

During June two factors, one more obvious than the other, were tilting the balance of forces in the favour of the Allies. The first, and the more visible, was the Americans. By 22 June there were nineteen American divisions on the Western Front, fourteen of which were in the French sector. Because of the crisis on the Aisne some American divisions had already been committed to battle and Foch judged them to have performed well. The realisation that the American army could become a major factor during 1918 (something he had hitherto doubted) seems to have cheered Haig considerably. The second factor was the influenza pandemic. As GHQ's intelligence staff were aware, this was already hitting the Western Front. Indeed, Brigadier Edgar Cox, Haig's intelligence chief, was an early victim. He was knocked out by it for much of June and did not return to duty until mid-August. But generally the influenza seems to have struck the underfed Germans harder than the Allies, and to have been one of the factors sapping their offensive power during June. By 14 June, German offensive efforts against the French army had practically ground to a halt.[61]

Though naturally relieved by the relaxation of German pressure, Haig was initially puzzled by it. On 21 June he thought it "hard to find a good reason for the enemy's delay in putting his attacks against us". Haig was still puzzled eleven days later when he told Derby, now British ambassador in Paris, that he was "considerably mystified" about German intentions. Yet when Haig conferred with Foch on Friday 28 June it is clear that both men were in a much more confident and cheerful frame of mind. They took heart from a recent speech by the German Foreign Minister Richard von Kuhlmann, which seemed to indicate that the German government had already abandoned hope of winning the sort of decisive military victory that would allow it to dictate terms to the Allies.[62]

Apparently sensing the possibility of a turning of the tide, Foch and Haig each developed offensive plans. Foch was considering a large-scale counter-offensive to be mounted in late August. Haig had approved, on 25 June, a small-scale attack by ten Australian battalions, incorporating four American companies, supported by tanks and aircraft in the vicinity of the village of Hamel, in the Fourth Army sector on the Somme.[63] Though sanctioned by Rawlinson and Haig, this operation was the brainchild of the Australian Corps, now commanded by Lieutenant-General Sir John Monash. Monash was an Australian civil engineer and, in peacetime, a militia officer of German–Jewish extraction. His performance in his first campaign, Gallipoli, had demonstrated some weaknesses in his front-line leadership under pressure. But he had done much better since his arrival on the Western Front, where meticulous planning, combined, some said, with a good deal of self-advertising, became his trademark.

Haig liked his air of confidence and aggressiveness and was instrumental in his rise to command the Australian Corps, which he had taken over in May when his predecessor, General Sir William Birdwood, went to command a reconstituted but very weak Fifth Army.[64] A visit to Australian Corps headquarters on 1 July confirmed Haig's view that:

Monash is a most thorough and capable commander who thinks out every detail and leaves nothing to chance. I was greatly impressed with his arrangements.[65]

Haig was right to be impressed. When the operation went ahead on 4 July the village of Hamel and over 1,000 prisoners were taken at modest cost and Fourth Army's hold on the Villers-Bretonneux Ridge was significantly improved. It is indicative of Haig's more relaxed and optimistic outlook by early July that some forty-eight hours after Hamel he went off for a few days' leave in London, where he was reunited with Doris and his infant son.[66]

By 4 July the French had spotted indications of another major German offensive in Champagne. Cox's team had noted much of the same evidence, but remained more worried about a renewal of German attacks on the Lys.[67] Eight days later Foch was certain the French army was about to be attacked in the Champagne sector east of Rheims. He demanded that two groups of four British divisions (eight in all) be sent south to Champagne. By Sunday 14 July Haig had despatched two of these divisions, but did so unwillingly:

And all this when there is nothing definite to show that the Enemy means to attack in Champagne. Indeed Prince Rupprecht still retains 25 divisions in reserve on the British front.

Haig wrote to Foch telling the Generalissimo plainly that he was misreading the situation. Haig was reluctant to send any more British troops to Champagne at this time. He adhered to his previous opinion that the Germans were likely to mount smaller attacks in Champagne and in Flanders to get the Allies to commit their reserves, but that their real breakthrough attempt would be mounted between Lens and Chateau Thierry. GHQ received a phone call from Wilson that night indicating that he and the War Cabinet were prepared to support Haig on this issue and allow him to use his discretion.[68] But on this issue the Germans proved Foch right and Haig wrong. They launched a major offensive on either side of Rheims, in the Champagne sector, at 4 a.m. on 15 July. While he remained worried about the substantial reserves still available to Rupprecht's Army Group, it was difficult for Haig to argue that anything on this scale was merely a diversion. When he had lunch with Foch at Mouchy le Chatel that day, he agreed to send another two divisions to

Champagne. But Foch was not, in any case, particularly desperate for British help. The French army, with American assistance, appeared to be coping well enough and Haig noted that: "Foch was in the best of spirits."[69]

For the next few days Haig remained nervous about the renewal of a German attack on his front; Flanders was now his particular anxiety. On 17 July he asked that Foch return the four British divisions that had been sent to Champagne. Foch, however, remained focused on the Champagne battle. The French mounted a major counter-offensive on 18 July, a battle that the British XXII Corps entered two days later. The Second Battle of the Marne, as it is now known, continuing into early August, became a major victory for the Allies, one in which the American army played a significant part. Some 29,000 German prisoners were taken as well as over 800 artillery pieces and mortars and 3,330 machine guns. Though it was not completely clear to everyone at the time, the tide had finally turned.[70]

Haig's generalship in the German offensives: assessment

How should we judge Haig's generalship during the German offensives of 1918? Obviously the initiative at this period was in German hands. Haig spent a lot of time trying to guess and second-guess German moves. He had a highly professional intelligence staff to help him, controlling a sophisticated intelligence-gathering apparatus. Yet reading German intentions was extremely difficult, at least in part because these intentions were ill-defined and constantly changing. Haig and his staff got the timing of *Michael* right and accurately predicted that Third and Fifth Armies would be the first to be hit. On the other hand, GHQ collectively seems to have been taken aback by the sheer scale and persistence of the German effort against these formations. *Mars* was very accurately predicted and effectively dealt with. But there was a definite intelligence failure over *Georgette* and a quite understandable doubt as to whether the German focus had definitely switched to the French army from late May onwards.

How well did Haig plan on the basis of the intelligence available? He and his staff seem to have been aware from February that in the event of a really big attack it was unlikely that Gough would be able to hold his Battle Zone. They had made a contingency plan for a general retreat to the Tortille and the Somme. But this by no means solved Gough's problems. He was given inadequate resources with which to fortify, in the time available, the rearward areas to which it was anticipated he might have to retreat. Admittedly Haig's forces were overstretched and the Fifth Army sector seemed less vital than those nearer the Channel ports.

Nevertheless it does appear that GHQ's contingency planning for the Fifth Army front was unrealistic. It was apparent that if Gough were attacked on any scale he would need prompt and massive French help. Yet Haig had opposed the idea of a General Reserve controlled by the staff at Versailles and his arrangements with Pétain for the latter to support his right flank in the event of trouble proved inadequate under the pressure of events.

That Haig apparently made no effort to speak to Gough on 21 March represents an error of judgement – indeed, a failure of leadership on his part. Combined with Lawrence's off-hand and detached attitude over the telephone, it gave Gough the feeling that GHQ was out of touch and that Fifth Army was being abandoned to its fate. This sense of abandonment may well have precipitated Gough's decision to permit his corps commanders to withdraw their forces from the Battle Zone at their own discretion, though it does not necessarily justify it. Once corps commanders started withdrawing on their own initiative and in the face, especially on the southern part of the front, of massive odds, the process became hard to control. Haig and his staff also failed to exercise any real control over Third Army. GHQ's instructions to Third Army before the offensive started were that the Flesquières Salient should be held as a "false front" and evacuated quickly when attacked. But, as we have noted, Byng manned the salient strongly and ordered his forces to hold in place. The tough initial resistance of Third Army seems to have been a major factor in causing Ludendorff to change his plan for *Michael*, shifting the main weight of the offensive to the south. But the evacuation of the Flesquières Salient belatedly and under intense pressure helped produce a partial collapse of the southern wing of Third Army by 24 March. That in turn resulted in the acute danger of an unbridgeable gap opening between Third Army and the battered and depleted Fifth Army to its right.

Haig's apparent complacency in the first couple of days of *Michael* (possibly attributable to an assumption that the Germans would soon switch their main effort to the Champagne sector) had turned to extreme alarm by Sunday 24 March. He had largely lost control of the situation and had become critically dependent on French help. Rarely a good communicator, even in his own language, he seems to have conveyed to Pétain the impression that the British army was collapsing and that he had despaired of holding Amiens. While Pétain still wanted to maintain contact with the British if possible, his priority, as he had spelt out to his own generals earlier in the day, was to cover Paris. The crisis of 24–26 March was, therefore, a desperate one, and without the intervention of Lloyd George, Milner, Wilson and Foch it is entirely possible that all Franco-British military co-operation might have collapsed, the British army been crushed and the war lost.

Haig's imperturbability is often reckoned to be amongst his greatest strengths. His nerves, however, seem to have been stretched very close to breaking point from 24–26 March, from 9–12 April and again from 25–28 April. Pétain was perhaps as close to cracking as Haig during the first of these crises. Yet the French had done much to prop up the British army during *Michael* and *Georgette*, taking over what had been Fifth Army frontage and ultimately sending divisions as far north as Flanders. In the late April crisis, after the fall of Mount Kemmel, Foch proved more resolute than did Haig. Without Foch's exertion of his authority, Haig might well have abandoned the entire Ypres Salient including the ruins of the town. When the French came under massive attack, from 27 May, Haig was slow to reciprocate the support he had received. Admittedly he was commanding a significantly smaller army, much of which was already very badly mauled. Admittedly, too, his intelligence staff indicated that Rupprecht's Army Group, directly facing his forces, continued to possess a substantial reserve. These factors give some justification to his apparent lack of generosity. Yet Haig arguably never had the right instinct or aptitude to be a good alliance general in crises of this magnitude. At such times his vision tended to narrow and it took the British government's continuing, albeit limited and conditional, support for Foch's authority to ensure the alliance's survival.

In the succession of crises in spring and early summer 1918, therefore, Haig's performance was not especially impressive. His leadership, especially in relation to Gough, at the opening of *Michael* was arguably downright weak, and most of the spring fighting was a series of "soldiers' battles" over which he exercised only very modest degrees of control. Yet, however close to it he might have been at certain times, he had not collapsed psychologically and had not issued panic-stricken orders. Despite the British government's generally poor view of his performance and indeed of his brainpower, he had somehow ridden out the crisis and, rather amazingly, was still in command.

19   The final campaign

German vulnerability in summer 1918

By mid-summer 1918 the Germans on the Western Front were in very serious trouble. Between 21 March and 25 June the length of the front they held had increased from 390 kilometres to 510. Over the same period they had suffered about one million casualties, so the numbers available to hold the extended front had significantly declined. German military organisation and method had ensured that casualties were disproportionately heavy amongst just the elite troops and combat leaders that were now so desperately needed.[1] The Germans had launched their offensives from sophisticated and powerful systems of fortification in which they had invested massive amounts of capital and labour (their own and that of the people whose territory they had conquered) over many months. By contrast, much of the front they occupied in late June, July and early August was fortified only in the most rudimentary way.

German troops had been told that their spring offensives would prove decisive and bring peace. When, in late March, despite dramatic advances, final victory had proved elusive and they were ordered to start digging trenches again, morale began to dip. By late June disillusionment and demoralisation had set in with a vengeance. Discipline was in sharp decline. Many were genuinely sick with influenza, but there also seems to have a certain amount of malingering and avoidance of duty, for which the epidemic provided cover. Overstretched, undernourished, tired and, in some cases, apathetic, the Germans did not do enough work to strengthen the positions they now held. It did not help that, while Ludendorff kept postponing his next offensive in Flanders (codenamed *Hagen*), he did not order a general transition to a defensive posture until 2 August. Even then he insisted on continuing preparations for a number of limited offensives, including a modified *Hagen*. Having shot its bolt, the German high command's best chance of preserving the army through the months ahead was to pull it back to the powerful fortifications left behind in the spring while getting the government to make realistic peace moves. But this would have meant open acknowledgement of the failure of the spring offensives and Ludendorff was not ready to make such an admission.[2]

British offensive plans

The British contribution to the Second Battle of the Marne, the battle that marks the turn of the tide of war on the Western Front in 1918, was relatively small and (on Haig's part) reluctant. In the first week of that battle, Haig's principal preoccupation was the possibility of Prince Rupprecht's Army Group renewing its offensive against Plumer's Second Army in Flanders, north of the Lys. Because of his anxiety about Plumer's front, Haig was eager to secure the return of the four British divisions sent to the Marne sector even before they had taken part in the fighting.[3]

Foch was eager for offensive action on the British front to complement that on the Marne. Haig was, indeed, planning some offensive action. But its extent and timing would depend on German moves. On 21 July Haig explained to Lieutenant-General Sir John Du Cane, the principal British liaison officer with Foch, that:

In view of Rupprecht's large reserves I cannot attack on the Kemmel front unless the enemy first attacks and is repulsed. If his reserves remain on my front, I will carry out local attacks: if they go, I am preparing an operation in the south ...[4]

It was not until 23 July that Haig became reasonably confident that the German offensive in Flanders would not be renewed. Needing reserves earmarked for it to contain the Marne counter-offensive, Ludendorff had actually decided to cancel *Hagen* four days earlier.[5]

The idea of an "operation in the south" arose out of the Australian successes. The mainstay of Rawlinson's Fourth Army, the Australian Corps, had exploited poorly fortified German positions immediately south of the Somme with a policy of constant aggressive raiding and with the somewhat larger operation at Hamel on 4 July. The German Second Army had responded feebly, indicating that its troops were thin on the ground and shared the demoralisation becoming widespread in the German army by this stage.[6] In contrast with some of Haig's other generals, who seem to have been somewhat war-weary and cautious, both Sir John Monash, the Australian Corps commander, and Rawlinson at Fourth Army were full of aggressive ambition. Monash, recently appointed to corps command, had yet to mount a really big attack that would demonstrate the full power of his formation and the full scope of his own military talents. After a mixed but generally very disappointing performance on the Somme in 1916, Rawlinson had been on the sidelines throughout

1917. Like Monash he now wanted to prove his generalship with a major victory east of Amiens.[7]

On 5 July, immediately after the Battle of Hamel, Rawlinson suggested to Haig that Fourth Army now prepare a much larger attack. Haig encouraged this and, on 13 July, Lawrence instructed Rawlinson to submit a plan. Haig then ordered Horne and Byng to prepare some relatively minor attacks on the First and Third Army fronts. The main object of these preparations was, as Haig explained to Rawlinson during a visit to Fourth Army on Tuesday 16 July, "to attract the attention of the Enemy". The "*main operation*" was to be mounted by the Fourth Army east of Amiens between the Somme and the much smaller River Luce, a few miles to the south. To optimise his chances of success, Rawlinson wanted another strong corps to attack alongside the Australians. He asked for the Canadian Corps. Haig agreed, provided he could get the XXII Corps back from the Marne. Haig also said he would ask Foch to ensure the co-operation of Debeney's First French Army south of the Luce.[8]

Rawlinson sent his plan to GHQ the next day: 17 July. What Rawlinson and his Fourth Army staff seems originally to have intended was a short, sharp, opportunistic blow, taking advantage of the weakness of the Germans in the Amiens sector. Rawlinson aimed to "assure the safety of Amiens" by "driving the enemy out of shell range of the town". The most he appears to have hoped for was "the possibility of inflicting a serious blow on the enemy at a time when his morale will be low owing to the failure of the Champagne offensive".

The operational method proposed was, quite explicitly, a scaled up version of Hamel that also drew some inspiration from the opening blow of the Cambrai offensive on 20 November 1917. Surprise was the key. The two most powerful corps in Haig's command, the Australian Corps and the Canadian Corps, would strike a clearly identified German weak spot before the Germans realised that the Canadian Corps was in the area. The III Corps would attack simultaneously, immediately north of the Somme, where it was intended to cover the left flank of the Australian Corps. To help maintain surprise there was (as at Cambrai and Hamel) to be no preliminary artillery bombardment. But intense counter-battery fire and a creeping barrage were to be delivered from Zero hour for the infantry attack. Tanks and low-flying aircraft were to assist the infantry advance.

Though Haig had suggested involving Debeney's First French Army (on Fourth Army's right flank), Rawlinson was opposed to the idea. French involvement would, he believed, make it "almost impossible" to maintain secrecy. Rawlinson, moreover, wanted to keep the planning simple. French involvement would complicate it.[9] But Rawlinson soon found himself overruled. Under pressure from higher authority he found his simple plan becoming rather more elaborate and the aims of the operation more grandiose, yet the time allocated to prepare it considerably reduced.

On 24 July Haig attended a conference with Foch at his headquarters at Bombon Chateau. Pétain and Pershing were also present. Foch approved the operation east of Amiens, seeing it as part of a larger scheme to regain the initiative and open some important north–south railway lines that the German offensives had closed. At a further conference on 26 July Haig and Foch insisted that the French First Army should play a substantial part in the operation, something that General Marie Debeney, the Army commander, who was present with Rawlinson at the conference, did not particularly want. At this stage Rawlinson was planning to attack on Saturday 10 August. On 28 July, Foch sent Haig a letter requesting that it be brought forward by two days. Foch wanted to keep up the pressure on the Germans after their defeat on the Marne and was apparently anxious that they would pull back from their exposed positions in front of Amiens before Rawlinson's blow was struck. Haig immediately agreed to attack on 8 August and Rawlinson was informed of the change that evening.[10] The rescheduling upset Fourth Army's carefully worked out timetables of preparation for the attack. Rawlinson may have sworn under his breath, but made no official protest.

In the last few days before the offensive began there was also tension between Haig and Fourth Army HQ over the scope and intent of the operation. Rawlinson and his Fourth Army staff still seem to have conceived it as a short, sharp, opportunistic strike with limited aims and of very limited duration. Haig, on the other hand, was thinking in more grandiose terms. On 29 July he and Lawrence saw all the Army commanders except Rawlinson (who was too busy preparing his attack) for a "pep talk" combined with a briefing on strategy and tactics. Haig told his generals that Foch believed they had "turned the corner" and proceeded to give them an outline of his counter-offensive plans. Haig seems to have anticipated that much of the fighting for the rest of 1918 would be of the nature of "open warfare" and insisted that "Army commanders must do their utmost to get troops out of the influence of *Trench* methods."[11] Haig thus wanted the big offensive east of Amiens to be more open-ended than the Fourth Army commander and his staff originally intended. He pressed Rawlinson to aim at reaching the Chaulnes–Roye line: about twelve miles from the startline for the attack and five miles beyond Rawlinson's deepest objective at this stage. Haig then wanted exploitation towards Ham, a further fifteen miles away.[12] The same sort of tension that had often existed between GHQ and Fourth Army in 1916, especially during the planning for the opening round on the Somme, thus showed signs of reappearing in the second half of 1918.

The main difference in August 1918 was that Haig's intervention did not require Rawlinson significantly to alter his plan for the first day of his attack. Given German weakness in his sector and the very powerful strike force that he was assembling, Rawlinson had set very ambitious aims for the first day even before Haig's intervention. He was aiming at an advance of seven miles or more on 8 August.[13] Even Haig would have had to admit that it was unlikely that troops could go much further than that in the first twenty-four hours. On the issue of action after 8 August, Rawlinson showed his usual reluctance to confront Haig. But it is possible that, remembering the damaging nature of some of Haig's 1916 interventions and anxious at the prospect of an open-ended offensive with grandiose objectives, the Fourth Army staff would have preferred to close the operation down quite quickly after Z-day.

All involved were convinced that the initial blow must come as a surprise and the most elaborate means were used to maintain the secrecy. There was a good deal of active deception and the direst threats of retaliation were made against anyone who, being captured and interrogated, betrayed any useful information to the enemy. The concentration of force for the attack was immense. The number of artillery pieces in Fourth Army was doubled from about 1,000 to about 2,000. About 800 aircraft of the Royal Air Force (formally established on 1 April 1918) were made available to support the offensive and a further 1,104 French aircraft. Some 534 tanks were assembled as well as a battalion of armoured cars. The four divisions of the Canadian Corps, transferred from the First Army, were moved into position with only hours to spare before the attack. The whole thing was an exercise in logistics and administration of formidable complexity. That it was accomplished quite smoothly and with a remarkable degree of secrecy is tribute to the sophistication of British staff work by this period of the war.[14] Secrecy was crucial, as if the Germans had gained any clear idea of what was coming they could have taken a number of relatively simple counter-measures. A pre-emptive withdrawal, even of a mile or so, would have wrecked the whole Fourth Army plan. Even the large-scale relocation of batteries would have largely negated the counter-battery programme, which was a crucial element in it. The deployment of substantial reserves (which were still available at this stage) to the Amiens sector in good time could have drastically reduced the operation's impact. Such precautions remained largely neglected, however, and, when hit, the German Second Army manifested all the symptoms of surprise.

It was almost inevitable that there would be some mishaps in preparing an operation of this complexity. A strong German formation, the 27th

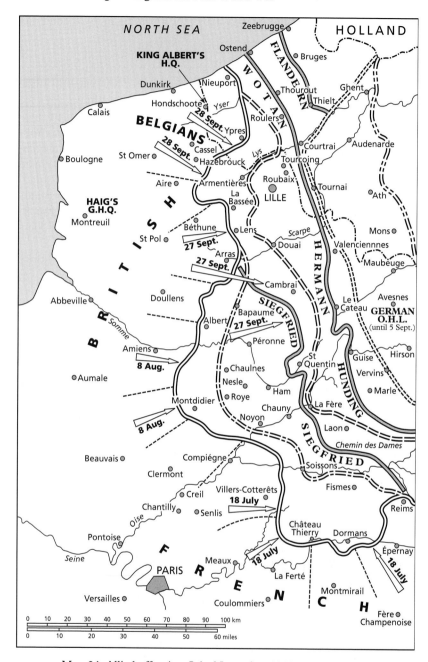

Map 24. Allied offensives July–November 1918

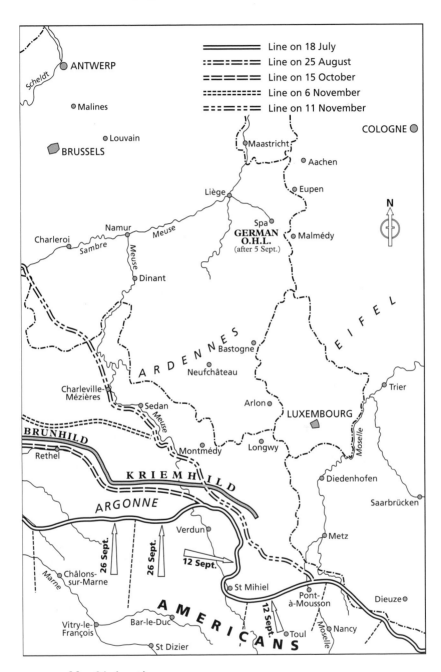

Map 24. (cont.)

Wuerttemberg Division, had recently arrived on the British III Corps' front, immediately north of the Somme. Elements of this formation mounted an attack on Tuesday 6 August, just as the 18th Division was shifting its position in preparation for the offensive. Some ground was lost and some prisoners taken. Some of the latter probably knew details of the forthcoming offensive. There is no evidence that the Germans learned anything from the prisoners taken, but their attack did somewhat disrupt III Corps' arrangements. A counter-attack designed to recover the lost ground the following day was only partly successful and left troops involved somewhat exhausted before the main operation began.[15]

The King came to GHQ on Wednesday 7 August. Compared with his previous visit in March, he was in a much more optimistic frame of mind. He also brought the welcome news that Lloyd George now seemed more favourably disposed towards Haig (though, in point of fact, the Prime Minister had not yet given up on finding another commander-in-chief). In the hours leading up to the great Fourth Army attack Haig was clearly very anxious. He found both his VIP guests, George V and the French President, Raymond Poincaré, irritating, dismissing Poincaré as a mediocrity and considering that his sovereign talked too much. Visiting Fourth Army's HQ at Flexicourt that afternoon probably helped to relieve the tension in Haig's mind. Rawlinson pronounced himself satisfied that the Germans were "in ignorance of the impending blow", despite the Canadian Corps having been moved into the Fourth Army area the previous night. When Haig saw Sir Arthur Currie, commanding the Canadian Corps, the same afternoon he found him in good heart and eager to contribute to the offensive. Whether it was necessary, at this juncture, for Haig pointedly to have "reminded Currie" that his corps had yet been but little engaged that year while the rest of the army was "fighting for its life" seems at least open to question.[16]

The Battle of Amiens: 8–11 August 1918

Haig spent that night in his headquarters train at Wiry au Mont Station. When he awoke on the morning of Thursday 8 August things were going well. Fourth Army had passed the night without untoward incident and opened its attack at 4.20 a.m., while it was still dark. Infantry and tanks followed an impressive creeping barrage, while an intense counter-battery effort that made full use of excellent aerial photographs silenced a high proportion of the German artillery. Just before noon a staff car took Haig and Davidson to Flexicourt to confer with Rawlinson. Though Butler's III Corps was meeting tough resistance and making slow progress north of the Somme, south of that river, where the Australians and the Canadians were making the main thrust, "the situation had developed more favourably" than GHQ had "dared even to hope". Indeed, so thoroughly were German field fortifications breached that both armoured cars and cavalry were able to conduct highly effective exploitation. After returning to his headquarters train for lunch, Haig then went to see Debeney of First French Army, who was also under his command for this particular operation. Though Haig could not avoid the temptation to enter some disparaging comment on French performance in his diary, Debeney's Army too had met with considerable success. Foch came to see Haig at 6 p.m., delighted with the victory unfolding. There were many signs of panic on the part of the Germans, who were "blowing up dumps in all directions and streaming eastwards" and there were seemingly vast hauls of prisoners and captured guns. Progress on the left, in the III Corps' sector, had been less than hoped for, but the main thrust of the offensive had always been intended to be south of the Somme. In that sector, where the Australian and Canadian Corps attacked, as much as eight miles had been gained in the day. Generally Allied losses had been very moderate for a major day of a major attack.[17]

A darker side to a highly successful day was the exceptionally heavy loss suffered by the Royal Air Force (RAF), which had been formed by uniting the Royal Flying Corps and the Royal Naval Air Service on 1 April. In the early stages of the attack the RAF played a useful role in supporting the advance of the ground forces and wrought havoc with retreating German troops. But then its effort was switched to attacks on the Somme bridges. These were tempting targets. Had they been destroyed it would have been difficult for German reinforcements to arrive and for routed Germans to escape. But the RAF did not really have equipment suitable for destroying them. In its efforts to do so it became vulnerable to German fighter reinforcements, which were arriving with impressive speed. The 8 August 1918 became one of the worst days of loss to British air forces in the whole course of the war, with the loss of forty-five aircraft and fifty-two others damaged beyond repair. By evening four airmen were known to be dead, nineteen wounded and fifty-seven missing. It has never been clear who originated the order to switch RAF effort, during the afternoon, to attacks on the Somme bridges. Though Haig mentions no such intervention in his diary, some have suspected that he was responsible and it does bear the hallmarks of the sort of overexcitement and overambition that often gripped him on the first day of a major offensive. But whether or not it originated with GHQ, the order to concentrate on the bridges during the afternoon was certainly passed through Major-General J. M. Salmond, Trenchard's successor in command of air forces on the Western Front. Had Salmond definitely insisted that his service lacked the technology to break the bridges, it seems unlikely that Haig would have overruled him. Salmond never protested that Haig had done this, so it seems that he must at least share responsibility for what one historian has termed a "black day" for the RAF.[18]

As frequently occurred on the second day of an offensive, on Friday 9 August Fourth Army was somewhat slow in renewing its attack. Troops were inevitably tired and artillery support and co-operation with flanking forces difficult to co-ordinate. A further factor was that, on 8 August, Rawlinson had promised Currie the 32nd Division, one of three British divisions held in GHQ reserve behind the Fourth Army, to help him renew his attack the following day. For reasons that have never been properly explained, Major-General Archibald Montgomery, Rawlinson's chief of staff, countermanded the order the following morning. It is at least possible that Montgomery wished to stick with the original Fourth Army concept of a limited offensive. He may not have wanted to press the advance too far and perhaps wished to keep reserves in hand to deal with potential counter-attacks. As the Canadians had been ordered to take the lead in renewing the offensive on Friday 9 August, confusion over this matter seems to have been a major source of delay. Yet some further progress was eventually made on 9 August and, by early evening, the prisoner count had climbed to over 16,000.[19]

Foch, who had by this stage had ordered the French Third Army on Debeney's right to join the fight, came to see Haig at 11 a.m. on 10 August and urged him to press on to the Noyon–Ham–Péronne line and take bridgeheads over the Somme. Haig was aware that resistance was stiffening and had some doubts about this mission. Yet, for the time being, he complied with Foch's wishes and transmitted to Currie of the Canadian Corps Foch's demand that he go for bridges. Apparently against his own better judgement, Currie agreed to try.[20] By that evening, however, many of the attacking troops were exhausted and strong German reinforcements had arrived. Fourth Army's advance gradually ground to a halt.

Rawlinson told Haig on Sunday 11 August that both the Australian and the Canadian Corps were meeting vigorous German counter-attacks. He suggested that there should be a pause in major offensive operations on the Fourth Army front and that Byng's Third Army on his left should mount an attack in the direction of Bapaume. Haig consented to this. Though Foch was initially disappointed and annoyed, Haig stood firm and gained his reluctant consent. Fourth Army issued orders that afternoon that there would be a pause in major operations until 15 August. Though it was not clear to all participants at the time, the Battle of Amiens was over. It had been a dramatic Allied victory. British Fourth Army and French First Army claimed slightly fewer than 30,000 prisoners between

17. A crowd of German prisoners taken by the Fourth Army in the Battle of Amiens in August 1918. With the permission of The Trustees of the Imperial War Museum, London.

them and captured over 400 guns. Fourth Army had suffered about 22,000 total casualties but only 4,000 of these had certainly been killed.[21]

Widening the offensive: Albert, the Scarpe and Péronne

Haig saw Byng on the morning of Sunday 11 August 1918 and told him to prepare an attack in the Bapaume direction. The instruction was repeated at a conference Haig held with Byng, Rawlinson, Debeney and Elles of the Tank Corps at Fourth Army's HQ at 3.30 p.m. the following day. On Thursday 15 August, Third Army and Fourth Army and French First Army were to attack together at dawn. Haig promised Byng reinforcement of 200 tanks, four infantry divisions and two cavalry divisions. He hoped that this renewed offensive would secure Chaulnes and the high ground east of Royes.[22] Twelve days were, however, to elapse before the next really major British attack. The exhausted Fourth Army was not ready to resume the offensive on 15 August. Currie argued strongly against it. Rawlinson passed on Currie's concerns and Haig gave way. Nor was

Byng in any rush. He had gained great plaudits for the Vimy Ridge operation on 9 April 1917 and for the success of 20 November 1917 at Cambrai. But since then he had received the shocks of the German 30 November counter-attack and the *Michael* offensive. Arguably, he had dangerously mishandled the latter. There are indications that these experiences had left him chastened and somewhat battle shy. In any case the Germans began a limited, voluntary withdrawal on the Third Army front on 15 August, which Byng had to follow up before he could mount an attack.[23]

Even when this German withdrawal had ceased and it was possible for Third Army to prepare a set-piece attack, Byng did so in a spirit of great caution, intending to make only a very short advance. Visiting Third Army's HQ on 19 August, Haig insisted that Byng extend the scope of the operation, that he should aim at breaking the German front and, having done so, advance on Bapaume. After nine months of doubt and anxiety following the German counter-offensive at Cambrai on 30 November 1917, Haig now appeared to have his old confidence back. He urged Byng that:

Now is the time to act with boldness, and in full confidence that, if we only hit the Enemy hard enough, and continue to press him, that he will give way and acknowledge that he is beaten.[24]

A successful attack by General Mangin's Tenth French Army on 20 August seemed to underline Haig's message. Byng, however, was conscious of weaknesses in his own forces and was in a cautious mood. When Third Army attacked at 4.55 a.m. on 21 August, the Germans appeared to be taken by surprise and Byng's men took 2,000 prisoners for relatively slight loss. But this attack did not break the German front. Indeed, it did little more than crumple the forward defence zone. Its advance was checked at Achiet le Grand, where the 63rd (Royal Naval) Division encountered serious resistance.[25] This was a fairly minor success. But to Haig's intense annoyance Byng announced at about 10.30 that night that he did not intend to continue the operation the following day. He pleaded that very hot weather had exhausted his troops and that artillery needed to be brought forward before the attack could be resumed.

It is by no means certain that Byng would have resumed offensive operations at all quickly had Haig not intervened. But Haig did, expressing "the wish that the attack be resumed at the earliest possible moment". Haig had thus far enjoyed a good relationship with Byng. But Byng would have realised that he could not necessarily expect to remain in command of an Army much longer if he ignored Haig's "wish". The cautious,

18. Haig reviewing Canadian troops following the Battle of Amiens. With the permission of The Trustees of the Imperial War Museum, London.

hesitant spirit in which Byng had attacked on 21 August was, however, by no means confined to him. That same day Haig had told the Minister of Munitions, Winston Churchill, who was paying a visit to GHQ, that "we ought to do our utmost to get a decision this autumn". Most of those in authority in London, however, were not expecting the decisive stage to arrive until some time in 1919 and Churchill's munitions production programmes were framed on that assumption.[26]

While Fourth Army resumed offensive operations on Thursday 22 August, Byng intended Third Army to consolidate its modest gains of the previous day. Von Below, commanding the German Seventeenth Army, which confronted Byng's Third, seems to have misread the situation. Apparently thinking he had beaten off the worst that Byng could throw at him on Wednesday 21 August, he mounted a general counter-attack the following morning. Third Army defeated it easily, inflicting heavy casualties on the Germans in the process. When Byng resumed his offensive on Friday 23 August, von Below's forces crumpled. After Third Army's hesitant start, the Battle of Albert (as this was later termed) proved the BEF's second great victory of the month. Between first light on 21 August and 6 p.m. on 24 August nearly 10,000 German prisoners passed into Third Army's cages.[27]

Albert was, perhaps, a more significant triumph than Amiens. The latter had been obtained through a unique concentration of the BEF's two biggest and most powerful corps (each of which had a high proportion of hardened, veteran troops) against a clearly identified German weak spot. Third Army had identified no such particular enemy vulnerability on its own front. Its own forces consisted, with the single exception of the New Zealand Division, of formations from the mother country, most of which had been battered in the German spring offensives. Battle casualties had been replaced with large numbers of young, inexperienced conscripts. That such troops could win so impressive a victory suggested not only the decline of the once-mighty German army, but also the effectiveness of British technology and tactics, and of the operational methods by which these were being combined and employed.

The proficiency of British artillery, especially in counter-battery work and the delivery of creeping barrages, had now become proverbial. In the battles over the next few months the British would often (though not always) dispense with preliminary bombardments in order to achieve surprise, relying on suppressive fire during the attack itself. In the opening stages of a big attack the British would often cloak themselves in darkness or would make heavy use of smoke. As well as knowing how to make full use of creeping barrages, British infantry had become appreciative of the support of tanks, and tank crews had learnt much about assisting the infantry. The best infantry, including the better divisions from the mother country as well as the much-vaunted Dominion troops, knew how to use their own weaponry to press forward when it was reasonable to do so, even in the absence of close artillery support. Finally, the ground troops enjoyed excellent assistance from an air arm which, though now theoretically a separate service, still saw its primary role as assisting the army almost regardless of the loss to itself. The accuracy of the artillery was heavily dependent on target acquisition, through both aerial photographs and direct observation, by the RAF, and in major attacks tanks and infantry were often assisted by RAF contact patrols and low-flying attack.[28]

Even before his second August victory was complete, Haig tried to imbue all his Armies with his conception of the opportunities that now beckoned. Late on the night of Thursday 22 August he sent a telegram to all his Army commanders. Key paragraphs are worth quoting:

I request that Army commanders will without delay bring to the notice of all subordinate leaders the changed conditions in which operations are now being carried on ...

The methods which we have followed, hitherto, in our battles with limited objectives when the enemy was strong, are no longer suited to his present condition ...

To turn the present situation to account the most resolute offensive is everywhere desirable. Risks which a month ago would have been criminal to incur must now be incurred as a duty.

It is no longer necessary to advance in regular lines and step by step. On the contrary, each division should be given a distant objective which must be reached independently of its neighbour and even if one's flank is thereby exposed for the time being.

Reinforcements must be directed against the sectors where our troops are gaining ground not where they are checked ...

The situation is most favourable: let each one of us act energetically and without hesitation push forward to our objective.[29]

The impact on the Army commanders and their staff of what Haig had to say here was probably limited by his track record of overoptimistic forecasts. Indeed, even at this stage, his imagination seems to have been running well ahead of events. On 23 August, Haig noted, in response to an order given by Byng, that he wanted "the cavalry kept together as a corps for strategical objectives in view of the possibility of the rapid disintegration of the Enemy". Over the next few weeks he would repeatedly state to the War Office that large-scale cavalry exploitation might soon be possible, demanding that Sir Henry Wilson make more mounted troops available to him. While the German army was certainly deteriorating, it had not yet reached the stage of disintegration. There was no opportunity for the large-scale use of cavalry on the Third Army front. Divisional commanders told Haig that same day that "hostile machine guns" were causing "much trouble".[30] By 24 August, the Germans on the Third Army front were in full retreat and days later their command sanctioned a fairly deep withdrawal on the fronts of the British Third and Fourth Armies and the French First Army. But the Germans skilfully covered their retreat with rearguards including substantial numbers of field guns and machine guns, composed of the most determined and reliable of their troops.[31]

The high price still being paid by his forces was brought home to Haig on 24 August by news of the death of a young officer who had become a personal friend. George Black had been in charge of a detachment from 17th Lancers, which formed Haig's mounted escort. He had been good for Haig's personal morale: "always so cheerful and happy even when things looked darkest". He had, however, transferred to the Tank Corps on the grounds that he wanted to fight. His tank had been hit and he had died of wounds the previous day. Haig noted that he was a "great loss to me and all of us".[32]

Sadness at Black's loss did not, however, diminish Haig's enthusiasm for continuing the offensive. He intended to do this with another leftward extension of major offensive efforts, bringing in Horne's First Army. Haig originally hoped that First Army would he able to envelop the right flank of the Germans facing Third Army, but the German withdrawal on the Third Army front made this more difficult. First Army's offensive (later known as the Battle of the Scarpe) nevertheless went ahead on 26 August and made good progress.[33] Yet how much longer Haig's forces could maintain offensive efforts on this scale had to be regarded as questionable. There was little evidence that the authorities at home endorsed Haig's belief in the possibility of victory in 1918. The War Office was insisting that, owing to a shortage of men, Haig's force of sixty-one divisions must be reduced by at least seven in the course of 1918. By 1919 he would be reduced to only thirty-two "active" British divisions with a further twelve "replacement divisions", together with ten Dominion divisions: a total of 54.[34]

Initially, Haig was less upset by this than might have been expected. For another day or two he hoped to have the use of some American divisions that had been training with British assistance in his sector of the front. But by 27 August it was becoming clear that Pershing, anxious to create a great concentrated American army under his own command, would not permit this. The Americans had for some time been preparing a major assault on the St Mihiel Salient, though Haig did not think much of that idea, wanting concentric, mutually supporting offensive movements "on Cambrai, on St Quentin and from the south on Mezières".[35]

The approach to the Hindenburg Line: 24 August–24 September 1918

From 24 August the Germans were withdrawing on the front of the British Third and Fourth Armies and from 26 August the First Army's offensive on the Scarpe was pushing them back, north of Arras to the Drocourt–Quéant Line, or, as the Germans called it, the Wotan Position. Ludendorff was hoping to anchor his front on the Wotan Position: a northward extension of the main Hindenburg Line (the Siegfried Position). Haig's plan was to assault and break the Drocourt–Quéant Line without delay almost as soon as First Army reached it: unhinging German forces further south and obliging them to continue their retreat. Recent victories made it very difficult to sack Haig at this stage, but he had not overcome Lloyd

George's mistrust of him. At the Prime Minister's instigation Wilson sent Haig a telegram labelled "personal":

Just a word of caution in regard to incurring heavy losses in attacks on the Hindenburg Line [an expression which Wilson seems to have used loosely, intending to include the Drocourt–Quéant line] as opposed to losses when driving the enemy back to that line. I do not mean to say that you have incurred such losses, but I know the War Cabinet would become anxious if we received heavy punishment in attacking the Hindenburg Line without success.[36]

Wilson followed this up next day with a letter couched in similar terms, but giving a fuller explanation. Haig seems to have realised that these messages were not sent on Wilson's personal initiative, but had originated with the War Cabinet itself. He was indignant. The War Cabinet was not forbidding an attack on the Hindenburg Line in 1918, and if that position were to be captured, would clearly be happy to share the credit. If things went wrong, however, it would endeavour to deny responsibility, blame Haig and, perhaps, sack him. While that attitude does seem rather contemptible, the context cannot be ignored. In 1916 and, more particularly, in 1917, Haig had done much to bring upon himself the lack of government trust that these messages conveyed. Moreover, he had just conveyed a rather similar message to his own subordinates.

By 29 August, First Army confronted the Drocourt–Quéant Line, while Fourth Army was nearing Péronne on the Somme. First Army intended to attack the Drocourt–Quéant Line on 2 September. On 31 August, however, Haig "sent Lawrence to see Horne and Currie" and tell them that he had "no wish to attack the Quéant–Drocourt Line if they are in any doubt about taking it".[37] By the time First Army successfully attacked that position, as scheduled, Fourth Army had already begun to unhinge the new German front further south, in the Mont St Quentin-Péronne sector, starting on 31 August. These latter operations were the inspiration of the ambitious and super-aggressive Australian Corps commander, Sir John Monash, rather than that of Haig or Rawlinson. Within a few days the Australians had made it quite impossible for the Germans to hang on in this sector.[38]

Haig, however, was apparently concerned that the Australians might wear themselves out prematurely. He noted in his diary on 1 September that at this stage he was "opposed to doing more attacking than was absolutely necessary. Our object is to keep the battle going as long as possible until the Americans can attack in force." He and Foch were beginning to plan a "General Offensive" (eventually mounted in late September) in which Belgian, British, French and American forces would all attack simultaneously. Contrary to his assessments earlier in the year, Haig, along with Foch, was now expecting that the American Army would play a crucial role:

The decisive moment will arrive when the Americans attack in force. The British Army must still be able to attack then, and to have the means of exploiting the victory and making it decisive. I therefore wish the Cavalry Corps to be kept as strong as possible ...[39]

By Tuesday 3 September the First Army (with the Canadian Corps playing the leading role) had secured the Drocourt–Quéant Line. Haig noted in his dairy that "The Enemy seems in full retreat today on the whole front from Lens to Péronne." It seemed clear that the Germans must fall back to the Hindenburg Line. In a surge of somewhat excessive optimism, Haig began to doubt whether they would even remain long on the latter position. They might, he considered, fall back to Namur and the Meuse. The following day Foch remarked in an after-lunch chat that he believed "the German is nearing his end". Haig noted that since 1 August "we British alone have captured over 72,000 prisoners and 700 guns".[40]

By this stage Haig had lost his chief of intelligence, Brigadier-General Edgar Cox. That unfortunate officer, out of action with influenza for much of June, drowned bathing in the sea on 26 August. On 8 September, however, Haig received an encouraging briefing from his temporary replacement, Colonel Butler. Later the same day Haig told Churchill, who was paying another visit to GHQ, that he expected the war to be won by the following spring at the latest, perhaps within the next couple of months. Haig urged that Churchill organise his munitions production programmes with this in view. Meanwhile, GHQ was working out with Foch arrangements for the "General Offensive" to be mounted in late September.

The British Fourth Army was intended to break the Hindenburg Line (*Siegfried Stellung*) in the first few days of this offensive. But this was only the strongest of a series of German defensive positions still confronting Haig's forces. By Sunday 8 September Fourth Army had still not quite reached what Rawlinson termed the "Main Hindenburg System" in the St Quentin Canal sector. Fourth Army's advance came to a halt in front of a fortified line that ran through Epehy, a few miles to the west. Before confronting the Main Hindenburg System, it would have to overcome three lesser defensive lines, all fairly formidable in themselves, the last of which Rawlinson termed the Advanced Hindenburg System. Rawlinson's troops, and especially the Australian Corps, had been engaged in fighting of extraordinary intensity for much of the last month. Units were depleted and tiredness evident. Over lunch on Sunday 8 September, therefore, Rawlinson asked Haig for the 6th Division from the GHQ reserve, but Haig, who wanted to keep some reserves for the "General Offensive", turned him down.[41]

Intending that the Allies offensive efforts would reach a climax over the next few weeks and believing that the end of the war would soon follow,

Haig crossed the Channel on Monday 9 September. He intended to convey this message to the government and urge that they send him all available resources immediately. (Unfortunately for his credibility he had made the same argument during the Third Battle of Ypres and it had then turned out to be based on false premises.) Speaking to Milner at the War Office on Tuesday 10 September, he asked that all reserves held in the United Kingdom and "men already marked for the Navy should for the next 6 months be sent to Army" at once. Munitions programmes should be focused on maximising his forces' equipment in the immediate future. Nothing that would take more than a few months to deliver was worth bothering with:

Within the last four weeks we had captured 77,000 prisoners and nearly 800 guns! There has never been such a victory in the annals of Britain ... The discipline of the German Army is quickly going, and the German officer is no longer what he was. It seems to me to be the beginning of the end. From these and other facts I draw the conclusion that the Enemy's troops will not await our attacks in even the strongest positions.

If we act with energy now, a decision can be obtained in the very near future.

Haig got the impression that Milner "fully agreed"[42] but this seems not to have been the case.[43] Given Haig's track record it is hardly surprising that Milner and his ministerial colleagues remained sceptical about his prognoses. Over the next few weeks his judgements of the balance of forces and the prospects for decisive victory were, indeed, to prove inconsistent and unreliable. Lunching at Buckingham Place the following day, Haig saw that, while the King was optimistic and determined to "continue the war until the Germans [were] completely broken", even he had not grasped the full magnitude of recent British victories. There can be little doubt that Haig was now paying the price for GHQ's overoptimism in the Charteris era and its efforts to "spin" the press at that time. Having lost confidence in Haig and GHQ after Third Ypres and Cambrai, and understandably wary of trumpeting false victories, journalists and editors were now underplaying very real ones.[44]

Shortly before he left for London, Haig had requested a report from each of his Army commanders, these to include comments on German "dispositions and probable intentions" and recommendations for the future conduct of "deliberate operations" by British forces. Their choices were circumscribed. In his dealings with Foch, Haig had already virtually committed his forces to an effort to break the Hindenburg Line by the end of the month. What Haig really wanted was to know how the Army commanders thought that they could contribute to that aim. Byng, perhaps trying to make up for his seeming lack of offensive spirit earlier in the campaign, was the first to reply and did so in pugnacious terms. He thought German morale poor, declaring that many German troops would "surrender if they dared: many fight extremely badly", but he advocated breaching the Hindenburg Line as quickly as possible as he thought the Germans might recover if given time to rest behind it. Horne and Rawlinson were a little slower to respond, each replying on 11 September. Horne thought his best policy was to support Byng's advance towards Cambrai. Rawlinson favoured mounting, as soon as possible, an attack that would carry his forces to within striking distance of the Main Hindenburg System. He thought they would need a period of rest before assaulting that position.[45]

On Thursday 12 September Byng mounted an attack (later known as the Battle of Havrincourt) that moved Third Army a little closer to the Main Hindenburg System. The Americans successfully attacked the St Mihiel Salient (from which the Germans were trying to withdraw) that same day. Six days later Rawlinson mounted an attack designed to bring Fourth Army within striking distance of the Main Hindenburg System, an operation later known as the Battle of Epéhy. For this Fourth Army employed three corps: Butler's III, Monash's Australian and Sir Walter Braithwaite's IX Corps, which had just come under Rawlinson's command. Fourth Army was supported by elements of Third Army on its left and the French First Army on the right. Fourth Army was most successful in the centre, in the Australian Corps's sector, where all objectives were taken, but less successful on the flanks. However, there were a series of further operations up to 27 September which secured most, though not all, of the ground Rawlinson wanted before assaulting the Main Hindenburg System.[46]

The General Offensive

With Fourth Army having closed up to the Main Hindenburg System, the stage was set for the opening of the long-planned General Offensive. The attacks were intended to be converging in order to give the best possible mutual support. Haig had encouraged that idea and had pressed for the main American operation of the General Offensive to be in the Meuse–Argonne sector, rather a follow-up to the pinching out of the St Mihiel Salient. Yet it is doubtful whether either Foch or Haig really counted on executing any particular scheme of manoeuvre. Haig thought, in late August, that Foch's basic strategy was "a simple straightforward advance by all the troops on the Western front and to keep the enemy on the move!" John Du Cane, Foch's principal British liaison officer, expressed the Generalissimo's intentions for the General Offensive as "Everyone is to attack ... as soon as they can, as strong as they can, for as long as they can." Adopting this approach, Foch appears to have reasoned that the Germans were bound to crack somewhere. They were, however, strongest in terms of relative numbers in the centre, where they faced the British, which was also the sector in which they also had the most powerful fortifications.[47]

The General Offensive began gradually with the opening, at 11.30 p.m. on Wednesday 25 September, of the preliminary bombardment for the great Franco-American attack in the Meuse-Argonne sector. The infantry assault, on a 44-mile front, equally divided between the forces of the two nations, commenced at 5.25 the following morning. But Haig's hope that this Franco-American effort would draw off German forces before the British assault on the Main Hindenburg System was to be disappointed. Pershing's part in the general offensive, on which both Foch and Haig had heavily counted, had ground to a halt within a couple of days. In the short-term, it proved difficult to restart and the next major American effort would not be until 4 October. Despite numerical superiority of 7:1 (or even 9:1 according to some estimates) the Americans could not break German resistance in their sector until the beginning of November.[48]

On Friday 27 September, First Army, with the Canadian Corps as its spearhead, attacked across the Canal du Nord, supported by Third Army on its southern flank. On Saturday 28 September the Belgian Army and the Plumer's Second Army (brought together, since 9 September, as the Group of Armies in Flanders under the Belgian King) joined the offensive. By the standards of 1917, progress was simply astonishing. Within a few days more ground was captured than in months at Third Ypres. Allied losses were, moreover, amazingly light by 1917 standards and the yield in terms of German prisoners and guns captured extremely gratifying.

After a preliminary bombardment, commencing at 10 p.m. on 26 September, Fourth Army attacked the Main Hindenburg System at 5.50 a.m. on Sunday 29 September. In the sector where the St Quentin Canal ran through a long tunnel, two divisions of the II American Corps, which had very recently joined Fourth Army, were used to open the attack, with Australian divisions passing through them in the course of the morning. Progress in the northern part of the tunnel sector was very limited though somewhat greater in the southern part. The most remarkable success, however, was that of Lieutenant-General Sir Walter Braithwaite's IX Corps, which, with the 46th (North Midland) Division as its spearhead, crossed an open section of canal immediately to the south of the tunnel. Braithwaite's operation was a late addition to the Fourth Army plan, and Monash, Fourth Army's principal planner for this particular attack, had been very sceptical of its merits. Fourth Army had a very hard fight that day, but by its end the Main Hindenburg System had been thoroughly ruptured.[49]

Though Haig had played a part in planning the General Offensive, his role, as it unfolded from 26–29 September, was little more than that of a spectator. The rapid breakdown of the American offensive in the Meuse-Argonne sector was a serious disappointment and the concept of all the Allied Armies simultaneously and continuously attacking until victory was won was soon abandoned. On the other hand, Haig heard from Foch on 26 September that (owing to an Allied offensive in the Balkans) the Bulgarians were dropping out of the war. Though neither Foch nor Haig knew it at the time, this news, coming on top of recent defeats on the Western Front, caused Ludendorff, at least temporarily, to lose his nerve. He demanded that the Kaiser's government should seek an immediate cease fire. Byng and Rawlinson, who met Haig at Third Army's headquarters on Tuesday 1 October, told him that it was merely a question of "continuing our pressure" to ensure a German collapse. Haig seemed to acknowledge that, given the apparent confidence and competence of his subordinate commanders, his own role had now contracted. Byng and Rawlinson "agreed that no further orders [from Haig] were necessary and both would be able to carry on without difficulty".[50]

There were, however, some less encouraging signs in early October. Both the Belgians and the Americans were in difficulty with their logistics and American tactical naivety had been cruelly exposed. Fourth Army managed to overcome the Beaurevoir Line (the reserve line to the Main Hindenburg System and the last heavily fortified position the Germans had on the Western Front) by 5 October. But this proved to be the last action in which Australian infantry were involved. The Australian Corps had been Fourth Army's principal spearhead from 8 August to late September. Even in an exhausted condition it had played a major role in breaking the Beaurevoir Line. But the Australians' invaluable contribution to the Allies' cause had come at enormous cost. Exhausted, the last of their infantry withdrew from the fighting for a desperately needed rest, never to return to action in this war.

But events were to indicate that there was more to Fourth Army than the Australian Corps. The British IX and XIII Corps were now proving highly effective and the American II Corps would make an important contribution until mid-October, when it too dropped out exhausted. On Sunday 6 October Haig was cheered by news that the Central Powers were seeking an armistice. On Tuesday 8 October a combined offensive by the Third and Fourth Armies broke the German front again and this was soon followed by the fall of Cambrai to Canadian troops of First Army. Even Lloyd George felt obliged to send a telegram of congratulations.[51]

On Thursday 10 October Haig met a cheerful, optimistic Foch, who gave him a copy of suggested armistice terms that he was sending to the Supreme War Council. According to these, German troops would be allowed to return to Germany with their rifles and officers with their swords. But, as Haig noted, Foch's terms amounted, in all matters of real substance, to unconditional surrender. There is no indication that, at this stage, Haig disagreed with such a policy. Discussing Foch's proposals with Herbert Lawrence after dinner at GHQ that night, Haig, however, discovered that his Chief of the General Staff:

> seemed in a pessimistic mood and foresaw many dangers ahead. He said "the British Army is doing all the fighting, the French will do nothing and the American Army is quite incapable of doing anything" and so on. If the Enemy were to counter-attack us, we would find ourselves in a difficult position!
>
> I assured him that the enemy has not the means nor the will-power to launch a counter-attack strong enough to affect even our front line troops. We have got the Enemy down, in fact he is a beaten army, and my plan is to go on hitting him as hard as we possibly can until he begs for mercy.
>
> Lawrence has a cold and is looking at things in a gloomy way tonight. I think the situation highly satisfactory, and the results of our victories will be *very far reaching* ... The Enemy is in such a state that we can run all kinds of risks without any chance of Enemy hitting back in any force.[52]

Haig knew, however, that he had been wrong in the past when insisting that the German army faced imminent collapse. Only two days later he heard that a determined counter-attack by a German rearguard had temporarily checked the advance of Lieutenant-General Shute's V Corps in Third Army. While this incident was not at all serious in itself, and while Haig tried to dismiss it, it may have reminded him of Lawrence's prognosis and, to some extent, played on his mind.[53] Over the next few days, a slight logistical pause was needed on the fronts of the Third and Fifth Armies "to complete ... railway communications on the Cambrai-Le Cateau front". Meanwhile, Plumer's Second Army, at this stage part of the Allied Group of Armies in Flanders, and thus not directly under Haig's command, took part in another highly successful attack, later known as the Battle of Courtrai, commencing on Monday 14 October.[54]

The Battle of the Selle and Haig's attack of pessimism: mid-October to early November 1918

On Thursday 17 October Fourth Army mounted a major attack in the Le Cateau sector, supported by Third Army on its left. This was the opening move of what was later known as the Battle of the Selle. The British had failed to achieve much surprise in this instance, and the Germans had reinforced the Le Cateau sector quite strongly. Resistance in some parts of the front was fierce and there were numerous counter-attacks. Yet even on this hard-fought first day, Fourth Army gained ground and took 4,000 prisoners. Haig's diary entry for 17 October indicates no particular dismay at the intensity of the fighting and, over the next few days, the Battle of the Selle would turn into one of the greatest victories in British history. Yet something odd happened in Haig's mind at this time. He suddenly became much more pessimistic. The instigator of this shift in his perception seems to have been Herbert Lawrence.

Before retiring to bed on the night of 17 October, Haig (who was due to go to London next day) spoke to Lawrence about the terms on which an armistice should be offered to the Germans. Lawrence's views were apparently unchanged since their conversation a week earlier. He believed it was in Britain's interests to end the war in 1918. He clearly did not think it possible to beat the Germans into complete submission over the next couple of months and reasoned that the armistice terms should "not be too exacting".[55] The previous week Haig had dismissed Lawrence's views as excessively gloomy, the result of his having a cold. He had then insisted that:

We have got the Enemy down, in fact he is beaten Army and my plan is to go on hitting him as hard as we possibly can until he begs for mercy.

By the time he met Sir Henry Wilson at the War Office, just after 10 a.m. on Saturday 19 October, Haig had, however, totally changed his tune. He was now humming Lawrence's. When Wilson said that "the Germans should be ordered to lay down their arms and retire to the east bank of the Rhine", Haig responded that "in that case there would be no armistice, and the war would continue for at least another year!" Wilson and Haig, accompanied by Davidson, then proceeded to Downing Street. Lloyd George asked Haig's views on armistice terms. Haig replied that "they must greatly depend on the answers given to two questions:

(1) Is Germany now so beaten that she will accept whatever terms the Allies may offer?
(2) Can the Allies continue to press the Enemy sufficiently vigorously during the coming winter months to cause him to with draw so quickly that he cannot destroy the railways, roads etc?

The answer to both questions is negative. The German Army is capable of retiring to its own frontiers, and holding that line if there should be any attempt to touch the *honour* of the German people.

The situation of the Allied Armies is as follows:

French Army worn out, and has not been fighting latterly. It has been freely said that "war is over" and "we don't want to waste our lives now that peace is in sight".

American Army is disorganised, ill equipped and ill trained. Good officers and NCOs are lacking.

The British Army was never more efficient but has fought hard, and it lacks reinforcements. With diminishing effectives moral is bound to suffer.

French and American Armies are not capable of making a serious offensive *now*. British alone can bring the enemy to his knees.

In the coming winter, Enemy will have some months for recuperation and absorption of 1920 class, untouched yet. He will be in a position to destroy all communications before he falls back. This will mean serious delay to our advance next year.

Haig outlined the armistice terms that he now favoured. The Germans were to evacuate France, Belgium and Alsace-Lorraine, but there was no mention of their having to lay down any arms. Haig's terms would apparently have left the German army in possession not only of small arms and officers' swords, but also its machine guns, mortars and artillery. He also advised setting "our face against the French entering Germany to pay off old scores". Haig apparently had no interest in forcing the Germans to evacuate any of territory they had occupied in Eastern Europe. Arthur Balfour, the Foreign Secretary, who joined the discussion part way through, seemed dismayed at this. But Haig endorsed the Prime Minister's opinion that "we cannot expect the British to go on sacrificing their lives for the Poles!"[56]

Haig was able to spend the Sunday at home, but returned to Downing Street on the morning of Monday 21 October. Some of the other official advice being given to the government favoured far greater toughness towards the Germans. Haig thought that Wilson wanted to demand the Germans' "complete surrender" and was inclined to attribute this to his wish to have justification for imposing conscription on Ireland, as a means of "pacifying" that country. Wilson did, indeed, favour conscription for Ireland (as had Haig at one time), but whether his advocacy of a tough line with Germany was directly related to his views on Ireland is less clear. The Navy's line was also much harder than that of Haig. Admiral Wemyss (the First Sea Lord) and Admiral Beatty (commanding the Grand Fleet) demanded that the Germans surrender practically their whole navy. The collapse of Turkey at this stage made even Lloyd George inclined to insist on harsher terms for a German armistice than Haig had advised.[57]

The fact that for most of the period from 18–22 October Haig was absent from GHQ while campaigning was in full swing is indicative of the extent to which his GHQ staff and the Armies could now run the war without him. Victory on the Selle was followed by another short period of pursuit. As for much of the Hundred Days' campaign, Haig, Lawrence and the operations branch at GHQ needed to intervene but little in what his Armies were doing. Directions were occasionally issued on such matters as the optimum use of tanks: a scarce resource in constant demand.[58] The allocation of tanks and GHQ's artillery and aviation assets between Armies had to be determined, and corps and divisions sometimes redistributed between them. From time to time arrangements needed to be made for co-ordinated assaults by more than one Army on the same day.[59] It is, however, doubtful whether Haig's personal intervention was required even for this, except perhaps to make arrangements with Foch when the close co-operation of the French army was also required.

GHQ had two further British offensives scheduled for early November. But Haig's diary and correspondence suggest that his principal preoccupations in late October were not the planning of these, which could safely be delegated to other hands, but rather his relations with his allies and the terms of the armistice to be offered to the Germans. One of the matters over which he expended a great deal of energy now seems extraordinarily petty in relation to the real issues of the day.

Since 9 September Haig had retained only four of the British Armies under his personal command. To facilitate Foch's "General Offensive", he had, as we have noted, authorised the integration of Plumer's Second Army with the Belgian Army in a Flanders Army Group theoretically commanded by the Albert, King of the Belgians, but actually by the latter's French chief of staff, General Degoutte. By late October Haig was pronouncing himself "disgusted at the almost underhand way in which the French are trying to get hold of part of the British Army" and was demanding the return of Second Army to his own control.

Certainly Plumer and his staff had sometimes found Degoutte a bit officious and awkward to deal with. But it is difficult to avoid the conclusion that Haig's preoccupation with the Second Army issue had far more to do with his own *amour propre* than with improving the operational effectiveness of Allied forces. The spirit in which he pursued it was certainly not conducive to harmonious feeling amongst the Allies at this critical time. Annoyed with Foch and his chief of staff, General Weygand, on 24 October Haig by his own account told them "a few 'home truths'". He insisted that "when all is said and done, the British army has defeated the Germans this year and I am responsible to the British government for the handling of British troops not Foch". Writing to Foch on 27 October, he pronounced that the failure to return Second Army to his direct control struck at the foundation of his position as British commander-in-chief, surely something of an exaggeration.[60]

On Friday 25 October Brigadier-General Clive, who had replaced Cox as intelligence chief at GHQ, briefed Haig on the strategic situation. Clive was clearly aware, at least in broad outline, of the potentially revolutionary climate in Germany:

He considers that the internal situation of Germany is serious, and that the German Government fears Bolshevism may get the upper hand and all law and order be at an end.

But, according to Haig, Clive proceeded to make the convoluted argument that the Bolshevik threat might lead to the fall of the relatively moderate government of Prince Max of Baden and thus the "militarists would return to Power and begin a life and death struggle". The very political instability of Germany, therefore, made it more dangerous and provided another reason for offering moderate armistice terms. When arguing for such terms at a senior Allied conference at Foch's HQ later that day, however, Haig found himself in a minority of one. Though only a couple of days earlier Pershing had appeared to agree with Haig, he now concurred with Foch and Pétain that the Allies should insist on occupation of the left bank of the Rhine as the price of cease-fire. Haig was dismayed:

I felt the Enemy might not accept the terms Foch proposed because of military necessity only – and it would be very costly and take a long time (2 years) to enforce them, unless the internal state of Germany compels the Enemy to accept them. We don't know much about the internal state of Germany – and so to try to impose such terms seems to me really a gamble which may come off or it may not.

In late October, when most others could sense that the Germans were at breaking point, Haig was anxious that the war might continue for several further months. He therefore felt a strong need to have the Australian Corps back in action and practically told his Adjutant-General that the Australians were shirking. This was an utterly outrageous accusation against a valiant corps that had bled itself white in the British Empire's service. Australia had suffered a higher proportion of casualties in relation to its numbers at the front than any other nation in the Empire and only New Zealand had a higher proportion in relation to size of population. Apparently oblivious to this, Haig insisted that he would take up the matter of the Corps' inaction with W. M. Hughes, the Australian Prime Minister.

The Australian Corps, however, was the one part of Haig's forces that had experienced disciplinary problems in 1918 serious enough to be characterised as mutiny. Traditionally these disturbances have been attributed to unit amalgamations as division were reduced from twelve battalions to nine. But the real story seems to have been more complicated and very much more serious. The Corps had been pushed past breaking point, not so much by Haig, GHQ or Fourth Army as by its intensely ambitious and aggressive commander, one of whose weaknesses was a high degree of isolation from his men. In fact the Australian Corps' withdrawal from action had been at the personal insistence of Hughes, who had threatened to sack Monash if this were not done. Perhaps blinded by Monash's bravura, Haig had evidently lost touch with an important part of the army he commanded. He clearly did not realise the shattered condition to which this once-formidable formation had now been reduced.[61]

Since 18 October Haig had been arguing that the Germans were far from complete defeat. If the Allies wanted a ceasefire in 1918 they would have to offer moderate terms. But events were making that position increasingly untenable. Meeting with Milner and Henry Wilson at Versailles on Sunday 27 October, Haig reasonably concluded that the intelligence recently received of Ludendorff's resignation spelt "a German retreat to the frontier and an armistice". By Tuesday 29 October he was admitting to Lloyd George, who had come to confer with the French government, that "the collapse of Austria makes Germany's position hopeless". Yet, while recognising that the "military situation is more in our favour today", Haig was unwilling to change the advice he had given ten days earlier. The Germans should be offered moderate armistice terms, at least as far as their land forces were concerned.[62] It is difficult to discern any sound reasoning behind this. It seems like intellectual obstinacy – the unwillingness to admit that advice so recently tendered had been based on false premises.

Meeting his Army commanders at Cambrai on Thursday 31 October, Haig again recorded his opinion that "the Enemy has not been sufficiently beaten as to cause him to accept an ignominious peace". No Army commander openly dissented, though whether this represented the true opinion of all is not clear. Haig's Army commanders' meetings had generally been conducted essentially as "orders groups" at which the commander-in-chief exerted his authority. Dissent had seldom been encouraged and free and frank discussion was not the norm. Practically everyone in the British forces was, indeed, weary of war, but it does not appear that all felt that this was quite the moment to end it. Two major offensives were planned for the next few days: a First Army and Third Army attack in the Valenciennes sector due to start the next morning, 1 November; and a massive combined attack by First, Third, Fourth and First French Armies on 4 November. One of the corps commanders, Lieutenant-General Godley of XXII Corps, told Haig that:

Enemy is fighting a good rearguard action, but he [Godley] hopes that no Armistice will be arranged until after his next 2 operations, viz. tomorrow and 4 November![63]

On the day of the first of the major attacks to which Godley had alluded, Haig was at a Supreme War Council meeting at Versailles. The Council decided to insist on Armistice terms much tougher than Haig had advocated. The Germans would have to hand over the great bulk of their artillery, locomotives and rolling stock, and allow the Allies to cross the

Rhine. Haig reluctantly agreed that the collapse of Turkey and Austria made it quite possible that the Germans would accept these terms. But having made premature predictions of the moral collapse of his opponents for more than two years, he now insisted, with breathtaking perversity, that "the determined fight put up by the Enemy today shows that the German Army is not yet *demoralised*!"[64] It is difficult to understand what led him to that conclusion. His First and Third Armies had won a relatively easy victory. In some critical parts of the front the Germans surrendered quite readily on Friday 1 November, and by the following day were in full retreat across practically the whole sector attacked. Fourth Army's attack on 4 November (later known as the Battle of the Sambre) was an even greater success. German resistance was initially fierce in some places, but was everywhere very brittle. As Haig himself commented:

The Enemy seems to have placed all his strength in his front line. Consequently when this was overcome he had no reserves in rear with which to oppose our advance.

Even as late as this, however, Haig was trying to show the War Office and the British government the darker side of the picture. The Belgians and most of the French army, he insisted, had virtually ceased to fight.[65] The British and the still-somewhat-green Americans were, in this assessment, practically on their own.

The German collapse and the Armistice

By Tuesday 5 November the Germans were in full retreat on the fronts of the British First, Third and Fourth Armies. Only rear guards opposed the British advance. By Saturday 9 November all the British Armies reported that the Germans were in full retreat. The same thing was happening in the French and American sectors. British advance guards had difficulty keeping up with the pace of the German retreat. On the same day the British picked up German radio broadcasts indicating that the Kaiser had abdicated.[66]

For weeks the Germans had been wrecking railways as they fell back. As British railheads were a long way behind the advancing troops it was clearly going to be difficult to keep them supplied if the Germans continued retreating at the same rate over the next few weeks. It has thus sometimes been suggested that logistical problems would have prevented the Allies consummating their victory in 1918 had the Germans not signed an armistice when they did.[67] It is, however, at least arguable that logistics had become almost an irrelevance by the first week in November. The Allies' victory was already won. There was mutiny in the German

19. Haig with his Army Commanders. With the permission of The Trustees of the Imperial War Museum, London.

fleet and revolution in some of the towns. In late October Ludendorff was sacked for insubordination and a level of mental instability that had resulted in judgements even more wildly fluctuating than those of Haig. On Monday 6 November General Gröner, who replaced him as *de facto* commander-in-chief, advised the Chancellor that the German army was likely to disintegrate if an armistice were not secured by the following Saturday. Its utter moral exhaustion, which Haig had so often predicted but could not recognise when it was finally happening, was now, in Gröner's analysis, an established fact.[68]

The Armistice was arranged in a railway carriage in the Forest of Compiègne. There were no real negotiations. The German delegates (civilians cynically tasked to sign what was bound to be a humiliating agreement in order to save the army's face) were presented with tough terms and told to take them or leave them. Rather horrified, they referred them to Hindenburg (still the Chief of the General Staff) and the government they represented. But no one saw any reasonable prospect for continued resistance. At 5.05 a.m. on Monday 11 November, therefore, they signed a ceasefire agreement timed to come into effect at 11 a.m. Notifying the British Armies of the impending armistice, GHQ insisted that no fraternisation with the enemy would be permitted. If German troops approached British lines they were to be warned off by fire. If they persisted they were to be shot. The cessation was not unexpected and British troops' initial reaction was generally subdued. There were more vigorous and noisy celebrations that night. The war, or at least the fighting of it, was over.

In retrospect, given our awareness of the "stab in the back" myth that some Germans were able to construct (and some, perhaps, even to believe), it may seem that the Allies let the German army off the hook too easily. But at the time both Haig and the Germans themselves considered the terms harsh to the point of brutality. The German army salvaged some dignity by retaining small arms and officers' swords. But it salvaged practically nothing else. Artillery pieces and most machine guns were handed over, as were bridgeheads over the Rhine. The Germans, as both sides clearly understood, were now naked before their enemies. The Allies could impose any peace they chose. The Armistice, in all but name and outward form, was in fact an unconditional surrender.[69]

Finally Haig conceded that:

The state of the German Army is ... very bad and the discipline seems to have become so low that the orders of the officers are not obeyed ...[70]

Haig in the Hundred Days: Assessment

The sorry state of the German army was certainly not a sudden development. Yet for a period of about a fortnight, from 18 October, Haig had expended much effort trying to persuade everyone of importance in the Allied camp of the precise opposite: that the forces opposing him were fighting with undiminished resolution and vigour. He was still trying to convince himself of this up to 4 November. From circa 22 August to circa 10 October, on the other hand, he had been trying to persuade everyone, slightly prematurely, that the German army was on the brink of collapse. Consistency is sometimes reckoned one of Haig's cardinal qualities.[71] If, however, his judgement had been consistent in 1918, it was only in the strange sense of being consistently erratic. His fluctuating assessments do not appear to have reflected those of his principal intelligence officers. Neither Cox nor Clive had the influence with him that Charteris had once enjoyed and, perhaps trying to learn the lesson of the latter's fall, both were consistently cautious. The reality was that Haig had an excitable temperament (which a carefully controlled exterior merely masked) combined with an intellect that offered him rather limited penetration into the fog of war.[72]

Yet despite his misjudgements, from 8 August to 11 November Haig had commanded the largest army the British Empire was ever to put in the field (about 1.8 million men) through an uninterrupted series of the greatest land victories in British history. Since July Haig's army had taken 186,000 prisoners (more than the French and the American armies combined) and captured more than 2,840 guns. The most important French contribution had been in the Second Battle of the Marne during July. If one views what British historians term the "Hundred Days" (8 August–11 November) alone, the British Empire's contribution bulks still larger. It came at a high price. Casualty figures always have to be treated with some caution, but Haig's Armies are estimated to have suffered approximately 379,000. This included at least 67,000 fatalities with over 30,000 counted as missing or prisoners.[73]

The argument of a distinguished historical partnership that Haig's personal role in conducting military operations had diminished by the Hundred Days certainly has validity.[74] By August 1918 there was a great deal of operational, tactical and administrative skill at GHQ, in the Armies and in subordinate formations. In matters of detail Haig needed to intervene relatively little. His pre-war military education had taught him that it was better to delegate the execution of military missions provided that subordinates were up to their tasks. For most of the Hundred Days he apparently concluded that most of them were – an assessment emphatically endorsed by some modern scholars.[75] It would, however, be going far too far to conclude that, by the Hundred Days, Haig had become an irrelevance. He commanded the most combat-effective of the Allied armies at this period in the war and there were few, if any, others who had the authority and determination to use the instrument with such vigour.

The initiative for the Amiens attack, mounted on Thursday 8 August, appears to have come from lower down: from Rawlinson and his Fourth Army staff and, perhaps, from Monash and the Australian Corps. But it could not have developed into the signal victory actually won without Haig's eager backing. In the widening of the British offensive, moreover, and the gradual setting of the whole front in motion with a series of massive offensive blows, his role was crucial. Haig's subordinate commanders were not all greyhounds in the slips in August 1918. Byng, in particular, showed initial signs of war-weariness and inertia. It took an effort of will on Haig's part to overcome this. It was only after the Battle of Albert that the ball really started rolling and the Allied campaign started to develop a momentum of its own.

Haig's co-operation with Foch was also crucial in shaping and mounting the "General Offensive" that started in late September. Though that combined effort did not work out as planned, it still played a useful part in shoving the Germans a bit further towards final collapse. By the time Haig's intense, sometimes excessive, optimism of August and September gave way to excessive pessimism in mid-October his most vital contribution had already been made. His role in bringing the war to an end in 1918 had, indeed, been vital. Without him, or some other British commander-in-chief equally determined and authoritative, it is more than likely that it would have dragged on well into the following year. A 1919 victory campaign in which the American army played the leading role might have led to a peace that American statesmanship played a larger part in shaping and the American people felt more interest in preserving. That might have worked out better for everyone in the long run. On the other hand, as Haig feared, the continuation of the war for another few months might have spread Red revolution through most of Europe. These, however, are mere counter-factual speculations. For better or worse, Haig had played a significant part in shaping the actual outcome.

Haig's homecoming and the demobilisation crisis

In the immediate aftermath of the Armistice Haig and Sir Henry Wilson engaged in a bout of fulsome mutual congratulations. Past tensions between them seemed to be forgiven, if not forgotten. Haig was far more generous in his appreciation of Wilson's help during 1918 than he had been of Robertson's at any stage in the war. The ill feeling between Lloyd-George and Haig, however, went so deep that even a victorious end to the war could not relieve it. Indeed, it seemed to get worse.

On 18 November 1918 the War Office sent Haig a telegram conveying the Prime Minister's offer of a peerage. But it seemed indicative of what Lloyd George actually thought of his contribution to victory that, whereas Marlborough and Wellington had gained dukedoms, Haig was offered a mere viscountcy: three rungs down the aristocratic ladder and almost the lowest form of lordly life. As Haig's official biographer later pointed out, a viscountcy was the "normal reward" that the "least distinguished Secretary of State" would get on retirement. As Haig himself noted, Sir John French had been made a viscount after being "*recalled* from the command of the Armies in France for *incompetence*". Given that Lloyd George had a very precise understanding of the honours system, of which he was a notorious manipulator, Haig found it difficult not to see the offer as something of an insult.[1]

Haig wanted and thought he deserved a peerage. But an earldom was the least he would accept. He also wanted a very substantial financial award to help him maintain the lifestyle befitting that rank. He was not above haggling to get what he wanted, even from the government of a nation whose circumstances had been reduced by war. But he did so very skilfully, seeming to hold the moral high ground throughout. The reason he gave for rejecting the Prime Minister's offer was that it was impossible for him to accept an award until the government had made financial provision for disabled officers and men.

Please express my very grateful thanks to the Prime Minister for the signal honour for which he has been kind enough to recommend me. I can hope however that he will allow all question of reward for me to stand over until he has been able to fix the allowances for disabled officers and men ...[2]

There is reason to believe that Haig was genuinely concerned about disabled ex-servicemen, thinking it quite wrong that they should be forced to rely on charity. When, a few months earlier, Doris had suggested making a £5,000 charitable donation to help disabled officers, Haig had been cautious about such immediate personal largesse, but had promised "not only money, but all the energy which I may have left after the war is over to help disabled Officers and men who have suffered in this war".[3]

Haig's refusal immediately to accept a viscountcy clearly vexed Lloyd George and put the government in an awkward position. Henry Wilson was given the job of overcoming Haig's objections. He pointed out that Admiral Sir David Beatty, commander of the Grand Fleet, had accepted the government's offer and that it would be "a wholly false situation, generally misunderstood by the public and distressing to the King if only Beatty was honoured at this moment". Without Haig's acceptance of his peerage it would, indeed, be impossible to make an award to Beatty. Haig was unmoved by this argument, even when put by the King himself, as it was during a royal visit to France on 27 November.[4] Relations between Haig and Lloyd George were, indeed, so poor that Haig may have taken a positive pleasure in the annoyance caused.

In his war memoirs, published in the 1930s, Lloyd George would give Foch most of the credit for the victories won by the British Armies in the final phase of the war. Haig, he implied, only became competent when reduced to the status of a subordinate commander under Foch's direction.[5] That version of events was already strongly implied in a parade that Lloyd George's government organised in London, mainly in Foch's honour, for 1 December. Haig was invited to take part but "heard that [he] was to be in the fifth carriage along with General Henry Wilson". He also heard that he was not to be invited to the reception afterwards. His involvement in this parade was, moreover, to represent his official return to London after the war. Haig felt that this was an effort to "belittle the British army" and that it was "more of an insult than I could put up with even from the PM".[6]

Haig's outlook at this time may well have been darkened by the knowledge that his infant son was ill from the influenza pandemic, which had killed, amongst millions of others, the housemaid at the Haigs' Kingston Hill home. In any case he decided that he wanted nothing to do with any "triumphal ride with Foch or with any pack of foreigners, through the streets of London, mainly in order to add to L.G.'s importance and help him in his election campaign". He refused to take part unless positively ordered to do so by the Army Council, one of his grounds being that the parade was to be held on a Sunday – the Presbyterian Sabbath. Some of the key personnel in the War Office realised the folly of pressing the issue and Haig was conspicuous by his absence from the parade. In his diary Haig waxed rhetorical:

Was ever such an insult prepared for the welcome of a general on his return from commanding an Army in the field during 4 long years of war? Yet this is the Prime Minister of England's view of what is fitting.[7]

On 8 December Haig took part in a major French victory celebration at Metz. For this occasion he raised no objection to being in the fourth carriage, along with Pershing. During the proceedings he accepted, from Pétain, the baton of a Marshal of France. Eight days later he went by train to Cologne where a ceremony was held to mark the establishment of a British zone of occupation on the Rhine. In a short speech he indicated his "hope that in our time of victory we may not lose our heads, as the Germans lost theirs after 1870 – with the result that we are here".[8]

Haig and his Army commanders made their official return to England on Thursday 19 December. They crossed to Dover and went from there by train to Charing Cross station, where the Duke of Connaught (representing the King) and Lloyd George met them at 1 p.m. The War Cabinet, the Army Council and such old friends as Sir Evelyn Wood and Herbert Asquith formed part of the official reception, and Haig's sister Henrietta was present in the crowd. It is indicative of the relaxed and joyous spirit of the occasion that Haig managed to give her a kiss while in the middle of inspecting the guard of honour mounted by the Grenadiers. Haig had little opportunity to chat with friends and admirers at the station, as he and his party were whisked into royal coaches for the journey to Buckingham Palace. Queen Alexandra (widow of Edward VII and Queen Mother) was waiting with Doris and Haig's children at Marlborough House. As the coach drew level with that building he had the driver stop. Doris and their daughters came out to the carriage and Queen Alexandra gave him flowers. Haig noted that:

The route was not lined with troops. The reception was essentially a *welcome by the people* without any official interference and I could not help feeling how the cheering from the great masses of all classes came from their hearts. As ADC to King Edward I have taken part in many functions, but never before have I seen such crowds, or such wholehearted enthusiasm.

That such an official welcome for the leaders of the Army had taken place at all, Haig believed, was owing to the influence of the Palace. He thanked the King for his "thoughtfulness and his personal intervention". He then talked at length with the King and his secretary, Lord Stamfordham, about issues including government responsibility for the disabled and his peerage. It was 5 p.m. before Haig and Doris were able to get back to their Kingston Hill home. Haig was then hoping for a quiet evening, but he found a huge crowd (mostly workers from the nearby Sopwith aircraft factory and their families) waiting for him. They were carrying torches and were accompanied by three bands. Haig made a short speech and watched as the multitude paraded past his house. Never really the impassive figure of legend, Haig was overjoyed:

Today ... has been a red letter one in my life. To receive such a spontaneous welcome all the way from the coast to my house at Kingston Hill shows how the people of England realise what has been accomplished by the Army and myself. This more than compensates me for the difficulties put in my way and the coldness displayed towards me by the Prime Minister.[9]

After spending Christmas with his family Haig was involved in official receptions in London for the American President. He dined at the palace on 27 December and lunched at the Mansion House the following day, where he heard Woodrow Wilson speak. Many of Wilson's audience on the latter occasion were politicians whose attention was somewhat distracted by breaking news of the results of the General Election in which the Lloyd George coalition won a landslide victory. Haig, however, seems to have listened closely to Wilson. He was wary of the President's idealism, sceptical of his League of Nations concept and regarded his emphasis on self-determination and democracy as excessive. He doubted whether Wilson was truly a practical man. Yet dinner with the President and Prime Minister at Downing Street on the evening of 28 December seems to have passed off smoothly enough.[10]

It is misleading to portray Haig as a fount of wisdom, sadly neglected, on the matter of the peace. It is true that he had humanitarian instincts: he did not want to see the German economy wrecked or the German people suffering unnecessarily. He thought that allowing the French to exact revenge on the Germans for their wartime sufferings would be a grave mistake.[11] With regard to Germany's political future, however, he seems to have lacked any clear and consistent vision.

Before the war he had feared Germany's aggressive intentions.[12] During it he had referred, disapprovingly, to German "militarism" and "militarists".[13] But after Germany's defeat he seems to have had little enthusiasm for Woodrow Wilson's policy of democratisation.[14] Though that was certainly not his opinion throughout the war, in the winter of 1917–1918 and again in October 1918 he had sometimes indicated that he wanted, or was prepared to accept, a very moderate peace.[15] After the Armistice, however, he came to doubt that a united Germany of over 70 million people was compatible with European security and suggested it needed to be broken up into several smaller states.[16] Interesting from a biographical viewpoint, Haig's rather muddled ideas on the post-war settlement of Europe were not sought by the British government and had no influence on the course of events.

Before Haig's return to France Lord Milner held a dinner in his honour at the Senior Service club in Pall Mall on 30 December. The party consisted mainly of senior army officers from the War Office and GHQ, with three of the Army commanders also present. Haig thought it "a very friendly gathering". There were speeches after dinner in which Milner praised Haig and his army: "the greatest ... the Empire has ever produced". Haig responded by praising the War Office's wartime work. He named all four of the current military members of the Army Council (including Henry Wilson) as having been particularly helpful. Haig thought his speech had been "very well received".[17]

This may have been generally true, but he had given acute offence to one of the most senior of his military colleagues. Deliberately or otherwise, he said not a word in praise of "Wully" Robertson. Robertson never publicly broke with Haig and largely ignored their wartime differences when he wrote his memoirs. But he was not the man to take this kind of slight (intended or otherwise) in complete silence. "I'll never go farting with 'aig again," he is reported to have remarked as he left the dinner.[18] Haig's behaviour towards him had indeed reeked (and not for the first time) of a combination of gross insensitivity and gross ingratitude.

Haig, however, emerges with some credit with regard to the most important issue with which he had to deal upon his return to France: demobilisation. The government was understandably concerned about the social consequences of discharging large numbers of soldiers who might not be able to find work. It therefore developed a scheme to release first those who could show that they had jobs to go to. But this meant allowing men who had joined latest to leave soonest and vice versa. Haig had warned against this scheme when it was first proposed in November 1917. It might seem to reward unpatriotic behaviour (the delaying of enlistment), might be perceived as unfair and could easily lead to trouble.[19]

The government's demobilisation scheme came into force on 7 January. On 9 January Haig telegraphed the War Office indicating that his army's morale was in danger of disintegration if the scheme were not changed. Trouble was not, indeed, long delayed. Towards the end of the month there was a mutiny in Calais. Haig's reaction was uncompromising. He had the camp at the centre of the outbreak surrounded by loyal troops. He insisted that order be restored immediately and by all necessary means: if that meant shooting rioters, he sanctioned it. Men of Brigadier-General Henry

Sandilands's 104th Brigade marched in with fixed bayonets, arrested three ringleaders and crushed the mutiny.[20]

The army was still, at least technically, on active service. Thinking that a stern example was needed, Haig wanted to have the ringleaders shot. Winston Churchill, who had replaced Lord Milner as Secretary of State for War, counselled moderation, arguing that the general public would only accept executions in cases in which military indiscipline put other men's lives in danger. Initially incensed at Churchill's interference, Haig contemplated overriding his wishes. But he soon calmed down. There were no executions as a result of this incident and the government reversed its policy on demobilisation, removing the major sources of grievance.[21]

Meanwhile, negotiations with the government on the peerage and pension issue were proceeding apace. Philip Sassoon went to Downing Street on 23 February 1919 to negotiate on Haig's behalf. Haig was doubtless still seriously concerned about the issue of pensions for the disabled. But he was also keenly interested in having a very substantial pension for himself. Indeed, he refused to accept a peerage unless it were accompanied by sufficient money to allow him to live in the style befitting a peer without financial anxiety for the rest of his life. As he had already refused the rank of viscount it was clear that he expected to live at least like an earl. Sassoon suggested a grant of £250,000. Lloyd George was prepared to concede £100,000 and that, together with the earldom, became the basis of the settlement worked out over the next few months. In addition, a voluntary public subscription raised sufficient money to purchase, on the new earl's behalf, the house at Bemersyde, where one branch of his family had long lived.[22]

By the spring the discipline crisis was over. Demobilisation was proceeding smoothly. Churchill was impressed with Haig's understanding of his soldiers' sensitivities on this issue and his prescience about the trouble it had caused. He must also have been aware of Haig's staunch anti-Bolshevism. The government had some anxieties about unrest in the United Kingdom and this combination of qualities perhaps made Haig seem suitable for the role of Commander-in-Chief Home Forces, to which he was appointed in April 1919. Handing over the Rhine Army to Plumer on 2 April, he said his farewells to Poincaré, Clemenceau and Pétain in Paris and to Pershing at Chaumont before embarking from Boulogne to Dover on 5 April.[23]

On 8 April Haig had an interview at the Palace. He agreed with his sovereign that the abolition of full dress uniforms for the regular army (a proposed economy measure) was a bad idea that would hurt recruiting. He then introduced a hobbyhorse he had been riding for the last couple of years:

I urged the King to press for the formation of a great-minded Imperial Church to embrace all our Churches except the Roman Catholics. This would be the means of binding the empire together ... Empires of the past had disappeared because there was no church or religion to bind them together. The British Empire will assuredly share the same fate at no distant date unless an Imperial Church is speedily created to unite us all in the service of God.[24]

Haig's official biographer insists that his omission of Roman Catholics from his proposed imperial church resulted from his knowledge of their aversion to all forms of oecumenicalism that they did not control, rather than from any prejudice against them. Actually Haig was, to some degree, hostile to Catholicism, if not to individual Catholics. Yet, as the same writer quite reasonably points out, he was by no means a died-in-the-wool Presbyterian bigot. Indeed, he was something of a free thinker in religious matters who later supported a revised Anglican prayer book in the House of Lords: generally considered rather High Church.[25]

Command of Home Forces, earldom and another child

On 15 April 1919 at the Horse Guards Haig took over the command of Home Forces from "Wully" Robertson. The hand-over appears to have been most perfunctory, reflecting, perhaps, the distinct lack of warmth between the generals at this stage in their careers. Haig initially appears to have considered the risk of serious domestic disorder to be rather slight. One of his first acts was to cut working hours for his headquarters staff. Over the next few days his time seems to have been taken up mainly by a series of major ceremonial occasions, including a procession of Australian troops through London on Anzac Day (25 April), after which he and Doris stayed for the weekend at Windsor castle. On 7 May he went off with Lady Haig on a three-week triumphal tour of Scotland. Presented with the freedom of all the principal Scottish cities, he seems to have revelled in the popular acclaim that he everywhere encountered. On 14 May 1919 he addressed the University of St Andrews, which had made him rector. He compared Britain's position in the world to that of Athens under Pericles, discoursed on the national character and ideals, and gave his imperial church idea another airing.[26]

Following the signature of peace with Germany, the government ordered a victory parade through London, in which Foch and Pershing would participate, for 19 July. Though he was feeling unwell, running a high temperature and far from sure that he could remain in the saddle throughout the procession, Haig did not want to be left out. In the event his health held up and he got through the day without incident. According to Lord Haldane's memoirs, Haig concluded this triumphal day with a generous and considerate act. Haldane had been unable publicly to participate in the celebration of victory. During the war the gutter press had pilloried him for his admiration for German culture and philosophy. He had been insulted in the street and had, as a result, largely eschewed public appearances. According to Haldane's account, Haig went to see him at his house in Queen Anne's Gate after the parade. Haig said little and left quickly but presented Haldane with a recently printed copy of his war despatches. After Haig's departure Haldane found it inscribed: "To Viscount Haldane of Cloan the greatest Secretary of State for War England has ever had ...". While Haldane's version of the timing of this event has been questioned, there can be no doubting Haig's continuing admiration for a statesman who was both a Liberal and an intellectual.[27]

On 6 August 1919 Haig received his £100,000 grant. Two months later he became an earl. As we have noted, Haig was not the passive recipient of these awards. They had been extracted through a process of haggling. Lady Haig, however, had doubts about Haig's accepting a large financial grant[28] and she was not alone. In late July, Haig's fellow Scot, Lord Murray of Elibank, who had got to know Haig a little while visiting GHQ during the war, had taken the extraordinary step of writing to Haig counselling against his accepting such an award. Haig had, Murray argued, saved the nation in war. He might be required to save it again in a troubled peace. Murray, however, believed that the working classes deeply resented the inequality that grants of this sort represented and, for the sake of maintaining his moral authority and influence, pleaded that Haig should reject it.[29]

Haig responded that he had refused to accept any award until he could be sure that ex-soldiers would be looked after. But

had no wish to appear to be setting myself up as superior to all the rest, and too superior to accept reward. Nor did I wish to join the Bolshevists by refusing the title which the King proposed to give me! Moreover any further refusal to accept the reward on my part won't benefit the ex-soldier. The Govt. has promised to do its duty in the matter – indeed the whole country is now behind me in its determination to see that these gallant fellows and their dependants are *properly* treated.[30]

Haig's period as Commander-in-Chief Home Forces proved not to be as uneventful as he had hoped. There was a good deal of industrial unrest and some disturbances on the streets. To his credit, he found the use of British troops to control British civilians deeply unpleasant. When a general strike seemed likely to grow out of a dispute involving the railwaymen in September 1919, he insisted on observing the strictest constitutional propriety, using the army as little as possible and only when specifically requested to do so by the civil power. He seems to have felt that any open display of military power would be provocative and ordered that

troops should be kept concealed as long as possible and should only appear when the civil authorities required their help. As soon as the necessity for action was over troops must be withdrawn at once out of sight.[31]

In the event, and to Haig's intense relief, there was no general strike in 1919. Another piece of good news was the birth of his fourth child, and third daughter, Irene, on 7 October. Three months later the post of Commander-in-Chief Home Forces was abolished. In January 1920, Haig effectively retired from the army, though, as a Field Marshal, he remained on the active list.

Retirement: Bemersyde, the Legion and the shaping of history

Commander-in-Chief Home Forces was not just Haig's final military appointment but his last official post of any kind under the crown. This might appear surprising. He was not yet fifty-nine and apparently in good health. He was occasionally spoken of as a possible Viceroy of India or Governor-General of Canada, but nothing came of this. His taciturn nature and poor skills in face-to-face communication would, perhaps, have rendered him somewhat unsuitable for a pro-consular career. Moreover, while he remained an ardent imperialist, his primary interests were now domestic. He seems genuinely to have wished to spend more time with his family, and through his work with war veterans he wanted to help the United Kingdom make the transition from war to an orderly and contented peace.

He was hoping to do these things while based at Bemersyde: the house in the Border country that was purchased on his behalf in 1921 from money raised by public subscription. The house needed major restoration and he only moved in on 15 March 1924. At Bemersyde he devoted much effort to developing the gardens, became an elder of the local church and enjoyed some pleasant times in the company of his family. Though the present second earl records some fond memories of his father, it seems that fatherhood was exercised in the emotionally rather distant, Victorian upper-class style. For long periods, even after the war, Haig's offspring apparently saw little of him: indeed, of either parent. His son remembers much childhood loneliness. When he was with his children, moreover, he could be very demanding. His daughters resented his old-fashioned insistence that they ride side-saddle and that they travel unusually long distances in this rather awkward fashion.[32]

As a peer, he was to attend carefully to some issues debated in the upper house, but showed no inclination to move to the centre of the political stage. His lack of talent as a public speaker and a lack of aptitude for the cut and thrust of debate would almost certainly have rendered him even less effective in domestic politics than in a pro-consular role. He would not, moreover, have fitted easily into the post-war political landscape. Much as he despised Lloyd George he had even less regard for the Liberal/Labour opposition. In the election of late 1918 he had voted for the government, though with a distinct lack of enthusiasm. When the Conservative Party broke with Lloyd George in 1922, precipitating his fall, Bonar Law remained its leader, and he and Haig had never held one another in high esteem. Thinking that both Bonar Law and his successor, Stanley Baldwin, were weak leaders, Haig feared moral decline and social revolution. It is, therefore, not altogether surprising that when he met Mussolini on a visit to Italy in 1926 (the year of the General Strike in Great Britain) he expressed some naive admiration for the *Duce's* approach to government.[33]

Haig's genuine Christianity and his conceptions of decency and fairness would probably have been enough to prevent him from becoming a true fascist. But it is worth emphasising how much he had to lose from any breakdown of the social order or from the accession to power of a government of the far Left – the sort of consideration that led many on the Continent to embrace fascism. In his final years, even more than in his earlier life, he was member of a wealthy, well-connected elite. He was Colonel of four regiments and Honorary Colonel of a fifth. He sat on the board of a number of major commercial enterprises including the Royal Bank of Scotland, the Fife Coal Company and the London and North-Eastern Railway, as well as John Haig Distillers.[34] It is reasonable to suppose that these positions afforded him a considerable income on top of his normal military pension and the interest on what was left, after the restoration of Bemersyde, of his £100,000 special award.

After his retirement from the army, therefore, Haig held many positions and was committed to a variety of activities. But there is no doubt that, from 1920 onwards, ex-servicemen (officers and other ranks) became an important preoccupation and absorbed an increasing amount of his time. Immediately after the war a number of ex-servicemen's associations had been established. Haig wished in so far as possible to amalgamate them into a single organisation that could speak for all veterans and campaign for their welfare. Haig did not intend this "British Legion" to be completely apolitical. He advocated "imperial" politics: promulgating patriotism, comradeship and the idea of the British Empire as a force for good in the world. While bolstering the monarchy and the fundamentals of the social order, he wanted, however, to keep aloof from the party fray. Partly because it might weaken the political objectives he had in mind, he had some concerns about the establishment of a separate organisation for ex-officers, which might "withdraw the real leaders from the ex-service men", and "divide officers and men into two camps". Yet an Officers' Association was in fact formed and its identity not wholly merged into that of the British Legion: the latter formally established in June 1921.[35]

Haig worked hard to promote unity amongst ex-servicemen, but so did many others. It is misleading to describe him the Legion's founder: a claim he never made for himself. He did, however, become the Legion's first National President and this was a position he held up to the time of his death. Lord Murray's fear that the acceptance of a handsome financial award for his wartime services would destroy his moral authority was not realised. The generally tolerant and deferential British public of this period evidently continued to accept massive inequalities of sacrifice and reward as part of the natural order of things. Haig went on to promote, with some success, the unification of veterans' movements in the Empire too, and to have these affiliated with the Legion, under his own leadership. To this end he visited South Africa in 1921 and Canada in 1925, the former visit leading to the creation of the British Empire Ex-Service's League with Haig as Grand President.[36]

During the 1920s, therefore, Haig led a life much more public, involving interaction with a larger cross-section of his fellow-countrymen, than he had ever previously experienced. He was in constant demand to speak to branches of the Legion and to public gatherings commemorating the war. He had never been any good at public speaking. According to some accounts he never got any better at it and found it a bit of a strain. His official biographer suggests that, in addition to making appearances and giving talks, he laboured through mountains of correspondence, ignored medical advice to reduce his commitments and, ultimately, through over-work, gave his life for the Legion.[37]

Haig's work for veterans and for the public commemoration of the war effort is worthy of respect. But the suggestion that he ultimately martyred himself through excessive exertion of this sort seems an exaggeration. Recent researches indicate that he attended personally only to a modest amount of Legion correspondence and that he did not write most of the talks he gave. His lifestyle in retirement seems, on the whole, to have been active but pleasant and healthy, including as it did much golf, fishing, shooting, hunting and riding.[38] When he died, he was not far past normal retirement age for most British males. Just to earn a basic living, many men of his age-group had to perform far more arduous work than any required of Douglas Haig at this stage in his life.

Controversy over Haig's part in the conduct of the war had, of course, raged during its course. It never altogether ceased. Haig generally avoided *open* personal involvement. But John Charteris, his former intelligence chief and an early biographer, went far too far in claiming that:

He never publicly gave expression to any extenuation or defence of his policy, nor did he ever authorise one word to be written in contradiction of accusations and criticisms levelled against him in the post-war flood of controversial literature. He appeared to watch with complete calm the gradual drawing aside of the curtain which had hidden and still partially hides many of the episodes of the war.[39]

In reality Haig was active behind the scenes in trying to influence the historical record in his own favour. In 1919 Lord French revealed in a passing remark in his controversial memoir, *1914*, that in early August that year Haig had advised against the immediate despatch of an Expeditionary Force to the Continent.[40] In a letter to the War Office Haig insisted that French was distorting the record. He had merely argued that part of the Expeditionary Force should be retained in Britain in order to assist with the training of an expanding army.[41] Though apparently soon prevailed upon to change his mind, there can be little doubt that Haig had argued initially very much as French had reported.[42] In this instance he protested too much.

Also in 1919, Haig had his private secretary, Lieutenant-Colonel J. H. Boraston, prepare for publication an edition of his wartime despatches. Boraston used rows of asterisks to indicate where the government had censored them. He also prepared slips containing the censored material. These were not included in the published version, but would allow serious researchers eventually to reconstruct the despatches as Haig had originally intended them to be read. The following year Haig asked Kiggell and Lawrence to write a lengthy "Memorandum on Operations on the Western Front 1916–18": essentially the Haig/GHQ version of the war. Eight copies were made and strategically placed with, amongst others, the King, Sir James Edmonds, the official historian, and the trustees of the British Museum.[43]

Yet it seems that he soon felt the need for a more immediate literary defence of his reputation. He encouraged Boraston and a former war correspondent, G. A. B. Dewar, to write a two-volume work entitled *Haig's Command*. Offering a view of the conduct of the war on the Western Front from the perspective of a loyal Haig supporter at GHQ, it appeared in 1922.[44] From the outset Haig also took a strong and sustained interest in the Official History, which was being compiled under the aegis of the Committee of Imperial Defence. He conducted an extensive correspondence with James Edmonds: the principal historian. Edmonds apparently felt that he owed much to Haig for having rescued his career after he had suffered a form of breakdown during the retreat from Mons, and there is some evidence that he allowed his early volumes to be biased in Haig's favour.[45]

Death and mourning

Haig died, apparently of a heart attack, on the night of Sunday 29 January 1928, while staying at his sister Henrietta's Kensington home after attending a Boy Scout rally at Richmond-upon-Thames. His wife, who was not with him at the time, believed that his end was hastened by a hunting accident a few days earlier. According to her account, his horse swung its head back after jumping a fence, hitting him in the face, breaking several of his teeth and causing a suspected minor fracture to the jaw. Though he looked pale, medical advice was that the fracture would heal itself. He therefore decided to proceed with his normal schedule and the Scout rally was one of the items on it.[46]

His post-war life had been rather short, but remarkably successful. He had left his family fairly secure financially. He had founded an earldom (which, at the time of writing, his son still holds) and had acquired the medieval seat of the Haig family (where, at the time of writing, the Second Earl still lives). He had, along with many others, lobbied, with some success, for the decent treatment of ex-servicemen. He had been able to exert a paternalistic, benevolent, but conservative influence over the ex-servicemen's movement. There can be little doubt that this contributed something to national stability at a difficult time. While controversy about his generalship had never ceased, at the time of his passing his image in the eyes of most of the British public was bathed in the afterglow of the Armistice and enhanced by the generally dignified and responsible way in which he had conducted himself subsequently.

Until 3 February Haig's coffin lay in state at St Columba's Church (where Haig had normally worshipped while staying in London), when it was carried to a memorial service at Westminster Abbey. From Westminster it went by train to Edinburgh where it again lay in state at St Giles's Cathedral before burial in a private ceremony at Dryburgh Abbey, near Bemersyde. Haig's passing was a major national event. Some 20–25,000 mourners filed past his coffin each day that it lay at St Columba's. The queue to enter St Giles's stretched for a mile in bitterly cold and wet weather. Local memorial services took place nationwide and were extremely well attended. Haig had died a national hero.[47]

Conclusion

The preceding pages have contained much severe criticism, as well as some praise, of Douglas Haig. In concluding it seems sensible first to review the qualities that allowed him to rise to be commander-in-chief of the largest army that the British have ever put in the field, to hold this position for the three years and to die honoured as a national hero.

The superficial can be very important, especially in armies. Haig presented the right image: the very model of a modern army officer. Strikingly handsome as a young man, he made the best of his genetic inheritance by being fastidious about diet, exercise and personal grooming: habits he had acquired even before he entered the army. He had an excellent seat on a horse and, given his equestrian knowledge and financial circumstances, the animal was likely to be well chosen and very well cared for: this too being important to his image. Good manners and strict self-control were fundamentals of his Victorian upbringing, though, in his case, they were imposed upon a nature that remained rather passionate, excitable and volatile. The need for a sense of purpose, and the character and determination to fulfil it, were values he thoroughly absorbed. Haig exuded character and determination and, together with a sometimes-deceptive appearance of calm, these characteristics tended to give him great natural authority.

Though the intensity of his religious conviction may not have been constant throughout his life, he seems genuinely to have believed in God and to have been influenced, to some degree, by Christian ethics. Proud of being Scottish, he also believed passionately in Great Britain, the monarchy and the Empire. He pursued a profession not really out of financial necessity, but because he accepted that it was a moral duty to lead a purposeful life. He married relatively late, and may have done so to please his royal patrons rather than out of strong personal inclination. But he proved intensely uxorious and his wife thought him an excellent husband. As a father he seems to have been emotionally distant by modern standards, and he was frequently absent. But his son has written fondly of him and treasures his memory.

Haig appears to have made an effort to apply moral standards to his professional life, though his values were somewhat different from those prevalent in the Britain of the early twenty-first century. Not having a profoundly reflective or critical mind, he seems rarely to have doubted that Great Britain was in the right, even in a war as morally dubious as the one in South Africa between 1899 and 1902. In the counter-guerrilla phase there, he approved of and applied what some called "methods of barbarism" without this seeming to trouble his conscience. He did not, however, exult in violence for its own sake and, in the final analysis, did not believe that might was necessarily and intrinsically right. Though an ardent imperialist, he did not view the British Empire simply as a system of exploitation by which the nation enriched itself. In common with Rudyard Kipling and so many others of his generation he saw it as a powerful force for good in the world.

While he could sometimes show anger and frustration in wartime, he had no real hatred of his country's enemies. He was more than willing to be reconciled with them when they had ceased to pose a threat. Though a force under Smuts's command had cut up C squadron of his own regiment near Tarkastad, he seems to have had no resentment against Smuts as a member of the War Cabinet in 1917 and 1918, and, indeed, seems to have dealt with him quite amicably. Similarly, while he saw himself as an enemy of German militarism, there is no sign of his becoming caught up in the hysterical hatred of Germany that wartime propaganda promoted. He wanted no acts of vengeance against Germany when the fighting stopped and seemed eager to spare the German people unnecessary suffering.

Born into privilege and a standard of living that was extremely high in relation to that of the vast majority of his countrymen, he accepted these things as his right and was socially and politically conservative, fearing radical change. Yet, by the standards of his time, some of his public and private attitudes were distinctly enlightened. His conception of the British Empire as a force for good was accompanied by seemingly enlightened views on race. Years before the First World War he advocated granting commissions to Indians and gradually preparing India for full self-government within the Empire. Though he may not have been entirely free of anti-Semitic prejudices in his younger years, in his maturity he had Jewish friends, trusted a Jewish private secretary with his most vital business and backed an officer of German-Jewish background to command the Australian Corps. While he retained enough petty snobbery to be irritated (at least sometimes) by William Robertson's plain plebeian manner of speech, he was not at all opposed to men rising by effort and ability, as Robertson had done, from humble origins to senior positions in the nation and Empire. In the interests of national unity and the war effort

Haig was prepared to welcome to his headquarters the working-class leader and former radical, Ben Tillett, and treat him with courtesy and respect.

Like most people, Haig had no definite, clearly defined political philosophy. His attitudes varied in the course of his life. During the South African War he expressed disillusionment with parliamentary politics as leading to government too weak and indecisive to deal such imperial emergencies. In South Africa he seemed briefly to develop attitudes verging on the militarism he later frowned upon in regard to Germany. For most of his career, however, he seems to have been politically rather correct. Though a royalist, he accepted that the British monarchy was constitutional and limited. Though it is often claimed that he despised politics, and was contemptuous of politicians as a breed, that is far too simplistic a view; it gives him insufficient credit for the shrewdness, the degree of worldly wisdom, without which he could not have climbed so high and remained there for any length of time.

Haig seems to have had no particular party affiliation. He was perfectly happy to carry through army reforms for a Liberal government that many considered dangerously radical. Richard Haldane, a Liberal intellectual in politics, was one of the men he most admired, and, while recognising Asquith's weaknesses as a war leader, he had a considerable respect for him too. Haig enjoyed much better relations with these Liberal Imperialists than he was able to achieve with any of the major Tory statesmen before or during the First World War. Though Haig had a degree of prejudice against Catholicism considered as an international political force, he seems not to have been a religious bigot. While sympathetic to the Ulster Unionists in 1914, he wanted the army to stay above the political fray and wanted to defuse the Ulster-Curragh crisis without overtly opposing a Liberal government that he had hitherto loyally served.

Most of Haig's basic attitudes and beliefs, therefore, were not bad ones by contemporary standards, perhaps not even by modern liberal standards. But this is not a hagiography and he was no saint. In his youth he had no particular vocation, and, while he was probably of somewhat above-average intelligence, his academic aptitude was, perhaps, too limited for the learned professions. He might have drifted had his sister Henrietta not prevailed upon him to pursue a military career. But once he had decided to do so, he became obsessively ambitious. In the early part of his military career, while working hard to charm and impress superiors, he could appear to be a martinet in his dealings with underlings. Still a captain in his late thirties, there are some signs of his becoming frustrated and disillusioned. Staff College, and at last meeting the royal family, seem to have made a real difference. But when he was in the Sudan in 1898 he was still desperate to attract attention and to gain credit for his insights, and did so by making extremely bold criticisms of Kitchener in his letters to Wood. Later, in South Africa, his criticisms of superiors as transmitted to the Prince of Wales through his sister smacked of disloyalty to such an extent that the Prince of Wales told Henrietta to get him to tone them down.

After years of frustrated ambition Haig had become, by 1898, a fierce in-fighter in the internal politics of the army and he became increasingly skilful at this. How much his financial loan to Sir John French had to do with the success of his subsequent career is difficult to say, but it has the appearance of a canny move. It was from the South African War onwards that his career really took off, but it did not do so as a result of any notable success as a commander in the field. His reputation was that of a zealous and efficient staff officer with the right connections. He had command of mobile columns in the counter-guerrilla phase, but there is no suggestion that he was responsible for running to earth any major commando or capturing any significant Boer leader. Given his assiduous attention to self-publicity, we would have heard of it if he had any such achievement to his credit. Very likely the explanation for the lack of notable success, as well as for the lack of any major disaster of that kind that damaged other careers, was a degree of caution and hesitancy that would remain a feature of his operations in 1914.

The royal connection certain seems to have played a major part in the rapid development of Haig's career after the South African War. He reinforced that connection by marriage and his acquisition of a key War Office post appears to have been owing to the influence of Esher: a professional courtier. He was able to impress men of intelligence and insight like Esher and Haldane with his professional knowledge and dedication. Yet his military ideas were generally of the most commonplace kind and he pushed his defence of the *arme blanche* far too far. As a military administrator too he had weaknesses. His toleration for very long hours of office work was limited and during his time at the War Office he went sick for many weeks. According to Haig himself, his deputy, Launcelot Kiggell, did a lot of the hard work while he was Director of Staff Duties. Haig came to appreciate the advantages of having officers like Kiggell around him: men who had an enormous capacity for detailed administrative work but who were happy to remain in the protective shade of a more assertive superior. He would employ quite a number of that type at GHQ.

Haig was ambitious enough to want to go to the very top and that almost inevitably involved senior command appointments. But in a longish military career before 1914 his aptitude for command in war had been tested only to a very limited degree. The British army between the South African

War and the First World War was trying to rapidly modernise and make itself more efficient, and the manoeuvres of 1912 were part of that. Most commentators, including those personally loyal to him, agreed that the exercise and the conference afterwards exposed weaknesses in Haig, in terms of both field command and the ability to explain his military ideas to a lay audience. Yet nothing much was done about this. No mechanism was in place to provide extra training to overcome his deficiencies and when war broke out he still commanded Great Britain's most powerful military formation.

As a commander Haig is often thought to have been permanently and incurably overoptimistic. To say the least, this needs to be qualified, especially with regard to 1914 and 1918. In 1914 he approached the war in no very confident manner. He had some intelligent insights: anticipating a struggle that would be fairly long and very hard. But he was not sure that the British Expeditionary Force of 1914 was fit for purpose and was far from eager to experience the shock of battle with the German army (which he had rated very highly for many years) as part of that untested instrument. Though pride and ambition would have prevented his admitting it, after his 1912 experience it is by no means inconceivable that Haig harboured, in the deepest recesses of his mind, some doubts as to his own talent as a corps commander. His performance in the first, mobile weeks of the war indicated hesitancy, battle-shyness and a potentially dangerous narrowness of vision in a crisis. He looked after his own corps, but failed to offer proper co-operation and support to the much weaker II Corps. In 1914 and throughout the war it was one of his characteristics that, under great stress, he tended to exhibit a kind of autism, losing sight of the broader picture and becoming capable of seeing things only from his own immediate viewpoint.

Another, closely connected, aspect of Haig's 1914 performance was a willingness flagrantly to disregard orders, especially if he thought obeying them would endanger his forces. Evidently he believed that he had sufficient personal ascendancy over a weak commander-in-chief to get away with this. During the First Battle of Ypres his disobedience sometimes proved entirely justified. But his blatant disregard of a direct order to cover II Corps' retreat from Mons on 24 August 1914 still seems rather shocking, especially as he had left the weaker corps, with its newly arrived commander, to do practically all the fighting the previous day. Moving his own corps rapidly out of harm's way, on the morning of 24 August, he left Smith-Dorrien's relatively weak, already battle weary, and thus slower moving formation to resist German attacks largely alone for the second successive day. Haig's similar disregard of orders at the opening of the Marne counter-offensive, and his hesitancy practically throughout its course, reduced British effectiveness and made things easier for an enemy now in difficulty. He was still hesitant at the start of the Aisne fighting and perhaps lost the opportunity to gain the Chemin des Dames and cause the Germans even more serious problems.

Yet it was also on the Aisne, after I Corps' first real day of battle on 14 September 1914, that Haig's confidence started to grow and he began to find his feet as a corps commander. By far his most creditable performances in that role were during the First Battle of Ypres. In the early stages of that battle Haig's natural caution and hesitancy, and his willingness to disregard French's orders whenever he thought them inappropriate, paid off handsomely. Here, boldness, initiative and aggression were required much less than resolution, mental and physical resilience and self-control: all suits in which Haig was strong. In some ways he was fortunate too. At the start of the battle he commanded by far the strongest of the BEF's corps and, compared to other corps commanders, had a relatively short front to hold.

After a very unconvincing start as a corps commander on active service, Haig ended 1914 as something of a hero. But not all of the great strength of his career position at that stage derived from the strength of his performance. The death of Grierson had removed a potential rival. The very poor relationship between French and Smith-Dorrien meant that Haig was not censured for failure to lend reasonable support to II Corps at the start of active hostilities and Smith-Dorrien did not gain all the credit he deserved for having borne the brunt of the fighting at that time. There is also evidence that Haig, even in the course of the frantic events of 1914, was still playing army politics, implicitly criticising Smith-Dorrien behind his back and exacerbating French's mistrust of the II Corps commander, while gaining maximum publicity for his own successes.

Most historians have recognised that Haig had intellectual and temperamental difficulties in adjusting to the conduct of the continuous entrenched front confronting the Allies across most of the Western Front by spring 1915. He was, of course, by no means alone in that. Arguably, however, Haig's difficulties as a commander went deeper. The mobile phase in 1914 was surely just the sort of thing that his military training and education (including his cavalry background and Henderson's teaching of military history) had prepared him for. Yet in the few weeks of such mobile warfare that the British army experienced, he demonstrated very little flair for it. Certainly he had proved resolute in defence in a "soldiers' battle" in Flanders in autumn 1914, in which there had been relatively little mobility and manoeuvre. But it was reasonable to remain doubtful, as did, for example, Charles Repington of *The Times*, that field command was where Haig's talents really lay[1].

One of Haig's characteristics as a commander, however, was that with successive promotions, as his headquarters receded from the front, he became more confident and aggressive. This was nothing to do with physical courage. His conduct at First Ypres suggests that he had quite enough of that. It was a psychological quirk. An anxious, hesitant corps commander, who ignored orders if they seemed risky to carry out, became an operationally ambitious Army commander who brooked no nonsense from subordinates. The Army commander, in turn, became a commander-in-chief who, in 1916 and 1917, developed extremely grandiose strategic visions and sometimes seemed reckless with the lives of his troops in their pursuit.

Even Haig's admirers usually admit that his record as an Army commander in 1915 was rather dismal. Mounting offensives under mature trench warfare conditions, with the limited resources the British army then had, was naturally very difficult. But, in a staff paper of February 1915, even before the British army had mounted its first offensive under these conditions, William Robertson demonstrated that he had a fair intellectual grasp of the problem and could already suggest a reasonable approach: a series of limited attacks backed by concentrated artillery fire, designed to inflict loss on the enemy rather than to gain ground. After Neuve Chapelle, in March, Henry Rawlinson and John Du Cane suggested approaches on similar lines and did so in rather more detail. By mid-1916 a substantial proportion of the army's most senior officers came to favour this of kind of "step-by-step" approach. But Haig thought he had failed to achieve a complete breakthrough at Neuve Chapelle only because of insufficient vigour on the part of subordinate commanders. Complete breakthrough was what he continued to aim for in his most major operations, at least until the middle of 1917.

It is true that, after Givenchy, Haig did not want to mount any more substantial attacks on the Western Front in 1915. For reasons of alliance politics, however, Kitchener pushed him into it. Rather than simply putting on a reasonably good show to satisfy allies, however, Haig once again became fixated on the achievement of dramatic breakthrough and achieving serious strategic results. Apparently he could not come to terms with the idea of mounting a large-scale military operation that did not aim at significant strategic results, referring back to G. F. R. Henderson's lessons on that point. As had already been the case at Neuve Chapelle and Aubers Ridge and would often be the case in subsequent offensives, Haig became overexcited in the early stages of the Battle of Loos. He badly misread the first day of that battle and became responsible for a major, unnecessary debacle on its second.

Haig, however, followed this rather disastrous performance in the field, by some fine footwork in army politics combined with effective use of royal patronage. He cannot be given much credit for outmanoeuvring the tired, ill and already discredited Sir John French, but his politicking put him in a good position to rise when French fell. There is, however, evidence that the choice of French's successor was not automatic. It may have hung in the balance between Haig and Robertson for a day or two. (Robertson as commander-in-chief is one of the most interesting counterfactual speculations that might be entertained with regard to the British army on the Western Front.) Robertson and Haig formed a personal alliance to get rid of French and reduce the influence of Kitchener, but they were never really the harmonious double-act that both initially wished others to perceive.

Haig's and Robertson's levels of understanding of the Western Front environment were quite different, as were their preferred approaches to the conduct of operations there. Haig constantly referred back to his military education, to "principles" and to field service regulations. Robertson thought principles fine for textbooks and textbooks fine for the classroom, but that every war was different and that the field service regulations would have to be rewritten when this one was over. He advocated pragmatism and wanted the careful, step-by-step approach that he had first adumbrated in February 1915 applied to future offensive operations on the Western Front. There was, therefore, considerable tension in the Haig–Robertson relationship from the outset. Robertson became deeply frustrated at his inability to get Haig to listen to operational advice and Haig became irritated by Robertson's increasingly evident lack of confidence in him. In late June 1917 Haig would positively suggest to Lloyd George Robertson's removal from the War Office.

Not very reflective or self-critical, Haig practically never admitted mistakes and, much more seriously, had a considerable capacity for self-deception. He did not learn the real lessons of 25–26 September 1915 at Loos and this proved extremely serious in the planning for the Somme. The evidence is also overwhelming that Haig did not engender at GHQ an intellectually stimulating environment in which force structure, policy, plans and operational methods could be frankly debated in his presence. He was not opposed to innovation as such. He would have been perfectly happy for technology to provide him with a magic bullet (or, indeed, with a "death-ray") that would enable him to break the stalemate and win the war. But he did not want some of his fundamental ideas and preconceptions disturbed. Most crucially he found it almost impossible to think in terms of planning military operations that did not aim at achieving major strategic results within a fairly short period. He seems to have chosen the staff officers with whom he had the most regular contact from people who would implement his will without trying fundamentally to change his thinking.

Haig wanted GHQ to speak with a single voice: rational enough in itself. But there is little evidence that he and the senior members of his head-quarters discussed issues vigorously and freely amongst themselves before deciding what the GHQ line should be. The fairly frequent regular Army commanders' "conferences" that Haig instituted seem, moreover, to have had relatively little to do with conferring. They were far more in the nature of a mechanism for imposing his will on his "barons" than for considering and discussing their ideas. Haig's authoritarian approach to running his army may to some extent have been influenced by fear of dissent at Army-level joining with dissent at GHQ to bring about his overthrow: a process he had himself helped to instigate against Sir John French in autumn 1915.

On the Somme, in his first major campaign as commander-in-chief Haig was under no particular political pressure to achieve an early break-through. Indeed, he was under no pressure to breakthrough at all. Kitchener tried to warn him against attempting such a thing. Robertson, Rawlinson and Montgomery all wanted to adopt a cautious step-by-step approach and all the Fourth Army corps commanders agreed with them. But Haig still aimed at making a deep penetration into the German defences on the first day and achieving their complete rupture soon after. He had a very limited understanding of his artillery and the scheme of attack ultimately adopted fatally dissipated its fire.

The particular tragedy of 1 July 1916 in a military (as opposed to a humanitarian) sense was the squandering of some of the finest human material ever made available to a British commander. The men of Kitchener's Army were not the "scum of the earth enlisted for drink" on whom Wellington had been obliged to rely. The British Isles had, on a voluntary basis, brought forth the best they bred and placed them at Haig's disposal. It is perfectly true that, at the beginning of July 1916, many of these men were trained to only a very limited standard. It is also true that an Allied offensive was urgently and desperately needed to take the pressure off Verdun. It was, however, Haig's responsibility to use operational methods that would get the bulk of those attacking on the first day across No Man's Land alive and intact. They needed to be allowed to live long enough to learn something of the particular arts of war appropriate to north-west Europe in the early twentieth century. There was nothing intrinsically impossible about this. The holocaust of British infantry on 1 July 1916 was not a natural disaster or an act of God. It was a product of human error. Haig proceeded with an approach that practically all the sources of advice available to him indicated to be dangerously overambitious. It is, therefore, difficult to avoid the conclusion that the error was primarily his.

The Somme campaign of 1916, considered as a whole, was not a defeat for the Allies. It helped save Verdun, helped preserve the French army from collapse and wrested the initiative on the Western Front from the Germans. Some branches of the BEF, most notably the Royal Flying Corps and the artillery, developed great technical and tactical proficiency. The tactics of the infantry too became more sophisticated, though infantry performance remained very uneven. It is, however, impossible to conclude that Haig conducted the campaign well. His poor co-ordination of the efforts of his Armies, his lack of a sense of the importance of time in relation to the climate and of the likely impact of the weather on his operations are amongst the more obvious criticisms that can legitimately be made.

The success of the opening day of the next major British offensive, at Arras on 9 April 1917, was a dramatic contrast with 1 July 1916. Sometimes this has been used to illustrate the BEF's "learning curve" in the interval. Certainly a good deal had been learned about the art of the set-piece attack, though improvements in the quantity and quality of the army's equipment (especially artillery pieces and shell) were equally important. But what Haig had failed to learn was every bit as significant. Instead of adopting step-by-step methods, Haig tried to penetrate a deep German defensive system by a single set-piece attack followed by rapid exploitation. This did not work and ultimately wasted more British lives. Arras was, indeed, a worse conducted battle from a British point of view than the Somme had been. Apart from securing the Vimy Ridge, the Battle of Arras achieved practically nothing strategically and German losses were lower in relation to those of the Allies than those of the Somme. So badly was the Arras campaign conducted that British morale, which had survived the Somme reasonably well, dropped markedly in May 1917.

The fault was every bit as much Haig's as Allenby's. Arras was a three-Army battle on the British side. As had been the case with regard to the two British Armies on the Somme, Haig neither created an Army Group command to give proper operational direction and control, nor functioned effectively as an Army Group commander himself. GHQ, in 1916 and 1917, was not designed, organised and staffed appropriately to function effectively as Army Group headquarters. The staff at Montreuil was largely administrative and that at Beaurepaire essentially personal. Arguably Haig himself was overtasked: trying to function at too many different "levels of war" at once. When it came to the conduct of campaigns, he appeared in the role of an occasionally intervening back-seat driver rather than a competent Army Group commander giving steady, continuous and positive operational direction to subordinate Armies.

The Flanders fighting of 1917 (especially the phases that were under Plumer's and Harington's direction) was generally conducted considerably better than that of the Arras campaign. Third Ypres involved three Allied Armies under Haig's command: Anthoine's, Gough's and Plumer's. The General Staff at GHQ had learned an important lesson by this stage. The offensive needed to be controlled by a single commander. Though no Army Group system was *formally* established, Gough and Plumer was each successively made, in effect, Army Group commander, while retaining command of his own Army. Plumer, it is generally agreed, did the job a lot better than Gough. Unfortunately he became the victim of his own success as an overexcited Haig increasingly intervened from early October, in effect (and in a very *ad hoc* manner) supplanting Plumer in his informal role as an Army Group commander and demoting him to the status of a mere Army commander once more. The evidence of Haig's diary seems to the present writer to confirm Sir James Edmonds's view that by mid-autumn both Plumer and Gough wanted to stick with careful step-by-step methods ("the idea of continuing our attacks for limited objectives")[2] but that Haig, who still had grandiose visions of inflicting a decisive defeat on the Germans by the end of the year, overrode them. The main criticism that might be made of Plumer and Gough in October and November 1917 is that, though they each from time to time indicated to Haig the difficulties involved in continuing the offensive, each being somewhat afraid of him and being to some degree rivals in relation to each other, they failed consistently to maintain the united front to restrain him that the situation demanded.

Perhaps the most serious question about Third Ypres, however, is whether the British should have been conducting a major offensive in Flanders in late 1917 at all. Unlike either the Somme or Arras, Third Ypres was very much Haig's idea. It is quite clear from the primary sources that Haig's real aim was neither to distract attention from the French army nor to rescue the British Isles from the U-boat menace, but to break the German army and bring Germany to its knees by the end of 1917. In the circumstances (with Russia all but out of the war and most of the French and Italian armies in poor shape) this was of very doubtful realism. Third Ypres did the German army real damage and, had Haig been luckier with the weather, would have done it more. But in relation to their respective sizes, it did more damage to Haig's own army, the morale of which, in late 1917, sank dangerously low.

Haig misjudged the overall strategic situation in the second half of 1917 as badly as he had misread many of his battles. He believed Germany far closer to collapse than was actually the case. As Haig himself pointed out, it was wrong to blame Charteris for any such misjudgement. In the final analysis Haig was his own chief intelligence analyst, drawing his own conclusions. He had access to War Office intelligence as well as to Charteris's product, but he dismissed the former as excessively pessimistic. Haig's continued misreading of the strategic situation, when coupled with his desire to restore his credibility after Third Ypres, was an important factor in the launching of the Cambrai offensive. Cambrai perfectly illustrates his strengths and weaknesses as commander-in-chief: his openness to technical and tactical innovation on the one hand and his misreading of strategic and battlefield situations and tendency to the back-seat driving of his Army commanders on the other. The reverse of 30 November brought Haig's reputation to its nadir, or very close to it.

Haig, in the winter of 1917–1918, was in an extremely difficult position and it is interesting to see how he reacted to it psychologically. His best-laid plans had failed, his strategic illusions had been shattered, his army was demoralised, the press no longer trusted him, some of it was actively attacking him, the Prime Minister was trying to isolate and replace him and the initiative on the Western Front was in German hands. The last part of this was unavoidable. He had brought much of the rest of it on himself. As usual he made no admission of errors. Occasionally he made utterances about being prepared to go if the Prime Minister had lost confidence in him. Actually Haig knew that Lloyd George had long since lost whatever confidence in him he had ever had. Yet, while being prepared to drop the senior members of entourage and former allies like Robertson and Derby, Haig clung on anyway. After spending his adult life building a military career, such tenacity had, perhaps, become instinctive.

It would, however, be wrong to suggest that Haig's resolution was undiminished and his optimism undimmed. His confidence in achieving a crushing victory over Germany had, indeed, to a large extent deserted him by mid-winter 1917–1918. Indeed, fearing the exhaustion of Britain's remaining strength and the spread of Bolshevism, he was no longer sure that the pursuit of such a victory was worth the likely cost. He considered that a negotiated peace might be the best option. This was the common talk at GHQ, when Hankey and Smuts were there in January 1918. Haig was, therefore, reacting to the failure of his methods to achieve the objective he had hoped for not by admitting that his methods might have been inappropriate but by trying to get the objective changed.

Haig was not obliged to detail at this stage the sort of peace he would have been prepared to accept. It was all too hypothetical, and the formulation of war aims was not officially his business at all. Yet he made it clear that winter that he did not care who had Alsace or Trieste. After a renewed attack of pessimism in mid-October 1918, a diary account of a meeting with Lloyd George indicates that he had little interest in the fate of Poland. It might be surmised that he would have been prepared to leave the German Empire in control of much of its conquered territory in Eastern Europe. For the British, and in terms of maintaining a balance of power on the Continent, this would have been a disastrous outcome to the war. That Haig was apparently prepared to contemplate this sort of settlement with equanimity suggests a judgement as wayward in grand strategic as it often was in operational matters. It also suggests the extreme pressure that he had been under for so long and a considerable degree of war weariness. For the traditional picture of a somewhat unimaginative but imperturbable commander blessed (or cursed) with relentless, remorseless resolution, we substitute a portrait of a more normal human being who, by 1918, was tired, rather shaken, somewhat confused, subject to mood swings, oscillating in his strategic judgements and, at times, willing to abandon the pursuit of clear-cut, decisive victory in the terms in which he had earlier conceived it.

The weakness of Haig's army in relation to the front it held at the start of the German spring offensive placed the Allies' cause in great jeopardy. But that weakness was a product of both very heavy casualties at Third Ypres and of the crisis of British civil military relations that inevitably followed Third Ypres and Cambrai. For that civil–military crisis Haig was every bit as responsible as Lloyd George, perhaps more so. Haig's decision in February 1918 to leave Fifth Army exceptionally weak, while staying stronger further north, was a choice amongst a number of possible evils. Both GHQ's contingency planning for Fifth Army's retreat and the Franco-British contingency planning for its reinforcement were, however, inadequate and the leadership of Haig and his GHQ General Staff in their dealings with Gough in the first couple of days of the offensive proved weak. At that stage there was little or no evidence that Kiggell's exit and Lawrence's arrival had significantly improved GHQ's performance.

From 23–25 March 1918 Franco-British co-operation teetered on the brink of collapse. Haig and Pétain were roughly equally at fault. By the evening of 24 March the situation was out of Haig's control and it was absolutely necessary for others to intervene over his head. Haig's and the British army's survival of the German spring offensives owed much to French military assistance and especially to Foch's efforts. But it was a characteristic of Haig, to which we have already referred, that he had difficulty, during a crisis, in seeing things from any point of view other than his own. This trait made his relations with allies problematical. During the period of the German 1918 offensives his tone when referring to the French in his diary sometimes became very shrill, and when, in May, the Germans shifted to attacking the French, he was somewhat awkward about reciprocating the support he had earlier received.

Yet, while Haig was often disillusioned with the French as allies, it would be going too far to suggest that he suffered from a general Francophobia. In 1914 he worked well with some French generals, including Franchet d'Espèrey. Later he spent a good deal of time and effort trying, under the tutelage of a French officer, to learn to speak the French language. The nadir of Franco-British relations, in early 1917, during the Nivelle period, was far more Nivelle's fault than it was Haig's. Haig's relationship with Foch in 1918 had its tensions, sometimes very severe, but Haig was a great admirer of Clemenceau, who forms one of a number of significant exceptions to Haig's alleged contempt for politicians as well as to his dislike of the French.

It is rather amazing, all things considered, that Haig survived as commander-in-chief into mid-1918. But he did. Even more remarkable is the continuous run of great and cumulatively decisive victories won by his Armies between August and November. There had been so many disappointments, failures and outright debacles under Haig's command that the British War Cabinet, the CIGS and the press could hardly credit what was happening. Historians have often had the same problem. It seems unlikely that Haig had suddenly been transformed into a general of stellar quality and, while they may have constituted a factor of some significance, it is difficult to show precisely how changes in the personnel and organisation of the General Staff at GHQ influenced events at the front. To attribute all the success of the Hundred Days to Foch, however, would be very unconvincing. The methods employed by the BEF, by far the most effective Allied army at that period, were too specifically British.

What had changed most significantly was the overall situation on the ground. German casualties, exhaustion and demoralisation, the lower density with which the Germans were now holding their expanded front, that front's generally poor level of fortification and the shift in the balance of forces with the American appearance on the battlefield in strength were all factors. Its abundance of artillery and artillery ammunition, moreover, offered the BEF a degree of flexibility in the conduct of offensive operations that it had not hitherto enjoyed. It was able to mount major attacks on different sections of the front in quick succession, or even simultaneously. Haig, however, did play a vital role in the Hundred Days, mainly by getting a sustained offensive going after the Battle of Amiens: gradually bringing in all his Armies. Despite all the shocks that he and the BEF had suffered over the last couple of years, Haig had, very much to his credit, recovered sufficiently by late July and August to make a determined try for final victory in 1918 when he saw the opportunity beckon. He still had, moreover, the force of personality and the necessary personal authority to overcome the weariness and inertia in others that form part of what Clausewitz called "friction".

Haig had not, however, suddenly gained surety of touch as a commander. For one thing he was still subject to fits of overexcitement. On 22 August 1918 he issued a general order that suggested that the Germans were closer to disintegration than they really were at that stage, and which recommended operational methods that would have proved too reckless had his Armies tried generally to apply them. When things did not go quite as smoothly as he had hoped on the Selle on 17 October, however, Haig rather suddenly sank into a mood of pessimism in which he began to exaggerate the residual strength of the German army and to insist that very lenient terms be offered if the fighting was to end that year. It is perhaps the ultimate comment on Haig's ability to read battles and strategic situations, and on his sense of timing, that, after spending years predicting the imminent collapse of German military morale, when, in late October and early November 1918, it was finally happening, he failed to perceive it. Indeed, in that particular period, Haig was tending to downplay the impact of the victories that his own army was winning. He is thus, perhaps, to some degree responsible for the relative lack of popular celebration of these achievements to this day.

It seems impossible to make a case for Haig as one of history's great generals. In relation to most of the war it is difficult to see him as a good one. But is important to keep a sense of balance about this. The Western Front 1914–1918 was a time and place that tended to make nearly all generals look inadequate. Haig was not, of course, responsible for the war, and given that the British government had decided to intervene, it was practically inevitable that hundreds of thousands of British and British Empire troops would die in France and Flanders before final victory was attained. But that is not to say that the British army could not have waged the war on the Western Front more efficiently than it actually did and achieved equally good, or better, results in many of its battles at a some-what lower cost.

The systematic application of step-by-step methods (short advances backed by massive firepower) would almost certainly have been the best approach to offensive operations 1915–1917. That a number of generals had conceived this approach by the end of March 1915, and that a substantial proportion of the most important (Kitchener, Robertson, Rawlinson, Rawlinson's chief of staff, Montgomery and all the Fourth Army corps commanders) were prepared to adopt or endorse it by the middle of 1916, indicates that there was nothing wrong with the capacity of the British army as a whole to analyse and adapt. The biggest obstacle to its general adoption as the British army's *modus operandi* for much of the 1915–1917 period was Douglas Haig, who, for most of it, remained obsessed with decisive breakthrough.

Haig was almost certainly not the most suitable officer in the British army to take over from Sir John French as commander-in-chief in December 1915. Robertson, despite his lack of command experience, might have done better. So might a number of younger men who were only corps or divisional commanders in December 1915. In retrospect the means of selecting officers for the top command appointments, depending, as it did, so much on seniority, and influenced, as it still could be, by royal patronage, appears completely inadequate. That a debacle at Loos, for which he was primarily responsible, could help propel Haig into the top job seems especially bizarre. Yet, combined with much politicking and the assiduous support of the Palace, it did. Tenacity, resolution (not as unshaken as sometimes suggested) and a certain amount of luck enabled him to hold on to it until he could, quite genuinely, help to shape the final victory and go on to reap its rewards.

Notes

INTRODUCTION

1. A particularly crude example of this school of "thought" was the *Daily Express* article of 6 November 1998 under the headline "He led a million men to their deaths" and the accompanying editorial. D. Winter, *Haig's Command: A Reassessment* (London: Viking) 1991, is also very unbalanced in its treatment.

2. Popular beliefs are very hard to assess accurately, but see J. Bourne, "Haig and the Historians". In B. Bond and N. Cave (eds.) *Haig: A Reappraisal 70 Years* (Barnsley: Leo Cooper) 1999, pp. 1–3.

3. By 1961 John Terraine had formed the opinion that Haig was one of Britain's great military commanders: an opinion he was never to revise. See K. Simpson, "The Reputation of Sir Douglas Haig". In B. Bond (ed.) *The First World War and British Military History* (Oxford: Clarendon Press) 1991, pp. 152–5. A more recent remarkably whole-hearted endorsement of Haig's contribution to the British war effort 1914–1918 is W. Reid, *Architect of Victory: Douglas Haig* (Edinburgh: Birlinn) 2006.

4. On Liddell Hart and the "British Way in Warfare" school a useful summary is B. Bond, *Liddell Hart: A Study of His Military Thought* (London: Cassell) 1977, pp. 65–8. For a discussion of Lloyd George's use of similar arguments see A. Suttie, *Rewriting the First World War: Politics and Strategy 1914–18* (Basingstoke: Palgrave Macmillan) 2005, pp. 41–59 and pp. 198–203.

5. For an early statement of Terraine's view that "Winning the War was never conspicuously easier on a secondary front", see J. Terraine, *Haig: The Educated Soldier* (London: Hutchinson) 1963, pp. 146–47.

6. See, for example, the statement on this subject in R. Prior and T. Wilson, *Command on the Western Front: The Military Career of Sir Henry Rawlinson 1914–18* (Oxford: Blackwell) 1992, p. 3.

7. W. Churchill, *The World Crisis* (London: Thornton Butterworth) 1931, p. 379.

8. T. Travers, *How The War Was Won: Command and Technology in the British Army on the Western Front 1917–1918* (London: Routledge) 1992, pp. 154–74.

9. P. Griffith, *Battle Tactics of the Western Front: The British Army's Art of Attack 1916–18* (London: Yale) 1994, pp. 101–58; J.P. Harris, *Men Ideas and Tanks: British Military Thought and Armoured Forces 1903–1939* (Manchester: Manchester University Press) 1995, pp. 4–194; J.P. Harris, *Amiens to the Armistice: The BEF in the Hundred Days' Campaign 8 August – 11 November 1918* (London: Brassey's) 1998, *passim*.

10. It is widely considered that this revolution in scholarship began with the publication of S. Bidwell and D. Graham, *Firepower: British Army Weapons and Theories of War 1904–1945* (London: Allen and Unwin) 1982. The appearance of T. Travers, *The Killing Ground: The British Army, the Western Front and the Emergence of Modern Warfare 1900–1918* (London: Allen and Unwin) 1987 was another major academic event.

CHAPTER 1

1. Brigadier-General J. Charteris, *Field Marshal Earl Haig* (London: Cassell) 1929, pp. 1–2. D. Cooper, *Haig* (London: Faber) 1935, pp. 17–18. D. Scott, *The Preparatory Prologue: Douglas Haig, Diaries and Letters, 1861–1914* (Barnsley: Pen and Sword) 2006, pp. 1–11. J. Laver, *The House of Haig* (Markinch: John Haig and Co.) 1958, p. 41.
2. The statement that "Haig came from perhaps the oldest family on the Scottish border". In D. Woodward, "Sir William Robertson and Sir Douglas Haig", B. Bond and N. Cave, *Haig: A Reappraisal 70 Years On* (Barnsley: Leo Cooper) 1999, p. 66, is not altogether inaccurate, but is potentially misleading. Douglas Haig, the future Field Marshal, was a seventh generation descendent of Robert Haig, the oldest surviving son of James Haig, 17th Laird of Bemersyde. Because of the 17th Laird's financial mismanagement his son Robert did not succeed to the estate. The 17th Laird died in 1619, having transferred the estate to his brother William, the King's Solicitor of Scotland. The branch of the Haig family to which Douglas Haig belonged, which had been distilling whisky since the seventeenth century, was, during his early life, based in Fife and Edinburgh, not the Borders. Charteris, *Field Marshal Earl Haig*, p. 2. Scott, *Diaries and Letters*, pp. 10–11.
3. On a visit to Bemersysde in Haig's childhood see Countess Haig, *The Man I Knew* (Edinburgh: Moray Press) 1936, p. 315. On Haig's seldom referring to his connection with the Border family see Charteris, *Field Marshal Earl Haig*, pp. 1–2. Someone does, however, seem to have mentioned the Norman descent and the Bemersysde connection to the society columnists of the newspapers at the time of Haig's marriage in 1905. See "Ascot Romance: Engagement of General Haig and a 'Vivian Twin'", Acc. 3155/41, Haig Papers, National Library of Scotland (NLS).
4. D. Daiches, *Scotch Whisky: Its Past and Present* (London: Andre Deutsch) 1969, pp. 87–91. Laver, *The House of Haig*, pp. 1–43.
5. Laver, *The House of Haig*, pp. 48–9.
6. John Haig to Lady Haig, 16 February 1930, Acc. 3155/322 (a) and Rachel Haig to Douglas, 20 July 1877, MS 28001, Haig Papers. Laver, *The House of Haig*, p. 38. Countess Haig, *The Man I Knew*, p. 12. G. De Groot, *Douglas Haig, 1861–1928* (London: Unwin Hyman) 1988, pp. 9–10.
7. Countess Haig, *The Man I Knew*, pp. 11–12.
8. Charteris, *Field Marshal Haig*, p. 4.
9. Countess Haig, *The Man I Knew*, pp. 11–14. Charteris, *Field Marshal Haig*, p. 9.

10. Countess Haig, *The Man I knew*, pp. 14–15. O. F. Christie, *A History of Clifton College, 1860–1934* (Bristol: Arrowsmith) 1935, pp. 98–9. Rachel to Douglas Haig 15 July, 29 September, and 16 October 1875, 25 February, 28 February and 4 March 1879, MS 28001, Haig Papers, NLS.

11. Cooper, *Haig*, p. 19. Countess Haig, *The Man I knew*, p. 25.

12. Lord Askwith, "Haig at Oxford", *Oxford Magazine*, 23 February 1928, pp. 347–8. Charteris, *Field Marshal Haig*, pp. 6–7. Haig's diary 16 January and 18, 20 and 23 April 1883. De Groot, *Douglas Haigs*, pp. 20–3.

13. On religion and fortune-tellers see Charteris, *Field Marshal Haig*, pp. 4–6, 31–2, and Scott, *Diaries and Letters*, p. 287. On spiritualism see Haig's diary, 20 September 1906, 9 November 1907 and 24 November 1908, and De Groot, *Douglas Haig*, pp. 117–18. On clothes and women see Haig's diary 18, 23 and 28 April 1883, De Groot, *Douglas Haig*, pp. 23–4, Charteris, *Field Marshal Haig*, pp. 6–7 and Askwith, *Haig at Oxford*, pp. 347–8.

14. Countess Haig, *The Man I knew*, p. 32, Askwith, *Haig at Oxford*, p. 348.

15. On the friendship with the Hampshire landowner's son, see Charteris, *Field Marshal Haig*, p. 7. On the alleged pre-marital affair see W. Reid, *Douglas Haig: Architect of Victory* (Edinburgh: Berlinn) 2006, pp. 118–21. On the marriage, see Countess Haig, *The Man I knew*, *passim*. While commander-in-chief in France Haig wrote to his wife almost every day. The tone is consistently respectful and affectionate. Some letters, notably Haig to Lady Haig, 11 November 1918, are especially so.

16. Askwith, *Haig at Oxford*, p. 347, claims that Haig had already decided on an army career at the time of his arrival at Oxford. Scott, *Diaries and Letters* pp. 13–14, argues convincingly against this. Charteris, *Field Marshal Haig*, pp. 7–8, suggests that Haig was rather lacking in direction in his first two undergraduate years.

17. Scott, *Diaries and Letters*, p. 5. De Groot, *Douglas Haig*, p. 25.

18. On the Haig–Henrietta relationship see Charteris, *Field Marshal Haig*, pp. 3, 7, 8, Countess Haig, *The Man I knew*, p. 14 and Scott, *Diaries and Letters*, p. 5. On the Jamesons and their connection with the Haigs see also Laver, *The House of Haig*, pp. 48–9.

19. Haig diary, 6 and 14 March 1883. De Groot, *Douglas Haig*, pp. 25–6.

20. Cooper, Haig, pp. 32–3.

21. "The Register of Gentleman Cadets of the Royal Military College, 1806–1939", RMA Sandhurst archive, and S. Anglim, "Haig's Cadetship – A Reassessment", *The Wishstream, Journal of the Royal Military Academy Sandhurst, Vol. XLVI*, Autumn 1992, pp. 35–9.

22. Anglim, *Haig's Cadetship*, pp. 35 and 39. Charteris, *Field Marshal Haig*, p. 9.

23. Charteris, Field Marshal Haig, pp. 9–10. H. Harrison to Countess Haig, 17 April 1937, Acc. 3155/324(a), Haig Papers, NLS. De Groot, *Douglas Haig*, pp. 31–7.

24. On health, see Haig to Henrietta, 10 October and 3 November 1892, 6 May 1893 quoted in De Groot, *Douglas Haig*, pp. 13 and 15 and Scott, *Diaries and Letters* p. 27. On Haig's views on India's political future see Haig to Kiggell, 20 July 1911, 1/18, Kiggell Papers, Liddell Hart Centre for Military Archives, King's College London (LHCMA). On leaves and travel see Cooper, *Haig*, p. 36.

25. Charteris, *Field Marshal Haig*, pp. 10–11. De Groot, *Douglas Haig*, pp. 35–8.
26. Haig diary, 1 and 9 September 1892, 17 and 19 March and 4 April and 6 May 1893 and draft copy of Haig to War Office, n.d., Acc. 3155/6(e), Haig Papers, NLS. Cooper, *Haig*, pp. 37–9. J. Hussey, "'A Very Substantial Grievance' said the Secretary of State: Douglas Haig's Examination Troubles 1893", *Journal of the Society for Army Historical Research*, Vol. 74, 1996, *passim*. G. Mead, *The Good Soldier: The Biography of Douglas Haig* (London: Atlantic Books) 2007, pp. 66–8.
27. Cooper, *Haig*, p. 40.
28. Haig, "Report on the French Cavalry Manoeuvres in Touraine – September 1893", Acc. 3155/68, Haig Papers, NLS. Haig to Henrietta, 4 April, 4 May, 31 May and 9 June 1895. Cooper, *Haig*, pp. 40–3.
29. Haig, "Notes on German Cavalry, 1896", Acc. 3155/74, Haig Papers, NLS.
30. Evelyn Wood to Haig, 1 July 1895, Haig to Wood 9 July 1895, Acc. 3155/6(g), Haig Papers, NLS. De Groot, *Douglas Haig*, p. 45. Cooper, *Haig*, p. 44.
31. Cooper, *Haig*, p. 126.
32. Haig to Henrietta, 23 April and Haig to Wood, 9 July 1895 quoted in De Groot, *Douglas Haig*, pp. 42–3.
33. *Cavalry Studies* (London: Hugh Rees), 1907. Scott, *Diaries and Letters*, pp. 59–60.
34. Brigadier-General Sir James Edmonds, unpublished autobiography, chapter XIV, III/2/10, Edmonds Papers, Lidell Hart Centre for Military Archives, King's College London. G. Barrow to Wavell, n.d., Allenby 6/III, Allenby Papers, LHCMA. De Groot, *Douglas Haig*, p. 48.
35. B. Bond, *The Victorian Army and the Staff College* (London: Methuen) 1972, pp. 153–77, Charteris, *Field Marshal Haig*, p. 12. A recent edition of Henderson's classic work is G. F. R. Henderson, *Stonewall Jackson and the American Civil War* (New York: Da Capo) 1988. There is a copy of the original two-volume edition in the Haig papers, carefully annotated in Haig's script. On Henderson's prophecy of Haig's future see Haig to Edmonds 31 August 1911, quoted in Scott, *Diaries and Letters*, p. 61.
36. Bond, *The Victorian Army and The Staff College*, p. 147–77. Edmonds, Chapter XIV.
37. B. Wood and J. Edmonds, *A History of the Civil War in the United States 1861–5* (London: Methuen) 1905. Edmonds, Chapter XIV.
38. A. Green, *Writing the Great War: Sir James Edmonds and the Official Histories 1915–1948* (London: Frank Cass) 2003, pp. 21–43.
39. See, for example, Charteris's analysis of Haig's mental processes in Charteris, *Field Marshal Haig*, pp. 36–9.
40. T. Travers, *The Killing Ground: The British Army, The Western Front And the Emergence Of Modern Warfare, 1900–1918* (London: Allen and Unwin) 1987, pp. 85–91. P. Griffith, *Forward Into Battle: Fighting Tactics From Waterloo To Vietnam* (Chichester: Bird) 1985, pp. 43–74, suggests that the sorts of tactical idea that Haig picked up at Staff College in the 1890s were in the mainstream: neither backward by the standards of the rest of Europe nor fundamentally mistaken.
41. P. Magnus, *Kitchener: Portrait of an Imperialist* (London: Murray) 1958, pp. 77–83.

42. Wood to Haig, 13 April 1898, quoted in De Groot, *Douglas Haig*, p. 54. J. Marshall-Cornwall, *Haig as Military Commander* (London: Batsford) 1973, p. 11.

43. Haig's diary, 23 January 1898, quoted in Cooper, *Haig*, p. 51.

44. Haig to Henrietta, 6 and 11 February 1898. Haig to Wood, 14 February 1898. Haig's diary, 15 February 1898. Haig to Henrietta, 17 February 1898, Acc. 3155/6, Haig Papers, N.L.S. Scott, *Diaries and Letters*, pp. 68–72.

45. Haig to Henrietta, 2 March 1898, Haig diary, 13 and 17 March. Haig to Wood, 15 March 1898. On Kitchener's style of command see also Wood to Haig, 25 April 1898, Acc. 3155/6, Haig Papers, N.L.S. Scott, *Diaries and Letters*, pp. 74–8.

46. W. Churchill, *The River War: An Historical Account of the Reconquest of the Soudan (2 Vols.) Vol. I* (London: Longman) 1899, pp. 343–72.

47. Haig to Wood, 26 March 1898, Acc. 3155/6, Haig Papers, NLS. Scott, *Diaries and Letters*, pp. 79–81. Churchill, *The River War*, pp. 384–97.

48. Haig to Wood, 26 March 1898, quoted in Scott, *Diaries and Letters*, pp. 79–81.

49. Haig's diary, 5 April 1898, quoted in Scott, *Diaries and Letters*, pp. 83–4. Marshall-Cornwall, *Haig as Military Commander*, p. 29.

50. Churchill, *River War*, pp. 416–48. Scott, *Diaries and Letters*, pp. 83–5.

51. Haig to Wood, 29 April 1898, Acc. 3155/6, Haig Papers, NLS, Part of this letter is quoted in Scott, *Diaries and Letters*, pp. 86–7.

52. *Ibid.* Haig's diary, 13 April 1898. Scott, *Diaries and Letters*, p. 86. Churchill, *River War, Vol. II*, pp. 30–61.

53. Marshall-Cornwall, *Haig as Military Commander*, pp. 22–3.

54. Major-General Sir Frederick Maurice, *The Life Of General Lord Rawlinson of Trent* (London: Cassell) 1928, p. 38.

55. Haig's "Sudan diary", Friday 2 September, "Battle before Omdurman", p. 12, Acc. 3155/32(g). Scott, pp. 94–100. Churchill, *The River War, Vol. II*, pp. 107–200, and *My Early Life* (London: Odhams) 1958, pp. 122–36. R. french Blake, *The 17th /21st Lancers* (London: Hamish Hamilton) 1968, pp. 90–3.

56. Haig to Wood, 7 September 1898, Acc 3155/6 (g), Haig Papers, NLS. Scott, *Diaries and Letters*, pp. 102–3.

57. Marshall-Cornwall, *Haig as Military Commander*, p. 29.

58. R. Holmes, *The Little Field Marshal: A Life of Sir John French* (London: Weidenfeld and Nicolson) 1981, pp. 51–2 and *passim*.

59. *Ibid.* Haig to Henrietta, 16 May 1899. Scott, *Diaries and Letters*, pp. 112–13.

CHAPTER 2

1. T. Pakenham, *The Boer War* (London: Weidenfeld and Nicolson) 1979, pp. 100–14.

2. Haig diary, 23 September 1899. Haig to Henrietta, 26 September 1899. Haig's diary, 10 October 1899. G. De Groot, *Douglas Haig, 1861–1928* (London: Unwin Hyman) 1988, p. 71. R. Holmes, *The Little Field Marshal: A Life of Sir John French* (London: Weidenfeld and Nicolson) 1981, pp. 53 and 60.

3. "Notes on the Transvaal", n.d., Acc. 3155/38(i), Haig Papers, National Library of Scotland (NLS). Quoted in De Groot, *Douglas Haig*, p. 72.

4. *Ibid.* "Memorandum to General Forestier-Walker" [General Officer Commanding at the Cape], in Haig's diary, 13 October 1899, quoted in De Groot, *Douglas Haig*, pp. 71–3. A. Wessels, *Lord Roberts and the War in South Africa 1899–1902* (Stroud: Army Records Society/Sutton) 2000, p. 29.

5. Pakenham, *The Boer War*, pp. 125–32. Holmes, *The Little Field Marshal*, pp. 61–2.

6. Haig, "Diary of the Operations of the Cavalry in Natal", 20 and 21 October 1899, Acc. 3155/33, Haig Papers, NLS.

7. *Ibid.* Haig to Henrietta, 26 October 1899, quoted in De Groot, *Douglas Haig*, p. 74. Holmes, *The Little Field Marshal* pp. 11–14 and 63–7. J. Lee, *A Soldier's Life: General Sir Ian Hamilton 1853–1947* (London: Macmillan) 2000, pp. 48–51.

8. On French's reputation see Holmes, *The Little Field Marshal*, p. 67. On the rise of Haig's see Lord Roberts to Lord Kitchener, 4 May 1901, in Wessels, *Lord Roberts and the War in South Africa*, p. 177.

9. The quotation is from "Tactical Notes", n.d., on Elandslaagte in Acc. 3155/33. See also "Notes on Operations: 20 October to 2 November 1899", Acc. 3155/38(c), NLS.

10. Holmes, *The Little Field Marshal*, p. 69.

11. "Copy of telegram received from … Capetown 3.45 p.m., 1 November 1899", p. 34, "Diary of the Operations" and Haig to Henrietta, 3 November 1899, quoted in De Groot, *Douglas Haig*, pp. 74–5.

12. Holmes, *The Little Field Marshal*, pp. 71–2.

13. C. S. Goldman, *With General French and the Cavalry in South Africa* (London: Macmillan) 1902, pp. 34–69. "General French's Operations Round Colesberg", *The Times*, Saturday 5 May 1900. De Groot, *Douglas Haig*, pp. 76–7.

14. Pakenham, *The Boer War*, pp. 200–41.

15. French to Roberts, 18 January 1900, and Kitchener to French, 19 January 1900, Acc. 3155/6 (c), Haig Papers, N.L.S. Holmes, *The Little Field Marshal*, p. 85.

16. Roberts to Lord Lansdowne, 6 February 1900, Wessels, *Lord Roberts and the War in South Africa*, pp. 48–50. "Cavalry Division Diary", 10–15 February 1900, Acc. 3155/36, Haig Papers, N.L.S. Goldman, *With General French*, pp. 70–81.

17. "Cavalry Division Diary", 15 February 1900. "The March on Kimberley", *The Times*, Friday 6 April 1900. Haig to Henrietta, 22 February 1900, quoted in De Groot, *Douglas Haig*, p. 80. Goldman, *With General French*, pp. 73 and 81–97. Pakenham, *The Boer War*, pp. 321–8.

18. Pakenham, *The Boer War*, pp. 328–30.

19. "Cavalry Division Diary" 16 and 17 February 1900. Goldman, *With General French*, pp. 98–122.

20. Haig to Henrietta, 22 February 1900, quoted in De Groot, *Douglas Haig*, p. 82.

21. Haig to Lonsdale Hale, 2 March 1900, Acc. 3155/334 (e), Haig Papers, NLS.

22. Goldman, *With General French*, pp. 123–29.
23. Holmes, *The Little Field Marshal*, pp. 97–101. Haig to Henrietta, 16 March 1900, quoted in De Groot, *Douglas Haig*, pp. 82–3. Goldman, *With General French*, pp. 123–40.
24. De Groot, *Douglas Haig*, p. 84. Holmes, *The Little Field Marshal*, pp. 101–5.
25. Goldman, *With General French*, pp. 310–11. Wessels, *Lord Roberts and the War in South Africa*, pp. 89–94. De Groot, *Douglas Haig*, pp. 86–7.
26. Haig to Henrietta, 4 February 1900, 17 June and 15 August 1900, 9 September, 7, 18 and 26 December 1900, 20 January, 11 April and 7 September 1901, 13 July, 15 August and 17 September 1902. Quoted in De Groot, *Douglas Haig*, pp. 77–93. On executions of Boers captured in khaki see D. Scott (ed.) *Douglas Haig: The Preparatory Prologue 1861–1914, Diaries and Letters* (Barsnley: Pen and Sword) 2006, p. 197.
27. Roberts to Kitchener, 4 May 1901, Wessels, *Lord Roberts and the War in South Africa*, p. 177. De Groot, *Douglas Haig*, p. 90. R. french Blake, *The 17th/21st Lancers* (London: Hamish Hamilton) 1968, p. 98.
28. De Groot, *Douglas Haig*, p. 91. Scott, *Diaries and Letters*, pp. 196–7. French Blake, *The 17th/21st Lancers*, pp. 98–101.
29. Ian Hamilton suggested that Haig lacked vigour and daring in the handling of his forces in the anti-guerrilla phase. G. Mead, *The Good Soldier: The Biography of Douglas Haig* (London: Atlantic Books) 2007, pp. 121–22. Lee, *A Soldier's Life: General Sir lan Hamilton*, p. 66. As a rival of Haig's, Hamilton's objectivity may be questioned. But Sir John French thought Haig had failed to seize early opportunities in the big manoeuvres held in 1912 and Haig seems to have been a hesitant, somewhat battle-shy commander in the early stages of the 1914 campaign. So, at least to the present writer, Hamilton's comments ring true. The officer whose reputation was most conspicuously ruined by the South African War was Buller, whom Pakenham, to some degree, tries to rehabilitate – See *The Boer War*, pp. 456–8 and 535.
30. De Groot, *Douglas Haig*, pp. 95–6. Countess Haig, *The Man I Knew* (Edinburgh: Moray Press) 1936, pp. 31–2.
31. De Groot, *Douglas Haig*, p. 95.
32. *Ibid.*, pp. 96.
33. *Ibid.*, pp. 103. T. Heathcote, *The Military In British India: The Development of British Military Forces in South Asia 1600–1947* (Manchester: Manchester University Press) 1995, pp. 181–3.
34. Press reports of the engagement and marriage, one entitled "A wooing not long a-doing", are in Acc. 3155/41, Haig Papers, NLS. See also Countess Haig, *The Man I Knew*, pp. 32–8.
35. Countess Haig, pp. 317–18 and *passim*. Haig to Doris, 10 December 1916. De Groot, *Douglas Haig*, pp. 259–61 and 328–9.
36. French to Haig, 6 August 1905, Acc. 3155/334(e), Haig Papers, NLS.
37. Haig to Henrietta, 3 April 1906, quoted in De Groot, *Douglas Haig*, p. 116.
38. E. Spiers, "The Late Victorian Army". In Chandler and Bond (eds.) *The Oxford History of the British Army* (Oxford: Oxford University Press) 1994, pp. 202–3.

39. Esher to the King, 18 March 1903, in M. Brett and O. Esher (eds.) *Journals and Letters of Reginald Viscount Esher (4 Vols.) Vol. I* (London: Ivor Nicholson and Watson) 1934–1938, p. 391.

40. R. Haldane, *Richard Burdon Haldane: An Autobiography* (London: Hodder and Stoughton) 1931, p. 181 *passim*. Esher to Brett, 11 December 1911, in Brett, *Esher, Vol. 2*, pp. 126–7.

41. E. Spiers, *Haldane: An Army Reformer* (Edinburgh: Edinburgh University Press) 1980, pp. 118, 120–1.

42. D. Winter, *Haig's Command: A Reassessment* (London: Viking) 1991, pp. 32–3.

43. William M. Kuhn, "Brett, Reginald Balliol, 2nd Viscount Esher". In *Oxford Dictionary of National Biography, Vol. 7* (Oxford: Oxford University Press), 2004, p. 502.

44. Brigadier-General J. Charteris, *Field Marshal Earl Haig* (London: Cassell) 1929, pp. 36–8.

45. Haig to Henrietta, 18 February 1906, quoted in De Groot, *Douglas Haig*, p. 116.

46. Haig's diary, 9 June 1906. E. Spiers, *Haldane: An Army Reformer* (Edinburgh: Edinburgh University Press) 1980, pp. 150–1. Charteris, *Field Marshal Earl Haig*, pp. 36–7. Haldane, *An Autobiography*, p. 199.

47. Spiers, pp. 92–115. Haig to Esher, 9 September 1906, Acc. 3155/349(e), Haig Papers, NLS.

48. Haig's diary, 8 January 1907. Spiers, *Haldane*, pp. 85–101 and 92–105.

49. Spiers, *Haldane*, pp. 48–73 and 150–54. General Sir J. Marshall-Cornwall, *Haig as Military Commander* (London: Batsford) 1973, pp. 72–3.

50. Spiers, *Haldane*, pp. 116–34, esp. 120–8.

51. *Ibid.*, pp. 150–2.

52. *Field Service Regulations 1909, Part. I: Operations* (London: General Staff, War Office), esp. pp. 98–112. T. Travers, *The Killing Ground: The British Army, The Western Front and the Emergence of Modern Warfare 1900–1918* (London: Allen and Unwin), p. 68.

53. Quotation from "Report on the 1911 Indian Staff Tour", Acc. 3155/85, Haig Papers, NLS. Quoted in De Groot, *Douglas Haig*, p. 136.

54. D. Haig, *Cavalry Studies* (London: Hugh Rees) 1907, pp. 1–19. The most sympathetic treatment of late nineteenth and early twentieth century British arguments for cavalry cold steel is S. Badsey, "Fire and the Sword: The British Army and the *Arme Blanche* Controversy 1871–1921", Cambridge University PhD, 1982, *passim*.

55. *Cavalry Training, 1907* (London: General Staff, War Office) 1907, esp. pp. 185–192. *Field Service Regulations Part I*, pp. 12–13. S. Badsey, "Cavalry and Breakthrough Doctrine". In P. Griffith (ed.) *British Fighting Methods in the Great War* (London: Frank Cass) 1996, p. 145.

56. Marshall-Cornwall, *Haig as Military Commander*, p. 77. Charteris, *Field Marshal Earl Haig*, p. 45.

57. Haig noted, perhaps with some exaggeration, that Kiggell "did all the hard work for me when I was DSD", Haig to Kiggell, 5 April 1911, Kiggell 1/8, Kiggell Papers, Liddell Hart Centre for Military Archives, King's College London (LHCMA). On the illness see A. Duff Cooper, *Haig (2 vols.)*

(London: Faber and Faber) 1935–36, pp. 112–13. On "hypochondria" see I. Beckett, *Johnnie Gough V.C.: A Biography of Sir John Edmond Gough V.C., K.C.B, C.M.G.* (London: Tom Donovan) 1989, p. 147.

58. Haig diary, 15 March 1909 and Haig to Kiggell, 24 April, 27 April, 18 and 21 May and 3 July 1909, Kiggell 1/1, 2, 3, 4, Kiggell Papers, LHCMA. Countess Haig, *The Man I Knew*, pp. 71–3.

59. Cooper, *Haig*, p. 117. Countess Haig, *The Man I Knew*, p. 72.

60. Charteris, *Field Marshal Earl Haig*, pp. 50–2.

61. *Ibid.*, pp. 56–7.

62. Haig to Kiggell, 20 July 1911, Kiggell 1/18, Kiggell Papers, LHCMA. On Haig's friendship with Sir Pratap Singh see Scott, *Diaries and Letters*, pp. 72, 88, 243, 287, 288.

63. Haig to Kiggell, 18 May 1911, Kiggell 1/12. Haig to Kiggell, 7 December 1911, Kiggell 1/29, Kiggell Papers. LHCMA. Cooper, *Haig*, pp. 119–21.

64. Countess Haig, *The Man I Knew*, pp. 77 and 101. Marshall-Cornwall, *Haig as Military Commander*, p. 81.

65. Charteris, *Field Marshal Earl Haig*, p. 63. Countess Haig, *The Man I Knew*, pp. 107–08. De Groot, *Douglas Haig*, p. 140.

66. Haig to Kiggell, 25 May 1911, Kiggell 1/13, Kiggell Papers, LHCMA. Charteris, *Field Marshal Earl Haig*, pp. 66–7.

67. "Army Manoeuvres", *The Times*, 16 September 1912. Marshall-Cornwall, *Haig as Military Commander*, p. 83. For an account of the manoeuvres from the point of view of Haig's opponent see D. S. Macdiarmid, *The Life of Lieut. General Sir James Moncrieff Grierson* (London: Constable) 1923, pp. 244–8.

68. "Manoeuvres in East Anglia", *The Times*, 17 September 1912. Marshall-Cornwall, *Haig as Military Commander*, pp. 83–4.

69. "Report on Army Manoeuvres, 1912", TNA WO 279/47. The quotation about Haig's use of aviation in this exercise comes from A. Whitmarsh, "British Army Manoeuvres and the Development of Military Aviation, 1910–13", *War in History*, Vol. 14, No. 3 (2007). Further accounts of the exercise are found in "The King with his Army", *The Times*, 18 September 1912. "Army Manoeuvres at an End", *The Times*, 19 September 1912. "The Manoeuvres Conference", *The Times*, 21 September 1912.

70. Charteris, *Field Marshal Earl Haig*, pp. 65–6. "The Manoeuvres Conference", *The Times*, 21 September 1912.

71. Marshall-Cornwall, *Haig as Military Commander*, pp. 84–5. "The Army Exercise", *The Times*, Tuesday 23 September 1913, Thursday 25 September and Friday 26 September 1913. "The King on the Army Exercise", Saturday 27 September 1913, "The Army Exercise", Tuesday 30 September and Friday 10 October 1913.

72. R. Foster, *Modern Ireland 1600–1972* (London: Penguin) 1988, pp. 462–9. Beckett, *Johnnie*, pp. 149–150.

73. R. C. K. Ensor, *England 1870–1914* (London: Oxford University Press) 1964, pp. 473–7. R. Brade to Lieutenant-General Sir Arthur Paget, 14 March 1914, quoted in I. Beckett, *The Army and the Curragh Crisis* (London: Army Records Society/Bodley Head) 1986, p. 57.

74. Beckett, *Curragh*, pp. 8–9.

75. *Ibid.*, p. 12.
76. *Ibid.*, pp. 14–16.
77. Johnnie Gough to Haig, 20 March and Haig to Johnnie Gough, 21 March 1914, Acc. 3155/91(h), Haig Papers, NLS, and Beckett, *Johnnie*, pp. 160–1. On Haig and golf see Charteris, *Field Marshal Earl Haig*, p. 64.
78. Beckett, *Johnnie*, p. 164.
79. *Ibid.*, p. 165, Haig diary 21–27 March 1914, Acc. 3155/2, Haig Papers, NLS. Charteris, Field Marshal Earl Haig, pp. 712–3, Cooper, *Haig*, pp. 123–4.
80. French to Haig, 26 March 1914, Acc. 3155/91(h), Haig Papers, NLS. Holmes, *The Little Field Marshal* pp. 191–4. Beckett, *Johnnie*, p. 169.
81. Haig to Rothschild 13 October 1916, Acc. 3155/214(a), Haig Papers, NLS. Beckett, *Curragh*, p. 21.

CHAPTER 3

1. W. S. Churchill, *The World Crisis 1911–1914* (London: Thornton Butterworth) 1931, pp. 192–3.
2. J. P. Harris, "Great Britain". In R. F. Hamilton and H. H. Herwig (eds.), *The Origins of the First World War* (New York: Cambridge University Press) 2003, p. 279. E. Grey, *Twenty-Five Years (2 Vols) Vol. I* (London: Hodder and Stoughton) 1935, pp. 271–307.
3. Harris, "Great Britain", pp. 284–9.
4. *Ibid.*, pp. 289–90.
5. Grey, *Vol. II*, p. 20.
6. B. Wasserstein, *Herbert Samuel: A Political Life* (Oxford: Oxford University Press) 1992, pp. 162–4. Samuel personally believed that "The world is on the verge of a great catastrophe."
7. H. Nicolson, *King George The Fifth: His Life and Reign* (London: Constable) 1952, pp. 244–7. The King considered the war "a terrible catastrophe".
8. For the general hostility of the City of London to the idea of Britain's entering a European war see L. Albertini, *Origins of the War of 1914 (3 Vols.) Volume 3* (Oxford: Oxford University Press) 1957, p. 291.
9. J. Pollock, *Kitchener* (London: Constable) 1998, pp. 374–6.
10. Haig to Kiggell, 27 April 1909, Kiggell/1/2, Kiggell Papers, Liddell Hart Centre for Military Archives, King's College London (LHCMA).
11. T. Secrett, *Twenty-Five years with Earl Haig* (London: Jarrolds) 1929, p. 74. D. Cooper, *Haig* (London: Faber) 1935, p. 127. D. Scott, *The Preparatory Prologue: Douglas Haig Diaries and Letters 1861–1914* (Barnsley: Pen and Sword), pp. 325–6.
12. Haig to Haldane, 4 August 1914, quoted in Cooper, *Haig*, pp. 128–9.
13. J. Charteris, *Field Marshal Earl Haig* (London: Cassell) 1929, pp. 64–5.
14. Gary Mead's recent biography is informative and very frank on Haig and money. In 1905 Haig conferred slightly more than £600 a year on his wife as part of the marriage settlement. This was at a time when a typical factory worker earned £40 a year. Doris derived this income from a thousand shares in John Haig and Company, which were worth £10,000. G. Mead, *The Good Soldier: The Biography of Douglas Haig* (London: Atlantic Books) 2007,

pp. 141–2. On Haig's having the respect of other "great men" see J. Lees-Milne, *The Enigmatic Edwardian: The Life of Reginald 2nd Viscount Esher* (London: Sidgwick and Jackson)1986, p. 165, and R. Haldane, *Richard Burdon Haldane: An Autobiography* (London: Hodder) 1931, pp. 189–99.

15. D. S. Macdiarmid, *The Life of Lieut. General Sir James Moncrieff Grierson* (London: Constable) 1923, pp. 245–8.

16. Cooper, *Haig*, pp. 127–8.

17. M. Hankey, *The Supreme Command, 1914–18 (2 Vols.) Vol I* (London: Allen and Unwin) 1961, pp. 169–72. "Secretary's Notes of a War Council Held at 10 Downing Street", 5 August 1914, TNA PRO CAB 42/1.

18. W. Philpott, *Anglo-French Relations and Strategy on the Western Front 1914–18* (London: Macmillan) 1996, p. 11. G. Cassar, *Kitchener's War: British Strategy From 1914 to 1916* (Washington: Brassey's) 2004, pp. 24–5.

19. Extract from Haig's typescript "diary" for the period 29 July–5 August 1914, quoted in G. Sheffield and B. Bourne (eds.) *Douglas Haig: War Diaries and Letters 1914–1918* (London: Weidenfeld and Nicolson) 2005, p. 52. There is no manuscript diary for this period and the typescript "diary" is certainly of later, perhaps very much later, composition. In this instance, however, there is no reason to doubt the essential accuracy of Haig's recollections. "Secretary's Notes", TNA PRO CAB 42/1.

20. Haig's typescript diary, 5 August 1914. Cooper, *Haig*, pp. 130–1.

21. Haig to Haldane, 4 August 1914, quoted in Cooper, *Haig*, pp. 128–9.

22. G. De Groot, *Douglas Haig 1861–1928* (London: Unwin Hyman) 1988, p. 148. Viscount French, *1914* (London: Cassell) 1919, p. 6.

23. Wilson's diary, 5 August 1914, HHW 23, Wilson Papers, IWM. "Secretary's Note", TNA PRO CAB 42/1.

24. "Secretary's Notes of a War Council Held at 10 Downing Street, 6 August 1914", TNA PRO CAB 42/1. Cooper, *Haig*, pp. 133–4.

25. Wilson's diary, 12 August 1914, HHW 23, Wilson Papers, Imperial War Museum (IWM). G. Cassar, *The Tragedy of Sir John French* (Newark, Del.: University of Delaware) 1985, pp. 86–8.

26. Wilson's diary, 12 August. General Huguet, *Britain and the War* (London: Cassell) 1928, pp. 41–2.

27. Haig's diary, 14 August 1914.

28. *Ibid.*, 14 and 15 August 1914.

29. *Ibid.*, 16 August 1914.

30. *Ibid.*, 17 August 1914. Macdiarmid, *Grierson, passim*.

31. Cassar, *French*, pp. 94–9. R. Holmes, *The Little Field Marshal: A Life of Sir John French* (London: Weidenfeld and Nicolson) 1981, pp. 208–10.

32. Cassar, *French*, pp. 96–9.

33. "Talk with Edmonds", 11/1937/4, Liddell Hart Papers, LHCMA.

34. J. Edmonds, *Military Operations France and Belgium, 1914: Mons, The Retreat to the Seine, The Marne and the Aisne, August–October 1914* (London: Macmillan) 1933, p. 69.

35. I. F. W. Beckett, *Johnnie Gough V.C.: A Biography of Brigadier-General Sir John Edmond Gough V.C., K.C.B., C.M.G.* (London: Tom Donovan) 1989, pp. 176–7.

36. *Ibid.*, p. 177.
37. *Ibid.*, pp. 177–8.
38. Haig's diary (typescript version), 13 August 1914. Sheffield and Bourne, *War Diaries*, pp. 56–8.
39. *Ibid.* and Haig's diary (manuscript), 19 August 1914.
40. GHQ Operation Order No. 5, 20 August 1914, GHQ War Diary, TNA PRO WO 95/1.
41. H. Strachan, *The First World War, Vol. I: To Arms* (Oxford: Oxford University Press) 2001, pp. 212–19.
42. *Ibid.* and J. Edmonds, *August – October* 1914, pp. 52–4.
43. Strachan, *Vol 1: To Arms*, pp. 208–12. Edmonds, August – October 1914, pp. 33–7.
44. Extracts from the Diary of Lieutenant-General Sir E. S. Bulfin, who commanded the 2nd Brigade (1st Division) British Expeditionary Force 1914, TNA PRO CAB 45/140 (henceforth Bulfin's diary), 21 August 1914. N. Gardner, *Trial by Fire: Command and the British Expeditionary Force in 1914* (Wesport: Praeger) 2003, pp. 2–7 and 42–3. Cassar, *French*, pp. 104–7. Holmes, *The Little Field Marshal*, pp. 211–14.
45. Gardner, *Trial by Fire*, p. 42.
46. Edmonds, *August – October 1914*, pp. 66–8. The Cavalry Division War Diary, contains a note from Henry Wilson, O(A) 470/A137, 12.45 p.m., 21 August 1914: "Information you have acquired and conveyed to the C-in-C appears somewhat exaggerated. It appears that only mounted troops, possibly supported by Jager battalions are in your immediate [vicinity?]." TNA PRO WO 95/1096. Wilson was here apparently responding to telephone calls to GHQ by George Barrow, the Cavalry Division's intelligence officer. See Gardner, *Trial by Fire*, p. 42. Bulfin's diary, 22 August 1914, TNA PRO CAB 45/140.
47. E. Spears, *Liaison 1914: A Narrative of the Great Retreat* (London: Cassell) 2000, pp. 147–50.
48. Holmes, *The Little Field Marshal*, p. 216. "Narrative of Major A. E. Haig, 2nd Battalion, the King's Own Scottish Borderers, 13th Brigade, Vth Division. Position of 2nd Battalion K. O. Scottish Borderers on the MONS-CONDÉ CANAL, 22nd and 23rd August 1914", TNA PRO 45/196.
49. Cassar, *French*, pp. 106–7.
50. *Ibid.*, pp. 107–10.
51. Gardner, *Trial by Fire*, pp. 13–14 and 37.
52. Haig's diary, 23 August 1914. Haig to Smith-Dorrien, 5.35 p.m., 23 August, quoted in Cooper, *Haig*, pp. 144–5.
53. J. Terraine, *Mons* (London: Batsford) 1960, p. 104. Edmonds, *August – October 1914*, p. 91. I Corps War Diary, "BATTLE OF MONS, 23rd August 1914", TNA PRO 95/588. An undated report in I Corps War Diary: "1st Division at the Battle of Mons", indicates that the division suffered only one fatal casualty on 23 August and only three were wounded. All but one of these casualties had occurred in the divisional cavalry squadron: XV Hussars.
54. Haig's diary, 23 August 1914. Gardner, *Trial by Fire*, p. 44. Edmonds, *August – October 1914*, p. 91.
55. Holmes, *The Little Field Marshal*, pp. 216–17. Spears, *Liaison*, p. 174.

56. Holmes, *The Little Field Marshal*, pp. 217–19. Gardner, *Trial by Fire*, pp. 46–9. Haig's diary, 24 August 1914. GHQ to 1st Army (confusingly, at this stage in the war, GHQ sometimes referred to its two Army Corps as "Armies") 1.40 a.m., 24 August, TNA PRO WO 95/588.

57. Haig's diary, 24 August 1914. Beckett, *Johnnie*, pp. 180–1.

58. Haig's diary, 24 August. Gardner, *Trial by Fire*, pp. 48–50.

59. Haig's diary, 24 August.

60. 1st Division War Diary, 25 August 1914, TNA PRO WO 95/1227. 2nd Division War Diary, 25 August, TNA PRO WO 95/1283, I Corps War Diary, 25 August 1914, TNA PRO WO 95/588. Bulfin's diary, 25 August, TNA PRO CAB 45/140. Haig's diary 25 August 1914. Gardner, *Trial by Fire*, pp. 51–2.

61. Gardner, *Trial by Fire*, p. 52. Beckett, *Johnnie*, p. 183.

62. Haig's diary, 25 August 1914.

63. "Action at Landrecies, August 25–6 1914" and "6th Infantry Brigade Action at MAROILLES – August 25–6 1914", I Corps War Diary, TNA PRO WO 95/588. Haig's diary, 25 August.

64. "Talk with Edmonds", 7 December 1933, 11/1933/26, Liddell Hart Papers. Charteris, *At GHQ* (London: Cassell) 1931, p. 18.

65. Charteris, *At GHQ*, p. 19. Secrett, *Twenty-Five Years With Haig*, pp. 83–4.

66. Haig's "Note on Certain Statements by Mr. Fortescue which appeared in the Quarterly Review of October 1919", 18 December 1919, TNA PRO CAB 45/129. Charteris, p. 19.

67. Beckett, *Johnnie*, p. 183. Gardner, *Trial by Fire*, pp. 53–4. Haig's diary, 26 August 1914.

68. Charteris, *At GHQ*, p. 20. A. H. Burne to B. Liddell Hart, 8 December 1933, 1/131/32, Liddell Hart Papers, LHCMA.

69. Cassar, *French*, pp. 125–6. Holmes, *The Little Field Marshal*, p. 225. Gardner, *Trial by Fire*, p. 55.

70. Smith-Dorrien's diary, 26 August 1914, TNA PRO CAB 45/206. I. Beckett, *The Judgement of History: Smith-Dorrien, Lord French and 1914* (London: Tom Donovan) 1993, Appendix A, p. iv.

71. Haig's diary, 26 August. Cooper, *Haig*, p. 156. Edmonds, *August – October 1914*, p. 93.

72. Haig's diary, 26 August. Gardner, *Trial by Fire*, pp. 55–7. Holmes, *The Little Field Marshall*, pp. 223–5. "ACTION AT LE GRAND FAYT (Connaught Rangers)", W. S. Sarsfield, 29 August, 1914, TNA PRO WO 95/588.

73. Gardner, *Trial by Fire*, pp. 55–7. Beckett, *Judgement of History, passim*.

74. Haig's diary, 27 and 28 August 1914. "Rear Guard Action, ETREUX, 27th August, 1914", F. I. Maxse, 21 September 1914, TNA PRO WO 95/588. Spears, *Liason 1914*, p. 255.

75. Haig's diary, 28 August 1914. I Corps War Diary, 28 August 1914, TNA PRO WO 95/588.

76. Haig's diary, 29 August 1914. I Corps War Diary, TNA PRO WO 95/588. Strachan, *Vol 1: To Arms*, pp. 248–9. Duff-Cooper indicates that, on 28 August, Haig expressed willingness to give limited co-operation to Lanrezac's French Fifth Army for the counter-offensive on 29 August.

Cooper, *Haig*, pp. 160–3. Gardner, *Trial by Fire*, p. 61, appears to support this version. It may well be accurate. But there is tension (if not contradiction) between these accounts and the original, manuscript version of Haig's diary.

77. Haig's diary, 29–31 August 1914. I Corps War Diary 29–31 August 1914, TNA PRO WO 95/588. Beckett, *Johnnie*, pp. 184–5.
78. Beckett, *Johnnie*, p. 185. Haig's diary, 22 February 1915.
79. Beckett, *Johnnie*, p. 185. Secrett, *Twenty-Five Years with Haig*, p. 82.
80. Holmes, *The Little Field Marshall*, pp. 228–9. French to Kitchener, 31 August 1914, quoted in Edmonds, *August – October 1914*, p. 475.
81. Cassar, *Kitchener's War*, pp. 91–2.
82. Edmonds, *August – October 1914*, pp. 250–1.
83. *Ibid.*, p. 267.
84. Haig's diary, 2 September 1914.
85. *Ibid.*, 3 September 1914 and Haig to Lady Haig, 3 September 1914.
86. Haig's diary, 4 September 1914. Cooper, *Haig*, p. 165.
87. Haig's diary, 5 September 1914. Edmonds, *August – October 1914*, pp. 295–8.
88. Beckett, *Johnnie*, p. 185.
89. *Ibid.*, p. 184. Holmes, *The Little Field Marshal*, pp. 221–5. A. Green, *Writing the Great War: Sir James Edmonds and the Official Histories 1915–1943* (London: Frank Cass) 2003, pp. 38–41. Gardner, *Trial by Fire*, p. 37.

CHAPTER 4

1. D. Cooper, *Haig* (London: Faber and Faber) 1935, p. 167.
2. H. Strachan, *The First World War, Volume I: To Arms* (Oxford: Oxford University Press) 2001, pp. 242–62. N. Gardner, *Trial By Fire: Command and the British Expeditionary Force in 1914* (Westport, Conn.: Praeger) 2003, pp. 74–86.
3. A. F. Becke, *History of the Great War: Order of Battle, Part 4: The Army Council, GHQ's, Armies and Corps 1914–1918* (London: HMSO) 1945, pp. 147–8.
4. Strachan, *Vol 1: To Arms*, pp. 250–2.
5. E. Spears, *Liaison 1914* (London: Cassell) 2000, pp. 383–409. Cooper, *Haig*, p. 186.
6. Haig's diary, 4 and 5 September 1914.
7. *Ibid.* 5 September 1914. French's "Operations Order No. 17", 5 September 1914, GHQ War Diary, TNA PRO WO 95/1.
8. Haig's diary, 6 September 1914. 1st Division War Diary, 6 September 1914, TNA, WO 95/1227. Sir Henry Wilson's diary, 4–7 September 1914, IWM.
9. Haig's diary, 6 September 1914. Cooper, *Haig*, p. 168. Gardner, *Trial by Fire*, p. 77.
10. Haig's diary, 7–10 September 1914. I Corps War Diary, TNA PRO WO 95/1227.
11. Gardner, *Trial by Fire*, p. 83. J. Edmonds, *Military Operation: France and Belgium, 1914, Mons, the Retreat to the Seine, the Marne and the Aisne: August–October 1914* (London: Macmillan) 1933, pp. 364–6.

12. Haig's diary, 11 September 1914. GHQ War Diary, 11 September, TNA PRO WO 95/1.

13. Haig's diary, 11 and 12 September 1914. 1st Division War Diary, 11 and 12 September 1914, TNA. PRO WO 95/1227. Gardner, *Trial by Fire*, p. 85.

14. Edmonds, *1914, August to October*, p. 371.

15. Haig's diary, 13 September 1914. 1st Division War Diary, 13 September 1914, TNA WO 95/1227. "Operations of the 1st Corps on the River Aisne 13–20 September 1914", I Corps War Diary, TNA PRO WO 95/588.

16. D. Winter, *Haig's Command: A Reassessment* (London: Viking) 1991, p. 36.

17. Edmonds, *1914, August-October*, pp. 373–6 and 392–4.

18. GHQ Operations Order No. 24, 6 p.m., 13 September 1914, TNA PRO WO 95/1.

19. Haig's diary, 13 September 1914, "Operations of the 1st Corps on the River Aisne 13th to 30th September, 1914", Acc. 3155/215, Haig Papers, NLS. This document is also in 1st Corps War Diary, TNA PRO WO 95/588.

20. Haig's diary, 14 September 1914. "Operations of the 1st Corps", Acc. 3155/215, Haig Papers, NLS.

21. *Ibid.* "Extracts from the diary of Lieutenant-General Sir E. S. Bulfin, K.C.B., G.V.O., who Commanded the 2nd Brigade (1st Division) British Expeditionary Force 1914, 11 August, 1914 to 3 November, 1914", 14 September 1914, TNA PRO CAB 45/140. "Battle of the Aisne (Amended account. 12 Oct.)", in 1st Division War Diary, TNA PRO WO 95/1227.

22. "Battle of the Aisne", TNA PRO WO 95/1227. Edmonds, *August-October*, pp. 416–18. Gardner, *Trial by Fire*, pp. 86–8.

23. "Operations of the 1st Corps", p. 11, Acc. 3155/215, Haig Papers, NLS.

24. Haig's diary, 14 September 1914. Edmonds, *August–October*, p. 419.

25. Beckett, *Johnnie Gough, V.C.* (London: Tom Donovan) 1989, p. 185. Haig's diary, 4 September 1914.

26. Gardner, *Trial by Fire*, p. 99.

27. GHQ Operation Order No. 26, 15 September 1914, GHQ War Diary, TNA PRO WO 95/1.

28. D. Ascoli, *Mons Star: The British Expeditionary Force, 5 August–22 November 1914* (London: Harrap) 1981, p. 166. Gardner, *Trial by Fire*, p. 90.

29. Edmonds, *August-October*, pp. 456–62.

30. R. Doughty, *Pyrrhic Victory: French Strategy and Operations in the Great War* (London: Harvard) 2005, pp. 98–104.

31. J. Edmonds, *Military Operations: France and Belgium, 1914: Antwerp, La Bassée, Armentières, Messines and Ypres October–November 1914* (London: Macmillan) 1929, pp. 27–67.

32. G. Cassar, *The Tragedy of Sir John French* (Newark: University of Delaware Press) 1985, p. 154. R. Holmes, *The Little Field Marshal: A Life of Sir John French* (London: Weidenfeld and Nicolson) 1981, p. 242.

33. Joffre to French 1 October 1914, French Papers, IWM. R. Doughty, *Pyrrhic Victory: French Strategy and Operations in the Great War* (London: Harvard) 2005, pp. 101–2.

34. Edmonds, *August-October*, pp. 464–5.

35. Cassar, *French* p. 157.

36. *Ibid.*, pp. 157–161. Becke, *Part 4: The Army Council*, p. 155.

37. Haig's diary, 16 October 1914.

38. *Ibid.*, 19 October 1914. I Corps War Diary, 19 October 1914, TNA PRO WO 95/588.

39. I Corps War Diary, 20 October 1914, TNA PRO WO 95/588. Edmonds, *1914 October-November*, pp. 119–21.

40. Haig's diary, 20 October 1914.

41. *Ibid.*, 21 October 1914.

42. I. Beckett, *Ypres: The First Battle 1914* (London: Pearson) 2004, pp. 36–7 and 62–3. Gardner, *Trial by Fire*, p. 209.

43. Edmonds, *1914 August-October*, p. 426. Strachan, *Vol. 1. To Arms*, p. 262.

44. *Der Weltkrieg, Vol. V* (Berlin: Mittler) 1929 p. 279.

45. Cassar, *French*, pp. 162–3.

46. Haig's diary, 21 October 1914.

47. *Ibid.* and Edmonds, *October-November*, p. 163.

48. Haig's diary, 21 October 1914. Edmonds, *October-November*, p. 164. Beckett, *Ypres*, pp. 80–1.

49. Haig's diary, 21 October 1914. Beckett, *Ypres*, pp. 72–4.

50. *Ibid.*, 22 October 1914. *Ibid.*, p. 79.

51. Edmonds, *October-November*, p. 147.

52. Bulfin's diary, 22 October 1914, TNA PRO CAB 45/140. Edmonds, *October–November*, p. 183.

53. *Ibid.*, pp. 183–4 and Haig's diary, 22 and 23 October 1914.

54. I Corps War Diary, 23–28 October 1914. TNA WO 95/588. Ascoli, *Mons Star*, p. 216. Edmonds, *October-November*, pp. 188–9 and 194–5.

55. Haig's diary, 26 October 1914 and I Corps War Diary, 24–26 October 1914. TNA PRO WO 95/588. "1st Corps, Narrative of the Operations From 17 October to 11 November", Acc. 3155/215(g), Haig Papers, NLS. Edmonds, *October–November*, pp. 199–200. Gardner, *Trial by Fire*, pp. 157–8. C. T. Atkinson, *The Seventh Division 1914–1918* (London: John Murray) 1927, pp. 47–65.

56. Haig's diary, 27 October 1914. Gardner, pp. 164–5.

57. Beckett, *Ypres*, p. 95.

58. Edmonds, *October–November*, pp. 256 and 259. Haig's diary, 28 October 1914.

59. Haig's diary, 29 October 1914. I Division War Diary, TNA PRO WO 95/1227. I Corps War Diary, 29 October 1914, TNA PRO WO 95/589. C. Fitzclarence, "Report on Actions between October 27 and November 2 by the 1st Infantry Brigade", in 1st Division War Diary, TNA PRO WO 95/1227.

60. Cassar, *French*, p. 169. French to Kitchener, 29 October 1914, French Papers, IWM.

61. I Corps Operations Order No. 27, 5.50 p.m., 29 October 1914 and I Corps War Diary 30 October, TNA PRO WO 95/588. Haig's diary, 30 October 1914.

62. Edmonds, *October–November*, pp. 303–4.

63. I Corps War Diary, 31 October 1914, TNA PRO WO 95/588.

64. *Ibid.* and C. Fitzclarence, "Report on Actions", 1st Division War Diary, TNA PRO WO 95/1227.

65. Haig's diary 29–31 October 1914. I Corps War Diary, 31 October 1914, TNA PRO WO 95/588. Edmonds, *October–November*, pp. 323–4. I. F. W. Beckett, *Johnnie*, pp. 192–3.

66. Haig's diary, 31 October 1914. Holmes, *The Little Field Marshal*, p. 251.

67. Beckett, *Johnnie*, p. 193. J. Charteris, *At GHQ* (London: Cassell) 1931, p. 53.

68. Charteris, At GHQ, p. 53. Haig's diary, 31 October 1914.

69. Winter is the principal doubter of Haig's version. See *Haig's Command*, p. 36. J. Hussey, in his "A Hard Day At First Ypres: The Allied Generals and their Problems: 31 October 1914", *British Army Review*, Vol. 107, August 1994, p. 88, defends Haig's version of events.

70. Hussey, "Hard Day", and Haig's diary, 31 October 1914.

71. Haig's diary, 31 October 1914. Bulfin's diary, 31 October 1914, TNA PRO CAB 45/140. Edmonds, *October–November*, pp. 334–5. Gardner, *Trial by Fire*, pp. 222–3. Cooper, *Haig*, pp. 206–7.

72. Haig's diary, 1 November 1914. I Corps War Diary, I November 1914, TNA PRO WO 95/588. "1 Corps Narrative of Operations", Acc. 3155/215 (g), Haig Papers, NLS.

73. Haig's diary, 11 November 1914. Beckett, *Ypres*, pp. 165–73. Cassar, *French*, p. 177.

74. Beckett, *Ypres*, pp. 171–2.

75. Haig's diary, 12–20 November 1914. Gardner, *Trial by Fire*, p. 227. Beckett, *Johnnie*, pp. 194–6.

76. Beckett, *Ypres*, pp. 177–8.

77. Gardner, *Trial by Fire*, pp. 207–31.

CHAPTER 5

1. Haig's diary, 12–22 November 1914.

2. *Ibid.*, 22–27 November 1914.

3. Haig's diary, 1–15 December 1914, and J. Edmonds and G. C. Wynne, *Military Operations, France and Belgium, 1915: Winter 1914–15.* (London: Macmillan) pp. 16–19.

4. Haig's diary, 20 and 21 December. I. Beckett, *Johnnie Gough, V.C. A Biography of Brigadier-General Sir John Edmond Gough V.C., K.C.B., C.M.G* (London: Tom Donovan) 1989, p. 196. J. Charteris, *At GHQ* (London: Cassell) 1931, pp. 65–7 and 72. Edmonds and Wynne, *Winter 1914–15*, pp. 20–1 and 27–8. Haig's diary, 24 December 1914.

5. Haig's diary, 24 and 25 December 1914 and Haig to Rothschild, 26 December 1914, Acc. 3155/214(e), Haig Papers, NLS.

6. Beckett, *Johnnie*, p. 197. A. F. Becke, *Order of Battle, Part 4, The Army Council, GHQ's, Armies and Corps 1914–1918* (London: HMSO) 1945, pp. 71–3. Edmonds and Wynne, *Winter 1914–15*, p. 23. Charteris, *At GHQ*, p. 67. Haig's diary 26 December–1 February 1914.

7. Haig's diary, 18 December 1914 and 26–29 December 1914. Haig to Doris, 19 December 1914. K. Jeffery, *Field Marshal Sir Henry Wilson: A Political Soldier* (Oxford: Oxford University Press) 2006, pp. 141–4.

8. Haig's diary, 28 November and 1 December 1914.

9. Haig to Doris, 13 December 1914.

10. Haig's 15–18 December 1914.

11. *Ibid.*, 4 and 22 January 1914.

12. Charteris to his wife, 14 December 1914. Charteris Papers, Liddell Hart Centre for Military Archives (LHCMA) King's College London.

13. On 20 November 1914 French wrote to Kitchener of Haig's "marvellous tenacity and undaunted courage". *The Complete Despatches of Lord French 1914–1916* (London: Chapman and Hall) 1917, p. 119.

14. Haig's diary, 18 December 1914 and 25 and 26 January 1915.

15. *Ibid.*, 4 January 1914.

16. *Ibid.*, 29 December 1914. W. J. Philpott, *Anglo-French Relations and Strategy on the Western Front, 1914–18* (Basingstoke: Macmillan) 1996, pp. 54–67.

17. R. Doughty, *Pyrrhic Victory: French Strategy and Operations in the Great War* (Cambridge, Mass.: Belknapp Press of Harvard University Press) 2005, pp. 137–9.

18. Haig's diary, 25–29 January and 6 February 1915.

19. *Ibid.*, 5 February 1915. Robertson, "Memorandum on the Possibility of Undertaking Offensive Operations", 8 February 1915, GHQ to the Armies, OA 485, 9 February 1915 and First Army to GHQ, No. G.S. 37, 12 February 1915, TNA PRO WO 158/181. Doughty, *Pyrrhic Victory*, pp. 138–9.

20. The role of an Army commander had not been clearly defined in the British army at this period in the war. Possibly Haig's somewhat tentative initial approach to the job is best understood in this context. But whereas Sir John French wanted "Army" to be essentially an administrative organisation, Haig indicated that he did not wish to be overloaded with administrative detail and that he preferred to concentrate on operations and command. So the question as to why he was actually so reluctant to take direct personal charge of planning First Army's first offensive is still difficult to answer. I. Brown, *British Logistics on the Western Front, 1914–1919* (Wesport, Conn.: Praeger) 1998, p. 77. N. Barr, "Command in the Transition From Mobile to Static Warfare, August 1914 to March 1915". In G. Sheffield and D. Todman (eds.) *Command and Control on the Western Front: The British Army's Experience 1914–1918* (Staplehurst: Spellmount) 2004, p. 31. N. Lkoyd "With Faith and Without Fear": Sir Douglas Haig's Command of First Army During 1915", *The Journal of Military History*, Vol. 71, No.4, 1054–5. On Rawlinson's previous career and relationship with Haig, see N. Gardner, *Trial by Fire: Command and the British Expeditionary Force in 1914* (London: Praeger) 2003, pp. 14–15. See also F. Maurice, *The Life of General Lord Rawlinson of Trent* (London: Cassell) 1928, pp. 61–73 and 84–6.

21. R. Prior and T. Wilson, *Command on the Western Front: The Military Career of Sir Henry Rawlinson* (Oxford: Blackwell), p. 24.

22. Haig's diary, 22 February 1915 and "Memorandum on the Attack on Neuve Chapelle by First Army", n.d., para. 3, TNA PRO WO 158/261.

23. Prior and Wilson, *Command*, pp. 24–5.

24. Rawlinson's "Remarks on VIIIth Division Scheme", in IV Corps War Diary, January–February 1915, TNA PRO WO 95/707.

25. *Ibid.*

26. Haig's diary, 15 February 1915.

27. *Ibid.*, 5 March 1915.

28. *Ibid.*, 20–23 February 1915. Beckett, *Johnnie*, pp. 202–5.

29. Rawlinson, "The Attack on Neuve Chapelle", 21 February 1915, quoted in Prior and Wilson, *Command*, p. 28.

30. Haig's diary, 22 February 1915.

31. *Ibid.*, 23 February 1915.

32. Prior and Wilson, *Command*, pp. 29–31. Haig's diary, 25 February 1915.

33. R. Holmes, *The Little Field Marshal: A Life of Sir John French* (London: Weidenfeld) 1981, pp. 269–70. Doughty, *Pyrrhic Victory*, p. 140.

34. Haig's diary, 28 February 1915. GHQ to Haig (O.A.M 643), 27 February 1915, and Haig, "Memorandum" to GHQ, 28 February 1915, TNA PRO WO 158/181.

35. Haig's diary, 2 and 5 March 1915. "Notes on a Conference on 5/3/15", Appendix A to "Memorandum on the Attack on Neuve Chapelle by First Army", TNA PRO WO 158/261.

36. Prior and Wilson, *Command*, p. 32.

37. A detailed enumeration in the Royal Artillery's regimental history gives a grand total of 530 artillery pieces available for the Neuve Chapelle operation: M. Farndale, *History of the Royal Regiment of Artillery: Western Front 1914–18* (London: Royal Artillery Institution) 1986, pp. 86–7. Farndale's figures agree with those in Edmonds and Wynne, *Winter 1944–15*, p. 85, but not with those in the same volume's Appendix 2, pp. 36–67, which lists 358 pieces altogether. At least one type of weapon apparently used at Neuve Chapelle, the 60–pdr gun (Prior and Wilson, *Command*, p. 34, Farndale, *History of the Royal Regiment of Artillery*, pp. 84 and 88) is, however, not listed at all in this appendix. In a later work, one of the official historians indicated that 276 field and sixty-six heavy pieces undertook the preliminary bombardment. G. C. Wynne, *If Germany Attacks: The Battle in Depth in the West* (Westport, Conn.: Greenwood) 1976, p. 25.

38. Farndale, *History of the Royal Regiment of Artillery*, p. 88.

39. *Ibid.*, p. 86, and Edmonds and Wynne, *Winter 1914–15*, Appendix 16, pp. 390–1.

40. Haig's diary, 10, 24 February and 3 March 1915. Prior and Wilson, *Command*, p. 30.

41. Prior and Wilson, *Command*, p. 31.

42. Edmonds and Wynne, *Winter 1914–1915*, p. 82.

43. Haig's diary, 9 and 10 March 1915.

44. "Neuve Chapelle: Report on Operations", n.d., TNA PRO WO 158/374. 23 Brigade War Diary, Nov. 1914–May 1915, TNA PRO WO 95/1707.

45. J. Merewether and F. Smith, *The Indian Corps in France* (London: John Murray) 1919, pp. 2234–6. Edmonds and Wynne, *Winter 1914–1915*, pp. 93–4.

46. Edmonds and Wynne, *Winter 1914–1915*, pp. 102–3 and 114.

47. Haig's diary, 10 March 1915. Edmonds and Wynne, *Winter 1914–1915*, Appendix 18, p. 392.

48. Edmonds and Wynne, *Winter 1914–1915*, pp. 116–18. Haig's diary, 10 and 11 March 1915.

49. Haig's diary, 11 March 1915. 1st Army Operation Order No. 12, Edmonds and Wynne, *Winter 1914–1915*, Appendix 20, p. 393.

50. Haig's diary, 12 March 1915. 1st Army Operation Order No. 13, 12 March 1915, Edmonds and Wynne, *Winter 1914–1915*, p. 393. First Army War Diary, 12 March 1915, TNA PRO WO 95/154. Prior and Wilson, *Command*, pp. 66–7.

51. Edmonds and Wynne, *Winter 1914–1915*, p. 151. German casualties for Neuve Chapelle have caused no great controversy amongst historians. It seems widely accepted, even by fierce critics of the British military establishment (Prior and Wilson, *Command*, p. 68) that they were little different from British losses. However, for later British and Allied offensives on the Western Front, German casualty figures are very problematical indeed. They have been a cause of huge controversy since the publication of Churchill's *World Crisis* in the 1920s. Using official published statistics Churchill alleged a huge imbalance in the Germans' favour between Allied and German casualties on the Western Front. The Germans, however, apparently did not count, in the published figures that Churchill used, the lightly wounded likely to return to duty quickly. British official historians recognised this problem and generally gave much higher estimates of German casualties in their own work. For some battles, most notably for the Somme, it is now generally agreed that the figures for German casualties given in the British official history are excessively inflated, though Churchill's figures are certainly too low. Estimates of German casualties given in the present work are generally taken from what appear to be the most respectable and reliable modern English language sources. Where recent reputable scholars differ widely in their estimates, either the differences are spelt out or a sort of median position has been adopted. This, admittedly, is not very scientific. But the problems are too complex to be resolved in a military biography such as this. A recent and important scholarly discussion is J. McRandle and J. Quirk, "The Blood Test Revisited: A New Look at German Casualty Counts in World War I", *Journal of Military History*, Vol. 70, No. 3, July 2006. McRandle and Quirk make use of figures from the few surviving copies of a German medical history, known as the "Sanitats". These figures are substantially higher than the German statistics that Churchill used and apparently incorporate figures for the lightly as well the more seriously wounded. Applying Sanitats figures to the two most controversial Allied offensives, McRandle and Quirk estimate that German casualties for the Somme were approximately a third lower than those of the Allies and that German casualties for "Passchendaele" (one assumes that this means Third Ypres as a whole) were about a quarter lower than those of the Allies. This is interesting but hardly radical, tending roughly to confirm what most historians already believed. McRandle and Quirk point out that no one knows exactly how the Sanitats figures were complied and there are other difficulties with that set of statistics. Thus while they make an interesting contribution to the long-standing debates on German casualties, McRandle and Quirk make no claim to resolve them completely.

52. Haig's diary, 21 December 1914 and 4 February 1915.

53. "1st Army Summary of Casualties 10th to 16th and 17th of March", Appendix R to "Report on Operations of IV Corps from 1st March to 7th March, 1915", TNA PRO WO 95/154. Prior and Wilson, pp. 57–68.

54. Edmonds and Wynne, *Winter, 1914–1915*, pp. 148–57.

55. Charteris, *At GHQ*, pp. 84–5. Haig's diary, 10–17 March 1915.

56. Prior and Wilson, *Command*, pp. 49–55.

57. *Ibid.*, pp. 70–3.

58. Haig' diary, 16 March 1915.

59. *Ibid.*, 17 March 1915.

60. *Ibid.*, and Gardner, *Trial by Fire*, pp. 14–15.

61. Haig's diary, 21–26 March 1915.

62. Charteris, *At GHQ*, pp. 83–4.

63. *Ibid.*, p. 81.

64. Haig to GHQ, 28 February 1915, TNA PRO WO 158/181. Haig's diary, 2 and 5 March 1915. Robertson to Haig, 8 March 1915, TNA PRO WO 158/181. Prior and Wilson, *Command*, p. 51.

65. Robertson, "Memorandum on the Possibility of Undertaking Offensive Operations", 8 February 1915, TNA PRO WO 185/17. This memorandum was forwarded to Haig with Haig to GHQ, OAM 485, 9 February 1915, TNA PRO WO 185/181. Prior and Wilson, *Command*, p. 72.

66. Rawlinson to Wigram, 25 March 1915, Rawlinson Papers, National Army Museum (NAM). Quoted in Prior and Wilson, *Command*, p. 78.

67. Rawlinson to Kitchener, 1 April 1915, Rawlinson Papers, NAM.

68. Prior and Wilson, *Command*, p. 79.

69. Du Cane to Robertson: "Du Cane's Memo on Neuve Chapelle", 15 March 1915, TNA PRO WO 158/17.

CHAPTER 6

1. Charteris, *At GHQ* (London: Cassell) 1931, p. 82.

2. Haig's diary, 14 March, 18 March and 19 April 1915. Charteris, *At GHQ*, pp. 84–5.

3. Haig's diary, 19 April 1915 and R. Doughty, *Pyrrhic Victory: French Strategy and Operations in the Great War* (London: Harvard University Press) 2005, p. 156.

4. G. Cassar, *The Tragedy of Sir John French* (Newark, Del.: University of Delaware Press) 1985, pp. 218–20. Doughty, *Pyrrhic Victory*, pp. 157–8.

5. Doughty, *Pyrrhic Victory*, pp. 148–51.

6. Haig's diary, 24 April 1915. Charteris, *At GHQ*, p. 88.

7. Haig's diary, 30 April–May 1915. R. Holmes, *The Little Field Marshal: A Life of Sir John French* (London: Weidenfeld and Nicolson) 1981, pp. 282–5.

8. A. Becke, *Order of Battle, Part 4: The Army Council, GHQs, Armies and Corps 1914–1918* (London: HMSO) 1945, pp. 79, 161, 123. Haig was already being discussed in government circles as a future commander-in-chief in early April 1915, before Second Ypres. Charteris, *At GHQ*, p. 86.

9. First Army to its Corps, Divisions and Brigades, 13 April 1915, "Paper A: General Instructions for the Attack" and "Conference, 1st Army, 27th April, At Béthune", 30 April 1915, PRO WO 158/260. J. Edmonds, *Military*

Operations France and Belgium, 1915: Battles of Aubers Ridge etc. (London: Macmillan and HMSO) 1928, pp. 7–8 and Appendix 6, pp. 431–2. and 1st Army Operation Order, No. 22, 6 May 1915.

10. First Army to Corps, para. 2, 13 April 1915, TNA PRO WO 158/260.
11. Haig's diary 30 April 1915.
12. A. Bristow, *A Serious Disappointment: The Battle of Aubers Ridge 1915 and the Munitions Scandal* (Barnsley: Leo Cooper) 1995, pp. 47–8.
13. Edmonds, *1915: Aubers Ridge*, p. 9.
14. *Ibid.*, pp. 14–15.
15. *Ibid.*
16. R. Prior and T. Wilson, *Command on the Western Front* (Oxford: Blackwell) 1992, p. 85. M. Farndale, *History of the Royal Regiment of Artillery: Western Front 1914–18* (Royal Artillery Institution) 1986, pp. 104–6.
17. Prior and Wilson, *Command*, p. 85.
18. *Ibid.*, p. 86. Farndale, *History of the Royal Regiment of Artillery*, p. 104.
19. "1st Army Operations Order No. 22", 6 May 1915, Acc. 3155/172, Haig Papers, National Library of Scotland (NLS). Bristow, p. 57.
20. Haig's diary, 7–9 April 1915. Edmonds, *1915: Aubers Ridge*, p. 12.
21. Charteris, *At GHQ*, p. 91.
22. Letter home from 2nd Lieutenant B.U.S. Cripps, 17 May 1915, quoted in Bristow, *Disappointment*, p. 75.
23. Edmonds, *1915: Aubers Ridge*, pp. 22–3.
24. "8th Division Report on Operations, 9th and 10th May, 1915", pp. 9–11, TNA PRO WO 95/1672.
25. Haig to GHQ, "1st Army Weekly Report on Operations: 8th–14th May", p. 2, Acc. 3155/172, Haig Papers, NLS. Edmonds, *1915: Aubers Ridge*, p. 24. Bristow, *Disappointment*, pp. 104–5.
26. Bristow, *Disappointment*, p. 105.
27. "1st Army Weekly Report", pp. 2–3. Edmonds, *1915: Aubers Ridge*, pp. 24–5.
28. "1st Army Weekly Report", p. 3. Bristow, *Disappointment*, pp. 106–7. Edmonds, *1915: Aubers Ridge*, p. 25.
29. "1st Army Weekly Report", p. 4. Edmonds, *1915: Aubers Ridge*, p. 37.
30. *Ibid.*, p. 5.
31. *Ibid.*, pp. 4–5. H. Gough, *The Fifth Army* (London: Hodder and Stoughton) 1931, p. 84.
32. "1st Army Weekly Report", pp. 6–7. Haig's diary, 10 May 1915.
33. "1st Army Weekly Report", p. 1. Bristow, *Disappointment*, pp. 167–70.
34. Bristow, *Disappointment*, pp. 167–8.
35. Cassar, *French*, p. 235. Doughty, *Phyrric Victory*, pp. 159–62.
36. Holmes, *The Little Field Marshal*, pp. 287–92. Cassar, *French*, pp. 238–48. D. Woodward, *Lloyd George and the Generals* (London: Frank Cass) 2004, pp. 50–4. G. Cassar, *Asquith as War Leader* (London: Hambledon) 1994, pp. 91–110.
37. Haig's diary, 26 May 1915.
38. "The Offensive Under Present Conditions", 15 June 1915, TNA PRO WO 158/17, p. 5, indicates that the attacks of 9 May failed "not because there was not sufficient ammunition, but because the methods employed were not

correct". On the bombardment before Festubert see Edmonds, *1915: Aubers Ridge*, p. 53.

39. Prior and Wilson, *Command*, pp. 77–88, esp. p. 84.
40. General Ulysses Grant's conduct at the Battle of Cold Harbor in early June 1864 is an example of a general, whom most historians have tended to treat generously, making this kind of mistake. See B. Catton, *Takes Command: 1863–1865* (Edison, N.J.: Castle Books) 2000, pp. 257–69.
41. Haig's diary, 11 May 1915.
42. Holmes, *The Little Field Marshal*, p. 293. Edmonds, *1915: Aubers Ridge*, pp. 46–7.
43. Haig's diary, 10–15 May 1915. Edmonds, *1915: Aubers Ridge*, pp. 49–52.
44. Gough, *The Fifth Army*, pp. 85–7. Edmonds, *1915: Aubers Ridge*, p. 53 and "1st Army General Staff No. G.S. 82 (a)", 13 May 1915, Appendix 9 Edmonds, *1915: Aubers Ridge*, pp. 437–8.
45. Edmonds, *1915: Aubers Ridge*, pp. 52–3, and "1st Army Weekly Report On Operations Period: 15th–21st May", pp. 1–2, Acc. 3155/172, Haig Papers, NLS.
46. "1st Army Weekly Report", pp. 2–4, Edmonds, *1915: Aubers Ridge*, p. 58.
47. "1st Army Weekly Report", pp. 7–8. Edmonds, *1915: Aubers Ridge*, pp. 56–63. G. T. Atkinson, *The Seventh Division 1914–1918* (London: John Murray) 1927, pp. 167–73.
48. "1st Army Weekly Report", pp. 5–11, and Gough, *The Fifth Army*, pp. 88–9.
49. "1st Army Weekly Report", pp. 11–15, and "1st Army Weekly Report on Operations Period: 22/5–31/5", p. 1–6, Acc. 3155/172, Haig Papers, NLS.
50. Edmonds, *1915: Aubers Ridge*, pp. 76–9, and First Army's reports: 15–31 May 1915.
51. Doughty, *Phyrric Victory*, pp. 162–5. "1st Army Weekly Report: 22/5–31/5", pp. 9–10.
52. Haig's diary, 27 May and 1 June 1915.
53. *Ibid.*, 11 June 1915.
54. Rawlinson's diary, 4 June, quoted in Prior and Wilson, *Command*, p. 86.
55. IV Corps Operations Order No. 24, 7 June 1915, TNA PRO WO 95/709.
56. Prior and Wilson, *Command*, p. 97. Haig's diary, 13 June 1915.
57. Edmonds, *1915: Aubers Ridge*, pp. 93–4.
58. Prior and Wilson, *Command*, p. 98.
59. "Weekly Report on Operations: Period 15–21 June 1915", pp. 4–10, TNA PRO WO 95/156.
60. Edmonds, *1915: Aubers Ridge*, p. 97. Prior and Wilson, *Command*, p. 98.
61. Haig's diary, 25 June 1915.
62. Prior and Wilson, *Command*, p. 99.
63. Haig's diary, 16 June 1915.
64. *Ibid.*, 8–14 July 1915.
65. *Ibid.*, 14 July 1915.
66. *Ibid.*, 17 July 1915.

CHAPTER 7

1. Haig's diary, 25 June 1915.
2. *Ibid.*, and 30 July 1915.

3. First Army to GHQ, 23 July 1915, TNA PRO WO 95/156.
4. Haig's diary, 22 June 1915.
5. J. Edmonds, *France and Belgium, 1915 Battles of Aubers Ridge, Festubert and Loos* (London: Macmillan and HMSO) 1928, pp. 126–130. N. Lloyd, *Loos: 1915* (Stroud: Tempus) 2006, pp. 41–5.
6. Edmonds, *1915: Aubers Ridge*, pp. 83–138. Haig's diary, 12–22 June 1915.
7. Haig's diary, 14–22 June 1815.
8. R. Doughty, *Pyrrhic Victory: Strategy and Operations in the Great War* (Cambridge, Mass.: Belknapp Press of Horvard University Press) 2005, pp. 171–82.
9. Haig's diary, 19 June 1915.
10. *Ibid.*, 22 June 1915.
11. *Ibid.*, 22 June and 3 July 1915.
12. *Ibid.*, 9–17 July 1915.
13. First Army to GHQ, 23 July 1915, TNA PRO WO 95/156.
14. Haig's diary, 21 July 1915.
15. For Sir John French's short-term acceptance of Haig's proposal for a renewed Aubers attack see Haig's diary 2 August 1915. For his ultimate surrender to pressure from Joffre see Haig's diary, 7 August 1915.
16. R. Prior and T. Wilson, *Command on the Western Front: The Military Career of Sir Henry Rawlinson 1914–18* (London) 1992, p. 103. Haig's diary, 7 August 1915.
17. Haig's diary, 13 August 1915.
18. Joffre to French, 12 August 1915, Wilson Papers, Imperial War Museum (IWM) Quoted in Haig's diary, 14 August 1915. Cassar, *The Tragedy of Sir John French* (Newark: University of Delaware) 1985, pp. 254–6.
19. Wilson's diary, 14 August 1914, IWM. Cassar, *French*, p. 257.
20. Haig's diary, 17 August 1915.
21. *Ibid.*, 19 August 1915.
22. *Ibid.*
23. "Plan of Operations", 28 August 1915, TNA PRO WO 95/157.
24. Edmonds, *1915: Aubers Ridge*, p. 130. Haig's diary 31 August–25 September 1915.
25. Prior and Wilson, *Command*, pp. 108–111.
26. *Ibid.*, pp. 111–13.
27. Edmonds, *1915: Aubers Ridge*, pp. 163–7. Prior and Wilson, *Command*, p. 112. Haig to Robertson, 16 September 1915, TNA PRO WO 95/158.
28. D. Richter, *Chemical Soldiers: British Gas Warfare in World War I* (Barnsley: Leo Cooper) 1994, pp. 1–22.
29. *Ibid.*, pp. 22–37 and Haig's diary, 7 July 1915.
30. Richter, *Chemical Soldiers*, p. 36, and Haig's diary, 22 August 1915.
31. Richter, *Chemical Soldiers*, p. 39.
32. First Army, "Plan of Operations", 28 August 1915, TNA PRO WO 95/157.
33. "Précis of Conference: First Army Conference on Monday, 6th September 1915", TNA PRO WO 95/158. Cassar, *French*, p. 262. A. Becke, *Order of Battle: Part 4: The Army Council, GHQs, Armies and Corps 1914–1918* (London: HMSO) 1945, p. 131. Haig's diary 30 August–6 September 1915.
34. "Précis of Conference", TNA PRO WO 95/158.

35. "Notes on the Conference Held at Hinges at 10.30 a.m. on 6th September by the GOC, First Army", TNA PRO WO 95/158.

36. Haig's diary, 18 and 19 September 1915 and Haig to GHQ 19 September 1915, GS 164/21(a), TNA PRO WO 95/158.

37. Haig's diary, 1 September 1915. Becke, *Part 4: The Army Council*, p. 199. Lloyd, *Loos*, p. 64. Haig's diary, 18 and 19 September 1915.

38. On communication between Haig and GHQ over the positioning of XI Corps see Haig's diary 18 and 19 September 1915. Haig to GHQ, 19 September 1915, GS 164/21(a), TNA PRO WO 95/158. On French's poor health see Haig's diary, 1 September 1915 and Lloyd, p. 54.

39. Haig's diary 3–6 September 1915. J. Merewether and F. Smith, *The Indian Corps in France* (London: John Murray) 1919, pp. 400–1. Lloyd, *Loos*, p. 54.

40. Haig's diary, 19 September 1915.

41. First Army Operations Order No. 95, 19 September 1915, TNA PRO WO 95/158.

42. Haig's diary, 24–25 September 1915. Edmonds, *1915: Aubers Ridge*, pp. 168–70.

43. First Operations Order No. 95, 19 September 1915, TNA PRO WO 95/158. Edmonds, *1915: Aubers Ridge*, pp. 154–5, Cassar, *French*, p. 262. Lloyd, *Loos*, p. 55. G. C. Wynne, "The Affair of the 21st and 24th Divisions at Loos, 26th September 1915", *The Fighting Forces, Vol. II*, (1934), p. 32.

44. First Army Operations Order No. 95 and Edmonds, *1915: Aubers Ridge*, pp. 155–7.

45. Haig to Robertson, 16 September 1915, TNA PRO WO 95/158.

46. Haig's diary, 16 September 1915. Sir John French's insistence that Haig must attack on 25 September regardless of the weather and whether or not gas was used was reiterated in GHQ to First Army, OAM 868, 18 September 1915, TNA PRO WO 95/158.

47. Haig to GHQ, GS 164/17 (a), 18 September 1915, TNA PRO WO 95/158. Robertson to Haig, OAM 859, TNA PRO WO 95/158.

48. Edmonds, *1915: Aubers Ridge*, pp. 157–8.

49. *Ibid.*, pp. 158–61. On the defectiveness of First Army staff work in relation to the handling of reserves in particular see Lloyd, *Loos*, pp. 63–7.

50. Haig's diary, 24–25 September 1915. Richter, *Chemical Soldiers*, pp. 57–9.

51. Haig's diary, 25 September 1915. Edmonds, *1915: Aubers Ridge*, pp. 170–1. Lloyd, *Loos*, p. 126. E Wyrall, *The History of the Second Division, 1914–1918 (2 Vols.) Volume I: 1914–1916* (London: Nelson) 1921, p. 222.

52. Haig's diary, 25 September 1915. Richter, *Chemical Soldiers*, p. 59. Edmonds, *1915: Aubers Ridge*, pp. 171–3.

53. On "smoke helmets" see IV Corps to 1st, 15th and 47th Divisions, 3 September 1915, TNA PRO WO 95/711. Lloyd, *Loos*, p. 122. Edmonds, *1915: Aubers Ridge*, p. 173.

54. On German suspicions see Lloyd, *Loos*, p. 81. Richter, *Chemical Soldiers*, pp. 61–86.

55. Wyrall, *History of the Second Division*, pp. 223–30.

56. J. Ewing, *The History of the 9th (Scottish) Division* (London: John Murray) 1921, pp. 32–50. Lloyd, *Loos*, pp. 128–31.

57. "Narrative of the Operations of the 1st Division, 25th, 26th and 27th September, 1915", PRO WO 95/1229. "Report on the Operations of the IV Corps, 22nd September to 7th October 1915", pp. 1–5, TNA PRO WO 95/711.

58. "Report on the Operations of the IV Corps, 22nd September to 7th October 1915", TNA PRO WO 95/711. Edmonds, *1915: Aubers Ridge*, pp. 208–23.

59. J. Stewart and J. Buchan, *The 15th Scottish Division* (Edinburgh: Blackwood) 1926, pp. 17–42.

60. "Report on Operations of 47th Division, September 25th to October 2nd", 4 October 1915, TNA PRO WO 95/2698. A. Maude, *The 47th (London) Division 1914–1919* (London: Amalgamated Press) 1922, pp. 25–32.

61. Edmonds, *1915: Aubers Ridge*, pp. 265 and 282–4.

62. Haig's diary, 25 September 1915. Edmonds, *1915: Aubers Ridge*, pp. 272–87. G. C. Wynne, "The Affair of the 21st and 24th Divisions at Loos, 26th September 1915", *The Fighting Forces*, Vol. 11 (1934), pp. 30–3. All quotations in this paragraph are from Wynne's article. Wynne was one of the official historians, and the most outspoken in his criticism of British generalship. The article is based on both British and German sources.

63. "Handling of Reserves at the Battle of Loos: 2. Explanations of Certain Statements made in First Army's Weekly Report of 22nd to 30th September 1915 and 5. Narrative of the march of the Reserve Divisions on 25th September 1915 with map of Traffic Control Arrangements on this day", TNA PRO WO 106/390. "21st Division Operations of September 25th, 26th, and 27th", Forestier-Walker (GOC 21st Division) to IX Corps, 21 Div. G. 458, 10 October 1915 and Forestier-Walker to 2nd Corps, 21st Division G. 545, TNA PRO WO 158/263. Edmonds, *1915: Aubers Ridge*, pp. 282–9.

64. Edmonds, *1915: Aubers Ridge*, p. 283.

65. Lloyd, *Loos*, pp. 156–62. Wynne, "The Divisions at Loos", p. 30. Edmonds, *1915: Aubers Ridge*, pp. 262–7.

66. Lloyd, *Loos*, pp. 156–8. Edmonds, *1915: Aubers Ridge*, pp. 220–3 and 267.

67. Forestier-Walker to 2nd Corps, 21st Div. G. 545, para. 2, 15 October 1915, TNA PRO WO 158/263. Wynne, p. 32. Edmonds, *1915: Aubers Ridge*, pp. 177–8.

68. Edmonds, *1915: Aubers Ridge*, pp. 267–70.

69. C. T. Atkinson, *The Seventh Division 1914–18* (London: John Murray) 1927, pp. 217–18. Edmonds, *1915: Aubers Ridge*, pp. 300–4 and 306–7.

70. First Army to its corps, G. 184, 11.30 p.m., 25 September 1915, Acc. 3155/215, National Library of Scotland. Edmonds, *1915: Aubers Ridge*, p. 309.

71. Stewart and Buchan, *The 15th Scottish Division*, p. 42. Lloyd, *Loos*, p. 54.

72. "Narrative of the Operations of the 1st Division, 25th, 26th and 27th September 1915", TNA PRO WO 95/1229. "21st Division: Operations of September 25th, 26th and 27th", PRO WO 158/263. Haig's diary, 26 September. Stewart and Buchan, *The 15th Scottish Division*, pp. 43–5. Lloyd, *Loos*, pp. 163–87.

73. C. Headlam, *History of the Guards Division in The Great War 1915–1918 (2 Vols.) Vol. I* (London: John Murray) 1924, pp. 49–54. "Report on

Operations of the IV Corps, 22nd September to 7th October, 1915", pp. 10–13, TNA PRO WO 95/711.

74. Haig to GHQ, "First Army. Weekly Report on Operations. Period: 22nd–30th September 1915", 3 October 1915, Haig to GHQ, "First Army. Weekly Report on Operations. Period: 1st–7th October, 1915", 8 October 1915 and Haig to GHQ, "First Army. Weekly Report on Operations. Period: 8th–14th October, 1915", 16 October 1915, Acc. 3155/215, National Library of Scotland. Lloyd, pp. 190–212. Edmonds, *1915: Aubers Ridge*, pp. 369–70.

75. Edmonds, *1915: Aubers Ridge*, pp. 392–401.

76. Lloyd, *Loos*, pp. 69–70.

77. "This instruction is not, however, to be taken as preventing you from developing your attack deliberately and progressively, should you be of the opinion that the nature of the enemy's defences makes such a course desirable." GHQ to Haig, 23 August 1915, TNA PRO WO 95/157. Lloyd, *Loos*, p. 53.

78. Haig's diary, 14 July 1915.

79. *Ibid.*, 19 August 1915.

80. Edmonds, *1915: Aubers Ridge*, pp. 308–9.

CHAPTER 8

1. N. Lloyd, *Loos 1915* (Stroud: Tempus) 2006, pp. 163–87.

2. F. Maurice, *Haldane 1915–1928: The Life of Viscount Haldane of Cloan K.T.O. M.* (London: Faber and Faber) 1929, pp. 10–11.

3. R. Holmes, *The Little Field Marshal: A Life of Sir John French* (London: Weidenfeld and Nicolson) 1981, pp. 230–71.

4. D. Woodward, *Lloyd George and the Generals* (London: Frank Cass) 2004, pp. 59 and 65.

5. Haig's diary, 14 July 1915.

6. D. Woodward, *Field Marshal Sir William Robertson: Chief of the Imperial General Staff in the First World War* (Wesport: Praeger) 1998, p. 23.

7. Holmes, *The Little Field Marshall*, pp. 291–2.

8. G. Cassar, *Asquith as War Leader* (London: Hambledon) 1994, pp. 114 and 135.

9. Haig's diary, 17 October 1915.

10. *Ibid.*, 14 July, 19 August and 20 September 1915.

11. *Ibid.*, 14 July 1915.

12. Haig to Kitchener, 29 September 1915, TNA PRO 30/57/53.

13. Haig's diary, 9 October, Haig to Rothschild, 18 October, Haig's diary, 24 October 1915.

14. GHQ to Haig, OAM 77, 16 October 1915, Acc. 3155/177, Haig Papers, National Library of Scotland (NLS). Lloyd, *Loos*, p. 145. R. Prior and T. Wilson, *Command on the Western Front: The Military Career Of Sir Henry Rawlinson 1914–1918* (Oxford: Blackwell) 1992, pp. 125–6.

15. Kitchener to French 6 October and French to Kitchener 9 October, quoted in G. Cassar, *The Tragedy of Sir John French* (Newark: University of Delaware Press) 1985, pp. 273–4.

16. GHQ to Haig, OAM 77, 16 October 1915.

17. Holmes, *The Little Field Marshall*, pp. 305–9.
18. Haig's diary, 9 October 1915. Cassar, *French*, p. 275. Maurice, *Haldane*, pp. 17–18.
19. Haig's diary, 17 October 1915.
20. *Ibid.*
21. Woodward, *Robertson*, pp. 1–7, and Woodward, "Sir William Robertson and Sir Douglas Haig". In B. Bond and N. Cave (eds.) *Haig: A Reappraisal 70 Years On* (Leo Cooper: London) 1999, p. 66. Haig's diary, 13 February 1916.
22. Haig's diary, 14, 24, and 25 November 1915.
23. Woodward, "Sir William Robertson and Sir Douglas Haig", pp. 66–7. Haig's diary, 18 January 1916.
24. Esher's journal, 23 September 1916. Quoted in Woodward, "Sir William Robertson", p. 64.
25. Robertson signed GHQ to Haig (OAM 77), 16 October 1915, which presents the GHQ side of the GHQ/First Army controversy over Loos.
26. Esher's journal, 9 December 1915. O. Esher, *Journals and Letters of Reginald Viscount Esher, Vol. 3, 1910–1915* (London: Ivor Nicholson and Watson) 1938, p. 295.
27. Haig's diary, 24 October and 25 November 1915.
28. Cassar, *French*, p. 276. Haig's diary, 24 October 1915.
29. Haig's diary, 28 October 1915. H. Nicolson, *King George V: His Life and Reign* (London: Constable) 1952, pp. 267–8.
30. Cassar, *French*, p. 276.
31. Nicolson, p. 268, and Robertson to Haig, 15 November 1915, quoted in Woodward, *Lloyd George*, p. 79.
32. Asquith to Lord Selborne, 26 October 1915, MS 80, Selborne Papers, Bodleian Library, Oxford. Quoted in Cassar, *French*, pp. 275–6.
33. Haig's diary, 14 November 1915.
34. *Ibid.*, 23 and 24 November 1915.
35. *Ibid.*, 25 November 1915.
36. Esher's journal, 23 October–7 November 1915, Esher, *Journals and Letters*, pp. 281–9.
37. Esher's journal, 3 December 1915, Esher, *Journals and Letters*, pp. 290–2.
38. Stamfordham to Asquith, 2 December 1915, RA GV Q838/47, Royal Archives, Windsor.
39. Asquith to Stamfordham, 6 December 1915, RA GV Q838/52, Royal Archives, Windsor.
40. French to Asquith, 4 December 1915, Asquith Papers 28, Folio 251, Bodleian Library, Oxford.
41. Haig's diary, 10 December 1915.
42. Esher's journal, 4 December 1915, quoted in Woodward, *Robertson*, p. 23.
43. Asquith to Stamfordham, 6 December 1915, RA GV Q838/52, Royal Archives, Windsor.
44. Woodward, *Robertson*, p. 24.
45. Hankey's diary, 14 December 1915. Quoted in S. Roskill, *Hankey: Man of Secrets (3 Vols.) Volume I: 1877–1918* (London: Collins) 1970, p. 238.

46. Becke, *Order of Battle: Part 4: The Army Council, GHQ's, Armies and Corps 1914–1918*, (London: HMSO) 1945, p. 11.

47. Haig's diary, 10–26 December 1915.

48. In response to Robertson's guarded criticism of Haig's handling of the early part of the Somme battle, Kiggell noted admiringly that in the face of disappointment and heavy losses: "Sir D.H. never turns a hair." Kiggell to Robertson, 14 July 1916, Robertson 7/6/56, Robertson Papers, Liddell Hart Centre for Military Archives, King's College London. J. Hussey, "Portrait of a Commander-in-Chief". In Bond and Cave, *Haig: A Reappraisal*, p. 27. N. Lytton, *The Press and the General Staff* (London: Collins) 1920, p. 67.

49. Hussey, *Portrait*, pp. 13–14. The phrase "mask of command" is borrowed from John Keegan. Keegan, *The Mask of Command* (London: Jonathan Cape) 1987, pp. 10–11.

50. J. Charteris, *Field Marshal Earl Haig* (London: Cassell) 1929, pp. 59–60.

51. Haig to Rothschild, 26 December 1914, Acc. 3155/214 (e), Haig Papers, NLS.

52. N. Cave, "Haig and Religion". In Bond and Cave, *Haig: A Reappraisal*, p. 243.

53. Haig's diary, 2 January 1916.

54. Cave, "Religion", pp. 249–52. J. Charteris, *At GHQ* (London: Cassell) 1931, p. 219.

55. Charteris, *At GHQ*, p. 181.

56. Haig's diary, 12 December and 21 December 1915.

57. Becke, *Part 4: The Army Council*, p. 71. John Bourne, "Charles Monro". In I. F. W. Beckett and S. J. Corvi (eds.) *Haig's Generals* (Barnsley: Pen and Sword) 2006, pp. 127–30.

58. Becke, *Part 4: The Army Council*, p. 99.

59. Woodward, *Robertson*, p. 29. T. Travers, *The Killing Ground: The British Army, The Western Front and the Emergence of Modern Warfare, 1900–1918* (London: Unwin Hyman) 1987, pp. 104–5, 115–118. S. Robbins, *British Generalship on the Western Front: 1914–18: Defeat Into Victory* (London: Frank Cass) 2005, pp. 118–19.

60. Haig's diary, 12 and 21 December 1915. Becke, *Part 4: The Army Council*, p. 11.

61. Woodward, *Robertson*, p. 29. Travers, *The Killing Ground* pp. 104–5.

62. Charteris, *Haig*, p. 382.

63. Becke, *Part 4: The Army Council*, p. 153.

64. Hussey, *Portrait*, p. 19.

65. I. Brown, *British Logistics on the Western Front 1914–1919* (Westport, Ct.: Praeger) 1998, pp. 109–53. *War Office, Statistics of the Military Effort of the British Empire 1914–1920* (London: HMSO) 1922, pp. 838–80. Hussey, *Portrait*, pp. 19–20.

66. Repington to Andrew Bonar Law, 16 November 1915. AJA Morris (ed.) *The Letters of Lieutenant-Colonel Charles à Court Repington CMG: Military Correspondent of The Times, 1903–1918* (Stroud: Sutton) 1999, pp. 239–41.

67. On early visits of politicians (F. E. Smith, Lloyd George and Bonar Law) to GHQ in Haig's time, see Haig's diary, 30 and 31 January 1916. On addressing ministers in London, see Haig's diary, 15 April 1916.
68. Hussey, *Portrait*, p. 17.
69. S. Badsey, "Haig and the Press". In Bond and Cave, *Haig: A Reappraisal*, pp. 176–95.
70. On ministers' right and duty to control campaigns, sometimes not exercised, see R. Prior and T. Wilson, *Passchendaele: The Untold Story* (New Haven: Yale) 1996, pp. 143–55.
71. Travers, *The Killing Ground*, p. 86.
72. Hubert Gough, a cavalry brigade commander in 1914 was an Army commander by 22 May 1916. Historians have not generally been too impressed with his performance at any of these levels of command. See, for example, G. Sheffield and H. McCartney, "Hubert Gough". In Beckett and Corvi, *Haig's Generals*, pp. 75–97.
73. On First Army's casualties under Haig's command see N. Lloyd, "With Faith and Without Fear", Sir Douglas Haig's Command of First Army During 1915", *The Journal of Military History 71*, October 2007, 1058. On "a series of clear tactical defeats" see J. Bourne, *Britain and the Great War, 1914–1918* (London: Edward Arnold) 1989, p. 38.
74. "G.S.O.", *GHQ (Montreuil-sur-Mer)* (London: Philip Allan) 1920, pp. 1–15.
75. *Ibid.*, pp. 36–7. Charteris, *At GHQ*, p. 143. S. Badsey, "Haig and the Press". In Bond and Cave, *Haig: A Reappraisal*, pp. 181 and 185.
76. *Ibid.*, pp. 36–47. Becke, *Part 4: The Army Council*, pp. 11–16. D. Todman, "The Grand Lamasery Revisited: General Headquarters on the Western Front, 1914–1918". In G. Sheffield and D. Todman, *Command and Control on the Western Front: The British Army's Experience 1914–18* (Staplehurst: Spellmount) 2004, pp. 39–70. I. Brown, *British Logistics on the Western Front 1914–1919* (Westport: Praeger) 1998, pp. 138–78. P. Griffith, *Battle Tactics of the Western Front: The British Army's Art of Attack 1916–18* (London: Yale) 1994, pp. 76–9. A. Geddes, "Major-General Arthur Solly-Flood, GHQ, and Tactical Training in the BEF, 1916–1918", MA dissertation, Centre for First World War Studies, University of Birmingham, September 2007.
77. Hussey, *Portrait*, pp. 13–14 and 16.
78. *Ibid.*, pp. 16–17.
79. *Ibid.*, p. 17.
80. Charteris, *Haig*, pp. 204–7. Hussey, *Portrait*, p. 18.
81. Robbins, *Defeat into Victory*, pp. 78–9.
82. Charteris, *Haig*, p. 382.
83. Becke, *Part 4: The Army Council*, pp. 24–6.
84. J.P. Harris, "Haig and the Tank". In Bond and Cave, *Haig: A Reappraisal*, pp. 105–45, and J. P. Harris, *Men, Ideas and Tanks: British Military Thought and Armoured Forces* (Manchester: Manchester University Press) 1995, pp. 47–194.
85. Haig's diary, 28 September, 1 November and 15 November 1916.
86. On Haig and the railway expert, Eric Geddes, see K. Grieves, "The Transportation Mission to GHQ, 1916". In B. Bond *et al. "Look To Your*

Front": Studies in the First World War (Staplehurst: Spellmount) 1999, pp. 63–78.

87. Haig's diary, 2 January, 9 January and 19 March 1916. See also G. DeGroot (ed.) "The Reverend George S. Duncan at GHQ, 1916–1918". In Guy, Thomas and DeGroot (eds.) *Military Miscellany I: Manuscripts from the Seven Years War, The First and Second Sikh Wars and the First World War* (Stroud: Sutton) 1996, pp. 265–434.

88. Charteris, *Haig*, pp. 36, 69. Travers, *The Killing Ground*, p. 104.

89. Travers, *The Killing Ground*, p. 104.

90. P. Simkins, "Haig and his Army Commanders". In Bond and Cave, *Haig: A Reappraisal*, p. 94.

91. Robbins, *Defeat into Victory*, pp. 72–3 and 118–19. For military and ministerial attitudes to Charteris see Derby to Haig, 7 December 1917, Acc. 3155/347, Haig Papers, NLS. The comment on Haig's general staff as a whole is from Esher's diary, 1 June 1916, quoted in Robbins, *Defeat into Victory*, p. 119.

92. Travers, *The Killing Grounds*, p. 107.

93. Haig's diary, 8 January 1916.

94. Haig's diary, 14 January 1916. Travers, *The Killing Grounds*, p. 106.

95. J. Bourne, "Charles Monro", M. Hughes, "Edmund Allenby". In Beckett and Corvi, *Haig's Generals*, pp. 12–33 and 122–40.

96. P. Simkins, "Herbert Plumer". In Beckett and Corvi, *Haig's Generals*, pp. 144–5.

97. Haig's diary, 18 February 1916.

98. Simkins, "Plumer", p. 141. "Talk with Edmonds", 11/1938/59, Liddell Hart Papers, Liddell Hart Centre for Military Archives, King's College London, Travers, p. 105.

99. C. Harington, *Plumer of Messines* (London: John Murray) 1935, p. 111.

100. By the end of September 1917, Plumer thought there was no real prospect of a collapse of German morale or of major strategic results flowing from the Third Ypres offensive. See Plumer to GHQ, G924, 30 September 1917, TNA PRO WO 158/250. Yet when Haig urged the continuance of this offensive, Plumer offered no serious dissent.

101. Travers, *The Killing Grounds*, p. 105. Simkins, "Haig and the Army Commanders", p. 85.

102. Instructions of the Secretary of State to the General Commanding-in-Chief British Armies in France, 28 December 1915. G. Sheffield and J. Bourne (eds.) *Douglas Haig: War Diaries and Letters 1914–1918* (London: Weidenfeld and Nicholson) 2005, Appendix Two, pp. 514–15.

103. Haig's diary, 26 February 1917.

104. Charteris, *Haig*, p. 152.

105. W. J. Philpott, *Anglo-French Relations and Strategy On The Western Front, 1914–18* (Basingstoke: Macmillan) 1996, p. 113.

106. Haig's diary, 23 December 1915.

107. Philpott, *Strategy*, pp. 99–100.

108. Haig's diary, 29 December 1915.

109. General Huguet, *Britain and the War: A French Indictment* (London: Cassell) 1928, pp. 189–201. E. Greenhalgh, *Victory Through Coalition: Britain and*

France during the First World War (Cambridge: Cambridge University Press) 2005, pp. 87–8 and 90–3. Philpott, *Strategy*, p. 99.

CHAPTER 9

1. Two able historians of Franco-British relations have recently had a remarkably ill-tempered debate on British aims. See E. Greenhalgh, "Why the British were on the Somme in 1916", *War in History*, Vol. 6, No. 2, (1999) pp. 14–173. W. Philpott, "Why the British were really on the Somme: A Reply to Elizabeth Greenhalgh", *War in History*, Vol. 9, No. 4 (2002) 446–71. E. Greenhalgh, "Flames over the Somme: A Retort to William Philpott", *War in History*, Vol. 10, No. 3 (2003), pp. 335–42.

2. British and French casualties are relatively non-controversial. German casualties have been the topic of heated debate. For recent discussions see C. Duffy, *Through German Eyes: The British and the Somme 1916* (London: Weidenfeld and Nicolson) 2006, p. 324, and G. Sheffield, *The Somme* (London: Weidenfeld and Nicolson) 2003, p 151.

3. G. Sheffield, pp. 155–60, sees the Somme as an important milestone on the road to ultimate Allied victory. J. Sheldon, *The German Army on the Somme 1914–1916* (Barnsley: Pen and Sword) 2005, pp. 398–9, argues a case for regarding it as a German victory.

4. "Written statement of the conference held at Chantilly, Dec 6th 1915: Conclusions come to at the conference", 6 December 1915, TNA PRO WO 106/1454.

5. W. J. Philpott, *Anglo-French Relations and Strategy on the Western Front 1914–18* (Basingstoke: Macmillan) 1996, p. 114.

6. Joffre to Haig, 25 December 1915, TNA PRO WO 158/14, and Philpott, *Anglo-French Relations*, pp. 114–15.

7. Haig's diary, 17 December 1915, Philpott, *Anglo-French Relations*, p. 115.

8. Haig to Joffre, OA 254, 31 December 1915, TNA PRO WO 158/14.

9. Philpott, *Anglo-French Relations*, pp. 116–17.

10. Haig's diary, 14 January 1916.

11. "Notes of an Interview with General Joffre at St Omer", 20 January 1916, Acc. 3155/213d, Haig Papers, NLS.

12. Joffre to Haig, 23 January 1916, TNA PRO WO 158/14.

13. Robertson to Haig, 28 January 1916, Acc. 3155/104, Haig Papers, NLS.

14. Haig to Joffre, OAD 344, 1 February 1916, TNA PRO WO 158/14.

15. Haig's diary 11 and 12 February 1916. Philpott, *Anglo-French Relations*, p. 119.

16. Haig's diary, 7 February 1916.

17. Haig's diary, 14 February 1916. Haig to George V, 15 February 1916, RA PS/GV/827/118, Royal Archives, Windsor.

18. Haig's diary, 19 and 20 February 1916. Charteris, *At GHQ*, p. 137.

19. Joffre to Haig, OAD 459/1, 22 February 1916, TNA PRO WO 158/14.

20. Haig to Joffre, 25 February 1916, TNA PRO WO 158/14.

21. Haig's diary, 28 February and 8 March 1916. Robertson to Haig, 6 March 1916, Acc. 3155/105, Haig Papers, NLS.

22. Haig's diary, 5 March, and Haig to Joffre, 6 March 1916, TNA WO 158/14.
23. Charteris, *At GHQ*, p. 141. Philpott, *Anglo-French Relations*, p. 123.
24. A. Wiest, *Passchendaele and the Royal Navy* (Westport, Connecticut: Greenwood) 1995, pp. 44–54. Philpott, *Anglo-French Relations*, pp. 123–6.
25. Haig's diary, 29 March 1916.
26. *Ibid.*
27. Robertson to Haig, 26 April 1916, Acc. 3155/105, Haig Papers, NLS. Haig's diary, 4 May 1916.
28. Haig's diary, 20 May 1916.
29. Charteris, *At GHQ*, p. 143.
30. Haig's diary, 26 and 27 May 1916.
31. *Ibid.*, 31 May 1916.
32. Charteris, *At GHQ*, pp. 136–7.
33. Haig's diary, 15 June 1916. Philpott, *Anglo-French Relations*, p. 126.
34. Charteris, *At GHQ*, p. 143.
35. Robertson, "Memorandum on the Possibility of Conducting Offensive Operations", 8 February 1915, PRO WO 158/17. D. Woodward, *Field Marshal Sir William Robertson: Chief of the Imperial General Staff in the Great War* (Wesport, Conn.: Praeger) 1998, pp. 12–15.
36. Robertson to Clive, 12 January 1916, RA Geo. V Q 838/71, Royal Archives, Windsor.
37. Robertson to Haig, 28 May 1916, Acc. 3155/106, Haig Papers, NLS.
38. Charteris, *At GHQ*, p. 143.
39. Haig to Robertson, 29 May 1916, Acc. 3155/106, Haig Papers, NLS.
40. War Committee Minutes, 7 June 1916, CAB 42/15/6. Haig's diary, 7–9 June 1916.
41. R. Prior and T. Wilson, *Command on the Western Front* (Oxford: Blackwell) 1992, p. 137. Becke, *Order of Battle*, Part 4: *The Army Council, GHQs, Armies and Corps 1914–1918* (London: HMSO) 1945, pp. 111–14.
42. Prior and Wilson, *Command*, p. 137. A. Simpson, *Directing Operations: British Corps Command on the Western Front 1914–18* (Stroud: Spellmount) 2006, p. 1.
43. Prior and Wilson, *Command*, p. 138.
44. Haig's diary, 12 December 1915.
45. Prior and Wilson, *Command*, p. 139.
46. Becke, *Part 4: The Army Council*, p. 101.
47. Rawlinson to Wigram, 27 February 1916, 5201/33/18, Rawlinson Papers, National Army Museum. Quoted in Prior and Wilson, *Command*, p. 139.
48. G. C. Wynne, *The Battle in Depth in the West* (London: Faber) 1940, pp. 100–1. "Plan for Offensive By Fourth Army", 3 April 1916, paras. 7–11, TNA PRO WO 158/233.
49. G. Sheffield, *The Somme* (London: Cassell) 2003, p. 27.
50. Rawlinson to GHQ, 3 April 1916, paras. 1 and 2, TNA PRO WO 158/233.
51. "Plans for Offensive by Fourth Army", 3 April 1916, TNA PRO WO 158/233.
52. *Ibid.*, para. 30.
53. *Ibid.*, para. 32.

54. *Ibid.*, para. 19.
55. Rawlinson to First Army, 21 June 1915, TNA PRO WO 95/710. Prior and Wilson, *Command*, p. 145.
56. "Plans for Offensive by Fourth Army", 3 April 1916, paras. 7, 18, 33 and 34. TNA PRO WO 158/233. Prior and Wilson, *Command*, pp. 161–2.
57. This is evident from Haig's marginal notes on the Fourth Army plan of 3 April and from an endnote dated 5 April and addressed to Kiggell.
58. Kiggell to Fourth Army, 12 April 1916, TNA PRO WO 158/233.
59. E. Greenhalgh, *Victory through Coalition: Britain and France during the First World War* (Cambridge: Cambridge University Press) 2005, p. 52.
60. Marginal notes by Haig on the Fourth Army plan of 3 April 1916, TNA PRO 158/233. Haig's diary, 5 April 1916. GHQ (Kiggell) to Fourth Army, 13 April 1916, TNA PRO WO 158/233.
61. Noel Birch to Edmonds, 8 July 1930, TNA PRO CAB 45/132. T. Travers, *The Killing Ground* (London: Allen and Unwin) 1987, pp. 138–9.
62. "Plan for an Offensive by the Fourth Army", 3 April 1916, para. 9, TNA PRO WO 158/233.
63. Prior and Wilson, *Command*, p. 150.
64. "Plans for an Offensive", 3 April 1916, para. 28, TNA PRO WO 158/233. This was reiterated in Rawlinson to GHQ, 19 April 1916, para. 6, TNA PRO WO 158/233.
65. This case is strongly argued in Prior and Wilson, *Command*, pp. 137–53. Sheffield, *The Somme*, pp. 37–41, seems to accept it, as does P. Hart in *The Somme* (London: Weidenfeld and Nicolson) 2005, pp. 64–70. Badsey is a dissenter, who suggests that the concept of deep penetration on the first day might have worked if Rawlinson had loyally implemented Haig's wishes. See S. Badsey, "Cavalry and the Development of Breakthrough Doctrine". In P. Griffith, *British Fighting Methods in the Great War* (London: Frank Cass) 1996, pp. 153–7.
66. Prior and Wilson, *Command*, p. 168.
67. Haig's diary, 21 June 1916.
68. *Ibid.*, J. Edmonds, *Military Operations, France and Belgium, 1916* (London: Macmillan) 1932, pp. 304–6. H. Gough, *The Fifth Army* (London: Hodder and Stoughton) 1931, pp. 134–6.
69. Prior and Wilson, *Command*, pp. 158–63.
70. Edmonds, *Military Operations*, pp. 300–1.
71. M. Farndale, *History of the Royal Regiment of Artillery: Western Front 1914–18* (London: Royal Artillery Institution) 1986, p. 142.
72. Farndale, *History of the Royal Regiment of Artillery*, p. 143, and Prior and Wilson, *Command*, pp. 155–6.
73. Farndale, *History of the Royal Regiment of Artillery*, pp. 144–7, and Simpson, *Directing Operations*, p. 30.
74. Farndale, *History of the Royal Regiment of Artillery*, pp. 145–6.
75. H. A. Jones, *The War in the Air, Vol II* (Oxford: Clarendon Press) 1928, pp. 175–6 and 207–20. Prior and Wilson, *Command*, pp. 171–2. Edmonds, *Military Operations*, pp. 120–4.
76. Prior and Wilson, *Command*, p. 173.

77. Rawlinson's diary, 30 June 1916, RWLN 1/5, Churchill College, Cambridge.
78. Prior and Wilson, *Command*, pp. 173–4.
79. Farndale, *History of the Royal Regiment of Artillery* pp. 146–8.
80. Becke, *Part 4: The Army Council*, pp. 25–6. Edmonds, *Military Operations*, p. 304.
81. Haig's diary, 1 July 1916.
82. M. Middlebrook, *The First Day on the Somme: 1 July 1916* (London: Allen Lane) 1971, pp. 107–71.
83. *Ibid.*, pp. 119 –122.
84. C. McCarthy, *The Somme: The Day By Day Account* (London: Cassell) 1993 pp. 16–33. R. A. Doughty, *Pyrrhic Victory: French Strategy and Operations in the Great War* (London: Belknap) 2005, p. 293.
85. McCarthy, *The Somme*, pp. 290–31. C. Duffy, *Through German Eyes and Nicholson* 2006, pp. 134–7.
86. Mc Carthy, *The Somme*, pp. 27–31. Duffy, *Through German Eyes*, pp. 130–55.
87. McCarthy, *The Somme*, pp. 16–25. Duffy, *Through German Eyes*, pp. 155–64.
88. Duffy, *German Eyes*, p. 165. Prior and Wilson, *Command*, p. 177.
89. Haig's diary, 1 July 1916. Prior and Wilson, *Command*, p. 182.
90. Haig's diary, 1 July 1916.
91. Prior and Wilson, *Command*, pp. 176–86.
92. Edmonds, *Military Operations*, pp. 344–5.
93. J. Ewing, *The History of the 9th (Scottish) Division 1914–1919* (London: John Murray) 1921, pp. 95–6. Kiggell to Fourth Army (OAD) 963, 4 June 1916 and Kiggell to Gough (OAD) 964, 4 June 1916 and "Army Commander's Remarks at the Conference held at Fourth Army Headquarters, 22nd June, 1916", para. 8, 24 June 1916, TNA PRO WO 158/233. Badsey, "Cavalry", pp. 154–6.
94. "Army Commander's Remarks … 22nd June, 1916", paras. 7–16, TNA PRO WO 158/233.
95. Doughty, *Phyrric Victory*, pp. 291–3. Edmonds, *Military Operations*, pp. 342–3.
96. Edmonds, *Military Operations*, pp. 342–5 and 369–70.
97. R. Prior and T. Wilson, *The Somme* (London: Yale) 2005, pp. 109–11.
98. *Ibid.*, p. 53.
99. Duffy, *Through German Eyes*, pp. 126–7.
100. Greenhalgh, pp. 60–2.
101. G. Cassar, *Kitchener: Architect of Victory* (London: William Kimber) 1977, pp. 476–80.
102. G. H. Cassar, *Kitchener's War: British Strategy From 1914 to 1916* (Washington D.C.: Brassey's) 2004, pp. 272–3. Cassar indicates Kitchener's wish for an offensive with limited objectives, in which Haig would carefully husband British manpower. It is, however, going too far to state that "Kitchener had no reason to suspect that Haig would misuse the BEF." Kitchener evidently did suspect Haig of an inclination towards reckless operational methods. But, as Cassar correctly indicates, he was in a poor position to do anything about it even before a German mine and the waters off the Orkneys ended his life.
103. Prior and Wilson, *The Somme*, pp. 1–34.

CHAPTER 10

1. Haig's diary, 1 and 2 July. C. Duffy, *Through German Eyes: The British and the Somme 1916* (London: Cassell) 2006, pp. 165–9. E. Greenhalgh, *Victory Through Coalition: Britain and France during the First World War* (Cambridge: Cambridge University Press) 2005, p. 55. R. Prior and T. Wilson, *Command on the Western Front: The Military Career of Sir Henry Rawlinson 1914–1918* (Oxford: Blackwell) 1992, p. 187.
2. Fourth Army Operations Order No. 3, 1 July 1916, Fourth Army Papers, Vol. 7, Imperial War Museum.
3. Haig's diary, 2 July 1916.
4. *Ibid.*, 1 and 2 July 1916.
5. *Ibid.*, 2 July 1916. GHQ to Rawlinson, OAD 37, 2 July 1916, TNA PRO WO 158/234.
6. Haig's diary, 3 July 1916. "Note of an interview between Sir D. Haig and General Joffre on 3 July 1916 at Val Vion. Also present Generals Foch and Kiggell", 4 July 1916, TNA PRO WO 158/14.
7. R. Foley, *German Strategy and the Path to Verdun: Erich von Falkenhayn and the Development of Attrition 1870–1916* (Cambridge: Cambridge University Press) 2005, pp. 250–5.
8. R. Doughty, *Pyrrhic Victory: French Strategy and Operations in the Great War* (London: Belknap) 2005, pp. 294–5. Greenhalgh, *Coalitiou*, pp. 64–5. Congreve (GOC XIII Corps) to Fourth Army, 15 July 1916, TNA PRO WO 158/234. W. Miles, *Military Operation France and Belgium, 1916: 2nd July to the end of the Battle of the Somme* (London: Macmillan) 1938, p. 67.
9. Becke, *Order of Battle: Part 4: The Army Council, GHQs, Armies and Corps 1914–18* (London: HMSO) 1945, p. 114. Haig's diary 2–6 July. Prior and Wilson, *Command*, p. 187. GHQ to Allenby, Gough and Rawlinson, OAD 52, 8 July 1916 and Fourth Army Operations Order No. 4, TNA PRO WO 158/234.
10. Haig's diary, 4 July. Advanced GHQ to Fourth Army, OAD 49, 6 July 1916, TNA PRO WO 158/234. Prior and Wilson, *Command*, p. 187.
11. Duffy, *Through German Eyes*, pp. 170–1.
12. Miles, 2 *July to the end of the Somme*, pp. 26–7 and 59–60. Foley, *German Strategy*, p. 251.
13. Of Ulster, Cyril Falls wrote: "The whole Province was plunged into mourning for its sons." C. Falls, *The History of the 36th (Ulster) Division* (London: McCaw, Stevenson, and Orr) 1922, p. 59. Hankey's diary, 3 July 1916, HNKY 1/1, Hankey Papers, Churchill College Cambridge.
14. Haig's diary, 1 July. Robertson to Maurice, 2 July 1916, D. Woodward (ed.) *The Military Correspondence of Field Marshal Sir William Robertson, Chief of the Imperial General Staff, December 1915–February 1918* (London: Bodley Head) 1989, p. 61. Hunter-Weston to Robertson, 2 July 1916, 7/5/26, Robertson Papers, LHCMA, King's College London (LHCMA).
15. D. Woodward, *Field Marshal Sir William Robertson* (Westport: Conn., Praeger) 1998, p. 53.
16. Robertson to Haig, 5 July 1916, Acc. 3155/107, Haig Papers, National Library of Scotland (NLS).

17. Robertson to Haig, 7 July 1916, 7/6/51, Robertson Papers, LHCMA.
18. Haig to Robertson, 8 July 1916, TNA PRO WO 158/21.
19. Haig to Robertson, 3 June 1916, Acc. 3155.106, Haig Papers, NLS. S. Badsey, "Haig and the Press". In B. Bond and N. Cave, (eds.) *Haig: A Reappraisal 70 Years On* (Barnsley: Leo Cooper) 1999, p. 184.
20. Haig's diary, 8 July 1916. Badsey, p. 184. Charteris, *At GHQ* (London: Cassell) 1931, pp. 12–153.
21. Haig to Lady Haig, 23 July 1916. Lady Haig to Alan Fletcher (an ADC), 29 July 1916, Acc. 3155/144, Haig Papers, NLS. Quoted in G. De Groot, *Douglas Haig 1861–1928* (London: Unwin Hyman) 1988, pp. 259–62.
22. Robertson to Kiggell, 5 July 1916, 8/4/65, Robertson Papers, LHCMA.
23. *Ibid.*
24. Robertson to Haig, 5 July 1916, Acc. 3155/107, Haig Papers, NLS.
25. Kiggell to Robertson, 14 July 1916, 7/6/56, Robertson Papers, LHCMA.
26. S. Robbins, *British Generalship on the Western Front 1914–18* (London: Frank Cass) 2005, pp. 121–5.
27. Henry Wilson's diary, July/August 1916, Imperial War Museum. Woodward, *Robertson*, p. 57.
28. Robertson to Haig, 8 March 1916, 7/6/30, Robertson Papers, LHCMA. Woodward, *Robertson*, pp. 29–33.
29. GHQ to Fourth Army, "Note of a discussion as to the attack on the LONGUEVAL plateau and the C-in-C's decision thereon", OAD 60, n.d., but apparently 12 July 1916, TNA PRO WO 158/234.
30. Prior and Wilson, *Command*, pp. 191–2.
31. Haig's diary, 10 and 11 July 1916.
32. OAD 60, TNA PRO WO 158/234.
33. *Ibid.*
34. "Notes of a Meeting at Querrieu on the 12th July 1916", OAD 63, and Kiggell to Montgomery, 12 July 1916, TNA PRO WO 158/234.
35. "Meeting at Querrieu", and Prior and Wilson, *Commands*, pp. 194–5.
36. Adv. GHQ to Fourth Army and Reserve Army, OAD 58, 12 July 1916, TNA PRO WO 158/234.
37. Miles, 2 *July to End of the Somme*, pp. 67–89. Duffy, *Through German Eyes*, p. 180.
38. Haig's diary, 14 July 1916.
39. On Repington's attitude to Haig: J. Grigg, *Lloyd George: From Peace to War 1912–1916* (London: Eyre Methuen) 1985, p. 378. On Lloyd George's role in arranging Northcliffe's visit: A. D. Cooper, *Haig*, Vol. I (London: Faber and Faber) 1935, pp. 340–3. On the visit itself: Haig's diary, 21–3 July 1916, and J. Charteris, *At GHQ*, pp. 156–8.
40. Robertson to Haig, 29 July 1916, 7/6/61, Robertson Papers, LHCMA.
41. Woodward, *Robertson*, p. 55.
42. Haig to Robertson, OAD 90, 1 August 1916, summarised in Haig's diary, 1 August 1916.
43. Robertson to Haig, 3, 5, 7 and 8 August 1916, Acc. 3155/107, Haig Papers, NLS.
44. Robertson to Stamfordham, 10 August 1916, quoted in D. Woodward (ed.) *Robertson, Correspondence*, p. 81.

45. Adv. GHQ to Fourth Army and Reserve Army, OAD 76, 13 July 1916, TNA PRO WO 158/234.
46. Miles, *July to the End of the Somme*, pp. 136–46.
47. Prior and Wilson, *Command*, pp. 202–4.
48. Miles, *July to the End of the Somme*, pp. 208–31. Sheffield, p. 101.
49. Robbins comments on the weaknesses of Haig's staff at pp. 119–20 and on the acute British shortage of trained staff officers at pp. 39–40. For the German use of an Army Group command on the Somme see Miles, 2 *July to the End of the Somme*, pp. 118 and 230.
50. Duffy, *Through German Eyes*, pp. 181–98, 385–92 and 305–19.
51. Joffre to Haig, 11 August 1916, and Haig to Joffre, 16 August 1916, TNA PRO WO 158/15.
52. Miles, 2 *July to the End of the Somme*, pp. 190–6. Prior and Wilson, *Command*, pp. 216–4.
53. GHQ to Fourth Army, OAD 116, 19 August 1916 and GHQ to Fourth Army, OAD 123, 24 August 1916, TNA PRO WO 158/235.
54. Prior and Wilson, *Command*, p. 225.
55. Haig's failure to understand the French sense of urgency about making the next big push is clearly illustrated in Haig to Robertson, 27 August 1916, 7/6/71, Robertson Papers, LHCMA. Probably writing before the Franco-British conference that day, Haig indicated that "The French have been tiresome lately. For some reason they (i.e. Joffre and Co.) have been pressing me to make a big attack *not later* than 6th September. I have told them that I will support them with a big attack on the 30th [and another about a fortnight later]. They try to make out that this will be 'too late' but exactly why they are not clear." For the conference at which Poincaré explained French reasoning, see Haig's diary, 27 August 1916.
56. On tanks see R. Prior and T. Wilson, *The Somme* (London: Yale University Press) 2005, pp. 47–8. J. P. Harris, *Men, Ideas and Tanks* (Manchester: Manchester University Press) 1995, pp. 47–8. See also "Preliminary Notes on Tactical Employment of Tanks (Provisional)" and "Tank Organisation and Equipment", August 1916, TNA PRO WO 158/235.
57. Rawlinson's diary, 26 August 1916, Rawlinson Papers, Churchill College, Cambridge. Rawlinson to Advanced GHQ, 28 August 1916, TNA PRO WO 158/235.
58. Rawlinson's diary, 28 August 1916, quoted in Prior and Wilson, *Command*, p. 230.
59. Haig's diary, 29 August 1916, and handwritten note dated 29 August on Rawlinson's draft plan of 28 August, TNA PRO WO 158/235.
60. Advanced GHQ to Rawlinson and Gough, OAD 131, 31 August 1916, TNA PRO WO 158/235.
61. Rawlinson to Advanced GHQ, 31 August 1916, TNA PRO WO 158/235. Prior and Wilson, *Somme*, pp. 216–8.
62. Haig's diary, 15 September 1916. Prior and Wilson, *Somme*, pp. 229–38. T. Pidgeon, *The Tanks At Fler: An Account of the First Use of Tanks in War at the Battle of Flers-Courcelette, The Somme, 15 September 1916* (Cobham: Fairmile Books) 1995.

63. Miles, 2 *July to the end of the Somme*, p. 344 and pp. 349–60. Haig's diary, 16 September 1916. C. McCarthy, *The Somme: The Day by Day Account* (London: Arms and Armour) 1993, pp. 113–15.

64. Miles, 2 *July to the end of the Somme*, p. 348. Prior and Wilson, *Command*, p. 246.

65. Prior and Wilson, *Command*, pp. 246–8.

66. Miles, 2 *July to the end of the Somme*, pp. 391–422. I. Beckett, "Hubert Gough, Neill Malcolm and Command on the Western Front". In Bond *et al.* "*Look to Your Front*": *Studies in The First World War* (Staplehurst: Spellmount) 1999, pp. 1–11. G. Sheffield, "An Army Commander on the Somme: Hubert Gough". In G. Sheffield and D. Todman, *Command and Control on the Western Front: The British Army's Experience 1914–18* (Staplehurst: Spellmount) 2004, pp. 391–422.

67. Haig's diary, 1 and 2 October 1916.

68. Duffy, *Through German Eyes*, pp. 242–3.

69. Prior and Wilson, *Command*, pp. 250–1, and McCarthy, *The Somme*, pp. 128–30. I. Brown, *British Logistics on the Western Front 1914–1919* (Westport, Conn.: Praeger) 1998, pp. 109–38. Charteris, *At GHQ*, pp. 172–3.

70. Prior and Wilson, *Command*, pp. 252–3.

71. Haig's diary, 1–18 October. Haig to Roberston, 7 October 1916, Acc. 3155/107, Haig Papers, NLS.

72. Prior and Wilson, *Command*, pp. 255–6.

73. Haig's diary, 23 October 1916. H. Gough, *The Fifth Army* (London: Hodder and Stoughton) 1931, p. 155.

74. Prior and Wilson, *Command*, pp. 256–7.

75. Miles, 2 *July to the end of the Somme*, pp. 476–510. Duffy, *Through German Eyes*, pp. 285–60. Gough, *The Fifth Army*, pp. 154–9.

76. Foley, *German Strategy*, pp. 250–8. Duffy, *Through German Eyes*, pp. 326–7.

77. Duffy, *Through German Eyes*, pp. 87–8 and 320–8.

CHAPTER 11

1. Haig's diary, 15–16, November 1916. W. J. Philpott, *Anglo-French Relations and Strategy on the Western Front 1914–18* (Basingstoke: Macmillan)1996, p. 129.

2. Haig's diary, 26–27 February 1917. A. Suttie, *Rewriting the History of the First World War: Lloyd George Politics and Strategy 1914–18* (Basingstoke: Palgrave Macmillan) 2005, p. 4.

3. R. C. K. Ensor, *England 1870–1914* (Oxford: Oxford University Press) 1936, pp. 413–18.

4. Haig's diary, 16 and 22 January 1916.

5. J. Charteris, *At GHQ* (London: Cassell) 1931, p. 133.

6. Haig to Robertson, 20 May 1916, and War Committee Minutes, 24 May 1916, TNA PRO CAB 42/14.

7. D. Woodward, *Field Marshal Sir William Robertson: Chief of the General Staff in the Great War* (Westport, Ct.: Praeger) 1998, pp. 24–5. Robertson to Lloyd George, 2 May 1916, quoted in D. Woodward, *The Military Correspondence of Sir William Robertson* (London: Bodley Head) 1989, p. 47. Writing to Haig

about the Somme campaign on 1 August 1916, Robertson stated that "L G is all right provided I can say *I* am satisfied..." Robertson 7/6/62, Robertson Papers, LHCMA.

8. On Geddes see I. M. Brown, *British Logistics on the Western Front 1914–1919* (Westport, Conn.: Praeger) 1998, pp. 131–53.

9. Haig's diary, 15 September 1916. Robertson to Haig, 9 October 1916, 7/6/80, Robertson Papers, LHCMA.

10. Robertson to Kiggell, 5 July 1916. 8/4/65, Robertson Papers, LHCMA. Haig's diary, I August 1916.

11. Robertson on the importance of their sticking together in Robertson to Haig, I/22/18, 24 January 1916, and again in Robertson to Haig, 8 March 1916, 7/6/30, Robertson Papers, LHCMA.

12. Robertson to Haig, 7 September 1916, Acc. 3155/108, Haig Papers, NLS.

13. Haig to Lady Haig, 13 September 1916.

14. Haig's diary, 17 September 1916.

15. G. De Groot, *Douglas Haig 1861–1928* (London: Unwin Hyman) 1988, pp. 264–5. J. Grigg, *Lloyd George from Peace to War 1912–1916* (London: Methuen)1985, pp. 381–3.

16. Robertson to Repington, 31 October 1916, 8/2/72, Robertson Papers, LHCMA.

17. Haig's diary, 7 and 10 October 1916. Robertson to Haig 9 October 1916, 7/6/80, Robertson Papers, LHCMA.

18. Haig's diary, 20 October and Haig to Lady Haig, 21 October 1916.

19. War Committee Minutes, 3 November 1916, TNA PRO CAB 42/23/4.

20. Haig's diary, 22 November 1916.

21. Grigg, *Lloyd George*, pp. 430–74.

22. Haig to Lady Haig, 6 December 1916, and Haig to Philip Sassoon, 8 December 1916 (quoted in P. Stansky, *Sassoon: The Worlds of Philip and Sybil* (London: Yale) 2003, p. 67).

23. Haig's diary, 18 November 1916.

24. Grigg, *Lloyd George*, p. 490.

25. Haig's diary, 15 December 1916.

26. Woodward, *Robertson*, pp. 80–6. Robertson to Lloyd George, 6 January 1917, quoted in Woodward, *Military Commander*, pp. 136–7.

27. R. A. Doughty, *Pyrrhic Victory: French Strategy and Operations in the Great War* (London: Belknap) 2005, pp. 318–22.

28. *Ibid.*, pp. 323–4.

29. Haig's diary, 20, 27 and 28 December 1916 and Haig to Lady Haig, 20 December 1916.

30. Nivelle to Haig, 21 December 1916, TNA PRO WO 158/37. Haig's diary 27 and 28 December 1916.

31. C. Falls, *Military Operations in France and Belgium, 1917* (London: Macmillan) 1940, p. 11. Haig's diary, 22 December 1916.

32. George V to Haig, 27 December 1916, quoted in A. D. Cooper, *Haig: The Second Volume* (London: Faber)1936, p. 14.

33. Memorandum to Army Commanders on Winter Policy, 18 November 1916, Acc. 3155/109, Haig Papers, NLS.

34. Minutes of the War Committee, 20 November 1916, TNA PRO CAB 42/24. "Precis of a meeting held in the CIGS's room, 23 November 1916", TNA PRO WO 158/22.
35. Nivelle to Haig, 2 January 1917, and Haig to Nivelle 6 January 1917, TNA PRO WO 158/37.
36. Haig's diary, 8–15 January 1916.
37. *Ibid.*, 15 January 1917. Hankey's diary, 15 January 1917, HNKY 1/1, Hankey Papers, Churchill College, Cambridge.
38. Haig's diary, 16 January 1917.
39. W. Robertson, *From Private to Field Marshal* (London: Constable) 1921, pp. 308–9.
40. Haig's diary, 18 January 1917.
41. Haig's diary, 7 February 1917.
42. *Ibid.*, 1 February 1917.
43. *The Times*, 15 February 1917.
44. Haig's diary, 18 and 22 February 1917, and Haig to Lady Haig, 22 February 1917.
45. Charteris, *At GHQ*, pp. 193–4.
46. *Ibid.* S. Badsey, "Haig and the Press". In B. Bond and N. Cave (eds.) *Haig: A Reappraisal 70 Years On* (Barnsley: Leo Cooper) 1999, pp. 186–7. N. Lytton, *The Press and the General Staff* (London: Collins) 1921, pp. 64–72.
47. Derby to Haig, 20 February 1917, Acc. 3155/347, Haig Papers, NLS.
48. Charteris, *At GHQ*, pp. 204–5.
49. Haig to Robertson, 26 December 1916, 7/6/98, Robertson Papers, LHCMA. I. M. Brown, *British Logistics on the Western Front 1914–1919* (Westport, Conn.: Praeger) 1998, pp. 155–9.
50. Haig's diary, 16 February 1916. Robertson to Haig, 14 February 1916, 7/7/7, and Robertson to Haig, 28 February 1917, 7/7/8, Robertson Papers, LHCMA.
51. J. Grigg, *Lloyd George: War Leader 1916–18* (London: Penguin) 2003, pp. 40–1. Hankey's diary, 25 February 1917, HNKY 1/1, Hankey Papers, Churchill College, Cambridge.
52. Haig diary, 26 February 1917. Hankey's diary, 26 February 1917, HNKY 1/1, Hankey Papers, Churchill College, Cambridge.
53. Grigg, *War Leader*, pp. 40–1.
54. Haig's diary, 27 February 1917. The account of the early morning meeting with Lyautey occurs in the typescript version of the diary, but not in the somewhat shorter manuscript version. While, in general, it is necessary to be extremely cautious about relying on Haig's typescript diary, there is no particular reason to think this account dishonest.
55. Haig to Robertson, 27 February 1917, quoted in A. D. Cooper, *Haig: The Second Volume* (London: Faber) 1936, p. 48.
56. Hankey's diary, 26 February 1917, HNKY 1/1, Hankey Papers, Churchill College, Cambridge. S. Roskill, *Hankey: Man of Secrets, Volume I* (London: Collins) 1970, pp. 362–4.
57. Grigg, *War Leader*, pp. 41–3.
58. Haig to Lady Haig, 28 February 1917.

59. Haig to King George V, 28 February 1917, and Stamfordham to Haig, 5 March 1917, quoted in G. de Groot, *Douglas Haig, 1861–1928* (London: Unwin Hyman) 1988, pp. 305–6.
60. Haig to Lady Haig, 2 March 1917.
61. Grigg, *War Leader*, p. 41.
62. Haig's diary, 28 February 1917.
63. Charteris, *At GHQ*, p. 197.
64. Haig's diary, 25 February 1917, and Haig to Lady Haig, 3 March 1917.
65. Falls, *Military Operations*, pp. 87–170.
66. Haig to Lady Haig, 2 March 1917.
67. Haig's diary, 2 March 1917.
68. Nivelle to Haig, 6 March 1917, TNA PRO WO 158/37, and Haig's diary 7 March 1917.
69. D. Woodward, *Lloyd George and the Generals* (London: Frank Cass) 2004, p. 151.
70. Hankey to Lloyd George, 7 March 1917, TNA PRO CAB 63/19. Hankey's diary, 10 March, HNKY 1/1, Hankey Papers, Churchill College, Cambridge.
71. Minutes of War Cabinet 91, para. 11a, 8 March 1917 and Minutes of War Cabinet 92, para. 9, 9 March 1917, TNA PRO CAB 23/2. Nivelle to Haig, 9 March 1917, HHW 2/87/2, Wilson Papers, IWM.
72. Haig's diary, 11 and 12 March 1917.
73. Woodward, *Lloyd George*, pp. 150–2.
74. Haig's diary, 12–14 March. Anglo-French Conference, 12–13 March 1917, TNA PRO CAB 28/2.
75. Woodward, *Lloyd George*, pp. 152–4.

CHAPTER 12

1. GHQ to the Army Commanders and the Cavalry Corps, O.A.D. 258, 2 January 1917, Appendix 6 to C. Falls, *Military Operations France and Belgium, 1916, 1917* (London: Macmillan) 1940.
2. While Winter's portrayal of the Haig–Nivelle relationship is complex and difficult to interpret, he seems to suggest that Haig was deceiving Nivelle as to true British intentions and holding back British support for the Allies' spring offensive. D. Winter, *Haig's Command: A Reassessment* (London: Viking) 1991, pp. 70–85.
3. J. Marshall-Cornwall, *Haig as Military Commander* (London: Batsford) 1973, p. 213.
4. R. A. Doughty, *Pyrrhic Victory: French Strategy and Operations in the Great War* (London: Belknap) 2005, pp. 337–41. E. Greenhalgh, *Victory Through Coalition: Britain and France during the First World War* (Cambridge: Cambridge University Press), pp. 145–7.
5. J. Charteris, *At GHQ* (London: Cassell) 1931, pp. 204–8. Haig to Robertson, 8 April 1916, 7/7/16, Robertson Papers, LHCMA.
6. Fourth Army intelligence summaries, 1 and 6 March 1917, PRO WO 157/180. Third Army intelligence summary, 7 March 1917, TNA PRO WO 157/150.

J. Beach, "British Intelligence and the German Army 1914–1918", PhD thesis, University of London, 2005, pp. 182–3.

7. Charteris, *At GHQ*, pp. 204–5, 207.
8. GHQ intelligence summary, 1 March 1917, TNA PRO WO 157/18 and Charteris to his wife, 27 March 1917 and 15 April 1917, Charteris papers, LHCMA. Beach, pp. 183–4.
9. Haig's diary, 13 April 1917.
10. *Ibid.*, 23 March 1917.
11. *Ibid.*, 24 March 1917.
12. GHQ, summary of information, 6, 7, 8, 9 April 1917, TNA PRO WO 157/19. Falls, *Military Operations*, pp. 174–6.
13. GHQ to First, Third, Fourth and Fifth Armies and the Cavalry Corps, 26 March 1917, O.A.D. 350, 26 March 1917, Falls, *Military Operations*, Appendix 26.
14. Haig's diary, 26 February 1917.
15. Falls, *Military Operations*, Appendix 11.
16. S. Robbins, "Henry Horne: First Army 1916–18". In Beckett and Corvi (eds.), *Haig's Generals* (Barnsley: Pen and Sword) 2006, pp. 97–121. D. Farr, *The Silent General: Horne of the First Army: A Biography of Haig's Trusted Great War Comrade in Arms* (Solihull: Helion) 2007, *passim*.
17. For discussions of the particular effectiveness of the Canadian Corps from spring 1917 onwards see C. Pugsley, *The ANZAC Experience: New Zealand, Australia and Empire in the First World War* (Auckland) 2004, pp. 165–203, and B. Rawling, *Surviving Trench Warfare: Technology and the Canadian Corps 1914–1918* (Toronto: University of Toronto Press) 1992, *passim*.
18. N. Gardner, "Julian Byng: Third Army, 1917–18". In Beckett and Corvi (eds.), *Haig's Generals*, pp. 54–67. Byng to Adv. GHQ, 10 August 1917, TNA PRO WO 158/311. P. Dickson "The End of the Beginning" and P. Brennan, "Julian Byng and Leadership in the Canadian Corps". In G. Hayes, A. Iarocci and M. Bechthold (eds.) *Vimy Ridge: A Canadian Reassessment* (Ontario: Wilfrid Laurier University Press) 2007, pp. 31–51 and 87–105.
19. Falls, *Military Operations*, pp. 302–3.
20. *Ibid.*, pp. 176–8.
21. M. Hughes, "Edmund Allenby: Third Army 1915–1917". In Beckett and Corvi, *Haig's Generals*, pp. 12–23.
22. Charteris, *At GHQ*, pp. 210–11.
23. Falls, *Military Operations*, pp. 177–9.
24. Hughes, *Edmund Allenby*, p. 24, and J. Nicholls, *Cheerful Sacrifice: The Battle of Arras 1917* (Barnsley: Pen and Sword Books) 1990, p. 25.
25. Falls, *Military Operations*, pp. 179–81.
26. *Ibid.*, pp. 179–82.
27. *Ibid.*, pp 192–3.
28. P. Hart, *Bloody April: Slaughter in the Skies over Arras, 1917* (London: Weidenfeld and Nicolson) 2005, p. 11 and *passim*. Falls, *Military Operations*, pp. 187–8.
29. Falls, *Military Operations*, pp. 186–8. M. Farndale, *History of the Royal Regiment of Artillery, Western Front 1914–18* (London: Royal Artillery Institution) 1986, pp. 164–6.

30. Falls, *Military Operations*, pp. 186–8.
31. Haig's diary, 5 April 1917. Falls, pp. 186–8.
32. A. F. Becke, *Order of Battle Part 4: The Army Council, G.H.Q.s, Armies, and Corps 1914–1918* (London: HMSO) 1945, pp. 24–6. Haig's diary, 9 April 1917.
33. Falls, *Military Operations*, pp. 201–36.
34. Haig's diary, 14 April 1917. Falls, p. 554.
35. Fergusson to Falls, 14 May 1937, TNA PRO CAB 45/116.
36. *Ibid.*
37. Haig to George V, 9 April 1917, PS/GV/Q 832/137, Royal Archives, Windsor, quoted in J. Bourne and G. Sheffield, *Douglas Haig: War Diaries and Letters 1914–1918* (London: Weidenfeld and Nicolson) 2005, p. 278.
38. Haig's diary, 10 April 1917.
39. Falls, *Military Operations*, p. 272.
40. *Ibid.*, p. 259.
41. "Copy of a Telegram to F.M.C. in C. from Secretary of State for War dated 10th April 1917", Acc. 3155/347, Haig Papers NLS. Robertson to Haig, 10 April 1917, 7/7/17. Robertson Papers, LHCMA. Charteris, pp. 212–13.
42. Falls, *Military Operations*, p. 273.
43. Third Army report to GHQ for 7–13 April 1917, Third Army No. GI4/55, 14 April 1917, TNA PRO WO 95/362. J. Walker, *The Blood Tub: General Gough and the Battle of Bullecourt, 1917* (Staplehurst: Spellmount) 1998, pp. 91–113. Falls, *Military Operations*, pp. 343–8.
44. G. Dewar and J. Boraston, *Sir Douglas Haig's Command* (London: Constable) 1922, pp. 257–62. A. Geddes, "Major-General Arthur Solly Flood, GHQ and Tactical Training in the BEF, 1916–1918", MA dissertation, Centre for First World War Studies, University of Birmingham, 2007, pp. 4–18. P. Griffith, *Battle Tactics of the Western Front: The British Army's Art of Attack 1916–18* (London: Yale University Press) 1994, pp. 76–9. C. McCarthy, "Queen of the Battlefield: The Development of Command, Organisation and tactics in the British Infantry Battalion during the Great War". In G. Sheffield and D. Todman (eds.) *Command and Control on the Western Front: The British Army's Experience 1914–18* (Staplehurst: Spellmount) 2004, pp. 173–93. Humphries, "Old Wine in New Bottles": A Comparison of British and Canadian Preparations for the Battle of Arras". In Hayes, Iarocci and Bechthold, *Vimy Ridge*, pp. 65–86. Farndale, *History of the Royal Regiment of Artillery*, pp. 348–9. Falls, *Military Operations*, p. 554.
45. Falls, *Military Operations*, pp. 274–8.
46. Farndale, *History of the Royal Regiment of Artillery*, pp. 172–3.
47. Falls, *Military Operations*, pp. 274–8 and 297–9.
48. Haig's diary, 12 April 1917.
49. Haig to Nivelle, 12 April 1917, TNA PRO WO 158/137.
50. Haig's diary, 13 April 1917.
51. *Ibid.*, 15 April 1917.
52. *Ibid.*, 14 April 1917. Falls, *Military Operations*, p. 378.
53. On Haldane's vitriolic relations with Allenby see A. Haldane, *A Soldier's Saga* (London: Blackwood) 1948, p. 344. For accounts of the generals' revolt see

Falls, *Military Operations*, p. 378, P. Simkins, "Haig and the Army Commanders". In B. Bond and N. Cave (eds.) *Haig: A Reputation 70 Years On* (Barnsley: Leo Cooper) 1999, p. 84, and Hughes, Edmund Allenby, p. 27. Edmonds admitted his part in bowdlerising Falls' already restrained official account: Edmonds to Acheson, 19 July 1950, TNA PRO CAB 103/113.

54. Information on the subsequent careers of the divisional commanders involved in the quasi-mutiny has been taken from Dr J. Bourne's database on British generals at the Centre for First World War Studies, University of Birmingham. Falls, *Military Operations*, p. 378. Haig's diary, 14 April 1917.

55. Haig's diary, 16 April 1917. Falls, *Military Operations*, p. 379.

56. Falls, *Military Operations*, pp. 379–82.

57. Charteris to his wife, 15 April 1917, Charteris Papers, LHCMA.

58. Doughty, *Pyrrhic Victory*, pp. 349–54.

59. Haig's diary, 17 and 18 April 1917.

60. *Ibid.*, 26 April 1917.

61. *Ibid.*, 18 April 1917.

62. Haig to Robertson, 19 April 1917, quoted in A. D. Cooper, *Haig: The Second Volume* (London: Faber and Faber) 1936, p. 90.

63. S. Roskill, *Hankey: Man of Secrets, Vol. I, 1877–1918* (London: Collins) 1970, pp. 378–9.

64. Haig's diary, 21 April 1917.

65. Robertson to Haig, 20 April 1917, 7/7/21, Robertson Papers, LHCMA.

66. *Ibid.*, 28 April 1917, 7/7/23, LHCMA.

67. Haig's diary, 20 and 24 April 1917.

68. *Ibid.*, 18 April and 24 April 1917.

69. On 28 April 1917 Robertson was worried about U-boats and reported that the War Cabinet was too: Robertson to Haig, 7/7/23, Robertson Papers, LHCMA. Derby had been very worried on the same subject when he wrote to Haig on 18 April, but was much less so when he wrote again on 27 May: Acc. 3155/347, Haig Papers, LHCMA. By early June Haig was dismissing the U-boat threat: Haig to the Army Commanders, O.A. 799, 5 June 1917, TNA PRO WO 158/311.

70. Haig to Army Commanders, O.A. 799, 5 June 1917, TNA PRO 158/311 and Haig's diary, 1 and 10 May 1917.

71. Haig's diary, 24 April 1917. "Record of a Conference held at NOYELLE VION at 11 a.m. on the 30th April 1917", OAD 426, 1 May 1917, TNA PRO WO 158/311.

72. Third Army War Diary, 20–27 April 1917, Third Army No. G. 14/72, 28 April 1917, TNA PRO WO 158/230.

73. Haig's diary, 24 April 1917. Falls, p. 141.

74. Haig's diary, 24 April 1917.

75. *Ibid.*, 26 and 27 April 1917.

76. Falls, *Military Operations*, pp. 41–2.

77. Third Army to GHQ, 27 April–4 May 1917, Third Army No. G14/80, TNA PRO 158/230.

78. "Record of a Conference held at NOYELLES VION at 11 a.m. on the 30th April 1917", OAD 426, TNA PRO WO 158/311.

79. Haig's diary, 30 April 1917.
80. Falls, *Military Operations*, pp. 430–3.
81. Third Army to GHQ, 27 April–4 May 1917, No. GI4/80, TNA PRO WO 158/230. Falls, *Military Operations*, pp. 433–54. Walker, *The Blood Tub*, pp. 137–50
82. Falls, *Military Operations*, pp. 471–81.
83. Walker, *The Blood Tub*, pp. 151–200.
84. Falls, *Military Operations*, pp. 556–8.
85. Nicholls, *Cheerful Sacrifice*, p. 211.
86. S. Badsey and P. Taylor, "Images of Battle: The Press, Propaganda and Passchendaele". In P. H. Liddle (ed.) *Passchendaele in Perspective: The Third Battle of Ypres* (Barnsley: Leo Cooper) 1997, p. 377.
87. On the "defeated enemy order coming too late", see G. C. Wynne, *If Germany Attacks: The Battle in Depth in the West* (Wesport, Conn.: Greenwood) 1976, p. 199. On Allenby's failure to restore his credibility see Haldane, *Soldiers' Saga*, p. 344.
88. Simkins, *Haig and the Army Commanders*, p. 84.
89. In December 1917 War Office intelligence estimated that in the Egypt–Palestine theatre the British had a rifle-strength of 96,000 against 21,000. See Lloyd George's remarks at the Cabinet Committee on Manpower, 1st Meeting, 10 December 1917, TNA PRO CAB 27/14.

CHAPTER 13

1. I. Passingham, *Pillars of Fire: The Battle of Messines Ridge, June 1917* (Stroud: Sutton) 1998, pp. 5–8.
2. P. Barton, P. Doyle, J. Vandewalle, *Beneath Flanders' Fields: The Tunnellers' War 1914–18* (Staplehurst: Spellmount) 2004, pp. 15–161.
3. J. Edmonds, *Military Operations in France and Belgium 1917, Vol. II, 7th June – 10th November* (London: HMSO) 1948, pp. 1–2 and Appendix 1, pp. 316–17.
4. Haig's diary, 26 December 1915.
5. Hunter-Weston, "A note on the projected landing at Ostende", 24 February 1916, quoted in A. Wiest, *Passchendaele and the Royal Navy* (Westport, Conn.: Greenwood) 1995, p. 47.
6. "General Sir Henry Rawlinson's Proposals for the Attack By The British Fourth Army On the Ypres Front", 27 February 1916, Appendix III, Edmonds, *1917, Vol. II*, p. 399.
7. Edmonds, *1917, Vol. II*, pp. 9–11.
8. GHQ to Second Army, 6 January 1917, TNA PRO WO 158/214.
9. Edmonds, *1917, Vol. II*, pp. 15–17 and "GHQ Instruction on the Formation of a Special Sub-Section Of The Operations Section Of The General Staff", 8 January 1917, Appendix VI, pp. 407–9.
10. Rawlinson to GHQ, 9 February 1917, TNA PRO WO 158/214.
11. Macmullen to Davidson, 15 January 1917, TNA PRO WO 158/214 and "Memorandum by Operations Section, General Staff", 14 February 1917, Appendix VII, Edmonds, *1917, Vol. II*, pp. 410–11.
12. Haig's diary, 30 April 1917. Edmonds, *1917, Vol. II*, pp. 18–19.

13. Cabinet Paper G.T. 477, 17 April 1917, TNA PRO CAB 24/10.
14. J. Grigg, *Lloyd George, War Leader 1916–1919* (London: Allen Lane) 2002, p. 155.
15. Haig's diary, 18 April 1917. Maurice to Haig, 18 April 1917 and Haig to Robertson, 19 April 1917.
16. Memorandum by Hankey, 18 April 1917, TNA PRO CAB 63/20.
17. "Record of a Conference held at NOYELLE VION at 11 a.m. on the 30th April, 1917", O.A.D. 426, 1 May 1917, TNA PRO WO 158/311.
18. Haig's diary, 30 April 1917.
19. *Ibid.*, 1 May 1917 and Haig to War Cabinet, 1 May 1917.
20. Grigg, pp. 158–9. D. Woodward, *Lloyd George and the Generals* (London: Frank Cass) 2004, pp. 162–70. War Cabinet Minutes, 1 May 1917, TNA PRO CAB 23/13.
21. Haig's diary, 3 May 1917.
22. Anglo-French Conference, 4–5 May 1917, TNA PRO CAB 28/2.
23. Haig's diary, 4 May 1917.
24. On Lloyd George at GHQ on 7 May see J. Charteris, *At GHQ* (London: Cassell) 1931, pp. 223–4. On the need for active French co-operation see Robertson to Haig, 14 May 1917, Acc. 3155/113, Haig Papers, NLS.
25. "Note of the proceedings of an Army Commanders' Conference held at DOULLENS on Monday the 7th May 1917, at 11 a.m.", O.A.D. 291/26, 7 May 1917, TNA PRO WO 158/311.
26. "For the personal information of Army Commanders and the Cavalry Corps Commander: Record of instructions issued verbally by the Field-Marshal Commanding-in-Chief ... ", O.A.D. 434, 7 May 1917, TNA PRO WO 158/311. Haig to Robertson, 16 May 1917, quoted in Wiest, *Passchendaele*, p. 93.
27. Esher to Robertson, 11 May 1917, quoted in Woodward, *Lloyd George*, p. 165.
28. Haig's diary, 18 May 1917. E. Greenhalgh, *Victory through Coalition: Britain and France during the First World War* (Cambridge: Cambridge University Press) 2005, p. 149.
29. Wilson to Haig, 20 May 1917, Acc. 3155/113, Haig Papers, NLS.
30. Wilson's diary, 2 June 1917, HHW 26, Wilson Papers, IWM.
31. Charteris, *At GHQ*, p. 225.
32. Haig's diary, 2 June 1917.
33. Woodward, *Lloyd George*, p. 169.
34. Advanced GHQ to Army Commanders, O.A.D. 799, 5 June 1917, TNA PRO WO 158/311.
35. C. Bean, *The Australian Imperial Force in France: 1917* (Sydney: Angus and Robertson) 1943, pp. 598–9. Edmonds, *1917, Vol. II*, pp. 90–5.
36. *Ibid.*, pp. 41–4.
37. Second Army, G.68, 10 March 1917, TNA PRO WO 158/215.
38. Edmonds, *1917, Vol. II*, pp. 41–9.
39. *Ibid.*, pp. 32–4.
40. Second Army to VIII, IX, X and II Anzac Corps, G. 68, 10 March 1917, with marginal notes by Haig. Second Army to GHQ G. 366, 20 March 1917 and GHQ to Second Army, O.A.D. 349, TNA PRO WO 158/215.

41. R. Prior and T. Wilson, *Passchendaele the Untold Story* (London: Yale) 1996, p. 58. "Second Army Operations Order No. 1", 10 May 1917 and "Second Army Operations Order No. 2", 19 May 1917, TNA PRO WO 158/215.

42. Edmonds, *1917, Vol. II*, p. 19. Prior and Wilson, *Passchendaele*, p. 58. Haig's diary, 20–24 May 1917.

43. Haig's diary, 22 May 1917.

44. GHQ to Plumer, 29 May 1917, TNA PRO WO 158/215.

45. Passingham, *Pillars of Fire*, pp. 94–109.

46. *Ibid.*, pp. 109–17.

47. *Ibid.*, pp. 117–26.

48. *Ibid.*, pp. 126–33.

49. Edmonds, *1917, Vol. II*, p. 87.

50. Local German commanders argued against an Army Group proposal to anticipate the British attack on the Ridge by withdrawal to the Oostaverne Position because they considered it untenable with the Ridge itself in British hands. Bean, *Australian Force*, pp. 598–9.

51. Edmonds, *1917, Vol. II*, pp. 87–8. Passingham, *Pillars of Fire*, pp. 163–5.

52. Haig's diary, 7 June 1917.

53. T. Travers, *The Killing Ground: The British Army, The Western Front And The Emergence Of Modern Warfare, 1900–1918* (London: Allen and Unwin) 1987, p. 105.

54. Haig's diary, 7 June 1917.

55. GHQ to Second Army, O.A.D. 458, 24 May 1917, TNA PRO WO 158/215. Haig's diary 8–14 June. Edmonds, *1917, Vol. II*, pp. 88–90.

56. Minutes of War Cabinet 156, 6 June 1917, TNA PRO CAB 23/3.

57. Note by Lord Milner, 7 June 1917 and Minutes of War Cabinet, 159A, 8 June 1917, TNA PRO CAB 23/16. "Forecast of the Arrival of American Land Forces in France" by Major-General Tom Bridges, 14 June 1917, TNA PRO CAB 27/7. Minutes of the Cabinet Committee on War Policy, 7th Meeting, 19 June 1917, TNA PRO CAB 27/6.

58. Minutes of War Cabinet 159, para. 13, 8 June 1917, TNA PRO CAB 23/3. Quoted in Woodward, *Lloyd George*, p. 170.

59. Woodward, *Lloyd George*, p. 172.

60. "Conference held at ABBEVILLE on the 7th June 1917 between General Foch and General Sir William Robertson", TNA PRO WO 106/1513.

61. Haig's diary, 9 June 1917.

62. *Ibid.*, 10 June 1917.

63. Robertson to Haig, 13 June 1917, Acc. 3155/114, Haig Papers, NLS.

64. "Memorandum on the Present Situation and Future Plans", Appendix XII, Edmonds, *1917, Vol. II*, pp. 423–7.

65. Haig's diary, 14 June 1917.

66. *Ibid.*, 17–19 June 1917. Cabinet Committee on War Policy, 7th Meeting, 19 June 1917, TNA PRO CAB 27/6.

67. Haig's diary, 19–25 June 1917.

68. Minutes of the Cabinet Committee on War Policy, 9th Meeting, 20 June 1917, TNA PRO CAB 27/6.

69. Hankey's diary, 30 June 1917, HNKY 1/3, Hankey Papers, Churchill College, Cambridge. Minutes of the Cabinet Committee on War Policy, 11th Meeting, 25 June 1917, TNA CAB 27/6. Haig's diary, 25 June 1917.

70. D. Woodward, *Field Marshal Sir William Robertson: Chief of the General Staff in the Great War* (Westport, Conn.: Praeger) 1998, p. 137.

71. Robertson to Kiggell, 5 July 1916, 814/65, and Robertson to Haig, 20 April 1917, 7/7/21, Robertson Papers, LHCMA.

72. Haig's diary, 9 May 1917.

73. *Ibid.*, 24 June 1917. K. Grieves, *Sir Eric Geddes: Business and Government in War and Peace* (Manchester: Manchester University Press) 1989, p. 41.

74. Haig's diary, 26 June 1917. Grieves, *Geddes*, p. 44.

75. K. Jeffery, *Field Marshal Sir Henry Wilson: A Political Soldier* (Oxford: Oxford University Press) 2006, pp. 192–5.

76. Woodward, *Lloyd George*, p. 172.

77. Haig's diary, 28 June 1917.

78. Jeffery, *Wilson*, p. 195.

79. Haig's diary, 26 June 1916. Woodward, *Lloyd George*, p. 182.

80. "Talk with Maurice Hankey, at United Service Club, 8 December 1932", 11/1932/45, Liddell Hart Papers, LHCMA.

81. Haig's diary, 25–27 June 1917.

CHAPTER 14

1. A. Becke, *Order of Battle Part 4: The Army Council, GHQs, Armies and Corps 1914–1918* (London: HMSO) 1945, p. 113.

2. G. Wynne, *If Germany Attacks* (Westport, Conn.: Greenwood) 1976, pp. 282–98. R. Prior and T. Wilson, *Passchendaele: The Untold Story* (London: Yale) 1996, pp. 71–3.

3. J. Bruce and K. Kelly, "The Royal Flying Corps and the Struggle for Supremacy over the Salient". In P. Liddle, *Passchendaele in Perspective: The Third Battle of Ypres* (Barnsley: Leo Cooper) 1997, pp. 159–65. M. Farndale, *History of the Royal Regiment of Artillery: Western Front 1914–18* (London: Royal Artillery Institution) 1986, p. 199.

4. J. Edmonds, *Military Operations France and Belgium 1917, Vol II 7 June – 10 November* (London: HMSO) 1948, pp. 139–41 and 147. CM, Carthy, "Queen of the Battlefield: The Development of Command, Organisation and Tactics in the British Infantry Battalions during the Great War". In G. Sheffield and D. Todman, *Command and Control on the Western Front: The British Army Experience 1914–18* (Staplehurst: Spellmount) 2004, pp. 173–93.

5. Fifth Army to its corps, S.G. 671/1, 7 June 1917, TNA PRO WO 158/249. Fifth Army to its corps, 27 June 1917, Appendix III in Edmonds, *1917, Vol. II*, pp. 431–2.

6. Edmonds, *1917, Vol. II*, p. 132.

7. Becke, *Part 4: The Army Council*, p. 12.

8. Davidson to Kiggell, 26 June 1917, TNA PRO 158/249.

9. J. Davidson, *Haig: Master of the Field* (London: Peter Nevill) 1953, pp. 29–30.

10. "Memorandum by Sir Hubert Gough", 26 (or 28?) June 1917, TNA PRO 158/249.

11. GHQ to Plumer, O.A.D. 415, 15 June 1917, TNA PRO 158/249.

12. Davidson, *Haig*, pp. 31–2. Edmonds, *1917, Vol. II*, p. 129.

13. Davidson, *Haig*, pp. 31–2.

14. H. Gough, *The Fifth Army* (London: Hodder and Stoughton) 1931, p. 198.

15. Haig's diary, 27–30 June 1917.

16. Fifth Army S.G. 657/49, 30 June, TNA PRO WO 158/249.

17. Edmonds, *1917, Vol. II*, p. 132.

18. Haig's diary, 7 and 12 July 1917 and "Conference at WATOU, 12/717", 12 July 1917, TNA PRO WO 158/249.

19. Becke, *Part 4: The Army Council*, p. 101.

20. Edmonds, *1917, Vol. II*, pp. 116–22.

21. J. Charteris, *At GHQ* (London: Cassell) 1931, pp. 234–5.

22. Edmonds, *1917, Vol. II*, p. 122. Haig to Robertson, 15 July 1917, 7/7/37, Robertson Papers, LHCMA.

23. Haig's diary, 11 and 28 July 1917.

24. *Ibid.*, 8, 11 and 28 July 1917. Farndale, *History of the Royal Regiment of Artillery*, pp. 199–201.

25. Haig's diary, 25–28 July. Farndale, *History of the Royal Regiment of Artillery*, p. 201.

26. Anthoine to Haig, 21 July 1917 and Kiggell to Gough, O.A.D. 567, 23 July 1917, TNA PRO WO 158/249. Charteris, *At GHQ*, p. 237.

27. Kiggell to the Armies, O.A.D. 571, 25 July 1917, TNA PRO WO 158/249.

28. Robertson to Haig, 30 June 1917, 7/7/33, Robertson Papers, LHCMA.

29. Robertson to Haig 6 July 1917, 8/5/20 and 18 July 1917, 7/7/38, Robertson Papers, LHCMA.

30. Haig to Robertson, 21 July 1917, Acc. 3155 No. 115, Haig Papers, NLS.

31. Robertson to Haig, 21 July 1917, 7/7/40, Robertson Papers, LHCMA.

32. Haig's diary 30 and 31 July 1917. Becke, *Part 4: The Army Council*, pp. 24–6.

33. Edmonds, *1917, Vol. II*, pp. 146–77.

34. Prior and Wilson, *Passchendaele*, p. 95. Adv. GHQ to First French Army, Fifth Army and Second Army, O.A.D. 581, 1 August 1917, TNA PRO WO 158/311. Haig to Robertson, "Report on the battle of 31st July, 1917, and its results", O.A.D. 589, 4 August 1917, Acc. 3155, No. 114, Haig Papers, NLS.

35. Haig's diary, 31 July 1917.

36. J. Stewart and J. Buchan, *The Fifteenth (Scottish) Division 1914–1919* (Edinburgh: William Blackwood) 1926, pp. 168–72. Haig's diary, 1 August 1917.

37. J. Hussey, "The Flanders Battle Ground and the Weather in 1917". In Liddle, *Passchendaele in Perspective*, pp. 140–58.

38. Prior and Wilson, *Passchendaele*, pp. 98–100.

39. Davidson, *Haig*, p. 35. Haig's diary, 2 August 1917. Gough, *The Fifth Army*, p. 199.

40. Kiggell to Gough, 7 August 1917, 4/114, Kiggell Papers, LHCMA and Kiggell to the Army Commanders, 7 August 1917, O.B./2089, TNA PRO WO 256/21. Haig's diary, 8 August 1917.

41. A. Farrar-Hockley, *Goughie: The Life of General Sir Hubert Gough GCB, GCMG, KCVO* (London: Hart Davis, MacGibbon) 1975, p. 223. G. H. F. Nicholls, *The 18th Division in the Great War* (London: Blackwood) 1922, pp. 214–26. Prior and Wilson, *Passchendaele*, pp. 101–2.

42. Haig's diary, 16 August 1917. Prior and Wilson, *Passchendaele*, pp. 101–4.

43. Haig's diary, 19–27 August 1917. Prior and Wilson, *Passchendaele*, pp. 106–8. "Report on Tank Operations, 19 August 1917", n.d., TNA PRO 95/92. "XVIII Corps Report On Operations, August 19th 1917", TNA PRO WO 95/951.

44. Farrar-Hockley, *Goughie*, pp. 227–9.

45. Cabinet paper, G.T. 1621, 4 August 1917, TNA PRO CAB 24/22.

46. Robertson to Haig, 9 August, 7/7/42, Robertson Papers.

47. Haig to Robertson, 13 August 1917, 7/7/44, Robertson Papers.

48. Haig's diary, 19 August 1917.

49. Haig's diary, 24 August 1917.

50. GHQ to Gough, 28 August 1917, TNA PRO WO 158/250.

51. *Ibid.*, O.A.D. 609, 28 July 1917 and "Notes on a Conference held at Cassel, at 11.30 a.m. on Thursday, 30th August 1917", TNA PRO 158/250. Farrar-Hockley, *Goughie*, pp. 230–2.

52. Haig to Robertson, "Memo. Pointing out the effect on present offensive operations of withdrawing guns from the Western front", 3 September 1917 and Haig to Robertson, 8 September 1917, Acc. 3155, No. 117, Haig Papers, NLS. Haig's diary, 1–11 September 1917.

53. G. Powell, *Plumer: The Soldiers' General* (Barnsley: Leo Cooper) 1990, pp. 210–14.

54. Edmonds, *1917, Vol. II*, pp. 239–77. J. Lee, "Command and Control in Battle; British Divisions on the Menin Road Ridge", 20 September 1917". In G. Sheffield and D. Todman (eds.) *Command and Control on the Western Front* (Staplehurst: Spellmount), 2004, pp. 119–38.

55. GHQ to Plumer and Gough, O.A.D. 628, 21 September 1917, TNA PRO WO 158/250 and Haig's diary, 21 September 1917.

56. Edmonds, *1917, Vol. II*, pp. 281–4.

57. *Ibid.*, pp. 284–95.

58. Haig's diary, 26 and 28 September 1917.

59. Edmonds, *1917, Vol. II*, p. 297. Prior and Wilson, *Passchendaele*, pp. 133–4.

60. Haig's diary, 2 October 1917.

61. Prior and Wilson, *Passchendaele*, pp. 134–9. Haig's diary, 4 October 1917.

62. Robertson to Haig, 13 September 1917, 7/7/51, Robertson Papers, LHCMA.

63. Haig's diary, 26 September 1917.

64. Robertson to Haig, 27 September 1917, 7/7/54, Robertson Papers, LHCMA.

65. Robertson to Haig, 9 October 1917, Acc. 3155, No 118, Haig Papers, NLS.

66. Prior and Wilson, *Passchendaele*, pp. 159–60. Farndale, *History of the Royal Regiment of Artillery*, p. 211.

67. Haig's diary, 7, 8, 9, 13 October 1917.

68. *Ibid.*, 4 October 1917.

69. Edmonds, *1917, Vol. II*, pp. 323–7.

70. Haig's diary 9 and 10 October. Prior and Wilson, *Passchendaele*, pp. 166–9.

71. *Ibid.*, 12 October 1917.
72. *Ibid.*, 15 October 1917. "The Manpower and Internal Conditions of the Central Powers: Note by the Director of Military Intelligence", W.P. 49, 1 October 1917 and manuscript comments by Haig dated 14 October. Haig to Robertson, O.A.D. 672, 16 October 1917, enclosing his own memorandum on "German Manpower and Moral", Acc. 3155 No. 18, Haig Papers, NLS.
73. Haig's diary, 13 October 1917.
74. A. M. J. Hyatt, *Sir Arthur Currie: A Military Biography* (Toronto: University of Toronto Press) 1987, pp. 68–83 and *passim*, and D. Oliver, "The Canadians at Passchendaele". In Liddle, *Passchendaele in Perspective*, pp. 255–71.
75. Edmonds, *1917, Vol. II*, pp. 349–52. Haig's diary, 26 October 1917.
76. Prior and Wilson, *Passchendaele*, pp. 175–7. Haig's diary, 30 and 31 October 1917.
77. Prior and Wilson, *Passchendaele*, p. 179.
78. GHQ to Rawlinson and Byng, O.A.D. 291/29, 13 December 1917, TNA PRO WO 158/311.
79. B. Bond, *The Unquiet Western Front* (Cambridge: Cambridge University Press) 2002, pp. 14, 18, 45–6.
80. On the recovery of French morale see Allain Bernède, "Third Ypres and the Restoration of Confidence in the Ranks of the French Army". In Liddle, *Passchendaele in Perspective*, pp. 88–101. On the French high command's lack of enthusiasm for Third Ypres see D. French, *The Strategy of the Lloyd George Coalition 1916–18* (Oxford: Clarendon) 1995, p. 126. On Haig's increasing emphasis on helping the French as a justification for Third Ypres after the fact see T. Travers, *How the War Was Won: Command and Technology in the British Army on the Western Front 1917–1918* (London: Routledge) 1992, p. 18.
81. Prior and Wilson, *Passchendaele*, p. 195. B. Bond, "Passchendaele: Verdicts, Past and Present". In Liddle, *Passchendaele in Perspective*, pp. 486–7. The estimate that Allied casualties at Third Ypres exceeded German by approximately a quarter is from J. Mc Randle and J. Quirk, "The Blood Test Revisted: A New Look At German Casualty Counts in World War I", *The Journal of Military History*, Vol. 70, No. 3, July 2006.
82. On the peculiar horror of some phases of Third Ypres see Edmonds, *1917, Vol. II*, pp. 208–10, and P. Liddle, "Passchendaele Experienced: Soldiering in the Salient during the Third Battle of Ypres". In Liddle, *Passchendaele in Perspective*, pp. 305–6. On its impact on British army morale see D. Woodward, *Lloyd George and the Generals* (London: Frank Cass) 2004, p. 230, and Prior and Wilson, *Passchendaele*, p. 196. On its effect on the Germans, see G. Werth, "Flanders 1917 and the German Soldier". In Liddle, *Passchendaele in Perspective*, pp. 324–32. On the greater proportional impact on the British than on the Germans: D. Stevenson, *1914–1918: The History of the First World War* (London: Allen Lane) 2004, pp. 336–7.

CHAPTER 15

1. B. Millman, *Pessimism and British War Policy 1916–1918* (London: Frank Cass) 2001, pp. 176–98.

2. Bonar Law to Lloyd George, 18 August 1917, quoted in D. Woodward, *Lloyd George and the Generals* (London: Frank Cass) 2004, p. 200.

3. Haig's diary, 12 March 1917 and 26 December 1917.

4. Milner to Curzon, 17 October 1917, quoted in Millman, *Pessimism*, p. 130.

5. Millman, *Pessimism*, pp. 112–54.

6. Haig to Robertson, 13 August 1917, I/33/44, Robertson papers, LHCMA. Haig's diary, 15 October 1917. Woodward, *Lloyd George*, p. 200.

7. Derby to Haig, 20 February 1917, Acc. 3155, No. 347, Haig Papers, NLS.

8. S. Badsey and P. Taylor, "Images of Battle: The Press Propaganda and Passchendaele". In P. Liddle (ed.) *Passchendaele in Perspective: The Third Battle of Ypres* (Barnsley: Leo Cooper) 1997, p. 377.

9. Robertson to Haig, 15 September 1917, I/23/51, Robertson Papers, LHCMA.

10. J. Bourne, *Britain and the Great War 1914–1918* (London: Edward Arnold) 1989, pp. 209–10.

11. J. Charteris, *At GHQ* (London: Cassell) 1931, pp. 253–4.

12. Haig's diary, 12 September 1917.

13. Woodward, *Lloyd George*, pp. 223–5.

14. Badsey and Taylor, "Images of Battle", pp. 383–5.

15. *Ibid.*, p. 387.

16. Robertson to Haig, 13 June 1917, Acc. 3155, No. 114, Haig Papers, NLS.

17. D. Stevenson, *1914–1918: The History of the First World War* (London: Allen Lane) 2004, pp. 377–9.

18. G. Powell, *Plumer, The Soldier's General: A Biography of Field Marshal Viscout Plumer of Messines* (Barnsley: Leo Cooper) 1990, p. 234.

19. Haig's diary, 7 November 1917.

20. Minutes of War Cabinet 259A, 30 October 1917, TNA PRO CAB 23/13.

21. Haig's diary, 4 November 1917.

22. *Ibid.*, 10 November 1917.

23. J. Edmonds, *Military Operations, France and Belgium, 1917, Vol. II* (London: HMSO) 1948, p. 360.

24. J. Grigg, *Lloyd George: War Leader, 1916–1918* (London: Allen Lane) 2002, pp. 285–6 and pp. 287–9.

25. Woodward, *Lloyd George*, pp. 225–7.

26. Haig's diary, 14 November, and Haig to Lady Haig, 14 and 18 November 1917.

27. T. Travers, *How The War Was Won: Command and Technology in the British Army on the Western Front 1917–1918* (London: Routledge) 1992, p. 19. J. F. C. Fuller, *Memoirs of an Unconventional Soldier* (London: Nicholson and Watson) 1936, pp. 168–219.

28. Tank Corps War Diary, 3 and 4 August 1917, TNA PRO WO 95/92. Elles, "Project for the Use of Tanks on the First Army Front", 18 September 1917, TNA PRO WO 158/835. J. P. Harris, *Men, Ideas and Tanks: British Military Thought and Armoured Forces 1903–1939* (Manchester: Manchester University Press) 1995, pp. 108–10. C. B. Hammond, "The Theory And Practice of Tank Co-operation With Other Arms", PhD thesis, University of Birmingham, 2005, pp. 179–83.

29. J. Williams, *Byng of Vimy: General and Governor-General* (London: Leo Cooper) 1992, pp. 172–3.

30. *Ibid.*, p. 174, and W. Miles, *Military Operations in France and Belgium 1917: The Battle of Cambrai* (London: HMSO) 1948, pp. 4–5.

31. Miles, *Cambrai*, p. 6.

32. *Ibid.*, pp. 6–7.

33. Woollcombe to Elles, 23 August 1917, IV Corps, No. H.R.S. 1-A, with attached "Project for a Surprise Attack on the Flesquières-Havrincourt Ridge", TNA PRO WO 158/396.

34. Miles, *Cambrai*, pp. 7–8.

35. Haig's diary 16 and 17 September 1917.

36. Miles, *Cambrai*, p. 9, and Haig's diary, 13 October 1917.

37. "Draft Scheme for operation GY", Third Army No. G.Y. 1/1, 25 October 1917, TNA PRO WO 95/366.

38. Byng to Advanced GHQ, 10 August 1917, TNA PRO WO 158/311.

39. Miles, *Cambrai*, pp. 17–19.

40. Williams, *Byng*, p. 182. Miles, *Cambrai*, p. 18.

41. GHQ to Byng, O.A.D. 690, 3 November 1917. Miles, *Cambrai*, pp. 17–18.

42. Miles, *Cambrai*, p. 19.

43. "Operation GY", 13 November 1917, Appendix 1, in Miles, *Cambrai*, pp. 306–9.

44. Miles, *Cambrai*, p. 10.

45. G. A. B Dewar and J. H. Boraston, *Sir Douglas Haig's Command* (London: Constable) 1929, p. 389.

46. Williams, *Byng*, p. 182. Haig to Robertson, 15 November 1917.

47. Haig's diary, 12–16 November 1917.

48. "Notes on Conference Held At Headquarters Tank Corps on 25th and 26th October 1917", Section 4, Training with Infantry", I/BCI/2/15, Fuller Papers, LHCMA. "Tank and Infantry Operations Without Methodical Artillery Preparation", 30 October 1917, section 9, TNA PRO WO 95/92. Hammond, "Theory and Practice of Tank Co-operation", p. 185.

49. Haig's diary, 19 November 1917.

50. IV Corps No. 17/4/2G "Operation G.Y.", 14 November 1917, IV Corps Operations Order No. 320, 15 November 1917. III Corps Operations Order No. 224, 16 November 1916, TNA PRO WO 158/319. C. Falls, *The History of the 36th Ulster Division* (London: McCaw, Stevenson and Orr) 1922, pp. 144–9.

51. Third Army, "Operation G.Y.", para. 6. VI Corps Operations Order No. 23, 15 November 1917. VII Corps Order No. 197, 18 November 1917, TNA WO 158/319.

52. Cavalry Corps: "Report on operations commencing 20th November 1917", 13 December 1917, TNA PRO WO 158/316. Anglesey, Marquis of *A History of the British Cavalry 1816–1919, Vol. 8: The Western Front 1915–1918* (Barnsley: Leo Cooper) 1997, pp. 107–11.

53. M. Farndale, *History of the Royal Regiment of Artillery: Western Front 1914–18* (London: Royal Artillery Institution), pp. 216–21.

54. IV Corps Order No. 320, 15 November 1917, TNA PRO WO 158/319.

55. Farndale, *History of the Royal Regiment of Artillery*, p. 219.
56. Miles, *Cambrai*, pp. 46–51.
57. IV Corps, "Havrincourt – Bourlon Wood Operation, 20th–25th November 1917, Narrative of Operations", n.d., TNA PRO WO 158/319. F. W. Bewsher, *The History of the 51st (Highland) Division 1914–18* (Edinburgh: Blackwood) 1921, pp. 245–50. Hammond, "Theory and Practice of Tank Co-Operation", pp. 205–9. J. L. Gibot and P. Gorczynski, *En Suivant Les Tanks: Cambrai 20 Novembre–7 Decembre 1917* (Privately published) 1997, pp. 54–8.
58. "Summary of III Corps Operations for the month of November 1917", n.d., TNA PRO WO 158/319.
59. De Pree to Wilson, 14 December 1918, HHW 2/87/38, Wilson Papers, IWM. Cavalry Corps, "Report on operation", and Anglesey, *British Cavalry*, pp. 113–41.
60. III Corps, "Summary of Operations" and IV Corps, "Havrincourt – Bourlon Wood". Miles, *Cambrai*, pp. 88–91. Williams, *Byng*, pp. 192–3.
61. Haig's diary, 20 November 1917.
62. Miles, *Cambrai*, pp. 91–3.
63. *Ibid.*, pp. 23–4 and 90–1. Haig's diary, 20 November 1917.
64. Haig's diary, 21 November 1917. IV Corps, "Summary of Operations, from 20th to 28th November, 1917", n.d., TNA PRO WO 158/397. III Corps, "Summary of Operations for the Month of November 1917", TNA PRO WO 158/319.
65. Haig's diary, 21 November 1917.
66. *Ibid.*, 22 November 1917.
67. De Pree to Wilson, 14 December 1917, HHW 2/87/38, Wilson Papers, IWM. Haig's diary, 23 November 1917.
68. Haig's diary, 24 November 1917.
69. *Ibid.*, 25–28 November 1917.
70. On failures of communication, command and control in Third Army see Jeudwine to Vaughan, 22 December 1917, TNA PRO WO 158/320. On the fightin see Third Army, "Cambrai: Narrative of operations on 30th November", n.d., and "Narrative – 12th Division", n.d., TNA PRO WO 158/316. See also C. Headlam, *The Guards Division in The Great War, Vol. II* (London: John Murray) 1924, pp. 2–14.
71. Byng to GHQ, 18 December 1917, para. 8, TNA PRO WO 158/320. Farndale, *History of the Royal Regiment of Artillery*, p. 223.
72. W. Moore, *A Wood Called Bourlon: The Cover-up After Cambrai* (Sutton: Stroud) 1998, pp. 165–80.
73. Haig's diary, 30 November 1917.
74. On GHQ's arrangement of reinforcements and plea to the French see Miles, pp. 221–2. On blaming the reverse on incompetence and lack of resolution at junior levels see Byng to GHQ, 18 December 1917, para. 9, TNA PRO WO 158/320. On Byng's version being endorsed by GHQ and communicated to London, see Moore, *Bourlon*, pp. 171–2.
75. Haig's diary, 1 December 1917.
76. *Ibid.*, 2 and 3 December 1917.
77. *Ibid.*, 2, 5 and 19 December 1917.

78. Miles, *Cambrai*, pp. 273–4. S. Badsey, "Haig and the Press". In B. Bond and N. Cave, *Haig: A Reappraisal 70 Years On* (Barnsley: Leo Cooper) 1999, pp. 188–9.

79. See, for example, J. Terraine, *Douglas Haig: The Educated Soldier* (London: Hutchinson) 1963, pp. 381–3.

CHAPTER 16

1. W. Moore, *A Wood Called Bourlon: The Cover-up after Cambrai, 1917* (Stroud: Sutton) 1998, pp. 165–80.

2. S. Badsey, "Haig and the Press". In B. Bond and N. Cave (eds.), *Haig: A Reappraisal 70 Years On* (Barnsley: Leo Cooper) 1999, p. 189.

3. Though Robertson had been generally quite pessimistic about the strategic situation in late 1917, there is some evidence to suggest that Haig's success in the early stages of the Cambrai battle had temporarily brightened his mood. On 23 November 1917 he told ministers that "Germany's military power might be a good deal less than … we had thought to be the case." But he was, of course, soon to regret this brief seeming partial endorsement of the Charteris/Haig view of the world. R. Prior and T. Wilson, *Passchendaele: The Untold Story* (London: Yale University Press) 1996, pp. 188–90. On the bell-ringing see J. Charteris, *At GHQ* (London: Cassell) 1931, p. 290.

4. Haig's diary, 4 November 1917. C. Repington, *The First World War, Vol. II* (London: Constable) 1920, p. 148.

5. Moore, *Bourlon*, p. 165.

6. Minutes of War Cabinet 292, 5 December 1917, TNA PRO CAB 23/4. D. Woodward, *Lloyd George and the Generals* (London: Frank Cass) 2004, p. 231.

7. War Cabinet 292, TNA PRO CAB 23/4. G. De Groot, *Douglas Haig 1861–1928* (London: Unwin Hyman) 1988, p. 353.

8. Haig to Robertson, 9 December 1917, quoted in De Groot, *Douglas Haig*, p. 353.

9. Robertson to Haig, 11 December 1917, Acc. 3155, No. 120, Haig Papers, NLS.

10. Charteris, *At GHQ*, p. 272.

11. Badsey, "Haig and the Press," pp. 189–90.

12. J. Williams *Byng of Vimy: General and Governor-General* (Barnsley: Leo Cooper) 1992, p. 168. Woodward, *Lloyd George*, p. 232.

13. Charteris, *At GHQ*, p. 273.

14. Woodward, *Lloyd George*, p. 232.

15. Derby to Haig, 7 December 1917, Acc. 3155, No. 347, Haig Papers, NLS. Haig's diary, 9 December 1917.

16. Haig to Lady Haig, 23 November 1917.

17. Haig's diary, 9 December 1917.

18. Haig to Derby, 10 December 1917, quoted in De Groot, *Douglas Haig*, p. 354.

19. Haig's diary, 9 December and 14 December 1917.

20. Moore, *Bourlon*, pp. 168–9.

21. Moore, *Bourlon*, pp. 168 and 173.

22. Woodward, *Lloyd George*, pp. 230–1.

23. Haig's diary, 15 and 16 December 1917.

24. Becke, *Order of Battle, Part 4: The Army Council, GHQs, Armies and Corps 1914–1918* (London: HMSO) 1945, p. 12.

25. Byng to GHQ, 18 December 1917, TNA PRO WO 158/320.

26. Moore, *Bourlon*, p. 171. Williams, *Byng*, pp. 204–8.

27. Becke, *Part 4: The Army Council*, pp. 145, 153, 175.

28. Charteris, *At GHQ*, p. 267. Anglesey, *A History of British Cavalry 1816–1919* (Barnsley: Leo Cooper) 1997, p. 102.

29. Haig to Lady Haig, 14 December 1917.

30. Charteris, *At GHQ*, pp. 277–87.

31. G. Sheffield and J. Bourne, *Douglas Haig: War Diaries and Letters 1914–1918* (London: Weidenfeld and Nicolson) 2005, p. 38.

32. Robertson to Kiggell, 5 July 1917, 8/4/65, and Kiggell to Robertson, 14 July 1917, 7/6/56, Robertson Papers, LHCMA.

33. Kiggell to Gough, 7 August 1917, 4/114, Kiggell Papers, LHCMA.

34. Haig's diary, 20 December 1917.

35. *Ibid.*, 1 January 1918.

36. Becke, *Part 4: The Army Council*, p. 11.

37. *Ibid.*, p. 12.

38. *Ibid.*, p. 145.

39. *Ibid.*, p. 11.

40. S. Robbins, *British Generalship on the Western Front: Defeat into Victory* (London: Frank Cass) 2005, pp. 115 and 119–21.

41. J. M. Bourne, "Lawrence, Sir Herbert Alexander". In *Dictionary of National Biography, Vol. 32*, (Oxford: Oxford University Press), pp. 829–30, and Robbins, *Defeat into Victory*, pp. 119–20. Desmond Morton was the ADC who claimed that Haig hated to be told anything that conflicted with his preconceptions. Quoted in De Groot, *Douglas Haig*, p. 295.

42. Haig's diary, 26 December 1917.

43. "Memorandum on the Question of an extension of the British front", 15 December 1917, M.P.C., TNA PRO CAB 27/14.

44. Woodward, *Lloyd George*, p. 230. S. Badsey and P. Taylor, "Images of Battle: The Press, Propaganda and Passchendaele". In P. H. Liddle (ed.) *Passchendaele in Perspective: The Third Battle of Ypres* (Barnsley: Leo Cooper) 1997, p. 377. "The Morale of the British Army on the Western Front 1914–1918", Occasional Paper 2, Institute for the Study of War and Society, De Monfort University, Bedford, 1996. American officers attached to GHQ in December 1917 concluded that morale in the ranks of the British Army was "very low". See J. Beach, "British Intelligence and the German Army 1914–1918", PhD thesis, University of London, 2005, p. 249.

45. Haig's diary, 7 December 1917.

46. Charteris, *At GHQ*, p. 273.

47. *Ibid.*, p. 274.

48. Woodward, *Lloyd George*, p. 235. "Manpower for the Army: Memorandum by the Army Council with reference to the request of the Prime Minister for

concrete proposals as to how more men are to be obtained for the Army", 27/Gen. No. 6622, Appendix 1, Army Council 239th Meeting, 3 December 1917, TNA PRO WO 163/22.

49. D. French, *The Strategy of the Lloyd George Coalition* (Oxford: Clarendon) 1995, pp. 171–92.
50. Woodward, *Lloyd George*, pp. 232–9.
51. French, *Strategy*, pp. 171–95.
52. Woodward, *Lloyd George*, pp. 234, 238, 241–2, 244.
53. Memorandum by Hankey, paras. 42 and 43, 18 April 1917, TNA PRO CAB 63/20.
54. Haig's diary, 23 December 1917 and 2 January 1918.
55. Woodward, *Lloyd George*, p. 240.
56. Haig's diary, 28 December 1917.
57. *Ibid.*, 2 January 1918.
58. *Ibid.*, 7 January 1918. Minutes of War Cabinet 316A, 7 January 1918, TNA PRO CAB 23/13.
59. Haig's diary, 9 January 1918.
60. *Ibid.*, 10 January 1918.
61. French, *Strategy*, p. 186.
62. Haig's diary, 3 October 1917.
63. *Ibid.*, 14 January 1918.
64. Woodward, *Lloyd George*, p. 246.
65. Hankey diary, 18 January 1918, HNKY 1/3, Hankey Papers, Churchill College, Cambridge.
66. De Groot, *Douglas Haig*, p. 361.
67. Haig to Lady Haig, 2 January 1918.
68. Hankey to Lloyd George, 22 January 1918, quoted in Woodward, *Lloyd George*, p. 246.
69. J. Grigg, *Lloyd George: War Leader 1916–1918* (London: Penguin) 2003, pp. 380–3.
70. Woodward, *Lloyd George*, pp. 245–7.
71. *Ibid.*, p. 246.
72. Haig's diary, 26 January 1918.
73. Repington to Bonar Law, 16 November 1915, in A. J. A. Morris, *The Letters of Lieutenant-Colonel Charles à Court Repington CMG: Military Correspondent of The Times 1903–1918* (Stroud: Sutton) 1999, pp. 239–40.
74. Charteris, *At GHQ*, p. 157.
75. Woodward, *Lloyd George*, pp. 246–7. Haig's diary 27 January 1918.
76. Haig's diary, 29 January–2 February, and Haig to Lady Haig, 31 January 1918.
77. *Ibid.*, 2 February 1918.
78. Derby to Haig, 7 February 1918, and Haig to Derby 9 February 1918.
79. Haig's diary, 9 February 1918.
80. *Ibid.*, 11 February 1918.
81. *Ibid.*, 13 February 1918.
82. *Ibid.*, 15 February 1918.
83. *Ibid.*, 16 February 1918.
84. *Ibid.*, 17 February 1918.

85. Grigg, *War Leader*, p. 419.
86. Haig to Lady Haig, 14 January 1918.
87. Haig's diary, 17 February 1918.
88. *Ibid.*, 18 February 1918.
89. Woodward, *Lloyd George*, p. 274.
90. Becke, *Part 4: The Army Council*, p. 7.
91. Haig's diary, 19 February 1918.

CHAPTER 17

1. J. Charteris, *At GHQ* (London: Cassell) 1931, p. 273 and Appendix A, "Note on German Intentions", 6 December 1917. "The influence of increased strength on German intentions during 1918", Ia/43614, 7 January 1918. "Statement regarding present situation on Western front as given at the Conference of Army Commanders held at DOULLENS at 10 a.m. on 16th February 1918", O.A.D. 291/31, 17 February 1918. "Statement regarding the present situation on Western front as given at the Conference of Army Commanders held at DOULLENS on Saturday, 2nd March, 1918", O.A.D. 291/32/4, 3 March 1918. "Record of a Conference of Army Commanders held at DOULLENS on Saturday, 2nd March, 1918", O.A.D. 291/32/3, 3 March 1918, TNA PRO WO 158/311.
2. Charteris, *At GHQ*, pp. 273–4. Haig's diary, 14 March 1918. At a meeting at Downing Street on this date Haig said that, by June, he would have a desperate shortage of men "if [*sic*] the Enemy attacked".
3. Haig's diary, 19 March 1918.
4. *Ibid.*, 2 March 1918.
5. *Ibid.*, 7 and 9 January 1918. D. Woodward, *Lloyd George and the Generals* (London: Frank Cass) 2004, p. 235.
6. J. Edmonds, *Military Operations, France and Belgium 1918: The German March Offensive and its Preliminaries* (London: Macmillan and HMSO) 1935, pp. 47–56 and Appendix 7. Woodward, *Lloyd George*, pp. 301–2. M. Kitchen, *The German Offensives of 1918* (Stroud: Tempus) 2001, pp. 46–7.
7. Woodward, *Lloyd George*, p. 236.
8. *Ibid.*, p. 231.
9. Edmonds, *1918: The German March Offensive*, p. 52.
10. "Report of the Cabinet Committee on Manpower", 9 January 1918, TNA PRO CAB 24/4. Woodward, pp. 235–6. Edmonds, *1918: The German March Offensive*, p. 51.
11. Haig's diary, 29 March 1918.
12. R. F. Foster, *Modern Ireland: 1600–1972* (London: Allen Lane) 1988, pp. 487–90.
13. D. French, *The Strategy of the Lloyd George Coalition 1916–1918* (Oxford: Clarendon) 1995, pp. 182–7. Haig's diary, 23 December 1917, 10 March 1918.
14. Woodward, *Lloyd George*, p. 238.
15. Kitchen, *German Offensives*, pp. 58 and 79. "Note on the situation on the 2nd March 1918", Ia/46599, HQ Third Army (General Staff), section 5, p. 5, TNA PRO WO 158/311.

16. Haig's diary, 13 January 1918.

17. *Ibid.*, 18–21 January 1918.

18. Edmonds, *1918: The German March Offensive*, pp. 103–8, 142. Edmonds gives 192 as the figure for German infantry divisions on the Western Front on 21 March 1918. G. Fong's useful article, "The Movement of German Divisions to the Western Front 1917–1918", *War in History*, Vol. 7, No. 2, 2000, p. 209, gives a figure of 191.

19. "Memorandum on Defensive Measures Issued With O.A.D. 291/29 dated 14th December 1917", TNA PRO WO 158/311.

20. "Record of a Conference of Army Commanders held at Doullens at 10 a.m. 16th February, 1918", para. viii, TNA PRO WO 158/311.

21. Edmonds, *1918: The German March Offensive*, pp. 48 and 114–16. E. Greenhalgh, *Victory Through Coalition: Briatin and France during the First World War* (Cambridge: Cambridge University Press) 2005, pp. 188–9, gives some credit to Lloyd George's "pique" explanation for Haig's keeping the Fifth Army sector so weak.

22. A. F. Becke, *Order of Battle, Part 4: The Army Council, GHQs, Armies and Corps 1914–1918* (London: HMSO) 1945, p. 113.

23. H. Gough, *The Fifth Army* (London: Hodder) 1931, pp. 221–6.

24. *Ibid.*, pp. 227–31. Edmonds, *1918: The German March Offensive*, pp. 94–6 and Appendix 2, "Gough to GHQ S.G. 675/41, 1 February 1918".

25. Gough, *The Fifth Army*, pp. 232–3. Edmonds, *1918: The German March Offensive*, Appendix 12.

26. Lawrence to Gough, O.A.D. 781, 9 February, TNA PRO WO 158/311.

27. Gough, *The Fifth Army*, pp. 235–6.

28. Haig's diary, 13–15 February 1918.

29. Gough, *The Fifth Army*, p. 223. Derby to Haig, 5 March 1918, Acc. 3155/347, Haig Papers, NLS.

30. Gough, *The Fifth Army*, pp. 237–9.

31. "Record of a Conference held at Doullens at 10 a.m. 16th February 1918", O.A.D. 291/31, 17 February 1918. "Statement regarding present situation on Western front as given at the Conference of Army Commanders held at Doullens at 10.a.m. on 16th February 1918", 17 February 1918, TNA PRO WO 158/311. Lawrence to Byng, 12 February 1918, TNA WO 158/226.

32. Haig's diary, 25 February 1918.

33. French, *Strategy*, pp. 219–21.

34. Haig's diary, 2 March 1918. "Record of a Conference of Army Commanders held at Doullens on Saturday, 2nd March, 1918", O.A.D. 291/32/3, 3 March 1918. "Statement regarding the present situation on Western front as given to the Conference of Army Commanders held at Doullens on Saturday, 2nd March, 1918", O.A.D. 291/32/4, 3 March 1918. "Note on the Situation on the 2nd March 1918", Ia/45399, 3 March 1918, TNA WO 158/311.

35. Haig's diary, 2 March 1918. For a discussion of German deception planning at this period see D. French, "Failures of Intelligence: The Retreat to the Hindenburg Line and the March 1918 Offensives". In M. Dockrill and D. French, (eds.) *Strategy and Intelligence: British Policy during the First World*

War (London: Hambledon) 1996, pp. 67–95. Oddly, French does not discuss the principal deception that plagued the Allies until 25 March: the belief that a big German attack was imminent in the Champagne sector.

36. Kitchen, *German Offensives*, pp. 39–40.
37. O.A.D. 291/32/3, 3 March 1918, TNA PRO WO 158/311.
38. "Statement regarding present situation", para. 8, 17 February 1918, TNA PRO WO 158/311.
39. Haig's diary, 4 December 1917. "The Influence Of Increased Strength On German Intentions During 1918", Ia 436/4, 7 January 1918, TNA PRO WO 158/311.
40. J. M. Beach "British Intelligence and the German Army 1914–1918", PhD thesis, University of London, 2005, p. 248.
41. Edmonds, *1918: The German March Offensive*, Appendix 2.
42. Haig to Derby, 4 March 1918.
43. Haig's diary, 6 March 1918. R. Doughty, *Pyrrhic Victory: French Strategy and Operations in the Great War* (London: Belknap) 2005, pp. 413–14.
44. Haig's diary, 7–9 March 1918.
45. *Ibid.*, 12–14 March 1918.
46. *Ibid.*, 15 March 1918. Haig to War Office, O.B. 1937, 1 November 1916, 7/6/87, Robertson Papers, LHCMA.
47. D. Cooper, *Haig: The Second Volume* (London: Faber) 1936, p. 242. Haig's diary, 16 March 1918.
48. Haig's diary, 18 and 19 March 1918.
49. *Ibid.*, 21 March 1918.
50. Beach, *British Intelligence*, pp. 244–5.
51. Kitchen, *German Offensives*, pp. 62–6.
52. This argument is advanced in A. Simpson, *Directing Operations: British Corps Command On The Western Front 1914–18* (Stroud: Spellmount) 2006, pp. 131–4.
53. The quotation is from Captain Bond of 199th Infantry Brigade HQ in M. Middlebrook, *The Kaiser's Battle, 21 March 1918: The First Day of the German Spring Offensive* (London: Allen Lane) 1978, p. 156. Kitchen, *German Offensives*, pp. 62–7.
54. Haig's diary, 21 March 1918.
55. Greenhalgh, *Victory*, pp. 186–8. Simpson, *Directing Operations*, p. 142.
56. Gough, *The Fifth Army*, pp. 270–2.
57. Fifth Army Order No. 44, 9.45 p.m., 21 March 1918, TNA PRO WO 158/252.
58. Gough, *The Fifth Army*, p. 271.
59. Fifth Army, OB/A5555, 10.45 a.m., 22 March 1918, TNA PRO WO 158/252.
60. Simpson, *Directing Operations*, pp. 142–5.
61. Fifth Army Order, 9.57 p.m., 22 March 1918, TNA PRO WO 158/252. For a favourable interpretation of Maxse's decision making during the March crisis see J. Baynes, *Far From a Donkey: The Life of General Sir Ivor Maxse* (London: Brassey's) 1995, pp. 184–204. J. Williams, *Byng of Vimy: General and Governor-General* (Barnsley: Leo Cooper) 1983, p. 222.

62. Haig's diary, 22 March 1918. Haig to Pétain, 22 March 1918, TNA PRO 158/48.
63. Gough, *The Fifth Army*, p. 271.
64. Third Army War Diary, 21–24 March 1918, TNA PRO WO 158/369. "Short Account of Operations of Third Army From 21st March to 30th April 1918", n.d., TNA PRO WO 95/370.
65. GHQ to Byng, O.A.D. 291/29, 13 December 1917, TNA PRO WO 158/311. GHQ to Third Army, 10 March 1918, TNA PRO WO 158/226.
66. Lt. Col. Dill to Davidson, 11 February 1918 and Lawrence to Byng, 12 February 1918, TNA PRO WO 158/226.
67. Williams, *Byng*, pp. 223–7. A. H. Maude, *The 47th (London) Division* (London: Amalgamated Press) 1922, pp. 158–65.
68. "PROCES VERBAL of Conference between F.M. Commander-in-Chief and General Pétain, March 23rd, 1918, at 4 p.m.", O.A.D. 786, 23 March 1918, TNA PRO WO 158/48. Haig's diary, 23 March 1918. Greenhalgh, *Victory*, pp. 192–4.
69. "Record of a Conference held at the Commander-in-Chief's house at 7 p.m. on 23rd March 1918", O.A.D. 785, 23 March 1918, TNA WO 158/311.
70. Haig's diary, 23 March 1918.
71. "Conference at DURY at 11 p.m., Sunday, March 24th 1918", n.d., TNA PRO WO 158/48. Doughty, *The Fifth Army*, pp. 435–6.
72. Haig to Lady Haig, 22, 23 and 24 March 1918. Haig's diary 23 and 24 March 1918. Beach *British Intelligence*, pp. 250–2.
73. Haig's diary, 24 March 1918. Doughty, *The Fifth Army*, pp. 436–7.
74. Haig's diary, 25 March 1918.
75. E. Greenhalgh, "Myth and Memory: Sir Douglas Haig and the Imposition of Allied Unified Command in March 1918", *Journal of Military History*, Vol. 68, No. 3, July 2004, *passim*. J. Grigg, *Lloyd George: War Leader, 1916–1918* (London: Allen Lane) 2002, pp. 450–1. C. E. Callwell, *Field-Marshal Sir Henry Wilson Bart., G.C.B., D.S.O: His Life and Diaries, Vol. II* (London: Cassell) 1927, p. 75.
76. K. Jeffery, *Field Marshal Sir Henry Wilson: A Political Soldier* (Oxford: Oxford University Press) 2006, p. 220. Callwell, *Bart*, p. 76. Wilson diary, 24 March 1918, HHW 27, Wilson Papers, IWM.
77. Haig's diary, 25 March 1918. H. Høiback, *Command and Control in Military Crisis: Devious Decisions* (London: Frank Cass) 2003, pp. 38–45. Wilson diary, 25 March 1918, HHW 27, Wilson Papers, IWM. Callwell, *Bart*, p. 77.
78. Haig's diary, 25 March 1918. D. T. Zabecki, *The German 1918 Offensives* (New York: Routledge) 2006, p. 149.
79. Haig's diary, 26 March 1918. "Record of first conference held at DOULLENS, at 11 a.m., 26th March 1918", O.A.D. 793, 26 March 1918, TNA PRO WO 158/226.
80. Williams, *Byng*, p. 232. Edmonds, *1918: The German March Offensive*, p. 532.
81. "Record of Second Conference held at DOULLENS, at 11.40 a.m., 26th March 1918", O.A.D. 794, 26 March 1918, TNA PRO WO 158/226.
82. Haig's diary, 26 March 1918. "Record of Third Conference held at DOULLENS at 12 noon, 26th March 1918", O.A.D. 795, 26 March 1918,

TNA PRO WO 158/226. After seriously attacking Haig's typescript diary account of events of 24 and 25 March, Høiback, *Command and Control*, p. 53, essentially confirms Haig's version of the elevation of Foch at the third Doullens meeting on 26 March.

83. Haig's diary, 26 March 1918. Wilson's diary, 26 March 1918, HHW 27, IWM. Callwell, *Wilson*, p. 78.

84. Haig's diary, 29 March and 3 April 1918.

85. Gough, *The Fifth Army*, pp. 305–7.

86. Doughty, *Phyrric Victory*, pp. 438–9. Gough, *The Fifth Army*, pp. 310–11.

87. Edmonds, *1918: The German March Offensive*, pp. 518–20.

88. Kitchen, *German Offensives* pp. 85–92. Zabecki, *1918 Offensives*, pp. 113–14, downplays logistical breakdown as a cause of ultimate German failure and plays up Ludendorff's indecisiveness and poor decision making.

89. *Ibid.*, p. 79.

90. *Ibid.*, pp. 76–8.

91. Beach, *British Intelligence*, p. 253.

92. Zabecki, *1918 Offensives*, pp. 113–73, esp. pp. 154–5. Williams, *Byng*, pp. 234–5. Haig's diary, 28 March 1918.

93. Middlebrook, *The Kaiser's Battle*, pp. 334–58. Kitchen, *German Offensives*, p. 94.

94. Edmonds, *1918: The German March Offensive*, p. 533.

95. For a passionate defence of Fifth Army's fighting record by a contemporary see S. Sparrow, *The Fifth Army in March 1918* (London: John Lane) 1931, *passim.*

CHAPTER 18

1. Haig's diary, 2 April 1918. J. Beach, "British Intelligence and the German Army 1914–1918", PhD thesis, University of London, 2005, p. 253.

2. F. Foch, *Memoirs of Marshal Foch* (London: Heinemann) 1931, pp. 291–303.

3. Haig's diary, 26 March 1918.

4. *Ibid.*, 26 and 29 March 1918.

5. R. Prior and P. Wilson, *Command on the Western Front: The Military Career of Sir Henry Rawlinson* (Oxford: Blackwell) 1992, p. 286. H. Gough, *The Fifth Army* (London: Hodder and Stoughton) 1931, p. 315. Becke, *Order of Battle, Part 4: The Army Council, GHQs, Armies and Corps 1914–1918* (London: HMSO) 1945, p. 111.

6. Haig's diary, 29 March 1918. Becke, *Part 4: The Army Council*, p. 111.

7. Becke, *Part 4: The Army Council*, p. 119.

8. Haig's diary, 3 April 1918.

9. A. Farrar-Hockley, *Goughie: The Life of Sir Hubert Gough GCB, GCMG, KCVO* (London: Hart-Davis, Mac Gibbon) 1975, pp. 313–22.

10. Haig's diary, 5 April 1918.

11. Farrar-Hockley, *Goughie*, p. 324.

12. J. French, *The Strategy of the Lloyd George Coalition* (Oxford: Clarendon) 1995, p. 233.

13. Hankey's diary, 8 April 1918, quoted in French, *Strategy*, p. 233.

14. Wilson's diary, 8 April 1918, HHW 27, IWM. C. Callwell, *Field-Marshal Sir Henry Wilson: His Life and Diaries, Vol. II* (London: Cassell) 1927, p. 88.
15. D. Todman, "The Grand Lamasery Revisited: General Headquarters on the Western Front". In G. Sheffield and D. Todman, *Command on the Western Front: The British Army's Experience 1914–18* (Staplehurst: Spellmount) 2004, pp. 58–66.
16. Haig's diary, 1 April 1918.
17. *Ibid.*, 3 April 1918.
18. *Ibid.*
19. Haig's diary, 6 April 1918, and Haig to Foch, 6 April, quoted in D. Cooper, *Haig: The Second Volume* (London: Faber) 1936, pp. 268–9. Kitchen, *The German Offensives of 1918* (Stroud: Tempus) 2001, p. 99.
20. Haig's diary, 7 April 1918. The idea of a counter-offensive to disengage Amiens had already been in Foch's mind for a few days. GHQ to Byng and Rawlinson, O.A.D. 806, 4 April 1918, TNA PRO WO 158/226.
21. Kitchen, *German Offensives*, pp. 96–7.
22. Haig's diary, 8 and 9 April 1918.
23. Beach, "British Intelligence", pp. 254–5.
24. Horne to GHQ, First Army No. G.S. 1167, 14 June 1918. "Portuguese Corps, Second Division, Battle of the Lys, 9th April 1918, Summary of Events by Divisional Commander, General Gomes da Costa", n.d., and Haking to First Army, XI Corps, 16 August 1918, TNA PRO WO 158/75.
25. Kitchen, *German Offensives*, p. 102.
26. Haig's diary, 9 April 1918.
27. Kitchen, *German Offensives*, pp. 102–3.
28. D. Zabecki, *The German 1918 Offensives A Case Study in the Operational Level of War* (London: Taylor and Frances) 2006, p. 188. Haig's diary, 10 April 1918.
29. Zabecki, *1918 Offensives*, p. 189. Haig's diary, 11 April 1918.
30. J. Edmonds, *France and Belgium, 1918, March to April* (London: Macmillan) 1937, Appendix 10.
31. E. Greenhalgh, *Victory through Coalition: Britain and France During the First World War* (Cambridge: Cambridge University Press) 2005, pp. 206–7. Kitchen, *German Offensives*, pp. 103–6.
32. Haig's diary, 12 and 13 April 1918.
33. Callwell, *Wilson*, pp. 89 and 92. Greenhalgh, *Victory*, p. 203. Haig's diary, 14 April 1918.
34. Zabecki, *1918 Offensives*, p. 194. Kitchen, *German Offensives*, pp. 106–7.
35. Haig's diary, 15 April 1918.
36. Kitchen, *German Offensives*, p. 117. Zabecki, *1918 Offensives*, p. 194.
37. Haig's diary, 18 and 19 April 1918.
38. *Ibid.*, 26 December 1917 and 28 April 1918.
39. T.H. O'Brien, *Milner: Viscount of St. James's and Capetown 1854–1925* (London: Constable) 1979, pp. 287–90.
40. Haig's diary, 19 April 1918.
41. Kitchen, *German Offensives*, pp. 117–19.
42. *Ibid.*, pp. 119–21. Haig's diary, 25 and 26 April 1918.

43. Kitchen, *German Offensives*, p. 128.

44. Haig's diary, 27 April–May 1918.

45. Kitchen, *German Offensives*, p. 126. Beach, *British Intelligence*, pp. 257–9.

46. J. Grigg, *Lloyd George: War Leader 1916–1918* (London: Allen Lane) 2002, pp. 489–512.

47. D. Woodward, *Lloyd George and the Generals* (London: Frank Cass) 2004, p. 299.

48. Maurice's own version of events is contained in "The Story of the Crisis of May, 1918". In N. Maurice (ed.) *The Maurice Case* (Barnsley: Leo Cooper) 1972, pp. 91–116. Haig to Lady Haig, 7 May 1918.

49. Woodward, *Lloyd George*, pp. 303–4.

50. Haig to Lady Haig, 11 May 1918.

51. Haig's diary, 28 May 1918.

52. R. Doughty, *Pyrrhic Victory: French Strategy and Operations in the Great War* (London: Belknap) 2005, pp. 449–52.

53. Haig's diary, 28 May 1918.

54. Kitchen, *German Offensives*, pp. 150–4.

55. Haig's diary, 31 May 1918. Beach, *British Intelligence*, p. 261.

56. Haig's diary, 1 June 1918.

57. *Ibid.*, 3 June 1918. Cooper, *Haig*, pp. 306–8.

58. Haig's diary, 4 June 1918.

59. *Ibid.*, 7 June 1918.

60. *Ibid.*, 13 and 18 June 1918.

61. Beach, *British Intelligence*, p. 262. Haig's diary, 18 and 22 June 1918.

62. Haig's diary, 21 and 28 June and 31 July 1918. D. Dutton (ed.) *Paris 1918– The War Diary of the British Ambassador, the 17th Earl of Derby* (Liverpool: Liverpool University Press) 2001, pp. 76–9.

63. Haig's diary, 25 June 1918. P. A. Pedersen, *Monash and Military Commander* (Melbourne: Melbourne University Press) 1985, pp. 226–33. Haig's diary, 25 June 1918.

64. R. Rhodes-James, *Gallipoli* (London: Batsford) 1965, pp. 271–3. G. Serle, *John Monash: A Biography* (Melbourne: Melbourne University Press) 1982, pp. 292–324.

65. Haig's diary, 1 July 1918.

66. *Ibid.*, 4–6 July 1918.

67. Beach, *British Intelligence*, p. 263.

68. Haig's diary, 14 and 15 July 1918.

69. Kitchen, *German Offensives*, pp. 182–7. Haig's diary, 15 July 1918.

70. Doughty, *Pyrrhic Victory*, pp. 470–5.

CHAPTER 19

1. H. Strachan, "The Morale of the German Army, 1917–18", H.Cecil and P. Liddle (eds.) *Facing Armageddon: The First World War Experienced* (Barnsley: Leo Cooper) 1996, pp. 390–8.

2. *Ibid.*, and M. Kitchen, *The German Offensive of 1918* (Stroud: Tempus) 2001, pp. 202–22. An excellent summary of German military difficulties at this period

is to be found in W. Deist, "The Military Collapse of the German Empire: The Reality behind the Stab-in-the-Back Myth", *War in History*, Vol. 3, No. 2, 1996, pp. 186–207.

3. Haig's diary, 15–17 July 1918.
4. *Ibid.*, 20 July 1918.
5. *Ibid.*, 23 July 1918. Kitchen, *German Offensives* pp. 220–1.
6. P. Pedersen, *Monash as Military Commander* (Melbourne: Melbourne University Press) 1985, pp. 222–32.
7. *Ibid.*, pp. 233–7. G. Serle, *John Monash: A Biography* (Melbourne: Melbourne University Press) 1982, pp. 337–43. R. Prior and T. Wilson, *Command on the Western Front: The Military Career of Sir Henry Rawlinson 1914–18* (Oxford: Blackwell) 1992, pp. 301–8.
8. J. P. Harris, *Amiens to the Armistice: The BEF in the Hundred Days' Campaign, 8 August–11 November 1918* (London: Brassey's) 1998, pp. 59–86. Haig's diary, 16 July 1918.
9. Rawlinson to GHQ, 220 (G), 17 July 1918, TNA PRO WO 158/241.
10. Haig's diary, 24–28 July 1918.
11. *Ibid.*, 29 July 1918.
12. *Ibid.*, 5 August 1918. Prior and Wilson, *Command*, p. 303.
13. Rawlinson to GHQ, 220 (G), 17 July 1918, TNA PRO WO 158/241.
14. Harris, *Amiens*, pp. 59–86.
15. A. Montgomery, *The Story of the Fourth Army in the Battles of the Hundred Days: August 8th to November 11th 1918* (London: Hodder and Stoughton) 1919, pp. 26–7. G. H. F. Nichols, *The 18th Division in the Great War* (Edinburgh: Blackwood) 1922, pp. 339–45.
16. Haig's diary, 7 August 1918.
17. *Ibid.*, 8 August 1918. Montgomery, *Fourth Army*, pp. 30–51.
18. Harris, *The BEF*, pp. 100–2. W. Raleigh and H. A. Z. Jones, *The War in the Air, Vol. VI* (Oxford: Clarendon Press) 1937, pp. 433–68. P. Griffith, *Battle Tactics of the Western Front: The British Army's Art of Attack 1916–18* (London: Yale University Press) 1994, pp. 156–7.
19. *Ibid.*, pp. 108–13. J. Edmonds, *Military Operations France and Belgium 1918, Vol. IV* (London: HMSO) 1947, pp. 93–118.
20. Haig's diary, 10 August 1918.
21. Prior and Wilson, *Command*, pp. 327–36. Fourth Army Operations Order, 20/6 (G), 12 August 1918, TNA PRO WO 158/241.
22. Haig's diary, 11 August 1918.
23. Prior and Wilson, *Command*, pp. 332–7. Harris, *Amiens*, pp. 119–26. A. M. J. Hyatt, *General Sir Arthur Currie: A Military Biography* (Toronto: Toronto University Press) 1987, p. 117. Haig's diary, 15 August 1918.
24. Haig's diary, 19 August 1918.
25. *Ibid.*, 20 and 21 August 1918. Harris, *Amiens*, pp. 121–33.
26. Haig's diary, 21 August 1918.
27. Harris, *Amiens*, pp. 131–43.
28. *Ibid.*, pp. 23–57. Griffith,. P. Simkins, "Co-Stars or Supporting Cast? British Divisions in the 'Hundred Days', 1918". In P. Griffith, *British Fighting Methods in the Great War* (London: Frank Cass) 1996, pp. 50–70.

29. Haig to the Armies, O.A.D. 911, 22 August 1918, TNA PRO WO 158/241.

30. Haig's diary, 23 August 1918. Haig to Wilson, 1 September 1918, HHW 2/7/11 and 24 September 1918, HHW 2/78/18, Wilson Papers, IWM.

31. Edmonds, *1918, Vol IV*, pp. 310–13. Montgomery, *The Fourth Army*, pp. 86–95.

32. Haig's diary, 24 August 1918.

33. *Ibid.*, 26 August 1918. Edmonds, *1918, Vol. IV*, pp. 297–347.

34. Haig's diary, 27 August 1918.

35. *Ibid.*, 27–29 August 1918.

36. Wilson to Haig, 31 August 1918, quoted in Edmonds, *1918, Vol. IV*, p. 383. D. Woodward, *Lloyd George and the Generals* (Newark: University of Delaware Press), p. 331.

37. Haig's diary, 31 August and 1 September 1918. Haig to Wilson, 1 September 1918, HHW 2/78/10, Haig to Wilson 1 September 1918, HHW 2/78/11, Wilson Papers, IWM.

38. Prior and Wilson, *Command*, pp. 342–3. Montgomery, *The Fourth Army*, pp. 96–113. Serle, *Monash*, pp. 353–7.

39. Haig's diary, 1 September 1918.

40. *Ibid.*, 3 and 4 September 1918.

41. *Ibid.*, 4 September 1918.

42. *Ibid.*, 9 and 10 September 1918.

43. Woodward, *Lloyd George*, pp. 332–3.

44. Haig's diary, 11 September 1918. S. Badsey, "Haig and the Press". In *Haig: A Reappraisal 70 Years On* (Barnsley: Leo Cooper) 1999, pp. 188–90.

45. Byng to GHQ, 9 September 1918, TNA PRO WO 158/311. Horne to GHQ, 11 September 1918, TNA PRO WO 158/191. Rawlinson to GHQ, 11 September 1918, TNA PRO WO 95/43.

46. Edmonds, *1918, Vol. IV*, pp. 469–96. D. Smythe, *Pershing: General of the Armies* (Bloomington: Indiana University Press) 1986, pp. 179–89. Montgomery, *The Fourth Army*, pp. 114–46.

47. Harris, *Amiens*, pp. 147–9.

48. Smythe, *Pershing*, pp. 190–244.

49. S. Schreiber, *The Shock Army of the British Empire: The Canadian Corps in the Last 100 Days of the Great War* (Westport: Conn., Praeger) 1997, pp. 95–104. J. Edmonds and R. Maxwell-Hyslop, *Military Operations, France and Belgium 1918, Vol. V* (London: HMSO) 1947, pp. 1–93. Haig's diary, 26 September–1 October 1918.

50. Haig's diary, 1–9 October 1918. Harris, *Amiens*, pp. 182–202.

51. Haig's diary, 6–11 October. Smythe, *Pershing*, pp. 190–201. Edmonds and Maxwell-Hyslop, *1918, Vol. V*, pp. 185–202.

52. Haig's diary, 10 October 1918.

53. *Ibid.*, 12 October 1918.

54. *Ibid.*, 12–14 October. Edmonds and Maxwell-Hyslop, *1918, Vol. V*, pp. 185–211.

55. Rawlinson's diary, 17 October 1918, RWLN 1/11, Rawlinson Papers, Churchill College, Cambridge. Montgomery, *The Fourth Army*, pp. 209–38. Edmonds and Maxwell-Hyslop, *1918, Vol. V*, pp. 295–385. Haig's diary, 17 October 1917.

56. Haig's diary, 19 October 1918.
57. Haig's diary, 21 October 1918. On Wilson and Irish conscription see K. Jeffery, *Field Marshal Sir Henry Wilson: A Political Soldier* (Oxford: Oxford University Press) 2006, pp. 196–7 and 222–3.
58. Lawrence to the Armies, O.A. 109, 1 September 1918, TNA PRO WO 158/ 832. J. P. Harris, *Men, Ideas and Tanks: British Military Thought and Armoured Forces, 1903–1939* (Manchester: Manchester University Press), pp. 184–9.
59. See, for example, GHQ to Horne, Byng and Rawlinson, 5 October 1918, TNA PRO WO 158/242.
60. Haig's diary, 24–27 October 1918.
61. Haig's diary, 25 October 1918. The issue of disturbances in the Australian Corps in September 1918 seems still to be sensitive in Australia. It seems never to have been fully explored in print. Scholarly writings by Antipodean authors, however, contain plenty of hints. Serle, *Monash*, pp. 361–2 and 369, admits that some mutinies resulted from the troops being driven too hard. Problems of physical and moral exhaustion are emphasised in C. Pugsley, *The ANZAC Experience: New Zealand, Australia and Empire in the First World War* (Auckland: Reed) 2004, pp. 272–7, and J. G. Fuller, *Troop Morale and Popular Culture in the British and Dominion Armies 1914–1919* (Oxford: Clarendon Press) 1990, pp. 24–5 and 50–2.
62. Haig's diary, 27–29 October 1918.
63. *Ibid.*, 31 October 1918.
64. *Ibid.*, 1 November 1918.
65. *Ibid.*, 4 November 1918. Haig to Wilson, 4 November 1918, enclosing a report on recent French military operations dated 1 November, HHW 2/78/ 21, Wilson Papers, IWM.
66. Haig's diary, 5–9 November 1918.
67. For various views on logistics in the closing stages of the campaign see Montgomery, *The Fourth Army*, pp. 260–1, Edmonds and Maxwell-Hyslop, *1918, Vol. V*, pp. 613–15. Montgomery's account appears the most pessimistic about the possibility of maintaining the advance.
68. Edmonds and Maxwell-Hyslop, *1918, Vol. V*, pp. 515–17. Gröner's conclusion as to the hopeless state of the German army (as recorded in the British Official History) is confirmed in Deist, *The Military Collapse of the German Empire*, p. 204. By early November the "leadership could count on scarcely a dozen divisions classified as 'fully combat-ready' or 'combat capable' in the whole area from the Belgian coast to the Upper Rhine. The army was a shadow of its former self." The front was of gossamer fragility, held, as the German Crown Prince put it, by a "spider's web of fighters".
69. D. Stevenson, *1914–1918: The History of the First World War* (London: Allen and Unwin) 2004, pp. 496–8. GHQ to the Armies, O.A.D. 953 and 953/1, TNA PRO WO 158/243. Harris, *Amiens*, pp. 285–6.
70. Haig's diary, 11 November 1918.
71. The last chapter of G. De Groot's biography of Haig is entitled "Consistent to the End". G. De Groot, *Douglas Haig, 1861–1928* (London: Unwin Hyman) 1988, pp. 396–407.

72. This interpretation (the lack of any close relationship during the Hundred Days between Haig's fluctuating judgement of the German capacity to resist and the intelligence with which he was provided) is based on a reading of the Late 1918 chapter of J. M. Beach's "British Intelligence and the German Army 1914–18", PhD thesis, University of London, 2005. It is, however, this author's interpretation, not necessarily Dr Beach's.

73. P. Simkins, "'Building Blocks': Aspects of Command and Control at Brigade level in the BEF's Offensive Operations, 1916–1918". In G. Sheffield and D. Todman (eds.), *Command and Control on the Western Front: The British Army's Experience 1914–18* (Staplehurst: Spellmount) 2004, p. 165. Edmonds and Maxwell-Hyslop, *1918 Vol. V*, p. 557. Harris, *Amiens*, pp. 291–5.

74. Prior and Wilson, *Command*, p. 305.

75. In a letter of 20 September 1918 Haig told Wilson that "we have a surprisingly large number of *very capable* Generals". HHW 2/78/16, Wilson Papers, IWM. For a modern endorsement of that position see J. M. Bourne, "The BEF's Generals on 29 September 1918: An Empirical Portrait with Some British and Australian Comparisons". In P. Dennis and J. Grey (eds.) *1918: Defining Victory* (Canberra: Department of Defence) 1999, pp. 96–114.

CHAPTER 20

1. Haig to Wilson, 15 November 1918, HHW 2/78/23, Wilson Papers, IWM. War Office to Haig, 18 November 1918, Acc. 3155/216, Haig Papers, NLS. Haig's diary, 19 November 1918. Haig to Lady Haig, 21 November 1918. D. Cooper, *Haig: The Second Volume* (London: Faber) 1936, p. 410.

2. The quotation is from Haig to Milner, n.d. (but probably 19 November 1918), Acc. 3155/216, Haig Papers, NLS. Haig's diary, 19 November 1918.

3. Haig to Lady Haig, 30 July and 4 October 1918.

4. Wilson to Haig, 20 November 1918, and Haig to Wilson, 21 November 1918, Acc. 3155/216. Haig's diary, 27 November 1918. Countess Haig, *The Man I Knew* (Edinburgh: The Moray Press) 1936, pp. 244–5.

5. D. Lloyd George, *War Memoirs of David Lloyd George*, Vol. VI (London: Ivor Nicholson and Watson) 1936, pp. 3125–52 and 3473–8. Lloyd George used the index of his war memoirs to concentrate an exceptionally violent assault on Haig's reputation.

6. Haig's diary, 30 November 1918.

7. Countess Haig, *The Man I Knew*, p. 248. Haig to Sir Clive Wigram, 1 December, PS/GV/K1387/7, Royal Archives, Windsor. Haig's diary, 30 November 1918.

8. Haig's diary, 16 December 1918, and O. Elton, *C.E. Montagu: A Memoir* (London: Chatto and Windus) 1929, p. 230, quoted in G. Sheffield and J. Bourne, *Douglas Haig: War Diaries and Letters 1914–18* (London: Weidenfeld and Nicholson) 2005, p. 491.

9. Haig's diary, 19 December 1918.

10. *Ibid.*, 27 and 28 December 1918.

11. *Ibid.*, 19 October and 27 November 1918, and 11 and 12 February 1919.

12. Haig memorandum on German intentions towards Persia and India, 2 April 1911, Acc. 3155/89, Haig Papers, NLS.
13. Interview with Haig printed in *The Times*, 15 February 1917. Haig's diary, 25 October 1918.
14. Haig's diary, 28 December 1918.
15. *Ibid.*, 19 March and 19 October 1918.
16. *Ibid.*, 26 January 1919.
17. *Ibid.*, 30 December 1918.
18. "Talk with Maurice Hankey at United Service Club", 8 November 1932, 11/1932/43, Liddell Hart Papers, LHCMA. K. Jeffery, *Field Marshal Sir Henry Wilson: A Political Soldier* (Oxford: Oxford University Press) 2006, p. 228.
19. Haig's diary, 3 November 1917 and 8 January 1919.
20. Haig's diary, 28 January 1919. M. Gilbert, *Winston S. Churchill, Vol. IV: 1916–22* (London: Heinemann) 1975, pp. 181–93.
21. Haig's diary, 1 February 1919. Gilbert, *Churchill*, pp. 193–6. Jeffery, *Wilson*, pp. 230–1.
22. R. Blake (ed.) *The Private Papers of Douglas Haig 1914–1919* (London: Eyre and Spottiswoode) 1952, pp. 357–8. Cooper, *Haig*, p. 411. D. French, "Sir Douglas Haig's Reputation 1918–1928: A Note", *The Historical Journal*, Vol. 28, No. 4, 1985 953.
23. Haig's diary, 2 April 1919.
24. Cooper, *Haig*, pp. 413–14.
25. *Ibid.*, pp. 414–15. Haig's diary, 15 October 1917.
26. *Ibid.*, pp. 415–16.
27. *Ibid.*, p. 117. R. Haldane, *Richard Burdon Haldane: An Autobiography* (London: Hodder and Stoughton), 1929, pp. 287–9. Doubts about Haldane's version of events are referred to in W. Reid, *Douglas Haig: Architect of Victory* (Edinburgh: Berlinn) 2006, pp. 490–91.
28. Haig to Lady Haig, 26 February 1919.
29. Lord Murray of Elibank to Haig, 25 July 1919, Acc. 3155/3147/1–25, NLS.
30. Haig to Lord Murray of Elibank, 27 July 1919, Acc. 3155/3147/1–25, Haig Papers, NLS.
31. Cooper, *Haig*, pp. 418–19.
32. Countess Haig, *The Man I Knew*, pp. 280 and 315. Cooper, *Haig*, pp. 413 and 418–19. French, "Reputation", p. 953. Reid, *Architecht*, p. 495. Earl Haig, *My Father's Son* (Barnsley: Leo Cooper) 2000, pp. 10–25.
33. Haig's diary, 14 December 1918. G. De Groot, *Douglas Haig, 1861–1928* (London: Unwin and Hyman) 1988, p. 405. Haig to J. Allison, 27 February 1926, Acc. 3155/337 (k), Haig Papers, NLS.
34. French, "Reputation", p. 953.
35. De Groot, *Haig*, p. 403. N. Barr and G. Sheffield, "Douglas Haig, the Common Soldier and the British Legion". In B. Bond and N. Cave (eds.) *Haig: A Reappraisal Seventy Years On* (Bamsley: Leo Cooper) 1999, p. 229.
36. Barr and Sheffield, *Haig: Common Soldier*, pp. 230–1. Cooper, *Haig*, pp. 426–8.
37. Cooper, *Haig*, p. 423.

38. Barr and Sheffield, *Haig: Common Soldier*, p. 230. Countess Haig, *The Man I Knew*, pp. 282 and 316.
39. J. Charteris, *Field-Marshal Earl Haig* (London: Cassell) 1929, pp. 374–5.
40. Lord French, *1914* (London: Constable) 1919, p. 6.
41. Haig to the War Office, 4 April 1919, 71/13/2, Boraston Papers, IWM.
42. Wilson diary, 5 August 1914, HHW, 23, Wilson Papers, IWM. "Secretary's note of a War Council held at 10 Downing Street", 5 August 1914, TNA PRO CAB 42/1/2.
43. "Operations on the Western Front 1916–18", 30 January 1920, Acc. 3155/213 (a), Haig Papers, NLS. French, p. 956.
44. Haig to Boraston, 21 and 23 June 1921, 71/13/3, Boraston Papers, IWM. G. A. B. Dewar and J. H. Boraston, *Sir Douglas Haig's Command 1915–1918*, *2 Vols.* (London: Constable) 1922.
45. Haig to Edmonds, 26 January 1923 and 22 April 1927, TNA PRO CAB 45/183. French, "Reputation", p. 959. D. French, "Sir James Edmonds and the Official History: France and Belgium". In Brian Bond (ed.) *The First World War And British Military History* (Oxford: Clarendon Press) 1991, pp. 70–86.
46. Countess Haig, *The Man I Knew*, pp. 318–19. Cooper, *Haig*, p. 433.
47. D. Todman, "'Sans peur and sans reproche': The Retirement, Death and Mourning of Sir Douglas Haig, 1918–28", *The Journal of Military History*, Vol. 67, No. 4, October 2003, 1085–6 and *passim*.

CONCLUSION

1. Repington to Bonar Law, 16 November 1915, A. J. A. Morris, *Letters of Lieutenant-Colonel Charties à Court Repington CMG: Military Correspondent of The Times, 1905–1908* (Stroud: Sutton) 1999, pp. 239–40.
2. Haig's diary, 2 October 1917.

Select Bibliography

ARCHIVAL SOURCES

BODLEIAN LIBRARY, OXFORD

Earl of Oxford Papers
Viscount Milner Papers

CHURCHILL COLLEGE, CAMBRIDGE

Maurice Hankey Papers
Lord Rawlinson Papers

IMPERIAL WAR MUSEUM

Fourth Army Papers
J. H. Boraston Papers
Sir Henry Horne Papers
Sir Henry Wilson Papers
Viscount French Papers

LIDDELL HART CENTRE FOR MILITARY ARCHIVES, KING'S
COLLEGE LONDON

Sir Edmund Allenby Papers
John Charteris Papers
Sir James Edmonds Papers
Sir Launcelot Kiggell Papers
Sir Basil Liddell Hart Papers
Sir Archibald Montgomery-Massingberd Papers
Sir William Robertson Papers

NATIONAL ARCHIVES (PUBLIC RECORD OFFICE, KEW)

CAB 23 War Cabinet Minutes
CAB 27 War Cabinet Committee Papers
CAB 42 War Council (and successors) Papers

CAB 45 Official Historians' correspondence
WO 95 War Diaries
WO 157 Intelligence Files
WO 158 Military Headquarters Papers
WO 159 Lord Kitchener's Private Office Papers
WO 256 Haig Papers
WO 279 Reports on Manoeuvres and Conferences

NATIONAL ARCHIVES

Sir Henry Rawlinson Papers

NATIONAL LIBRARY OF SCOTLAND

Sir John Davidson Papers
Earl Haig Papers
Sir Herbert Lawrence Papers

ROYAL ARCHIVES

George V Papers

PUBLISHED PRIMARY SOURCES: DIARIES, LETTERS, DESPATCHES

I. F. W. Beckett (ed.) *The Army and the Curragh Incident, 1914* (London: Bodley Head) 1986

R. Blake (ed.) *The Private Papers of Douglas Haig 1914–1919* (London: Eyre and Spottiswoode) 1952

J. H. Boraston (ed.) *Sir Douglas Haig's Despatches* (London: Dent) 1919

M. V. Brett and O. Esher (eds.) *Journals and Letters of Reginald Viscount Esher (4. Vols.)* (London: Ivor Nicholson and Watson) 1934–1938

J. Charteris, *At GHQ* (London: Cassell) 1931

D. Dutton (ed.) *Paris 1918; The War Diary of the 17th Earl of Derby* (Liverpool: Liverpool University Press) 2001

J. Ferris (ed.) *The British Army and Signals Intelligence during the First World War* (Stroud: Alan Sutton) 1992

J. French, *The Despatches of Lord French* (London: Chapman and Hall) 1917

A. J. Guy, R. N. W. Thomas and G. De Groot (eds.) *Military Miscellany I* (Stroud: Sutton) 1997

K. Jeffery (ed.) *The Military Correspondence of Field Marshal Sir Henry Wilson 1918–1922* (London: Bodley Head) 1985

A. J. A. Morris (ed.) *The Letters of Lieutenant-Colonel Charles à Court Repington CMG: Military Correspondent of The Times, 1903–1918* (Stroud: Sutton) 1999

D. Scott (ed.) *Douglas Haig: The Preparatory Prologue 1861–1914, Diaries and Letters* (Barnsley: Pen and Sword) 2006

G. Sheffield and J. Bourne (eds.) *Douglas Haig: War Diaries and Letters* (London: Weidenfeld and Nicolson) 2005

A. Wessels (ed.) *Lord Roberts and the War in South Africa 1899–1902* (Stroud: Sutton) 2000

D. Woodward (ed.) *The Military Correspondence of Field-Marshal Sir William Robertson: Chief Imperial General Staff December 1915–February 1918* (London: Bodley Head) 1989

BOOKS AND ARTICLES SPECIFICALLY ABOUT DOUGLAS HAIG

S. J. Anglim, "Haig's Cadetship: A Reassessment", *The Wishstream: The Journal of the Royal Military Academy Sandhurst*, Vol. XLVI, Autumn 1992, pp. 35–9

G. Arthur, *Lord Haig* (London: Heinemann) 1931

G. R. Askwith, "Haig at Oxford", *Oxford Magazine*, 1928

B. Bond and N. Cave (eds.) *Haig: A Reappraisal 70 Years On* (Barnsley: Leo Cooper) 1999. (This book contains a collection of scholarly articles on Haig's career, including one by the present writer. For reasons of space these articles are not separately listed.)

J. Charteris, *Field Marshal Earl Haig* (London: Cassell) 1929
  Haig (London: Duckworth) 1933

J. Davidson, *Haig Master of the Field* (London: Peter Nevill) 1953

G. De Groot, *Douglas Haig 1861–1928* (London: Unwin Hyman) 1988

G. A. B. Dewar and J. H. Boraston, *Sir Douglas Haig's Command 1915–1918* (2 Vols., London: Constable) 1929

A. Duff Cooper, *Haig* (2 Vols., London: Faber and Faber) 1935–6

G. S. Duncan, *Haig As I Knew Him* (London: Allen and Unwin) 1966

D. French, "Sir Douglas Haig's Reputation, 1918–1928: A Note", *The Historical Journal*, Vol. 21, No. 4, Dec. 1985

E. Greenhalgh, "Myth and Memory: Sir Douglas Haig and the Imposition of Allied Unified Command in March 1918", *Journal of Military History*, Vol. 68, No. 3, July 2004

Haig, The Countess, *The Man I Knew* (Edinburgh: The Moray Press) 1936

Haig, The Earl, *My Father's Son* (Barnsley: Leo Cooper) 2000. (This work is an autobiography of the second Earl Haig, but contains valuable personal recollections of his father.)

J. Hussey, "Douglas Haig, Adjutant: Recollections of Veterans of the Seventh Hussars", *Journal of the Society for Army Historical Research*, Vol. 73, 1995
  "Of the Indian Rope Trick, the Paranormal and Captain Shearer's Ray–Sidelights on Douglas Haig", *British Army Review*, Vol. 112, No. 4, 1996
  "'A Very Substantial Grievance' said the Secretary of State: Douglas Haig's Examination Troubles, 1893", *Journal of the Society for Army Historical Research*, Vol. 74, 1996

N. Lloyd, "'With Faith and Without Fear': Sir Douglas Haig's Command of First Army During 1915", *The Journal of Military History*, Vol. 71, No. 4, October 2007

J. Marshall-Cornwall, *Haig as Military Commander* (London: Batsford) 1973

G. Mead, *The Good Soldier: The Biography of Douglas Haig* (London: Atlantic Books) 2007

W. Reid, *Architect of Victory: Douglas Haig* (Edinburgh: Birlinn) 2006

T. Secrett, *Twenty-Five Years With Earl Haig* (London: Jarrolds) 1929

K. Simpson, "The Reputation of Douglas Haig". In B. Bond (ed.) *The First World War and British Military History* (Oxford: Clarendon Press) 1991

E. K. G. Sixsmith, *Douglas Haig* (London: Weidenfeld and Nicolson) 1976

J. Terraine, *Douglas Haig: The Educated Soldier* (London: Hutchinson) 1963

D. Todman, "Sans peur and sans reproche: The Retirement Death and Mourning of Sir Douglas Haig", *The Journal of Military History*, Vol. 67, No. 4, October 2003

P. Warner, *Field Marshal Earl Haig* (London: Bodley Head) 1991

A. Wiest, *Haig: The Evolution of a Commander* (Washington D.C.: Potomac Books) 2006

D. Winter, *Haig's Command: A Reassessment* (London: Viking) 1991

OFFICIAL HISTORIES

The official histories of three countries: Australia, Canada and the United Kingdom have been used in the writing of this book. The individual volumes consulted are referred to in the notes and it seems unnecessary to list each volume separately here. In the case of the United Kingdom, however, elements of three distinct series have been used.

AUSTRALIA

C. E.W. Bean *The Official History of Australia in the War of 1914–1918: The Australian Imperial Force in France* (Sydney: Angus and Robertson) 1943

CANADA

G. W. L. Nicholson, *The Official History of the Canadian Army in the First World War: Canadian Expeditionary Force 1914–1919* (Ottowa: Queens Printer) 1962

UNITED KINGDOM

A. F. Becke, *History of the Great War: Order of Battle, Part 4, The Army Council, GHQs, Armies and Corps 1914–1918* (London: HMSO) 1945

Sir James Edmonds (ed.) *Official History of the Great War: Military Operations, France and Belgium 1914–18 (14 Vols. plus appendices and maps)* (London: Macmillan and HMSO) 1922–48

Sir W. Raleigh and H. A. Jones, *The War in the Air: Being the Story of the Part Played in the Great War by the Royal Air Force (6 Vols.)* (Oxford: Clarendon Press) 1922–37

CORPS, DIVISIONAL AND REGIMENTAL HISTORIES

C. T. Atkinson, *The Seventh Division 1914–1918* (London: John Murray) 1927

F. W. Bewsher, *The History of the 51st (Highland) Division 1914–1918* (Edinburgh: William Blackwood) 1921

A. D. Ellis, *The Story of the Fifth Australian Division* (London: Hodder and Stoughton) 1920

J. Ewing, *The History of the 9th Scottish Division 1914–1919* (London: John Murray) 1921

C. Falls, *The History of the 36th Ulster Division* (London: M'Caw, Stevenson and Orr) 1922

M. Farndale, *History of the Royal Regiment of Artillery: Western Front 1914–1918* (London: Royal Artillery Institution) 1986

R. L. V. ffrench Blake, *The 17th/21st Lancers* (London: Hamish Hamilton) 1968

C. Headlam, *The History of the Guards Division in The Great War (2 Vols.)* (London: John Murray) 1924

A. Maude (ed.) *The 47th London Division 1914–1919* (London: Amalgamated Press) 1922

J. W. B. Merewether and F. Smith, *The Indian Corps in France* (London: John Murray) 1919

G. H. F. Nichols, *The 18th Division in the Great War* (London: William Blackwood) 1922

S. Spallow, *The Fifth Army in March 1918* (London: John Lane)

S. Stewart and J. Buchan, *The Fifteenth (Scottish) Division 1914–1919* (Edinburgh: William Blackwood) 1926

E. Wyrall, *The History of the Second Division 1914–1918 (2 Vols.)* (London: Thomas Nelson) 1921

OTHER PUBLISHED WORKS

L. Albertini, *Origins of the War of 1914 (3 Vols.)* (Oxford: Oxford University Press) 1957

Anglesey (Marquis of), *A History of the British Cavalry (8 Vols.) Vol. 8: The Western Front, 1915–1918, Epilogue, 1919–1939* (Barnsley: Leo Cooper) 1997

D. Ascoli, *Mons Star: The British Expeditionary Force* (London: Harrap) 1981

C. Barnett, *The Swordbearers: Studies in Supreme Command in the First World War* (London: Eyre and Spottiswoode) 1963

P. Barton, P. Doyle and J. Vandewalle, *Beneath Flanders Fields: The Tunnellers' War 1914–18* (Staplehurst: Spellmount) 2004

J. Baynes, *Far From A Donkey: The Life of General Sir Ivor Maxse KCB, CVO, DSO* (London: Brassey's) 1995

I. F. W. Beckett, *Johnnie Gough, V.C.* (London: Tom Donovan) 1989
    The Judgement of History: Sir Horace Smith-Dorrien, Lord French and 1914 (London: Tom Donovan) 1993
    Ypres: The First Battle, 1914 (Harlow: Pearson Education) 2004

I. F. W. Beckett and S. Corbi (eds.) *Haig's Generals* (London: Pen and Sword) 2006

S. Bidwell and D. Graham, *Firepower: British Army Weapons and Theories of War 1904–1945* (London: Allen and Unwin) 1982

B. Bond, *The Victorian Army and the Staff College 1854–1914* (London: Eyre Methuen) 1972
    Liddell Hart: A Study of His Military Thought (London: Cassell) 1977
    The First World War and British Military History (Oxford: Clarendon Press) 1991

The Unquiet Western Front: Britain's Role in Literature and History (Cambridge: Cambridge University Press) 1992

B. Bond *et al.*, *"Look To Your Front": Studies in The First World War* (Staplehurst: Spellmount) 1999

J. M. Bourne, *Britain and the Great War 1914–1918* (London: Edward Arnold) 1989

A. Bristow, *A Serious Disappointment: The Battle of Aubers Ridge, 1915 and the Subsequent Munitions Scandal* (London: Leo Cooper) 1995

I. M. Brown, "Not Glamorous But Effective: The Canadian Corps and the Set-Piece Attack, 1917–1918", *The Journal of Military History*, Vol. 58, No. 3, July 1994

    British Logistics on the Western Front 1914–1919 (Wesport, Conn., Paeger) 1998

C. E. Callwell, *Field-Marshal Sir Henry Wilson: His Life and Diaries (2 Vols.)* (London: Cassell) 1927

G. H. Cassar, *Kitchener: Architect of Victory* (London: William Kimber) 1977

    The Tragedy of Sir John French (Newark, Del.: University of Delaware Press) 1985

    Asquith as War Leader (London, Hambledon) 1994

    Kitchener's War: British Strategy From 1914 To 1916 (Dulles, Va., Brassey's) 2004

B. Catton, *Takes Command: 1863–1865* (Edison, N.J.: Castle Books) 2000

H. Cecil and P. H. Liddle, *Facing Armageddon: The First World War Experience* (Barnsley: Leo Cooper) 1996

D. Chandler and I. Beckett (eds.) *The Oxford History of the British Army* (Oxford: Oxford University Press) 1994

O. F. Christie, *A History of Clifton College 1860–1934* (Bristol: Arrowsmith) 1935

R. Churchill, *Lord Derby: "King of Lancashire"* (London: Heinemann) 1959

W. S. Churchill, *The River War: An Historical Account of the Reconquest of the Soudan (2 Vols.)* (London: Longman) 1899

    The World Crisis (London: Thornton Butterworth) 1931

    My Early Life (London: Odhams) 1958

A. Clayton, *Paths of Glory: The French Army 1914–18* (Cassell: London) 2003

G. Corrigan, *Mud, Blood and Poppycock* (London: Cassell) 2003

D. Daiches, *Scotch Whisky: Its Past and Present* (London: Andre Deutsch) 1969

W. Deist, "The Military Collapse of the German Empire: The Reality Behind the Stab-in-the-Back Myth", *War in History*, Vol. 3, No. 2, 1996

P. Dennis and J. Grey, *1918: Defining Victory* (Canberra: Army History Unit) 1999

M. Dockrill and D. French (eds.) *Strategy and Intelligence: British Policy during the First World War* (London: Hambledon) 1996

R. A. Doughty, *Pyrrhic Victory: French Strategy and Operations in the Great War* (Cambridge, Mass.: Belknap Press of Harvard University Press) 2005

C. Duffy, *Through German Eyes: The British and the Somme 1916* (London: Wiedenfeld and Nicolson) 2006

O. Elton, *C. E. Montagn: A Memoir* (London: Chatto and Windus) 1929

R. C. K. Ensor, *England 1870–1914* (Oxford: Oxford University Press) 1936

O. Esher, *Journals and Letters of Reginald Viscount Esher*, Vol. 3, 1910–1915 (London: Ivor Nicholson and Watson) 1938

C. Falls, *Military Operations in France and Belgium, 1917* (London: Macmillan) 1940

D. Farr, *The Silent General: Horne of the First Army* (Solihull: Helion) 2007

A. Farrar-Hockley, *Goughie: The Life of General Sir Hubert Gough* (London: Hart-Davis, MacGibbon) 1975

N. Fergusson, *The Pity of War* (London: Allen Lane) 1998

F. Foch, *The Memoirs of Marshal Foch* (London: Heinemann) 1931

R. T. Foley, *German Strategy and the Path to Verdun: Erich von Falkenhayn and the Development of Attrition 1870–1916* (Cambridge: Cambridge University Press) 2005

G. Fong, "The Movement of German Divisions to the Western Front, Winter 1917–1918", *War in History*, Vol. 7, No. 2, 2000

P. Fraser, *Lord Esher: A Political Biography* (London: Hart Davis) 1973

D. French, *British Strategy and War Aims: 1914–1916* (London: Allen and Unwin) 1986

   "The Meaning of Attrition 1914–1916", *English Historical Review*, 1988

   "Watching the Allies; British Intelligence and the French Mutinies of 1917", *Intelligence and National Security*, Vol. 6, No. 3, 1991

   The Strategy of the Lloyd George Coalition 1916–1918 (Oxford: Clarendon Press) 1995

   "'Had we Known how bad Things were in Germany we might have got Stiffer Terms', Great Britain and the German Armistice". In M. F. Boemeke, G. D. Feldman and E. Glaser (eds.) *The Treaty of Versailles: A Reassessment after 75 Years* (Cambridge: Cambridge University Press) 1998

D. French and B. H. Reid, *The British General Staff: Reform and Innovation, 1890–1939* (London: Frank Cass) 2002

J. French, *1914* (London: Constable) 1919

R. F. Foster, *Modern Ireland: 1600–1972* (London: Allen Lane) 1988

J. F. C. Fuller, *Memoirs of an Unconventional Soldier* (London: Nicholson and Watson) 1936

J. G. Fuller, *Troop Morale and Popular Culture in the British and Dominion Armies 1914–1918* (Oxford: Clarendon Press) 1990

N. Gardner, *Trial By Fire: Command and the British Expeditionary Force in 1914* (Westport, Conn.: Praeger) 2003

J. L. Gibot and P. Gorczynski, *En Suivant Les Tanks: Cambrai 20 Novembre–7 Decembre 1917* 1997

M. Gilbert, *Winston S. Churchill 1874–1965, Vol. IV, 1916–1922* (London: Heinemann) 1975

C. S. Goldman, *With General French and the Cavalry in South Africa* (London: Macmillan) 1902

A. M. Gollin, *A Proconsul in Politics: A Study of Lord Milner in Opposition and Power* (London: Anthony) 1964

J. Gooch, "The Maurice Debate 1918", *Journal of Contemporary History*, Vol. 3, No. 4, 1968

   The Plans of War: The General Staff and British Military Strategy c.1900–1916 (London: Routledge and Kegan Paul) 1974

H. Gough, *The Fifth Army* (London: Hodder and Stoughton) 1931

A. Green, *Writing the Great War: Sir James Edmonds and the Official Histories 1915–1948* (London: Frank Cass) 2003

E. Greenhalgh, "'Parade Ground Soldiers': French Army Assessments of the British on the Somme in 1916", *Journal of Military History* Vol. 16, No. 2, 1999

"Why the British were on the Somme in 1916", *War in History*, Vol. I, No. 2, April 1999

"Hames over the Somme: A Retort to William Philpott", *War in History*, Vol. 10, No. 3, 2003

Victory Through Coalition: Britain and France During the First World War (Cambridge: Cambridge University Press) 2005

E. Grey, *Twenty-Five years (2 Vols.)* Vol. 1 (London: Hodder and Stoughton) 1935

K. Grieves, *Sir Eric Geddes: Business and Government in War and Peace* (Manchester: Manchester University Press) 1989

P. Griffith, *Battle Tactics of the Western Front: The British Army's Art of Attack 1916–18* (London: Yale) 1994

Forward into Battle: Fighting Tactics from Waterloo to Vietnam (Chichester: Bird) 1995

P. Griffith (ed.) *British Fighting Methods in the Great War* (London: Frank Cass) 1996

J. Grigg, *Lloyd George: From Peace To War 1912–1916* (London: Methuen) 1985

Lloyd George: War Leader 1916–1918 (London: Penguin) 2003

"G. S.O", *GHQ (Montreuil-Sur-Mer)* (London: Philip Allan) 1920

B. Gudmundsson, *Stormtroop Tactics: Innovation in the German Army, 1914–1918* (Westport, Conn.: Praeger) 1989

On Artillery (Westport, Conn.: Praeger) 1993

D. Haig, *Cavalry Studies* (London: Hugh Rees) 1907

A. Haldane, *A Soldier's Saga: The Autobiography of General Sir Aylmer Haldane* (Edinburgh: William Blackwood) 1948

R. Haldane, *Richard Burdon Haldane: An Autobiography* (London: Hodder and Stoughton) 1929

R. F. Hamilton and H. H. Herwig, *The Origins of World War I* (Cambridge: Cambridge University Press) 2003

M. Hankey, *The Supreme Command 1914–18 (2 Vols.)* (London: Allen and Unwin) 1961

C. Harington, *Plumer of Messines* (London: John Murray) 1935

Tim Harington Looks Back (London: John Murray) 1940

J. P. Harris, *Men, Ideas and Tanks: British Military Thought and Armoured Forces* (Manchester: Manchester University Press) 1995

(with Niall Barr), *Amiens to the Armistice: The BEF in the Hundred Days' Campaign, 8 August–11 November 1918* (London: Brassey's) 1998

J. P. Harris and Sanders Marble, "The 'Step-by-Step Approach': British Military Thought and Operational Method on the Western Front 1915–17", *War in History*, Vol. 15, No. 1, Jan. 2008

P. Hart, *The Somme* (London: Weidenfeld and Nicolson) 2005

Bloody April (London: Weidfenfeld and Nicolson) 2005

G. Hayes, A. Iarocci and M. Bechthold (eds.) *Vimy Ridge: A Canadian Reassessment* (Ontario: Wilfrid Laurier University Press) 2007

C. Hazlehurst, *Politicians at War July 1914 to May 1915: A Prologue to the Triumph of Lloyd George* (London: Jonathan Cape) 1970

T. A. Heathcote, *The Military In British India: The Development Of British Land Forces 1600–1947* (Manchester: Manchester University Press) 1995

H. Herwig, *The First World War: Germany and Austria-Hungary, 1914–1918* (London: Arnold) 1997

H. Høiback, *Command and Control in Military Crisis: Devious Decisions* (New York: Frank Cass) 2003

R. Holmes, *The Little Field Marshal: A Life of Sir John French* (London: Weidenfeld and Nicolson) 1981

    Tommy: The British Soldier on the Western Front 1914–1918 (London: Harper Collins) 2004

M. Hughes and M. Seligmann (eds.) *Leadership in Conflict 1914–1918* (Barnsley: Leo Cooper) 2000

V. Huguet, *Britain and the War: A French Indictment* (London: Cassell) 1928

A. M. J. Hyatt, *General Sir Arthur Currie: A Military Biography* (Toronto: University of Toronto Press) 1987

K. Jeffery, *Field Marshal Sir Henry Wilson: A Political Soldier* (Oxford: Oxford University Press) 2006

D. Judd and K. Surridge, *The Boer War* (London: John Murray) 2002

J. Keegan, *The Mask of Command* (London: Jonathan Cape) 1987

M. Kitchen, *The German Offensives of 1918* (Stroud: Tempus) 2001

W. M. Kuhn, "Brett Reginald Balliol, 2nd Viscount Esher". In *Oxford Dictionary of National Biography*, Vol. 7 (Oxford: Oxford University Press) 2004

J. Laver, *The House of Haig* (Markinch: John Haig and Co.) 1958

J. Lee, *A Soldier's Life: General Sir Ian Hamiliton 1853–1947* (Basingstoke: Macmillan) 2000

J. Lees-Milne, *The Enigmatic Edwardian: The Life of Reginald 2nd Viscount Esher* (London: Sidgwick and Jackson) 1986

B. Liddell Hart, *The Real War 1914–1918* (London: Faber and Faber) 1930

P. H. Liddle (ed.) *Passchendaele in Perspective: The Third Battle of Ypres* (Barnsley: Leo Cooper) 1997

N. Lloyd, *Loos 1915* (Stroud: Tempus) 2006

D. Lloyd-George, *War Memoirs* (London: Ivor Nicholson and Watson) 1933–6

E. Ludendorff, *My War Memoirs 1914–1918, 2 Vols.* (London: Hutchinson) n.d.

N. Lytton, *The Press and General Staff* (London: Collins) 1921

D. S. Macdiarmid, *The Life of Lieutenant General Sir James Moncrieff Grierson* (London: Constable) 1923

P. Magnus, *Kitchener: Portrait of an Imperialist* (London: John Murray) 1958

F. Maurice, *The Life of General Lord Rawlinson of Trent* (London: Cassell) 1928

    Haldane 1915–1928: The Life of Viscount Haldane of Cloan K. T. O. M. (London: Faber and Faber) 1929

N. Maurice (ed.) *The Maurice Case* (Barnsley: Leo Cooper) 1972

C. McCarthy, *The Somme: The Day-by-Day Account* (London: Arms and Armour) 1993

    Passchendaele: The Day-by-Day Account (London: Arms and Armour) 1995

    "Queen of the Battlefield: The Development of Command, Organisation and Tactics in the British Infantry Battallions during the Great War". In

G. Sheffield and D. Todman, *Command and Control on the Western Front: The British Army Experience 1914–18* (Staplehurst: Spellmount) 2004

J. McRandle and J. Quirk, "The Blood Test Revisited: A New Look at German Casualty Counts in World War I", *Journal of Military History*, Vol. 70, No. 3, July 2006

C. Messenger, *Call To Arms: The British Army 1914–18* (London: Weidenfeld and Nicolson) 2005

M. Middlebrook, *The First Day on the Somme* (London: Allen Lane) 1971
   The Kaiser's Battle, 21 March 1918: The First Day of the German Spring Offensive (London: Allen Lane) 1978

W. Miles, *Military Operations France and Belgium, 1916: 2nd July to the End of the Battle of the Somme* (London: Macmillan) 1938

A. R. Millett and W. Murray (eds.) *Military Effectiveness Vol. I: The First World War* (Boston: Allen and Unwin) 1988

B. Millman, *Pessimism and British War Policy 1916–1918* (London: Frank Cass) 2001

A. Montgomery, *The Story of the Fourth Army in the Battles of the Hundred Days: August 8th–November 11th 1918* (London: Hodder and Stoughton) 1919

W. Moore, *A Wood Called Bourlon: The Cover-up after Cambrai* (Sutton: Stroud) 1998

J. Nicholls, *Cheerful Sacrifice: The Battle of Arras 1917* (Barnsley: Pen and Sword Books) 1990

H. Nicolson, *King George The Fifth: His Life and Reign* (London: Constable) 1952

T. H. O'Brien, *Milner: Viscount Milner of St. James's and Cape Town 1854–1925* (London: Constable) 1979

T. Pakenham, *The Boer War* (London: Weidenfeld and Nicolson) 1979

A. Palazzo, *Seeking Victory on the Western Front: The British Army and Chemical Warfare in World War I* (London: University of Nebraska Press) 2000

I. Passingham, *Pillars of Fire: The Battle Of The Messines Ridge 1917* (Stroud: Sutton) 1998

P. A. Pedersen, *Monash as Military Commander* (Melbourne: Melbourne University Press) 1985

W. J. Philpott, *Anglo-French Relations and Strategy on the Western Front 1914–1918* (Basingstoke: Macmillan) 1996
   "Why the British were really on the Somme: A reply to Elizabeth Greenhalgh" *War in History*, Vol. 9, No. 4, 2002, 446–71

T. Pidgeon, *The Tanks at Flers (2 Vols.)* (Cobham: Fairmile Books) 1995

J. Pollock, *Kitchener* (London: Constable) 1998

G. Powell, *Plumer: The Soldiers' General* (Barnsley: Leo Cooper) 1990

R. Prior and T. Wilson, *Command on the Western Front: The Military Career of Sir Henry Rawlinson 1914–18* (Oxford: Blackwell) 1992
   Passchendaele: The Untold Story (London: Yale) 1996
   The Somme (London: Yale) 2005

C. Pugsley, *The Anzac Experience: New Zealand , Australia and Empire in the First World War* (Auckland: Reed) 2004

B. Rawling, *Surviving Trench Warfare: Technology and the Canadian Corps 1914–1918* (Toronto: University of Toronto Press) 1992

C. Repington, *The First World War, Vol. II* (London: Constable) 1920

R. Rhodes James, *Gallipoli* (London: Batsford) 1965

D. Richter, *Chemical Soldiers: British Gas Warfare in World War I* (London: Leo Cooper) 1992

S. Robbins, *British Generalship on the Western Front 1914–18: Defeat into Victory* (London: Frank Cass) 2005

W. Robertson, *From Private To Field-Marshal* (London: Constable) 1921
  Soldiers and Statesmen 1914–1918 (2 Vols.) (London: Cassell) 1926

S. Roskill, *Hankey: Man of Secrets (3 Vols.) Vol. 1* (London: Collins) 1970

M. Samuels, *Doctrine or Dogma: German and British Infantry Tactics in the First World War* (London: Frank Cass) 1992
  Command or Control? Command, Training and Tactics in the British and German Armies, 1888–1918 (London: Frank Cass) 1995

S. B. Schreiber, *Shock Army of the British Empire: The Canadian Corps in the Last 100 Days of the Great War* (Wesport, Conn.: Praeger) 1997

G. Serle, *John Monash: A Biography* (Melbourne: Melbourne University Press) 1982

G. Sheffield, *Forgotten Victory: The First World War–Myths and Realities* (London: Headline) 2001
  The Somme (London: Cassell) 2003

G. Sheffield (ed.) *Leadership and Command: The Anglo-American Military Experience Since 1861* (London: Brassey's) 1997

G. Sheffield and D. Todman (eds.) *Command and Control on the Western Front: The British Army's Experience 1914–18* (Staplehurst: Spellmount) 2004

J. Sheldon, *The German Army on the Somme 1914–1916* (Barnsley: Pen and Sword) 2005

P. Simkins, *Kichener's Army* (Manchester: Manchester University Press) 1988

A. Simpson, *Directing Operations: British Corps Command on the Western Front 1914–18* (Stroud: Spellmount) 2006

D. Smythe, *Pershing: General of the Armies* (Bloomington: Indiana University Press) 1986

J. Snyder, *The Ideology of the Offensive: Military Decision Making and the Disasters of 1914* (London: Cornell University Press) 1984

D. Sommer, *Haldane of Cloan, His Life and Times, 1856–1928* (London: George Allen and Unwin) 1960

E. L. Spears, *Prelude to Victory* (London: Jonathan Cape) 1939

E. Spears, *Liaison 1914* (London: Cassell) 2000

E. M. Spiers, *Haldane: An Army Reformer* (Edinburgh: Edinburgh University Press) 1980

P. Stansky, *Sassoon: The Worlds of Philip and Sybil* (New Haven, Conn.: Yale University Press) 2003

D. Stevenson, *1914–1918: The History Of The First World War* (London: Allen Lane) 2004

H. Strachan, *European Armies and the Conduct of War* (London: Allen and Unwin) 1983
  "The Battle of the Somme and British Strategy", *Journal of Strategic Studies*, Vol. 21, No. 1, 1998

The First World War, Vol. I: To Arms (Oxford: Oxford University Press) 2001

The First World War: A New Illustrated History (London: Simon and Schuster) 2003

A. Suttie, *Rewriting the First World War: Lloyd George, Politics and Strategy 1914–18* (Basinstoke: Palgrave Macmillan) 2005

J. Terraine, *Mons* (London: Batsford) 1960

The Road to Passchendaele: The Flanders Offensive of 1917 (Barnsley: Leo Cooper) 1977

D. Todman, *The Great War: Myth and Memory* (London: Hambledon) 2005

D. F. Trask, *The AEF and Coalition War Making 1917–1918* (Lawrence, Kansas: Kansas University Press) 1993

T. Travers, "The Offensive and the Problem of Innovation in British Military Thought, 1870–1915", *Journal of Contemporary History*, Vol. 13, 1978

"Technology Tactics and Morale: Jean Bloch, the Boer War and British Military Theory 1900–1914", *Journal of Modern History*, Vol. 51, 1979

The Killing Ground: The British Army, the Western Front and the Emergence of Modern Warfare, 1900–1918 (London: Unwin Hyman) 1987

How The War Was Won: Command and Technology in the British Army on the Western Front (London: Rouledge) 1992

"Could the Tanks of 1918 Have Been War-Winners for the British Expeditionary Force?", *Journal of Contemporary History*, Vol. 17, No. 3, July 1992

J. Turner, *British Politics and the Great War: Coalition and Conflict 1915–1918* (Yale: London) 1992

J. Walker, *The Blood Tub: General Gough and the Battle of Bullecourt, 1917* (Staplehurst: Spellmount) 1998

B. Wasserstein, *Herbert Samuel: A Political Life* (Oxford: Oxford University Press) 1992

A. Whitmarsh, "British Army Manoeuvres and the Development of Military Aviation, 1910–1913", *War in History*, Vol. 14, No. 3, 2007

A. Wiest, *Passchendaele and the Royal Navy* (Wesport, Conn.: Greenwood) 1995

J. Williams, *Byng Of Vimy: General and Governor-General* (Barnsley: Leo Cooper) 1983

B. Wood and J. Edmonds, *A History of the Civil War in the United States 1861–5* (London: Methuen) 1905

D. R. Woodward, "Did Lloyd George Starve the British Army of British Men Prior to the German Offensive of March 1918", *Historical Journal*, Vol. 27, 1984

Field Marshal Sir William Robertson, Chief of the Imperial General Staff in the Great War (Westport, Conn.: Prager) 1998

Lloyd George and the Generals (London: Frank Cass) 2004

G. C. Wynne, "The Affair of the 21st and 24th Divisions at Loos, 26th September 1915", *The Fighting Forces*, Vol. 11, 1934

If Germany Attacks: The Battle in Depth in the West (London: Faber and Faber) 1940

D. T. Zabecki, *The German 1918 Offensives: A Case Study in the Operational Level of War* (London: Taylor and Francis) 2006

UNPUBLISHED THESES

S. Badsey, "Fire and the Sword: The British Army and the *Arme Blanche* Controversy 1871–1921", PhD thesis, University of Cambridge, 1982

J. Beach, "British Intelligence and the German Army, 1914–1918", PhD thesis, University of London, 2005

A. Geddes, "Major General Arthur Solly Flood, GHQ and Tactical Training in the BEF, 1916–1918", MA Dissertation, Centre for First World War Studies, University of Birmingham, 2007

C. B. Hammond, "The Theory and Practice of Tank Co-operation with other Arms on the Western Front During the First World War", PhD thesis, University of Birmingham, 2005

W. S. Marble, "The Infantry cannot do with a Gun Less: The Place of Artillery in the BEF, 1914–1918", PhD thesis, University of London, 1998

Index